MW00709673

Ada

A Developmental Approach

Ada

A Developmental Approach

Second edition

Fintan Culwin
South Bank University

PRENTICE HALL
_London   New York   Toronto   Sydney   Tokyo   Singapore
Madrid   Mexico City   Munich   Paris_

First published 1992
2nd edition published 1997 by
Prentice Hall Europe
Campus 400, Maylands Avenue
Hemel Hempstead
Hertfordshire, HP2 7EZ
A division of
Simon & Schuster International Group

© Prentice Hall Europe 1992, 1997

All rights reserved. No part of this publication may be reproduced,
stored in a retrieval system, or transmitted, in any form, or by any
means, electronic, mechanical, photocopying, recording or otherwise,
without prior permission, in writing, from the publisher.

Typeset in 10 on 12pt Sabon
by Mathematical Composition Setters Ltd, Salisbury, Wilts

Printed and bound in Great Britain by
Hartnolls Limited, Bodmin, Cornwall

Library of Congress Cataloging-in-Publication Data

Culwin, Fintan.
    Ada, a developmental approach / Fintan Culwin. – 2nd ed.
        p.   cm.
    Includes index.
    ISBN 0-13-264680-3 (pbk. : alk. paper)
    1. Ada (Computer program language)   I. Title.
QA76.73.A35C85   1996
0055.13'3–dc20   96-7971
                                                  CIP

British Library Cataloguing in Publication Data

A catalogue record for this book is available from
the British Library

ISBN 0-13-264680-3 (pbk)

---

1   2   3   4   5   01   00   99   98   97

This one is for
Hazel and Bernadette ...

Contents

Preface   xv

Section I   An Introduction to Software Development   1

Chapter 1   Software development in context   3
              Software artefacts   4
              Software engineering as the production of quality artefacts 6
              The production process   8
              Learning to be a software developer   11
              EXERCISES   12

Chapter 2   The structure of simple Ada programs   13
              A first program   13
              A second specification   24
              Producing a program   32
              EXERCISES   36

Chapter 3   Using packages and subprograms   39
              The package ADA.TEXT_IO   39
              Object diagrams, data flow diagrams,
                 subprogram declarations and package specifications   44
              Using ADA.TEXT_IO   45
              The package ADA.TEXT_IO.INTEGER_IO   47
              Subprogram calls and parameter modes   51
              EXERCISES   52

Chapter 4   Developer supplied packages   53
              The *TransactionCounter* object   53
              The *TransactionCounter* data flow diagrams and subprogram
                 declarations   55
              The public parts of the *TransactionCounter* package
                 specification   57
              A program to demonstrate the *TransactionCounter* package 58
              The private part of the package specification and the package
                 body   66

Contents

		Building and maintaining the executable	71
		EXERCISES	72
Chapter 5	Extending data types		74
		The *CashRegisters* extension	74
		The *RoomMonitor* extension	83
		Procedures and functions	88
		EXERCISES	91
Chapter 6	Selection in programs		92
		Selection in programs	93
		Two way sequential selections	93
		Three way sequential selections	97
		Other forms of sequential selections	98
		Nested selections	101
		An alternative implementation of the *NestedDemo* specification	105
		The *or* Boolean operator	107
		An alternative to using **if**	109
		A warning on overcomplexity	113
		EXERCISES	115
Chapter 7	Iteration in programs		116
		A first indefinite iteration specification	116
		An alternative design and implementation	121
		A second specification	125
		Definite iterations	128
		A second definite iteration specification	132
		The equivalence of indefinite and definite iteration	138
		EXERCISES	140
Chapter 8	Developing an application		141
		The application specification	141
		The construction plan	142
		Extending the class hierarchy	143
		The *Parking Ticket Office* application	156
		Constructing the executable	168
		EXERCISES	171
Section II	An Introduction to Developing Software		173
Chapter 9	Ada numeric types		175
		Integer data types	175
		Real data types	189
		EXERCISES	197

Chapter 10	Character, string and enumeration types	
	Character types	
	Strings	
	Enumeration types	~~220~~
	Ada's simple data types	231
	EXERCISES	231
Chapter 11	The user interface	233
	User interface design	233
	Exception processing	240
	EXERCISES	246
Chapter 12	Abstract data types	247
	An abstract data type requirement	247
	The *JulianDate* specification	250
	The Ada *JulianDate* package specification file	257
	The Ada *JulianDate* package definition file	261
	A client program	279
	EXERCISES	279
Chapter 13	Testing software	281
	Exhaustive testing	281
	Testing rationale	282
	The process of testing	283
	The *black box* rationale in practice	286
	Comparison of methods and techniques	301
	Software development or software assembly	302
	EXERCISES	303
Chapter 14	Production and debugging	305
	Production planning	305
	Tracing and debugging	315
	Debugging	331
	EXERCISES	332
Chapter 15	Software documentation	333
	The technical documentation	333
	Technical documentation for reusable components	339
	EXERCISES	340
Chapter 16	Standard packages	342
	The standard packages	343
	Instantiation and generic packages	344
	The package ADA.CALENDAR	346
	The package COMMAND_LINE	349
	The packages ADA.NUMERICS.FLOAT_RANDOM and ADA.NUMERICS.DISCRETE_RANDOM	352

The packages ADA.NUMERICS.ELEMENTARY_FUNCTIONS
and ADA.NUMERICS.GENERIC_ELEMENTARY_
FUNCTIONS   356
The package ADA.STRINGS and its child packages   357
The package ADA.TEXT_IO.EDITING   370
EXERCISES   372

Section III   **Arrays, Recursion, Access Types and Files**   **375**

Chapter 17   Iteration in structure: arrays   377
Declaring constrained arrays   377
Array aggregate values   381
Declaring unconstrained arrays   382
Attributes of arrays   384
Using arrays   385
An example array program   389
EXERCISES   393

Chapter 18   Two (and more) dimensional arrays   395
Declaring two dimensional constrained arrays   395
Declaring two dimensional unconstrained arrays   400
Two dimensional array aggregates   401
Two dimensional array attributes   402
Higher dimensional arrays   403
Using two dimensional arrays   404
EXERCISES   416

Chapter 19   Recursion   417
Recursion in everyday life   417
Recursive subprograms   419
Recursion and data structures   427
Mutual recursion   430
Recursion and iteration   432
EXERCISES   433

Chapter 20   Access types   434
Dynamically allocated access variables   434
A first example program   437
Access values and static variables   445
Class wide access types   448
Pointers to subprograms   451
EXERCISES   455

Chapter 21   Text files   456
The structure of text files   457
Text file management and use   459

| | Example text file programs | 468 |
| | *EXERCISES* | 483 |

Chapter 22	Sequential files and direct files	485
	Sequential files	486
	Direct files	499
	EXERCISES	514

| ***Section IV*** | **Object Oriented Programming** | **515** |

Chapter 23	Encapsulated static variables	517
	An example ESV specification	518
	The design of the coin hopper	519
	The *CanDispenser* client	528
	EXERCISES	534

Chapter 24	Programming by extension revisited	536
	Specification analysis and class design	537
	The analysis and design of the library hierarchy	538
	The design and implementation of the common base of the	
	hierarchy	539
	The hierarchy in retrospect	561
	EXERCISES	562

Chapter 25	Heterogeneous data structures	564
	The class hierarchy overview	564
	The *LibraryLists* type	565
	The *EditableLists* type	567
	The *ListableLists* type	576
	A client program	579
	The *SearchableLists* type	585
	The *IssueableLists* type	588
	The client program revisited	591
	EXERCISES	594

Chapter 26	Ordering and storing heterogeneous structures	595
	The *OrderedLists* type	595
	Writing heterogeneous lists to, and reading from, backing	
	store	601
	An overview of the hierarchies and *LibraryDemonstration*	
	client	607
	Object oriented programming	612
	EXERCISES	616

| *Chapter 27* | Generic program units | 617 |
| | A first example | 617 |

Contents

	Generic searching	620
	Generic packages	626
	EXERCISES	639

Chapter 28	Homogeneous generic hierarchies	641
	The homogeneous generic list class hierarchy	641
	The abstract *GeneralLists* type	642
	The abstract *BoundedLists* type	644
	The abstract *PrintableLists* type	648
	The non-abstract *OrderedLists* type	650
	Instantiating and using the hierarchy	657
	A second instantiation	661
	EXERCISES	663

| **Section V** | **Algorithms, Metrics, Testing and Production** | **665** |

Chapter 29	Algorithms and programming by contract	667
	Algorithms	667
	Formal and informal algorithm analysis	669
	Formal statements of an algorithm's specification	670
	Programming by contract	672
	Enforcing the contract	676
	The ADA.EXCEPTIONS standard package	679
	Assertions and contract enforcement in practice	682
	EXERCISES	683

Chapter 30	Measuring software	685
	The order of an algorithm	685
	Simple dynamic measurement	698
	EXERCISES	703

Chapter 31	Flowgraphs and white box testing	705
	Flowgraph analysis	705
	Flowgraphs and texting	713
	More complex flowgraphs	719
	EXERCISES	723

Chapter 32	Small scale software metrics	724
	The reasons for measurement	724
	Measuring the complexity of a specification	726
	Static metrics	728
	Dynamic measurements	733
	EXERCISES	738

| Chapter 33 | Large scale metrics | 740 |
| | General large scale metrics | 740 |

	Medium scale metrics	743
	Usability metrics	746
	Metrics in context	750
	EXERCISES	752
Chapter 34	Testing and production	753
	Testing concluded	753
	Production processes	763
	EXERCISES	766
Appendix A	Other resources	767
Index		769

Preface

From the preface of the first edition (1992):

> The impetus for this book came from a question asked by a student at the
> end of an introductory lecture. The lecturer had just recommended that the
> students taking the course would require access to three separate books: one
> book was a reference manual for the programming language; one was
> concerned with program design; and one was concerned with software
> development, including testing The question asked by the student was
> reasonable and, given students' incomes, predictable: which of the three
> books was most important? The question does not have an easy answer ...

The first edition was an attempt to produce a book which answered the student's
question, using Ada '83 as the programming language. From the comments on the
first edition the prediction I made in the preface, 'In writing this book, I am aware
that I will fail to satisfy many people', was partially correct. Although I have had
some negative opinions the overwhelming response, and the number of copies
sold, indicated that I managed to provide an answer to most parts of the student's
question and provided a resource which many tutors, students and developers have
found very valuable.

Since the first edition *object oriented development* (OOD) has become
established as the prevalent paradigm of programming in the 1990s. Ada '83
provided limited support for OOD and *object oriented programming* (OOP), but
the need for additional support for this style of development had already been
recognized. In 1995 a revised Ada standard, ANSI/ISO/IEC-8652:1995,
commonly known as Ada '95, was approved. The revision added a number of
facilities to Ada '83, possibly the most important of which was support for OOP.

Pedagogically this raised an important question, one which currently has no
consensual answer from the global community of software development educators.
The question can be briefly phrased as 'Object first or object last?'. Should the
process of learning software development start with traditional imperative/structured
programming, which reflects the educational experience of the current generation of
tutors? Or should the process now start with a consideration of objects in order to
emphasize their importance to modern software development practice?

When I started preparing the second edition I was of the object last opinion. However, when I introduced objects half way through an initial draft, I realized that it invalidated much that I had already advocated. Moving objects further forward to about one-quarter of the way through the draft alleviated, but did not solve, the problem. I became convinced of the necessity of an object first approach and the published version of the book reflects this.

The preface of the first edition critiqued most existing software development textbooks on educational and pedagogic grounds, and stated three important educational considerations which I intended to abide by:

• Abstraction is only possible from concrete foundations.

• Presentation of a construct does not guarantee that it has been cognitively assimilated, merely that it may have been accommodated.

• The development of a new cognitive structure can only be made if prerequisite structures are already in place.

The second edition continues to stress these educational principles. It also respects the major pedagogic critique that while the overwhelming majority of introductory texts exhort the reader to design before implementing, the vast majority then proceed without presenting any design considerations. As with the first edition, an essential feature of this book is the presentation of designs, in the form of Booch style object diagrams and JSP schematics, for almost every piece of code presented. The reasoning behind this approach is that whilst computer languages wax and wane in popularity, essential design skills will remain applicable.

Section I of the book commences with two chapters which are little changed from the first edition, introducing some essential concepts. Chapter 3 then introduces the use of a pre-supplied package and of the facilities which it provides. This allows an initial extendible data type, commonly known as an object, to be introduced in Chapters 4 and 5 before the imperative concepts of selection and iteration are introduced in Chapters 6 and 7. Section I concludes with a consolidation of all the concepts by additional extensions to the initial object, which involve selection and iteration. Tutors who are less convinced of the merits of an object first approach may care to direct their students to a more imperative sequence of study following the sequence of Chapters 1, 2, 6, 7, 3, 4, 5 and 8.

Section II commences, in Chapters 9 and 10, with an introduction to Ada's pre-declared data types. The importance of the user interface is then introduced in Chapter 11 before developer supplied data types, from Section I, are consolidated in Chapter 12. This section continues with considerations of testing, production and debugging and documentation in Chapters 13, 14 and 15, before concluding with an introduction to Ada's standard packages.

Section III introduces, in its first two chapters, internal iterative data types in the form of arrays, before considering recursion and access types in Chapters 19 and 20. The section concludes with an introduction to external iterative data types in the form of files, in Chapters 21 and 22.

Section IV returns to the theme of OOD and OOP by first introducing encapsulated static variable designs and implementations, before revisiting extendible types in Chapter 24. Iterative container objects are then introduced in Chapters 25 and 26, before generic considerations are presented in Chapter 27, allowing the section to conclude with an introduction to generic iterative container objects.

Section V consolidates the theme of software engineering by introducing algorithms, algorithm measurement, flowgraphs and white box testing, metrics, including OOP and usability metrics, before revisiting testing and production considerations.

One other very significant development has taken place since the publication of the first edition. The Internet has mushroomed from a quiet backwater, largely populated by computing academics, into a torrential river attracting millions to its banks. The largest factor fuelling this growth has been the development of the World Wide Web (The Web). The potential for this medium for education and training has been widely commented upon and a Web service to support this book is located at South Bank University (SBU), at the URL given below. The site contains the entire text of the book as well as some chapters which did not, for various reasons, make it into the published edition. All the source code presented in the book, and much other material which is used at SBU to support its courses, is available on the site.

The site also contains hyperlinks to many other Ada resources. The most useful of these might be locations where a free Ada '95 development environment called *gnat* can be located. At the time of writing *gnat* is available for MS-DOS, many flavours of Unix and there are plans to make it available on Macintosh computers. The software in this book was developed using the *gnat* environment and tested with *Linux*, a free Unix, and also with MS-DOS. In order for source code filenames to conform to MS-DOS restrictions they had to be 'krunched' down to *eight* characters. These names are given at the start of each source code listing in the book, following the full name, as the *k8* name.

Although all the source code in the book has been checked and tested and each chapter has been read and commented upon by a number of people, it would be very naïve to assert that all errors and inconsistencies have been removed. All I can do is apologize in advance to any reader who encounters an error and ask that they e-mail details to me at the address below. In return I will collect and place a list of errors on the Web site.

This book has taken about two years to produce, during which time I have had support, encouragement and criticism from a large number of people. The greatest in number and most enthusiastic in support are the students who have endured the draft versions, with particular thanks to Bill, John, Toby and Danny who started the process of transferring the text onto the Web. Pete Chalk took it upon himself to critique each chapter in detail, as it was produced, again when each section was completed and, for one or two particularly difficult chapters, seemingly innumerable times. Thanks are also due to the technical support at SBU particularly Ewan

Harley and John Shanks. Helen Martin provided editorial support for the first edition for which I am still grateful, Jackie Harbor undertook this onerous task for this edition. Many errors which would otherwise have plagued the book were caught at the copy-editing stage by Neville Hankins.

From the last paragraph of the preface to the first edition:

> Finally I have to thank Leah, Seana and Maria, who put up with less of a father or a lover than they might otherwise have had, particularly during many long weekends when a rational person would have shredded the entire text.

They have now been through the process for a third time and still provide patient and loving support. I promise them that this will be the last time...until the next time! The final thank you is in the form of an apology: whilst I was struggling with a particularly difficult chapter a friend phoned and an incautious conversation may have caused her many problems...

Mérþ ykir leitt ef ég hef sœrt þig.

fintan@sbu.ac.uk
http://www.scism.sbu.ac.uk/~fintan

SECTION I

An Introduction to Software Development

CHAPTER 1
Software development in context

This book is concerned with introducing the techniques by which *software artefacts* can be produced using the programming language Ada '95. Although Ada Lovelace, in honour of whom the Ada programming language is named, is credited with developing the first program in 1843, *software development* did not become economically significant until about 1950 and did not become widespread until about 1970. Since then software, and software related activity, have grown to an estimated 20% of the North American and European economies. All indications are that this proportion will continue to grow into the twenty-first century.

This growth has been achieved despite the fact that much of the software produced has been of a rather dubious quality, and that its production processes have been at worst chaotic and on average poorly managed. These problems became glaringly apparent in the early 1970s when some very expensive software development projects had to be abandoned and the possibility of humans being killed or injured by software failure became apparent. To start to solve these problems the theories and practices from the large scale production of other artefacts were applied to the production of software, leading to the emergence of a discipline called *software engineering*.

One consequence of this focus on the engineering of software was the development of the initial Ada language, known as Ada '83, in the early 1980s. The intention was to produce an environment which encouraged developers to apply the established principles of good software engineering practice. These practices were further developed through the 1980s and the early 1990s, most noticeably with the development of *object oriented programming* (*OOP*), and the revised language Ada '95 provides support for this style of development.

Software development is a complex activity. It will take the rest of this section, and subsequently the book, to start to explain exactly how complex this activity is and from these considerations to obtain an understanding of what is required to become an effective *software developer*. One rather simple answer to the question 'What is software development?', is that software development is the activity of designing, producing and maintaining software artefacts. This is a rather tautological answer but it gives rise to an easier initial question, 'What is a software artefact?'.

3

Software artefacts

A dictionary definition of *artefact* is 'Product of human art and workmanship...'. This term has been deliberately chosen as, although the body of knowledge which underpins software engineering is often called *computer science*, the current practice of software production is more akin to a *black art*. That is, an arcane activity practised by the initiated which can only be passed on to the uninitiated by a long and tortuous apprenticeship. The black arts of the medieval alchemists gave raise in due course to the modern sciences of medicine and chemistry, and their engineering expressions in pharmacy and chemical engineering. An honest appreciation of current software development practice might conclude that it is somewhere between being a black art and an engineering discipline.

A software artefact is a component of a system which instructs a computer to perform some specified task; the most obvious component would be a complete program. A less obvious, but potentially more useful, component would be a module which can be assembled with other modules to produce a complete program. This distinction can be clarified by a comparison with electronic artefacts. An electronic artefact can be a complete product, for example a portable telephone or a computer. Or an electronic artefact can be a microchip which can be assembled with other artefacts such as other microchips, circuit boards, power supplies, microphones, etc., to produce a complete product.

Both types of software component embody instructions from the software developer to the computer which, when followed, will achieve some specified task. This can be compared with the situation where one person (the *instructor*) gives a set of instructions to a second person (the *instructee*) which, when followed, will allow the instructee to achieve some specified task. There are several requirements which have to be satisfied before the instructions can be successfully transmitted and performed:

- The instructor must know how to perform the task.

- The two people must have a common language.

- The two people must have some means of communication.

- The instructions must be given at a suitable level.

- The sequence of instructions has to be planned.

The person giving the instructions must know how to perform the task. This may sound obvious, but it is not enough for the instructor simply to relay a set of instructions. Unless the instructor has a sufficient understanding of how to perform the task he or she will be unable to expand and explain the instructions if the instructee has difficulty in understanding them.

The two people must have a common language and they must have *some means of communication.* Another obvious point but the language can take many forms including *natural languages* such as English, non-verbal languages such as those used by scuba divers, visual languages such as the diagrams which accompany self-assembly furniture and abstract languages such as knitting patterns or algebra. Likewise the means of communication can take many forms, including face to face interaction, telephone calls, live video connections, published instruction manuals and letters or e-mails. For a given task different combinations of language and communication mechanism may be more or less effective, and some combinations may make the process very difficult or even impossible.

The instructions must be given at a suitable level. This level is determined by the abilities of the instructee. For example, the sequence of instructions for the preparation of a cheese sauce might start with 'First prepare a roux' if the instructee was known to be a qualified chef. If the instructee was known to be a novice at cooking the first instruction might be 'Gently melt 50 grams of butter in a heavy bottomed saucepan'.

The sequence of instructions has to be planned. Although the instructions for a simple task could be successfully given by a very skilled communicator with an expert knowledge of the domain, in most cases the instructions would have to be planned. For a complicated task it would be essential for the instructor to spend some time planning the sequence in which the instructions should be given. For a particularly complicated, or important, task it would also be advisable for the planned sequence to be tried out with some representative instructees to make sure that they work as the instructor intends.

The communication between a software developer and a computer which results in the production of a software artefact can be analyzed with these considerations. The developer must have an adequate knowledge of how to perform the task. The meaning of adequate in this context will be explained below after the other criteria have been considered.

The language used is a computer programming language, such as Ada. These languages are abstract languages which are more precise than natural languages but, like algebra, can be very difficult for many people to become proficient in. Communication is usually achieved by the developer typing a set of instructions in the computer language at a terminal and then asking the computer if it under-stands them. The initial reply from the computer will only indicate if the instructions seem to be in the correct language. Once this has been confirmed the computer will follow the instructions and, unless an impossible instruction is given, the developer must then decide if the computer has understood them.

The level of instructions which can be given to the computer is asinine. Using the cooking example above the equivalent first instruction to a computer would be on the level of explaining exactly where to locate the butter. Software artefacts which are intended to be assembled by a developer might, in the same comparison, provide a pre-packaged set of instructions for the construction of a roux. This would allow the developer using the component to issue the first instruction at a much higher level, for example 'First prepare a roux'.

Because of the very low level at which the instructions have to be given to the computer it is absolutely essential that the developer has a very detailed knowledge of the task and of the techniques by which it can be performed. Even then it is essential that the developer plans the sequence of actions before expressing them to the computer. The process of translating the developer's ideas into a computer language, issuing them to a computer and deciding if they have been correctly expressed, is so tedious that pre-planning so as to avoid as many errors as possible is imperative.

A set of instructions which if expressed precisely and followed carefully achieves some defined purpose is known as an *algorithm*. A knowledge of the nature and properties of algorithms, and the acquisition of a collection of common algorithms, are an essential part of becoming a software developer. Accordingly a large part of this book is essentially concerned with algorithms.

Software engineering as the production of quality artefacts

The production of a software artefact by the communication of instructions between a developer and a computer, as described above, takes place within a much broader context. A complete description of this context would require a book at least as long as this one. Appendix A lists several standard software engineering textbooks which provide a much more complete description of the context. This part of this chapter will only provide an initial mention of some considerations. Some of these will be further expanded through the rest of this book.

A software system has some defined requirement which it has to satisfy. The statement of the task is known as its *specification* and the production of a complete and consistent specification is the first stage in developing a software artefact. One of the most fundamental aspects of the production process is to ensure that the artefact will meet its specification when it is produced.

A software system is a complex product and, in the vast majority of cases, requires a team of developers to co-operate together in order to produce it in a timely manner. As a team product it requires production management in order to ensure that the activities of the subteams and individuals are co-ordinated, so that as their products are assembled they will work effectively together towards satsifying the specification.

A team of skilled software developers brought together to produce a software artefact usually have to be paid. Thus a software product is an economic product which requires an initial investment, has to be produced to an agreed budget and has to recoup its costs.

The users of a software artefact may be the human end-users or they may be other software artefacts. For human users there are ergonomic considerations which should be taken into account in order to produce a user interface which allows the user to operate the system as effectively and efficiently as possible. For an artefact which is intended to be used by other software artefacts it must conform to an agreed protocol for communication between them.

The product will usually have to satisfy some external constraints. These constraints may be related to how usable it is to the end-user, how robust it is, how quickly it performs its task or how much storage the artefact and/or its data requires.

An artefact is a unique product which implies that its development is not a mechanistic process but requires some degree of human creativity. An artefact has a *life span* and a *life cycle*, and it has an initial stage where it is commissioned, specified, designed and constructed. During its use it will require maintenance and at some stage it will be abandoned or replaced. Of these stages the maintenance stage has been shown to be the most expensive. The initial stage should take this into account and make sure that further changes, additions, extensions and other modifications can be easily accomplished.

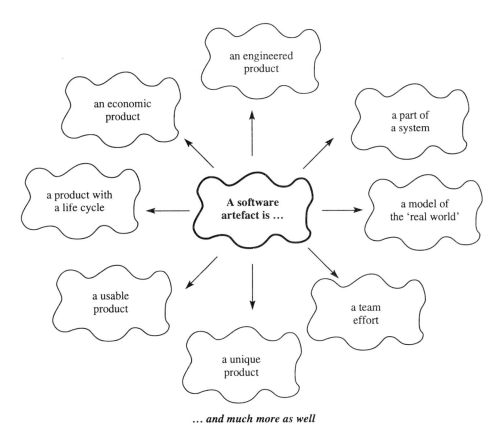

... and much more as well

Figure 1.1 A software artefact is ...

An artefact is a model of some aspect of the 'real world' which exists beyond the computer system. A model provides only some aspects of what it is modelling. For example, a model aircraft in a travel agent's shop window provides an accurate scale model of a real aircraft, but is totally incapable of flying. A sheet of paper folded into a dart does not physically resemble any aircraft but provides a model which can be used to illustrate some aspects of aerodynamics. A software artefact has to model the aspects of the real world with which it is concerned in an accurate and effective manner.

These considerations are summarized in Figure 1.1, whose most important statement is that 'it is much more as well'.

The production process

The first activity in the production of any software artefact is to investigate the possibility of not producing it at all! Assuming that a specification for the artefact has been produced, it may be that an artefact satisfying the specification already exists. If so it might be more sensible and cost effective to purchase, or obtain, the existing artefact than to go to the expense and trouble of reproducing it. Even if no existing artefact satisfies the complete specification it might be that one satisfies, or nearly satisfies, a part of it. Again it would be more sensible and cost effective to use, or adapt, the existing component and use it for a part of the product than to construct it entirely from scratch.

The most fundamental advice which can be given for the production process is to practise *software assembly* rather than *software construction*. As the processes of producing a robust and reliable software artefact are so complex and expensive it is preferable to assemble from existing artefacts rather than to construct entirely from scratch. The contents of this book will provide an initial set of components which are intended to be reused in a large number of situations. Appendix A includes details of where other collections of reusable components can be located. The process of learning to become an effective software developer should involve learning how to use these *software repositories*.

However, even when an artefact is largely being constructed from existing components, the developer will be required to produce some part of the product. This may be an adaptation of an existing component to make it more suitable for the specification and/or the production of the *glue* which holds the reused components together, or even construction of components from scratch. Production, or modification, should always be approached with some plan of the processes which will be followed.

There are two basic approaches to the software production process: *waterfall* and *spiral*. The waterfall approach represents an ideal situation which is rare in actual practice, but provides a goal which the spiral approach should attempt to move towards. Waterfall production assumes that the entire production process can be broken up into a number of distinct stages, each of which can be completed before the next stage is started. The phrase *waterfall* implies that once a stage has been completed it cannot be easily returned to. Just as, when travelling down a river, it is possible to go over a waterfall but very difficult to return back up it. The waterfall production process is illustrated in Figure 1.2.

The major stages involved in this production process are to produce the *specification*, then to *design* the software, then to *build* the software and finally to *test* the product. This production process assumes that it is possible to complete each of these stages without making any mistakes. This is occasionally possible: skilled and experienced developers may be able to produce an artefact in this manner if it is similar to artefacts which they have already produced. However, these situations rarely exist, and mistakes are invariably made in all of the production stages. When a mistake is made the stage where the error was originally made, and all succeeding stages, have to be repeated. Thus a mistake in constructing the original specification will require a redesign, rebuild and repetition of the testing. If a mistake was made in the testing, which indicated a fault in software which did not exist, then only a corrected test needs to be repeated. The problems with the waterfall method are that in practice is very difficult to achieve, and when applied the costs involved in repeating stages are huge.

In contrast the *spiral* process recognizes that errors will be made in all stages of the production process and proceeds on this basis. A diagram of the spiral method is given in Figure 1.3. Here it is admitted that it is very unlikely that all stages can be correctly completed on the first attempt, and it is planned that each stage will be returned to following experience of the succeeding stages.

The solid lines on the spiral indicate the optimal path, a specification leads to a design, which leads to the building of the software which leads to testing the software. Following this a possible return to the specification stage is allowed for, but an extension to the design is expected followed by an extension to the build and then to the test. The spiral will continue until the artefact is released, but the process is never considered completely finished as the spiral continues into the maintenance phase. The dashed paths on the diagram indicate that this process may be circumvented and experience with the design may influence the specification

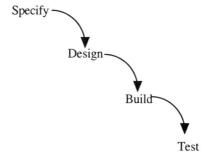

Figure 1.2 The waterfall production process.

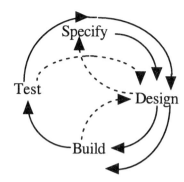

Figure 1.3 The spiral production process.

before a build is attempted. Likewise experience with the build may require changes in the design or experiences with testing may require a redesign.

The spiral technique does not assume the entire product to be constructed in a single cycle. The first version of the artefact would be very primitive and succeeding cycles would add additional facilities, steadily making the artefact more complex. When this style of development is used it is important that each time the product is tested, all the previous tests are reapplied before the new facilities are tested. This is to make sure that the changes which have been made in the current cycle do not cause the artefact to fail a test which it once passed.

What is common between the two techniques is an insistence that design will always precede a build. The possibility of just building without first designing, or extending a design, is not allowed. If this was allowed it would be expected that in the vast majority of cases the product would have an unacceptably low quality.

The spiral process is more suited to the way in which most developers have been observed to work in most situations. It is suitable when the developer has an incomplete understanding of the specification or the facilities of the developmental tools, including the language, are not fully understood. This is much more akin to the situation experienced by the novice developer and thus the recommended production process for novices is a spiral not a waterfall. The technique is commonly known as a *design, build, test, design, build, test ...* process.

The product of the developmental process, whatever technique is used, is a software artefact. This comprises the program component itself, and also documentation to accompany it. This documentation should record not only the product by presenting its design, its implementation in the programming language and the testing which was performed upon it; it should record the production process indicating who developed it, why it was developed, when and where it was developed and what problems were encountered in its development. These documents will be essential during the maintenance phase of the artefact's life cycle, which, as mentioned above, is the most expensive part of the cycle. Without a design any changes to the implementation will be very difficult to accomplish. As changes are made during maintenance details of them should be added to the documentation so that it always provides an accurate description of the current status of the artefact.

One of the major errors made by novice developers is to neglect the documentation aspects of a development process. This is in part caused by the more fundamental error of failing to produce a design before attempting to produce an implementation. The process of 'documentation' in this situation consists of faking a design after inelegant program code has been produced. In contrast the completion of a design before an implementation is attempted allows self-documentation to take place. The design will be of use as the software is constructed and, as it is developed in parallel with the artefact, will always accurately reflect it.

Learning to be a software developer

So far this chapter has concentrated upon the processes followed by professional developers. Novice developers are in a different situation and cannot be expected to have the experiences of producing specifications, designs and building and testing code which an experienced developer has assimilated from training and experience. The contents of this book will provide the training aspects of an initial course in software development. In order to learn how to develop software effectively, a novice developer will also have to assimilate the experiences of actually producing software artefacts. It is not possible to learn about software development by reading a book; in order to learn about developing software the experiences of developing software are also required.

Even with the initial exercises in this first section the full software development process should be followed. There is a temptation to regard the only product of a novice exercise to be the code and consequently the other aspects of software development, design, documentation and testing are omitted. This can lead to the establishment of bad habits and the only skill obtained from the exercises is the production of code by composition at the terminal. This 'skill' consists of making a large number of changes to code, without adequate thought or reflection, until the product appears to work. The code produced by this technique is likely to be of a very low quality.

A longer term effect of not following the full development process with the initial exercises is that the skills which will be required for large programs are not practised, and honed, on the initial exercises. For the end of chapter exercises in this introductory section, the full development process is really not required as an effective program can be produced, even by a novice, without a design. However, for the more complex exercises in the remaining parts of the book design is an absolute prerequisite and the skills which will be obtained from fully completing the exercises in the initial section will be essential.

Software development is a complex cognitive skill and the process of learning any skill can be summarized in the Confucian proverb:

> You tell me and I forget,
> You show me and I remember,
> I do it and I understand.

The text of this book will do the telling and some aspects of the showing. The experiences of completing the end of chapter exercises will provide the understanding.

EXERCISES

1.1 In order to learn to develop software it will be necessary to write and compile programs on a computer system. In order to prepare for this make sure you know how to use the system. In particular, make sure that you can edit text files, print text files and store files in directories.

CHAPTER 2
The structure of simple Ada programs

Having explained what a program is in some detail in the previous chapter, this chapter will concentrate upon the structure of two simple Ada programs. The first program is a very untypical program in that it has no input from the user and the output from the program is exactly the same no matter how many times it is executed. It is included here only to illustrate the structure of the source code from which a program is constructed. The second program is a little more typical in that it requires some input from the user and the output of the program will differ every time the program is run, depending upon what the user inputs. Although this program is trivial, it will be presented as a complete development exercise, starting with a *specification* and continuing with a *data design* and a *program design* before the Ada source code which implements the design is presented.

If either of these programs were really needed, or more likely if programs of a similar complexity were needed, a complete design process would not be followed by experienced programmers. They would be much more likely just to implement the program directly. For novice developers this temptation should be avoided as it is only by practising design skills on simple specifications, such as these, that the skills can be cultivated and then be available for use on the more complicated specifications which follow.

A first program

In order to write any program a specification for the program must exist. In order to introduce the basic form of an Ada program a very simple specification will be used. A program is required which when executed will produce the following output on the terminal:

```
The answer to life,
the universe and everything is -
forty two.
```

A very useful answer, though not a very useful program. An Ada program which would implement this specification might be as follows:

```
0001    -- Filename UltimateAnswer.ada (k8 ultimate.adb).
0002    -- Introductory Ada program for Section I Chapter 2.
0003    --
0004    -- Fintan Culwin, v0.1, Jan 1997.
0005
0006    with ADA.TEXT_IO;
0007    use  ADA.TEXT_IO;
0008
0009    procedure UltimateAnswer is
0010
0011       TheAnswer : constant STRING := "forty two.";
0012
0013    begin -- UltimateAnswer
0014       PUT_LINE( "The answer to life, ");
0015       PUT_LINE( "the universe and everything is -");
0016       PUT_LINE( TheAnswer );
0017    end UltimateAnswer;
```

The numbers on the left of the program listing are the *line numbers*; they are not required by Ada and are included here in order to allow each line of the program to be easily referred to in the text.

The difference between words in the listing which are shown in **bold**, words which are shown in CAPITALS, and words which are shown in italic with *EmbeddedCapitals* will be explained later in this section. The line numbers, the **bold** effect and the *italic* effect ***must not*** be used for the production of programs. A version of this program in a suitable format for actual use would be as follows:

```
-- Filename UltimateAnswer.ada (k8 ultimate.adb).
-- Introductory Ada program for Section I Chapter 2.
--
-- Fintan Culwin, v0.1, Jan 1997.

with ADA.TEXT_IO;
use  ADA.TEXT_IO;

procedure UltimateAnswer is

   TheAnswer : constant STRING := "forty two.";

begin -- UltimateAnswer
   PUT_LINE( "The answer to life, ");
   PUT_LINE( "the universe and everything is -");
   PUT_LINE( TheAnswer );
end UltimateAnswer;
```

The program heading

The heading of the program is in lines 0001 to 0008. Lines 0001 to 0004 are strictly not part of the Ada program, although they are part of the listing. These lines start with the Ada term '--', which is a double hyphen (or minus sign). This term is an instruction to the compiler to ignore the rest of the line. Text such as this in program listings is known as a ***comment***. Comments are included in program listings so that anybody reading the listing can make better sense of it.

The comments in this example program are the minimum comments which should be included in any program. The first comment should be used to identify the operating system filename indicating where the program text is stored. Two names are given in this and the other programs in this book. The first name is the full name for the source code file that should be used in environments, such as Unix, Windows 95 or Macintosh OS, which support arbitrarily long filenames. The alternative name, identified as the k8 name, is for the MS-DOS environment where filenames are limited to eight characters (k8 indicates *k*runched to *eight* characters).

The second comment should give some indication of the contents of the file and why it was produced. The remaining comments should identify the programmer who initially developed the code, the date on which the program was written and its version number. The intention of including these comments can be summarized as where?, why?, what?, when?, who?.

Lines 0006 and 0007 are required by this program as it will be required to produce some text output; text output is composed of a sequence of characters. An Ada program does not know how to produce any output unless it has access to suitable facilities. The lines '**with** ADA.TEXT_IO; **use** ADA.TEXT_IO;' will allow this Ada program access to facilities for the input and output of text information. Including this line in the header of any Ada program will allow all parts of the program to input and output text information. A clause such as this in a program header is known as a ***context clause***. Line 0008 is the final line of the program header; an Ada program is composed of a number of parts. The simplest of these parts is a known as a ***procedure***, so a simple program such as this is composed of a single procedure. Line 0008 identifies the start of a procedure, which in this case is also the program, and gives it a name. The name is '*UltimateAnswer*', and has been invented by the programmer. The rules for inventing names will be given later in this section.

The header also contains lines 0005 and 0008. These lines are very important, although they contain nothing and Ada will do nothing with them. They are included to make the program easier to read, as they indicate where different parts of the program start and finish. The person who reads a program the most is the person who is developing the program; thus it is in the developer's interest to make the program listing as readable as possible by the use of blank lines and comments where appropriate. For the same reasons it also helps to make the program more reusable and maintainable.

This heading can be used as a template for the heading lines of simple programs. The only parts which will change will be the program name and the comments. More complex programs may input and output information other than text information. Examples of context clauses which will allow the program to access suitable facilities for the input and output of non-text information will be given as they are required in the rest of this section.

The program declarations

The declarations part of this program is between lines 0010 and 0012. In this program there is only one declaration made, the declaration of a **constant**. A constant is an object used within a program whose value will not change as the program executes.

Each constant has to have a name, a data type and a value. The name of the constant is given first followed by a colon ':'. In this example the name of the constant, which is invented by the programmer, is '*TheAnswer*'. The reserved word '**constant**' follows the colon to indicate that this is a constant declaration and is followed by the data type of the constant, in this example 'STRING'. Objects of the data type STRING can be used to hold information composed of a sequence of characters.

Constants have to be given a value as they are declared; the value is indicated by the symbol ':=', which can be read here as 'has the value of', and is followed by the actual value. String values are indicated in Ada programs by enclosing them within double quote marks '"'. This string contains a total of ten characters, the five characters of the word "forty", the three characters of the word "two", the single space character which separates them, and the full stop which terminates the string.

This line illustrates the usage of **bold**, CAPITALS and *EmbeddedCapitals* in the program listings presented in this book. The meaning of these different styles will be made clear below in the section on program layout conventions.

In a more complex program there might be many constants declared, each of which is a separate program object. It is useful to produce a summary table of all the program objects used in a program. The table can then be used as a reference for which objects have been declared, what values they have and what they will be used for within the program. A table of constants for this example program would be as follows:

Program Constants

Name	Type	Value	Notes
TheAnswer	STRING	"forty two."	The ultimate answer

The declarations section of the program also includes lines 0010 and 0012, which are blank lines included to make the program listing more readable.

The program statements

The final part of the program is between lines 0013 and 0017; these are the *statements* which tell Ada what actions to perform when the program is executed. In this program the executable part consists of a sequence of three 'PUT_LINE' statements.

The three statements are enclosed between a **begin**/**end** pair on lines 0013 and 0017. A **begin**/**end** pair in an Ada program listing is used to mark the start and end of a particular part of the program. The **begin**/**end** pair in this program delineate the start and end of the procedure *UltimateAnswer*. As this is the procedure which identifies the program it is known as the ***program procedure***. As there can be many **begin**/**end** pairs in an Ada program it is important to adopt a convention to indicate what they mark the start and end of.

The **begin** on line 0013 has been commented as the start of the procedure *UltimateAnswer*, which, being the only procedure of the program, is also the start of the program. The **end** on line 0017 could have been expressed simply as 'end,'. Ada allows an **end** which marks the end of a procedure to include the name of the procedure as part of its syntax. Alternatively the name of the procedure can be included as a comment following the semicolon symbol ';' which marks the end of the procedure, that is 'end; -- *UltimateAnswer*'.

It is recommended that the name of the procedure be included as a comment accompanying a procedure's **begin**, and be included within the syntax of the **end**, as shown in the example program. A very common novice error when adopting this convention is to omit the comment which forms part of the **begin** line and, when Ada complains about the resulting syntax, to terminate the line with a semicolon:

```
correct                        incorrect
begin -- UltimateAnswer        begin UltimateAnswer;
```

If this mistake is made then the program will compile, but on execution will apparently do nothing. The program will probably come to an end with an error message after some considerable time or more likely will have to be interrupted from the terminal. The reasons for this behaviour are too complex to explain at this stage. The error is known as an ***infinite recursive loop***, and will be explained in Chapter 19.

The 'PUT_LINE' statement is one of the methods used by Ada to output text information. It is one of the facilities in ADA.TEXT_IO to which this program gained access by using the context clause on lines 0006 and 0007 of the listing. The effect of the PUT_LINE statement, when it is executed, is to output anything within the brackets which form part of the PUT_LINE statement on the terminal screen and then advance the cursor to the next line of the terminal.

In lines 0014 and 0015 of this program the brackets contain *string literals*. String literals are sequences of characters which are contained between the opening and closing double quote marks '"'. A string literal was also used in line 0011 to supply a value for the STRING constant. The effect of these lines when they are executed by Ada is to output the sequence of characters between the quote marks but not to output the quote marks themselves.

In line 0016 the PUT_LINE brackets contain *TheAnswer*. This is not a string literal as it is not included between double quotes; it is the name of the constant declared in line 0011 as having the value "forty two.". The PUT_LINE statement will display the value of the constant, in this case 'forty two.'.

If a PUT_LINE statement does not contain a literal then it may contain the name of a program object. What will be printed out is not the name of the program object but the value which it contains. To understand what happens, Ada can be thought of as trying to obey the PUT_LINE statements as instructions. For the first two statements the opening and closing quotes indicate that the literal contained within the quotes is to be output on the screen. For the last statement the absence of quotes indicates that a program object is being referred to. Ada takes the name of the object from the statement and looks it up in the data tables to see if this object is known. In this case the object *TheAnswer* is known, and its value can be found in the table. Once its value has been found it is output on the screen. If the object is not known then Ada will report it as an error when compilation is attempted.

Each of the PUT_LINE statements is a complete Ada statement and is terminated with a semicolon ' ; '. The end of the program follows line 0017 of the listing, which includes a semicolon to terminate the procedure. The declaration of a constant on line 0011 requires a semicolon to terminate it. The context clause on lines 0006 and 0007 consists of two declarations, a **with** and a **use**, each of which requires a semicolon to terminate it.

When this program is executed by the computer the sequence of statements which form the executable part of the program are each obeyed, in the sequence specified in the listing. The effect of the execution of the three PUT_LINE statements is to output the three lines of text, as shown in the specification. The execution of the last PUT_LINE statement completes the program and control is returned from the program to where the program was invoked from, most probably the operating system or an integrated development environment.

This concludes the initial discussion of the *UltimateAnswer* program. Before the second program is introduced some general comments will be made about the construction of Ada source code.

Program layout conventions

There are very few rules imposed by Ada upon how an Ada program listing has to be laid out. There are, however, advantages in having conventions which define exactly how a program text should be laid out. For example, within a team of programmers, if all the programmers use the same convention for program layout, it makes it easier for the programs to be read by all team members. The conventions for program layout used in this book will be introduced throughout the text.

In the program listings in this book **bold** lower case text will be used for Ada reserved words. These are words which Ada reserves for her own use, and cannot be used for any other purpose within an Ada program. A complete list of Ada reserved words is given in Table 1.1. The use of **bold** to emphasize Ada reserved words is used to make the reserved words easier to recognize in the program listings. Program listings which are intended to produce programs should not attempt to reproduce the bold effect.

CAPITALIZED text is used for words which have a pre-defined meaning to Ada. These meanings can be changed by a program, but should not be changed unless it is certain that a change of meaning is required. The most important of these words are given in Table 1.2.

All other words in an Ada program are invented by the programmer to provide identifiers for various objects in the program. These words are shown in program listings using an *EmbeddedCapital* style. Where the identifier consists of a single word, for example '*total*', it is typed with an initial capital – '*Total*'. It is more usual for multiple word identifiers to be used for example '*total tax to pay*'. In this

Table 1.1 Ada reserved words

abort	abs	abstract	accept	access
aliased	all	and	array	at
begin	body	case	constant	declare
delay	delta	digits	else	elsif
end	entry	exception	exit	for
function	generic	goto	if	in
is	limited	loop	mod	new
not	null	of	or	others
out	package	pragma	private	procedure
protected	raise	range	record	rem
renames	requeue	return	reverse	select
separate	subtype	tagged	task	terminate
then	type	until	use	when
while	with	xor		

Table 1.2 Some Ada words with a pre-defined meaning

BOOLEAN	CHARACTER	CLOSE	CREATE	DELETE
FALSE	FLOAT	GET	INTEGER	NATURAL
NEW_LINE	OPEN	PUT	PUT_LINE	POSITIVE
READ	RESET	SKIP_LINE	STRING	TEXT_IO
TRUE	WRITE			

case the spaces have to be removed from the phrase but to mark the start of each separate word an initial capital is used – '*TotalTaxToPay*'. When identifiers are referred to within the text of the book they are shown in *italic*. As with the bold effect for reserved words this is to assist in recognizing programmer supplied identifiers and the italic effect should not be used for production listings.

The guidelines for inventing names will be introduced later in this chapter. Although the convention for using upper case, lower case and embedded capitals will be followed in this text and recommended as good program layout style, it is not important to Ada. In most circumstances Ada does not regard the case of a character as important, so line 0011 of the program listing could have been typed as:

```
tHeansWer : cOnStAnT strING := 'forty two';
```

although it would not seem sensible to do so. The major exception to this is the content of string literals, where the case of the characters is preserved by Ada when the literal is stored or output.

Program layout conventions will also be used to determine how many statements can be included within one line of text, where on the line a statement should start, where comments should be included within program listings and where blank lines should be used in listings.

These conventions will be introduced throughout the rest of this book. In general the following conventions are recommended:

- Only one statement or declaration should be included on a single line of text, but two statements can sometimes be included where they are short and closely related in their meaning or function.

- Lines will be indented (moved to the right) to show groups of statements which comprise different parts of the program. In the example program above lines 0014, 0015 and 0016 have been indented three characters to the right, to indicate that they comprise the executable statements of the procedure.

- Comments should be included at the start of programs to identify where?, what?, why?, who?, when?. They should also be included to make clear the meaning of any statements or declarations whose meaning is not clear from their identifiers or position in the listing. There are many other places where comments should be included, which will be introduced as they are met.

- Blank lines should be used to separate parts of the program, allowing them to be more easily recognized when program listings are being read.

Names in programs

There are many places in a program where the programmer has to invent names for objects. In the example program above a name was required for the program itself and for the constant which was used in the program. These names are known as *identifiers*; there are a number of rules for constructing identifiers. Some of these rules are imposed by Ada, some are suggestions which are included in order to make program listings more readable.

Identifiers should be as meaningful as possible without being verbose. For example, neither

> *s1* nor *TheFirstStudentOnTheList*

are regarded as being good identifiers in terms of style. The first, '*s1*' is too short to be meaningful and the second too long to be convenient. Better identifiers might be:

> *Student1* or *FirstStudent*

This rule is a style requirement not an Ada requirement. Ada does not impose any restrictions on the minimum length of an identifier; in the example just cited, the identifier could simply be '*S*'.

Ada does not place any restriction on the maximum length of an identifier but some compilers, particularly those on microcomputers, do not distinguish different names beyond a certain number of characters. If a compiler will only distinguish different identifiers on the basis of the first eight characters then it will be unable to distinguish between these three identifiers:

```
Student11      Student12      Student13
↑↑↑↑↑↑↑↑       ↑↑↑↑↑↑↑↑       ↑↑↑↑↑↑↑↑
12345678       12345678       12345678
```

Ada will regard all these identifiers as being *Student1*. Consequently you should ensure that the identifiers you use in your program can be distinguished by the compiler you are using. A more usual limit is 31 or 32 characters, which is large enough for most people to construct unique meaningful identifiers.

Spaces are not allowed in identifiers but multiple word identifiers are encouraged, using the embedded capital convention to remove the spaces:

```
not allowed      The ultimate answer
allowed          TheUltimateAnswer
```

Programmer defined names are not allowed to conflict with Ada reserved words, so using the following as identifiers is not allowed:

> *Constant   Procedure*

Non-reserved Ada words which have a pre-defined meaning can be used as identifiers, so the following would be allowed as identifiers:

```
String      Put_line
```

Using these as identifiers either gives them a different meaning from their pre-defined meaning or adds an additional meaning to their existing meaning or meanings. Giving a different meaning should be avoided unless it is certain that a redefinition is actually required. Adding an additional meaning is a very powerful Ada facility which will be introduced in due course.

Constants in programs

Constants should be used in a program wherever there is a value which is not going to change within the program. The following are examples of numeric constants which might be declared:

Name	Type	Value	Notes
YardsToMiles	INTEGER	1760	No. of yards in one mile
WeeksInaYear	INTEGER	52	No. of weeks in one year
MaxNoStudents	INTEGER	80	Max No. of students in a class
Pi	FLOAT	3.142	Pi, geometric constant
LitresToPints	FLOAT	0.568	No. of litres in 1 pint
PintsToLitres	FLOAT	1.7606	No. of pints in 1 litre
ExitChoice	CHARACTER	'x'	Menu option to leave program
Greeting	STRING	"Hello"	Standard greeting, change to "Bonjour" etc. for internationalization

Declared constants have two advantages. The first is that where they are used in calculations, the name of the constant can be used in place of the value allowing the meaning of the program to become clearer:

```
ImperialVolume := MetricVolume * 0.568;
ImperialVolume := MetricVolume * LitresToPints;
```

Without fully understanding the meanings of these statements, it should be clear that the second version of the statement is more meaningful than the first version.

The second advantage of constants is that should the value of a constant have to be changed only a single change to the text of the program is needed. In the example above, if the maximum number of students is increased to 100, then only the declaration of the constant will have to be changed. The program should be constructed so that changing the value in the constant declaration will cause other changes in the program, but will ensure that the program still works correctly.

One of the principles which was introduced in the previous chapter to differentiate between well constructed programs and poorly constructed programs was the ease with which the program could be reconfigured when a change is required. The appropriate use of constants will allow such reconfiguration to be more easily accomplished.

Constants are only constant within the time that a program is being executed. In the examples above some of the constants will never change, for example the number of yards in a mile. Other constants may change during the life cycle of the application; for example, greater accuracy may be required in the value of Pi, or the maximum number of students may increase. However, whilst a program is executing the value of a program constant cannot be changed.

An alternative program listing

This is an alternative program which will behave in exactly the same way as the first program:

```
0001    -- Filename AlternativeUltimateAnswer.ada (k8 alternat.adb).
0002    -- Alternative introductory Ada program,
0003    -- developed for Section I Chapter 2.
0004    -- ONLY.
0005    -- Fintan Culwin, v0.1, Jan 1997.
0006
0007    with ADA.TEXT_IO;
0008    use  ADA.TEXT_IO;
0009
0010    procedure AlternativeUltimateAnswer is
0011
0012       MessageLine1 : constant STRING := "The answer to life,";
0013       MessageLine2 : constant STRING :=
0014                              "the universe and everything is -";
0015       TheAnswer    : constant STRING := "forty two.";
0016
0017    begin -- AlternativeUltimateAnswer
0018       PUT( MessageLine1 ); NEW_LINE;
0019       PUT( MessageLine2 ); NEW_LINE;
0020       PUT( TheAnswer );    NEW_LINE;
0021    end AlternativeUltimateAnswer;
```

There are several differences between the two programs:

- All string literals are now declared as string constants.

- Each PUT_LINE has been replaced with a sequence of PUT and NEW_LINE. (An example of where two statements can appear on the same line.)

- Extra spaces have been included to line up similar parts of the program listing. (This is intended to aid readability.)

- An overlong line has been split over two lines at a convenient point. (This is also intended to aid readability.)

The important point about this alternative implementation is not the differences between it and the first implementation. The point is that alternative implementations are possible. For any program specification there is always more than one possible implementation; for a complex specification there will be a large number of possible implementations. It is not sufficient for a programmer to produce an implementation which merely appears to fulfil the specification; it is also necessary for the programmer to produce a 'good' implementation.

This implies that there must be methods of examining alternative implementations and measuring the 'goodness' of the alternatives. Methods of measuring the goodness of program designs and implementations do exist; the intent in this book is to introduce methods which will ensure good designs are produced, and consequently that good programs are implemented from them.

A second specification

The specification for a second program might be that when the program is executed it might produce an interaction with the user as follows:

```
Most Ultimate Answer
The answer to life, the universe and everything is 42
How many universes are there 17
The answer to life, the universes and everything is 714
```

In this example interaction the items shown in bold may change every time the program is executed, and the parts which are bold and underlined indicate the inputs which the user might supply. If the program were executed a second time the user might reply that there were 23 universes in which case the output of the program would be 966.

To develop a program from this specification there are two design stages to go through before the code can be produced. The design stages are to design the data and subsequently to design the program.

The data design

The data design for the first program consisted only of constant program objects, which were defined as parts of the program which would not change no matter how many times the program was executed. Additionally this program has a requirement for the design of *variables*. These are the data objects which might change every time the program was executed.

One technique for starting to identify the variables which are required for a program is to identify those parts of the interaction which may change every time the program is executed. From the example interaction above there are two parts of the program which may change: the input representing the number of universes and the output indicating the most ultimate answer. Using this understanding of the specification, the constant and variable tables for the program which is about to be produced might be:

Program constants

Name	Type	Value	Notes
ProgramTitle	STRING	"Most Ultimate Answer"	Title for the program
InitialPrompt	STRING	"The answer to life, the universe and everything is"	Prompt for the initial output of the simple answer
SimpleAnswer	INTEGER	42	The value of the simple answer
InputPrompt		"How many universes are there"	Prompt for input of number of universes
MostUltimate Prompt	STRING	"The answer to life, the universes and everything is"	Prompt for the output of the most ultimate answer

Program variables

Name	Type	Initial value	Notes
NumberOfUniverses	INTEGER	??	Input from user
MostUltimateAnswer	INTEGER	??	Calculated and output to user

A variable table differs from a constant table by the renaming of the value column to initial value. A variable, like a constant, has to have an identifier, a data type and a note explaining its use. Unlike a constant it does not have to be given a value as it is declared, although for some specification it may have an initial value. In this design neither variable has an initial value and this is indicated by the double question mark in the initial value column. The appropriate data type for both these variables is INTEGER, a pre-declared data type which can contain numeric values without any decimal parts.

Following the completion of the data design, the design of the program can continue with the program design.

The program design

Program design commences by indicating that the program consists of a single component called *MostUltimateAnswer*:

Most Ultimate Answer

As this is too complex to be written directly in Ada, it is ***refined*** into a number of smaller, simpler components:

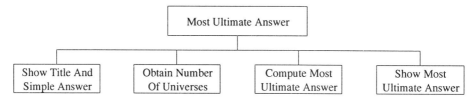

This design now states that in order to do the program *MostUltimateAnswer* it is first necessary to show the title and the simple answer, then obtain the number of universes, then compute the most ultimate answer before finally showing the most ultimate answer. If all four of these activities are carried out in the sequence suggested then the program specification will have been fulfilled, as can be confirmed by referring to the specification above.

Each of the first level subsidiary components has to be checked in turn in order to determine if they are suitable for implementation directly as Ada statements, or if they require further refinement. The first component, *ShowTitleAndSimple-Answer*, can be refined into two components, *ShowTitle* and *ShowSimpleAnswer*:

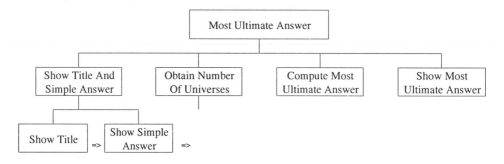

Likewise the second first level component *ObtainNumberOfUniverses* will have to be refined into two components, *ShowInputPrompt* and *AcceptNumber-OfUniverses*. And the final component will have to be refined into two components, *ShowMostUltimateAnswerPrompt* and *ShowMostUltimateValue*. This produces the final design as

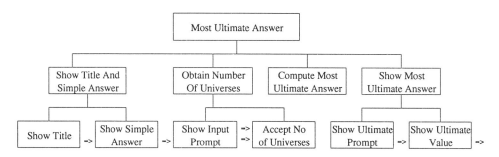

The third first level component, *ComputeMostUltimateAnswer*, does not require any further refinement as it can be implemented directly as a single Ada statement. Refinement of any design component has to continue until the components into which it is refined into are sufficiently simple to be implemented as a single Ada statement, or a very simple sequence of Ada statements.

This design technique presents a problem to novice programmers designing their initial programs as the facilities of the Ada language are unknown and the level to which designs have to be refined is consequently unknown. The only solution to this 'chicken and egg' problem is to study the design decisions which are made in a number of simple programs and, more importantly, to design and implement a number of simple specifications. As was emphasized in the introductory chapter the only way to learn how to do software development is to develop software.

The final design presented above indicates by the use of input and output symbols (=>), those components which output information from the program to the terminal and those which accept information from the keyboard. The final design can be read using a ***top-down–left–right*** rule where each component is read from left to right with each refined component having its components read, before the next component at the same level is read. Applying this rule to the design above it can be read as

> In order to perform the program *MostUltimateAnswer* it is necessary first to perform the component *ShowTitleAndSimpleAnswer*. In order to perform the component *ShowTitleAndSimpleAnswer* it is necessary first to perform the component *ShowTitle* followed by the component *ShowSimpleAnswer*. After performing the component *ShowTitleAndSimpleAnswer* the component *ObtainNumberOfUniverses* is performed by performing the components *ShowInputPrompt* and *AcceptNoOfUniverses*. Following *ShowTitleAndSimpleAnswer* the component *ComputeMostUltimateAnswer*

is performed, and finally the component *ShowMostUltimateAnswer* is performed by performing *ShowMostUltimatePrompt* and *ShowMostUltimateValue*.

The design components can be categorized as either **elementary components**, which appear at the periphery of the design and are not refined further; or **structural components** which appear inside the design and are refined into either further structural and/or elementary components. If the sequence in which the **elementary components** are performed is extracted from this reading of the design they appear in the following sequence:

>*ShowTitle*
>*ShowSimpleAnswer*
>*ShowInputPrompt*
>*AcceptNoOfUniverses*
>*ComputeMostUltimateAnswer*
>*ShowMostUltimatePrompt*
>*ShowMostUltimateValue*

When compared with the illustrative interaction, this indicates that the design will correctly perform its specification. This **design review** at this stage in the production process is essential. The next stage in program development is the production of the source code and any flaws in the design will result in errors in the code which is produced. It is much simpler and cheaper to remove errors from a program at the design stage than after the code has been produced, and one technique to discover design errors is carefully to 'walk through' the design following its operations by reading it as above.

The program code

The implementation of this design as an Ada source code program might be as follows:

```
0001    -- Filename MostUltimateAnswer.ada (k8 mostulti.adb).
0002    -- Introductory Ada program for Section I Chapter 2,
0003    -- including the use of INTEGER variables.
0004    --
0005    -- Fintan Culwin, v0.1, Jan 1997.
0006
0007    with ADA.TEXT_IO;
0008    use  ADA.TEXT_IO;
0009
0010    procedure MostUltimateAnswer is
0011
```

```
0012      package IntegerIO is new TEXT_IO.INTEGER_IO( INTEGER );
0013      use IntegerIO;
0014
0015      ProgramTitle      : constant STRING :=
0016                                  "Most Ultimate Answer";
0017      InitialPrompt     : constant STRING :=
0018         "The answer to life, the universe and everything is ";
0019      InputPrompt       : constant STRING :=
0020                                  "How many universes are there ";
0021      MostUltimatePrompt : constant STRING :=
0022         "The answer to life, the universes and everything is ";
0023
0024      SimpleAnswer      : constant INTEGER := 42;
0025
0026      NumberOfUniverses  : INTEGER;
0027      MostUltimateAnswer : INTEGER;
0028
0029   begin -- MostUltimateAnswer
0030      -- Show Title And Ultimate Answer
0031      -- Show Title
0032      SET_COL( 10); PUT_LINE( ProgramTitle);
0033      NEW_LINE( 2);
0034
0035      -- Show Simple Answer
0036      PUT( InitialPrompt);
0037      PUT( SimpleAnswer); NEW_LINE;
0038
0039      -- Obtain Number Of Universes
0040      -- Show Input Prompt
0041      PUT( InputPrompt);
0042      -- Accept Number of Universes
0043      GET( NumberOfUniverses); SKIP_LINE;
0044
0045      -- Compute Most Ultimate Answer
0046      MostUltimateAnswer := SimpleAnswer * NumberOfUniverses;
0047
0048      -- Show Most Ultimate Answer
0049      -- Show Most Ultimate Prompt
0050      PUT( MostUltimatePrompt);
0051      -- Show Most Ultimate Value
0052      PUT( MostUltimateAnswer); NEW_LINE;
0053
0054   end MostUltimateAnswer;
```

The first part of the listing comprising the header comments and the program's context clause are identical to those of the program 'UltimateAnswer' given earlier in this chapter.

The first part of the program declarations, on lines 0012 and 0013, prepares the program for the input and output of INTEGER values. Ada does not know how to input and output values of the pre-declared type INTEGER, but the package ADA.TEXT_IO contains within it facilities for the *instantiation* of a suitable package. Line 0012 creates an instance of (hence instantiation) a general purpose package called INTEGER_IO contained within the package TEXT_IO which can be used for the input/output of INTEGER values. A full explanation of the meaning of instantiation from general purpose (*generic*) packages cannot be given at this stage; all that can be said is that whenever a program has a requirement for the input and output of INTEGER values line 0012 has to be included within the program's declarations. Once the new package has been instantiated it can be brought into direct visibility by the use of a **use** clause, as shown on line 0013.

The program declarations continue on lines 0015 to 0022 with the declarations of the STRING constants which were designed in the data table and are comparable with the declaration of STRING constants in the previous program. Line 0024 declares the INTEGER constant, *SimpleAnswer*, its type is specified as INTEGER and its value is expressed as an INTEGER literal (42).

The declarations conclude with the declaration of the two INTEGER variables, *NumberOfUniverses* and *MostUltimateAnswer*. The absence of the reserved word **constant** indicates that these are variables and as they do not have an initial value no value is specified. The state of the three INTEGER objects, *SimpleAnswer*, *NumberOfUniverses* and *MostUltimateAnswer*, following their declaration can be visualized as:

SimpleAnswer		*NumberOfUniverses*		*MostUltimateAnswer*
42		??		??
INTEGER		INTEGER		INTEGER

Each object has: a name, shown in italics at the top of the diagram; a data type, shown at the bottom of the diagram; and a value, shown in the middle of the diagram. The value of *SimpleAnswer* is constant and this is indicated by the heavy lines around the value part of the diagram.

The body of the program procedure, *MostUltimateAnswer*, between lines 0029 and 0051 has been heavily commented using the component names from the design. This allows a design and implementation to be easily cross referenced, although it could be argued that the number of comments in this implementation is excessive.

The first part of the body, on lines 0030 to 0033, implements the design component *ShowTitle*. It starts on line 0032 with the use of a facility called SET_COL (set column) from ADA.TEXT_IO which ensures that the output of the program title starts at column 10 of the terminal, as indicated by the visualization above. The title itself is output by use of PUT_LINE, and is separated by two lines from the rest of the interface by use of the ADA.TEXT_IO facility NEW_LINE.

The output of the *SimpleAnswer* follows: the *InitialPrompt* is output to the terminal by use of the ADA.TEXT_IO, PUT facility rather than use of the PUT_LINE facility. The difference between these two facilities is that PUT_LINE will advance to the next line of the terminal after the string has been output, but PUT will remain on the same line. The PUT facility from *IntIO* is used to output the value of the INTEGER constant *SimpleAnswer*. PUT_LINE cannot be used here as it only exists in the package ADA.TEXT_IO and cannot be used for the output of INTEGER values. However, the same effect, of moving the terminal output on to the next line, can be accomplished by the use of NEW_LINE as shown in line 0037. If PUT_LINE were used in program line 0036 then the *InitialPrompt* and the value of *SimpleAnswer* would be on different output lines, as shown below:

```
The answer to life the universe and everything is
42
```

This is not as acceptable to the user as having both items on the same output line, as shown in the user interface design, and accomplished by use of PUT on program line 0036.

Lines 0039 to 0043 implement the component *ObtainNumberOfUniverses*; the first part of this component, *ShowInputPrompt* is implemented using the ADA.TEXT_IO PUT facility as discussed above. Line 0043 accepts from the user the value of the *NumberOfUniverses* by making use of the *IntIo* facility GET. When Ada reaches this part of the listing she will stop and wait for the user to input an INTEGER value from the keyboard. The INTEGER value input will be stored in the variable mentioned as a part of the GET, in this example *Number-OfUniverses*. Assuming that the user inputs the value 17, the state of the three program objects shown above will change to

SimpleAnswer		NumberOfUniverses		MostUltimateAnswer
42		17		??
INTEGER		INTEGER		INTEGER

The listing continues with the implementation of the component *Compute-MostUltimateAnswer* on line 0046. This Ada statement can be read as: 'The value of *MostUltimateAnswer* becomes equal to the value of *SimpleAnswer* multiplied by the value of *NumberOfUniverses*.' When this statement is obeyed by Ada, the

31

value of the three program objects becomes

SimpleAnswer
42
INTEGER

NumberOfUniverses
17
INTEGER

MostUltimateAnswer
714
INTEGER

The program listing concludes with the component *ShowMostUltimateAnswer*, whose implementation is comparable with the implementation of *ShowSimple-Answer* on lines 0035 to 0037, before concluding on line 0054.

Producing a program

The programs above can be regarded as handwritten program listings. In order to execute them on a computer there are a number of stages to go through. These stages depend upon the computer system and the compiler which is being used. The combination of machine and compiler is called the ***environment***.

One class of environment is known as an ***integrated environment***, where the programmer works from a 'work-bench' which provides the developer with access, via pull-down menus, to all the tools which are required for the development of Ada programs. An example of an integrated environment, the GW/Gnat environment, is shown in Figure 2.1.

The alternative environment is known as a ***command line*** environment where the developer has to invoke the separate tools, editors, compilers, linkers and run time support from an operating system command line.

The command line environment which will be considered here is DEC Ada on a VAX series computer. The details of the process may change for other environments, but the processes will be largely the same. In order to implement a simple program on the VAX there are various stages to go through: these are summarized in Figure 2.2.

EVE is an editor; it is used to make the source file. In this example the source file will be called *Program.ada*. The source file contains the text of the program, that is a copy of the program instructions given above in a machine readable format. There are other editors which could be used to produce the source file. Which editor is used is not important; what is important is that a text file containing the text of the program is produced by the editor.

The text file *Program.ada* is then used by the Ada compiler to produce an *OBJ*ect file *Program.obj*. The object file is a translation of the Ada text program into a form which a particular computer can understand; this process is known as compilation. The file produced by the compiler *Program.obj* does not contain all the instructions which are required for the program to run. There is a standard set of computer instructions which have to be added to any program so that it can run

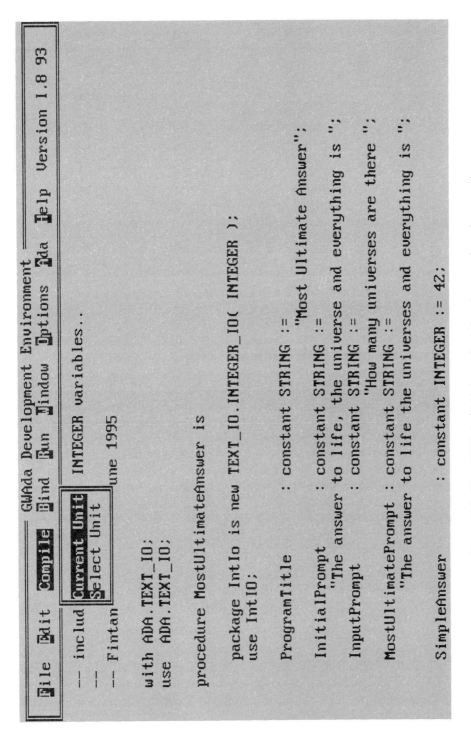

Figure 2.1 The GWAda/Ed integrated development environment.

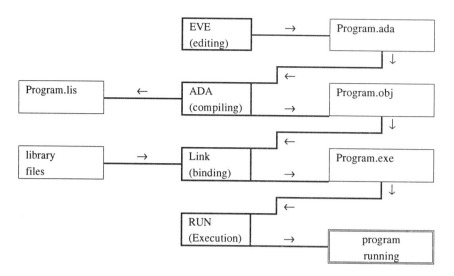

Figure 2.2 The VAX Ada command line environment.

on a particular machine. In the example program above the instructions for the output of text information will also have to be added to the object file.

The addition of these instructions to the program instructions is performed by the *LINK*er. The linker takes the file *Program.obj* as input and links it to the standard set of instructions which can be found in the library files. The product of the linker is an *EXE*cutable file called *Program.exe*. The process of linking is also known as binding when Ada executables are being produced.

Having produced the executable file it can then be executed by the computer using the RUN command. The complete sequence of instructions in the VAX environment might be as follows:

```
$EVE program.ada   -- edit the program to produce
                   -- the text file
          -- editing session here
$ADA program.ada   -- compile the program to produce
                   -- the object file
$ACS LINK program -- link the object file to produce
                   -- the executable
$RUN program       -- run the executable
         -- program execution here
```

If an integrated environment is being used the separate stages outlined above still have to be followed, either by activating the tools individually from the menu bar or by using a menu option which will attempt to apply all the tools in sequence, stopping the sequence if any errors occur.

The figure above shows a very unusual situation as it implies that the source file will compile correctly with no errors reported on the first attempt. This is not usually the case; in most cases, the program will not compile correctly on the first attempt.

Assuming the program design and the intended implementation are correct the most common reason why a program will not compile correctly is due to typing errors made as the source file was entered. The reasons why the program would not compile correctly will be displayed on the terminal screen as the program fails compilation.

In these cases the errors have to be identified and interpreted. It is useful to have a *LIS*ting file produced by the compiler which contains the program text and the errors which were detected. A *LIS*ting file, usually called *Program.lis,* can be produced by most compilers.

Using the listing file the errors reported can be interpreted and the changes to the source code decided upon. The editor can then be used on the source file to make the changes required, and the changed source file can then be submitted to the compiler again.

There is no guarantee that the source file will now be error free; compilation will probably indicate that there are still errors. This process of attempted compilation, re-editing of the source file and another compilation attempt can (and does) take place indefinitely. It can be a time consuming and frustrating process. There are methods of reducing the time spent at this stage:

- The program should not be designed at the terminal. Many novice programmers do not produce adequate designs and attempt to compose the program as they are sitting at the terminal. This is rarely a successful practice. The time spent in perfecting the design on paper will be repaid by an easier production of the program at the terminal.

- Program listings should initially be produced from the program design in a handwritten form. The handwritten version can then be carefully checked for errors before entering the program using the editor.

- If (or more likely when) the first compilation attempt fails a hard copy of the listing file should be obtained. The listing file contains a copy of the program and the error messages which were produced by the compiler. The corrections should be made by hand on the listing file, before taking it back to the editor and re-editing the source file.

This does seem as if it would take more time than just sitting at a terminal and entering the program or correcting the errors. However, it is easier to spot and correct errors when the whole program is visible on a listing, than when only a small part of the program can be seen on the screen at one time.

Some integrated environments will automatically activate the editor, positioning the editing cursor at the location of the first error and displaying the appropriate error message in a separate window. These facilities are so convenient to use that the danger of attempting to implement or correct a program at the terminal can become overwhelming. The advice to generate a program listing and make corrections on paper before entering them into the computer must be emphasized when using an integrated environment.

EXERCISES

2.1 Comment upon the suitability or otherwise of the following constant identifiers. For unsuitable identifiers suggest an alternative.

Constant	Suggested identifier
Conversion factor between pounds and dollars	*PTD*
The speed of light	*c*
The cost per unit of electricity used	*UnitCost*
The fastest marathon time	*Record*
The number of smarties in a tube	*TheNumberOfSmartiesInaTube*

2.2 The following is the (simulated) output of a VAX Ada compiler including compilation error messages. Identify and correct each error to produce a correct version of the program.

```
1-- filename WrongOne.ada
2-- Trivial Ada program containing deliberate errors,
3-- for Section I Chapter 2 of Ada book.
4--
5-- Fintan Culwin, v0.1, Jan 1997
8
6 with ADA.TEXT_IO; use ADA.TEXT_IO;
7
8 procedure WrongOne is ;
........................1
%ADAC-E-IGNOREUNEXP, (1) Unexpected ";" ignored
9
10 msg1 : STRING constant := 'Data design + ';
.............................1...........2............3
 %ADAC-E-LEXAPOST, (2) Invalid apostrophe ('); possible
    unterminated character literal or string literal
    delimited by apostrophe (') instead of by quotation
    marks (")
 %ADAC-E-LEXAPOST, (3) Invalid apostrophe ('); possible
    unterminated character literal or string literal
    delimited by apostrophe (') instead of by quotation
    marks (")
```

```
%ADAC-E-FOUNDEXP, (1) Found reserved-word "constant" when
                                          expecting one
  of { "delta" "digits" "range" "renames" "'" "("
                                          "." ":=" ";" }
%ADAC-I-IGNOREDECLL, (1) Declaration ignored due to
  syntactic errors
11
12 begin WrongOne
...................1
%ADAC-E-INSSEMI, (1) Inserted ";" at end of line
13 PUT( "msg1 ");
14 PUT( "+ program design ");
15 PUT( " = programming.");
16 end Wrong1;
............1
%ADAC-E-PM_NAMDOENOTMAT, (1) Name Wrong1 does not match
WrongOne at line 8
```

2.3 The following is the (simulated) output of the *gnat* Ada compiler including compilation error messages. Identify and correct each error to produce a correct version of the program.

```
1 -- filename WrongToo.ada
2 -- Trivial Ada program containing deliberate errors,
3 -- for Section I Chapter 2 of Ada book.
4 --
5 -- Fintan Culwin, v0.1, Jan 1997
6
7 procidure WrongToo is;
"wrongtoo.adb", line 7: error: Incorrect spelling of
keyword
"procedure"'
"wrongtoo.adb", line 7: error: declaration expected
8
9    MessageOne : constant STRINF :=
                              "Ada error messages are";
"wrongtoo.adb', line 9: error: "STRINF" is undefined
10    MessageTwo : constant STRING :=
                              "Not always very helpful";
"wrongtoo.adb", line 10: error: missing string quote
11    ErrorCount : constant STRING := "eight ";
12
13 begin -- WrongToo
14    PUT_LINE( MessageOne );
"wrongtoo.adb", line 14: error: "PUT_LINE" is undefined
15    PUT_LINE( MessageTwo );
16    PUT( "This program contains at least ");
```

```
"wrongtoo.adb", line 16: error: "PUT" is undefined
17    PUT( ErrorCount, "errors ");
"wrongtoo.adb", line 19: error: invalid parameter list in
 call
18    PUT("and is only 20 lines long");
19    NEW_LINE;
"wrongtoo.adb", line 19: error: "NEW_LINE" is undefined
20 end WrongToo;
```

2.4 Using the corrected listings from Exercises 2.2 and 2.3, learn how to use your Ada environment by entering, compiling and running the programs. This will also allow you to find out if you can manage to detect and correct all the errors.

CHAPTER 3
Using packages and subprograms

The exercises from the previous chapter should have indicated that the construction of software is a laborious and error prone activity. One of the most effective ways to make the development of software less laborious is to make use of software components which have already been developed. In the previous chapter this was illustrated when the *standard package* ADA.TEXT_IO was used for the input and output of information.

This chapter will provide a more formal introduction to the contents of the ADA.TEXT_IO package in order both to introduce its input/output facilities, but more importantly to introduce the use of packages and of the facilities which they contain.

The package ADA.TEXT_IO

ADA.TEXT_IO is a large and complex package and only a small part of it will be introduced in this chapter. Most of the remaining parts of the package will be introduced throughout the rest of the book. ADA.TEXT_IO is an example of a *standard package*, which are the packages which every implementation of Ada is obliged to provide. Thus it can be guaranteed that every Ada environment will supply a version of every standard package. It can also be guaranteed that facilities supplied by these packages will be identical in every environment.

The ADA.TEXT_IO object diagram

One of the easiest ways to see what is provided by ADA.TEXT_IO, or by any other package, is to examine, or construct, an *object diagram*. A very simplified object diagram for the ADA.TEXT_IO package might be as follows:

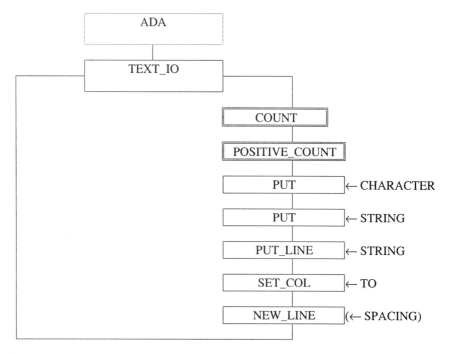

The diagram indicates, at the top, that the package TEXT_IO is a ***child package*** of a package called ADA which is assumed to exist. The package ADA does not actually exist; it is simply assumed to exist in order to provide a ***parent package*** for a number of standard packages, including TEXT_IO. As the package ADA does not actually exist it is shown on the diagram with dotted lines.

The facilities which are publicly exported by ADA.TEXT_IO are shown on the right hand side of the object diagram crossing the line which encloses the inside of the package. The first two things which are exported are ***data types***, as indicated by the double lined boxes. The types are called COUNT and POSITIVE_COUNT. The other five things which are exported are ***subprograms***, indicated by the simple boxes and the arrowed ***data flow*** going into the boxes. Data types can be thought of as objects which can contain information and subprograms can be thought of as actions which can be applied to the objects.

ADA.TEXT_IO subprogram data flow interface diagrams

More detailed information concerning the ADA.TEXT_IO subprograms can be provided by ***subprogram data flow interface diagrams***, more conveniently known as *data flow diagrams*. The data flow diagrams for the first subprogram from the object diagram above would be

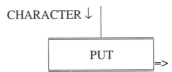

Output the value of CHARACTER on the terminal, with no <RETURN>.

This data flow diagram indicates by the double horizontal lines, and the capitalized name, that this subprogram is pre-declared. The name of the subprogram is PUT, the arrowed data flow at the top of the diagram indicates that it always needs to be supplied with a single CHARACTER value, and the double lined arrow at the right indicates that it will output some information to the terminal.

The data flow may be labelled with either the name of the object being passed to the subprogram or its type, depending upon which makes the most sense. The note under the diagram gives some indication of what actions the subprogram will do when it is used. In this explanation it indicates that the character output will not be followed by a <RETURN> so that subsequent output will appear on the same line.

The data flow diagrams for the next three subprograms are similar to that given above:

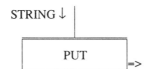

Output the value of STRING on the terminal, with no <RETURN>.

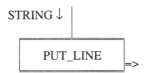

Output the value of STRING on the terminal, followed by a <RETURN>.

Output spaces to the terminal until the next output will appear
at column TO, even if that means moving on to the next line.

The data flow diagram for the last subprogram, NEW_LINE, differs in having its data flow enclosed in brackets:

If SPACING is supplied output that many <RETURN>s,
otherwise output a single <RETURN>.

The brackets indicate that NEW_LINE may, or may not, be supplied with a value for SPACING. If SPACING is supplied it will be an integer value and the subprogram will output that number of <RETURN>s. Otherwise, if a value for SPACING is not supplied a single <RETURN> will be output.

ADA.TEXT_IO subprogram declarations

More detailed information concerning the subprograms can be obtained by constructing or reading the subprogram *declarations*. These are written in Ada and give both the names of the data flow objects and also their data type. A subprogram can be either a **procedure** or a **function**. For reasons which will be given later, all of the subprograms in the object diagram above are procedures. The procedure declarations are as follows:

```
procedure PUT( ITEM : in CHARACTER);
-- Output the value of ITEM to the terminal,
-- with no <RETURN>.

procedure PUT( ITEM : in STRING);
-- Output the value of ITEM to the terminal,
-- with no <RETURN>.

procedure PUT_LINE( ITEM : in STRING);
-- Output the value of ITEM to the terminal,
-- followed by a single <RETURN>.

procedure SET_COL( TO : in POSITIVE_COUNT);
-- Output spaces to the terminal until the next
-- character output will appear at column TO,
-- even if that means moving onto the next line.

procedure NEW_LINE( SPACING : in POSITIVE_COUNT := 1);
-- Output SPACING <RETURN>s to the terminal.
```

The ADA.TEXT_IO package specification

The final way in which the facilities of the ADA.TEXT_IO package may be expressed is in its *package specification.* This is also written in Ada and collects together the declaration of the data types, the subprogram declarations and possibly other facilities as well. The package specification file for the simplified ADA.TEXT_IO package may be as follows:

```
0001    -- Filename ADA.TEXT_IO_.pkg (k8 a-text_i.ads).
0002    -- Supposed package specification for a simplified
0003    -- ADA.TEXT_IO standard package.
0004    --
0005    -- Produced for the Ada book Section I Chapter 3.
0006    -- Fintan Culwin, v0.1, Jan 1997.
0007
0008    package ADA.TEXT_IO is
0009
0010        type COUNT is range 0 .. INTEGER'LAST;
0011        subtype POSITIVE_COUNT is COUNT range 1 .. COUNT'LAST;
0012
0013        procedure PUT( ITEM : in CHARACTER);
0014        -- Output the value of ITEM to the terminal,
0015        -- with no <RETURN>.
0016
0017        procedure PUT( ITEM : in STRING);
0018        -- Output the value of ITEM to the terminal,
0019        -- with no <RETURN>.
0020
0021        procedure PUT_LINE( ITEM : in STRING);
0022        -- Output the value of ITEM to the terminal,
0023        -- followed by a single
0024
0025        procedure SET_COL( TO : in POSITIVE_COUNT);
0026        -- Output spaces to the terminal until the next
0027        -- character output will appear at column TO,
0028        -- even if that means moving onto the next line.
0029
0030        procedure NEW_LINE( SPACING : in POSITIVE_COUNT := 1);
0031        -- Output SPACING <RETURN>s to the terminal.
0032
0033    end ADA.TEXT_IO;
```

The **type** and **subtype** declarations on lines 0010 and 0011 make available a specialized INTEGER type which is used by the ADA.TEXT_IO subprograms. The reasons for using a specialized INTEGER type, instead of using the pre-declared INTEGER type, will be fully explained in Section II.

Object diagrams, data flow diagrams, subprogram declarations and package specifications

The previous part of this chapter has presented the facilities of the ADA.TEXT_IO package in four different ways: object diagrams, data flow diagrams, subprogram declarations and package specifications. This part of the chapter will attempt to explain why there are so many different representations and which representation is most useful under which circumstances.

The most obvious difference between the representations is that two, subprogram declarations and package specifications, are expressed in Ada, and two, object diagrams and data flow diagrams, are expressed using a visual notation. The visual notations are more suitable for a rapid visual inspection to obtain an overall indication of the facilities of a package or a subprogram. The Ada representations are required for compilation and, when the associated comments are also considered, give the most detailed information concerning the facilities.

Another difference is one of scale: object diagrams and package specifications represent the contents of an entire package. Data flow diagrams and subprogram declarations give information concerning a single subprogram. Object diagrams and package specifications also give a more complete indication of the contents of a package. In addition to subprograms they will include information concerning data types, and other facilities yet to be introduced, which may be provided by a package.

The discussion on the various representations has so far concentrated upon using them to gain an understanding of the contents of a pre-supplied package. They can also be used when a ***developer declared package*** is being produced. The two visual notations are useful for sketching and refining a design, which could start with an object diagram whose actions do not have the data flow specified. A data flow interface diagram is then useful for the detailed design of the data flow required by each subprogram. The types of the data flows may then indicate that a data type has to be supplied by the package, and this information can be fed back into a refinement of the object diagram.

Once the data flow interface diagrams have been finalized, each diagram can then be used to produce its corresponding subprogram declaration. The processes of transforming a data flow interface diagram into a subprogram declaration, or vice versa, are amongst the most mechanical and thus easiest of activities involved in software development.

Likewise the subprogram declarations produced at this stage will be required when the package specification is constructed. The object diagram will indicate what other facilities will have to be included in its public declarations.

Before leaving the topic of visual notations, the relationship between the *JSP diagrams* introduced in the previous chapter and the various notations introduced in this chapter will be explained. The subprogram interface diagrams describe *what* data flow interface a subprogram has. The notes associated with the diagram and the comments with the *declaration* give additional details of *what* actions the subprogram perform. There is an additional Ada component required by a sub-program – its *definition*. This expresses to Ada not *what* the subprogram does, but *how* it does it. All but the simplest subprograms will require a corresponding JSP diagram to design, or to describe, the actions of the subprogram.

In a similar way the *public* part of a package specification states only *what* facilities a package supplies. Two additional parts, the *private* part of the package specification and the *package body*, express *how* the package implements these facilities. Details of the public and private parts of package specifications and of package bodies will be given in the next chapters when developer declared packages are introduced.

Using ADA.TEXT_IO

The section above gave a description of the facilities which are contained within the standard package ADA.TEXT_IO; this part of the chapter will describe the techniques by which the facilities can be used. A package makes public a set of facilities which can be used by other software components which are being assembled, or produced, to construct an application. The component which makes use of the facilities supplied by a package is said to be a *client* of that package. So the example programs from the previous chapter could be said to be client programs of ADA.TEXT_IO.

A client program makes use of the subprogram facilities of a package by *calling* the subprograms. The client can assume that the package will do *what* it stated it would do in its package specification; it need not be concerned with *how* the package accomplishes this.

In the program *MostUltimateAnswer* in the previous chapter the design component *ShowTitle* was implemented as follows:

```
0032   SET_COL( 10); PUT_LINE( ProgramTitle );
0033   NEW_LINE( 2);
```

This program fragment contains three calls to three of the subprograms supplied by ADA.TEXT_IO: SET_COL, PUT_LINE and NEW_LINE. The calls are accomplished by using the name of the subprogram in a program statement and following the name with the *actual* data flow which will match the *formal* data flow in the declarations.

The procedure declaration of the first subprogram, called SET_COL, indicates that it requires a single data flow of the type POSITIVE_COUNT. The call of SET_COL in this fragment supplies the INTEGER value 10 to match this data flow.

As POSITIVE_COUNT is a specialized INTEGER type, Ada is able to accept this value as being of a suitable type. When the program procedure *MostUltimateAnswer* starts execution its first action is to pass ***flow of control*** to the ADA.TEXT_IO SET_COL procedure and wait for flow of control to be passed back to it.

The concept of flow of control is used by the developer to indicate to Ada which is the next action to be performed. The action of calling the SET_COL procedure can be visualized on a flow of control diagram:

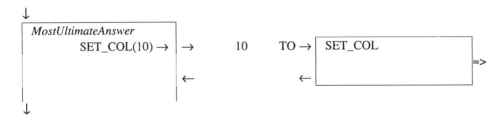

The diagram indicates that flow of control is initially passed to *MostUltimate-Answer* when the user starts the program executing. *MostUltimateAnswer* immediately passes control to SET_COL, passing 10 as the actual data flow value which is received by SET_COL in its TO formal data flow. Flow of control then remains with SET_COL for a period of time, during which it produces output on the terminal. While SET_COL is active, *MostUltimateAnswer* is also active, but suspended and waiting for flow of control to be returned from SET_COL. The suspension of *MostUltimateAnswer* is indicated by its dotted lines. When SET_COL finishes, flow of control is passed back to *MostUltimateAnswer* which can then continue its actions.

The flow of control diagram would continue with the calls of PUT_LINE and NEW_LINE:

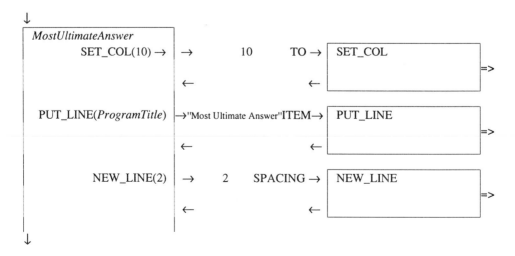

When PUT_LINE is called the actual data flow supplied is the **constant** STRING *ProgramTitle*; what is actually passed is the value of the string "Most Ultimate Answer". This value is received by PUT_LINE in its formal ITEM data flow and is output before control is returned to the *MostUltimateAnswer* program procedure.

Flow of control continues with a call of NEW_LINE, which is comparable with the call of the previous two procedures, and when it returns control to the program procedure flow of control will continue with the remaining instructions.

The interplay of flow of control between programs and subprograms, and between subprogram and subprogram, together with the associated passing of data in the actual and formal data flows is central to the understanding and subsequently the production of Ada programs. What has been described so far as data flows are more commonly known as *parameters*. The value, variable or constant which is supplied by the caller of a subprogram is known as the *actual parameter* and the object into which it is received by the called subprogram is known as the *formal parameter*.

The package ADA.TEXT_IO.INTEGER_IO

In the previous chapter the program *MostUltimateAnswer* introduced the *instantiation* of the package ADA.TEXT_IO.INTEGER_IO for the input and output of the pre-declared INTEGER type. The ADA.TEXT_IO specification, given in the previous part of this chapter, included the declaration of a new INTEGER type, POSITIVE_COUNT, and it was stated that the reasons for declaring new INTEGER types would be given in the next section.

The design and instantiation of ADA.TEXT_IO.INTEGER_IO

As there can thus be a large number of INTEGER types, rather than a single INTEGER type, Ada supplies a general facility for the input and output of INTEGER types in general and no specific facility for the input and output of the pre-declared INTEGER type. This general facility has to be tailored for the input and output of a specific type in the process of instantiation. The instantiation, and subsequent bringing into **use**, of the ADA.TEXT_IO.INTEGER_IO package for the pre-declared INTEGER type was given in the program *MostUltimateAnswer* as follows:

```
0012   package IntegerIO is new TEXT_IO.INTEGER_IO( INTEGER);
0013   use IntegerIO;
```

This instantiation can be thought of as creating a package whose simplified object diagram would be as follows:

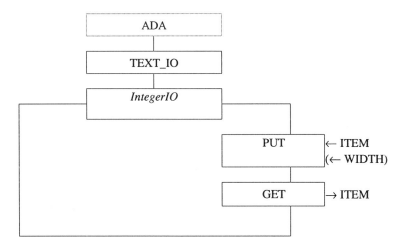

The diagram indicates that the package *IntegerIO* is a child of the package TEXT_IO which is itself a child of the supposed package ADA. The italicization of *IntegerIO* and the use of initial capitals indicates that this name has been chosen by the developer and is not pre-declared.

The package supplies two subprograms, both procedures, one called PUT which will output an INTEGER value and one called GET which will input an INTEGER value. The data flow interface diagrams and subprogram declarations for these actions are as follows:

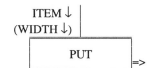

Output a representation of the INTEGER value ITEM on the terminal,
using at least WIDTH characters with no <RETURN>.

```
procedure PUT( ITEM  : in INTEGER;
               WIDTH : in FIELD := DEFAULT_WIDTH );
```

Input an INTEGER value from the terminal, passing it out in
ITEM ignoring any <RETURN>. Raise
CONSTRAINT_ERROR or DATA_ERROR if a problem occurs.

```
procedure GET( ITEM : out INTEGER );
```

The data type FIELD is another specialized INTEGER type and DEFAULT_ WIDTH is a pre-declared value of this type. Both of these are declared in ADA.TEXT_IO and ADA.TEXT_IO.INTEGER_IO, but have been omitted from the object diagrams for the sake of clarity.

The PUT **procedure** will out*Put* a representation of the INTEGER value supplied using at least the number of characters specified in the optional parameter WIDTH. If WIDTH is not specified in the call the default value is usually in the order of eight characters. If the value specified for WIDTH is too small for the value of the integer to be output, for example the value 3456 which would require at least four characters, Ada will ignore the specified value for WIDTH and will use the minimum number of characters required to output the entire value.

The GET **procedure** is in some sense the reverse of the PUT **procedure**. It will accept a sequence of characters from the terminal and attempt to convert them into an INTEGER value, returning the value in the ***out only*** ITEM parameter. If the sequence of characters cannot be converted into an INTEGER value, for example the sequence *"help"*, then Ada will **raise** a DATA_ERROR **exception**. Alternatively if an INTEGER value is supplied, but it is too large for the precise INTEGER type, for example 99999999999999999999 which in most environments is too large for the pre-declared INTEGER type, Ada will raise a CONSTRAINT_ERROR exception. For the simple programs which are being developed in this section any raising of an exception will halt the program. The techniques which can be used to ***handle*** an exception when it is raised will be introduced in the next section.

The supposed package specification for the package *IntegerIO* would be as follows.

```
0001    -- Filename ADA.TEXT_IO.IntegerIO_.pkg (k8 a-te-int.ads).
0002    -- Supposed package specification for a simplified
0003    -- ADA.TEXT_IO.INTEGER_IO standard package, instantiated
0004    -- with the pre-declared INTEGER type.
0005    --
0006    -- Produced for the Ada book Section I Chapter 3.
0007    -- Fintan Culwin, v0.1, Jan 1997.
0008
0009    package ADA.TEXT_IO.IntegerIO is
0010
0011       procedure PUT( ITEM  : in INTEGER;
0012                      WIDTH : in FIELD := DEFAULT_WIDTH);
0013       -- Output a representation of the INTEGER value
0014       -- ITEM on the terminal using at least WIDTH characters
0015       -- with no <RETURN>.
0016
0017       procedure GET( ITEM : out INTEGER);
0018       -- Input an INTEGER value from the terminal, passing it
0019       -- out in ITEM ignoring any <RETURN>. Raise
                                               CONSTRAINT_ERROR
```

```
0020          -- or DATA_ERROR if a problem occurs.
0021
0022    end ADA.TEXT_IO.IntegerIO ;
```

Using *IntegerIO*

The design component *ObtainNumberOfUniverses* from the *MostUltimateAns-wer* program illustrated the use of the GET **procedure** from the *IntegerIO* instantiated package. The implementation of the design was as follows:

```
0040    -- Show Input Prompt
0041    PUT( InputPrompt);
0042    -- Accept Number of Universes
0043    GET( NumberOfUniverses); SKIP_LINE;
```

The call of PUT on line 0041 uses as an actual parameter the STRING constant *InputPrompt*; this allows Ada to decide that the STRING version of the PUT **procedure** from the ADA.TEXT_IO package should be used. The call of the GET **procedure** on line 0043 uses as an actual parameter the INTEGER variable *NumberOfUniverses*; this allows Ada to decide that the INTEGER version of the GET **procedure** from the *IntegerIO* instantiated package should be used.

The *flow of control* diagram for the execution of this part of the program, assuming that the user inputs the value 17, is as follows:

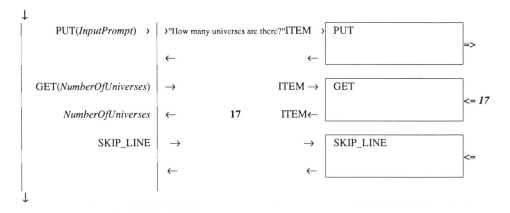

The call of PUT shown at the top of the diagram is comparable with the call of PUT_LINE shown above. The call of GET differs, as the parameter is *out only* and receives a value from GET as opposed to supplying a value as with PUT. When GET is called by the program procedure the *actual parameter* supplied is *NumberOfUniverses*, but no data are passed. Within GET the value (17) is obtained from the user and held in the *formal parameter* ITEM. When flow of control is passed back to the program procedure the value in ITEM is transferred into *NumberOfUniverses*. The effect of this pattern of activity is to store the value which the user inputs in the variable *NumberOfUniverses*.

The GET procedure will only accept the characters '1' and '7' from the terminal keyboard. However, the user has to indicate that he or she has finished typing a line of input with a <RETURN> key press. This <RETURN> character is still waiting to be accepted by the Ada program and may well cause problems the next time the program attempts to obtain any input. The call of SKIP_LINE on line 0043 of the program fragment will cause flow of control to be passed to the ADA.TEXT_IO SKIP_LINE procedure which will accept and throw away the <RETURN> character.

The implementation of the design component *ShowUltimateValue* from the *MostUltimateAnswer* program contains a call to the *IntegerIO* PUT **procedure**:

```
0052    PUT( MostUltimateAnswer); NEW_LINE;
```

This call of the *IntegerIO* PUT **procedure** will output the value of the variable *MostUltimateAnswer*, which, assuming the user input the value 17, would be 714. The flow of control diagram for this part of the program procedure would be as follows:

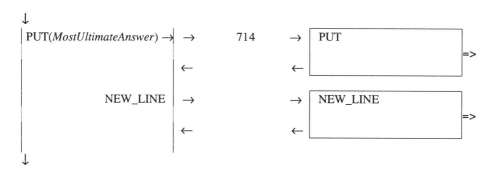

When NEW_LINE is called no value is specified for the optional SPACING parameter, and thus no data flow is shown. NEW_LINE will output the default single <RETURN> as it executes.

Subprogram calls and parameter modes

The explanations of the various ADA.TEXT_IO and ADA.TEXT_IO.*IntegerIO* subprograms given in this chapter are valuable in their own right. However, they have been introduced at this point in the book in order to introduce the subprogram call and parameter passing mechanisms.

The programs introduced in the previous chapter were very small, up to about

50 lines; the smallest realistic program would contain thousands, or many thousands, of lines. In these circumstances it would be almost impossible to construct the program without dividing it into a number of packages, and each package would contain a number of subprograms. A realistic program would also involve the use of packages, and the subprograms which they contain, which have already been developed. Thus the mechanisms by which flow of control, and data, are passed between subprograms are fundamental to the software development process.

The two modes of data flow, *in only* and *out only*, which have been introduced in this chapter are complemented by a third mode, *in out*, which will be introduced in the next chapter where the design and implementation of a package by the developer will be introduced.

EXERCISES

3.1 Produce a complete flow of control diagram for the *MostUltimateAnswer* program from Section I Chapter 2.

3.2 Explore the facilities offered by ADA.TEXT_IO by using it to produce a page of output which makes use of SET_COL and NEW_LINE to space out the information.

3.3 Explore the use of the optional WIDTH parameter in the *IntegerIO* PUT procedure by setting it to different values for the output of the same INTEGER value.

3.4 Explore the behaviour of the *IntegerIO* GET procedure when the user inputs a series of characters which cannot be recognized as an INTEGER value, and when the value supplied is too large an INTEGER value for Ada to cope with.

3.5 Look forward to Section II Chapter 16, where the package specifications of a number of standard packages are given. Without looking at the data flow interface diagrams and object diagrams given in the chapter, attempt to translate them yourself.

CHAPTER 4

Developer supplied packages

The previous chapter introduced techniques for the representation and usage of pre-supplied packages, and the facilities which they provide. This chapter will continue the introduction to the development of software from separate modules by introducing the techniques by which a developer supplied package can be designed, constructed and used. The construction and use of packages, and the facilities which they contain, will be an important theme of the rest of the book. Consequently the contents of this chapter are vital to understanding nearly all of the chapters which follow.

The *TransactionCounter* object

Many different application specifications have a requirement for counting the number of times that something occurs. Examples might include: the number of times a door is opened, the number of vehicles which pass a junction or the number of radioactive particles detected by a Geiger counter. A more obvious application might be to model a mechanical hand-held counter which has a numeric display, a button which increments the value of the display, a button which decrements the value of the display and a button to clear the display. These devices are commonly used to count people as they enter a room or building, by clicking the increment button whenever a person passes the entrance.

The *TransactionCounter* object diagram

A model of this hand-held device, which will be known as a *TransactionCounter*, can be described by an object diagram:

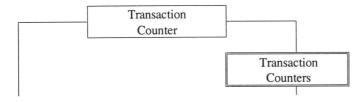

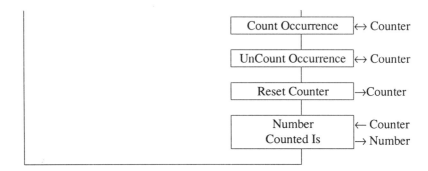

This object diagram can be read in the same way as the object diagrams which were introduced in the previous chapter. This diagram describes the facilities which are supplied by an object called *TransactionCounter*; it supplies a data type called *TransactionCounters* and the subprograms which can be used with instances of the type. The combination of a data type and associated subprograms is one of the most common uses of packages when developing Ada programs. The data type itself is used to provide a model of an ***object*** from the ***real world***, in this case a hand-held transaction counter, and the subprograms are used to model the ***actions*** which can be performed upon an instance of that object.

The diagram above indicates that there are only four actions which can be performed upon a *TransactionCounters* instance in a program which makes use of the object. These are: to count an occurrence (*CountOccurrence*), to uncount an occurrence (*UnCountOccurrence*), to reset the counter to zero (*ResetCounter*) and to find out how many occurrences it has counted (*NumberCountedIs*).

The diagram also introduces the convention that the singular form of the noun which describes the object (*TransactionCounter*) is used as the object diagram's title. But the plural form (*TransactionCounters*) is used for the data type exported by the object diagram. This convention is used because there is only a single object diagram, but an application design can contain many instances of the object.

In out data flow

The object diagram also introduces the third data flow mode, ***in out***, which was mentioned at the end of the previous chapter. This mode is shown on object diagrams as a data flow with a double headed arrow. ***In out*** data flow allows the value of the actual parameter being passed in the data flow to be changed. In the previous chapter the example of ***in only*** data flow in the PUT procedures allowed the subprogram to receive, but not to change, the value of an actual parameter. The ***out only*** data flow, used in the GET procedure, supplied a value to an actual parameter, but did not receive a value in the parameter. The third mode, ***in out***, combines these two modes by both supplying a value to, and receiving a value from, the actual parameter. The effect of this on the part of the program calling the subprogram is that the value of the variable used as the actual parameter may be changed when the subprogram is called.

In the *CountOccurrence* action above this is clearly required. If a *Transaction-Counters* object is being used to count people as they enter a building, the subprogram will have to change the value of the *TransactionCounters* object supplied to it. This implies that it will have to receive the value in order to increment it by one, and then supply the changed value back. The *UnCountOccurrence* action requires **in out** data flow for the same reason.

The *ResetCounter* action will supply a new value for the *TransactionCounter* which is passed to it, but will not need to know its old value before resetting it. Thus this action requires an **out only** data flow. The *NumberCountedIs* action will need to receive the value of the *TransactionCounter* which is passed to it, but will not change the value in any way. Thus this action requires an **in only** data flow. A fuller explanation of these data flow modes will be given below, when a program which makes use of the *TransactionCounter* package is developed and its execution explained.

The *TransactionCounter* data flow diagrams and subprogram declarations

The development of the *TransactionCounter* package should continue with the refinement of the actions from the object diagram into subprogram data flow interface diagrams, and from them into subprogram declarations. This is presented here as a single distinct step, but during the actual development the design of an object may require a number of refinements.

An initial sketch of the object diagram might result in an attempt to produce data flow diagrams, and descriptions of their operations, which indicate that a proposed action is better implemented as two or more distinct actions – or that an action is missing from the diagram, or that a data type is missing from the diagram, or there is some other fault in the diagram. This discovery will result in the object diagram having to be changed, which will result in a second set of data flow diagrams, which might themselves reveal faults, which requires a third version of the object diagram, and so on.

The techniques which can be used in an attempt to circumvent this process will be introduced later in the book. However, design nearly always proceeds by successive refinement, even for skilled and experienced developers, and the only way in which design skills can be learned is by practising the design process. It is much easier and cheaper to refine a design than it is to refine the Ada code once the design has been implemented, and thus the time spent producing a design is rarely wasted.

The data flow diagrams and subprogram declarations for the *Transaction-*

Counter actions are as follows:

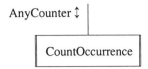

```
procedure CountOccurrence( AnyCounter :
                                in out TransactionCounters);
-- Count an occurrence by incrementing AnyCounter by one.
```

```
procedure UnCountOccurrence( AnyCounter :
                                in out TransactionCounters);
-- Uncount an occurrence by decrementing AnyCounter by one.
```

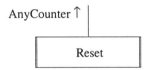

```
procedure ResetCounter( AnyCounter:out TransactionCounters);
-- Reset the value of AnyCounter to zero.
```

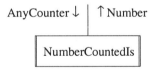

```
function NumberCountedIs( AnyCounter : in TransactionCounters)
                                        return NATURAL;
-- Find out the number of occurrences counted.
```

The reasons why *CountOccurrence*, *UnCountOccurrence* and *ResetCounter* are declared as **procedures** and *NumberCountedIs* is declared as a **function** will be explained in the next chapter. The data type NATURAL which is returned from the *NumberCountedIs* **function** is an INTEGER **subtype** which can only take values greater than or equal to zero. This subtype is used in preference to the INTEGER type itself, as the detailed consideration of the design of this version of the *TransactionCounter* object decided that it could not be used to count a negative number of occurrences.

The subprogram boxes are shown with double vertical lines as the subprograms are under development in the software component currently being described. The ADA.TEXT_IO subprograms used in the previous chapter were shown with double horizontal lines as they were pre-declared, and thus not under development in the current design.

The public parts of the *TransactionCounter* package specification

The next stage in the development of the *TransactionCounter* package is to produce the **public** part of the package specification. A second **private** part of the specification will be given below, where the reasons for having a public and private part will be introduced.

Most of the public part of the specification has already been produced, when the subprogram declarations were constructed from the interface diagrams. Only the declaration of the package itself and of the *TransactionCounters* data type has to be added. The public part of the *TransactionCounter* package specification might be as follows:

```
0001   -- Filename TransactionCounter_.pkg (k8 transact.ads).
0002   -- First developer supplied package containing an
0003   -- extendible data type, which counts occurrences.
0004   --
0005   -- Written for Ada Book Section I Chapter 4.
0006   -- Fintan Culwin, v0.1, Jan 1997.
0007
0008   package TransactionCounter is
0009
0010      type TransactionCounters is tagged private;
0011
0012      procedure CountOccurrence( AnyCounter :
0013                                   in out TransactionCounters);
0014      -- Count an occurrence by incrementing AnyCounter by one.
0015
0016      procedure UnCountOccurrence( AnyCounter :
0017                                   in out TransactionCounters);
0018      -- Uncount an occurrence by decrementing AnyCounter by one.
0019
0020      procedure ResetCounter( AnyCounter : out
0021                                   TransactionCounters);
0021      -- Reset the value of AnyCounter, to zero.
0022
```

```
0023      function NumberCountedIs( AnyCounter : in
                                    TransactionCounters) return NATURAL;
0024
0025      -- Find out the number of occurrences counted.
0026
0027   private
0028
0029      type TransactionCounters is
               Private details omitted for the moment!
0035
0036   end TransactionCounter;
```

The package specification commences with comments identifying who, what, why, when and where, as was explained in previous chapters. The package itself commences on line 0008 with the statement that this is the declaration of a **package** called *TransactionCounter*, the **end** of the package declaration is on line 0036. The package itself is divided into the ***public*** part between lines 0008 and 0026 and the **private** part between lines 0027 and 0036. All the types, subtypes, subprograms and other facilities which are shown as being made available by the object diagram have to be declared in the ***public*** part of the package specification.

The public declaration of the *TransactionCounters* data type states that it is a **tagged private** type. The reasons for declaring the type in this way will be introduced in the next chapter and developed throughout the rest of the book. Briefly a **tagged** declaration implies that the type can be extended, and a **private** declaration prevents programs which are using the type from performing any actions on instances on the type which are not included in the package specification. The remainder of the public part of the package specification contains the subprogram declarations which have already been derived from the interface diagrams given above.

A program to demonstrate the *TransactionCounter* package

The development of the *TransactionCounter* package could continue with the production of the **private** part of the package specification and of the package body. However, in order to emphasize that a program which makes use of the facilities of a package needs only to know about the public part of the specification, a demonstration program will be developed before the contents of the private part and the package body are given. A program which makes use of a package is known as a ***client*** of the package, and so the program which is about to be developed is known as a client of the *TransactionCounter* package.

This program will demonstrate the correct operation of all four actions which are supplied by the package. This is not the same as saying that this program will test the package. Although a demonstration is a necessary part of testing, by itself it is not sufficient. The techniques which are required to test a package, or a program, will be introduced in Section II.

The JSP design of the *TransactionCounterDemonstration* program is as follows:

Transaction Counter Demonstration program

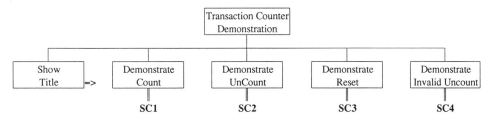

This design indicates that in order to demonstrate the *TransactionCounter* a title has to be shown, then the *CountOccurrence* action has to be demonstrated, then the *UnCountOccurrence*, then the *ResetCounter* action and finally a demonstration of an invalid *UnCountOccurrence* action. In order not to make this design too complicated each of the four major components has been cross referenced to its own structure chart, shown on the diagram as **SC1**, **SC2**, **SC3** and **SC4**. To complete the design of the program each of these components will have to have its own design produced.

The *DemonstrateCount* component

SC1: Demonstrate Count

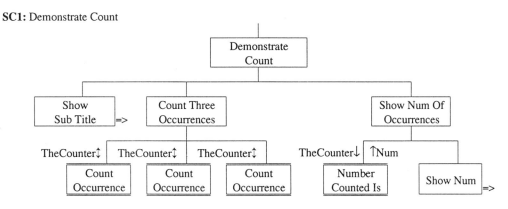

This design indicates that the demonstration of the *CountOccurrence* action will first count three occurrences and will then show the number of occurrences. In order to count three occurrences the subprogram *CountOccurrence* has to be called three times, passing it a *TransactionCounters* parameter identified as

TheCounter. In order to show the number of occurrences the *NumberCountedIs* subprogram is called, passing *TheCounter* as its **in only** parameter, and the value returned, shown as *Num*, is then output to the terminal.

If both *CountOccurrence* and *NumberCountedIs* are working correctly then the number of occurrences reported should be three. On the design the calls of the subprograms supplied by the *TransactionCounter* package are shown with double horizontal lines as they are external to the software component which is currently being designed. The implementation of this part of the design and of the preceding comments, context clause and declarations might be as follows:

```
0001   -- Filename TransactionDemonstration.ada (k8 transdem.adb).
0002   -- Non-interactive client to demonstrate the
0003   -- TransactionCounter object.
0004   --
0005   -- Written for Ada book Section I Chapter 4.
0006   -- Fintan Culwin, v0.1, Jan 1997.
0007
0008   with ADA.TEXT_IO, TransactionCounter;
0009   use  ADA.TEXT_IO, TransactionCounter;
0010
0011   procedure TransDem is
0012
0013       package IntegerIo is new ADA.TEXT_IO.INTEGER_IO( INTEGER);
0014       use IntegerIo;
0015
0016       TheCounter    : TransactionCounters;
0017       NumberCounted : NATURAL;
0018
0019   begin -- TransDem
0020       NEW_LINE( 2);
0021       SET_COL( 15);
0022       PUT_LINE( "Transaction Counter Demonstration");
0023       NEW_LINE( 2);
0024
0025       PUT_LINE( "Counting three transactions ..");
0026       CountOccurrence( TheCounter);
0027       CountOccurrence( TheCounter);
0028       CountOccurrence( TheCounter);
0029       NumberCounted := NumberCountedIs( TheCounter);
0030       PUT( NumberCounted, WIDTH =>1);
0031       PUT_LINE( " transactions have been counted. ");
```

The context clauses, on lines 0008 and 0009, bring the standard package ADA.TEXT_IO and the developer supplied package *TransactionCounter* into use. The declarative region of the program procedure, *TransDem*, on lines 0011 to 0018, instantiates INTEGER_IO as the output of NATURAL INTEGER values will be required. A variable object of the *TransactionCounters* type, called *TheCounter*, is then declared. This object will have a default value of zero counted occurrences, as will be shown when the **private** part of the package specification is introduced. A variable called *NumberCounted* of the INTEGER subtype NATURAL is also declared; its use will be described below.

The executable part of the program procedure starts with the output of a title for the program on lines 0020 to 0023 and a subtitle for the counter demonstration part on line 0025. The design component *CountThreeOccurrences* is then implemented on lines 0026 to 0029 as three calls of the *CountOccurrence* procedure, passing as the actual parameter the variable *TheCounter*. A flow of control diagram for this part of the program would be as follows:

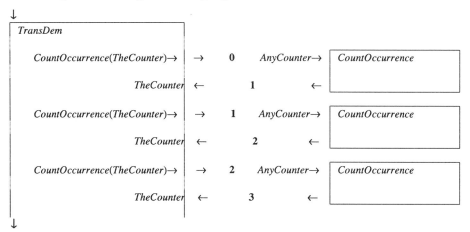

The *TransDem* program is shown on the left of the diagram and passes control to and from the *CountOccurrence* subprogram on the right of the diagram three times. Each time it passes the variable object *TheCounter* as the actual parameter, which is received into the formal parameter *AnyCounter*. The *CountOccurrence* subprogram increments the value of the parameter and passes the incremented value back to the *TransDem* program where it is received back into the *TheCounter* variable. The data flow shows the number of counted occurrences contained in *TheCounter* as it is passed back and forth. The flow of control diagram would continue with the calls on lines 0029 to 0031:

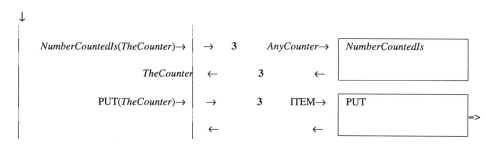

PUT_LINE("*Transactions counted*")→	→"*Transactions counted*"→	PUT_LINE
↓	← ←	=>

When it is executed the output of this part of the program, assuming the package does what it says it does in the specification, would be as follows:

```
          Transaction Counter Demonstration

     Counting three transactions ..
     3 transactions have been counted.
```

The *Demonstrate UnCount* component

The design of the *Demonstrate UnCount* part of the program might be as follows:

SC2: Demonstrate UnCount

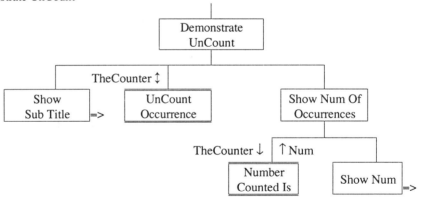

This design indicates that to demonstrate the *UncountOccurrence* action, after a subtitle has been output, the *UncountOccurrence* subprogram is called once, following which the same sequence of actions as was used in the *Demonstrate Count* component is used to output the new value of *TheCounter*. If *Uncount-Occurrence* is working correctly, and *NumberCountedIs* is assumed to be working correctly from its previous demonstration, then the value output should be one less than the previous output. The implementation of this design in the *TransDem* program might be as follows:

```
0035   NEW_LINE( 2);
0036   PUT_LINE( "Uncounting one transaction ..");
```

```
0037    UnCountOccurrence( TheCounter);
0038    NumberCounted := NumberCountedIs( TheCounter);
0039    PUT( NumberCounted, WIDTH =>1);
0040    PUT_LINE( " transactions have been counted. ");
```

A flow of control diagram for this part of the program might be as follows:

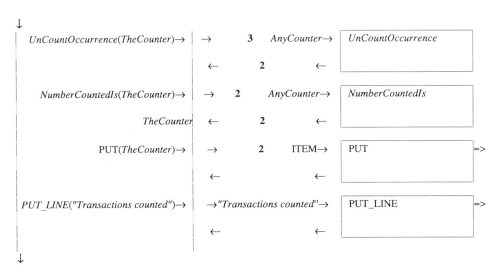

When it is executed the output of this part of the program, assuming the package does what it says it does in the specification, would be as follows:

```
Uncounting one transaction ..
2 transactions have been counted.
```

The *Demonstrate Reset* component

The design of the *Demonstrate Reset* part of the program might be as follows:

SC3: Demonstrate Reset

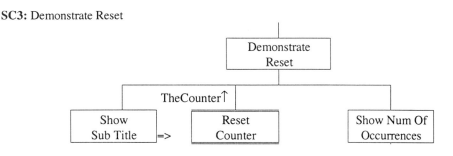

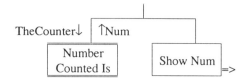

This design is essentially identical to the design of the *Demonstrate UnCount* component given above. Its implementation might be as follows:

```
0042   NEW_LINE( 2);
0043   PUT_LINE( "Resetting the counter .." );
0044   ResetCounter( TheCounter);
0045   NumberCounted := NumberCountedIs( TheCounter);
0046   PUT( NumberCounted, WIDTH =>1);
0047   PUT_LINE( " transactions have been counted. " );
```

The flow of control diagram for this part of the program would be as follows:

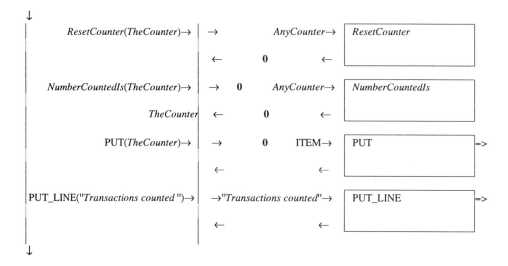

The call of *ResetCounter* shown at the top of the diagram does not show any value being passed into the subprogram, as the parameter is passed in **out only** mode. In this mode the calling part of the program receives a new value from the subprogram, but does not supply a value to it.

When it is executed the output of this part of the program, assuming the package does what it says it does in the specification, would be as follows:

```
Resetting the counter ..
0 transactions have been counted.
```

The *Demonstrate Invalid Uncount* component

The final part of the demonstration client is designed to demonstrate what happens when an invalid operation is attempted. The design of the *TransactionCounter* object made an explicit decision that the counter would not be designed to count a negative number of occurrences; this part of the demonstration attempts to do exactly this.

The design and implementation of this part of the client are essentially identical to that of *Demonstrate UnCount* and *Demonstrate Reset*:

SC4: Demonstrate Invalid Uncount

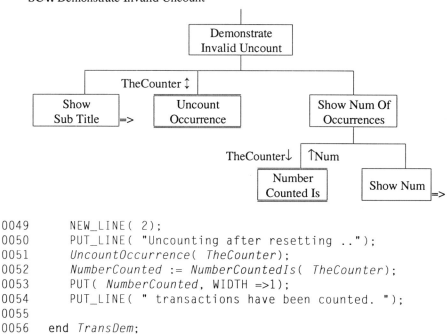

```
0049       NEW_LINE( 2);
0050       PUT_LINE( "Uncounting after resetting ..");
0051       UncountOccurrence( TheCounter);
0052       NumberCounted := NumberCountedIs( TheCounter);
0053       PUT( NumberCounted, WIDTH =>1);
0054       PUT_LINE( " transactions have been counted. ");
0055
0056   end TransDem;
```

The output of this part of the program, when it was executed within the **gnat** environment, was as follows:

```
Uncounting after resetting ..
raised Constraint_Error
```

The program never gets as far as executing lines 0052 onwards, because Ada detects an error when an attempt is made to uncount a transaction on line 0051. As the *TransactionCounters* object has just been reset (to zero) this would lead to a negative number of occurrences and so an **exception** is **raised** and the program is stopped. The precise name of the exception which is raised is CONSTRAINT_ ERROR, and this is indicated in the output produced by the **gnat** run time environment. There are techniques, to be introduced in Section II, which a developer can use to *handle* an exception, and prevent the program from stopping when one is raised.

The private part of the package specification and the package body

The **private** part of the package specification must be completed before the client program can be compiled. All three parts of the application, the client program, the package specification and the package body, will have to be completed before the executable can be linked and executed. It would have also been possible to have constructed the package body before the client.

The private part of the package specification

The contents of the private part of the package specification are as follows:

```
0027    private
0028
0029        type TransactionCounters is tagged
0030        record
0031            NumberOfOccurrences : NATURAL := 0;
0032        end record;
0033
0034    end TransactionCounter;
```

This states that instances of the *TransactionCounters* type contain a single *data attribute*, whose name is *NumberOfOccurrences*, whose data type is NATURAL and which has the initial value zero. Whenever an instance of the *Transaction-Counters* type is created this will ensure that it indicates that zero occurrences have been counted.

One technique for illustrating, or designing, a data object is to use a JSP *data structure* diagram. The diagram for this data type would be as follows:

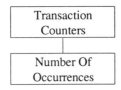

This JSP data structure diagram can be read in exactly the same way as the JSP *program structure* diagrams which were introduced in the previous chapter. It shows that the *TransactionCounters* data type is composed of a sequence of a single component, *NumberOfOccurrences*. More complex data types which contain more than one data attribute will have a more complex data structure diagram.

A data structure diagram is used to design, or illustrate, the structure of an *object* and as such should only contain *nouns* or *noun phrases*. A program structure diagram is used to design, or illustrate, the *actions* which will be performed upon an object and as such should only contain *verbs* or *verb phrases*. The use of data structure and program structure diagrams, and the advantages of having a single notation for both, will be explained throughout the rest of the book.

One other way of visualizing the structure of a *TransactionCounters* object is to use a diagram of the structure of the instance, similar to those used for the simple variables in the previous chapter. A diagram of the *TheCounter* variable immediately after it was declared in the demonstration client above might be as follows:

TheCounter
NumberOfOccurrences   0   NATURAL
TransactionCounters

The diagram indicates that the *TheCounter* variable, of the *TransactionCounters* type, contains a single data component called *NumberOfOccurrences* of the subtype NATURAL with the value zero.

As the *TransactionCounters* type is declared **private** in the public part of the specification, these details of the actual structure of the type are invisible to clients of the package. However, they are fully visible to the package body, which will make extensive use of the knowledge. The visibilities of the client and the body are shown in Figure 4.1.

The diagram indicates that the client programs can only see the contents of the public part of the package specification, but that the package body can see the entire contents of the package specification. The diagram also indicates that the client program has no knowledge of the package body and that the package body has no knowledge of the client.

The package body

The package body of the *TransactionCounters* package contains the *definitions* of the subprograms which were *declared* in the public part of the package

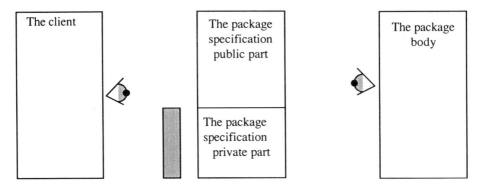

Figure 4.1 Visibilities between package specifications, package bodies and client programs.

specification. The subprogram declaration states *what* a subprogram does and what parameters it requires. The subprogram definition states *how* the subprogram implements its declaration. Using the diagram above it can be seen that a client thus knows *what* a package subprogram does, but not *how* it does it.

The first part of the *TransactionCounters* package body, including the definition of the first subprogram, *CountOccurrence*, is as follows:

```
0001    -- Filename TransactionCounter.pkb (k8 transact.adb).
0002    -- First developer supplied package body containing an
0003    -- extendible data type, which counts occurrences.
0004    --
0005    -- Written for Ada Book Section I Chapter 4.
0006    -- Fintan Culwin, v0.1, Jan 1997.
0007
0008
0009    package body TransactionCounter is
0010
0011       procedure CountOccurrence( AnyCounter :
0012                            in out TransactionCounters) is
0013       begin -- CountOccurrence
0014          AnyCounter.NumberOfOccurrences :=
0015                         AnyCounter.NumberOfOccurrences +1;
0016       end CountOccurrence;
```

The package body starts with the usual comments and on line 0009 declares that this is the declaration of the **package body** of the *TransactionCounter* package. There is no context clause required as the implementation of the subprograms in the body is not dependent upon any external resources. Likewise, there are no instantiations as there is no input or output of values in the package body.

The declaration of the *CountOccurrence* subprogram is given on lines 0011 to

1016. The declaration of a **procedure** in a package body is in many ways similar to the declaration of a program procedure in a client program. It is bounded by the '**procedure** *ProcName* **is**' on lines 0011 and 0012, and the '**end** *ProcName;*' on line 0016. The procedure itself is divided into a declarative part, which in this example is empty, and the executable part which is indicated by the '**begin** -- *ProcName*' on line 0013. The major difference is that this procedure, unlike a program procedure, has parameters and these have to be stated following the declaration of the name of the procedure, on lines 0011 and 0012.

The executable part of the procedure implements the procedure's specification of counting an occurrence by incrementing the *NumberOfOccurrences* component of the *AnyCounter* parameter. The statement on lines 0014 and 0015 can be read as follows:

> Take the value of the *NumberOfOccurrences* component of the *AnyCounter* object, add 1 to it, and store the resulting value back in the *NumberOf Occurrences* component of the *AnyCounter* object.

When the client program, given above, calls the *CountOccurrence* procedure for the first time passing *TheCounter* as the actual parameter, the sequence of actions can be illustrated as in Figure 4.2.

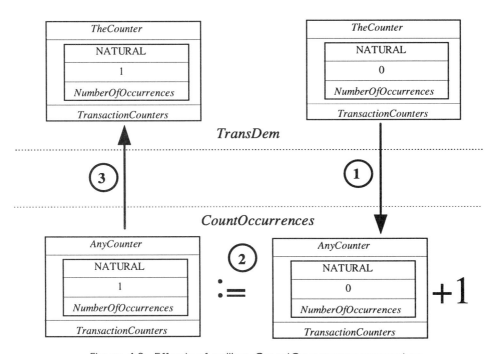

Figure 4.2 Effects of calling *CountOccurrence* procedure.

The first action, shown as **1** on the diagram, is when the *TransDem* program procedure passes flow of control to the *CountOccurrences* subprogram, and uses as an actual parameter *TheCounter* which, as it has just been declared, has counted zero occurrences. Within *CountOccurrences* the actual parameter, *TheCounter*, is received as the formal parameter *AnyCounter* and the value in *AnyCounter* is incremented to one as a result of the assignment statement, shown on the diagram as **2**. When *CountOccurrences* comes to an end, flow of control is passed back to the program procedure, shown on the diagram as **3**. As the parameter is declared with ***in out*** mode the new value of the formal parameter, *AnyCounter*, is passed back to the actual parameter, *TheCounter*. The effect on the *TransDem* main program is that the variable, *TheCounter*, has been changed so that it indicates that a single occurrence has been counted.

The remaining procedures in the package body are essentially identical to the *CountOccurrence* procedure. Their implementation might be as follows:

```
0019    procedure UnCountOccurrence( AnyCounter :
0020                                    in out TransactionCounters) is
0021    begin -- UnCountOccurrence
0022       AnyCounter.NumberOfOccurrences :=
0023                          AnyCounter.NumberOfOccurrences -1;
0024    end UnCountOccurrence;
0025
0026
0027    procedure ResetCounter( AnyCounter :
0028                                    out TransactionCounters) is
0029    begin -- ResetCounter
0030       AnyCounter.NumberOfOccurrences := 0;
0031    end ResetCounter;
```

The *ResetCounter* procedure declares its parameter with ***out only*** mode, and thus does not receive a value when it is called. Within the procedure no reference can be made to any existing value and this procedure simply assigns the value zero to its *NumberOfOccurrences* component, effectively resetting the counter to zero.

The package body concludes with the definition of the *NumberCountedIs* function:

```
0034    function NumberCountedIs( AnyCounter : in
                                TransactionCounters) return NATURAL is
0035
0036       begin -- NumberOfOccurrences
0037          return AnyCounter.NumberOfOccurrences;
0038       end NumberCountedIs;
0039
0040    end TransactionCounter;
```

A function, as indicated in its declaration, has to **return** a value, in this case a value of type NATURAL. This implementation **returns** the value of the *Number-OfOccurrences* component of the formal parameter, *AnyCounter*. This component is declared in the private part of the package specification as being of the NATURAL subtype and, as the procedures above have demonstrated, will always contain the number of occurrences which have been counted.

Building and maintaining the executable

At this stage all three components of the *TransDem* application, the *Transaction-Demonstration* client, the *TransactionCounter* package specification and the *TransactionCounter* package body, exist as source code. In order to produce the executable all three of these components will have to be compiled and then linked. The **order of compilation** of an executable which is constructed from a number of different sources can be deduced from a **dependency diagram**. The dependency diagram for this application is as shown in Figure 4.3.

A component at the end of an arrow on a dependency diagram is dependent upon the prior existence of the component at the head of the arrow. Thus both the client program and the package body are dependent upon the package specification. The client is dependent because it makes use of the facilities which are exported by the package specification and if they change it may also have to change. The package body is dependent upon the specification as it has to implement the facilities which are declared in the specification, and if they change it will have to change. The converse of this consideration is that as nothing is dependent upon both the client and the package body, any changes made to either of these will have no effect upon any other components.

A program component which is dependent upon another program component becomes **obsolete** when a change is made to the component which it is dependent

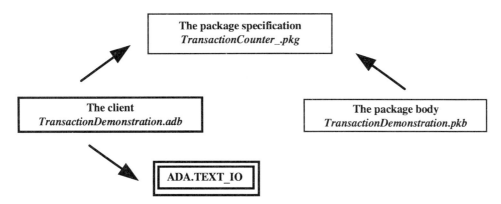

Figure 4.3 Dependencies of the transaction demonstration client.

upon. Thus in the diagram above if any changes are ever made to the package specification, both the client program and the package body will become obsolete. An executable cannot be produced if any of its components are obsolete and the linker will refuse to produce the executable in these situations.

These considerations also lead to the order of compilation requirement. A component can only be used to produce an executable if there is no possibility that it could be obsolete. Thus it can only be compiled after all the components which it is dependent upon have already been compiled. In this example the package specification must be compiled first, following which either the package body or the client program can be compiled. Once all three components have been successfully compiled they can be linked together to produce the executable.

During maintenance any changes made to any of the components may cause other components to become obsolete. For example, if a change is made to the specification, both the package body and the client program will become obsolete. When the change is made and the specification recompiled, both dependent components will also have to be compiled before a new executable can be produced. However, if either the body or the client is changed only the changed component will require recompilation before a new executable can be produced.

The dependency diagram above also indicates that the client program is dependent upon the standard package ADA.TEXT_IO, but as this can never change it can never become obsolete because of this dependency. The instantiation of INTEGER_IO to produce *IntegerIO* is not shown on this diagram as the instantiation takes place within the program procedure, so this is solely the concern of the client.

EXERCISES

4.1 Obtain the source code for the software described in this chapter, then compile and run the demonstration client.

4.2 Design and implement a more extensive test of the *TransactionCounter* client, for example to count more occurrences or to intermix more calls of *CountOccurrence*, *UnCountOccurrence* and *ResetCounter*. Does this increase your confidence in the correct implementation of the package? If it does, how much further demonstration would be required to give 100% confidence?

4.3 Construct a flow of control diagram illustrating the complete execution of the extended demonstration client from Exercise 4.2.

4.4 Edit the package specification file, for example by adding an additional comment that it has been changed, and then attempt to link the executable without recompiling the body or the client in order to demonstrate obsolescence.

4.5 Add a new action *CountTenOccurrences* to the *TransactionCounter* package which will count ten occurrences when it is called. Amend the demonstration client to allow this new action to be demonstrated.

CHAPTER 5
Extending data types

The production of software artefacts can be enormously simplified if existing components, in the form of packages and the facilities which they provide, can be used rather than having to construct new components from scratch. However, it is often the case that no existing component quite satisfies the requirements of the artefact under construction. The facility of allowing certain existing data types to be extended is intended to address this problem. If an extendible component can be located which satisfies some of the requirements, the missing requirements can then be added by extension.

This chapter will start the introduction of this facility by extending the *TransactionCounters* data type which was developed in the previous chapter. Two extensions of the type will be presented: a *CashRegisters* data type which implements a simple model of a cash register and a *RoomMonitors* data type which implements a more abstract concept of an object which can be used to monitor the number of people in a room.

It is only possible to extend a data type which was originally declared as a **tagged** type, and as this is potentially an extremely powerful facility all types should be declared **tagged** in case extension is ever required. A non-**tagged** declaration should only be made if it is certain that the type will never have to be extended.

The *CashRegisters* extension

The first extension to the *TransactionCounters* data type will produce a model of a *CashRegister*. As an extended *TransactionCounter*, a *CashRegister* **is a** *TransactionCounter* and **inherits** all the operations which can be performed upon a *TransactionCounter*. The occurrences which a *CashRegisters* instance counts are the number of times a deposit is made into the register. Each time a deposit is made a *transaction* will have to be counted, and the amount of money deposited will have to be added to the amount of money in the register. Other additional requirements of the model are to determine the total amount of money in the register and to reset the register by setting the number of transactions and the total amount of money in the register to zero.

The *CashRegister* object diagram

The object diagram for the *CashRegister* is as follows:

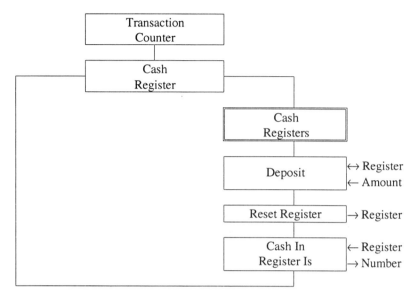

This object diagram indicates, at the top, that the *CashRegister* object is an extension of the *TransactionCounter* object. The facilities provided by the object are the *CashRegisters* type itself and three actions: to deposit an amount of money (*Deposit*), to reset the register (*ResetRegister*) and to find out the amount of money in the register (*CashInRegisterIs*).

The *CashRegister* interface diagrams and subprogram declarations

The data flow interface diagrams and subprogram declarations for the actions supplied by the *CashRegister* object are as follows:

```
AnyRegister ↕
   Amount ↓
┌──────────────────┐
│     Deposit      │
└──────────────────┘
```

```
procedure Deposit( AnyRegister : in out CashRegisters;
                   Amount      : in FLOAT);
-- Deposit Amount of money in AnyRegister and count a
-- transaction.
```

AnyRegister ↑ |

| Reset Register |

```
procedure ResetRegister( AnyRegister : out CashRegisters);
-- Reset AnyRegister setting the number of transactions and
-- the amount of money to zero.
```

AnyRegister ↓ | ↑ Cash

| Cash In
Register Is |

```
function CashInRegisterIs( AnyRegister : in CashRegisters)
                                            return FLOAT;
-- Find out the total amount of money in AnyRegister.
```

The *CashRegister* package specification

The implementation of the object design as a package specification file, including the **private** part, is as follows:

```
0001    -- Filename CashRegister_.pkg (k8 cashregi.ads).
0002    -- Extension to the TransactionCounter package to
0003    -- produce a CashRegister object.
0004    --
0005    -- Written for Ada Book Section I Chapter 5.
0006    -- Fintan Culwin, v0.1, Jan 1997.
0007
0008    with TransactionCounter;
0009    use  TransactionCounter;
0010
0011    package CashRegister is
0012
0013       type CashRegisters is new TransactionCounters with private;
0014
0015       procedure Deposit( AnyRegister : in out CashRegisters;
0016                          Amount      : in      FLOAT);
0017       -- Deposit Amount of money in AnyRegister and count a
0018                                                   transaction.
0019       procedure ResetRegister( AnyRegister : out CashRegisters);
0020       -- Reset AnyRegister setting the number of transactions
0021       -- and the amount of money to zero.
0022
```

```
0023      function CashInRegisterIs( AnyRegister : in CashRegisters)
0024                                              return FLOAT;
0025      -- Find out the total amount of money in AnyRegister.
0026
0027   private
0028
0029      type CashRegisters is new TransactionCounters with
0030      record
0031         CashInRegister : FLOAT := 0.0;
0032      end record;
0033
0034   end CashRegister;
```

The declaration of the *CashRegisters* data type in the public part of the specification states that the *CashRegisters* type is an extension of the *TransactionCounters* type, and that the details of the extension are hidden in the **private** part of the specification. It is possible to make a *public* extension to a **tagged** type, by publicly stating the details of the extension, but for the reasons explained in the previous chapter **private** data types and extensions should always be favoured. The public part of the package specification also includes the three subprogram declarations produced above.

The **private** part of the package specification gives full details of the extension to the data type. The extension adds a second data attribute, called *CashInRegister* of the pre-declared FLOAT data type with a default value of 0.0, to the *TransactionCounters* type in order to produce the *CashRegisters* type. The JSP structure chart for this extended type is as follows:

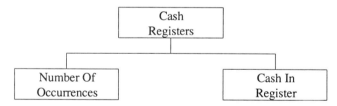

The diagram indicates that each *CashRegisters* instance contains two components. The first, *NumberOfOccurrences*, is inherited from the *TransactionCounters* type; the second, *CashInRegister*, is supplied by the extension. A visualization of a newly created instance of the *CashRegisters* type, called *TheRegister*, might be as follows:

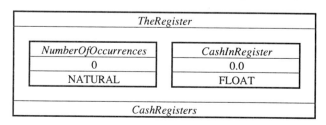

The *CashRegisterDemonstration* client

As with the explanation of the *TransactionCounters* type in the previous chapter a client program will be presented before details of the package body are given, in order to reinforce the consideration that the client is dependent upon the specification and independent of the body. The design of the demonstration client, called *CashRegisterDemonstration*, is as follows:

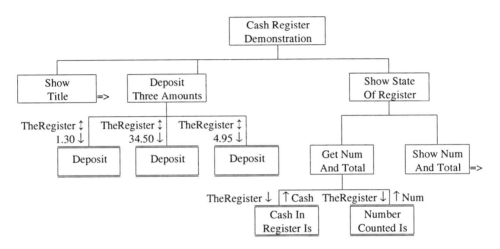

The design indicates that in order to test the *CashRegister* object, three *Deposits*, of 1.30, 34.50 and 4.95, will be made and following this the state of the register will be shown. If the object has been implemented correctly the state of the register should indicate that it has a total of 40.75 from three transactions. The implementation of this design might be as follows:

```
0001    -- Filename CashRegisterDemonstration.ada (k8 cashrdem.adb).
0002    -- Non-interactive client to demonstrate the
0003    -- CashRegister object.
0004    --
0005    -- Written for Ada book Section I Chapter 5.
0006    -- Fintan Culwin, v0.1, Jan 1997.
0007
0008    with ADA.TEXT_IO, TransactionCounter, CashRegister;
0009    use  ADA.TEXT_IO, TransactionCounter, CashRegister;
0010
0011    procedure CashRDem is
0012
0013        package IntegerIO is new ADA.TEXT_IO.INTEGER_IO( INTEGER);
0014        package FloatIO  is new ADA.TEXT_IO.FLOAT_IO( FLOAT);
```

```
0015        use IntegerIO, FloatIO;
0016
0017        TheRegister       : CashRegisters;
0018        NumberOfDeposits : NATURAL;
0019        TotalAmountTaken : FLOAT;
0020
0021   begin -- CashRegisterDemonstration
0022      NEW_LINE( 2);
0023      SET_COL( 15);
0024      PUT_LINE( "Cash Register Demonstration");
0025      NEW_LINE( 2);
0026
0027      PUT_LINE( "Depositing 1.30, 34.50 and 4.95 ..");
0028      Deposit( TheRegister, 1.30);
0029      Deposit( TheRegister, 34.50);
0030      Deposit( TheRegister, 4.95);
0031
0032      TotalAmountTaken := CashInRegisterIs( TheRegister);
0033      NumberOfDeposits := NumberCountedIs( TheRegister);
0034      PUT( TotalAmountTaken, FORE=>1, AFT>2, EXP=>0);
0035      PUT( " has been taken in ");
0036      PUT( NumberOfDeposits, WIDTH =>1);
0037      PUT_LINE( " deposits. ");
0038
0039   end CashRDem;
```

The context clause has to bring into **use**: ADA.TEXT_IO for the output of the prompts, *TransactionCounter* as one of its facilities will be directly used and *CashRegister* as its facilities will be extensively used. The declarative region instantiates INTEGER_IO and FLOAT_IO as output of a NATURAL INTEGER value and a FLOAT value will be required. The declarative region also declares: a variable instance of the *CashRegisters* type called *TheRegister*, a NATURAL variable called *NumberOfDeposits* and a FLOAT variable called *TotalAmountTaken*.

The executable part of the program implements the design directly: after the output of the program title and the subtitle for the three deposits, the *Deposit* subprogram is called three times each time passing *TheRegister* as the actual *CashRegisters* parameter and a literal FLOAT value as the *Amount* parameter.

The second part of the design is implemented on lines 0032 to 0037. On line 0032 the *CashRegister CashInRegisterIs* function is called and the value returned, containing the total amount of money in the register, is stored in the *TotalAmountTaken* FLOAT variable. On line 0033 the *TransactionCounter NumberCountedIs* function is called. The actual parameter of the *NumberCountedIs* function in the *TransactionCounter* specification stated that it required a parameter of the *TransactionCounters* type. *TheRegister* is acceptable as an actual parameter as the *CashRegisters* type is derived from the *TransactionCounters* type by extension. A *CashRegisters* instance ***is a*** *TransactionCounters* instance with additional components added. The value returned from the *NumberCountedIs* function is stored in the *NumberOfDeposits* variable.

Subsequently, on lines 0034 to 0037 the values of the two variables, *TotalAmountTaken* and *NumberCountedIs*, are output to indicate the state of the register. A flow of control diagram for the last call of *Deposit* and the calls of *CashInRegisterIs* and *NumberCountedIs* might be as follows:

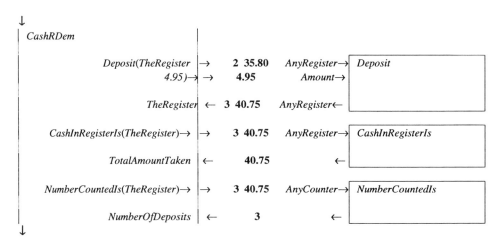

The first call, to *Deposit*, shows two data flows, corresponding to the *Any-Register* and *Amount* formal parameters. The actual parameter used for the *AnyRegister* data flow is the value of *TheRegister* which contains two data attributes, the *NumberOfTransactions* and *CashInRegister*. Accordingly two values are shown on this data flow which reflect the state of *TheRegister* after the first two deposits, two transactions and a cash total of 35.80. The second data flow at the start of the call is the amount being deposited, 4.95. The data flow at the end of the call of deposit shows the changed state of the *AnyRegister* parameter, now indicating three transactions and a cash total of 40.75.

The two remaining subprogram calls return the appropriate values retrieved from the actual *TheRegister* parameter. The call of *CashInRegisterIs* returns 40.75 and *NumberCountedIs* returns 3. The output of the program when it is executed is as follows:

```
                    Cash Register Demonstration

        Depositing 1.30, 34.50 and 4.95 ..
        40.75 has been taken in 3 deposits.
```

This would seem to indicate that the object is operating correctly.

The *CashRegister* package body

The first part of the package body, including the definition of the *Deposit* procedure is as follows:

```
0001    -- Filename CashRegister.pkb (k8 cashregi.adb).
0002    -- Extension to the TransactionCounter package to
0003    -- produce a CashRegister object.
0004    --
0005    -- Written for Ada Book Section I Chapter 5.
0006    -- Fintan Culwin, v0.1, Jan 1997.
0007
0008    package body CashRegister is
0009
0010       procedure Deposit( AnyRegister : in out CashRegisters;
0011                          Amount      : in      FLOAT) is
0012       begin -- Deposit
0013          AnyRegister.CashInRegister :=
0014                          AnyRegister.CashInRegister + Amount;
0015          CountOccurrence( AnyRegister);
0016       end Deposit;
```

The implementation of the *Deposit* procedure commences by adding the value of the *Amount* formal parameter to the *CashInRegister* component of the *Any-Register* parameter, and stores the resulting value back in the same component. The effect is to increase the value of the *CashInRegister* component by the value of *Amount*. Following this the *TransactionCounters CountOccurrence* action is called which, as explained in the previous chapter, will increment the *Number-OfOccurrences* component by one. The provision of an actual parameter of the *CashRegisters* type when the formal parameter is declared as being of the *TransactionCounters* type is acceptable to Ada as was explained in the discussion of the client program above.

A visualization of the flow of control and data within this subprogram, when it is called for the third time in the demonstration client above, might be as shown in Figure 5.1.

At point 1 *TheRegister* is passed from the program procedure *CashRDem* as an actual parameter to *Deposit*, where it is received at point 2 in the formal parameter *AnyRegister*. The first action in *Deposit* adds the *Amount* (4.95) to the *CashInRegister* component, shown at point 3. The *Deposit* parameter variable *AnyRegister* is then passed as the actual parameter to the *CountOccurrence* subprogram where it is received at point 4. *CountOccurrence* can only see the parameter as a *TransactionCounters* variable, and cannot see any components which have been added by extension. The *NumberOfOccurrences* component is incremented producing point 5, and the value is passed back to *Deposit* where it is

81

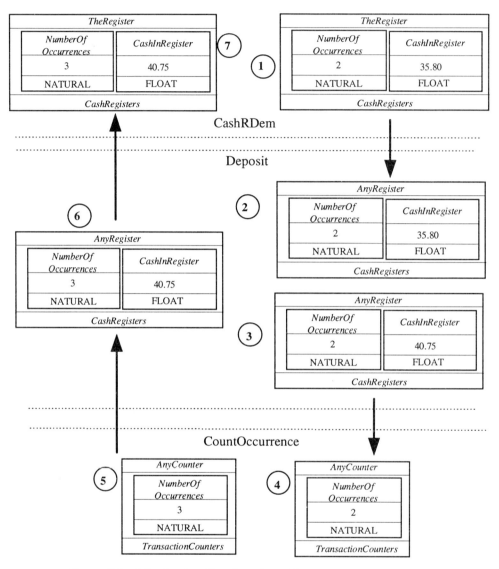

Figure 5.1 Effects of calling the *CountOccurrence* procedure.

received at point 6. The object is then immediately passed back to the program procedure *CashRDem* where it is received back into *TheRegister* at point 7.

The remaining part of the package body is as follows:

```
0019    procedure ResetRegister( AnyRegister : out CashRegisters)
                                                              is
0020    begin -- ResetRegister
```

```
0021           AnyRegister.CashInRegister := 0.0;
0022           ResetCounter( AnyRegister);
0023        end ResetRegister;
0024
0025
0026        function CashInRegisterIs( AnyRegister : in CashRegisters)
0027                                                 return FLOAT is
0028        begin -- CashInRegisterIs
0029           return AnyRegister.CashInRegister;
0030        end CashInRegisterIs;
0031
0032     end CashRegister;
```

The *ResetRegister* procedure sets the *CashInRegister* component to zero and then calls the *TransactionCounter ResetCounter* procedure passing the *AnyRegister* parameter onwards to have its occurrence counter reset to zero. The *CashInRegisterIs* function is implemented in a similar manner to the *TransactionCounter NumberOfOccurrencesIs* function, returning the value of the component *CashInRegister* as the amount of money in the register.

It may seem that the calls of the *TransactionCounter* procedures in the definitions of the *CashRegister* procedures may be unnecessary, as the *NumberOfOccurrences* component of the *AnyRegister* parameter could be manipulated directly. This has not, and should not, be done as the actions of transaction counting are performed by the *TransactionCounter* package and although the actions in this example are very straightforward this may not always be the case. Where an action has been implemented by a package subprogram that action should then always be used and direct access to the data attributes should be avoided.

The *RoomMonitor* extension

A second extension to the *TransactionCounter* object will be briefly presented, partly in order to reinforce the concept of developing a new object by extension, but also to introduce an object which models a concept which has no physical counterpart. The *TransactionCounter* object was introduced as a model of a hand-held transaction counter and the *CashRegister* as a model of a very simple cash register. The *RoomMonitor* object which will be introduced in this part of the chapter has no obvious physical existence. As such it is much more typical of the software *objects* which are customarily produced by developers.

The intention of the *RoomMonitor* is that it might form a part of the software of the system which is attached to the entrances of many shops and other public places. Every time a person enters, or leaves, the shop they are detected by a physical device, for example by opening a barrier or breaking an invisible beam.

Sophisticated room monitoring systems are able to store and extract much information from the data obtained, such as the total number of people who entered the shop, the current number of people in the shop, the maximum number of people ever in the shop and the average time which people spent in the shop. The simplified *RoomMonitor* object which will be presented in this chapter will only be able to produce the first two pieces of information from this list. Of course the additional requirements could always be added by extension.

The collection of three objects and the relationships between them can be represented on a ***class hierarchy diagram***. The class hierarchy diagram for the ***class*** of three data types ***rooted*** at the *TransactionCounters* type is as follows:

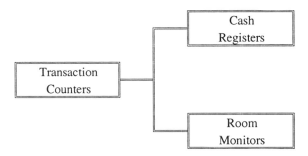

The diagram shows the ***parent/child*** relationships between the various types and for a more complex hierarchy is a useful diagram to explain the relationships, to indicate what objects are available from the collection and to decide the best place to add a new object to the hierarchy.

A discussion of the reasons for the design and implementation of the *Room-Monitor* would repeat all of the points made for the design and implementation of the *CashRegister* above. Accordingly the design and implementation will be presented with minimal comment, and no client program will be presented. The construction of a client and a trace of its execution will be left as an end of chapter exercise.

The *RoomMonitor* object diagram

The object diagram for the *RoomMonitor* is as follows:

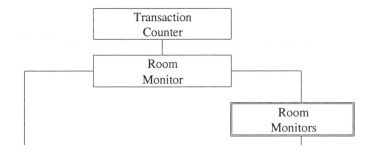

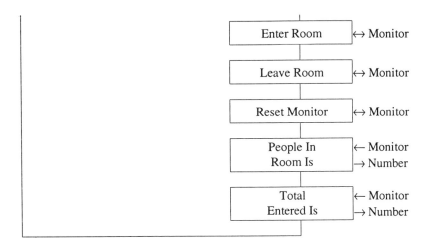

The *RoomMonitor* interface diagram and subprogram declarations

The *RoomMonitor* subprogram interface diagrams and declarations, derived from the object diagram above, are as follows:

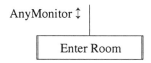

```
procedure EnterRoom( AnyMonitor : in out RoomMonitors);
-- Count a person entering a room.
```

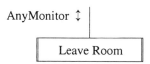

```
procedure LeaveRoom( AnyMonitor : in out RoomMonitors);
-- Count a person leaving the room.
```

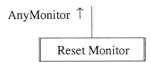

```
procedure ResetMonitor( AnyMonitor : out RoomMonitors);
-- Reset the monitor by setting all attributes to zero.
```

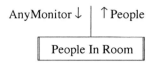

```
function PeopleInRoomIs( AnyMonitor : in RoomMonitors)
                                        return NATURAL;
-- Find out the number of people currently in the room.
```

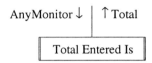

```
function TotalEnteredIs( AnyMonitor : in RoomMonitors)
                                        return NATURAL;
-- Find out the total number of people who have entered the room.
```

The *RoomMonitor* package specification

The package specification file, including the **private** part, derived from the object diagram and interface diagrams above, is as follows:

```
0001   -- Filename RoomMonitor_.pkg (k8 roommoni.ads).
0002   -- Extension to the TransactionCounter package to
0003   -- produce a RoomMonitor object.
0004   --
0005   -- Written for Ada Book Section I Chapter 5.
0006   -- Fintan Culwin, v0.1, Jan 1997.
0007
0008   with TransactionCounter;
0009   use  TransactionCounter;
0010
0011   package RoomMonitor is
0012
0013      type RoomMonitors is new TransactionCounters with private;
0014
0015      procedure EnterRoom( AnyMonitor : in out RoomMonitors);
0016      -- Count a person entering a room.
0017
0018      procedure LeaveRoom( AnyMonitor : in out RoomMonitors);
0019      -- Count a person leaving the room.
0020
0021      procedure ResetMonitor( AnyMonitor : out RoomMonitors);
0022      -- Reset the monitor by setting all attributes to zero.
0023
```

```
0024        function PeopleInRoomIs( AnyMonitor : in RoomMonitors)
0025                                          return NATURAL;
0026        -- Find out the number of people currently in the room.
0027
0028        function TotalEnteredIs( AnyMonitor : in RoomMonitors)
0029                                          return NATURAL;
0030        -- Find out the total number of people who have entered
0031                                                       the room.
0032    private
0033
0034        type RoomMonitors is new TransactionCounters with
0035        record
0036            TotalEntered : NATURAL := 0;
0037        end record;
0038
0039    end RoomMonitor;
```

The JSP data structure diagram and a visualization of a *RoomMonitors* instance would be as follows:

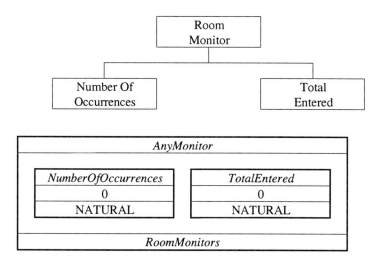

The *RoomMonitor* package body

```
0001    -- Filename RoomMonitor.pkb (k8 roommoni.adb).
0002    -- Extension to the TransactionCounter package to
0003    -- produce a RoomMonitor object.
0004    --
0005    -- Written for Ada Book Section I Chapter 5.
0006    -- Fintan Culwin, v0.1, Jan 1997.
```

```
0007
0008    with TransactionCounter;
0009    use  TransactionCounter;
0010
0011    package body RoomMonitor is
0012
0013       procedure EnterRoom( AnyMonitor : in out RoomMonitors) is
0014       begin -- EnterRoom
0015          AnyMonitor.TotalEntered := AnyMonitor.TotalEntered +1;
0016          CountOccurrence( AnyMonitor);
0017       end EnterRoom;
0018
0019
0020       procedure LeaveRoom( AnyMonitor : in out RoomMonitors) is
0021       begin -- LeaveRoom
0022          UnCountOccurrence( AnyMonitor);
0023       end LeaveRoom;
0024
0025
0026       procedure ResetMonitor( AnyMonitor : out RoomMonitors) is
0027       begin -- ResetMonitor
0028          AnyMonitor.TotalEntered := 0;
0029          ResetCounter( AnyMonitor);
0030       end ResetMonitor;
0031
0032
0033       function PeopleInRoomIs( AnyMonitor : in RoomMonitors)
0034                                              return NATURAL is
0035       begin -- PeopleInRoomIs
0036          return NumberCountedIs( AnyMonitor);
0037       end PeopleInRoomIs;
0038
0039
0040       function TotalEnteredIs( AnyMonitor : in RoomMonitors)
0041                                              return NATURAL is
0042       begin -- TotalEnteredIs
0043          return AnyMonitor.TotalEntered;
0044       end TotalEnteredIs;
0045
0046    end RoomMonitor;
```

Procedures and functions

In the implementation of the subprograms from the three packages in this and the
previous chapter, the reasons for deciding between implementation as a **procedure**

and as a **function** have not been given. If a subprogram interface diagram has:

- only one *out only* data flow,

- any number, including zero, of *in only* data flows,

- no *in out* data flows, and

- no terminal input or output,

then the subprogram can, and should, be declared as a **function**. If any of these rules do not apply then the subprogram must be declared as a **procedure**. A **procedure** could be declared wherever a **function** is possible. For example, the *RoomMonitor PeopleInRoomIs* **function** could have been implemented as follows:

```
procedure PeopleInRoomIs( AnyMonitor : in  RoomMonitors;
                          People     : out NATURAL );
```

Using the **function** implementation a fragment of a client demonstration program might be as follows:

```
CurrentlyInRoom := PeopleInRoomIs( TheMonitor);
PUT( "There are "); PUT( CurrentlyInRoom, WIDTH=>1);
PUT_LINE( " people in the room.");
```

If implementated as a **procedure** this would become

```
PeopleInRoomIs( TheMonitor, CurrentlyInRoom);
PUT( "There are "); PUT( CurrentlyInRoom, WIDTH=>1);
PUT_LINE( " people in the room.");
```

The converse possibility, that any **procedure** can always be implemented as a **function**, is not true as any *in out* data flow, or more than one *out only* data flow, will prevent it being a **function**.

There are two major reasons why implementation as a **function** is favoured over implementation as a **procedure**. The first is that as the parameters to a **function** must be *in only* it is immediately obvious from reading the subprogram call that the values of the actual parameters cannot have been changed by the call. This is not the case for a **procedure** as it can have *in out* parameters, and thus it can only be confirmed that an actual parameter cannot have been changed by having a knowledge of the **procedure's** declaration.

The second reason is that as a **function** has a value it can be used in some situations in a more direct manner than the equivalent **procedure**. For example, the first program fragment above could have been implemented as follows:

```
PUT( "There are "); PUT( PeopleInRoomIs( TheMonitor),
                                           WIDTH=>1);
PUT_LINE( " people in the room.");
```

The role of the variable *CurrentlyInRoom* in the first two fragments is to hold the value returned from the subprogram for a moment until it is sent to the terminal by the call of the *IntegerIO* PUT procedure on the next line. The revised version uses the call of the **function** as the actual parameter of the PUT procedure. This is acceptable as the PUT procedure has a formal *in only* data flow and only a value, not an object, is required.

This revised implementation reduces the number of variables which might have to be declared, but at the expense of an increased subprogram call complexity. Although this style of implementation has some advantages, and many advocates, it adds complexity to the subprogram calls and can obscure the meaning of the code. Consequently, in general, this style will not be used in the rest of this book.

The set of subprograms which is inherited by a data type and those which are declared in association with the data type in a package specification are known as the *primitive operations* of the data type. There is no simple mechanism which can be used to remove an action from this set of operations and this can lead to some potential problems. For example, the *CashRegister's* **primitive operations** include both the *Deposit* action and the *CountOccurrence* action. The intention of the *CashRegister* model is that the only time a transaction is counted is when a deposit is made. However, it is possible for the *CountOccurrence* procedure to be called by a client program which would increment the number of transactions without a deposit being made. The techniques by which this potential insecurity in the *CashRegister* object can be removed will be introduced when development by extension is considered in further detail in Section IV.

For a data type which is declared **private** in the *public* part of a package specification, the primitive operations also include assignment, equality testing and inequality testing. Assignment of one *CashRegister* or *RoomMonitor* value to an object presents no problems, but equality and inequality testing does. As the *CashRegisters* and *RoomMonitors* data types have two data attributes, two values of the same type are only considered equal if they have the same values in both components. Thus a *CashRegister* which has taken 13.47 in three transactions is only considered equal to one which has also taken 13.47 in three transactions. It is not considered equal to one which has taken 13.47 in two transactions, nor to one which has taken 14.37 in three transactions. This problem in equality testing will be considered at the end of the next chapter, after selective control structures have been introduced.

In addition to declaring a data type **private** it is also possible to declare a data type **limited private** in the public part of a package specification. In this case assignment, equality testing and inequality testing are not allowed for objects of the type and the set of primitive operations is limited to those inherited or declared in the package specification. A **limited private** data type is occasionally more appropriate than a **private** declaration, but in most circumstances declaring a type **private** is preferred.

EXERCISES

5.1 Obtain the source code for the *CashRegister* package and client. Construct a *dependency diagram* for the client and use it to determine an *order of compilation* for the client. Then build and execute the client.

5.2 Extend the *CashRegister* demonstration client so that two *CashRegisters* variables are declared. After making some deposits into the first variable, assign its value to the second variable and show the state of both variables in order to confirm the correct operation of the assignment action.

5.3 Design and implement a demonstration client for the *RoomMonitor* package and repeat Exercises 5.1 and 5.2 with it. Then construct a *flow of control* diagram which includes calls of all four of the subprograms supplied with the object.

5.4 Reimplement either the *CashRegister* or *RoomMonitor* packages replacing all **functions** with equivalent **procedures**. Reimplement the appropriate demonstration client and execute it to demonstrate the equivalence of the two implementations.

5.5 Reimplement either the *CashRegister* or *RoomMonitor* demonstration using the calls of functions directly in the PUT procedures and avoiding the declaration and use of the simple variables. Execute the reimplemented client to demonstrate the equivalence of the two implementations.

5.6 Extend the *CashRegister* type to produce a *ChangeGivingCashRegister*. The change giving *Deposit* action will require two *in only* parameters indicating the value to be deposited and the amount tendered; it should also have an *out only* parameter indicating the amount of change. For example, if the value to be deposited is 7.34 and 10.00 is tendered the change due would be 2.66. Adapt the *CashRegisterDemonstration* program to demonstrate the extended object.

CHAPTER 6
Selection in programs

All parts of the software which has been developed in the previous chapters were designed as sequences of instructions. The sequences were expressed in the program structure charts and in the derived source code. Essentially a sequence of instructions to the computer says do this, followed by this, followed by this.... If this was the only method available to instruct a computer, programming would be impossible. There are two other major techniques for instructing a computer to perform actions, *selection* and *iteration* (*repetition*). Selection involves instructing the computer to decide between two, or more, possible courses of action. Iteration involves instructing the computer to repeat a sequence of actions a number of times.

Although the previous chapters have emphasized the construction of programs from a number of separately compiled program modules, in order to illustrate the design, construction and use of software components which use selection and iteration, a simpler form of construction where the subprograms of the program procedure are defined in the same source code file will be used. Although this technique is more convenient for small, simple specifications, it should be remembered that the technique is not scalable to more realistic specifications and that it limits the potential reusability of subprograms. For these, and for other reasons, these techniques should not be relied upon and the construction of applications from separate modules should be practised.

This chapter will introduce the design and use of selection; the following chapter will introduce iteration. These facilities will then be used extensively throughout the rest of the book. The behavioural complexity of software is very largely due to the effects of selection and iteration. Consequently the greatest care should be taken to ensure that they are designed and implemented correctly at the outset. Should they be incorrectly implemented the behaviour of the software will not be as required by the specification, and the cost of locating and correcting the faulty selection or iteration will far outweigh the costs of constructing it correctly in the first instance.

Selection in programs

In order to introduce selection a number of small, simple specifications will be given and implemented, each of which will progressively introduce a more complex form of selection. In order to make this process more manageable only the salient parts of the implementation will be given for some of the example programs. The full source code of all the programs in this chapter is available; details of how to obtain it are given in Appendix A.

Two way sequential selections

A simple initial specification to illustrate selection is

> The program will invite the user to type '*y*' to indicate *yes* or '*n*' to indicate *no*. The program will then confirm the input as '*yes*' or '*no*'. In this version of the program it will be assumed that the user will always input either '*y*' or '*n*' and the upper case equivalents ('*Y*' or '*N*') will not be accepted.

This specification will be refined throughout this chapter, and the next, in order to become more realistic. When fully developed it will provide a design template for similar simple interactions with the user.

As was advised in previous chapters one technique to assist with interpreting a specification is to construct a user interface for it. As this specification has two alternative behaviours, two versions of the user interface will have to be illustrated:

```
        Yes No Demo 1

Please enter 'y' for yes or 'n' for no Y

You said Yes.


        Yes No Demo 1

Please enter 'y' for yes or 'n' for no n

You said No.
```

A design for a program to implement this specification, omitting the component which outputs the title of the program, might be as follows:

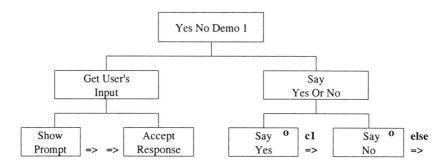

c1: If user entered 'y'.

The first part of the design, *GetUsersInput*, is directly comparable with the design of similar components in previous chapters. The second part of the design, *SayYesOrNo*, is a selective component which consists of two optional components. The component *SayYesOrNo* can be read as: '*SayYesOrNo is a selection between the component SayYes and the component SayNo controlled by condition 1 (c1)*'.

The option symbol (**o**) in the top right hand corner of the *SayYes* and *SayNo* components indicates that they are optional. Every optional component has to be keyed with either a condition number (e.g. **c1**), or for the last optional component **else** can be used as a key. A selective component of a design is the component which is refined into a number of options, the options themselves are not the selection. In the design above *SayYesOrNo* is the selective component. *SayYes* and *SayNo* are the optional components of the selection, but are not themselves selections.

Each condition in a design has to be expressed in a condition key which forms part of the design. The expression of the condition must be such that it is either true or false, and should be a natural language (i.e. English) sentence or phrase. Any phrase which is under certain conditions neither true nor false cannot be used.

The interpretation of the behaviour of this design component is that if the condition is true, the component *SayYes* will be performed and the component *SayNo* will be ignored. **Else** the condition must be false, so the component *SayNo* will be performed and the component *SayYes* will be ignored. On this design, if the user enters '*y*' when requested, the condition will be true and the component *SayYes* will inform the user that he or she said yes. If the user did not enter '*y*' then, according to the specification, the user must have entered '*n*'; the condition will be false and the component *SayNo* will inform the user that he or she said no.

To continue the design process, after completing and validating the design a data table should be constructed. This design requires only one variable object:

Program variables for *YesNoDemo1*

Name	Type	Initial value	Notes
UsersResponse	CHARACTER	?	The user's response, either 'y' or 'n'

The pre-declared data type CHARACTER is capable of containing a single character. The ? in the initial value column indicates that the value of the variable is unknown when it is declared, not that it contains a question mark. An implementation of this design might be as follows:

```
0001    -- Filename YesNoDemo1.ada
0002    -- Initial selection demonstration program.
0003    -- Written for Ada Book Section I Chapter 6.
0004    --
0005    -- Fintan Culwin, v0.1, Jan 1997.
0006
0007    with ADA.TEXT_IO;
0008    use  ADA.TEXT_IO;
0009
0010    procedure YesNoDemo1 is
0011
0012        UsersResponse : CHARACTER;
0013
0014    begin -- YesNoDemo1
0015        -- Output title.
0016        PUT_LINE(" Yes No Demo 1"); NEW_LINE(2);
0017
0018        -- Get user's input.
0019        PUT("Please enter 'y' for yes, or 'n' for no ");
0020        GET( UsersResponse); SKIP_LINE;
0021
0022        NEW_LINE( 2);
0023
0024        -- Say yes or no.
0025        if UsersResponse = 'y' then
0026            PUT_LINE("You entered Yes.");
0027        else
0028            PUT_LINE('You entered No.');
0029        end if;
0030    end YesNoDemo1;
```

The implementation of the selection component, *SayYesOrNo*, is on lines 0025 to 0029 and makes use of the Ada **if** control structure, configured as a two way selection with a default option. The general form of this configuration of the **if** structure is

```
if Condition then
   -- first actions
else
   -- second actions
end if;
```

The reserved words **if** and **end if** are used to delineate the extent of the control structure. The condition from the design is implemented as an Ada expression between the reserved words **if** and **then**. Between the **then** and the **else** reserved words are the actions which form the left hand component of the selection, and between the **else** and the **end if** reserved words are the actions which form the right hand component of the selection.

It is a style requirement, not an Ada requirement, that the statements which comprise the optional components of the design are indented by three character spaces relative to the **if/else/end if** terms. The indentation is intended to indicate to anyone reading the source code that these statements are under the control of the **if** structure. The person who reads the source code the most is the person who is developing the software, and the commonest reasons for reading it are either to determine what the software is doing or to attempt to work out why the software is not working correctly. In either case the use of indentation to indicate the extent of control structures will greatly assist both these endeavours. Consequently the rigorous use of indentation as the source code is constructed is very strongly advocated.

In the program above the condition is implemented as '*UsersResponse* = "y"', and can be read as " *(if) the value of the character variable UsersResponse is equal to the character value 'y'*". The operator symbol '=' should be read as '*is equal to*' and should not be confused with the assignment symbol ':=', read as '*becomes equal to*'. The *is equal to* operator will compare the value of the left hand expression, which in this case is the value of the character variable *UsersResponse*, with the value of the right hand expression, which in this case is the character literal '*y*'. If the two values are equal the expression will evaluate true, otherwise it will evaluate false. In the example above if the user entered '*y*', the value of *UsersResponse* will be '*y*', the expression will be true and the first PUT_LINE which says yes to the user will be executed. If the user entered '*n*', the value of *UsersResponse* will be '*n*', the expression will be false and the second PUT_LINE which says no to the user will be executed.

Three way sequential selections

A simple change to the specification might be

> The program will invite the user to type '*y*' to indicate yes or '*n*' to indicate no. The program will either confirm the input as '*yes*' or '*no*', or will inform the user that he or she has said neither yes nor no.

The user interface will now have a third possible outcome:

```
          Yes No Demo 2

     Please enter 'y' for yes or 'n' for no i

     You said neither Yes nor No.
```

The data table requires no changes and a design for this program might be as follows:

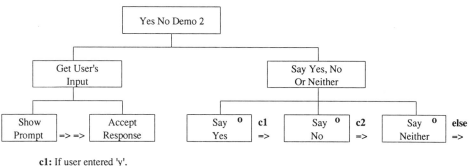

c1: If user entered 'y'.
c2: If user entered 'n'.

The decision has been extended to a three way selection with two conditions and a default third alternative. The interpretation of this design now is that if the first condition is true the component *SayYes* will be performed and the other two components will be ignored. Otherwise, if the first condition is false the second condition will be evaluated and if it is true the component *SayNo* will be performed and the component *SayNeither* ignored. Otherwise, if both condition 1 and condition 2 are false then the component *SayNeither* will be performed. Under any circumstances only one of the three optional components will ever be performed.

The data design, the context clause and the implementation of *GetUsers-Response* will not differ significantly from the *YesNoDemo1* program given above. The implementation of the component *SayYesNoOrNeither* would be as follows:

```
0025        if UsersResponse = 'y' then
0026            PUT_LINE("You entered Yes.");
0027        elsif UsersResponse = 'n' then
0028            PUT_LINE("You entered No.");
0029        else
0030            PUT_LINE("You entered neither Yes nor No.");
0031        end if;
0032    end YesNoDemo2;
```

The implementation of the three way decision involves extending the original **if/else/end if** structure into an **if/elsif/else/end if.** The second condition from the design is inserted into the simpler structure following the first actions as an **elsif** *Condition2* **then** clause followed by the actions which are controlled by the second condition, before the **else** which introduces the default actions.

The behaviour of this **if** structure is comparable with the description of the design given above. If the user enters '*y*', the value of *UsersResponse* will be '*y*', the condition on line 0025 will be true and the message on line 0026 will be output. Otherwise, if the user enters '*n*', the value of *UsersResponse* will be '*n*', and the condition on line 0025 will be false causing the condition on line 0027 to be evaluated; this condition will be true and the message on line 0028 will be output. Otherwise, if the user enters anything other than '*y*' or '*n*', the conditions on lines 0025 and 0027 will both be false causing the default message on line 0030 to be output.

Other forms of sequential selections

The extension of the two way selection to a three way selection can be taken further. For example, a five way selection could be designed as

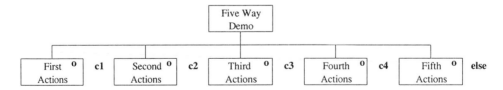

and implemented using an extended **if/elsif/else/end if** structure as

```
        if    Condition1 then
            -- first actions
```

```
elsif Condition2 then
   -- second actions
elsif Condition3 then
   -- third actions
elsif Condition4 then
   -- fourth actions
else
   -- fifth actions
end if;
```

The interpretation of this design and of the implementation is comparable with the interpretation of the three way selection above. Each condition is tested in turn and if any evaluates true the actions associated with it are performed. If none of the four conditions is true then the default actions, the fifth actions, are performed. Under all circumstances only one of the optional components will be performed.

With a sequential selection it is not always required that the last option is performed by default. For example, a four way sequential selection with no default final option could be designed as

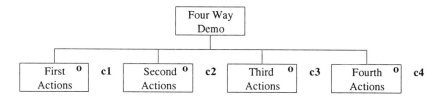

and implemented as

```
if Condition1 then
   -- first actions
elsif Condition2 then
   -- second actions
elsif Condition3 then
   -- third actions
elsif Condition4 then
   -- fourth actions
end if;
```

The difference between this form of selection design and the previous one is that if all conditions evaluate false, none of the actions will be performed. However, if any of the conditions evaluate true then only one of the actions will be performed. Should two, or more, of the conditions evaluate true then only the actions associated with the first condition that evaluates true will be executed.

A further, but not very common, design option is a one way selection whose design and implementation would be:

```
if Condition1 then
   -- only actions
end if;
```

In this design and implementation if the condition is true then the actions will be performed, otherwise the condition must be false and the actions are ignored.

One final form of sequential selection is a sequence of simple selections. The design and implementation of this form of selection, as a sequence of three simple selections, would be

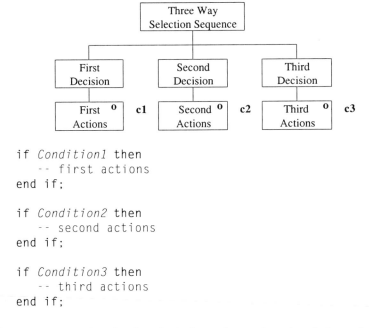

```
if Condition1 then
   -- first actions
end if;

if Condition2 then
   -- second actions
end if;

if Condition3 then
   -- third actions
end if;
```

In this structure each selection is independent of each of the others. As each condition and action is independent of the others, if the condition associated with any action evaluates true those actions will be performed. Thus this differs from the strict sequential decisions in that it is possible that any number of the actions, including none of the actions, may be taken.

Nested selections

A nested selection design extends a sequential selection design by replacing the actions associated with one of the optional components with a further selection. To illustrate this concept further a simple specification suitable for implementation as a nested selection will be developed. The specification is

> The program will first ask the user to indicate his or her gender by entering either '*m*' for *m*ale or '*f*' for *f*emale. It may be assumed that the user's input will always be either '*m*' or '*f*'. The program will continue by asking the user to input his or her age as an integer value, it may be assumed that the user will always enter a suitable integer value.
>
> The program will then categorize the user as:
>
> a male pensioner
> a male non-pensioner
> a female pensioner
> a female non-pensioner
>
> For the purposes of this program the current UK rules for pensioner status will be used: these are 65 years or older for a male and 60 years or older for a female.

A user interface design, combining all possible outcomes, for this specification might be

```
            Nested Selection Demo

    Please enter 'm' for male or 'f' for female  m or f
    Please enter your age in years                  ii

    You are a {male/male} [non] pensioner.
```

The user interface indicates that in reply to the first question the user will either enter '*m*' or '*f*'; and in response to the second question a two digit integer. The output indicates that the program may categorize the user as male or female, and as a non-pensioner or pensioner.

A suitable design for this program might be as follows

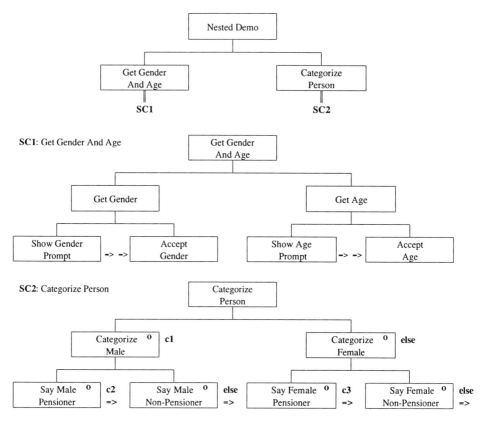

c1: If gender is male.
c2: If older than male retirement age.
c3: If older than female retirement age.

This design has been divided into three structure charts in order to allow it to fit on to the page and, more importantly, to assist with understanding the design by dividing a complex chart into three simple charts. The continuation charts are labelled **SC1** and **SC2** (structure chart 1 and 2) and are cross referenced to the main chart as shown. The designs in the main chart and **SC1** should be comprehensible from the designs which have been previously presented.

SC2 introduces the notation for a nested selection. It consists of a simple two way selection with a default alternative, which decides between males and females on the basis of condition 1. Each of the optional components of this selection are themselves two way selections with default alternatives. Thus the component *CategorizeMale* is both an optional component of the *CategorizePerson* selection and is itself a selection between the components *SayMalePensioner* and *SayMaleNonPensioner*.

The interpretation of the design is that if the user indicates male, the component *CategorizeMale* is performed and the component *CategorizeFemale* is ignored. When *CategorizeMale* is performed, if the user's age indicates that the user is older than the male retirement age the component *SayMalePensioner* is performed and the component *SayMaleNonPensioner* is ignored. The full actions of the decision structure can be better represented in the form of a **truth table**:

Truth table for *CategorizePerson*

Gender	Age	Action
male	>=male retirement age	Say Male Pensioner
male	<male retirement age	Say Male Non-Pensioner
female	>=female retirement age	Say Female Pensioner
female	<female retirement age	Say Female Non-Pensioner

The truth table validates the action of the design in a more compact and comprehensible manner than the equivalent continuation of the written decision in the previous paragraph. As was emphasized in the introduction to this chapter it is essential that the action of selections should be shown to be correct at the design stage as otherwise an incorrect program will be produced from the design. The costs involved in the correction of an incorrect program far outweigh the costs involved in validating a design by the careful construction of a decision table.

A data design for this program might be as follows:

Program constants for *Nested Selection Demo*

Name	Type	Value	Notes
MaleRetirementAge	INTEGER	65	Retirement age for males
FemaleRetirementAge	INTEGER	60	Retirement age for females

Program variables for *Nested Selection Demo*

Name	Type	Value	Notes
Gender	CHARACTER	?	Person's gender, 'm' for male or 'f' for female
Age	INTEGER	?	Person's age in years

The implementation of this design might be as follows:

```
0001    -- Filename NestedDemo.ada
0002    -- Nested selection demonstration program.
0003    -- Written for Ada Book Section I Chapter 6.
```

```
0004    --
0005    -- Fintan Culwin, v0.1, Jan 1997.
0006
0007    with ADA.TEXT_IO;
0008    use  ADA.TEXT_IO;
0009
0010    procedure NestedDemo is
0011
0012       package IntegerIO is new ADA.TEXT_IO.INTEGER_IO( INTEGER);
0013       use IntegerIO;
0014
0015       MaleRetirementAge   : constant INTEGER := 65;
0016       FemaleRetirementAge : constant INTEGER := 60;
0017
0018       Gender : CHARACTER;
0019       Age    : INTEGER;
0020
0021    begin -- NestedDemo
0022       -- Output title.
0023       PUT_LINE("          Nested Demo"); NEW_LINE(2);
0024
0025       -- Get gender and age.
0026       PUT("Please enter 'm' for male, or 'f' for female ");
0027       GET( Gender); SKIP_LINE;
0028       PUT("Please enter your age in years            ");
0029       GET( Age); SKIP_LINE;
0030
0031       NEW_LINE( 2);
0032
0033       -- Categorize person.
0034       if Gender = 'm' then
0035          if Age >= MaleRetirementAge then
0036             PUT_LINE("You are a male pensioner.");
0037          else
0038             PUT_LINE("You are a male non-pensioner.");
0039          end if;
0040       else
0041          if Age >= FemaleRetirementAge then
0042             PUT_LINE("You are a female pensioner.");
0043          else
0044             PUT_LINE("You are a female non-pensioner.");
0045          end if;
0046       end if;
0047    end NestedDemo;
```

The implementation of the nested **if** structure on lines 0034 to 0046 follows the design closely. The first selection structure, identified on the design as *Categorize-Person* is implemented as the outermost **if/else/end if** structure on lines 0034,

0040 and 0046. The first nested selection, identified on the design as *Categorize-Male*, is implemented as the **if/else /end if** structure on lines 0035 to 0039. This nested **if** structure is the first action component of the outermost **if** and consequently indented by three spaces from the outermost **if**. The action components of this nested **if**, the PUT_LINE statements on lines 0036 and 0038, are indented by three spaces relative to the nested **if**, and consequently are nested by two indents, six characters, from the outermost **if**. The second action component of the outermost **if**, identified on the design as *CategorizeFemale*, is likewise implemented as an **if/else/end if** structure on lines 0041 to 0045, and is indented from the outermost if by three character spaces. The actions of this inner **if**, the PUT_LINE statements on lines 0042 and 0044, are double indented by six characters from the outermost **if**.

As was emphasized in the discussion of sequential **if** structures above, the use of indentation is a very important aspect of relating implementations to designs, in order to assist with readability and thus with maintenance activities.

The execution of the nested **if** structure is comparable with the discussion of the interpretation of the design above. If the user enters '*m*' in response to the first question, the condition on line 0034 will be true, the actions on lines 0035 to 0039 will be executed and the actions on lines 0041 to 0045 ignored. If the user does not enter '*m*', then it is assumed that the user must have entered '*f*', the condition on line 0034 will be false, the actions on lines 0041 to 0045 will be executed and the actions on lines 0035 to 0039 ignored.

Assuming that if the user entered '*f*' in response to the first question, then the value which the user has entered in response to the second question will determine the value of the expression on line 0040. The condition on this line can be read as " *(if) the value of the INTEGER variable Age is greater than or equal to the value of the INTEGER constant FemaleRetirementAge*". To trace this statement it is first assumed that the user indicated an age of 59, in which case the condition can be interpreted as "*59 > = 60*", which is false and which will cause the message on line 0043 to be output. Alternatively if the user indicated an age of 60, the condition would be "*60 > = 60*", which is true and which will cause the message on line 0041 to be output. If the user had entered '*m*' in response to the first question, the ages 64 and 65 could be used to validate the first nested **if** on lines 0034 to 0038. The reasons why the values 59 and 60, and 64 and 65, are the most appropriate age values to test the nested **if** statement will be made clear in the chapters on testing which follow later in the book.

An alternative implementation of the *NestedDemo* specification

An alternative implementation of the *NestedDemo* specification would involve a redesign of the second structure chart from the design above:

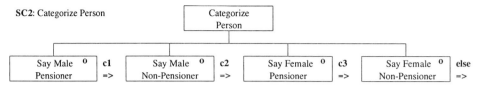

SC2: Categorize Person

c1: If gender is male and aged equal to or older than male retirement age.
c2: If gender is male and aged younger than male retirement age.
c3: If gender is female and aged equal to or older than female retirement age.

The design has been changed from a nested **if** to a four way sequential **if** with a default option. The design for this alternative can be argued to be simpler than the original design, as it avoids the use of nested structures and contains fewer boxes. It could also be argued that the revised design is more complex as in the original design there was never more than a two way decision. The reimplementation of this part of the program would be:

```
0034   if Gender = 'm' and Age >= MaleRetirementAge then
0035      PUT_LINE("You are a male pensioner.");
0036   elsif Gender = 'm' and Age < MaleRetirementAge then
0037      PUT_LINE("You are a male non-pensioner.");
0038   elsif Gender = 'f' and Age >= FemaleRetirementAge then
0039      PUT_LINE("You are a female pensioner.");
0040   else
0041      PUT_LINE("You are a female non-pensioner.");
0042   end if;
```

Although the relative complexity of the designs is not clear, the implementation of the decisions in the program code is clearly more complex in the reimplemented program. Each decision now consists of two subdecisions connected by a Boolean **and** operator. Each subdecision will evaluate as either true or false and the **and** operator will combine the two subdecisions according to the **and** rule:

and

Left expression	Right expression	Resulting value
False	False	False
False	True	False
True	False	False
True	True	True

The reasons why the **and** operator is described as a Boolean operator will be made clear in a later chapter. Assuming that the user indicated a 60 year old female, the first decision on line 0034 will be made by first evaluating the two subdecisions. The left hand subdecision, "*Gender* = '*m*'" would be equivalent to "'*f* = '*m*'" which is false. The right hand decision would be equivalent to "*60* > = *65*", which is false. The table above indicates that false **and** false is false. As the condition on line 0034 is false the statement on line 0035 will be ignored and the decision on line 0036 will be made. This decision will be made by first making the left subdecision, which is "*Gender* = '*m*'", which will be false as shown above. The right hand decision on line 0036 is equivalent to "*60* < *65*", which is true. The table indicates that the result of false **and** true is false. As the condition on line 0036 is false the statement on line 0037 will be ignored and the decision on line 0038 will be made.

The left hand subdecision on line 0038 is "*Gender* = '*f*'", which is equivalent to "'*f* = '*f*'", which is true. The right hand subdecision is "*Age* > = *Female-RetirementAge*", which is equivalent to "*60* > = *60*", which is true. The table indicates that true **and** true is true. As the condition on line 0038 is true the action on line 0039 will be performed, informing the user that the user is a female pensioner. The entire **if** structure will then terminate and following that the program will come to an end.

A similar trace could be made for a 65 year old male, a 64 year old male and a 59 year old female in order to demonstrate the equivalence of this implementation and to the previous implementation. As the two implementations are equivalent in their behaviour, any decision regarding which is the 'better' implementation of the specification must be made on the differences between the designs and the implementations. As was explained above, there is no clear difference in the designs, but as the second implementation involves the use of the **and** Boolean operator it can be regarded as more complex. A useful design heuristic is to implement specifications in a manner which is as complex as it needs to be, with due regard to maintainability, but no more complex. On this basis the first implementation is to be favoured, but with regard to the simplicity of these designs and implementations there is very little to choose between them.

The *or* Boolean operator

The previous section introduced the use of the Boolean **and** operator. The other common Boolean operator which can be used to connect two subdecisions together is the **or** operator. The truth table for this operator is

or

Left expression	Right expression	Resulting value
False	False	False
False	True	True
True	False	True
True	True	True

An amendment to the second specification given in this chapter will provide an opportunity to illustrate the use of the **or** operator, and will also make the specification more realistic:

> The program will invite the user to type either '*y*' or '*Y*' to indicate *yes*, or either '*n*' or '*N*' to indicate *no*. The program will either confirm the input as '*yes*' or '*no*', or inform the user that he or she has said neither yes nor no.

The design will only require the conditions to be amended:

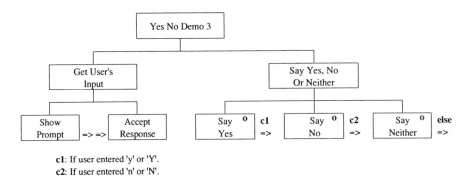

c1: If user entered 'y' or 'Y'.
c2: If user entered 'n' or 'N'.

The reimplementation of the relevant part of the program would be:

```
0025      if UsersResponse = 'y' or UsersResponse = 'Y' then
0026          PUT_LINE("You entered Yes.");
0027      elsif UsersResponse = 'n' or UsersResponse = 'N' then
0028          PUT_LINE("You entered No.");
0029      else
0030          PUT_LINE("You entered neither Yes nor No.");
0031      end if;
0032   end YesNoDemo2;
```

This part of the program can be traced to demonstrate its operation by assuming that it would be run five times with the values '*y*', '*Y*', '*n*', '*N*' and '*x*' input. The value '*x*' was chosen as representative of any character other than '*y*', '*Y*', '*n*' or '*N*' and has no other significance.

If the user inputs '*y*', the left hand subdecision on line 0025 would evaluate to "'*y*' = '*y*'", which is true, and the right hand subdecision would evaluate to "'*Y*' = '*y*'", which is false. The value of true **or** false is true and this will result in the message on line 0026 being output. If the user had entered '*Y*' the decision would have evaluated to false **or** true, which is also true.

If the user inputs '*n*', the decision on line 0025 would evaluate to false **or** false, which is false. This will cause the statement on line 0026 to be ignored and the decision on line 0027 to be made. The left hand subdecision on this line will evaluate to "'*n*' = '*n*'", which is true, and the right hand subdecision would evaluate to "'*n*' = '*N*'", which is false. The combined decision, true **or** false is true, and will cause the statement on line 0028 to be output. If the user had input '*N*', the decision on line 0025 would still have been false causing the decision on line 0027 to be made. This decision would have evaluated to false **or** true, which is also true.

Finally if the user has input '*x*' the combined decision on line 0025 would evaluate to "'*x*' = '*y*' **or** '*x*' = '*Y*'", which is false **or** false, which is false. This false result will cause the decision on line 0027 to be made. The combined decision on line 0027 would evaluate to "'*x*' = '*n*' **or** '*x*' = '*N*'", which is false **or** false, which is also false. This false result on line 0027 will cause the default message on line 0029 to be output.

An alternative to using if

Under some circumstances it is preferable to implement a sequential selection from a design by the use of a **case** structure rather than an **if/elsif/end if** structure. This section will introduce and develop a specification making use of the **case** structure before concluding by describing the circumstances where a **case** structure is preferable to an **if** structure. The specification for the demonstration program is as follows:

> The program will invite the user to type in a single character and will then tell the user if it is: lower case alphabetic ('a' .. 'z'), upper case alphabetic ('A' .. 'Z'), a digit ('0' .. '9'), a punctuation character ('.' ',' ':') or any other character.

The user interface for this program, known as *Character Classifier*, is as follows:

```
        Character Classifier

    Please enter a single character ?

    That is {lower case | upper case | a digit |
                    punctuation | unknown }
```

A data design for this specification would be as follows:

Program variables for *Character Classifier*, program procedure

Name	Type	Value	Notes
UsersReply	CHARACTER	?	The character the user input

A design for this program might be as follows:

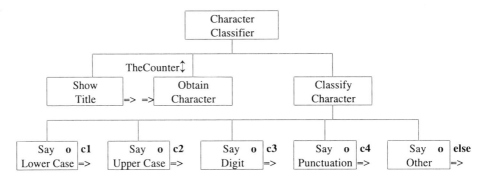

c1: If the character is lower case.
c2: If the character is upper case.
c3: If the character is a digit.
c4: If the character is punctuation.

The basis of the design of the selective component, *ClassifyCharacter*, does not differ from the five way selection with a default alternative given above. The *ObtainCharacter* component could be refined, in a similar manner to previous 'obtain components', but such a refinement does not add anything useful to the design. The implementation of this design might be as follows:

```
0001    -- Filename CharacterClassifier.adb (characte.adb).
0002    -- Program to illustrate the use of the case selective
0003    -- control structure.
0004    --
0005    -- Written for Ada book Section I Chapter 6.
0006    -- Fintan Culwin, v0.1, Jan 1997.
0007
0008    with ADA.TEXT_IO;
0009    use  ADA.TEXT_IO;
0010
0011    procedure CharacterClassifier is
0012
0013        UsersReply : CHARACTER;
```

```
0014
0015    begin -- CharacterClassifier
0016        NEW_LINE( 2);
0017        SET_COL(15); PUT_LINE( "Character Classifier");
0018        NEW_LINE( 2);
0019
0020        PUT( "Please enter a single character ");
0021        GET( UsersReply); SKIP_LINE;
0022        NEW_LINE(2);
0023
0024        case UsersReply is
0025        when 'a' .. 'z' =>
0026            PUT_LINE( "That is a lower case alphabetic character.");
0027        when 'A' .. 'Z' =>
0028            PUT_LINE( "That is an upper case alphabetic character.");
0029        when '0' .. '9' =>
0030            PUT_LINE( "That is a digit character.");
0031        when '.' | ',' | ';' | ':' =>
0032            PUT_LINE( "That is a punctuation character.");
0033        when others =>
0034            PUT_LINE( "That is an unknown character.");
0035        end case;
0036    end CharacterClassifier;
```

The section structure is implemented on lines *0024* to *0035* using a **case** structure whose general form is as follows:

```
case SelectionExpression is
when SelectionValue(s) =>
    -- actions
{when SelectionValue(s) =>
    -- actions
}
{when others =>
    -- actions
}
end case;
```

A **case** structure is delineated in source code by the use of the **case/end case** reserved word markers. The *SelectionExpression* which follows the **case** reserved word controls the selection, and the value of this expression must be of a ***discrete type***. A discrete type is a data type whose values can be precisely listed. For example, the INTEGER type is discrete as it has the sequence .. 1, 2, 3, 4 .., the CHARACTER type is also discrete as it has the sequence .. 'a', 'b', 'c', 'd', .. . The FLOAT data type is not discrete as it has no defined sequence; the next value after 1.0 might be 1.1 or 1.01 or 1.001, and so on.

The body of the **case** structure consists of at least one **when** clause. Each **when** clause defines a set of values from the discrete sequence; the definition expression is shown in the general form as *SelectionValue(s)*. The set can be expressed in a number of different ways: for example, if the *SelectorExpression* is of the type CHARACTER, the following *SelectionValue(s)* would define the sets as indicated:

Selection Value(s)	Characters in the set
`case 'A'`	Upper case A only
`case 'A' | 'a'`	Upper and lower case A
`case 'A' .. 'E'`	Upper case A, B, C, D & E
`case 'A' .. 'E' | 'a' .. 'e'`	Upper and lower case A, B, C, D & E
`case 'f' ..'h' | 'X'`	Lower case f, g & h and upper case X

The construction of a *SelectionValue(s)* expression can make use of the '|' operator which can be read as *and*, and the '..' operator which can be read as *range*. Thus the third expression in the table above can be read as "*the set consists of the characters in the range* 'A' *to* 'E' *and* the characters in the *range* 'a' *to* 'e'".

Each *SelectionValue(s)* expression is followed by the '=>' symbol, which is used to indicate the end of the expression and to introduce the actions which are controlled by the expression. As indicated above these actions are under the control of the **case** structure and consequently are indented by three characters. The actions can consist of any sequence of Ada statements.

The behaviour of the **case** structure, when it is executed, is to determine the value of the *SelectionExpression* and then to execute the actions which are associated with the *SelectionValue(s)* set which contains the determined value. It is a requirement of the **case** structure that every possible value of the *Selection-Expression*'s type occurs exactly once in the *SelectionValue(s)* sets. In many situations, as indicated in the program above, the number of values which control actions is only a small subset of all the possible values. In these situations the last *SelectionValue(s)* expression can be specified as **when others**, and defines a default set of values whose members are those not explicitly indicated in all previous *SelectionValue(s)* expressions. Where there are no actions associated with these default values, the actions to be performed can be specified as **null**. This is the Ada **null** statement and when executed by Ada causes nothing to happen.

In the example above the character supplied by the user will be used as the *SelectionExpression* and it will match one of the **when** clauses on lines 0025, 0027, 0029, 0031 or 0033, causing the appropriate message to be output to the user.

A **case** structure can always be replaced with an equivalent **if/elsif/else/end if** structure, but the converse is not always possible. In some situations the use of a **case** structure is preferable as it allows complex Boolean expressions from an **if** structure to be replaced with a simpler *SelectionValue(s)* expression in a **case** structure. For example, the equivalent **elsif** statement for the fourth expression in the table above would be

```
elsif ( AnyCharacter >= 'f' and AnyCharacter <= 'h')
      or (AnyCharacter = 'X') then
```

A comparison of these two expressions should be sufficient to illustrate the advantages of using a **case** structure in preference to an **if** structure where such a replacement is possible. A **case** structure can only replace an **if** structure when the value of a single discrete variable, or expression, is being used to control the selection.

A warning on overcomplexity

It was stressed at the start of this chapter that the behavioural complexity of software is very largely due to the effects of selections and iterations. The consequence of this consideration is that selections, and iterations, should be constructed with extreme care and attention to detail. As described above the Boolean expressions which are used in selections should be tested, by the use of trace tables, as they are designed and constructed to ensure that the decisions which they are implementing are appropriate to the specification.

For reasons concerned with human cognitive abilities the complexity of selections should be limited. Although a design such as the following could be constructed.

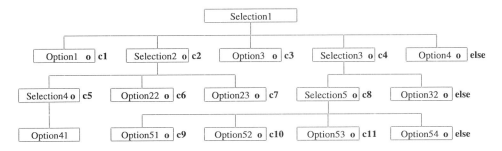

Such a design could be implemented in Ada by systematically transcribing it:

```
if cl then
    Option1;
elsif c2 then
    if c5 then
        Option41;
```

```
          elsif c6 then
              Option22;
          elsif c7 then
              Option23;
          end if;
      elsif c3 then
          Option3
      elsif c4 then
          if c8 then
              if c9 then
                  Option51;
              elsif c10 then
                  Option52;
              elsif c11 then
                  Option53;
              else
                  Option54;
              end if;
          else
              Option32;
          end if;
      else
          Option4
      end if
```

The construction of a truth table for this structure, which is a prerequisite for validating that it will perform according to specification, would be very difficult, and even when constructed would be impossibly difficult to comprehend. As the construction of such a structure would be extremely difficult and error prone it would be likely that such a structure would behave incorrectly during testing and the difficulties involved in initial debugging and subsequent maintenance would be horrendous.

The solution to the problem above is to modularize the design, possibly by implementing Selections 2 and 5 as subprograms which hide the complexity of their implementation, in this case a selection, within themselves. This redesign would then give three separate subprograms, each of which contains only a fraction of the original complexity and each of which is consequently easier to implement, debug and maintain.

There must come a point between the complexity of the selection structures which were designed and implemented earlier in this chapter and the horrendous structure above, where the selection is so complex that it should not be implemented without a modularization. This point is not very precise but a useful rule of thumb is to decide that a structure containing between five and nine *cognitive chunks* should be split. A *cognitive chunk* can be defined in this situation as an option within a selection structure or an operator within a Boolean expression. The range five to nine has been determined by cognitive psychologists who have experimentally determined that an average human is capable of attending to 'seven plus or minus two' simultaneous pieces of information. A selection structure which contains more than nine simple selections and/or decisions, or more than five more complex selections and/or decisions, will be incapable of being understood by an average human developer and can be predicted to be a potential trouble spot during construction and maintenance.

EXERCISES

6.1 Many specifications offer the user a menu of choices keyed with 'a', 'b', 'c', etc. Using the design of the *YesNoDemo2* program given in the chapter, design a demonstration program which will offer the user a range of choices and then accept a character. The program should then indicate which option the user has selected from the choices, or inform the user that the choice is invalid. The number of available choices should be determined by a CHARACTER constant.

6.2 A bus company will allow people aged under 5 or over 65 to travel for free, those aged between 5 and 15 to travel for half price and all others to pay the full price. Design and implement a program which will ask people for their age and then inform them of the rate they will have to pay on the bus.

6.3 A security company will only employ people between the ages of 21 and 50; additionally males have to be at least 1.80 metres and females at least 1.70 metres tall. Design and implement a program which asks people for their age, gender and height and then informs them if they are or are not employable. If they are not employable a reason must be given.

6.4 Reimplement the *Character Classifier* program from the chapter making use of an **if** structure instead of a **case** structure.

6.5 If you implemented Exercise 6.1 making use of a **case** structure reimplement it making use of an **if** structure, otherwise reimplement it making use of a **case** structure.

6.6 Are there any detectable differences between the two programs from Exercises 6.1 and 6.5 from the user's point of view? If not, does it matter whether a **case** or an **if** structure was used in the implementation?

CHAPTER 7
Iteration in programs

The previous chapter introduced selection control structures; this chapter will introduce iterative control structures, collectively known as *loops*. Iterative control allows a part of the program to be repeated a number of times. The word *iteration* is used instead of the word *repetition* as repetition implies that a sequence of actions controlled by the loop will be executed at least once, whilst iteration implies that the actions may not be executed at all.

There are two forms of iteration. *Definite iteration* is where the number of times a part of the program will be executed can be determined by the program immediately before the iterative structure is encountered. This includes the situation where the number of times can be determined from the specification. *Indefinite iteration* is where the number of times cannot be determined until the iterative structure is encountered.

There are two iterative structures in Ada corresponding to definite and indefinite loops. Definite loops are implemented using the Ada **for** structure; indefinite loops use the **while** structure. In most situations the specification or the design indicates which form of loop is most appropriate. Where the choice is not clear, an indefinite loop can always be used to simulate a definite loop, but the converse is not always the case. This chapter will start by considering the more general of the two structures, indefinite loops, before considering definite loops.

A first indefinite iteration specification

In the specifications presented in the previous chapter it was assumed that the user would always input an acceptable value when asked. More realistic specifications would never make this assumption and would have to allow for the possibility that the user would not do as asked. An extended specification of the *YesNoDemo* specification from the previous chapter might be as follows:

> The program will invite the user to type 'y' or 'Y' to indicate *yes* or to type 'n' or 'N' to indicate *no*. If the user types in any other character he or she will be reminded that only 'y', 'Y', 'n' or 'N' is acceptable and the input requested again. This process will continue until the user has input an acceptable character.
>
> The program will then confirm the input as 'yes' or 'no' before finishing.

A user interface for this specification might be as follows:

```
Yes No Demo 4

Please enter 'y' for yes or 'n' for no i
Only 'Y', 'y', 'N' or 'n' should be typed.

Please enter 'y' for yes or 'n' for no h
Only 'Y', 'y', 'N' or 'n' should be typed.

Please enter 'y' for yes or 'n' for no y

You said yes.
```

The interaction above could have continued with the user making any number of unacceptable responses when requested, before concluding with the user typing one of the four acceptable characters. The data design for this program does not change from the previous versions:

Program variables for *YesNoDemo4*

Name	Type	Initial value	Notes
UsersResponse	CHARACTER	?	The user's response, either 'y' or 'n'

A design for this specification might be as follows:

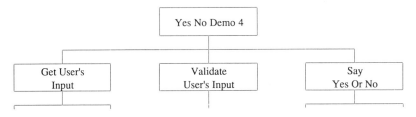

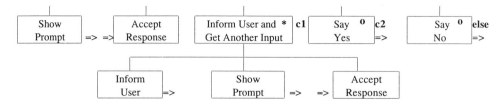

c1: While the user entered an unacceptable response.
c2: If the user's response indicated yes.

The basis of the design is first to input a response from the user, to validate the response and then to indicate to the user if the response was yes or no. The implementation of the validation component may require a sequence of actions to be repeated a number of times and this identifies it as an iterative component of the design.

An iteration on a design is indicated as a component which is refined into an iterated component. The iteration of the iterated component is indicated by an asterisk ('*') on the design. In the design above the component *ValidateUsers-Input* is the iteration, the component *InformUserAndGetAnotherInput* is the iterated component. The asterisk in the top right hand corner of the *InformUser-AndGetAnotherInput* box indicates that it is iterated, and may be executed zero or more times.

Every iteration on a program design must be keyed with a condition number which will express the conditions under which the component will be iterated. As with conditions which express selections, an iteration condition should be expressed as a natural language phrase and not as an Ada phrase. For indefinite iterations the condition phrase should always begin with the word 'while'.

The interpretation of an iterative design is that the iterated component will be performed for as long as the condition is true. The design above indicates that the iterated component will be executed for as long as the user's response is unacceptable. This implies that if the user inputs an acceptable response when asked for the first time, the condition will be false and the iterated component will not be executed at all.

Should the user not supply an acceptable response when asked for the first time, the condition will be true and the component will iterate. The effect of executing the iterated component is to inform the user that the response is unacceptable and to obtain a second response. At the end of the sequence which forms the body of the iteration the condition is evaluated for a second time. If the second response is also unacceptable then the condition will still be true and the body of the loop will iterate for a second time. Alternatively if the second response is acceptable the condition will be false and the loop will terminate.

Should the second response be unacceptable and the loop iterates for a second time, the condition will be evaluated for a third time at the end of the loop. This may cause the loop to be iterated for a fourth time and subsequently possibly for a fifth time, and so on. What is certain is that, however the component *SayYesOrNo* is reached, the user's response is guaranteed to be acceptable. The implementation of this design as an Ada program might be as follows:

```
0001    -- Filename YesNoDemo4.ada (k8 yesnode4.adb).
0002    -- First indefinite iteration demonstration program,
0003    -- incorporating the YesNoDemo2 selection from sIc6.
0004    -- Written for Ada Book Section I Chapter 7.
0005    --
0006    -- Fintan Culwin, v0.1, Jan 1997.
0007
0008    with ADA.TEXT_IO;
0009    use  ADA.TEXT_IO;
0010
0011    procedure YesNoDemo4 is
0012
0013        UsersResponse : CHARACTER;
0014
0015    begin -- YesNoDemo4
0016        SET_COL(15); PUT_LINE("Yes No Demo 4");
0017        NEW_LINE(2);
0018
0019        -- Get user's input.
0020        PUT("Please enter 'y' for yes, or 'n' for no ");
0021        GET( UsersResponse); SKIP_LINE;
0022
0023        while UsersResponse /= 'y' and
0024              UsersResponse /= 'Y' and
0025              UsersResponse /= 'n' and
0026              UsersResponse /= 'N'        loop
0027            -- Inform user and get another response.
0028            PUT_LINE("Only 'Y', 'y', 'N' or 'n' should be typed.");
0029            NEW_LINE;
0030            PUT("Please enter 'y' for yes, or 'n' for no ");
0031            GET( UsersResponse); SKIP_LINE;
0032        end loop;
0033
0034        -- Say yes or no.
0035        NEW_LINE( 2);
0036        if UsersResponse = 'y' or UsersResponse = 'Y' then
0037            PUT_LINE("You entered Yes.");
0038        else
0039            PUT_LINE("You entered No.");
0040        end if;
0041    end YesNoDemo4;
```

The iteration is implemented as a **while** loop control structure between lines 0023 and 0032. The general form of an Ada **while** loop is:

```
while BooleanCondition loop
   -- Statements to be iterated
end loop;
```

The scope of the **while** loop is delineated by the reserved words **while** and **end loop**. The *BooleanCondition* which controls the behaviour of the loop is enclosed between the **while** and **loop** reserved words at the start of the loop. There can be any number of Ada statements forming the body of the loop between these two terms. As indicated above it is strongly suggested that the body of the loop is indented by three characters relative to the **while** and **end loop** markers.

The behaviour of the **while** loop structure is that the condition is first evaluated and if it evaluates false the loop terminates without the body of the loop being executed at all. Otherwise the condition must have evaluated true and the body of the loop is executed, following which the condition is re-evaluated with the same consequences as when the condition was evaluated for the first time.

In the program above the **while** loop condition is expressed on lines 0023 to 0026 and consists of four relational expressions connected by three Boolean **and** operators. Ada evaluates this expression by first determining the result of the first relational expression and **and**ing this result with the result of the second relational expression. This **and**ed result is subsequently **and**ed with the third relational expression, whose result is subsequently **and**ed with the fourth relational expression to produce the result of the complete expression.

The outcome of this process is, as will be demonstrated below, that the entire expression will evaluate true if all four relational expressions evaluate true and will evaluate false if any of the relational expressions evaluate false. The effect of the expression is that if the user supplied one of the four acceptable characters the corresponding relational expression will evaluate false and the entire test will be false. However, if the user inputs an unacceptable character all of the relational expressions will evaluate true and the entire expression will be true. This can be demonstrated by use of a truth table:

Users-Response	Relational expression on line				Boolean expression
	0023	0024	0025	0026	
'y'	false	true	true	true	false
'Y'	true	false	true	true	false
'n'	true	true	false	true	false
'N'	true	true	true	false	false
'x'	true	true	true	true	true

As with the description of *YesNoDemo2* in the previous chapter the value 'x' has been chosen as being other than one of the acceptable characters and has no other significance. The behaviour of the program can be further illustrated by the use of a program trace table, assuming that the user will first input the value '*h*' followed by the value '*n*'.

Line number	UsersReponse	Boolean expression	Notes
0015	?		Initial value
0017	?		Title output
0020	?		Prompt output
0021	'h'		First response accepted
0023–0026	'h'	true	Loop condition evaluated for the first time
0028–0029	'h'		Message output
0030	'h'		Prompt output
0031	'n'		Second response accepted
0032	'n'		End of loop structure
0023–0026	'n'	false	Loop condition evaluated for the second time
0035	'n'		Spare lines output
0036	'n'	false	If condition evaluated
0039	'n'		Message output
0040	'n'		End of if structure
0041	'n'		End of program

An alternative design and implementation

An alternative design for the specification given above might be as follows:

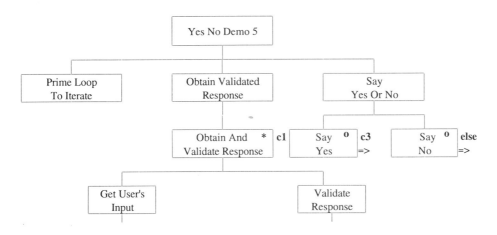

c1: While the user's response is unacceptable.
c2: If the user's response is unacceptable.
c3: If the user's response indicated yes.

The essential difference between this and the previous design is that in this design it is guaranteed that the body of the loop will be executed at least once, yet in the previous design it is possible that the body of the loop will never be executed.

In this design the first component of the design has the responsibility of ensuring that the loop iteration condition will succeed when it is evaluated for the first time. The body of the loop first obtains a response from the user and then validates the response, outputting a message to the user if the character typed in is unacceptable. Following the validation the loop iteration condition is evaluated for a second time and, if the response is unacceptable, the body of the loop will be executed for a second time.

This iterative process will continue indefinitely until the user inputs an acceptable character, whereupon the validation component will not output a message and the loop will terminate. The responsibility for ensuring that the loop iteration condition will evaluate true when it is tested for the first time is achieved by specifying an initial value for the variable *UsersResponse* as it is declared. The amended data table for this program might be as follows:

Program variables for *YesNoDemo5*

Name	Type	Initial value	Notes
UsersResponse	CHARACTER	'x'	The user's response either 'y', 'Y', 'n' or 'N', initial value chosen to be unacceptable, to prime loop

A program based on the design above might be as follows:

```
0001    -- Filename YesNoDemo5.ada (k8 yesnode5.adb).
0002    -- Second indefinite iteration demonstration program,
0003    -- indicating alternative approach to YesNoDemo4
                                              specification.
0004    -- Written for Ada Book Section I Chapter 7.
0005    --
0006    -- Fintan Culwin, v0.1, Jan 1997.
0007
0008    with ADA.TEXT_IO;
```

```
0009    use  ADA.TEXT_IO;
0010
0011    procedure YesNoDemo5 is
0012
0013        UsersResponse : CHARACTER := 'x'; -- Prime loop to
                                                        iterate.
0014
0015    begin -- YesNoDemo5
0016        SET_COL( 15); PUT_LINE("Yes No Demo 5");
0017        NEW_LINE(2);
0018
0019        while UsersResponse /= 'y' and
0020              UsersResponse /= 'Y' and
0021              UsersResponse /= 'n' and
0022              UsersResponse /= 'N'      loop
0023
0024           -- Get the user's response.
0025           PUT("Please enter 'y' for yes, or 'n' for no ");
0026           GET( UsersResponse); SKIP_LINE;
0027
0028           -- Possibly say no good.
0029           if UsersResponse /= 'y' and
0030              UsersResponse /= 'Y' and
0031              UsersResponse /= 'n' and
0032              UsersResponse /= 'N'      then
0033              PUT_LINE("Only 'Y', 'y', 'N' or 'n' should be
                                                        typed.");
0034              NEW_LINE;
0035           end if;
0036        end loop;
0037
0038        -- Say yes or no.
0039        NEW_LINE( 2);
0040        if UsersResponse = 'y' or UsersResponse = 'Y' then
0041           PUT_LINE("You entered Yes.");
0042        else
0043           PUT_LINE("You entered No.");
0044        end if;
0045    end YesNoDemo5;
```

In this listing the component *PrepareLoopToIterate* has been implemented as the assignment of a default value to the variable *UsersResponse*. A trace of this program using the same test data as was used in the trace of the program *YesNoDemo4* above will demonstrate the equivalence of the two implementations of the specification:

Line number	UsersResponse	Boolean expression	Notes
0015	'x'		Initial value
0017	'x'		Title output
0019–0022	'x'	true	Loop condition evaluated for the first time
0025	'x'		Prompt output
0026	'h'		First response accepted
0029–0032	'h'	true	If condition evaluated
0033–0034	'h'		Message output
0035	'h'		End of **if** structure
0036	'h'		End of loop structure
0019–0022	'h'	true	Loop condition evaluated for the second time
0025	'h'		Prompt output
0026	'n'		Second user's response accepted
0029–0032	'n'	false	If condition evaluated
0035	'n'		End of **if** structure
0036	'n'		End of loop structure
0019–0022	'n'	false	Loop condition evaluated for the third time
0039	'n'		Spare lines output
0040	'n'	false	If condition evaluated
0043	'n'		Message output
0044	'n'		End of **if** structure
0045	'n'		End of program

A comparison of the behaviour of this program under trace and the previous program will indicate that they behave identically. A consideration of the behaviour of both programs with a more extensive range of inputs would confirm their equivalence.

As the two designs are identical in behaviour when implemented, the advantages of one design over the other should be considered. Using the criterion of **cognitive complexity** introduced at the end of the previous chapter, the second design is clearly more complex. The first design contains only an iteration and a selection, the second contains an iteration and two selections.

Additionally the purpose of the first component of the designs, *GetUsersInput* in the first and *PrimeLoopToIterate* in the second, is considered as preparing the state of the variable *UsersResponse* prior to the testing of the loop condition for the first time. The purpose of the assignment of a character obtained from the user in the first implementation is clear; the reason for assigning the value '*x*' in the second is not obvious and would require an explanatory comment in the source code.

The first design uses the **while** loop structure as a ***true while*** loop, preserving the possibility that it may iterate zero times. The second design uses the loop as a *repeat loop*, which must iterate at least once. A repeat loop design can always be refined into a **while** loop design, but a **while** loop design cannot always be refined into a repeat loop design. In keeping with the philosophy of preferring the most general design techniques, *true while* loop designs are to be favoured over *repeat loop* designs.

A second specification

To continue the introduction of indefinite loops, and to consolidate the use of the extended data types from Chapter 5, an iterative client making use of the *RoomMonitors* type will be developed. The specification for this client will be as follows:

> The program will allow the user to record and control the number of people entering and leaving a room. The user will be able to press '+' when a person enters the room, '−' when a person leaves the room, '=' to find out how many people are currently in the room and 'q' to quit the program. Any other characters will be ignored.

A user interface design for this specification might be as follows:

```
                Room Control
+ + + + + + + + + + + + =
There are 12 people in the room.
+ + + − − − ? > 1 − − =
There are 10 people in the room.
+ + + + + − − + + + + + q
There were 18 people in the room when the program stopped.
```

A data design for this program might be as follows:

Program variables for *RoomControl*

Name	Type	Initial value	Notes
InRoom	*RoomMonitors*	0	The people in the room
CurrentChar	CHARACTER	?	The current character from the user
NumberInRoom	NATURAL	?	The number of people in the room

A program design might be as follows:

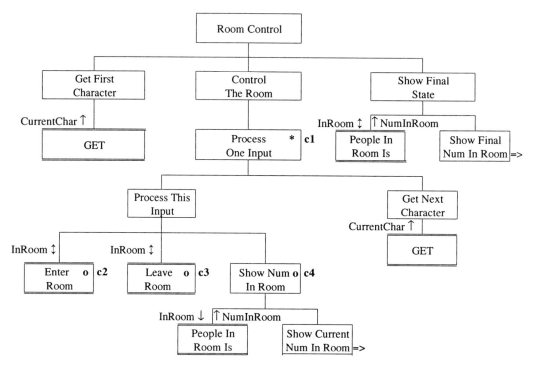

c1: While the user has not asked to stop the program.
c2: If the user indicates a person has entered the room.
c3: If the user indicates a person has left the room.
c4: If the user asks for the number of people in the room.

The iterative basis of the design is very similar to that of *YesNoDemo4* given above. The first character supplied by the user is obtained outside the loop and should it be a '*q*', the loop will never iterate, concluding the program with a message that there were zero people in the room.

Otherwise the program will iterate by first processing the character. If the character is '+' the *RoomMonitors EnterRoom* procedure will be called, if it is '−' the *RoomMonitors LeaveRoom* procedure will be called, if it is '=' the *Room-Monitors PeopleInRoomIs* function will be used to obtain the number of people in the room, which is subsequently output. The final action within the loop is to obtain the next character from the user, and if this is not a '*q*', to iterate again. The entire loop will terminate when the user enters '*q*' and the terminal component of the program will show the final state of the room.

The implementation of this design might be as follows:

```
0001    -- Filename RoomControl.ada (k8 roomcont.adb)
```

```
0002    -- Program to illustrate an iterative client of
0003    -- an extended data type.
0004    --
0005    -- Written for Ada book Section I Chapter 7.
0006    -- Fintan Culwin, v0.1, Jan 1997.
0007
0008    with ADA.TEXT_IO, RoomMonitor;
0009    use  ADA.TEXT_IO, RoomMonitor;
0010
0011    procedure RoomControl is
0012
0013       package IntegerIO is new ADA.TEXT_IO.INTEGER_IO( INTEGER);
0014       use IntegerIO;
0015
0016       InRoom            : RoomMonitors;
0017       CurrentCharacter  : CHARACTER;
0018       NumberInRoom      : NATURAL;
0019
0020    begin -- RoomControl
0021       NEW_LINE( 2);
0022       SET_COL( 15); PUT_LINE( "Room Control");
0023       NEW_LINE( 2);
0024
0025       GET( CurrentCharacter);
0026
0027       while CurrentCharacter /= 'q' loop
0028          case CurrentCharacter is
0029          when '+' =>
0030             EnterRoom( InRoom);
0031          when '-' =>
0032             LeaveRoom( InRoom);
0033          when '=' =>
0034             NumberInRoom := PeopleInRoomIs( InRoom);
0035             PUT( "There are "); PUT( NumberInRoom, WIDTH =>1);
0036             PUT_LINE( " people in the room.");
0037          when others =>
0038             null;
0039          end case;
0040
0041          GET( CurrentCharacter);
0042       end loop;
0043
0044       NumberInRoom := PeopleInRoomIs( InRoom);
0045       PUT( "There were "); PUT( NumberInRoom, WIDTH =>1);
0046       PUT_LINE( " people in the room when the program
                                                  stopped.");
0047    end RoomControl;
```

Tracing the effect of this program as it executes will be left as an end of chapter exercise.

Definite iterations

A definite iteration is a suitable design approach when the number of times that a component of the design will have to be iterated can be determined either from the specification, or by the program immediately before the start of the iteration. To illustrate the construction and use of definite iteration a program for the following specification will be developed:

> The program is to display a table indicating the sales tax to be paid and the total sale price of all purchase prices from £1.00 to £20.00 in steps of £1.00.

A user interface for this program, assuming a sales tax rate of 17.5%, might be as follows:

```
                Sales Tax Ready Reckoner

{          1         2         3         4         }
{1234567890123456789012345678901234567890123456789o}
  Purchase Price      Sales Tax            Sale price

          1.00          0.17                  1.17
          2.00          0.35                  2.35
           :             :                     :
           :             :                     :
         20.00          3.50                 23.50
```

The lines between the program title and the table headings are not part of the user interface; they are column numbers which have been included in this interface design to assist with the layout of the table. They indicate that the columns of numbers will start at column positions 1, 21 and 41 and that the decimal points of the numbers will be at column positions 6, 26 and 46. A suitable design for this program might be as follows:

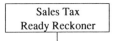

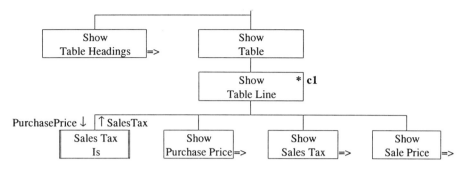

c1: Twenty times.

The same design notation which was used to indicate indefinite iteration, an asterisk in the top right hand corner, is used to indicate definite iteration. The component *ShowTable* is the iteration, and the iterated component is *ShowTable-Line*. The difference between definite and indefinite iteration is in the expression of the iteration condition which, for a definite iteration, states the number of times the component will be iterated and consequently does not start with the word 'while'.

The design indicates that the amount of sales tax will be calculated by a call to a subprogram called *SalesTaxIs*. This subprogram has a single **in only** parameter and a single **out only** parameter, which makes it suitable for implementation as a **function**, as explained earlier. This subprogram will be implemented as a **function** contained within the program procedure, rather than as a function contained within a separate package. The full implications of this style of implementation will be discussed in the next chapter.

The data flow interface diagram, and subprogram declaration, for this function might be as follows:

Price ↓ | ↑ TaxDue

Sales Tax
Is

```
function SalesTaxIs( Price : in FLOAT) return FLOAT;
```

The definition of this function will be given below. A data design for the program might be as follows:

Program constants for *SalesTaxReadyReckoner*, program procedure

Name	Type	Value	Notes
SalesTaxRate	FLOAT	0.175	The rate of sales tax (17.5%)

Program variables for *SalesTaxReadyReckoner*

Name	Type	Initial value	Notes
ThisLine	INTEGER	?	The loop parameter
PurchasePrice	FLOAT	?	The cost of a purchase
SalesTax	FLOAT	?	The sales tax to be paid on the purchase price
SalePrice	FLOAT	?	The cost of a purchase including sales tax

The meaning of the description of the variable *ThisLine* as the loop parameter will be made clear below. The implementation of this design might be as follows:

```
0001   -- Filename SalesTaxReadyReckoner.ada (k8 salestax.adb).
0002   -- Program to display a table of purchase prices,
0003   -- sales tax and consequent sale prices.
0004   --
0005   -- Written for Ada book Section I Chapter 7.
0006   -- Fintan Culwin, v0.1, Jan 1997.
0007
0008   with ADA.TEXT_IO;
0009   use  ADA.TEXT_IO;
0010
0011   procedure SalesTaxReadyReckoner is
0012
0013      package FloatIo is new ADA.TEXT_IO.FLOAT_IO( FLOAT);
0014      use FloatIo;
0015
0016      SalesTaxRate : constant FLOAT := 0.175;
0017
0018      PurchasePrice : FLOAT;
0019      SalesTax      : FLOAT;
0020      SalePrice     : FLOAT;
0021
0022      function SalesTaxIs( Price : in FLOAT) return FLOAT is
0023      begin -- SalesTaxIs
0024         return Price * SalesTaxRate;
0025      end SalesTaxIs;
0026
0027   begin -- SalesTaxReadyReckoner
0028      -- Do title and table headings.
0029      SET_COL(15);
0030      PUT_LINE("Sales Tax Ready Reckoner");
0031      NEW_LINE;
0032      SET_COL(  1); PUT("Purchase Price");
0033      SET_COL( 21); PUT("Sales Tax");
0034      SET_COL( 41); PUT("Sale Price");
```

```
0035        NEW_LINE( 2);
0036
0037        -- Do table body.
0038        for ThisLine in INTEGER range 1 .. 20 loop
0039            PurchasePrice := FLOAT( ThisLine);
0040            SalesTax      := SalesTaxIs( PurchasePrice);
0041            SalePrice     := PurchasePrice + SalesTax;
0042
0043            SET_COL( 1);  PUT( PurchasePrice, FORE=>5, AFT=>2,
                                                        EXP=>0);
0044            SET_COL( 21); PUT( SalesTax,      FORE=>5, AFT=>2,
                                                        EXP=>0);
0045            SET_COL( 41); PUT( SalePrice,     FORE=>5, AFT=>2,
                                                        EXP=>0);
0046      end loop;
0047    end SalesTaxReadyReckoner;
```

The definite loop in this program is implemented using the Ada **for** structure between lines 0038 and 0046. The general form of the **for** loop structure is

```
for LoopParameter in {reverse} {IndexType range}
                    LowExpression .. HighExpression loop
        -- body of the loop;
    end loop;
```

The parts of the general expression in curly brackets '{ }' are optional and need not always be used. The indication of an *IndexType* is not always required if Ada has sufficient clues from the data types of *LowExpression* and *HighExpression*. However, it is always useful for the developer to indicate the required type explicitly, which must always be a ***discrete type***. A discrete type, as explained in the previous chapter, is one which has a defined sequence.

The actions of Ada when executing a **for** loop are first to create a variable called *LoopParameter* of *IndexType* and initialize it to the value of *LowExpression*. The value of *LoopParameter* is then tested against the value of *HighExpression* and if it is less than or equal to the value of *HighExpression* the body of the loop is executed. If the value of *LoopParameter* is greater than the value of *HighExpression* the loop is terminated without the body being executed. Assuming that the initial test causes the body of the loop to be executed, following execution of the loop, the value of *LoopParameter* is incremented to the next value in the discrete sequence and the test is re-evaluated to decide if the loop should iterate again or terminate. The effect of the entire structure is that the *LoopParameter* counts forwards from *LowExpression* to *HighExpression* within the scope of the loop.

As the variable *LoopParameter* is created by Ada as part of the execution of the **for** statement, there is no need for the programmer to declare it in a declarative program region prior to the loop. Also, even though *LoopParameter* is described as being a variable the programmer cannot change its value within the loop; within the body of the loop the *LoopParameter* has to be treated as if it were a constant. The *LoopParameter* should be included in the data design but should not be explicitly declared as a variable in the listing.

When the **reverse** option is used in the **for** syntax the loop is executed backwards. That is, the value of *LoopParameter* is initialized to the value of *HighExpression* and is decremented to the previous value in the discrete sequence at the end of each execution of the loop body, and with appropriate changes to the tests applied. The effect is that the loop counts backwards from *HighExpression* to *LowExpression*.

In the example given above the value of the *LoopParameter*, *ThisLine*, is initialized to 1 and is incremented by 1 until it has the value 20. Thus the loop is executed 20 times with *ThisLine* having successive values 1, 2, 3, ..., 20. The format of *LowExpression* and *HighExpression* in this example is as INTEGER literals; other possible formats include constants, variables, function calls and complex expressions. Examples of these alternative formats will be met later in the book.

Within the body of the loop the value of the INTEGER loop parameter, *ThisLine*, is assigned via type conversion to the FLOAT variable *PurchasePrice*. It is not possible to use the variable *PurchasePrice* as the loop parameter, avoiding the necessity of type conversion, as in

```
-- This is not possible!
for PurchasePrice in FLOAT range 1.00 .. 20.00 loop
```

The loop parameter has to be of a discrete type and, as explained in the previous chapter, FLOAT is not a discrete type.

Having obtained a value for *PurchasePrice*, the value of the *SalesTax* and *SalePrice* can be computed and displayed as a line of the table. The effect of the loop is to compute and display the sales tax and sale price of all values between 1.00 and 2.00 in steps of 1.00, thus satisfying the specification.

The computation of *SalesTax* involves a call of the *SalesTaxIs* function which is defined on lines 0022 to 0025. The implementation of the function computes the sales tax due by multiplying the value of the *in only* parameter *Price* by the value of the constant *SalesTaxRate*. The resulting value is then returned as the value of the function call.

A second definite iteration specification

An extension to the specification given above will illustrate the use of a definite loop where the number of times that the loop will iterate is not known until the program is executing.

The program is to display a table indicating the sales tax to be paid and the total sale price of all purchase prices between two values input by the user. The table is to be displayed in reverse order.

A user interface design for this specification might be as follows:

```
            Sales Tax Ready Reckoner 2

Please enter the lower  value 30
Please enter the higher value 36

Purchase Price    Sales Tax    Sale Price

     36.00          6.30         42.30
     35.00          6.13         41.13
       :              :            :
       :              :            :
     30.00          5.25         35.25
```

There is no reason why the table is presented in reverse order, apart from providing an opportunity to provide an example of driving a definite loop in reverse. A high level design for this specification might be

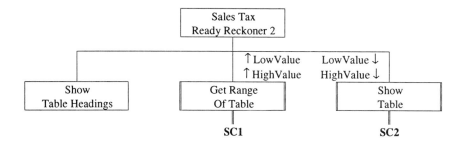

The interaction with the user to input the lower and higher values of the table's range has been designed as a call to the subprogram *GetRangeOfTable*, whose design is as follows:

SC1: Get Range Of Table

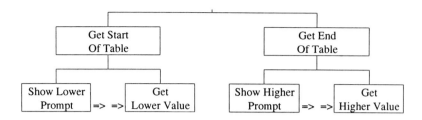

This design makes no attempt to ensure that the higher value is in fact greater than the lower value and it is assumed that the user will always correctly comply with the instructions. The design of the *ShowTable* component might be as follows:

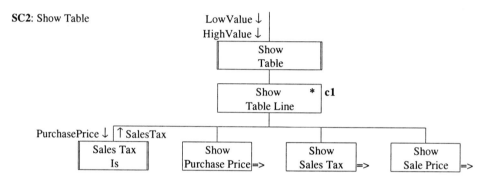

c1: For all values between HighValue and LowValue.

The major difference between this subprogram design and the design component for the output of the table in *SalesTaxReadyReckoner* above is in the expression of the condition. The **LowExpression** and **HighExpression** limits of the loop are now not INTEGER literals, but the value of the actual parameters, which were previously obtained from the user. The implementation of this refined design might be as follows:

```
0001    -- Filename SalesTaxReadyReckoner2.ada (k8 salesta2.adb).
0002    -- Program to display a reversed table of purchase prices,
0003    -- sales tax and consequent sale prices, between a range
0004    -- supplied by the user.
0005    --
0006    -- Written for Ada book Section I Chapter 7.
0007    -- Fintan Culwin, v0.1, Jan 1997.
0008
0009    with ADA.TEXT_IO;
0010    use  ADA.TEXT_IO;
0011
0012    procedure SalesTaxReadyReckoner1 is
0013
```

```
0014    package IntegerIO is new ADA.TEXT_IO.INTEGER_IO( INTEGER);
0015    use IntegerIO;
0016
0017    package FloatIO is new ADA.TEXT_IO.FLOAT_IO( FLOAT);
0018    use FloatIO;
0019
0020    SalesTaxRate : constant FLOAT := 0.175;
0021
0022    LowValueOfTable  : INTEGER;
0023    HighValueOfTable : INTEGER;
0024
0025
0026    procedure GetRangeOfTable( LowValue  : out INTEGER;
0027                               HighValue : out INTEGER ) is
0028
0029       LocalLow  : INTEGER;
0030       LocalHigh : INTEGER;
0031
0032    begin -- GetRangeOfTable
0033       PUT( "Please enter the lower value ");
0034       GET( LocalLow);
0035
0036       PUT( "Please enter the higher value ");
0037       GET( LocalHigh);
0038
0039       LowValue  := LocalLow;
0040       HighValue := LocalHigh;
0041    end GetRangeOfTable;
0042
0043
0044    function SalesTaxIs( Price : in FLOAT) return FLOAT is
0045    begin -- SalesTaxIs
0046       return Price * SalesTaxRate;
0047    end SalesTaxIs;
0048
0049
0050    procedure ShowTable( Lower  : in INTEGER;
0051                         Higher : in INTEGER) is
0052
0053       PurchasePrice : FLOAT;
0054       SalesTax      : FLOAT;
0055       SalePrice     : FLOAT;
0056
0057    begin -- ShowTable
0058       SET_COL( 1); PUT("Purchase Price");
0059       SET_COL( 21); PUT("Sales Tax");
0060       SET_COL( 41); PUT("Sale Price");
0061       NEW_LINE( 2);
```

```
0062
0063            -- Do table body.
0064            for ThisLine in reverse INTEGER range
0065                                          Lower .. Higher loop
0066              PurchasePrice := FLOAT( ThisLine);
0067              SalesTax      := SalesTaxIs( PurchasePrice);
0068              SalePrice     := PurchasePrice + SalesTax;
0069
0070              SET_COL( 1);
0071              PUT( PurchasePrice, FORE=>5, AFT=>2, EXP=>0);
0072              SET_COL( 21);
0073              PUT( SalesTax,      FORE=>5, AFT=>2, EXP=>0);
0074              SET_COL( 41);
0075              PUT( SalePrice,     FORE=>5, AFT=>2, EXP=>0);
0076            end loop;
0077        end ShowTable;
0078
0079
0080    begin -- SalesTaxReadyReckoner2
0081        -- Do title and table headings.
0082        SET_COL(15);
0083        PUT_LINE("Sales Tax Ready Reckoner");
0084        NEW_LINE;
0085
0086        GetRangeOfTable( LowValueOfTable, HighValueOfTable);
0087        ShowTable(       LowValueOfTable, HighValueOfTable);
0088    end SalesTaxReadyReckoner2;
```

There are now three subprograms contained within the program procedure. A
subprogram map of this implementation might be as follows:

```
┌─────────────────────────────────────────────────────┐
│                                                     │
│   procedure SalesTaxReadyReckoner1                  │
│                                                     │
│      ┌──────────────────────────────────────┐       │
│      │   procedure GetRangeOfTable( ~ ) is   │       │
│      │   begin -- GetRangeOfTable            │       │
│      │   end GetRangeOfTable;                │       │
│      └──────────────────────────────────────┘       │
│                                                     │
│      ┌──────────────────────────────────────┐       │
│      │   function SalesTaxIs( ~ ) is         │       │
│      │   begin -- SalesTaxIs                 │       │
│      │   end SalesTaxIs;                     │       │
│      └──────────────────────────────────────┘       │
│                                                     │
└─────────────────────────────────────────────────────┘
```

136

```
procedure ShowTable( ~ ) is



  begin -- ShowTable
  end ShowTable;


begin -- SalesTaxReadyReckoner1
end SalesTaxReadyReckoner1;
```

The subprogram map shows that the three subprograms, *GetRangeOfTable*, *SalesTaxIs* and *ShowTable*, are completely contained within the program procedure *SalesTaxReadyReckoner1*. The sequence of **declaration**, though not of **definition**, is significant. As the subprogram *ShowTable* has to call *SalesTaxIs*, *SalesTaxIs* has to be declared before *ShowTable*. In this style of implementation the **declaration** of a subprogram and the **definition** of the subprogram are combined into a single definition.

The three variables *PurchasePrice*, *SalesTax* and *SalePrice,* which were declared as variables of the program procedure in the previous implementation, have been declared as variables of the subprogram *ShowTable* in this implementation. A variable declared within a subprogram has a **scope** of that subprogram only and is not visible outside the boundaries of the subprogram, as indicated on the subprogram map. The use of local variables is in keeping with the design principle of keeping as much information as local as possible.

The program procedure obtains the bounds of the table from a call of *GetRangeOfTable* and these values are passed into the *ShowTable* procedure as the formal parameters *Lower* and *Higher*. Within the procedure they are specified as the range limits of the **for** control structure; thus the limits of the iteration are determined by the values input by the user. Despite the instruction that the loop is to iterate in reverse, indicated by the use of the **reverse** keyword in the **for** structure, the range is still specified from *LowExpression* to *HighExpression*. A common error would be to express a reversed loop as:

```
for ThisLine in reverse INTEGER range Higher .. Lower loop;
```

The action of a reversed loop is to initialize the value of the loop parameter to the value of the *HighExpression* and test the value of the loop parameter against the value of the *LowExpression*, terminating without executing the body of the loop if the value is lower. Otherwise the body of the loop is iterated, the value of the loop parameter is decremented and the test is made again with the same consequences.

If the loop is mis-implemented as shown above, the initial value of the loop parameter is first set to the value of *Lower*, tested against the value of *Higher* and

137

as the value of *Lower* is lower than *Higher*, the loop will terminate without iterating. The same effect will occur if the loop is correctly implemented and the user inputs a *lower* value which is higher than the *higher* value when asked.

The equivalence of indefinite and definite iteration

It was mentioned above that a definite iteration can always be implemented using an indefinite (**while**) construct, but an indefinite iteration cannot be implemented with a definite (**for**) construct. To illustrate this, the following listing is the *SalesTaxReadyReckoner* program reimplemented using the indefinite construct:

```
0001   -- Filename SalesTaxReadyReckoner3.ada (k8 salesta3.adb).
0002   -- Program to display a table of purchase prices,
0003   -- sales tax and consequent sale prices. Used to
0004   -- illustrate the equivalence of definite and
0005   -- indefinite iteration
0006   --
0007   -- Written for Ada book Section I Chapter 7.
0008   -- Fintan Culwin, v0.1, Jan 1997.
0009
0010   with ADA.TEXT_IO;
0011   use  ADA.TEXT_IO;
0012
0013   procedure SalesTaxReadyReckoner2 is
0014
0015      package FloatIo is new TEXT_IO.FLOAT_IO( FLOAT);
0016      use FloatIo;
0017
0018      SalesTaxRate  : constant FLOAT := 0.175;
0019
0020      PurchasePrice : FLOAT;
0021      SalesTax      : FLOAT;
0022      SalePrice     : FLOAT;
0023
0024    function SalesTaxIs( Price : in FLOAT) return FLOAT is
0025    begin -- SalesTaxIs
0026       return Price * SalesTaxRate;
0027    end SalesTaxIs;
0028
0029   begin -- SalesTaxReadyReckoner3
0030      -- Do title and table headings.
0031      SET_COL(15);
```

```
0032        PUT_LINE("Sales Tax Ready Reckoner");
0033        NEW_LINE;
0034        SET_COL(  1); PUT("Purchase Price");
0035        SET_COL( 21); PUT("Sales Tax");
0036        SET_COL( 41); PUT("Sale Price");
0037        NEW_LINE( 2);
0038
0039        -- Do table body.
0040        PurchasePrice := 1.0;
0041        while PurchasePrice <= 20.0 loop
0042           SalesTax  := CalculateSalesTax( PurchasePrice);
0043           SalePrice := PurchasePrice + SalesTax;
0044
0045           SET_COL( 1); PUT( PurchasePrice, FORE=>5, AFT=>2, EXP=>0);
0046           SET_COL(21); PUT( SalesTax,      FORE=>5, AFT=>2, EXP=>0);
0047           SET_COL(41); PUT( SalePrice,     FORE=>5, AFT=>2, EXP=>0);
0048           PurchasePrice := PurchasePrice + 1.0;
0049        end loop;
0050     end SalesTaxReadyReckoner3;
```

The reimplementation has replaced the loop parameter *ThisLine* with explicit manipulation of the program variable *PurchasePrice*. The **for** loop is replaced with a **while** loop and the value of the control variable is explicitly tested against a terminating condition to control the loop. The value of the control variable has to be explicitly initialized prior to the start of the loop, by being set to the initial value 1.0. Within the body of the loop the last action is to increment the value by 1.0. A trace of this version will confirm that the two implementations are equivalent with regard to the specification.

The most common error when constructing an indefinite iteration is not to ensure that the condition controlling the loop will at some stage evaluate false. This will cause the loop to iterate continuously. This fault is very noticeable if the body of the loop has some output and no input, as the output from the program will scroll off the top of the terminal. If the body of the loop has some input then the fault will be less noticeable, but the repeated request for input beyond the stage where the loop should have terminated will be noticed by the developer when testing the program. When a faulty loop has no input or output the fault can be very difficult to locate. The symptom is that the program apparently freezes, with no input being requested or output being produced. The program will have to be interrupted and terminated by a command from the terminal, but the location of the fault may consequently be very difficult to locate.

As with the selection structures introduced in Chapter 6, the construction of an indefinite loop should always be done with extreme care. The Boolean control condition should be carefully validated to ensure that it is correct, and the manipulation of the control variables in the body of the loop should be carefully examined to ensure that at some stage the loop is guaranteed to terminate.

EXERCISES

7.1   Produce a flow of control diagram, similar to those in Chapters 3 and 4, for a run of the *RoomControl* program given in the chapter.

7.2   Reimplement the *GetRangeOfTable* subprogram from the *SalesTaxReady-Reckoner1* program so that it will iterate, with suitable messages, until the user inputs a higher value which is shown to be higher than the lower value.

7.3   Reimplement the program from Exercise 6.1 so that the program will iterate until a valid menu choice has been obtained.

7.4   Reimplement *SalesTaxReadyReckoner2* making use of a **while** loop.

7.5   An investment scheme will run for ten years and offer a rate of interest determined by the initial investment. An investment of less than £1000 will be called a *Silver* investment and a rate of 5% is offered. An investment of between £1000 and £10 000 will be called a *Gold* investment and a rate of 6% is offered. An investment of more than £10 000 will be called a *Platinum* investment and a rate of 7.5% is offered. The program should output a table indicating the value of the investment each year.

7.6   Reimplement the program from Exercise 7.5 so that the nature of the investment (*Silver*, *Gold* or *Platinum*) is determined each year.

7.7   Reimplement the program from Exercise 7.4 so that the program iterates until the value of the original investment has more than doubled.

CHAPTER 8
Developing an application

This final chapter of this introductory section will attempt to draw together its key ideas by demonstrating how a complete, but very simple, application can be constructed. Its development will involve the further extension of the class hierarchy which was developed in Chapters 4 and 5. The adaptation of the iterative user interface designs from Chapter 7 using indefinite loops and definite loops will be illustrated. The selection structures from Chapter 6 will be used both in the client program and in the extended data types.

The facility of including subprograms within the program procedure, which was briefly introduced in Chapter 7, will be used more extensively in this application. The implications and limitations of this facility will also be discussed.

The application specification

A parking ticket payment office can only be entered when the clerk at the desk releases the door. Once inside the office people join a queue to pay their parking fines, which can be paid in cash, by cheque or by credit card. After each person has paid the fine, the clerk will open the door to allow the person who has paid the fine to leave and anyone waiting to enter. The program is to finish as soon as there is no one waiting.

The software is to simulate the administration of this system and is to produce a report at the end which will detail the number of fines and the total amount which has been paid by cash, by cheque and by credit card. It should also indicate the total number of fines paid and the maximum number of people who were waiting in the queue.

The specification can be clarified by the construction of a user interface:

```
                    Parking Ticket Office

How many people are waiting to enter at the start? 2

    There are 2 people in the queue.

    Pay fine by:
        a. Cash
        b. Cheque
        c. Credit card
    Please enter method a
    Please enter amount of fine 10.25

    How many people are waiting to enter? 0

    There are 1 people in the queue.

    Pay fine by:
        a. Cash
        b. Cheque
        c. Credit card
    Please enter method c
    Please enter amount of fine 35.60

    How many people are waiting to enter? 0

A total of 45.85 was taken in 2 fines.
A maximum of 2 people were waiting.
    10.25 was taken in 1 cash payments.
    0.00 was taken by cheque.
    35.60 was taken by 1 credit card payment.
```

If after the first fine had been paid there had been three people waiting to enter, the number of people waiting when the menu was presented for the second time would have been four. This would have caused the menu to iterate at least another four times. And, assuming that no one else entered the office during this time, the maximum number of people waiting in the queue would have also been four.

The construction plan

This specification has been artificially constructed to ensure that the resources which were previously developed in this section would be suitable for reuse with it. For an arbitrary specification the first stage in the construction plan would be to search for resources which could possibly be used in its construction. A major part of becoming a software developer is the collection of a library of generally reusable components and of learning how to obtain, evaluate and adapt components from commercial suppliers, or located in public domain repositories.

For the *Parking Ticket Office* specification it is obvious that the requirement to monitor the number of people in the office can largely be met by the *RoomMonitor* object from Chapter 5. However, the current development of that object does not allow for the maximum number of people ever in the room to be obtained from it, and so a further refinement is indicated.

The requirement to accept and store amounts of money is largely met by the *CashRegister* object from Chapter 5. However, it does not have the capability of keeping separate accounts for cash, cheque and credit card transactions, and some further development will be required.

With these two extended objects available the main client program can be considered. The major requirement would seem to be a *menu/dispatch* system. The program fragments developed in the previous two chapters for selection and iteration have prepared the way for the development of a suitable design and implementation, although this menu/dispatch design and implementation will have to be developed almost from scratch in this chapter. When it has been developed, its design will be available for use in any other client program which requires a menu/dispatch facility. Thus for an arbitrary specification this component could also be assumed to be available.

The plan for the construction of the *Parking Ticket Office* application has three major stages.

- Extend the *RoomMonitor* object to produce a *MaximumRoomMonitor*.

- Extend the *CashRegister* object to produce a *MultipleCashRegister*.

- Build the client program making use of a standard *menu/dispatch* design.

Extending the class hierarchy

The extension of the existing components will produce the following *class hierarchy*:

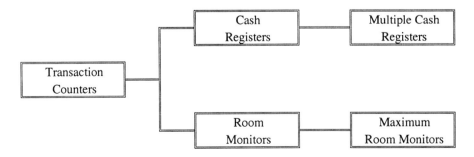

Both of the new types on this hierarchy will have to be developed, using the same techniques as were introduced in Chapters 4 and 5. Once constructed each type will have to have its correct operation demonstrated by a client demonstration program, before it is released for use with the *Parking Ticket Office* client.

The *MaximumRoomMonitor* object

The *MaximumRoomMonitor* object is the simpler of the two extensions and will be presented first. The object diagram for this extension is as follows:

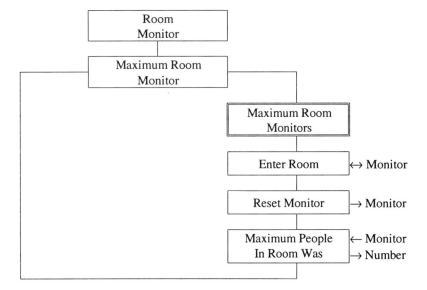

The extension **overrides** two existing actions, *EnterRoom* and *ResetMonitor*. These will require new implementations as the action of entering a room may change the maximum number of people ever in the room and resetting the monitor will have to reset this attribute. One new action, to find out the maximum number of people ever in the room (*MaximumPeopleInRoomWas*), is also introduced at this stage.

The **primitive operations** of the *MaximumRoomMonitors* type also include those which are inherited from its parent type *RoomMonitors*; these are *LeaveRoom*, *PeopleInRoomIs* and *TotalEnteredIs*. None of these actions require changes, by being overridden, as they do not have any effect upon the maximum number of people in the room. It also inherits *CountOccurrence* and *UnCountOccurrence* from the *TransactionCounters* type, but these actions should never be used. Techniques will be introduced later in the book which will allow non-required actions such as these to be hidden from clients.

The data flow interface diagrams and subprogram declarations for the *MaximumRoomMonitors* actions are as follows:

```
procedure EnterRoom( AnyMonitor : in out MaximumRoomMonitors);
-- Count a person entering a room and possibly update maximum.
```

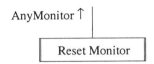

```
procedure ResetMonitor( AnyMonitor : out MaximumRoomMonitors);
-- Reset the monitor by setting all attributes to zero.
```

```
function MaximumPeopleInRoomWas( AnyMonitor : in
                                        MaximumRoomMonitors)
                                    return NATURAL;
-- Find out the maximum number of people ever in the room.
```

The package specification derived from this design might be as follows:

```
0001    -- Filename MaximumRoomMonitor_.pkg (k8 maxroomm.ads).
0002    -- Extension to the RoomMonitors type to add the capability
0003    -- to record the maximum number of people in the room.
0004    --
0005    -- Written for Ada Book Section I Chapter 8.
0006    -- Fintan Culwin, v0.1, Jan 1997.
0007
0008    with RoomMonitor;
0009    use  RoomMonitor;
0010
0011    package MaximumRoomMonitor is
0012
0013        type MaximumRoomMonitors is new RoomMonitors with private;
0014
```

```
0015      procedure EnterRoom( AnyMonitor : in out
                                        MaximumRoomMonitors);
0016      -- Count a person entering a room and possibly update
                                                     maximum.
0017
0018      procedure ResetMonitor( AnyMonitor : in out
                                        MaximumRoomMonitors);
0019      -- Reset the monitor by setting all attributes to zero.
0020
0021      function MaximumPeopleInRoomWas( AnyMonitor : in
0022                                        MaximumRoomMonitors)
0023                                        return NATURAL;
0024      -- Find out the maximum number of people ever in the room.
0025
0026
0027   private
0028
0029      type MaximumRoomMonitors is new RoomMonitors with
0030      record
0031         MaximumEver : NATURAL := 0;
0032      end record;
0033
0034   end MaximumRoomMonitor;
```

The implementation of the *MaximumRoomMonitors* type in the **private** part of the specification introduces a new data attribute called *MaximumEver*, of the subtype NATURAL with the default value zero. The data structure diagram and visualization of this extended data type are as follows:

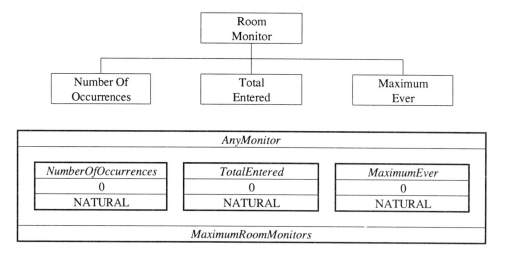

The overriding *EnterRoom* action will have to ensure that the *MaximumEver*

attribute always contains a record of the maximum number of people ever in the room. This can be ensured by checking the current *MaximumEver* value against the number of people currently in the room and updating it if necessary. The design and implementation of the *MaximumRoomMonitors EnterRoom* action are as follows:

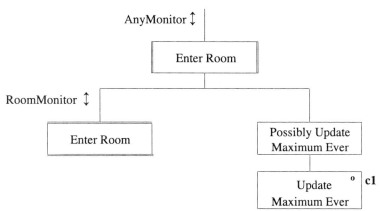

c1: If number in room now greater than the maximum ever recorded.

```
0010    procedure EnterRoom( AnyMonitor : in out
                                  MaximumRoomMonitors) is
0011    begin -- EnterRoom
0012        EnterRoom( RoomMonitors( AnyMonitor));
0013        if PeopleInRoomIs( AnyMonitor) > AnyMonitor.MaximumEver then
0014            AnyMonitor.MaximumEver := PeopleInRoomIs( AnyMonitor);
0015        end if;
0016    end EnterRoom;
```

The procedure first calls the *RoomMonitors EnterRoom* action making use of **type qualification** to ensure that the correct version of *EnterRoom* is used. It then uses the *RoomMonitors PeopleInRoomIs* function to obtain a value to test against the current *MaximumEver* value. If the number of people now in the room is greater than the maximum recorded so far, the value of *MaximumEver* is updated using the *PeopleInRoomIs* function. It would have been possible to have implemented this design making direct use of the *NumberOfOccurrences* data attribute which is directly visible, as follows:

```
0010    procedure EnterRoom( AnyMonitor : in out
                                  MaximumRoomMonitors) is
0011    begin -- EnterRoom
0012        EnterRoom( RoomMonitors( AnyMonitor));
0013        if AnyMonitor.NumberOfOccurrences >
                                  AnyMonitor.MaximumEver then
```

```
0014          AnyMonitor.MaximumEver := AnyMonitor.NumberOfOccurrences;
0015       end if;
0016    end EnterRoom;
```

However, this second version does not convey the meaning of the program code as clearly and advice has already been given, at the end of Chapter 5, that where there is an established subprogram to perform some action it should always be used in preference to direct access of data attributes. The reasoning behind this advice is concerned with the effective maintenance of class hierarchies.

The other two overridden actions can be implemented without requiring designs:

```
0018    procedure ResetMonitor( AnyMonitor : out
                                        MaximumRoomMonitors) is
0019    begin -- ResetMonitor
0020       AnyMonitor.MaximumEver := 0;
0021       ResetMonitor( RoomMonitors( AnyMonitor));
0022    end ResetMonitor;
0023
0024
0025    function MaximumPeopleInRoomWas( AnyMonitor : in
0026                                          MaximumRoomMonitors)
0027                                          return NATURAL is
0028    begin -- MaximumPeopleInRoomWas
0029       return AnyMonitor.MaximumEver;
0030    end MaximumPeopleInRoomWas;
```

The *ResetMonitor* procedure first resets the data attribute introduced by this extension and then calls the *RoomMonitors ResetMonitor* procedure. The *MaximumPeopleInRoomWas* function simple returns the value of the *Maximum-Ever* data attribute.

The demonstration client for this extended object can be based upon the demonstration client used for the *RoomMonitors* type. All the existing demonstrations should be unchanged by the extensions and additional demonstrations of the *MaximumPeopleInRoomWas* function would have to be included. The reimplementation of the client and practical demonstration of the efficacy of the implementation will be left as an end of chapter exercise.

The *MultipleCashRegister* object

This extension is a little more complex than the *MaximumRoomMonitors* extension given above. The object diagram for the *MultipleCashRegisters* type is as follows:

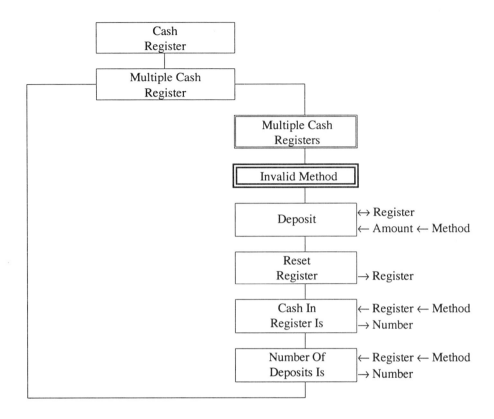

This design overrides the *Deposit*, *ResetRegister* and *CashInRegisterIs* actions of its parent *CashRegisters* type; it also adds a new action, *NumberOfDepositsIs*. All of these actions, apart from *ResetRegister*, require a *Method* parameter to indicate which payment method, cash, cheque or credit card, is being used. This implementation will use the value of a CHARACTER parameter, called *Method*, to communicate this information. Possible values for *Method* are: '*a*' for *a*ll, '*c*' for *c*ash, '*q*' for che*q*ue and '*r*' for c*r*edit card.

It is possible for a client to use a value other than these which would indicate a fault in the client program. In these cases the *MultipleCashRegisters* actions will **raise** an **exception** to indicate the faulty call. The name of the exception which will be raised is *InvalidMethod* and this is shown on the object diagram as being exported. The double heavy lines on the object diagram indicate that an exception is being supplied by the package. There is a much better technique for indicating the *Method* of payment involving the use of enumerated types; this facility will be introduced in the next section.

The data flow interface diagrams and subprogram declarations derived from this object diagram are as follows:

AnyRegister $\updownarrow$
Amount $\downarrow$
Method $\downarrow$

Deposit

```
procedure Deposit( AnyRegister : in out MultipleCashRegisters;
                   Amount      : in     FLOAT;
                   Method      : in     CHARACTER);
-- Deposit Amount by Method in AnyRegister. Method must be 'c'
-- for cash, 'q' for cheque or 'r' for credit card; otherwise
-- an InvalidMethod exception will be raised.
```

AnyRegister $\uparrow$

Reset Register

```
procedure ResetRegister( AnyRegister : out
                                      MultipleCashRegisters );
-- Reset the register by setting all amounts and counters
-- to zero.
```

AnyRegister $\downarrow$ $\uparrow$ Amount
Method $\downarrow$

Cash In
Register Is

```
function CashInRegisterIs
                ( AnyRegister : in MultipleCashRegisters;
                  Method      : in CHARACTER)
                                            return FLOAT;
-- Find out the amount of cash deposited in AnyRegister by
                                                Method.
-- Method must be 'a' for all, 'c' for cash, 'q' for cheque,
-- 'r' for credit card; otherwise an InvalidMethod exception
-- will be raised.
```

AnyRegister $\downarrow$ $\uparrow$ Number
Method $\downarrow$

Number Of
Deposits Is

```
function NumberOfDepositsIs
                ( AnyRegister : in MultipleCashRegisters;
                  Method      : in CHARACTER)
                                            return NATURAL;
```

```
          -- Find out the number of deposits made into AnyRegister by
                                                                Method.
          -- Method must be 'a' for all, 'c' for cash, 'q' for cheque,
          -- 'r' for credit card; otherwise an InvalidMethod exception
          -- will be raised.
```

The package specification derived from this design is as follows:

```
0001      -- Filename MultipleCashRegister_.pkg (k8 multiple.ads).
0002      -- Extension to the CashRegister package to produce a
0003      -- CashRegister object capable of taking cash, cheques
0004      -- and credit cards.
0005      --
0006      -- Written for Ada Book Section I Chapter 8.
0007      -- Fintan Culwin, v0.1, Jan 1997.
0008
0009      with CashRegister;
0010      use  CashRegister;
0011
0012      package MultipleCashRegister is
0013
0014          type MultipleCashRegisters is new CashRegisters with
                                                                private;
0015
0016          InvalidMethod : exception;
0017
0018          procedure Deposit
                          ( AnyRegister : in out MultipleCashRegisters;
0019                        Amount      : in      FLOAT;
0020                        Method      : in      CHARACTER);
0021          -- Deposit Amount by Method in AnyRegister. Method must be 'c'
0022          -- for cash, 'q' for cheque or 'r' for credit card: otherwise
0023          -- an InvalidMethod exception will be raised.
0024
0025          procedure ResetRegister( AnyRegister : out
                                              MultipleCashRegisters);
0026          -- Reset the register by setting all amounts and counters
0027          -- to zero.
0028
0029          function CashInRegisterIs
                          ( AnyRegister : in MultipleCashRegisters;
0030                        Method      : in CHARACTER)
0031                                                      return FLOAT;
0032          -- Find out the amount of cash deposited in AnyRegister
                                                           by Method.
0033          -- Method must be 'a' for all, 'c' for cash, 'q' for cheque,
```

```
0034        -- 'r' for credit card; otherwise an InvalidMethod
0035        -- exception will be raised.
0036
0037
0038        function NumberOfDepositsIs( AnyRegister : in
0039                                            MultipleCashRegisters;
0040                              Method      : in CHARACTER)
0041                                           return NATURAL;
0042        -- Find out the number of deposits made into AnyRegister
                                                        by Method.
0043        -- Method must be 'a' for all, 'c' for cash, 'q' for cheque,
0044        -- 'r' for credit card; otherwise an InvalidMethod exception
0045        -- will be raised.
0046
0047
0048    private
0049
0050        type MultipleCashRegisters is new CashRegisters with
0051        record
0052            ByCash       : CashRegisters;
0053            ByCheque     : CashRegisters;
0054            ByCreditCard : CashRegisters;
0055        end record;
0056
0057    end MultipleCashRegister;
```

The public part of the package specification is comparable with the package specifications which have already been introduced, apart from the declaration of an **exception** on line 0016. The use of this exception will be explained below, when the implementation of the subprograms which might raise it is described.

In the **private** part the data attributes added by extension to the *CashRegisters* type to produce the *MultipleCashRegisters* type are themselves instances of the *CashRegisters* type. Each method of deposition has to maintain a separate count of the number of deposits and the total amount of money deposited. As this is exactly the requirement which the *CashRegisters* type was designed to accommodate, the simplest solution is to reuse its facilities in this way. A data structure diagram and visualization of it are as follows:

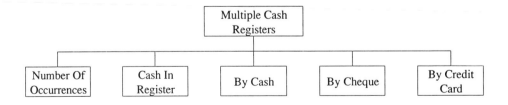

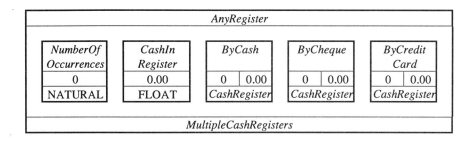

The visualization of the *AnyRegister* object is a little simplified. The three components which have been added by extension are instances of the *Cash-Registers* type and their internal structure should indicate two data components: *NumberOfOccurrences* of type NATURAL and *CashInRegister* of type FLOAT. Only the initial values of these components have been shown for the sake of clarity. The first two data components are inherited from the *CashRegisters* type and in the discussion below will be referred to as the **original register**. The three components added by extension will be referred to as the **extended registers**.

The design of the *Deposit* action is as follows:

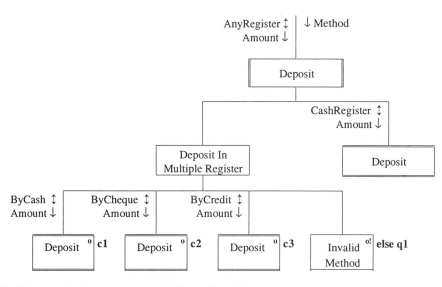

c1: If cash is deposited. **c3**: If a credit card is used.
c2: If a cheque is deposited. **q1**: Explicit InvalidMethod exception.

The basis of the design is first to make a deposit into one of the *CashRegisters* which have been added by extension, and then to make a deposit into the original cash register. Thus each extended register will contain details of its own transactions and the original register will contain details of all transactions.

However, the subprogram also has to allow for the possibility that it is called with a *Method* parameter which does not identify a valid extension register to deposit in. The selective design component *InvalidMethod* will detect this possibility and will be implemented explicitly to raise an *InvalidMethod* **exception**. A component which raises an exception has to be identified on a program structure chart with an exclamation mark (!) in the top right hand corner, and keyed with a *q* (for *q*uit). The *q* keys at the bottom of the chart have to state the name of the **exception** and if it is raised explicitly by the developer or implicitly when a subprogram is called. More details concerning the raising of exceptions and, more importantly, how to handle them will be given in the next section. The implementation of this design might be as follows:

```
0011    procedure Deposit( AnyRegister : in out MultipleCashRegisters;
0012                       Amount      : in FLOAT;
0013                       Method      : in CHARACTER) is
0014    begin -- Deposit
0015       case Method is
0016       when 'c' =>
0017             Deposit( AnyRegister.ByCash, Amount);
0018       when 'q' =>
0019             Deposit( AnyRegister.ByCheque, Amount);
0020       when 'r' =>
0021             Deposit( AnyRegister.ByCreditCard, Amount);
0022       when others =>
0023          raise InvalidMethod;
0024       end case;
0025       Deposit( CashRegisters( AnyRegister), Amount);
0026    end Deposit;
```

The **case** structure on lines 0015 to 0024 implements the four way selection of the design component *DepositInMultipleRegister*. Assuming that the value of *Method* is acceptable (i.e. 'c', 'q' or 'r') the *CashRegisters Deposit* action will be called passing one of the multiple registers added by extension; following this a *Deposit* will be made into the original register on line 0025.

However, if the *Method* parameter does not indicate a valid register then the default **case** option on line 0022 will be followed, and an *InvalidMethod* exception will be **raised** on line 0023. The effect of this is immediately to terminate the procedure without executing line 0025; hence a *q* for *q*uit on the design. Thus a deposit can only be made into the original register if a deposit has already been made into one of the extension registers. This will ensure that the *MultipleCash-Registers* object passed in the *AnyRegister* parameter will always be in a consistent state.

The *CashInRegisterIs* function has a somewhat similar design and implementation. The basis of the design is to indirect to the *CashRegisters CashInRegisterIs* function passing either the entire *MultipleCashRegisters* parameter or one of the

CashRegisters added by extension, depending upon the value of the *Method* parameter.

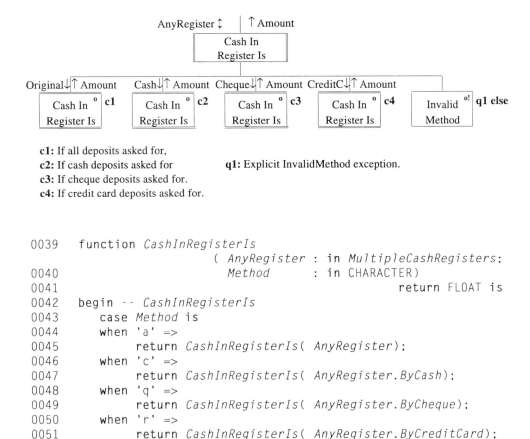

c1: If all deposits asked for,
c2: If cash deposits asked for   **q1:** Explicit InvalidMethod exception.
c3: If cheque deposits asked for.
c4: If credit card deposits asked for.

```
0039    function CashInRegisterIs
                      ( AnyRegister : in MultipleCashRegisters;
0040                    Method      : in CHARACTER)
0041                                      return FLOAT is
0042    begin -- CashInRegisterIs
0043       case Method is
0044       when 'a' =>
0045          return CashInRegisterIs( AnyRegister);
0046       when 'c' =>
0047          return CashInRegisterIs( AnyRegister.ByCash);
0048       when 'q' =>
0049          return CashInRegisterIs( AnyRegister.ByCheque);
0050       when 'r' =>
0051          return CashInRegisterIs( AnyRegister.ByCreditCard);
0052       when others =>
0053          raise InvalidMethod;
0054       end case;
0055    end CashInRegisterIs;
```

Type qualification is not required on line 0045, when the total amount of cash in the original register is requested. Ada has to decide if the *CashInRegisterIs* function in the *MultipleCashRegisters* or *CashRegisters* package is intended. As the *MultipleCashRegisters CashInRegisterIs* function requires a second parameter to indicate the payment method, the *CashRegisters CashInRegisterIs* function can be called. The extended registers are of the *CashRegisters* type and do not require qualification as there is only one possible *CashInRegisterIs* function for this type.

The design of the *NumberOfDepositsIs* function is essentially identical to that of the *CashInRegisterIs* function and the *ResetRegister* procedure does not merit a design. Their implementations are as follows:

```
0057   function NumberOfDepositsIs( AnyRegister : in
0058                                      MultipleCashRegisters;
0059                          Method      : in CHARACTER)
0060                                      return NATURAL is
0061   begin -- NumberOfDepositsIs
0062      case Method is
0063      when 'a' =>
0064          return NumberCountedIs( AnyRegister);
0065      when 'c' =>
0066          return NumberCountedIs( AnyRegister.ByCash);
0067      when 'q' =>
0068          return NumberCountedIs( AnyRegister.ByCheque);
0069      when 'r' =>
0070          return NumberCountedIs( AnyRegister.ByCreditCard);
0071      when others =>
0072        raise InvalidMethod;
0073      end case;
0074   end NumberOfDepositsIs;
0075
0076
0077   procedure ResetRegister( AnyRegister :
0078                           in out MultipleCashRegisters) is
0079   begin -- ResetRegister
0080      ResetRegister( CashRegisters( AnyRegister));
0081      ResetRegister( AnyRegister.ByCash);
0082      ResetRegister( AnyRegister.ByCheque);
0083      ResetRegister( AnyRegister.ByCreditCard);
0084   end ResetRegister;
```

As with the *MaximumRoomMonitors* extension the reimplementation of the *CashRegisters* demonstration client for the *MultipleCashRegisters* will be left as an end of chapter exercise.

The *Parking Ticket Office* application

Once the package specifications of the *MaximumRoomMonitors* and *Multiple-CashRegisters* extensions have been finalized the production of the *Parking Ticket Office* application can proceed.

The high level design and implementation

The high level design of this application might be as follows:

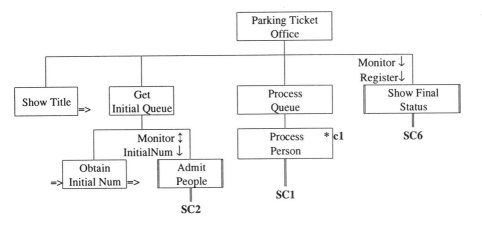

c1: While people remain in the queue.

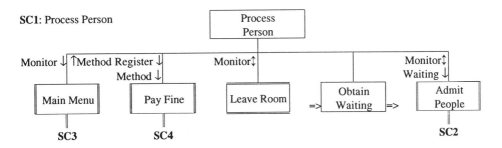

The basis of the design, after the initial number of people waiting have been admitted, is to process a person iteratively until the queue is empty. The program then terminates after showing the final status of the register and the monitor. In order to process a person the main menu is called to find out which method of payment is to be used, following which the fine is paid. The main iteration finishes by allowing one person to leave the room and then admits the number of people who are waiting to the queue.

A data table for this part of the program might be as follows.

Data Table for *Parking Ticket Office* application program procedure

Name	Type	Variables Initial value	Notes
ParkingRegister	*MultipleCashRegisters*	Default	The register to hold the fines in
OfficeMonitor	*MaximumRoomMonitors*	Default	To monitor the number of people waiting
NumberToEnter	NATURAL	?	The number of people joining the queue

157

| *PaymentMethod* | CHARACTER | ? | Character code for the type of payment, 'c', 'q' or 'r'. |

The high level design indicates that four local subprograms are required: *MainMenu*, *PayFine*, *AdmitPeople* and *ShowFinalStatus*. The partition of the design into subprograms was made in order to avoid having to write a program procedure which is too complicated, and in the hope that some of the subprograms may turn out to be reusable. In general each subprogram should be designed to do a simple straightforward task, and should consequently have a relatively simple design and implementation.

Where a similar task is being done in more than one part of the program, for example admitting an initial number of people and subsequently admitting people after each fine has been paid, implementation as a subprogram is also indicated. The partition of a design is a skill and, like all skills, can only be learned by practice. The data flow interface diagrams and subprogram declarations for these four subprograms are as follows:

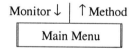

```
procedure MainMenu( TheMonitor : in MaximumRoomMonitors;
                MethodOfPayment : out CHARACTER);
-- Display a menu of payment options, preceded by the
-- number of people in the queue. Obtain a validated
-- payment choice from the user and return it in Method.
```

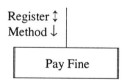

```
procedure PayFine
        ( TheRegister    : in out MultipleCashRegisters;
          PaymentMethod : in    CHARACTER);
-- Obtain the amount of fine from the user and deposit it into
-- the extended Register indicated by Method.
```

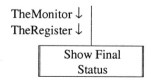

```
procedure ShowFinalStatus
              ( TheMonitor  : in MaximumRoomMonitors;
                TheRegister : in MultipleCashRegisters);
-- Display various attributes from TheMonitor and TheRegister.
```

TheMonitor ↕

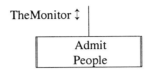

Admit
People

```
procedure AdmitPeople( TheMonitor : in out
                                      MaximumRoomMonitors);
-- Obtain the number of people waiting and admit them to
                                              the room.
```

Assuming the existence of these subprograms, the high level program procedure can be implemented as follows:

```
0001    -- Filename ParkingTicketOffice_.ada (k8 parkingt.adb).
0002    -- Client program to illustrate application construction
0003    -- by extension of existing objects.
0004    --
0005    -- Written for Ada book Section I Chapter 8.
0006    -- Fintan Culwin v 0.1, Jan 1997.
0007
0008    with ADA.TEXT_IO,
0009                      MaximumRoomMonitor, MultipleCashRegister;
0010    use  ADA.TEXT_IO,
0011                      MaximumRoomMonitor, MultipleCashRegister;
0012
0013    procedure ParkingTicketOffice is
0014
0015       package IntegerIO is new ADA.TEXT_IO.INTEGER_IO( INTEGER);
0016       package FloatIO  is new ADA.TEXT_IO.FLOAT_IO( FLOAT);
0017       use IntegerIO, FloatIO;
0018
0019       ParkingRegister : MultipleCashRegisters;
0020       OfficeMonitor   : MaximumRoomMonitors;
0021       PaymentMethod   : CHARACTER;
0022

       -- Local subprogram declarations and definitions omitted!

0140    begin -- ParkingTicketOffice
0141       NEW_LINE( 2);
0142       SET_COL( 15); PUT_LINE( "Parking Ticket Office");
0143       NEW_LINE( 2);
0144
0145       PUT( "How many people are waiting to enter at the start? ");
```

```
0146        AdmitPeople( OfficeMonitor);
0147
0148        while PeopleInRoomIs( OfficeMonitor) /= 0 loop
0149           MainMenu( OfficeMonitor, PaymentMethod);
0150           PayFine( ParkingRegister, PaymentMethod);
0151           LeaveRoom( OfficeMonitor);
0152           PUT( "How many people are waiting to enter? ");
0153           AdmitPeople( OfficeMonitor);
0154        end loop;
0155
0156        NEW_LINE( 2);
0157        ShowFinalStatus( OfficeMonitor, ParkingRegister);
0158
0159    end ParkingTicketOffice;
```

The context clause brings various packages into use. The list of required packages can only be decided once the detailed implementation of the subprograms has been completed and the location of the facilities which they use has been determined. Within the program procedure INTEGER_IO and FLOAT_IO are instantiated as the program will have to output and input both INTEGER and FLOATing point values. The declarative region also declares the variables from the data table above.

The implementation of the program procedure follows the designs given above. Following the output of the title, a prompt is issued before the *AdmitPeople* procedure is called. This call will admit the initial number of people into the room. The next component of the design is the iterative component *ProcessPeople* and is implemented as a **while** loop between lines 0148 and 0154. The loop will terminate when the number of people in the room is zero, as expressed in its control condition on line 0148. In real life the office would stop admitting people at a certain time and then process any people waiting in the queue. This method of terminating the program is used to simplify the example.

Within the loop *MainMenu* is called to obtain details of the payment method and this choice is passed to *PayFine*, which will obtain the amount of the fine from the user and deposit it. One person then leaves the room, on line 0151, before the people waiting to join the queue are admitted on lines 0152 to 0153, in a manner similar to lines 0145 to 0146. Once the loop has terminated the program concludes by calling the *ShowFinalStatus* procedure.

If it is assumed that the subprograms will perform in accord with the descriptions of their actions given with their declarations above, this design can be validated at this point by tracing the assumed states of the variable objects as the subprograms are called.

The *MainMenu* design and implementation

The design and implementation of a *menu/dispatch* system is a common requirement of a large number of programs. If this application were being developed by a skilled and experienced developer this part of the program could be quickly adapted from a standard design. The design of the *MainMenu* procedure is as follows:

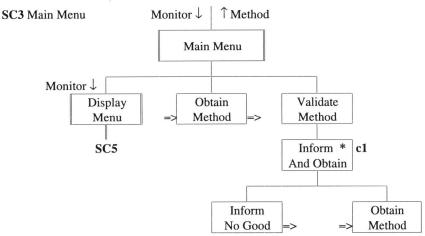

SC3 Main Menu

c1: While user's response is unacceptable.

This design is essentially identical to that given for the *YesNoDemo* programs in Chapter 7. The choices are displayed to the user and a response obtained. This response is then validated by an iterative component, which will inform the user that the response is unacceptable and ask for the input again. The presentation of the menu to the user is accomplished by a subprogram of the subprogram, called *DisplayMenu*. The design of this subprogram is as follows:

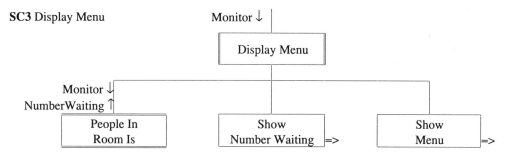

SC3 Display Menu

The data tables for these two subprograms are as follows:

Data Table for *Parking Ticket Office MainMenu* procedure

Name	Type	Constants Value	Notes
MinMenuChoice	CHARACTER	'a'	The minimum choice on the menu
MaxMenuChoice	CHARACTER	'c'	The maximum choice on the menu

Name	Type	Variables Initial value	Notes
TheMonitor	*MaximumRoomMonitors*	Default	Parameter: the number of people waiting
MethodOfPayment	CHARACTER	Default	Parameter: to receive the payment method
LocalChoice	CHARACTER	?	The chosen payment method

Data table for *Parking Ticket Office DisplayMenu* procedure

Name	Type	Variables Initial value	Notes
TheMonitor	*MaximumRoomMonitors*	Default	Parameter: the number of people waiting
NumberWaiting	NATURAL	?	Number of people obtained from *TheMonitor*

The implementation of this design is as follows:

```
0036    procedure MainMenu( TheMonitor      : in  MaximumRoomMonitors;
0037                        MethodOfPayment : out CHARACTER) is
0038
0039        MinMenuChoice : constant CHARACTER := 'a';
0040        MaxMenuChoice : constant CHARACTER := 'c';
0041
0042        LocalChoice   : CHARACTER;
0043
0044        procedure DisplayMenu( TheMonitor : in
0045                                      MaximumRoomMonitors) is
0046            NumberWaiting : NATURAL:= PeopleInRoomIs( TheMonitor);
0047
0048        begin -- DisplayMenu
0049            NEW_LINE( 2);
0050            SET_COL( 5); PUT( "There are ");
0051            PUT( NumberWaiting, WIDTH=>1);
0052            PUT_LINE( " people in the queue.");
0053            NEW_LINE;
0054            PUT_LINE( "Pay the fine by");
0055            SET_COL( 5); PUT_LINE( "a. Cash");
0056            SET_COL( 5); PUT_LINE( "b. Cheque");
0057            SET_COL( 5); PUT_LINE( "c. Credit card");
0058        end DisplayMenu;
0059
0060
```

```
0061    begin -- MainMenu
0062        DisplayMenu( TheMonitor);
0063        SET_COL( 5); PUT( "Please enter method ");
0064        GET( LocalChoice); SKIP_LINE;
0065        while LocalChoice < MinMenuChoice or
0066                LocalChoice > MaxMenuChoice loop
0067            SET_COL( 5); PUT( "You must enter a choice between ");
0068            PUT( MinMenuChoice); PUT( " and ");
0069            PUT( MaxMenuChoice); PUT_LINE( ".");
0070            SET_COL( 5); PUT_LINE( "Please try again!");
0071            SET_COL( 5); PUT( "Please enter method ");
0072            GET( LocalChoice); SKIP_LINE;
0073        end loop;
0074        MethodOfPayment := LocalChoice;
0075    end MainMenu;
```

On line 0046 the value of the variable *NumberWriting* is initialized upon declaration by a call of the *PeopleInRoomIs* function. If this were not done then the value of *NumberWaiting* would have to be initialized from a call in the body of the procedure. A trace of this procedure would be essentially identical to a trace of the *YesNoDemo* programs from Chapter 7.

The *PayFine* design and implementation

The design of the *PayFine* procedure is as follows:

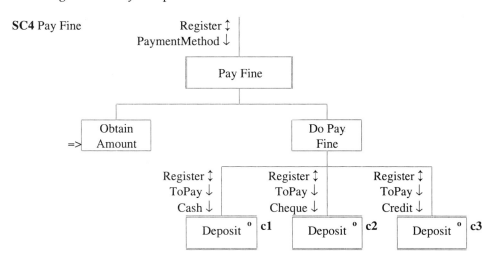

c1: If user indicates cash.
c2: If user indicates cheque.
c3: If user indicates credit card.

The basis of the design is to obtain the amount of the fine from the user and then to call the *MultipleCashRegisters Deposit* procedure indicating a *Cash* payment, a *Cheque* payment or a *Credit* card payment. The data table for this subprogram and its implementation might be as follows:

Data Table for *Parking Ticket Office PayFine* procedure

Name	Type	Variables Initial value	Notes
TheRegister	*MultipleCashRegisters*	Initialized	Parameter: to pay the fine into
PaymentMethod	CHARACTER	Initialized	Parameter: the payment method
ToPay	FLOAT	?	The amount of the fine

```
0080    procedure PayFine( TheRegister   : in out
                                          MultipleCashRegisters;
0081                       PaymentMethod : in CHARACTER) is
0082
0083       ToPay : FLOAT;
0084
0085    begin -- PayFine
0086       PUT( "Please enter amount of fine ");
0087       GET( ToPay); SKIP_LINE;
0088       case PaymentMethod is
0089       when 'a' =>
0090          Deposit( TheRegister, ToPay, 'c');
0091       when 'b' =>
0092          Deposit( TheRegister, ToPay, 'q');
0093       when 'c' =>
0094          Deposit( TheRegister, ToPay, 'r');
0095       when others =>
0096          null;
0097       end case;
0098    end PayFine;
```

The three way selection *DoPayFine* is implemented on the design as a **case** structure. A **case** structure has to account for all possible values of the selector expression. In this example this is a CHARACTER value and as only three possible values are used, a default do nothing option has been added in lines 0095 to 0096.

The *AdmitPeople* design and implementation

The design of the *AdmitPeople* procedure is as follows:

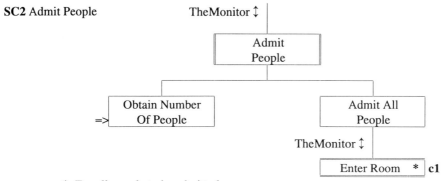

SC2 Admit People

TheMonitor ↕

Admit People

Obtain Number Of People

Admit All People

TheMonitor ↕

Enter Room * c1

c1: For all people to be admitted.

The basis of the design is to obtain from the user the number of people who wish to enter the room and then use this value to control a definite loop which repeatedly admits one person by calling the *MaximumRoomMonitors EnterRoom* procedure. The data table and implementation of this design might be as follows:

Data Table for *Parking Ticket Office AdmitPeople* procedure

Name	Type	Variables Initial value	Notes
TheMonitor	*MaximumRoomMonitors*	Initialized	Parameter: the people in the room
NumberToAdmit	NATURAL	?	The number of people to admit to the room

```
0024    procedure AdmitPeople( TheMonitor : in out
                                    MaximumRoomMonitors) is
0025
0026        NumberToAdmit : NATURAL;
0027
0028    begin -- AdmitPeople
0029        GET( NumberToAdmit); SKIP_LINE;
0030        for ThisPerson in 1 .. NumberToAdmit loop
0031            EnterRoom( TheMonitor);
0032        end loop;
0033    end AdmitPeople;
```

This procedure assumes that the prompt for the input on line 0029 has already been output before the procedure is called. Should the user enter zero in response to the prompt the bounds of the loop on line 0030 would be '*1 .. 0*', which would cause the loop to iterate zero times, admitting nobody. Otherwise the loop will iterate as many times as the value of *NumberToAdmit* and on each iteration *EnterRoom* will be called admitting one person.

The *ShowFinalStatus* design and implementation

The outline design of this subprogram is as follows:

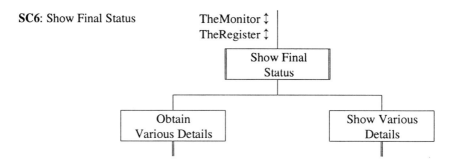

SC6: Show Final Status

There are nine pieces of information, which are listed in the data table below, which have to be retrieved from *TheMonitor* or *TheRegister* and shown to the user. A completion of this design would show that *ObtainVariousDetails* consists of a sequence of nine calls of various functions, and *ShowVariousDetails* a sequence of nine actions to output them.

The data table and implementation of this design are as follows:

Data table for *Parking Ticket Office AdmitPeople* procedure

Name	Type	Variables Initial value	Notes
TheMonitor	*MaximumRoomMonitors*	Initialized	Parameter: the people in the room
TheRegister	*MultipleCashRegisters*	Initialized	Parameter: containing the fines paid
NumberEntered	NATURAL	?	Total number of people who entered the room
MaximumWaiting	NATURAL	?	Maximum number waiting in the queue
PaidByCash	NATURAL	?	The number who paid in cash
PaidByCheque	NATURAL	?	The number who paid by cheque
PaidByCard	NATURAL	?	The number who paid by credit card
TotalAmountPaid	FLOAT	?	The total amount of fines
TotalByCash	FLOAT	?	The total amount paid in cash

TotalByCheque	FLOAT	?	The total amount paid by cheque
TotalByCard	FLOAT	?	The total amount paid by credit card

```
0101    procedure ShowFinalStatus( TheMonitor : in MaximumRoomMonitors;
0102                        TheRegister : in MultipleCashRegisters) is
0103
0104       NumberEntered  : NATURAL := TotalEnteredIs( TheMonitor);
0105       MaximumWaiting : NATURAL := MaximumPeopleInRoomWas(TheMonitor);
0106
0107    PaidByCash   : NATURAL := NumberOfDepositsIs( TheRegister, 'c');
0108    PaidByCheque : NATURAL := NumberOfDepositsIs( TheRegister, 'q');
0109    PaidByCard   : NATURAL := NumberOfDepositsIs( TheRegister, 'r');
0110
0111    TotalAmountPaid : FLOAT := CashInRegisterIs( TheRegister, 'a');
0112    TotalByCash     : FLOAT := CashInRegisterIs( TheRegister, 'c');
0113    TotalByCheque   : FLOAT := CashInRegisterIs( TheRegister, 'q');
0114    TotalByCard     : FLOAT := CashInRegisterIs( TheRegister, 'r');
0115
0116    begin -- ShowFinalStatus
0117       PUT( "A total of " );
0118       PUT( TotalAmountPaid, FORE=>1, AFT=>2, EXP=>0);
0119       PUT( " was taken in " );
0120       PUT( NumberEntered, WIDTH=>1); PUT_LINE( " fines.");
0121
0122       PUT( "A maximum of " );
0123       PUT( MaximumWaiting, WIDTH=>1);
0124       PUT_LINE( " people were waiting.");
0125
0126       PUT( TotalByCash, FORE=>1, AFT=>2, EXP=>0);
0127       PUT( " was taken in " ); PUT( PaidByCash, WIDTH=>1);
0128       PUT_LINE( " cash payments.");
0129
0130       PUT( TotalByCheque, FORE=>1, AFT=>2, EXP=>0);
0131       PUT( " was taken by " ); PUT( PaidByCheque, WIDTH=>1);
0132       PUT_LINE( " cheque payments.");
0133
0134       PUT( TotalByCard, FORE=>1, AFT=>2, EXP=>
0135       PUT( " was taken by " ); PUT( PaidByCard, WIDTH=>1);
0136       PUT_LINE( " card payments.");
0137    end ShowFinalStatus;
```

As with the *DisplayMenu* procedure above a small optimization of the design has been accomplished by initializing the nine local variables upon declaration to the values returned from various function calls.

Constructing the executable

The construction of the executable involves the assembly of the local subprograms within the *Parking Ticket Office* program and the compilation and linking of the various source code files.

Assembling the *Parking Ticket Office* program

A subprogram map of the *Parking Ticket Office* program is as follows:

```
procedure ParkingTicketOffice

     procedure AdmitPeople () is
     begin -- AdmitPeople
     end AdmitPeople ;


     procedure MainMenu( ~ ) is

          procedure DisplayMenu( ~ ) is
          begin -- DisplayMenu
          end DisplayMenu;

     begin -- MainMenu
     end MainMenu;


     procedure PayFine( ~ ) is
     begin -- PayFine
     end PayFine;


     procedure ShowFinalStatus( ~ ) is
     begin -- ShowFinalStatus
     end ShowFinalStatus;

begin -- ParkingTicketOffice
end ParkingTicketOffice;
```

The map indicates that not only can subprograms be contained within the program procedure, but also these subprograms can themselves contain subprograms. Although it is possible for this to be continued further, with the subprograms contained within subprograms themselves containing subprograms, and so on, such designs are cautioned against. As a rule of thumb only two levels of nesting, as in *DisplayMenu*, should be used. When deeper levels of nesting are used the resulting program will prove to be more difficult to maintain and the advantages of nesting are outweighed by maintenance problems.

The advantages of nesting subprograms are concerned with ***information hiding***. In the procedure map above the *DisplayMenu* subprogram is hidden within the *MainMenu* procedure and as it cannot be seen by any other subprograms it cannot be called by them.

Information hiding also applies to the data objects declared within subprograms. A nested subprogram can see all the declarations of its enclosing subprogram. In the example above a variable declared in the program procedure, for example *PaymentMethod*, can be seen by all nested subprograms, for example *MainMenu*, and also all of its nested subprograms, for example *DisplayMenu*. However, an enclosing subprogram cannot see the declarations of its nested subprograms. In the example above a variable declared in a subprogram, for example *LocalChoice* in *MainMenu*, cannot be seen by the program procedure *ParkingTicketOffice*.

The visibility of a data object can be divided into global and local scope. When the *PaymentMethod* variable of the program procedure is referenced in the program procedure it is being referenced in ***local scope***. If it were referenced in any of the subprograms it would be referenced with ***global scope***.

In the overwhelming majority of situations variable objects should only be referenced in local scope; global references should be banned unless there are compelling reasons to use them. If an object has to be passed from an enclosing to a nested subprogram it should be passed through the parameter mechanism. A very common error of novice developers is to reference variable objects with global scope by habit, and this prevents the parameter mechanism from ever being effectively learned.

The reason for effectively banning the use of global variables is to make each subprogram independent of all others. A global reference will prevent the subprogram from being taken out of the context in which it was first developed and reused in a different context. A subprogram dependent upon the existence of the global variable may not find a variable with the same name and meaning in its new context, preventing its easy or successful reuse.

Another common novice error in the development of nested subprogram implementations is to declare all parameters with ***in out*** mode. An ***in out*** parameter variable has no restrictions upon the way in which it can be used, an ***in only*** parameter can only be used as a value and an ***out only*** parameter can only be used as the destination of an assignment operation. As ***in out*** mode subsumes both *in only* and *out only* modes a subprogram can apparently be correctly implemented with incorrect parameter modes.

Compiling and linking the executable

The *Parking Ticket Office* application requires the following 11 source code files:

TransactionCounter_.pkg	The TransactionCounter specification
TransactionCounter.pkb	The TransactionCounter body
RoomMonitor_.pkg	The RoomMonitor specification
RoomMonitor.pkb	The RoomMonitor body
MaximumRoomMonitor_.pkg	The MaximumRoomMonitor specification
MaximumRoomMonitor.pkb	The MaximumRoomMonitor body
CashRegister_.pkg	The CashRegister specification
CashRegister.pkb	The CashRegister body
MultipleCashRegister_.pkg	The MultipleCashRegister specification
MultipleCashRegister.pkb	The MultipleCashRegister body
ParkingTicketOffice.ada	The client program

The production of a more realistic application would require an increased number of files. It is necessary to be very careful with the naming, storing, maintaining and archiving of the files which are used to build applications. The development of such techniques and the skills in applying them are an important part of learning to become a software developer.

The dependency diagram for the *Parking Ticket Application*, showing each package as a single component, is as follows:

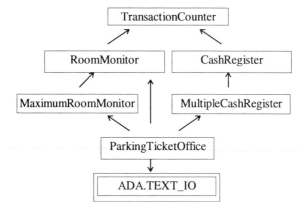

Each package body is only dependent upon its specification and has been omitted from this diagram for the sake of simplicity. This diagram gives one possible order of compilation as follows:

> TransactionCounter
> CashRegister
> MultipleCashRegister
> RoomMonitor
> MaximumRoomMonitor
> ParkingTicketOffice

The order of compilation refers to the package specifications; the corresponding package bodies can be compiled as soon as its specification has been compiled.

If any changes are made to any of the package specifications then any components which are dependent upon the changed specification will become obsolete and require recompilation before a new executable can be compiled. The Ada environment will always give a warning if an attempt is made to link an executable from an obsolete component. Most environments will also offer a facility to **make** an application by automatically recompiling all obsolete components and relinking the executable.

EXERCISES

8.1 Extend the *RoomMonitor* demonstration client and use it to demonstrate the correct implementation of the *MaximumRoomMonitor* extension.

8.2 Extend the *CashRegister* demonstration client and use it to demonstrate the correct implementation of the *MultipleCashRegister* extension.

8.3 Produce a flow of control trace table for an illustrative run of the *ParkingTicketOffice* application.

8.4 Reimplement the *MultipleCashRegister* object and the *ParkingTicketOffice* application to allow for payments to be made by a debit card.

8.5 Reimplement the *ParkingTicketOffice* application to make use of the *ChangeGivingCashRegister* from Exercise 5.6.

8.6 In order to reduce congestion a maximum of 15 people are allowed in the parking ticket office at any one time. Reimplement the *RoomMonitor* part of the hierarchy to introduce a *LimitedRoomMonitor* which supplies a Boolean function called *IsRoomFull* which will return true when the room is full. Reimplement the *ParkingTicketOffice* application to make use of this revised hierarchy.

8.7 Review the entire *TransactionCounters* hierarchy, including the *Change-GivingCashRegister* and *LimitedRoomMonitor* extensions, with a view to deciding if all extensions are in the correct relation to each other, that all actions are allocated to the most appropriate object, and if any actions or extensions are missing. What does this teach you about the initial design of a class hierarchy?

SECTION II

An Introduction to Developing Software

CHAPTER 9
Ada numeric types

The previous section informally introduced several Ada pre-declared data types. This chapter will start to introduce Ada data types formally. A **data type**, as defined in Section I, is a set of values and a set of operations which can be performed upon those values. Data types are used to declare the types of program objects, most obviously variables, which are then used to model some aspect of the 'real world'. Programmer declared data types were first met in Section I, where the extendible **tagged** types were introduced.

The pre-declared data types may not be the most appropriate for the modelling of a particular real world requirement. In these situations Ada allows for the declaration of additional, programmer declared, data types. These can be implemented as a **subtype** of an existing type, an extension of an existing **tagged** typed, or as a distinct **new type** based upon an existing type. A **subtype** identifies a range of an existing type for a particular purpose; however, objects of the base type and of the subtype remain compatible with each other. Objects of a new type are incompatible with objects of the base type from which the new type is derived. The intention is that groups of objects in the real world which are conceptually similar should be modelled using types and subtypes; groups of objects which are conceptually dissimilar should be modelled using distinct types. Both distinct types and subtypes inherit operations from the base type. A subtype will inherit all the base type's operations, a distinct type will only inherit a subset. A detailed description of the differences between subtypes and distinct types will be given in this and in the following chapter.

This chapter will introduce Ada's pre-declared numeric types, the following chapter will introduce Ada's pre-declared non-numeric types. Other data types will be introduced throughout this section and tagged types will be further considered in Section III.

Integer data types

Ada's integer data types are divided into **signed integer** and **modular integer** types. The only pre-declared integer data type is the INTEGER type which was used in the previous section. There are two pre-declared INTEGER subtypes, NATURAL and POSITIVE. The modular data types are intended for systems programming and other specialized areas of software development. The signed integer types will be considered in detail first, followed by a brief consideration of modular types.

In common terms an integer is a positive or negative value in the range minus to plus infinity, which does not have a decimal fractional part. However, values of Ada's INTEGER type can only take a finite range of integer values. The actual range is not defined in the Ada standard but is dependent upon the compiler being used.

Attributes of integer data types

The actual values of the lowest and highest integer value which can be represented by the compiler being used can be established by the use of ***attributes***. For any data type there are a number of different attributes which can be used to determine particular properties of that type. For the pre-declared INTEGER type the attribute FIRST will evaluate to the lowest value which Ada can represent and the attribute LAST to the highest value. The use of attributes is illustrated by the following program fragment:

```
-- assuming IntegerIO is in use
PUT("The lowest integer value is ");
PUT( INTEGER'FIRST ); PUT_LINE;

PUT("The highest integer value is ");
PUT( INTEGER'LAST ); PUT_LINE;
```

An attribute expression consists of the name of the data type, or for some attributes an object of the data type, followed by an attribute mark (') and the name of the attribute. An attribute expression, as with all Ada expressions, has a particular data type. For the INTEGER attributes FIRST and LAST the resulting value is of the type UNIVERSAL_INTEGER, a type which is compatible with any integer data type. The range of values of the INTEGER data type can be represented on a range diagram:

```
INTEGER <--------------------------------------->
        ^                                       ^
    INTEGER'FIRST                          INTEGER'LAST
```

Other INTEGER attributes include

Attribute	Name	Notes
PRED	predecessor	Returns preceding value (same as subtracting 1), or raises CONSTRAINT_ERROR for FIRST
SUCC	successor	Returns succeeding value (same as adding 1), or raises CONSTRAINT_ERROR for LAST
POS	position	Returns position in sequence, same as the value of the integer itself
VAL	value	Returns value of integer, same as the value of the integer itself
IMAGE	image	Returns a string containing a representation of the value
VALUE	value	Converts a string representation to an integer value, or raises DATA_ERROR for an invalid representation

Many of these attributes may seem superfluous, but they are provided for the INTEGER data type as it is a *discrete type* and make more sense for other discrete types such as CHARACTER. The meanings and use of these attributes will be explained in further detail in the next chapter.

Integer literals

STRING literals were introduced in Section I where they were used to initialize the value of a STRING constant, or were used as parameters of output procedures. Programs also have a requirement to specify literal values of other data types. The declaration of the INTEGER constant *SimpleAnswer* in the *MostUltimateAnswer* program in Section I Chapter 2 was as follows:

```
SimpleAnswer : constant INTEGER := 42;
```

Made use of the INTEGER literal '*42*'. Integer literals are expressed in Ada programs as a sequence of digit characters optionally preceded by a positive or negative sign. For large numbers it is not possible to include a comma to denote groups of thousands, an underscore has to be used instead:

```
usual form     not allowed     allowed
1234567        1,234,567       1_234_567
```

In some situations it is advantageous to express the integer value in a base other than base 10. Alternative bases can be used in literals by stating the base and then the value enclosed between hash (#) marks. The following all express the same integer value:

```
decimal    hexadecimal    octal       binary
12345      16#3039#       8#30071#    2#11000000111001#
```

Input and output of integers

Input and output of integers makes use of an instantiation of the generic package INTEGER_IO which is contained within the standard package TEXT_IO, which is itself contained within the package ADA. The instantiation can be accomplished using the following:

```
-- Assuming that ADA.TEXT_IO is at least withed.
package IntegerIO is new ADA.TEXT_IO.INTEGER_IO( INTEGER);
use IntegerIO;
```

This will create, and bring into direct visibility, a package called *IntegerIO* which is suitable for the input–output of values of the pre-declared INTEGER data type and of any subtypes whose base type is INTEGER. If a new type, as opposed to a subtype, is declared then it cannot make use of this instantiation and will have to instantiate its own specific input–output package:

```
-- Assuming that ADA.TEXT_IO is at least withed.
type NewIntegerType is range MinValue .. MaxValue;
package NewIntegerIO is new ADA.TEXT_IO.INTEGER_IO
                                        ( NewIntegerType);
use NewIntegerIO;
```

The location of such instantiations has implications concerning the resulting visibility of the instantiated package. All instantiations in Section I were within a unit's declarative region and have the effect of hiding the package inside the unit being produced. This allows the unit being produced to make use of the instantiated facilities, but other units have no knowledge of its existence.

The alternative would be to instantiate the package outside the scope of any program unit. This technically is a separate Ada *compilation unit* and places the newly instantiated package into the Ada program library. This location makes the instantiated unit available for any other program unit to make use of it in its context clause. A *compilation unit* is the smallest part of a source code file which could be compiled independently of the rest of the source code. An example of such an instantiation might be as follows:

```
0001   -- Filename IntegerDemo.ada (k8 integerd.adb).
0002   -- Example instantiation of i-o package outside the scope
```

```
0003    -- of a program procedure's or package's declarative region.
0004    -- And other examples of use of INTEGER data types.
0005    -- Ada book Section II Chapter 9.
0006
0007    -- Fintan Culwin, v0.1, Jan 1997.
0008
0009    -- This is a compilation unit in its own right!
0010    with ADA.TEXT_IO;
0011    package IntegerIO is new ADA.TEXT_IO.INTEGER_IO( INTEGER);
0012
0013    -- This is the context clause for the program procedure, which
0014    -- assumes that there is a package called IntegerIO in the
                                                                library.
0015    with ADA.TEXT_IO, IntegerIO;
0016    use  ADA.TEXT_IO, IntegerIO;
0017
0018    procedure IntegerDemo is
```

Some environments require that each compilation unit is submitted to the compiler as a separate source code file. These environments will refuse to compile the file above until it has been split into two files at line 0012.

The general advice is to make program units as independent as possible. A program unit which assumes that the instantiated package *IntegerIo* is in the library has a dependency upon that unit built into it. A program unit which makes no such assumptions and instantiates all required packages within its own scope avoids such a dependency and practises ***information hiding***. The only possible objection might be that the private instantiation of packages would increase compilation time and storage requirements. However, it is more important to ensure that software is robust and elegantly engineered than to save a little on system resources, and the advice is generally to practise private instantiations.

The instantiated INTEGER_IO packages supply two procedures, GET and PUT, for the input and output of integer values from and to the terminal respectively. The package also supplies other versions of the integer GET and PUT procedures for input–output to and from external files; these procedures will be introduced in a later chapter. There are also two further versions which can be used to input and output representations to and from strings, which will also be introduced in subsequent chapters.

The PUT procedure has an optional parameter WIDTH which can be used to control output formatting. By default the value of WIDTH is large enough for any integer value to be output and, as the largest possible integer value differs from compiler to compiler, the default value of WIDTH differs from compiler to compiler. If a value for WIDTH is specified and the representation requires fewer character spaces, the output is preceded by sufficient spaces to make it WIDTH characters wide. If the value of WIDTH is too small for the representation then the value is output using the minimum number of spaces required:

IntVar has the value 123456
WIDTH has the default value 12
¶ indicates a space

Procedure call	Output
`PUT(IntVar)`	¶¶¶¶¶¶123456
`PUT(IntVar, WIDTH => 10)`	¶¶¶¶123456
`PUT(IntVar, WIDTH => 15)`	¶¶¶¶¶¶¶¶¶123456
`PUT(IntVar, WIDTH => 6)`	123456
`PUT(IntVar, WIDTH => 1)`	123456

A second optional parameter, BASE, can be used to change the number base used to output the representation:

IntVar has the decimal value 123456
WIDTH has the default value 12
BASE has the default value 10
¶ indicates a space

Procedure call	Output
`PUT(IntVar)`	¶¶¶¶¶¶¶12345
`PUT(IntVar, BASE => 10)`	¶¶¶¶¶¶¶12345
`PUT(IntVar, BASE => 16)`	¶¶¶¶#16#3039
`PUT(IntVar, BASE => 8)`	¶¶¶¶#8#30071
`PUT(IntVar, BASE => 1)`	#2#11000000111001

The procedure GET will accept characters from the terminal, stopping when a character which cannot possibly be part of an integer value is input. If the sequence of characters is in the format of an integer literal, as described above, the value is assigned to the actual parameter specified in the GET procedure call. If the sequence of input cannot be recognized as a possible integer value then a DATA_ERROR exception is raised. If the value input is outside the defined range of values of the type or subtype of the specified variable then a CONSTRAINT_ERROR will be raised upon the assignment. Any characters remaining in the input stream, including the <ENTER> code, can be taken care of by using the SKIP_LINE procedure as described in Section I Chapter 4.

The GET procedure has an additional optional parameter called WIDTH. The default value of WIDTH is zero which causes the procedure to skip all input until a sign or digit character is encountered. If the value of WIDTH is non-zero then it indicates the maximum number of characters which are to be accepted.

For small simple programs it is also possible to output an integer value in decimal format by use of the IMAGE attribute. The IMAGE attribute takes an integer variable as a parameter and converts it into a string representation. This string representation can be output using TEXT_IO as opposed to INTEGER_IO instantiated package facilities:

```
-- This outputs integer values using only ADA.TEXT_IO.
PUT( INTEGER'IMAGE( IntegerVariable));
```

As this technique does not offer any facilities for formatting the output and does not provide for input of values, its use is discouraged unless a very simple output is required.

Integer subtypes

Not all real world integer objects which are required to be modelled in an Ada program require the full range of possible values. For example, a program which is counting the number of people on a bus would be better modelled by using an integer data type whose smallest value was zero. Similarly a program concerned with counting the number of seconds a process has taken might be better modelled by using an integer data type whose smallest value was one. Ada provides two pre-declared INTEGER *subtypes* called NATURAL and POSITIVE whose range of values are constrained to these smaller bounds:

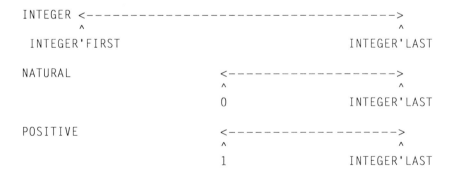

The design of these INTEGER subtypes can be illustrated on a Data Structure Diagram:

A data structure diagram is used to indicate the nature of the data objects which are being modelled, as opposed to program structure diagrams which are used to indicate the actions which a program will carry out on data objects. Consequently data structure diagrams should contain nouns or noun phrases and program structure diagrams should contain verbs or verb phrases. The diagrams above indicate that NATURAL and POSITIVE are subtypes of the INTEGER data type with ranges constrained as indicated. A double lined box is used on the data structure charts to indicate that this is the design of a subtype as opposed to a distinct type, which will be introduced shortly.

These subtypes are assumed to be declared in a package called STANDARD which is assumed to be **with**ed and **used** by all Ada program units. Their declaration in the package would be:

```
subtype NATURAL  is INTEGER range 0 .. INTEGER'LAST;
subtype POSITIVE is INTEGER range 1 .. INTEGER'LAST;
```

For a particular program requirement the pre-declared subtypes might not be appropriate. For example, a program specification may identify a real world object whose value can only be negative. In this situation it would be appropriate to declare a subtype whose values are restricted to negative integer values. Such a design and declaration might be

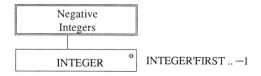

```
subtype NegativeIntegers is
                    INTEGER range INTEGER'FIRST .. -1;
```

Program objects such as constants, variables, parameters or functions can be declared to be of one of the specific subtypes, rather than of the *base type* INTEGER. This will allow Ada to monitor the values of these objects and to raise a CONSTRAINT_ERROR exception should any attempt be made to give them a value outside their declared range.

The intention is that as the program is intended to be an accurate model of the real world and as the range of the subtypes defines the values which the real world objects can have, then their values should never go outside this range. Should the value ever go outside this range then the program is in error and Ada is trying to be helpful by raising the exception. It may seem initially that the problem can be best solved by not using subtypes. However, this will not correct the program fault which is probably caused either by the programmer not understanding the specification or by a design fault. This behaviour by Ada is known as *strong type checking* and is one of the reasons why Ada is recommended for secure, reliable software.

Subtypes remain compatible with their base types and with other subtypes of the base type. This allows subtype values to be assigned or used in arithmetic, or other, expressions without the use of type conversion and also allows subtypes to share an input–output package instantiated for the base type. This implies that the two pre-declared subtypes NATURAL and POSITIVE, and the programmer declared subtype *NegativeIntegers*, are all compatible with each other and their base type INTEGER. All three subtypes, as well as the base type, can make use of the input–output package *IntegerIO* which was instantiated for the base type.

New INTEGER types

In addition to subtypes it is also possible, and in some cases desirable, to declare a completely new distinct integer data type rather than a subtype. The intention of subtypes is that they delineate a set of values within a greater range of possible values. A distinct type is intended for situations where a conceptually different set of values is being modelled.

An example may make this clearer. If a program is being developed for recording and analyzing the operations of a fleet of buses there may be a number of distinct integer concepts which have to be recorded. These concepts may include

the number of buses in the fleet;

the number of buses currently in operation;

the number of passengers on a particular bus;

the number of kilometres which a particular bus has travelled;

the route number;

the engine number.

A major part of the data design may now be to decide which of these concepts should be implemented using the pre-declared INTEGER type, the pre-declared INTEGER subtypes, new integer subtypes and distinct integer types. Some of these numbers, for example the route number or the engine number, are not numbers which are subject to arithmetic operations. Concepts such as the average route number or the sum of all the engine numbers do not seem to have any real world meaning. To model these kinds of numbers effectively a numeric type which does not have any arithmetic operations will have to be provided. This is only possible if the programmer specifies more explicitly exactly which operations are to be provided for a type. This is possible in the declaration of *abstract data types* which will be introduced in the next section.

If the concepts of *number of buses*, *distance travelled* and *number of passengers* are modelled using subtypes then they will remain compatible with each other; this will allow them to be used in expressions such as

```
NumberOfBuses := DistanceTravelled - NumberOnBoard;
```

The meaning of this expression is conceptually unclear, but as the data types of all three variables are compatible Ada will not object. A better model of the operation of buses might be produced by designing and declaring a series of distinct types and subtypes:

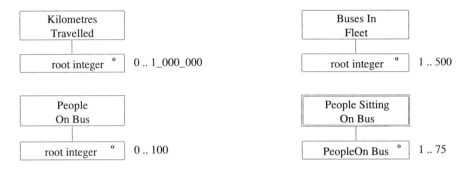

A single lined box on a data structure diagram is used to indicate the design of a distinct type, as opposed to subtype design which uses a double lined box. Thus the first three diagrams indicate that the types being designed are distinct types derived from INTEGER's base type which is a non-existent type called **root integer**. The last diagram indicates that the *PeopleSittingOnBus* is a subtype of the type *PeopleOnBus*, which is itself a distinct type derived from root integer.

```
        -- Distinct type for buses' odometer.
MinimumKilometresTravelled : constant := 0;
MaximumKilometresTravelled : constant := 1_000_000;
type KilometresTravelled is range
                            MinimumKilometresTravelled ..
                            MaximumKilometresTravelled;
        -- Distinct type for number of buses in fleet.
MinimumBusesInFleet : constant := 1;
MaximumBusesInFleet : constant := 500;
type BusesInFleet is range
            MinimumBusesInFleet .. MaximumBusesInFleet;
        -- Distinct type for number of passengers on a bus.
MinimumPeopleOnBus : constant := 0;
MaximumPeopleOnBus : constant := 100;
```

```
MaximumPeopleSittingOnBus : constant := 75;
type PeopleOnBus is range
                    MinimumPeopleOnBus .. MaximumPeopleOnBus;
subtype PeopleSittingOnBus is PeopleOnBus range
            MinimumPeopleOnBus .. MaximumPeopleSittingOnBus;
-- variables
DistanceTravelled : KilometresTravelled;
NumberOfBuses     : BusesInFleet;
BusesOnRoad       : BusesInFleet
NumberOnBoard     : PeopleOnBus;
StandingOnBoard   : PeopleOnBus;
SittingOnBoard    : PeopleSittingOnBus;
```

The expression given above

```
NumberOfBuses := DistanceTravelled - NumberOnBoard;
```

would now not be acceptable to Ada as the types of the three variables are incompatible. However, the type *PeopleOnBus* and its subtype *PeopleSitting-OnBus* are compatible with each other. Consequently the following statement would be allowed:

```
StandingOnBoard := NumberOnBoard - SittingOnBoard;
```

A distinct type inherits all operations from its base type, with the exception of input–output facilities contained within instantiated packages. Type conversion from a distinct type to the base type is always possible. Type conversion between two distinct types is also possible, but will raise a CONSTRAINT_ERROR if the value being converted is outside the declared range of the type which it is being converted to. Using distinct types the statement above could be rewritten as:

```
NumberOfBuses := BusesInFleet(DistanceTravelled) *
                 BusesInFleet(NumberOnBoard);
```

Although it is still not clear what the real world meaning of this calculation is, it now requires an explicit action by the programmer to make it acceptable, rather than being implicitly accepted by Ada. This will make it more likely that the operation makes sense in terms of the program's specification.

Relational operations on integer values

The six relational operators

Symbol	Name
=	is equal to
<>	is not equal to
>	is greater than
<	is less than
>=	is greater than or equal to
<=	is less than or equal to

can be used on values of compatible integer types without requiring type conversion. The resulting Boolean values are those expected from standard arithmetic rules. The Boolean membership operators **in** and **not in** are also pre-declared for integer values. The following expression evaluates to true if the value of *IntegerValue* is within the range 0 to 15 inclusive, and false otherwise:

```
IntegerValue in 0 .. 15;
```

The **not in** membership operator evaluates false when the **in** operator evaluates true and vice versa.

Arithmetic operations on integer values

The arithmetic operations which can be used with integer values are

Symbol	Name	Example
+	addition	$49 + 23 = 72$
–	subtraction	$49 - 23 = 26$
*	multiplication	$49 * 23 = 1127$
/	division	$49/23 = 2$ (23 goes into 49 two times)
rem	remainder	49 **rem** 23 = 3 (23 goes into 49 two times **remainder** 3)
* *	exponentiation	$49 * * 2 = 2401$ (49 to the power 2)
abs	absolute value	$abs(49) = 49$; $abs(-49) = 49$

There is also a small number of other arithmetic operations which mix integer and real types, which will be introduced below.

Modular integer types

There are no pre-declared modular types. Modular types differ from ***signed integer*** types largely by 'wrapping around' their range of values. For example:

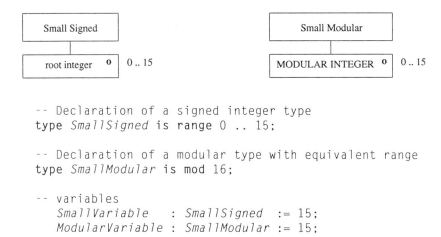

```
-- Declaration of a signed integer type
type SmallSigned is range 0 .. 15;

-- Declaration of a modular type with equivalent range
type SmallModular is mod 16;

-- variables
   SmallVariable   : SmallSigned  := 15;
   ModularVariable : SmallModular := 15;
```

This declares a new signed integer type whose objects can take values in the range 0 to 15 and a modular type with an equivalent range. The essential difference between the two types can be illustrated by the following attempted operation:

```
-- This will raise a CONSTRAINT_ERROR if
-- SignedVariable has the value 15.
SignedVariable := SignedVariable +1;

-- This is acceptable if
-- ModularVariable has the value 15.
ModularVariable := ModularVariable +1
```

When an attempt is made to increment the value of *SignedVariable* beyond the limits of its range a CONSTRAINT_ERROR is raised. When *ModularVariable* is incremented it wraps around to the start of its range. Thus the resulting value in *ModularVariable* following execution of the statement above is 0 and no exception is raised.

Modular types have all the pre-declared operations described for the signed types described above. The result of all arithmetic operations cannot cause a CONSTRAINT_ERROR; instead the modulo value (remainder after division) is assigned. Modular types are in part supplied for use by systems programmers where **bitwise** logical operations, **and, or** and **xor,** are important. These operations are supplied by Ada for use with modular types. The type *SmallModular* can be thought of as a four bit binary value. If the value of *ModularVariable* is assumed to be 12 (2#1010#) and the constant *Mask* has the value 7 (2#0111#), the result of the various operations would be

Operation	Expression	Result
not	**not** ModularVariable	(2#0101#)5
and	ModularVariable **and** Mask	(2#0010#)2
or	ModularVariable **or** Mask	(2#1111#)15
xor	ModularVariable **xor** Mask	(2#1101#)13

The **bitwise** operators apply the corresponding Boolean rule to each bit, or corresponding pairs of bits, in the operands. For example, the **xor** truth table is

xor

Left operand	Right operand	Resulting value
0	0	0
0	1	1
1	0	1
1	1	0

Which can be colloquially expressed as 'either but not both'. When the bitwise **xor** operator is applied to the two four bit values above, the resulting value is computed as

ModularVariable	1	0	1	0
Mask	0	1	1	1
xor result	1	1	0	1

The other examples using **not, and** and **or** can be illustrated using a similar table employing the truth tables presented in the previous section. Input–output facilities for modular types can be obtained by instantiating the package ADA.TEXT_IO.MODULAR_IO, for example:

```
-- Assuming that ADA.TEXT_IO is at least withed.
package SmallModularIO is new
                ADA.TEXT_IO.MODULAR_IO( SmallModular);
```

The use of modular types is not common in general purpose programs and will not be considered further.

Real data types

Real world numeric objects which have fractional values can be represented in an Ada program using one of the real data types *float*, *fixed* or *decimal*. A *float* data type specifies only the number of significant digits to be represented and does not guarantee any degree of accuracy over the entire range. A *fixed* data type specifies a degree of accuracy which has to be maintained over the entire range of the type. A *decimal* type combines a specification of significant digits and degree of accuracy. The most commonly used real data types are the float data types including the pre-declared type FLOAT. This part of the chapter will concentrate upon the float data types and will briefly consider the other possibilities at the end.

Attributes of float types

The attributes applicable to floating point types include

Attribute	Notes
FIRST	The lowest possible value
LAST	Largest possible value
DIGITS	The precision of the values

The values FIRST and LAST delineate the range of possible values, returning a value of type UNIVERSAL_FLOAT. The attribute DIGITS indicates the number of significant digits which the value can represent and returns a value of type UNIVERSAL_INTEGER. For the pre-declared type FLOAT the value of these attributes differs from compiler to compiler. The range diagram of the pre-declared FLOAT type compared with the pre-declared INTEGER type looks like this:

```
INTEGER                            <--->
FLOAT  <----------------------------------------------->
       ^                                              ^
    FLOAT'FIRST                              FLOAT'LAST
```

There is no suggestion that this diagram contains any meaningful scale, only that the range of INTEGER values is very much smaller than the range of FLOAT values. The diagram indicates that it is always possible to type-convert an INTEGER value to a FLOAT value; however, conversion of a FLOAT value to an INTEGER value will raise a CONSTRAINT_ERROR if the resulting INTEGER value is outside the range INTEGER'FIRST to INTEGER'LAST.

Floating point literals

Floating point literals can be represented in an Ada program either in conventional or standard form. A conventional form is a sequence of *possibly signed integer–decimal point–unsigned integer*: for example, 123.456, +12345.678, −123.456 or +0.0000123. The alternative form is *mantissa E exponent*: for example, 1.23456E2, +1.2345678E7, −1.23456E2 or +1.23E − 5.

Ada allows floating point literals to be expressed in either of these forms and allows the integer parts of the representation to use the embedded underscore convention: for example, +1.234_567_8E7. As with integer literals values need not be represented in decimal notation; alternative bases can be specified for the mantissa or the exponent or both.

Input and output of floating point values

Input and output of floating point values make use of an instantiation of the generic package FLOAT_IO which is contained within the standard package TEXT_IO, which is itself contained within the package ADA. The instantiation can be accomplished using the following:

```
-- Assuming that ADA.TEXT_IO is at least withed.
package FloatIO is new ADA.TEXT_IO.FLOAT_IO( FLOAT);
```

This will create a package called *FloatIO* which is suitable for the input–output of values of the pre-declared FLOAT data type and of any subtypes whose base type is FLOAT. If a new type, as opposed to a subtype, is declared then it cannot make use of this instantiation and will have to instantiate its own specific input–output package:

```
-- Assuming that ADA.TEXT_IO is at least withed.
type NewFloatType is digits 16;
package NewFloatIO is new ADA.TEXT_IO.FLOAT_IO( NewFloatType);
use NewFloatIO;
```

The instantiated FLOAT_IO packages supply versions of the GET and PUT procedures suitable for the input and output of floating point values. The floating point PUT procedure has three optional parameters: FORE, AFT and EXP. The parameter EXP has the default value 0 which causes real values to be output in conventional as opposed to exponent notation. Any non-zero positive value will cause the output to use exponent notation. The fields FORE and AFT are used to control the number of character places before and after the decimal point.

Examples of the use of this procedure are

FloatVar **has the value 1.234567**
¶ **indicates a space**

procedure call	output
PUT(FloatVar)	¶1.234567E+00
PUT(FloatVar, EXP => 0)	¶1.234567
PUT(FloatVar, AFT => 3, EXP= >0)	¶1.235
PUT(FloatVar, FORE=>5, AFT => 3, EXP= >0);	¶¶¶¶1.235

The GET procedure operates in a similar manner to the INTEGER GET procedure, accepting characters from the terminal until it can be decided that the sequence of characters does or does not represent a possible floating point value. If the input can represent a valid value the value is computed and assigned, otherwise a DATA_ERROR exception is raised. If the value assigned is outside the appropriate range then a CONSTRAINT_ERROR is raised.

The FLOAT GET procedure has an additional optional parameter called WIDTH. The default value of WIDTH is zero which causes the procedure to skip all input until a sign or digit character is encountered. If the value of WIDTH is non-zero then it indicates the maximum number of characters which are to be accepted.

The instantiated FLOAT_IO packages also supply versions of GET and PUT which are suitable for input and output to and from external files and to and from strings. These versions of the procedures will be introduced in subsequent chapters.

Float subtypes and distinct types

There are no pre-declared FLOAT subtypes, but programmer declared subtypes can be declared and used in much the same way as integer subtypes:

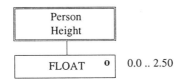

```
MinPersonHeight : constant := 0.0;
MaxPersonHeight : constant := 2.50;
subtype PersonHeight is FLOAT range
                MinPersonHeight .. MaxPersonHeight;
PatientHeight : PersonHeight;
```

Programmer declared new FLOAT types can be declared constrained or unconstrained. An unconstrained declaration specifies only the required precision and allows Ada to determine the largest possible range: for example:

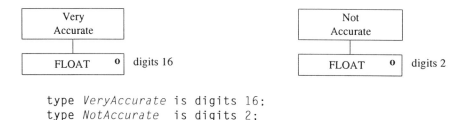

```
type VeryAccurate is digits 16;
type NotAccurate  is digits 2;
```

Values of the type *VeryAccurate* would have limited range with a high degree of precision. Values of the type *NotAccurate* would have a much greater range with only two digits of precision. It is more usual to specify a precision and a range. For example.

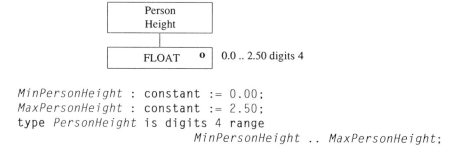

```
MinPersonHeight : constant := 0.00;
MaxPersonHeight : constant := 2.50;
type PersonHeight is digits 4 range
                    MinPersonHeight .. MaxPersonHeight;
```

The distinct type *PersonHeight* will have a four digit precision which allows the height of a person to be stored to the nearest tenth of a centimetre (e.g. 2.499). The design of a distinct floating point type requires decisions on the range of possible values and the precision with which it has to be stored. When an Ada program is compiled it may be that the compiler is unable to accommodate the range and precision requested. In this situation, as in all situations, Ada takes the safest action: that is, to abandon the compilation with a message informing the developer that the accuracy requested cannot be guaranteed.

Relational and arithmetic operations on float values

The six relational operators listed above, and the membership operators, can be applied to float values giving the expected Boolean results. Some care should be exercised with the use of relational operations on float values, as will be explained below.

The arithmetic operations which are pre-declared for float values are

Symbol	Name	Left op.	Right op.	Result	Example
+	addition	FLOAT	FLOAT	FLOAT	$1.2 + 2.3 = 3.5$
−	subtraction	FLOAT	FLOAT	FLOAT	$1.2 - 2.3 = -1.1$
*	multiplication	FLOAT	FLOAT	FLOAT	$1.2 * 2.3 = 2.76$
/	division	FLOAT	FLOAT	FLOAT	$1.2/2.3 = 0.522$
* *	exponentiation	FLOAT	INTEGER	FLOAT	$1.2 * * 3 = 1.728$
abs	absolute value	FLOAT	FLOAT	FLOAT	$abs(-1.2) = 1.2$

When an integer value is being used within a computer program it is represented and manipulated with absolute accuracy. Floating point numbers are not always represented within programs with absolute accuracy. There are some decimal floating point numbers which cannot be represented in decimal format: for example, $10/3 = 3.3333...$, $pi = 3.14159....$ When floating point values are represented in a computer program, they are subject to similar problems. Some values which can be represented accurately in decimal form cannot be represented accurately in binary form within the program, and vice versa. Floating point values are subject to rounding error when they are stored or manipulated by computer programs.

This can be demonstrated by the use of a simple program. Starting with the floating point value 1.00, divide it by 10_000.00 to obtain a representation of the value 1/10_000. Add this value to itself 10_000 times and then compare the resulting value with the value 1.00. By the logic of arithmetic the value should still be 1.00, but due to rounding errors it may be very close to, but not quite, 1.00. The design and implementation of this program might be

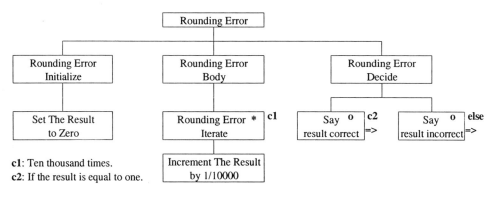

```
0001    -- Filename RoundingError.ada (k8 rounding.adb).
0002    -- Program to demonstrate the effects of rounding errors
0003    -- when floating point values are stored and manipulated.
0004    --
```

```
0005    -- Written for Ada book Section II Chapter 9.
0006    -- Fintan Culwin, v 0.1, Jan 1997.
0007
0008    with ADA.TEXT_IO;
0009    use  ADA.TEXT_IO;
0010
0011    procedure RoundingError is
0012
0013    package FloatIO is new ADA.TEXT_IO.FLOAT_IO( FLOAT);
0014    use FloatIO;
0015
0016       Zero              : constant FLOAT   := 0.0;
0017       TenThousand       : constant INTEGER := 10_000;
0018       One               : constant FLOAT   := 1.0;
0019       OneTenThousandth  : constant FLOAT   :=
0020                                     One / FLOAT( TenThousand );
0021
0022       TheResult : FLOAT := Zero;
0023
0024    begin -- RoundingError
0025       -- TheResult is equal to Zero
0026       for Counter in 1 .. TenThousand loop
0027          TheResult := TheResult + OneTenThousandth;
0028       end loop;
0029       -- TheResult is arithmetically equal
0030       -- to 1/10_000 * 10_000 = 1.0.
0031
0032       if TheResult = One then
0033          PUT_LINE("Isn't this what you expected!");
0034       else
0035          PUT_LINE("Isn't this a surprise!");
0036          PUT("One is        "); PUT( One,       EXP =>0);NEW_LINE;
0037          PUT("The result is "); PUT( TheResult, EXP =>0);NEW_LINE;
0038       end if;
0039    end RoundingError;
```

When this program was executed on a VAX computer the output was:

```
Isn't this a surprise!
One is        1.00000
The result is 0.99973
```

The difference in values between the expected result and the actual result is small, but it is sufficient for the equality test to fail. When floating point values are being manipulated within a computer program the possibility of rounding errors should be borne in mind and allowed for. In this situation the program could be amended so as not to test the result for equality with one, but tested for it being as close as to make no difference:

```
0001    -- Filename RoundingErrorCorrected.ada (k8 roundinc.adb).
0002    -- Program to demonstrate a technique to allow for
0003    -- the effects of rounding errors when floating point
0004    -- values are stored and manipulated.
0005    --
0006    -- Written for Ada book Section II Chapter 9.
0007    -- Fintan Culwin, v0.1, Jan 1997.
0008
0009    with ADA.TEXT_IO;
0010    use  ADA.TEXT_IO;
0011
0012    procedure RoundingErrorCorrected is
0013
0014        package FloatIO is new ADA.TEXT_IO.FLOAT_IO( FLOAT);
0015        use FloatIO;
0016
0017        Zero              : constant FLOAT   := 0.0;
0018        TenThousand       : constant INTEGER := 10_000;
0019        One               : constant FLOAT   := 1.0;
0020        OneTenThousandth  : constant FLOAT   :=
0021                                      One/ FLOAT( TenThousand );
0022        CloseEnough       : constant FLOAT   := 0.001;
0023
0024        TheResult  : FLOAT := Zero;
0025        Difference : FLOAT;
0026
0027    begin -- RoundingError
0028        -- TheResult is equal to Zero
0029        for Counter in 1 .. TenThousand loop
0030            TheResult := TheResult + OneTenThousandth;
0031        end loop;
0032        -- TheResult is arithmetically equal
0033        -- to 1/10_000 * 10_000 = 1.0.
0034
0035        Difference := abs( One - TheResult);
0036
0037        if Difference < CloseEnough then
0038            PUT_LINE("Isn't this what you expected!");
0039        else
0040            PUT_LINE("Isn't this a surprise!");
0041            PUT("One is        "); PUT( One,       EXP =>0);NEW_LINE;
0042            PUT("The result is "); PUT( TheResult, EXP =>0);NEW_LINE;
0043        end if;
0044    end RoundingErrorCorrected;
```

This version of the program gives the expected result and indicates a technique by which the problem of rounding errors can be allowed for.

Fixed and decimal types

The declaration of a float data type specified the number of digits of precision, and optionally a range of values, which are to be used by Ada when real values are stored. The alternative fixed declaration allows for an absolute accuracy to be specified. An example of a fixed data type declaration is

```
        ┌──────────────┐
        │   Person     │
        │   Height     │
        └──────┬───────┘
               │
        ┌──────────────┬───┐
        │   FLOAT      │ o │   0.0 .. 2.50 delta 0.001
        └──────────────┴───┘
```

```
MinPersonHeight : constant := 0.0;
MaxPersonHeight : constant := 2.50;
type PersonHeight is delta 0.001 range
                        MinPersonHeight .. MaxPersonHeight;
```

Unlike the declaration of float types the **range** clause is not optional. The **delta** clause specifies the accuracy with which the values are to be stored and manipulated throughout the entire range. This example is comparable with the declaration of the float type *PersonHeight* given above. Here again an accuracy of one-tenth of a millimetre is requested for the entire range.

The use of fixed types within Ada programs is largely comparable with the use of float types. Input–output facilities are obtained by instantiating the generic package ADA.TEXT_IO.FIXED_IO. The fixed PUT procedure has the same set of optional parameters as the FLOAT PUT procedure.

Ada '95 introduces a further fixed type known as a decimal type. An example of a decimal data type declaration is

```
┌──────────────────┐            ┌──────────────────┐
│  British Pounds  │            │   Italian Lira   │
└────────┬─────────┘            └────────┬─────────┘
         │                               │
┌────────────┬─────────────────┐ ┌────────────┬──────────────────────────┐
│            │ 0 ..            │ │            │ 0 ..                     │
│   REAL     │ 9_999_999_999_999_999.99 │   REAL     │ 9_999_999_999_999_999_999_ │
│            │ delta 0.01, digits 18 │ │            │ 999, delta 1.0, digits 22 │
└────────────┴─────────────────┘ └────────────┴──────────────────────────┘
```

```
type BritishPounds is delta 0.01 digits 18
                    range 0_000_000_000_000_000.00 ..
                        9_999_999_999_999_999.99;
type ItalianLira is delta 1.0 digits 22
                    range 0_000_000_000_000_000_000_000 ..
                        9_999_999_999_999_999_999_999;
```

The decimal type combines the specification of the number of significant digits in the **digits** clause with the requirement for fixed accuracy in the **delta** clause. As suggested in the example declarations, one intended use of decimal types is for the representation and manipulation of currency in specialized commercial applications. The use of decimal types within Ada programs is largely comparable with the use of float types. General input–output facilities for decimal types are obtained by instantiating the generic package ADA.TEXT_IO.DECIMAL_IO. Specialized facilities for the formatted output of decimal types are obtained by instantiating the generic package ADA.TEXT_IO.PICTURES.

The use of fixed and decimal types is more specialized than the use of float types and the characteristics and use of these types will not be considered further.

EXERCISES

9.1 Declare suitable **types** or **subtypes** for the following requirements:

(a) Examination scores which are whole numbers in the range 0 to 100.

(b) A proportions probability measure to six significant digits in the range 0.0 (impossible) to 1.0 (certain).

(c) An integer percentage probability measure in the range 0 (impossible) to 100 (certain).

(d) A correlation coefficient to four significant digits in the range −1.0 to +1.0.

9.2 The probability of an event can be expressed using one of the measures from Exercises 9.1(b) and 9.1(c). For example, the probability of obtaining a head when tossing a fair coin can be expressed as the proportion 0.500000 or the percentage 50. Design and implement a pair of functions which will convert a proportional probability into a percentage probability and vice versa.

9.3 Reimplement the *RoundingError* program making use of a fixed point instead of floating point values and attempt to demonstrate the effects of rounding errors on these types.

9.4 Design and implement an application which will allow the user to explore unsigned 16 bit modular hexadecimal arithmetic. This will require a modular integer type with the range of values 2^0 to 2^{16} and an interface which allows the user to input two four character hexadecimal values separated by an arithmetic operator $(+, -, /, *)$. The program should compute and then display the result in hexadecimal.

CHAPTER 10

Character, string and enumeration types

This chapter will complete the introduction to Ada's simple types by first introducing the text oriented CHARACTER and STRING types. The representation and manipulation of text information is as important, and possibly more prevalent, in the majority of commercial programs as the representation and manipulation of numeric information. Consequently an understanding of text oriented data types is at least as important as the understanding of numeric types presented in the previous chapter.

The introduction to text oriented types will be followed by an introduction to a very powerful facility to declare enumeration types. Enumeration types can be used to model more accurately some real world concepts, which are not very well represented by numeric or text based types. One particular pre-declared enumeration type is the BOOLEAN data type which will be formally introduced at the end of the chapter.

Character types

Ada data objects of the type CHARACTER can take a range of *single* character values; the range of characters from which this value can be selected is dependent upon the *collating sequence* which is used by the compiler.

What can cause a great number of problems for novice programmers is the relationship between the character '1' and the integer value 1. The character '1' is a mathematical symbol for the integer value 1. Different cultures have different symbols for '1'; however, all these different symbols represent the same mathematical concept of 1. Accordingly a computer system needs to represent the character symbol for '1', and needs to represent the integer value 1 (and also the real value 1.00). One of the available characters is used to represent the character symbol '1' and this has the type CHARACTER. This is distinct from the integer value 1 which has the type universal integer, and both of these are distinct from the real value 1.00 which has the type universal real.

Computers represent characters internally by using an integer numeric code, where each character is individually represented by a unique code. There are a number of coding conventions which computers can use, the commonest of these being ASCII. ASCII is an acronym for *American Standard Code for Information Interchange*; this coding convention is used by all Ada compilers.

In addition to the symbols for '0' .. '9', 'A' .. 'Z' and 'a' .. 'z', ASCII has a large number of other codes for other types of symbol, including some symbols which control the VDU or printer and as such have no visible representation. Such symbols are known as non-printing characters and include such codes as LF (*line feed*), BS (*back space*) and FF (*form feed*). The ASCII collating sequence has been in use since the earliest computers were developed. The initial ASCII specification, now known as ISO 646, has only 128 characters and is biased towards the English language character set. It cannot be used to represent some characters used in non-English languages such as diaeresis ('Ä' 'ä'), cedilla ('Ç' 'ç'), the ae diphthong ('Æ' 'æ') and many other characters and common symbols. The multiplication symbol used in computer programs is the asterisk (*) as there was no multiplication symbol in the original ASCII code and the use of a lower case X (x) would have been confusing. In an attempt to alleviate this situation the ASCII convention was extended to 256 characters allowing an additional 128 characters. The rules for how the additional 128 characters are to be used is expressed in ISO 8859-1, and the commonest implementation is ISO 6429 known informally as *Latin_1*. The first 128 characters of the ISO 8859-1 character set are identical to the original ASCII convention. A *Latin_1* code table is shown in Table 10.1.

The original ASCII convention used seven bits to encode a character ($2^7 = 128$), the *Latin_1* extension added a single bit ($2^8 = 256$) to use a complete byte. Although 256 characters are adequate for most romanized alphabets there are many other alphabets and character sets in use in the world. These include Arabic alphabets and Chinese, Japanese and Korean ideogram character sets, any one of which has more than 256 characters. At the time that the Ada '95 standard was being defined, a standardization of a 16 bit character set containing 65535 characters (ISO 10646) was also being produced. The first 256 characters of the ISO 10646 standard will conform to the ISO 8859-1 standard. However the full standardization of ISO 10646 was not available for inclusion in the initial Ada '95 standard (ISO 8652:1995).

Ada pre-declares two CHARACTER data types. The type CHARACTER is based upon an eight bit, 256 character, ISO 8859-1 definition. The type WIDE_CHARACTER is based upon a 16 bit, 65535 character, ISO 10646 definition. At the time of writing this book the use of WIDE_CHARACTER data type is not very common and as the conceptual differences between the CHARACTER and WIDE_CHARACTER types are not very great, only the CHARACTER data type will be considered in detail.

Table 10.1   An eight bit ASCII Latin_1 code table.

Literal	Name		Literal	Name
0		NUL	1		SOH
2		STX	3		ETX
4		EOT	5		ENQ
6		ACK	7		BEL
8		BS	9		HT
10		LF	11		VT
12		FF	13		CR
14		SO	15		SI
16		DLE	17		DC1
18		DC2	19		DC3
20		DC4	21		NAK
22		SYN	23		ETB
24		CAN	25		EM
26		SUB	27		ESC
28		FS	29		GS
30		RS	31		US
32	' '	Space	33	'!'	Exclamation
34	'"'	Quotation	35	'#'	Number_Sign
36	'$'	Dollar_Sign	37	'%'	Percent_Sig
38	'&'	Ampersand	39	'''	Apostrophe
40	'('	Left_Parenthesis	41	')'	Right_Parenthesis
42	'*'	Asterisk	43	'+'	Plus_Sign
44	','	Comma	45	'-'	Hyphen Minus_Sign
46	'.'	Full_Stop	47	'/'	Solidus
48	'0'		49	'1'	
50	'2'		51	'3'	
52	'4'		53	'5'	
54	'6'		55	'7'	
56	'8'		57	'9'	
58	':'	Colon	59	';'	Semicolon
60	'<'	Less_Than_Sign	61	'='	Equals_Sign
62	'>'	Greater_Than_Sign	63	'?'	Question
64	'@'	Commercial_At	65	'A'	
66	'B'		67	'C'	
68	'D'		69	'E'	
70	'F'		71	'G'	
72	'H'		73	'I'	
74	'J'		75	'K'	
76	'L'		77	'M'	
78	'N'		79	'O'	
80	'P'		81	'Q'	
82	'R'		83	'S'	
84	'T'		85	'U'	
86	'V'		87	'W'	
88	'X'		89	'Y'	
90	'Z'		91	'['	Left_Square_Bracket
92	'\'	Reverse_Solidus	93	']'	Right_Square_Bracket
94	'^'	Circumflex	95	'_'	Low_Line

Table 10.1   Continued.

	Literal	Name		Literal	Name
96	' ` '	Grave	97	'a'	LC_A
98	'b'	LC_B	99	'c'	LC_C
100	'd'	LC_D	101	'e'	LC_E
102	'f'	LC_F	103	'g'	LC_G
104	'h'	LC_H	105	'i'	LC_I
106	'j'	LC_J	107	'k'	LC_K
108	'l'	LC_L	109	'm'	LC_M
110	'n'	LC_N	111	'o'	LC_O
112	'p'	LC_P	113	'q'	LC_Q
114	'r'	LC_R	115	's'	LC_S
116	't'	LC_T	117	'u'	LC_U
118	'v'	LC_V	119	'w'	LC_W
120	'x'	LC_X	121	'y'	LC_Y
122	'z'	LC_Z	123	'{'	Left_Curly_Bracket
124	'|'	Vertical_Line	125	'}'	Right_Curly_Bracket
126	'~'	Tilde	127		DEL
128		Reserved_128	129		Reserved_129
130		Reserved_130	131		Reserved_131
132		IND	133		NEL
134		SSA	135		ESA
136		HTS	137		HTJ
138		VTS	139		PLD
140		PLU	141		RI
142		SS2	143		SS3
144		DCS	145		PU1
146		PU2	147		STS
148		CCH	149		MW
150		SPA	151		EPA
152		Reserved_152	153		Reserved_153
154		Reserved_154	155		CSI
156		ST	157		OSC
158		PM	159		APC
160		No_Break_Space	161	'¡'	Inverted Exclamation
162	'¢'	Cent_Sign	163	'£'	Pound_Sign
164	'¤'	Currency_Sign	165	'¥'	Yen_Sign
166	'¦'	Broken_Bar	167	'§'	Section_Sign Paragraph_Sign
168	'¨'	Diaeresis	169	'©'	Copyright_Sign
170	'ª'	Feminine_Ordinal_Indicator	171	'«'	Left_Angle_Quotation
172	'¬'	Not_Sign	173	''	Soft_Hyphen
174	'®'	Registered_Trade_Mark_Sign	175	'¯'	Macron
176	'°'	Degree_Sign Ring_Above	177	'±'	Plus_Minus_Sign
178	'²'	Superscript_Two	179	'³'	Superscript_Three
180	'´'	Acute	181	'µ'	Micro_Sign
182	'¶'	Pilcrow_Sign	183	'·'	Middle_Dot
184	'¸'	Cedilla	185	'¹'	Superscript_One
186	'º'	Masculine_Ordinal_Indicator	187	'»'	Right_Angle_Quotation
188	'¼'	Fraction_One_Quarter	189	'½'	Fraction_One_Half

(continued)

Table 10.1   Continued.

Literal		Name	Literal		Name
190	'¾'	Fraction_Three_Quarters	191	'¿'	Inverted_Question
192	'À'	UC_A_Grave	193	'Á'	UC_A_Acute
194	'Â'	UC_A_Circumflex	195	'Ã'	UC_A_Tilde
196	'Ä'	UC_A_Diaeresis	197	'Å'	UC_A_Ring
198	'Æ'	UC_AE_Diphthong	199	'Ç'	UC_C_Cedilla
200	'È'	UC_E_Grave	201	'É'	UC_E_Acute
202	'Ê'	UC_E_Circumflex	203	'Ë'	UC_E_Diaeresis
204	'Ì'	UC_I_Grave	205	'Í'	UC_I_Acute
206	'Î'	UC_I_Circumflex	207	'Ï'	UC_I_Diaeresis
208	'Ð'	UC_Icelandic_Eth	209	'Ñ'	UC_N_Tilde
210	'Ò'	UC_O_Grave	211	'Ó'	UC_O_Acute
212	'Ô'	UC_O_Circumflex	213	'Õ'	UC_O_Tilde
214	'Ö'	UC_O_Diaeresis	215	'×'	Multiplication_Sign
216	'Ø'	UC_O_Oblique_Stroke	217	'Ù'	UC_U_Grave
218	'Ú'	UC_U_Acute	219	'Û'	UC_U_Circumflex
220	'Ü'	UC_U_Diaeresis	221	'Ý'	UC_Y_Acute
222	'þ'	UC_Icelandic_Thorn	223	'ß'	LC_German_Sharp_S
224	'à'	LC_A_Grave	225	'á'	LC_A_Acute
226	'â'	LC_A_Circumflex	227	'ã'	LC_A_Tilde
228	'ä'	LC_A_Diaeresis	229	'å'	LC_A_Ring
230	'æ'	LC_AE_Diphthong	231	'ç'	LC_C_Cedilla
232	'è'	LC_E_Grave	233	'é'	LC_E_Acute
234	'ê'	LC_E_Circumflex	235	'ë'	LC_E_Diaeresis
236	'ì'	LC_I_Grave	237	'í'	LC_I_Acute
238	'î'	LC_I_Circumflex	239	'ï'	LC_I_Diaeresis
240	'ð'	LC_Icelandic_Eth	241	'ñ'	LC_N_Tilde
242	'ò'	LC_O_Grave	243	'ó'	LC_O_Acute
244	'ô'	LC_O_Circumflex	245	'õ'	LC_O_Tilde
246	'ö'	LC_O_Diaeresis	247	'÷'	Division_Sign
248	'ø'	LC_O_Oblique_Stroke	249	'ù'	LC_U_Grave
250	'ú'	LC_U_Acute	251	'û'	LC_U_Circumflex
252	'ü'	LC_U_Diaeresis	253	'ý'	LC_Y_Acute
254	'þ'	LC_Icelandic_Thorn	255	'ÿ'	LC_Y_Diaeresis

Types, subtypes and attributes of character data types

The following attributes are available for use with the CHARACTER data types:

Attribute	Name	Notes
FIRST	first	Returns the first character value of the data type, or subtype, specified

LAST	last	Returns the last character value of the data type, or subtype, specified
PRED	predecessor	Returns the preceding character in the collating sequence, or raises CONSTRAINT_ERROR for the first character
SUCC	successor	Returns the succeeding character in the collating sequence, or raises CONSTRAINT_ERROR for the last character
POS	position	Returns an integer value indicating the position of the character parameter in the collating sequence
VAL	value	Returns the character value whose location in the collating sequence is specified by the integer parameter
IMAGE	image	Returns a string containing a representation of the CHARACTER parameter
VALUE	value	Converts a string representation to a CHARACTER value

The last two of these attributes are not particularly useful for CHARACTER data types, but they are available by virtue of the CHARACTER type being discrete. In the preceding chapter where these attributes were listed for the INTEGER data type, attributes such as POS and VAL were not useful in that context.

Assuming the existence of the following types, subtypes and variable declarations

```
type     Capitals   is new CHARACTER range 'A' .. 'Z';
subtype DigitsCPF1 is      CHARACTER range '0' .. '9';

CharVar  : CHARACTER  := 'A';
Capital  : Capitals   := 'A';
Digit    : Digits     := '1';
```

then the value of the following attribute expressions will be

Expression	Value	Type
CHARACTER'FIRST	non-printing	CHARACTER
CHARACTER'LAST	'ÿ'	CHARACTER
Capitals'FIRST	'A'	*Capitals*
Capitals'LAST	'Z'	*Capitals*
Digits'FIRST	'0'	CHARACTER
Digits'LAST	'9'	CHARACTER
CHARACTER'SUCC(*CharVar*)	'B'	CHARACTER
CHARACTER'PRED(*CharVar*)	'@'	CHARACTER
Capitals'SUCC(*Capital*)	'B'	*Capitals*

Capitals'PRED(*Capital*)	Raises implicit CONSTRAINT_ERROR	
Digits'SUCC(*Digit*)	'2'	CHARACTER
Digits'PRED(*Digit*)	'0'	CHARACTER
CHARACTER'POS(*CharVar*)	65	universal integer
CHARACTER'VAL(*65*)	'A'	CHARACTER
Capitals'POS(*Capital*)	65	universal integer
Capitals'VAL(*65*)	'A'	*Capitals*
Digits'POS(*Digit*)	49	universal integer
Digits'VAL(*57*)	'9'	CHARACTER
CHARACTER'IMAGE('z')	'z'	STRING
CHARACTER'VALUE("z")	'z'	CHARACTER

The first character of the pre-declared CHARACTER data type has the ASCII value 0, which is the null character and cannot be printed. Two other points should be noted: first, that the POS and VAL attributes make use of the ordinal values of the base type and not the ordinal values of the new type, and thus *Capitals*'POS('A') is 65 not 0; second, taking the predecessor of the first value of a subtype, or the successor of the last value, will not automatically raise a CONSTRAINT_ERROR. The value obtained is of the base type and if there is a suitable value then no CONSTRAINT_ERROR will be raised, although if the value obtained is assigned to a variable of the subtype, then a CONSTRAINT_ ERROR will be raised upon assignment:

```
-- This will raise a CONSTRAINT_ERROR!
Digit := Digits'PRED( Digits'FIRST );
-- But this will not.
CharVar := Digits'PRED( Digits'FIRST );
```

Character literals and character input–output

The simplest way by which a character literal can be specified is to enter the literal directly into the source code enclosing it between single quote marks. For example, 'a', '¥', '®', etc. Alternatively most characters also have a name defined in the package ADA.CHARACTERS.LATIN_1. Table 10.1 lists the names defined in this package, together with their ASCII value and appearance. The name can be used in place of the equivalent literal, wherever the literal could be used:

```
-- Assuming that Country is a variable of an enumerated type
-- (see below), that CurrencySymbol is a CHARACTER variable and
-- that ADA.CHARACTERS.LATIN_1 is in use, then the following two
-- fragments are equivalent.
```

```
if Country := UK then              if Country := UK then(x)1
    CurrencySymbol := '£';            CurrencySymbol := POUND_SIGN;
elsif Country = Japan then         elsif Country = Japan then
    CurrencySymbol := 'Y';            CurrencySymbol := YEN_SIGN;
elsif Country = USA then           elsif Country = USA then
    CurrencySymbol := '$';            CurrencySymbol := DOLLAR_SIGN;
end if(x)1;                         end if;
```

The input and output of characters is accomplished by use of ADA.TEXT_IO, whose facilities have already been described. Relational operators, when applied to character values, make use of the underlying integer representation shown in Table 10.1. The membership operator (**in**) can also be used, with the bounds of the membership range being the characters included between the two values specified or the limits of the subtype specified. For example, the following two program fragments are equivalent:

```
if AnyChar in '0' . . '9' then     if AnyChar in Digits then
PUT( AnyChar);                     PUT( AnyChar);
PUT_LINE( " is a digit." );       PUT_LINE( " is a digit." );
end if;                            end if;
```

Pre-declared character subprograms

The package ADA.CHARACTERS.HANDLING contains a collection of subprograms which can be used to assist with the processing of character values. The first part of the collection contains BOOLEAN functions which can be used to categorize a CHARACTER value. For example, the function IS_LOWER can be used to determine if a character value is a lower case CHARACTER ('a' .. 'z'):

ITEM ↓ | ↑BOOLEAN

| IS_LOWER |

```
function IS_LOWER( ITEM : in CHARACTER) return BOOLEAN;
-- Returns TRUE if the value of ITEM is between 'a' and 'z'
-- inclusive, or between values 223 and 255 including
-- LC_German_Sharp_S or LC_Y_Diaresis; and FALSE otherwise
```

The BOOLEAN data type is a pre-declared data type which can take one of the values TRUE and FALSE, it will be introduced below. Other functions with a similar use include

Function	
IS_CONTROL	Returns TRUE if ITEM is a control character, i.e. value ranges 0 .. 31, 127 .. 161 in Table 10.1
IS_GRAPHIC	Returns TRUE if ITEM is a printable character, i.e. all characters other than control characters
IS_LETTER	Returns TRUE if ITEM is a letter, 'A' .. 'Z', 'a' .. 'z', or value ranges 192 .. 214, 216 .. 246 and 248 .. 245
IS_UPPER	Returns TRUE if ITEM is an upper case character, 'A' .. 'Z', or value ranges 192 .. 214 and 216 .. 221
IS_BASIC	Returns TRUE if ITEM is a basic letter, i.e. all letters excluding those with diacritical marks
IS_DIGIT	Returns TRUE if ITEM is between '0' .. '9' inclusive
IS_DECIMAL_DIGIT	Same as IS_DIGIT
IS_HEXADECIMAL_DIGIT	Returns TRUE if ITEM is a digit or in one of the ranges 'A' .. 'F' or 'a' .. 'f'
IS_ALPHANUMERIC	Returns TRUE if ITEM is a letter or a digit
IS_SPECIAL_GRAPHIC	Returns TRUE if ITEM is a graphic character, excluding alphanumerics
IS_ISO_646	Returns TRUE if ITEM is in the range 0 .. 127

The package also includes a collection of functions which can be used to convert between different possible sets of characters. For example, the function TO_LOWER will convert an upper case character into its lower case equivalent:

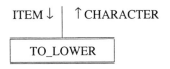

ITEM ↓ | ↑CHARACTER

TO_LOWER

```
function TO_LOWER( ITEM : in CHARACTER) return CHARACTER;
-- If ITEM is an upper case character, returns the equivalent
-- lower case character. Otherwise, returns the value of ITEM
-- unchanged
```

The other conversion functions are

Function	
TO_UPPER	If ITEM is lower case returns equivalent upper case character, otherwise returns ITEM unchanged LC_Y_Diaerisis and LC_German_Sharp_S do not have upper case equivalents

| TO_BASIC | If ITEM has a diacritical mark returns equivalent character without mark, otherwise returns ITEM unchanged |
| TO_ISO_646 | If ITEM is above value 127 returns either space or the value of an optional second character parameter. Otherwise returns ITEM unchanged |

Additionally there are other functions for conversion between CHARACTER and WIDE_CHARACTER data types.

Strings

Single characters are not used extensively in the real world, and consequently are not common in computer programs; it is much more common for an iteration of characters to be used. The programming term for an iteration of characters is a *string*. As strings are used so extensively in computer programs Ada provides a pre-declared data type, called STRING, to implement them. A data structure diagram for the STRING data type is

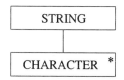

This data structure diagram indicates that a STRING is an indefinite iteration of CHARACTERs. A data structure diagram, unlike a program structure diagram, does not have to include the condition which constrains the iteration. This implies that a STRING can contain a minimum of zero characters and an unspecified maximum number of characters. String data types which have an indefinite number of characters are known as **unconstrained strings**. String data types which have a known number of characters are known as **constrained strings**. It is possible for a data type to be unconstrained, but an actual string value must have a known number of characters and thus has to be constrained.

As with the CHARACTER data types, there are two string data types, STRING and WIDE_STRING, of which only the simpler STRING data type will be considered in detail.

Designing and declaring string data types

The Ada pre-declared type STRING is capable of implementing string objects of differing lengths, and thus it is unconstrained. It is not possible to declare an object of the type STRING, without explicitly or implicitly declaring how many characters the created STRING is to contain; thus all instances of STRINGs are constrained. The best way of declaring a constrained STRING object is to declare an explicit constrained subtype with a suitable range and then to declare objects of the subtype. For example:

```
BigStringLength   : constant = 26;
SmallStringLength : constant = 4;

subtype String26s is STRING( 1 .. BigStringLength);
subtype String4s  is STRING( 1 .. SmallStringLength);
```

The effect of these subtype declarations is to make available structures which are composed of a defined number of characters. This can be shown in data structure diagrams for the subtypes as

The *String26s* type can be more conveniently visualized by considering it as a sequence of 26 characters:

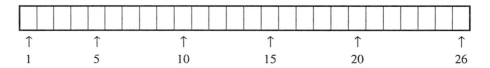

Each box in this structure is a place where a character can be stored. Any individual character can be identified by its position within the structure, indicated by the numbers below the structure.

The declaration above defines the structure of the data types *String26s* and *String4s*, but does not declare any data objects of these subtypes. To declare a data object of this type a variable declaration has to be made. If two variables of the type *String26s* called *Alphabet* and *Response* were required, the declarations might be as follows:

```
Alphabet,
Response : String26s;
```

It is also possible for string variables to be given a default value as they are declared. If it were required for a variable of subtype *String4s* called *LeftName* to be declared and given the value "Fred", and for another variable called *Right-Name* to be declared and set to spaces; the declarations might be

```
-- Assuming the package ADA.CHARACTER.LATIN_1 is in use.
LeftName  : String4 := "Fred";
RightName : String4 := ( others => SPACE );
```

The STRING expressions which are used to initialize the values of string variables have to be compatible with the objects which they are initializing. This means that a string literal has to contain exactly as many characters as the string is capable of containing. String literals are represented in Ada programs enclosed between double quotes ("), unlike character literals which are enclosed between single quotes ('). The first declaration above initializes the value of the variable from a string literal. The second initialization sets all characters, not explicitly given a value, to space characters, using the manifest name for the space character defined in the package LATIN_1. In this example no explicit values are mentioned, and thus all characters in the string are set to spaces.

It is also possible to define implicitly the length of the string variable upon declaration, for example:

```
MiddleName : STRING := "Jane";
```

This declaration implicitly defines the length of the string variable *MiddleName* to four characters, without first declaring an explicit subtype. This is a useful facility if all that is required is a small string variable which is to be formatted for output, but if more extensive manipulation of a string variable is envisaged the advice is always to declare an explicit subtype for it.

Attributes of strings

The following attributes are available for use with string types:

Attribute	Name	Notes
FIRST	first	The value of the lower bound of the string's index
LAST	last	The value of the upper bound of the string's index
LENGTH	length	The number of characters in the string
RANGE	range	Equivalent to the range string'FIRST .. string'LAST

The string attributes can be applied either to string data types or to string variables. Using the subtypes and variables declared above the use of the attributes can be illustrated:

Expression	Value	Type
Alphabet'FIRST	1	universal integer
Alphabet'LAST	26	universal integer
Alphabet'LENGTH	26	universal integer
Alphabet'RANGE	1 .. 26	universal integer range
String26s'FIRST	1	universal integer
String4s'LAST	4	universal integer
String26s'LENGTH	26	universal integer
String4s'RANGE	1 .. 4	universal integer range
LeftName'FIRST	1	universal integer
RightName'LAST	4	universal integer
MiddleName'LENGTH	4	universal integer
MiddleName'RANGE	1 .. 4	universal integer range

A **universal integer range** is an expression which can be used in a **for** loop to define the limits of the iteration. This is a very useful attribute whose use will be illustrated below.

Operations on strings

Assignment of string values can take place if the lengths of the two strings are equal. A value can be assigned from a string literal:

```
Alphabet := "abcdefghijklmnopqrstuvwxyz";
```

Following this assignment the state of the variable *Alphabet* can be visualized as

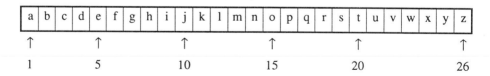

The contents of a string variable can also be the source of an assignment statement:

```
Response := Alphabet;
```

The effect of this statement would be to copy the values of all 26 characters in

Alphabet into all 26 characters in *Response*. If *Alphabet* had the value shown in the diagram above, following assignment *Response* would have the same value.

STRING assignments are only possible if the strings are of the same length. Consequently the following assignments are not possible:

```
-- These assignments are not allowed as the
-- strings are of different lengths.
LeftName := Response;
Alphabet := RightName;
```

It is possible to access an individual character from a STRING by specifying the position within the STRING where the character is located. So if the string *Alphabet* has the value shown above, then

```
Alphabet( 10) has the value 'j' and is of type CHARACTER
Alphabet( 17) has the value 'q' and is of type CHARACTER
```

The value inside the brackets which identifies that location of the character within the string is known as a **subscript** expression, and the process itself is known as **subscripting**. It is also possible to access a **slice** of a string by using a range subscript expression. For example:

```
Alphabet( 20..23) Has the value "tuvw" and has the
                        implicit type of a four character string

Alphabet( 4..9)   Has the value "defghi" and has the
                        implicit type of a six character string.
```

The slices have implicit types as shown. The types are said to be implicit as the subtypes do not have to be formally declared before the reference becomes valid. Using slices the following assignments are valid:

```
-- Assuming LeftName contains "FRED",
-- and RightName contains "    ".

LeftName := Alphabet( 20 .. 23);
-- LeftName now contains "tuwv".

RightName( 3 .. 4) := Alphabet( 11 .. 12);
-- RightName now contains " kl".

LeftName( 2 .. 4) := LeftName( 1 .. 3);
-- LeftName now contains "ttuw".
```

Accessing a character from a string or accessing a slice from a string can only be successfully performed where the INTEGER expressions used to specify the position of the character, or to specify the limits of the slice, are within the specified bounds of the string's declaration or implicit declaration. If this is not the case then a CONSTRAINT_ERROR will be raised.

Where the values which specify the bounds of the range of the slice are equal, as in *Alphabet*(10 .. 10), the slice is of the implicit type string of one character. A STRING of one character is not compatible with a CHARACTER object. It can be made compatible by use of type conversion. For example, *Alphabet*(10 .. 10) is of implicit type one character STRING and has the value "J". The type conversion of this value would be

```
CharVal := CHARACTER( Alphabet( 10 .. 10));
```

It is possible for a slice expression to reference an empty string. An empty string is a string containing zero characters and can be obtained when the value of the second index is less than the value of the first index. When an empty string is being referenced it is possible for the index values to lie outside the specified bounds of the string's declaration and not cause a CONSTRAINT_ERROR to be raised.

It is possible to join two strings together using the catenation operator (&). For example

```
MiddleName := Alphabet(1 .. 2) & Alphabet(25 .. 26);
```

which would cause *MiddleName* to have the value "abyz". The catenation can be used to join a CHARACTER and a STRING. For instance, the output of the message in the example of the CHARACTER membership operator above could have been expressed as

```
PUT_LINE( AnyChar & " is a digit character.");
```

Relational operators can be applied to STRING values. Unlike assignment it is possible for strings of differing lengths to be compared. The interpretation of the relations between the strings is made on the basis of the following rules.

For the *is equal* to operator corresponding characters from each string are compared using the character *is equal to* operation. If the strings are of identical lengths and all corresponding comparisons indicate that the strings contain the same characters in the same sequence then the operation evaluates TRUE.

If the left string is shorter than the right string and all corresponding characters are shown to be equal then it becomes a relation between an empty and a non-empty string; likewise if the right string is shorter than the left string the comparison becomes a comparison between a non-empty string and an empty string. Both of these *is equal to* comparisons involving empty strings will evaluate FALSE causing the entire expression to evaluate FALSE.

The *is not equal* to operator has the reverse logic to the *is equal* to operator. Some examples will clarify this:

```
"Freda" = "Freda" is TRUE        "Freda" /= "Freda" is FALSE
"Fred"  = "Freda" is FALSE       "Fred"  /= "Freda" is TRUE
"Freda" = "Fred"  is FALSE       "Freda" /= "Fred"  is TRUE
 "Fred" = "Fred"  is TRUE        "Fred"  /= "Fred"  is FALSE
```

For the *is less than* operator, corresponding characters from each string are compared until one character from the left string is shown to be less than the corresponding character from the right string, or one of the strings terminates. If any character from the left string can be shown to be lower than the corresponding right string character the expression evaluates TRUE.

If the left string is shorter than the right string and corresponding characters do not prove the less than relationship, then the comparison becomes a comparison between an empty string and a non-empty string; such a comparison is always TRUE. Likewise if the right string is shorter than the left string, the relation can become a comparison between a non-empty string and an empty string; such a comparison is always FALSE. The *greater than or equal* to operator has the reverse logic to the *is less than* operator. Some examples will clarify this:

```
"Freda" < "Freda" is FALSE       "Freda" >= "Freda" is TRUE
"Fred"  < "Freda" is TRUE        "Fred"  >= "Freda" is FALSE
"Freda" < "Fred"  is FALSE       "Freda" >= "Fred"  is TRUE
"Fred"  < "Fred"  is FALSE       "Fred"  >= "Fred"  is TRUE
```

The remaining relational operators *is greater than* and *is less than or equal to* can be deduced from the explanation of the *is less than* operator above. The empty string comparisons which may be required for strings of differing lengths are defined as

empty string	=	non-empty string	is FALSE
non-empty string	=	empty string	is FALSE
empty string	>	non-empty string	is FALSE
non-empty string	>	empty string	is TRUE
empty string	<	non-empty string	is TRUE
non-empty string	<	empty string	is FALSE

The remaining operators *is not equal to, is greater than or equal to* and *is less than or equal to* can be derived using the negation equivalencies of the relational operators. That is, *is not equal* to is not (*is equal to*), *is greater than or equal to* is not (*is less than*) and *is less than or equal to* is not (*is greater than*).

Input and output of string values

Procedures for the input and output of STRING values are contained within the package ADA.TEXT_IO. STRING output procedures have been used extensively in previous chapters. When a STRING expression is used as a parameter, the STRING version of the PUT procedure is used:

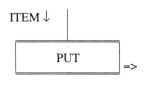

```
procedure PUT( ITEM : in STRING);
```

The effect of this procedure is to output all the characters of the string expression specified. When strings are being output it is possible to use PUT_LINE instead of PUT. PUT will leave the cursor on the same output line, PUT_LINE will use NEW_LINE to move the cursor on to the next line.

The procedures available for the input of strings are

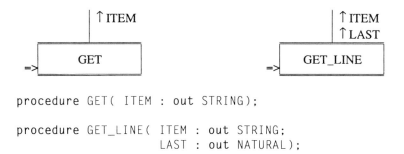

```
procedure GET( ITEM : out STRING);

procedure GET_LINE( ITEM : out STRING;
                    LAST : out NATURAL);
```

When the procedure GET is executed with a STRING parameter it will input from the terminal sufficient characters to initialize all the characters in the string; any <ENTER> codes within the sequence input from the terminal will be ignored. The GET procedure is not very useful for input from the terminal and should only be used for getting strings from an external file.

The GET_LINE procedure is more useful for obtaining STRING values from the terminal. When executed it will input characters from the terminal giving the character's value to successive characters in the string. The procedure will terminate when an <ENTER> code is input or when sufficient characters to fill the string have been input. The second output only parameter, called LAST, is of the NATURAL subtype and will effectively be set to the number of characters input.

If fewer characters are input than the string is capable of containing, then the characters in the string which have not been set from the terminal are left unchanged. If more characters are input than the string is capable of containing, the overflow characters are lost. If no characters are input then the value of LAST is effectively zero.

The value returned in LAST after the procedure call in the explanations above was said to be effectively the number of characters input or effectively zero as its value is set with respect to the lower bound of the string. When a slice is being used this bound is not necessarily 1. Some examples should make the behaviour of this procedure clear. Using the variable *LeftName* as declared above, with the initial value "FRED", in the statement GET_LINE(*LeftName*, *NumChar*), where *NumChar* is a variable of subtype NATURAL, the state of *LeftName* and *NumChar* with the following successive inputs would be

GET_LINE(*LeftName, NumChar*);		
Input	*LeftName*	*NumChar*
BETH	"BETH"	4
alberta	"albe"	4
SUE	"SUEe"	3
<ENTER>	"SUEe"	0

In the third example only three characters were input before the <ENTER> key was pressed. Consequently only the first three characters of *LeftName* were initialized and *NumChar* was set to 3; the fourth character of the string was left unchanged. In the last example the <ENTER> key was pressed without entering any characters. Consequently none of the characters in the string were changed and *NumChar* was set to 0. If the same inputs are repeated with the following use of the GET_LINE procedure the effects would be

GET_LINE(*Alphabet(10..13), NumChar*);		
Input	*LeftName*	*NumChar*
BETH	"BETH"	13
alberta	"albe"	13
SUE	"SUEe"	12
<ENTER>	"SUEe"	9

The interpretation of the returned value in the *NumChar* parameter from the

GET_LINE procedure should always be made with respect to the actual bounds of
the string provided as the STRING parameter.

The instantiated INTEGER_IO and FLOAT_IO packages contain additional
versions of the PUT and GET procedures which can be used for input and output,
from and to strings. The data flow diagrams and declaration of these procedures
are as follows:

```
VALUE ↓ | ↑ TO                    FROM ↓ | ↑ VALUE
(BASE) ↓ |                                | ↑ LAST
    ┌─────────────┐                    ┌─────────────┐
    │     PUT     │                    │     GET     │
    └─────────────┘                    └─────────────┘
```

```
procedure PUT( TO   : out STRING;
               ITEM : in  INTEGER;
               BASE : in  NUMBER_BASE := DEFAULT_BASE);
-- Output the representation of the value of ITEM into
-- the string TO, using the same rules for a PUT to the
-- terminal. WIDTH is considered equal to the length of TO.

procedure GET( FROM : in  STRING;
               ITEM : out INTEGER;
               LAST : out POSITIVE);
-- Input from the string into ITEM an integer value, using
-- the same rules as a GET from the terminal. LAST indicates
-- the last character which was taken from the string.
```

Examples of the use of these procedures will be given in the next section. They can
be used when the input and output format of a value differs from that usual for
INTEGER or real values.

The four procedures PUT, PUT_LINE, GET and GET_LINE can also be used to
output STRING values to an external file or to input strings from an external file;
this will be considered later in this section.

String subprograms

The package ADA.CHARACTERS.HANDLING contains a number of functions
for the processing of strings which are equivalent to some of the CHARACTER
subprograms introduced above:

Function	
TO_LOWER	STRING function taking a STRING parameter called ITEM, applies the TO_LOWER character function every character in the string

TO_UPPER	As for TO_UPPER using the TO_UPPER character function
TO_BASIC	As for TO_UPPER using the TO_BASIC character function
IS_ISO_646	A BOOLEAN function taking a STRING parameter called ITEM, returns TRUE if all characters in the string return TRUE when the IS_ISO_646 character function is applied, and FALSE otherwise
TO_ISO_646	As for TO_UPPER with an additional optional parameter with the default value space, calls the TO_ISO_646 character function for each character passing on the value of the optional parameter

There are additional string functions which are used to manipulate strings composed of WIDE_CHARACTERs. An additional package called ADA.-STRINGS.FIXED contains a collection of subprograms to assist with the manipulation of strings. It contains subprograms to trim, justify, count, search for substrings, delete substrings as well as various other operations.

Programmer declared subprograms can use parameters of the type STRING, or of a specific declared STRING subtype. One example will be provided here and additional examples will be used throughout the rest of the book.

The specification for this example subprogram is

A name should be presented to the user with a strict convention regarding the use of capital and lower case letters, for example "*Lady Augusta Ada Lovelace*". The rule is that each component of the name starts with an upper case letter and continues with lower case letters. There are exceptions such as "O'Brien" or "MacIntosh", but for the purposes of this exercise they will be ignored.

An interface diagram and subprogram declaration for this subprogram might be

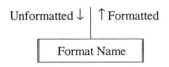

```
function FormatName( Unformatted : in STRING ) return STRING;
-- Returns a copy of the string supplied, formatted with
-- conventional initial capitals.
```

The type of the formal parameter of the function, *Unformatted*, is specified as the unconstrained type STRING. This will allow any constrained actual parameter to be used. If the function were to be declared with a formal parameter of an explicit constrained STRING subtype, then only an actual parameter whose length was equal to the length of the constrained formal parameter could be used. The use of an unconstrained parameter is clearly advantageous. The design of this subprogram might be

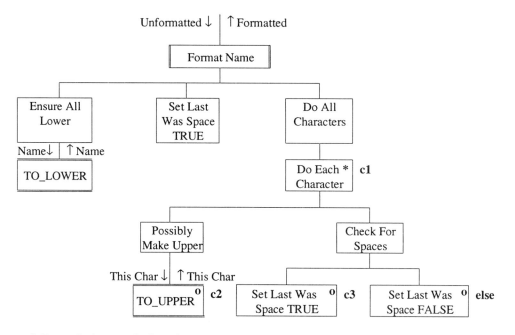

c1: For each character in the string.
c2: If the last character was a space.
c3: If the current character is a space.

The basis of the design is first to ensure that all characters in the string are lower case and then to iterate through the string setting each character which is preceded by a space to upper case. To accomplish this a BOOLEAN variable, *LastWasSpace*, is set TRUE or FALSE as each character is processed and used as the control expression of the selection structure. In order to ensure that the first character of the name is capitalized, *LastWasSpace* is set to true before the loop starts. When a BOOLEAN variable is used to record and communicate the state of the program in this manner it is known as a *flag*. The use of BOOLEAN variables will be introduced later in this chapter. The implementation of this function, assuming that the standard package ADA.CHARACTERS is **with**ed and **use**d, might be

```
0020    function FormatName( Unformatted : in STRING) return STRING is
0021
0022        LocalString : STRING( Unformatted'RANGE ) := Unformatted;
```

```
0023        LastWasSpace : BOOLEAN := TRUE;
0024
0025   begin -- FormatName
0026        LocalString := TO_LOWER( LocalString);
0027        for ThisChar in LocalString'RANGE loop
0028            if LastWasSpace then
0029                LocalString( ThisChar) :=
0030                    TO_UPPER( LocalString( ThisChar));
0031            end if;
0032            if LocalString( ThisChar) = SPACE then
0033                LastWasSpace := TRUE;
0034            else
0035                LastWasSpace := FALSE;
0036            end if;
0037        end loop;
0038        return LocalString;
0039   end FormatName;
```

The implementation of the function declares a local string variable, called
LocalString, whose bounds are set to those of the string passed into the function in
the formal parameter *Unformatted*. This is accomplished by using the RANGE
attribute applied to the formal parameter, and ensures that on each call of the
function the bounds of *LocalString* are set to those of the actual parameter passed.
The declaration of this variable also assigns it the value of the actual parameter.

The function commences by using the TO_LOWER string function to ensure
that all alphabetic characters in the local string are lower case. The main part of
the function is a definite iteration whose range is matched to that of the bounds of
the local string by use of the RANGE attribute. Within the body of the loop each
character is considered in turn by use of a subscript expression employing the value
of the loop parameter, *ThisChar*. If the *LastWasSpace* flag is set, the current
character is set to upper case using the character function TO_UPPER. The loop
concludes by setting the value of the flag to TRUE if the current character is a
space; this ensures that the flag is correctly set for the next iteration of the loop.
Finally outside the loop the value of *LocalString*, now formatted, is returned from
the function.

The use of this function can be demonstrated by use of a test harness:

```
0001   -- Filename FormatNameTest.ada (k8 formatna.adb).
0002   -- Test harness program for the FormatName function,
0003   -- written for Ada book Section II Chapter 10.
0004   --
0005   -- Fintan Culwin, v0.1, Jan 1997.
0006
0007   with ADA.TEXT_IO, ADA.CHARACTERS,
0008        ADA.CHARACTERS.HANDLING, ADA.CHARACTERS.LATIN_1;
0009   use  ADA.TEXT_IO, ADA.CHARACTERS;
```

```
0010          ADA.CHARACTERS.HANDLING, ADA.CHARACTERS.LATIN_1;
0011
0012    procedure FormatNameTest is
0013
0014        TestNameLength : constant INTEGER:= 40;
0015        TestNameString : STRING( 1 .. TestNameLength)
0016                                        := ( others => Space);
0017        NumCharEntered : NATURAL;
0018
        -- declaration and definition of FormatName assumed
0041
0042    begin -- FormatNameTest
0043        PUT_LINE("Format Name Test Program");
0044        NEW_LINE(2);
0045        PUT( "Please enter a name to test ");
0046        GET_LINE( TestNameString, NumCharEntered);
0047
0048        TestNameString( 1 .. NumCharEntered) :=
0049            FormatName( TestNameString( 1 .. NumCharEntered));
0050
0051        NEW_LINE(2);
0052        PUT_LINE("The formatted name is ");
0053        PUT_LINE( TestNameString( 1 .. NumCharEntered));
0054    end FormatNameTest;
```

This test harness demonstrates the use of the GET_LINE procedure and uses the returned value of the second parameter to delineate a slice of the string which is passed into the *FormatName* function. The *FormatName* function will return a string of the same size of the string passed in and this string is assigned into the same slice of the string which was passed, effectively replacing the slice of the string entered by the user.

Enumeration types

There are many real world data objects whose values do not fit into the ranges or subranges of Ada's pre-declared types. A common example of such a requirement is the representation of days of the week. This requirement can be expressed in a data structure diagram as follows:

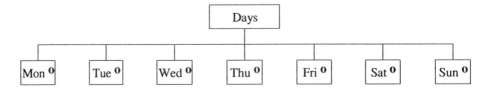

What is required is a data type called *Days* whose objects could take one of the values *Mon*, *Tue*, *Wed*, *Thu*, *Fri*, *Sat* or *Sun* as shown in the data structure diagram. Ada provides a facility for declaring a suitable type as an ***enumeration data type***. An enumeration data type is one where all the possible values which objects of the data type can take are listed (***enumerated***) in its declaration. Objects of this type can take the value of one of the possible values listed.

As with the data structure diagram for the STRING data type above, it is possible for an optional or selective component to be expressed on a data structure diagram without any condition. The diagram above asserts that this is the nature of the object and that an instance of the object can only have the values listed, and at any instant in time will only have one of the values. A program structure diagram, expressing actions, would have to have a condition indicating under what conditions the optional action will be taken.

Designing and declaring enumeration types

To declare an enumeration type, each of the values which an object of the type can take is represented by a symbolic name in an enumeration list. For example, the enumeration declaration of the *Days* type might be

```
type Days is ( Mon, Tue, Wed, Thu, Fri, Sat, Sun);
```

Data objects of type *Days* can take one of the values listed, mapping them explicitly onto the possible values of the data objects in the real world. The values used to express the values of the enumeration type are ***enumeration literals***; they are not strings and should not be enclosed within double quote marks ("). Having declared an enumeration type within a program it is possible to declare subtypes of the enumeration type. For example:

```
subtype WorkDays    is Days range Mon .. Fri;
subtype WeekendDays is Days range Sat .. Sun;

AnyDay  : Days;
WorkDay : WorkDays;
RestDay : WeekendDays;
```

The variable *AnyDay* is of type *Days* and can take any of the values expressed in the declaration of *Days*. The variable *WorkDay* is of the subtype *WorkDays* and can take a restricted range of *Days* values as expressed in its declaration. Likewise the variable *RestDay* is of the subtype *WeekendDays* and can only take one of the *Days* values *Sat* or *Sun*. As *WorkDay* and *RestDay* are both variables of a subtype of the base type *Days* they are compatible with the variable *AnyDay* which is of the type *Days*, without type conversion being necessary. For example:

```
AnyDay  := WorkDay;  -- Always valid.
AnyDay  := RestDay;  -- Always valid
WorkDay := AnyDay;   -- Valid if AnyDay is in Mon..Fri.
RestDay := AnyDay;   -- Valid if AnyDay is Sat or Sun.
WorkDay := RestDay;  -- Syntactically valid.
```

The last example is **syntactically** valid as the assignment is between two compatible subtypes. But it is **semantically** invalid as the ranges of the subtypes do not overlap and thus a CONSTRAINT_ERROR exception will always be raised when it is executed. Some compilers may be intelligent enough to spot the semantic error and issue a warning.

If the following two type declarations exist within the same program and both are in scope

```
type Colours  is ( Red, Orange, Yellow, Blue, Indigo, Violet);

type JudoBelts is ( White, Yellow, Orange, Green, Blue, Black);
```

then several of the enumeration literals are overloaded. The meaning of the enumeration literals *Yellow*, *Orange* and *Blue* could be of the type *Colours*, or could be of the type *JudoBelts*. An overloaded term is allowed in Ada, providing there is some way by which Ada can determine which meaning of the term is intended. For example:

```
Sky := blue;
```

is unambiguous if the variable *Sky* is declared to be of type *Colours*. However, in the following

```
for Something in Yellow .. Blue loop
```

the intended meaning is unclear. This could be interpreted as an attempt to construct a loop whose loop parameter is of type *Colours* or whose type is *JudoBelts*. The meaning should be made clear to Ada, and to the reader, by explicitly stating the base type as in

```
for ThisBelt in JudoBelts range Yellow .. Blue loop
```

A better expression of this requirement may be to declare an explicit subtype and use the subtype name to define the limits of the loop:

```
subtype Novices is JudoBelts range Yellow .. Blue;
for ThisBelt in Novices loop
```

Attributes of enumeration types

Enumeration types are *discrete*, and share the same set of attributes as other discrete types such as INTEGER or CHARACTER. These are

Attribute	Name	Notes
FIRST	first	Returns the first enumeration value of the data type, or subtype, specified
LAST	last	Returns the last enumeration value of the data type, or subtype, specified
PRED	predecessor	Returns the preceding enumeration value in the declaration list, or raises CONSTRAINT_ERROR for the first value
SUCC	successor	Returns the succeeding enumeration value in the declaration list, or raises CONSTRAINT_ERROR for the last value
POS	position	Returns an integer value indicating the position of the enumerated value in the declaration sequence
VAL	value	Returns the character value whose location in the declaration sequence is specified by the parameter
IMAGE	image	Returns a string containing a representation of the enumeration parameter
VALUE	value	Converts a string representation to an enumeration value

With the declaration of the types and subtypes above, the following are examples of the use of the enumeration attributes:

Expression	Value	Type
Days'FIRST	*Mon*	*Days*
Days'LAST	*Sun*	*Days*
Novices'FIRST	*Yellow*	*JudoBelts*
Novices'LAST	*Blue*	*JudoBelts*
Days'SUCC(*Wed*)	*Thu*	*Days*
Novices'PRED(*Orange*)	*Yellow*	*JudoBelts*
Days'SUCC(*Sun*)	implicit CONSTRAINT_ERROR	
Colours'PRED(*Red*)	implicit CONSTRAINT_ERROR	
Days'POS(*Mon*)	0	universal integer
WeekendDays'POS(*Sat*)	5	universal integer

223

Colours'VAL(2)	*Yellow*	*Colours*
Novices'VAL(1)	*Yellow*	*JudoBelts*
Days'VAL(8)	implicit CONSTRAINT_ERROR	
Novices'IMAGE(Blue)	"blue"	STRING
Colours'VAL("Blue")	*Blue*	*Colours*
Days'VAL("Blue")	implicit CONSTRAINT_ERROR	

Operations on enumeration types

The only operations which are pre-declared for enumeration types, apart from assignment, are the relational and membership operators. The implementation of these operations makes use of the order in which the enumeration literals appear in the enumeration type's declaration. Consequently all the following comparisons can be assumed to be true, if either *Colours* or *JudoBelts* is the intended type:

```
Wed = Wed  Black = Black    Sun /= Sat    Black /= White
Tue > Mon  Violet > Indigo Orange >= Orange White <= Yellow
Thu < Sun  White < Black    Fri <= Fri    Indigo <= Violet
```

The case of enumeration literals is not significant, so all the following expressions are also true:

```
blue = BLUE THU = thu OrAnGe >= oRaNgE
```

The value of the expression '*Orange* < *Yellow*' is dependent upon what type the values of *Orange* and *Yellow* are: for *Colours* the relation is true but for *JudoBelts* it is false. Ada must be able to decide this from the context. It is possible to use **type qualification** to indicate explicitly the type intended:

```
JudoBelts'( Orange) < JudoBelts'( Yellow) is FALSE
Colours'  ( Orange) < Colours'  ( Yellow) is TRUE
```

Type qualification, expressed as *Colours*'(*literal*), differs from **type conversion,** expressed as *Colours*(*literal*), in that type qualification simply expresses the programmer's intention regarding the type of the expression. Type conversion will cause the type of the value of the expression to be converted into a type which is compatible with the type requested which is not always the same as the type expressed in the conversion request.

The membership operator can be used with enumeration values. For example:

```
if Today in WeekendDays then
   PUT("Holiday ");
end if;
```

An enumeration type can be used as a loop parameter. For example, the following fragment of code will have the intended effect:

```
-- Assuming suitable i-o facilities are in use.
PUT( "The colours of the rainbow are " );
for ThisColour in Colours loop
   PUT( ThisDay, SET => LOWER_CASE );
   if ThisColour /= Colours'LAST then
      PUT( ", " );
   end if;
end loop;
PUT_LINE(".");
```

The use of input–output facilities for enumeration types will be introduced shortly. The output of this program fragment when executed would be

```
The colours of the rainbow are red, orange, yellow, green,
                                    blue, indigo, violet.
```

An enumeration value can be used as the selector in a **case** statement. For example, this program fragment will categorize a novice according to the colour of his or her belt:

```
-- Novice is a variable of subtype Novices.
case Novice is
   when Yellow          => PUT( "Beginner");
   when Orange | Green  => PUT( "Improving");
   when Blue            => PUT( "Expert");
end case;
```

Input and output of enumeration values

As with INTEGER and floating point types, Ada provides a general facility for the instantiation of packages tailored for the input and output of a particular enumeration type. The name of the general package is ENUMERATION_IO and it is contained within the package ADA.TEXT_IO. Using the types declared earlier in this section the creation of suitable enumeration input–output packages can be accomplished as follows:

```
-- Assuming that ADA.TEXT_IO is at least withed.
package DaysIO is new ADA.TEXT_IO. ENUMERATION_IO( Days);
use DaysIO;
-- Package DaysIO can be used with the Days type
-- and the subtypes WorkDays and WeekendDays.
```

```
package ColoursIO is new ADA.TEXT_IO.ENUMERATION_IO( Colours );
use ColoursIO;
-- Package ColoursIO can be used with the Colours type,
-- but not with the JudoBelts type.
```

The creation of such packages is not possible in a program until the enumeration types which they are to be tailored for have been declared. Once the package is declared a suitable scope for a **use** clause has to be found. If extensive use is being made for input and output of the enumeration values then an appropriate scope might be the entire scope of the enumeration type itself. If only local use is being made of the facilities then the scope of the **use** of the package should be restricted.

When a suitable package for input and output has been created, the two procedures GET and PUT configured for use with the enumeration type are accessible. The data flow diagram and subprogram declaration for the PUT procedure are as follows:

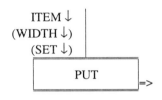

```
procedure PUT( ITEM  : in EnumerationType;
               WIDTH : in FIELD := DEFAULT_WIDTH ;
               SET   : in TYPE_SET := DEFAULT_SETTING );
```

EnumerationType is the type from which the input–output package has been instantiated. When called the PUT procedure will by default output the appropriate enumeration literal as a sequence of upper case characters, using as many characters as required for the representation of the literal. There are two optional parameters to the procedure. The first optional parameter is WIDTH, which can be used to specify the number of characters to be used. If the value of WIDTH specified is less than the number of characters required it will be ignored and the number of characters required for the literal will be output. If the value specified for WIDTH is greater than the number of characters required, it will be ignored and the value will be output using the minimum number of characters to express it.

The second optional parameter is SET which requires a value, which is itself an enumeration literal, to be specified. Possible values for this parameter are LOWER_CASE and UPPER_CASE. The default effect of this parameter, if no value is explicitly specified, is to output enumeration values in upper case. If the value of SET is specified as LOWER_CASE the value will be output in lower case. Some examples will make the effects of the procedure and its optional parameters

226

clearer:

AnyDay := Wed;	
Expression	**Output**
PUT(*AnyDay*);	WED
PUT(*AnyDay*, WIDTH => 2);	WED
PUT(*AnyDay*, WIDTH => 5);	WED¶¶
PUT(*AnyDay*, SET => LOWER_CASE);	wed
PUT(*AnyDay*, WIDTH => 5, SET => LOWER_CASE);	wed¶¶

In the second of these examples the requested value of WIDTH has been ignored as a minimum of three characters is required to output the value of *AnyDay*.

The GET procedure can be used to input enumeration values from the terminal. Its data flow diagram and declaration are as follows:

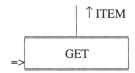

```
procedure GET( ITEM : out EnumerationType);
```

When the procedure is called it will accept characters from the terminal, ignoring leading spaces, until it can be determined if the sequence is, or is not, a valid enumeration literal of the base type of the parameter. If the sequence input is a valid enumeration literal, irrespective of the case of the characters, the actual parameter will be set to the value represented by the input. If the sequence of characters input is not a valid enumeration literal then a DATA_ERROR exception will be raised. If the formal parameter is a subtype and the sequence is a valid enumeration literal of its base type but is outside its declared range, a CONSTRAINT_ERROR will be raised.

The ENUMERATION_IO package also supplies versions of the GET and PUT procedures which can be used to input and output enumeration values from and to external files and to and from strings. The use of the string versions is comparable with the string GET and PUT, INTEGER and FLOAT procedures described above. The use of external files will be described in a later chapter.

Enumeration subprograms

A common operation required for some enumeration types is to increment the enumeration value, with the value which follows the last value in the enumeration list being defined as the first value of the enumeration list. For example, the value which follows *Sunday* in the real world is considered to be *Monday*. The attribute function SUCC will implement most of this requirement, but as noted above it will raise a CONSTRAINT_ERROR if the SUCCessor of the last element in the enumeration list is requested.

To implement this requirement a programmer declared enumeration function called *NextDay* would be required, which could be based on this design:

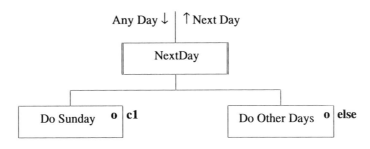

c1: If Any Day is Sunday.

This design can be implemented as:

```
0001    function NextDay( AnyDay : in Days) return Days is
0002
0003    begin -- NextDay
0004        if AnyDay = Days'LAST then
0005            return Days'FIRST;
0006        else
0007            return Days'SUCC( AnyDay );
0008        end if;
0009    end NextDay;
```

The implementation of this function has employed the use of the enumeration attributes FIRST and LAST to implement the *wrap around* decision. This makes the function more robust and more general. It is more robust as a change to the enumeration declaration, perhaps by declaring *Sun* as the first day and *Sat* as the last day, will not require any changes to be made to the function. It is more general as the implementation of the function can be used as the basis for any enumeration type which requires the *wrap around* successor behaviour.

The function also differs from most functions previously produced as it does not employ a function variable. Consequently it has two **return** statements and thus two places where flow of control can leave the function. For a function of this size and complexity, not using a function variable makes the implementation of the function more straightforward. When functions become larger or more complex then the use of a function variable, avoiding the possibility of multiple **returns**, is advocated as good style.

Where an enumeration type is declared which requires this wrap around behaviour two functions, one to return the next value in sequence and one to return the previous, should be implemented for use with the type. As has been mentioned, the full definition of a data type includes not only the values of the type but also the operations which can be performed upon the type. In the next section a method of encapsulating such developer declared values and operations within an Ada package to produce an abstract data type will be introduced.

Another pre-declared enumeration type

The pre-declared type CHARACTER is implemented in the package STANDARD as an enumeration type. The CHARACTER enumeration values are the characters themselves or for character values which are non-printing the character names shown in Table 10.1.

The other pre-declared enumeration type is BOOLEAN. Its implicit declaration in STANDARD would be

```
type BOOLEAN is (FALSE, TRUE);
```

This gives the interesting consideration that according to Ada FALSE is less than TRUE! The values of Boolean variables can be used wherever a Boolean value is required. For example, the relational expressions which were used in the previous section to control the actions of a selection or of an indefinite iteration could have been replaced with the name of a BOOLEAN variable.

The advantages of using a BOOLEAN variable can be illustrated by considering the changes which would have been required in the **if** structure of the *FormatName* function developed earlier in this chapter. Using a BOOLEAN variable this was expressed as

```
if LastWasSpace then
```

If a BOOLEAN variable was not used then the equivalent expression would have been

```
if ( (ThisChar = LocalString'FIRST)      or
     (LocalString( ThisChar -1) = SPACE)) then
```

As was emphasized repeatedly in the last section the construction and validation of the BOOLEAN expressions which control selections and iterations are amongst the most important aspects of the construction of effective and elegant source code. It should be apparent that the use of a BOOLEAN expression in this example

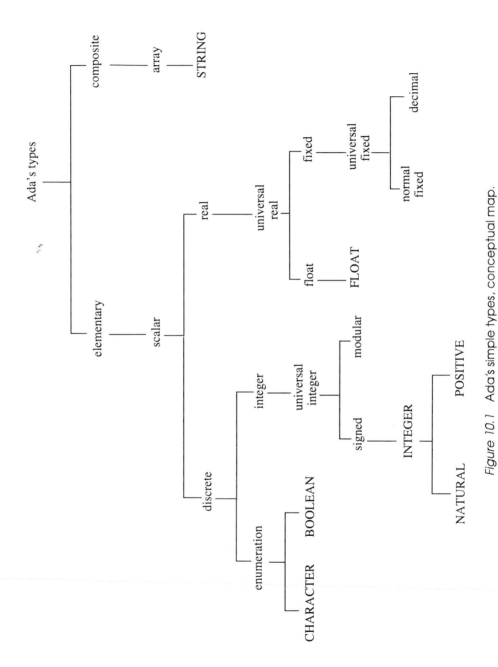

Figure 10.1 Ada's simple types, conceptual map.

simplifies the construction of the **if** control expression and thus should be a favoured technique.

Ada's simple data types

This concludes the introductory look at Ada's simple data types and the facilities they offer. A *conceptual map* of the types introduced in the last two chapters is given in Figure 10.1. It is not intended to be a complete or comprehensive diagram of all of Ada's types, but to put into relation with each other some of the types, subtypes and classes of types which have been discussed. The pre-declared types are shown capitalized.

EXERCISES

10.1 Implement a demonstration harness program which will use the character classifier functions to indicate if a character input by the user is, or is not, upper case, a digit, a punctuation character, etc.

10.2 A simple encryption scheme can be implemented by *shifting* each character up the ASCII table. For example, the character '*a*' can be shifted up the ASCII table by two characters and be encrypted as the character '*c*'. Design and implement an encryption function which will require a string parameter and a *shift value*. It should return a string where each character has been shifted by *shift value*. A decryption function will also be required to demonstrate that the encryption is reversible.

10.3 Design and implement a function which will count and return the number of words in a string. A word can be recognized as a sequence of alphabetic characters followed by a sequence of non-alphabetic characters which include at least one space or a punctuation character.

10.4 Adapt the *FormatName* function so that it will deal correctly with names such as *Sean O'Casey* or *Liam MacNichols*. Hint: for names like *O'Casey*, any punctuation character should prime the subprogram to capitalize the next character. However, for names like *MacNichols*, the three characters at the start of the name will have to be explicitly tested when the fourth character is considered.

10.5 Reimplement the *colours of the rainbow* program fragment to produce the following output:

> The colour of the rainbow are *red, orange, yellow,*
> *green, blue, indigo* and *violet.*

Each enumeration literal is followed by a comma apart from the penultimate one, which is followed by *and* and the ultimate one which is followed by a full stop. A general, not a particular, solution should be found so that the fragment can be quickly adapted to output the colours of judo belts or the names of the days of the week.

10.6 Return to the *MultipleCashRegister* type from Section I Chapter 8, and replace the CHARACTER parameter which indicates the deposit method with an enumeration type supplied by the package.

CHAPTER 11

The user interface

In the programs presented in the previous chapters the importance of designing the user interface at an early stage in the software production process was stressed for two reasons. The first reason was to assist the developer with fully understanding the specification. For most simple specifications it is likely that all aspects of the functionality of the software will be made available to the user and the construction of a user interface design will indicate to the developer if he or she has a sufficient understanding of the specification.

The second, more important, reason for the early design of the user interface is to ensure that the finished product will be acceptable to the sponsor, and to ensure that the users of the software will accomplish the tasks for which the software is being constructed. The user interface is the only part of the software which the user will directly experience and the difference between an acceptable user interface and an interface which is difficult to use can be the difference between success and failure of a development project when the software is deployed.

One aspect of the user interfaces which have so far been presented is unacceptable. Whenever the user has been asked to provide a specific input it has always been assumed that the user will provide one of the inputs which the software is designed to accept. Real users do not always behave in this manner and a request for a particular input may result in the user supplying something totally unexpected. For example, whenever a floating point value has been requested a user may provide an integer value expecting the software to assume that the decimal part is intended to be '.00'. With the programs which have been developed so far, such a response from the user has resulted in the *propagation* of a DATA_ERROR **exception** which has halted the program.

This chapter will commence with an overview of the techniques by which a user interface can be designed, evaluated and documented. The second part of the chapter will introduce techniques by which user input exceptions can be trapped and processed.

User interface design

The user interface is that part of a software component which accepts information from the user and which presents information to the user. It is best regarded as a conversation between two intelligent entities; a conversation between two entities is also known as a *dialog*. However, for the most part, the intelligence of currently available software is rather lacking in many attributes of intelligence which could be regarded as being human-like. The human side of the dialog, the user, cannot always be relied upon to demonstrate totally intelligent behaviour either. The resulting conversation is mediated by the interface designer when the interface is designed, and will take place each time the software is used.

A dialog is most satisfying when it is a conversation between equal intelligences with both parties of the conversation taking responsibility for initiating and maintaining the conversation, and both parties demonstrating respect for each other's needs and limitations. A well designed interface should ideally become virtually invisible to the user and will only become evident when there is some breakdown in the conversation. The role of the interface designer from this perspective is to specify how the conversation will take place, attempt to prevent breakdowns in the flow of the conversation and to establish techniques by which the flow of conversation can be re-established following a breakdown.

In order to do this in the most effective manner the interface designer has to have a detailed knowledge of human physical, perceptual and intellectual capabilities. These considerations could take an entire book of this length to introduce, and consequently only an introductory overview can be provided in this chapter. The conclusions of the considerations can be distilled into a number of *heuristic* rules. A heuristic rule is a rule which can be simply expressed, but the explanation of the rule is either too complex to be expressed or unknown.

The process of producing an effective program interface is an engineering task in its own right. Starting with establishing the requirements of the users of the software, a specification for the interface is produced. From the specification an initial design is produced, according to established heuristic rules, and the design is validated in some way. One possible method of validating a proposed design is to construct a *usability prototype* and have representative users operate the prototype whilst their behaviour is measured and subsequently their opinions are sought. A usability prototype is a 'mock-up' of the software where the interface is complete but aspects of the functionality of the software are missing, inelegant or simulated. Once a validated design for the interface is available it can be passed to the developers for implementation, together with the rest of the program. During the maintenance phase of the life cycle, the interface will be subject to continual review and modification as well as the rest of the program. These aspects of software development are starting to become so central to the production of effective software that a recognized role, known as a *usability engineer*, is starting to appear in professional development teams.

Styles of user interfaces

There are a number of different styles of user interface. Currently the most popular is possibly the *w*indows, *i*cons, *m*enus and *p*ointer (**WIMP**) style. This style of interface is used with Microsoft Windows, Apple computers and X Windows, and has become very acceptable to a wide variety of users. The techniques for the design and construction of such interfaces are beyond the scope of this book, although standard Ada toolkits supporting their construction are available.

Perhaps the easiest style of interface for a novice developer to design and construct is the simple ***menu driven*** style, an example of which is the *Shopping-Demo* program's interface from the previous section. In more complex programs this style may be developed into a hierarchical menu system, where the main menu leads to submenus which may themselves lead to sub-submenus, continuing down an indeterminate number of levels before the functionality of the program is available to the user. Although menu driven interfaces are easy for the developer to construct they are very restrictive to the user as the interface designer has to decide at the outset which options are to be accessed from which menus and in what sequence the options are to be presented.

The most immediately obvious alternative to the menu driven style is the ***command line*** style, where the user has to type in commands at a prompt. On an IBM compatible *p*ersonal *c*omputer (PC), the DOS interface is an example of a command line interface. A command line interface, as opposed to a menu driven interface, gives the user more opportunity to initiate and control the dialog. With the menu style the system decides which commands are available at any stage; with the command line style the user can issue any available command at any stage.

Menu driven interfaces tend to be favoured by inexperienced computer users who feel safer and more confident with the system taking more control of the interaction. Skilled computer users would prefer a command line system, as they feel constrained by having to navigate a hierarchical menu system to achieve an objective which could be achieved with a single command. This consideration provides several important clues for the design of effective interfaces. The first conclusion is that there is no one best interface for a given functional specification; the most appropriate interface depends upon the skills and experiences of the individual user. This leads to a second conclusion that an interface can be made more effective by allowing users to customize it to their own preferences. In the example above this might suggest that two alternative interfaces to a single program could be provided. A menu driven interface could be supplied for casual or inexperienced users and an alternative command line interface for habitual skilled users.

Criteria for evaluating, and guiding the design of, interfaces

There are many other possible styles of interface, besides the three mentioned above. For any interface style there are a number of criteria which can be applied to the evaluation of an existing interface, or used to assist in the design of a new interface. This part of the chapter will provide a whistle stop tour of some of the most important of these criteria. There is no indication in the sequence in which they are presented of any particular degree of importance.

Consistency is important in order that a user can learn an interface quickly and easily. Humans are very adept at pattern recognition and once a pattern in an interface has been recognized it can be used to predict the behaviour of parts of the interface which have yet to be explored. This advantage will be lost if parts of the interface are inconsistent with other parts of the interface.

This advantage can be exploited between applications as well as within applications. Particularly with the WIMP style of interface, there are established conventions for the way in which the conversations should be structured. An application which conforms to these conventions will be able to take advantage of the user's prior experience with other interfaces. These conventions are available as *style guides* which form part of the documentation of development toolkits.

For the menu driven interface examples of how consistency can be achieved include the order in which options are presented to the user or the positioning and key press required to exit from any menu. For a command line system it might include the way in which the commands are chosen and the syntax with which they are expressed.

The *memory load* of the user should be kept to a minimum. Humans have been shown to be capable of keeping only between five and nine 'chunks' of information available for immediate attention or recall. When designing an interface this consideration can be implemented by presenting information to the users on the screen rather than having them remember it. For example, in a menu driven interface the position of the current menu in the menu hierarchy could be indicated rather than have the user remember it. In a command line interface a facility to retrieve, edit and reissue previously used commands would save the user from the necessity of having to remember the syntax of a little used, recently issued command.

An ability to *undo* the effects of any action will encourage the user to explore the application and will in turn also improve the *learnability* of the interface. If an undo facility is always available the users will not feel that any mistakes which they make will have undue consequences. If there is no facility to undo the effects of any command then the users may feel worried that they may damage the information they are working with, or in some cases may even feel that they will somehow damage the computer itself. If an undo facility is made generally available, then there may be some actions which are so powerful that an undo cannot be offered. In such cases an explicit confirmation from the user should be obtained before the action is taken. An example of this can be found with the DOS delete file (*del*) command: when this command is issued to delete all files in a directory (*del* *.*) the interface will issue the message 'This will delete all files in the directory, are you sure (Y/N)?'.

A well designed *help system* is a necessity for all but the most simple interfaces. Help should always be available to a user's request and should be appropriate to the task which the user is currently attempting; this is known as ***context sensitive*** help. The help offered and the style of ***language used*** should be appropriate to the user of the application. Most applications are specialized to some area of activity, for example book keeping or train signalling. The language used in the help information should use the terms which are appropriate to the specialized activity of the application, and should not use the specialized language of software developers. This advice on the use of language should be extended to the text used in the interface itself, as well as the text used in the help system.

One important aspect of the use of language, which is often neglected, is to allow for the ***internationalization*** of the software. At the simplest level this would imply that none of the text used in the interface, or in the help system, should be ***hard coded*** into the software. Instead it should be loaded into the software from a resource file, or files, as the system is started. A suitable software design technique for this will be introduced in the next section of this book as an example of the use of an encapsulated static variable (ESV) module design.

Other aspects of internationalization include the character set which is used, details of which were introduced in the previous chapter. This consideration can be extended to the direction in which the text runs across the screen. For western languages this is always from left to right, but this is not always the case in all parts of the world. Support for non-left-to-right text layout is just becoming available as a standard part of computer systems. Other conventions which should be considered include the layout of such things as addresses, dates, times, numbers in general, phone numbers and currency. A previous chapter introduced the standard Ada package ADA.TEXT_IO.PICTURES which provides support for the specialized input–output formatting of numeric information. The next chapter will illustrate how internationalization considerations can be built into an abstract data type.

Internationalization considerations lead to the consideration of ***customization***. Users will feel ***empowered*** if they have the opportunity to change the interface to their own requirements and preferences. This could be as simple as allowing the user to choose screen colours and fonts. It could extend to allowing users to construct their own menu hierarchies in a menu driven system, or to define their own commands in a command line system. There are two potential problems with customization. It is possible that a user might customize an interface so much that it becomes unusable: 'pressed a black button on a black background which lit up a black error message on a black screen'[1]. Alternatively within an organization extensive customization may cause the situation where an application is so extensively customized to an individual's personal choices that it is not possible for another person to operate it. This might cause problems if the usual operator is not available for any reason.

Error management and error recovery: with even the best designed user interface there will be situations where the input provided by the user will not

---

[1] Douglas Adams *The Hitch Hiker's Guide to the Galaxy*.

seem to be appropriate. If these situations are considered as errors then the error is in the process of communication and should not be considered simply as a mistake by the user. Any unacceptable input should be detected as soon as possible after it has been provided, an explanation given to the user of why the system is unable to accept the input and a reinput, or an opportunity to abandon the current operation, requested. Many available systems contain very poor examples of error management, including the use of threatening language (*illegal input*), obscure messages (*system error 200234*) and late detection (*the information given three screens ago is unacceptable, please start again*).

Hidden support for experienced users attempts to reconcile the requirements of a novice user for a simple interface with the requirements of an experienced user for a powerful interface. For example, in a hierarchical menu system a common pair of operations may require navigation from one menu to a sibling menu, via the parent menu. This is acceptable to a novice user but there may also be a hidden menu option, that is one which is not advertised on the menu, which allows a skilled user who knows about it to access the second operation from the first menu, removing the need to navigate the menu hierarchy.

The problem with hidden support is in encouraging the transition from novice to expert behaviour. It is possible that the hidden option is documented in the user guide, but it is also known that user guides are rarely consulted after the initial learning phase, and then only to solve a particular problem rather than to extend knowledge of the interface. One solution to this problem which is just becoming available in commercial application is an *intelligent agent*, a software process which monitors the user's actions and attempts to predict the actions required to complete the task. Once it has a prediction it offers it to the user and asks permission to complete the task. Such an intelligent agent could identify when the user had become so familiar with the interface that the user would benefit from the knowledge of hidden options and inform the user of their existence. Alternatively the agent might create hidden options where the user was seen to perform a number of tasks in a definite sequence, or even reconfigure a menu to offer the sequence of actions from a single menu option.

The user documentation

Whatever style of interface is provided and whatever options it offers to the user some form of documentation will have to be provided with the software package which, as a minimum, introduces the interface to the user. The intended reader of the *user documentation* is the end-user of the software product. The software production process also produces *technical documentation*, the intended reader of which is an engineer who is maintaining the product. These are two totally different types of reader and require documents written in totally different styles. The production of technical documentation will be introduced later in this section. For large software development projects the user documentation may be produced by a *technical writer,* who is trained to be able to understand the complexities of software production and construction, and to be able to convey its operation to the user in a suitable manner. With smaller teams the technical writer and the usability engineer may be the same person, and for small teams or individual projects the user documentation will have to be written by a software engineer.

The user documentation is intended to be a guide for the user of the program. It must not be assumed that the user has any technical knowledge of computing, so the documentation should introduce the program to the user in terms that the user can understand. These terms should refer to the data objects and the processing of those objects as they are perceived by the user in the real world, rather than how they are perceived by the programmers developing the software.

The user documentation should commence with an overview of what processing the program is intended to do, using the terms employed by the user to describe the objects and actions rather than the terms which would be used by a developer. In the case of interactive programs the main part of the user documentation should be a tutorial introduction to the operation of the program's user interface.

Where a menu driven interface style is used this will take the form of an introduction to the various menus and options which are controlled by the menus. The functions of each menu option should be explained, in terms of either what other menus are accessed from that option or what data processing operations are possible from that option. The visual form of the menus should be included in the user guide. This is very useful for a user who is consulting the guide to solve a problem when operating the program. The terminal screen can be compared with the menus in the user guide to confirm that the correct place in the user guide has been found in order to resolve the problem which the user is experiencing.

Where a command line style of user interface is being used the organization of the user guide is more problematic. The basic syntax and form of all commands should be introduced to the user first, following which all commands should be described. The sequence of the commands could follow one of many possible patterns: alphabetically grouped by larger command classes (e.g. all input–output commands, all formatting commands, etc.), grouped according to tasks to be performed, or grouped according to frequency of operations, etc. Whatever organization is chosen it can be guaranteed that it will not satisfy all readers, so an index to cross reference all commands should also be supplied.

Wherever in the explanation of an operation or command an input is requested from the user, the precise format of the prompt which will be issued and of the input expected should be explained. This should include the meaning of the input to the program, the number of characters expected, the range of values allowed and if the <ENTER> key is required to terminate the input. If any error dialog is produced by the program during input, the possible error messages which could be produced should be listed. The meaning of each error message should be explained, and the action required to correct the error specified. Where an option or a command requests the program to provide some output, the format and meaning of the output should be similarly illustrated in the user guide.

For a complex program a large number of error or warning messages may be generated by the program. Including an alphabetic list of possible messages and cross referencing the list to the appropriate point in the user guide can be very useful to the user. Many user guides are only consulted when the user encounters a problem which is made apparent by the output of an error message. As the user guide and the user interface are the two places where the user has most interaction with the program, it is important to make both as supportive as possible.

Most of this documentation will be available from the user interface design which is produced in the first part of the program design phase. If the user guide is also produced at this stage it can be used in two ways. First, as it makes explicit the programmer's interpretation of the specification, the user guide can be shown to the sponsor of the program to confirm that the sponsor's interpretation and the programmer's interpretation are congruent. This will avoid the problem of the programmer producing a program which is different from the program which the sponsor wanted, or of producing a prototype which turns out to be totally unacceptable.

The other way in which the user guide can be used is during the production engineering of the software. As it is an explicit realization of the usability specification, it and the specification can be used to design the program structure and the user interactions. It can also be used to produce those aspects of the test plan which are solely concerned with the operation of the user interface. An example of this type of test plan was given in the previous chapter.

The user guide and the program should be congruent. If the user guide is used as the basis of the program design and implementation, then this will not be a problem. If for any reason the program has to be changed at a later stage, then the user guide will need to be updated to reflect these changes.

Exception processing

As was mentioned in the introduction to this chapter one unacceptable aspect of most of the user interfaces which have been developed so far has been that they have halted the program execution if the user supplied an unexpected input. This behaviour is unacceptable for a production quality interface and the techniques by which an interaction with the user can be used safely to obtain a validated input from the user are an essential part of a developer's knowledge.

In such cases the program is halted by the *propagation* of an unhandled **exception** which originated within the GET input procedure. In order to implement a secure input procedure within a program, design techniques and Ada facilities concerned with *exception handling* will have to be introduced. Although these techniques are being presented here in the context of accepting an input from the user, there are other situations where an exception can be raised, either *implicitly* by a pre-declared subprogram or *explicitly* by the developed code in response to some exceptional occurrence. The production techniques which will be introduced here for the handling of a response from the user are equally applicable to other situations where exceptions need to be handled.

Input of a validated price

To introduce the design and implementation of an *Exception handler* a *Shopping* program will be considered. The specification of an acceptable input procedure for the price of an item being purchased would require the user to input a floating point value, with two decimal places, greater than zero and less than or equal to some maximum value. Should the user not supply such an input the program should state that the input is unacceptable and request another input from the user. This process should continue until the user supplies an acceptable input, or until the user indicates that he or she wishes to abandon the operation.

When Ada is inputting a numeric value, or an enumerated value, using one of the pre-declared GET procedures, characters are accepted from the keyboard and stored in a buffer until either the <ENTER> key is pressed or it can be decided that what is being input is complete or unacceptable. When the series of characters input by the user represents a possible value of the data type being input, the characters in the buffer are converted into a value of the data type being input. In other situations Ada will **raise** an **exception**.

For a *PurchasePrice* the user might be requested to input a value of type FLOAT within the range 0.00 to 1000.00. It cannot be guaranteed that the user will input values according to the instructions given on the screen; in this example the user may do any of the following:

User's input	Comment
25.1	Accepted as a FLOAT with the value 25.10
48.50	Accepted as a FLOAT with the value 48.50
−1.00	Accepted as a FLOAT with the value −1.00, but too small for the application
1000.01	Accepted as a FLOAT with the value 1000.01, but too large for the application
48	Not accepted as INTEGER and FLOAT are incompatible, DATA_ERROR exception raised
<ENTER>	Not accepted as not a possible FLOAT value, DATA_ERROR exception raised
help	Not accepted as not a possible FLOAT value, DATA_ERROR exception raised
25.10.34	Accepted as a FLOAT with the value 25.10, characters '.', '3' and '4' left in the buffer

The program should accept the first two and the last of these without comment.

For the last possibility the additional characters can be discarded. In the third and fourth possibility the program should reject the value with an appropriate error message. In all other cases, where a DATA_ERROR exception is raised, the program should intercept the exception, issue an error message to the user and request a valid input. This will require a program design which makes use of *exception handling.*

The design of an exception handler

A suitable design for the input of a validated *PurchasePrice* is

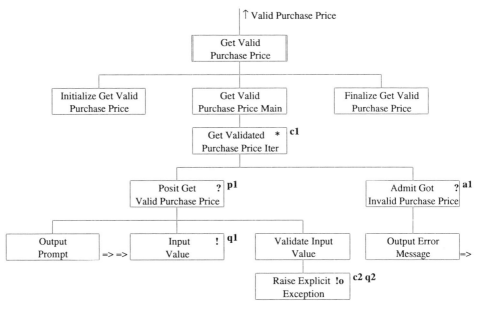

c1: While valid price not entered.   **a1**: Admit DATA_ERROR exception raised.
c2: If price outside allowed range.

                                       q1: Implicit DATA_ERROR.
p1: Assume input of value will be acceptable   **q2**: Explicit DATA_ERROR.

The high level parts of this design are in structure identical with the high level parts of the input designs given in the previous section. The difference lies within the body of the loop where a *posit/admit* design structure has been introduced to allow the implementation to intercept and handle exceptions. The basis of the design is to *posit* (*assume*) that everything will proceed normally and that no exceptions will be raised. The other part of the design *admits* that something went wrong and attempts to handle it. Within the body of the posit the places where an exception could be implicitly raised, or where an exception is explicitly raised, are marked with *q*uits. An implicit quit is an exception which is raised by a pre-declared subprogram, an explicit quit is one which is raised by the developer.

A *posit/admit* design must have a single posit and at least one admit alongside it. It is possible for multiple admit components to be present, each of which would attempt to handle a different exception. Within the body of the posit component these must be at least one, and there may be many, quits marked. The posit component box is marked on the design with a question mark ('?') and is keyed with a *p* for *p*osit. Each admit component is also marked with a question mark ('?') and is keyed with an *a* for *a*dmit. Each component which can raise an exception is identified with an exclamation mark ('!') and is keyed with a *q* for *q*uit. The condition for a quit in the condition list should indicate if the quit is implicit or explicit.

The implementation of an exception handler

The implementation of this design as an Ada procedure might be

```
0001    procedure GetValidPurchasePrice( ValidPrice : out FLOAT) is
0002
0003        IsValidPrice  : BOOLEAN := FALSE;
0004        PossiblePrice : FLOAT;
0005
0006    begin -- GetValidPurchasePrice
0007       while not IsValidPrice loop
0008          begin -- posit/ admit block
0009             PUT("Please enter the purchase price ");
0010             -- implicit exception may be raised here
0011             GET( PossiblePrice);
0012             if PossiblePrice < MinPrice or
0013                PossiblePrice > MaxPrice then
0014                   -- raise explicit exception
0015                   raise DATA_ERROR;
0016             end if;
0017             -- tidy up terminal buffer
0018             SKIP_LINE;
0019             IsValidPrice := TRUE;
0020          exception
0021             when DATA_ERROR =>
0022                SKIP_LINE;
0023                PUT("This value is invalid!"); NEW_LINE;
0024                PUT("Please enter a value ");
0025                PUT("(including decimal parts) between ");
0026                PUT( MinPrice, EXP=>0, FORE=>4, AFT=>2);
0027                PUT(" and ");
0028                PUT( MaxPrice, EXP=>0, FORE=>4, AFT=>2);
```

```
0029                NEW_LINE;
0030           end; -- posit/ admit block
0031      end loop;
0032      ValidPrice := PossiblePrice;
0033   end GetValidPurchasePrice;
```

This implementation assumes the existence of two global FLOAT constants called *MinPrice* and *MaxPrice* which delineate the range of valid prices and have the values 0.00 and 1000.00 respectively. The outermost level of this implementation is comparable with the implementation of input procedures developed in the previous section. This is to be expected because, as noted above, the high levels of the two designs are comparable. The differences in the designs, and consequently in the implementations, are within the scope of the loop.

The design indicates that the body of the loop consists of a ***posit/admit*** structure. This is implemented within the loop as an explicit ***begin/end*** pair with the ***exception*** keyword marking the end of the posit and the start of the admit parts.

The posit part follows the posit design and is implemented as a sequence of three components. The places where exceptions may be raised are commented; either an implicit raising when the GET procedure is called, or explicitly within the body of the **if** statement. Flow of control passes through this sequence of actions and, if no exception is raised, will then pass over the admit part of the structure to the end of the posit/admit block.

If an exception is raised then flow of control passes immediately from the place where it was raised to the start of the admit part. Within the admit part, flow of control may pass to the statements associated with a named exception handler. In this example the only named handler is for DATA_ERRORs, and any DATA_ERROR which is raised will cause the statements associated with the handler to be executed. If there is no named exception handler within the admit part, or if there is no admit part at all, flow of control moves to the next outermost block looking for an exception handler. This search for an exception handler will continue through the nested blocks and if at the outermost block, the program procedure, there is no exception handler the program will crash. This process of exceptions raising through the flow of control of a program is known as *propagation*. If there is an exception handler then, following execution of the handler code, flow of control continues with the statements following the **end** of the admit block.

In the example above, if an exception is raised, the statement on line 0019 which sets the BOOLEAN variable *IsValidPrice* to TRUE is not executed. Following execution of the exception handler, the first statement outside the admit block is an **end loop**. This will cause flow of control to return to the start of the loop, where the loop control condition is re-evaluated, and as *IsValidPrice* is still FALSE, will cause the loop to reiterate.

If an exception is not raised the value of *IsValidPrice* is set to TRUE, following which the admit part of the block is omitted. The **end loop** following the end of the admit block causes the loop control condition to be re-evaluated and as *IsValid-Price* is now TRUE, the loop terminates. Following termination of the loop the value of *PossiblePrice* is assigned to the parameter variable *ValidPrice* to be exported from the procedure.

A trace of the exception handler

A trace of the procedure will make the flow of control clearer. In this trace it is assumed that the user will first input *help*, then *1000.01*, then *56.00*.

Line	ValidPrice	PossiblePrice	IsValidPrice	User's input	Comments
0006	?	?	F	F	initial values
0007					loop test evaluates TRUE – loop iterates
0008					posit started
0009					prompt output for first time
0010				help	DATA_ERROR exception implicitly raised
0020					admit started
0021					admit handler found
0022					terminal buffer emptied
0023–29					error message output
0030					posit/admit block terminated
0031					loop block terminated
0007					loop condition evaluates TRUE – loop reiterates
0008					posit started
0009					prompt output for second time
0010		1000.01		1000.01	user's input accepted as FLOAT value
0012–13					**if** control condition evaluates TRUE
0015					DATA_ERROR exception explicitly raised
0020					admit started
0021					admit handler found
0022					terminal buffer emptied
0023–29					error message output
0030					posit/admit block terminated
0031					loop block terminated
0007					loop condition evaluates TRUE – loop reiterates
0008					posit started
0009					prompt output for third time

245

0010	56.00		56.00	user's input accepted as FLOAT value
0012–13				**if** control condition evaluates FALSE
0016				**if** body omitted
0018				terminal buffer emptied
0019		T		*IsValidPrice* set TRUE
0030				admit part of block skipped
0031				loop terminates
0007				loop condition evaluates FALSE – loop terminates
0032	56.00			value moved to *ValidPrice* for export
0033				procedure terminates

The only other thing to note in this procedure is the call of the SKIP_LINE procedure at appropriate points to empty the terminal buffer. When Ada accepts characters from the terminal keyboard, they are not transmitted until the <ENTER> key is pressed. SKIP_LINE is used to clear any unused characters from the buffer, leaving it empty for the next input request to start with an empty buffer. The trace indicates that SKIP_LINE is called if an exception is raised or if an exception is not raised.

EXERCISES

11.1 Use the criteria listed above to evaluate the user interface of a small commercial application that you are familiar with.

11.2 Adapt the interface of the *GetValidPurchasePrice* procedure so that it takes two additional optional parameters which delineate the range of acceptable values. The default values should the FIRST and LAST attributes of the type supplied.

11.3 Extend the interface from Exercise 11.2 so that it also requires two strings. The first, called *PromptString*, should be used as the input prompt and the second, called *DialogString*, for the error dialog.

11.4 Adapt, and demonstrate, the subprogram from Exercise 11.3 for the input of INTEGER values.

11.5 Adapt, and demonstrate, the subprogram from Exercise 11.3 for the input of an enumerated value.

CHAPTER 12
Abstract data types

Abstract data types were first introduced in Section I where they were used as a basis upon which an extendible type hierarchy was constructed. This chapter will revisit the design and implementation of an abstract data type, without consideration of extendability. The type which will be developed in this chapter will most probably not require extension, although in the next section it will be used as a component part of an extendible data type. Some of the information presented in this chapter has already been presented in Section I, but is repeated here in order to make this chapter complete in its own right.

Ada provides a facility by which a new data type can be completely specified by stating, or implicitly stating, the values which objects of the new type can take and by stating all the operations which an object of the new type can have performed upon it. Such a type is rather misleadingly known as an *abstract data type* (ADT). The name is misleading as it implies that the pre-declared types are themselves non-abstract. Even simple pre-declared data types, such as INTEGER, are themselves abstractions and thus their implementation within a compiler must be abstract. However, the term abstract data type is commonly used to mean a programmer declared type where a full set of values and actions is explicitly provided by the developer.

Once an ADT has been developed it can be used in an Ada program in almost exactly the same way as any of the pre-declared Ada types. This is a very powerful facility and one in which Ada excels. It is also one of the major ways by which the engineering requirement of reuse can be implemented. A correctly defined ADT should be available for immediate use by any program which requires program objects of the real world concept which the ADT is attempting to model. There are repositories of ADTs available and the fulfilling of an ADT requirement should commence with a search of repositories for a suitable type which could be used or adapted, rather than the construction of the type from scratch.

An abstract data type requirement

Many areas of activity have a requirement to represent calendar dates and to manipulate them, for example determining the number of days between two dates. This requirement was first articulated by a sixteenth century French scholar called Joseph Scaliger. Within astronomy it is necessary to be absolutely precise about the meaning of a date, the relationships between different dates and how many days there are between two given dates. Scaliger proposed a concept, which he called *Julian dates*, where days were numbered sequentially from day 1. Day 1 was arbitrarily defined as 1 January 4713 BCE[1], and subsequent days are numbered from then. Joseph Scaliger named the concept *Julian dates* in honour of his father Julius Caeser Scaliger; it has no other connection with Julius Caesar the Roman dictator.

The requirement can thus be loosely stated as a need to provide a data type called *JulianDates* which will store, represent and manipulate calendar dates in Julian dates format. In the interests of manageable simplicity this implementation will restrict the range of dates to 1 Jan 1900 to 31 Dec 2999 (730 485 days), which should be sufficient for the life span of any programs which make use of the ADT. In order to be developed further this vague statement of requirements will have to be refined into a precise specification of which operations are to be provided. For any ADT, one way to assist the precise definition of operations for the type is to consider possible operations from the following categories:

- Operations for the input and output of values of the type.

- Relational operations on the type.

- Arithmetic or pseudo-arithmetic operations.

- Operations to construct and/or deconstruct values of the type.

- Operations which are specific to the type being considered.

Considering each of these categories in turn, the following operations for *JulianDate* are proposed.

Operations for the input and output of values of the type

The input and output of dates should make use of the conventional representation of dates. Dates can be represented in a number of ways of which the following is a selection:

Thursday 19 Jan 1995   19/1/1995   1/19/1995

---

[1] BCE is *before common* era, also known as *before* Christ (BC). The current era is known as *common era* (CE), also known as *anno domini* (after Christ) (AD). The designations BCE and CE are preferred to BC and AD as they have no religious or cultural connotation.

There are many other possible representations, but again in the interests of manageable simplicity only the three possibilities above will be considered. The first of these representations will be known as a *Full* representation and the other two will be known as a *Sparse* representation. The difference between the two sparse representations is a difference between the *English (UK)* convention which is dd/mm/yyyy and the *American (USA)* convention which is mm/dd/yyyy.

The requirements can be more precisely specified by stating that the output of dates should allow output in *Full, European* or *American* formats. The input of dates should allow input in either *European* or *American* formats. This is an example of internationalization being considered at the outset of the design process.

Relational operations on *JulianDates*

The six relational operators (=, <>, >, <, >=, <=) all have a commonly understood real world meaning. Two dates are equal if they refer to the same day, one date is greater than another date if it identifies a day which occurred later and one date is less than another date if it identifies a day which occurred earlier.

Arithmetic or pseudo-arithmetic operations

It does not seem to make sense to add two *JulianDates* together. For example, there is no obvious meaning for *Mon 5 Apr 1993 + Wed 29 Mar 1995*. However, there is an obvious meaning for subtracting one date from another. For example, *Wed 29 Mar 1995 – Mon 5 Apr 1993* might be interpreted as the number of days between the two dates (723 days). If this interpretation of subtraction is accepted then the addition operation could be interpreted as the addition of an integer value to a date which will result in a date which is so many days in the future for positive integers, or in the past for negative integers.

Having decided that there are pseudo-arithmetic interpretations for addition and subtraction, multiplication and division can be considered. There does not seem to be any commonly accepted meaning of multiplication and division for dates, so these operations will not be implemented.

Operations to construct and/or deconstruct values of the type

A *JulianDate* can be constructed by inputting a value from the terminal, but this is not always appropriate or convenient. It should also be possible to construct a date from its component parts, by specifying the day of the month, the month and the year. It should also be possible to deconstruct a date, that is by supplying a *JulianDate* and having returned the day name, the day of the month, the month and the year.

This has the implication that the package will have to supply types to represent days (Mon, Tue, etc.), day numbers (in the range 1 to 31), month names (Jan, Feb, etc.), month numbers (in the range 1 to 12) and years (in this implementation 1900 to 2999).

Operations which are specific to the type being considered

This is the most difficult category to specify. For the *JulianDate* type an ability to determine the current day would be appropriate, as would operations which will determine the succeeding and preceding date of a given *JulianDate*.

This is also the place to consider anything which could go wrong with any of the operations which have been decided upon. Many of the operations suggested above could be attempted with or could result in inappropriate dates. For example, an attempt could be made to construct a *JulianDate* specifying an invalid date (e.g. 29 Feb 1995). These errors could be reported using a pre-declared exception; in this example CONSTRAINT_ERROR would seem appropriate. Alternatively an exception specific to the *JulianDate* type could be used. The decision in this requirement is to use a specific exception called *JulianDateError*.

The *JulianDate* specification

The preceding stage in producing the requirements for an ADT will provide an informal specification of the type which is to be constructed. The process continues with the production of an exact specification of the type which is to be constructed. The first of the specification documents is an **object diagram** which indicates exactly what types, operations and values the data type will supply. The object diagram for the *JulianDate* data type is

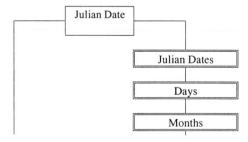

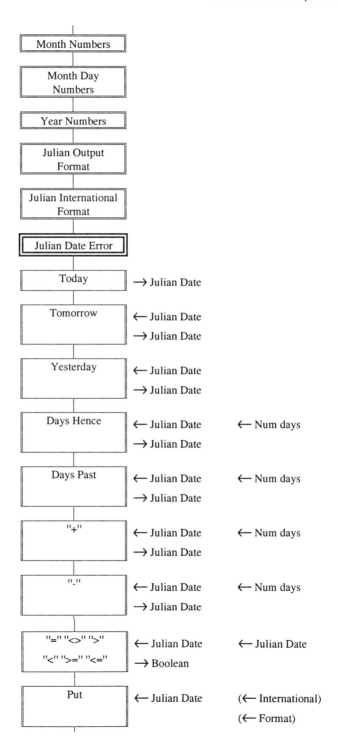

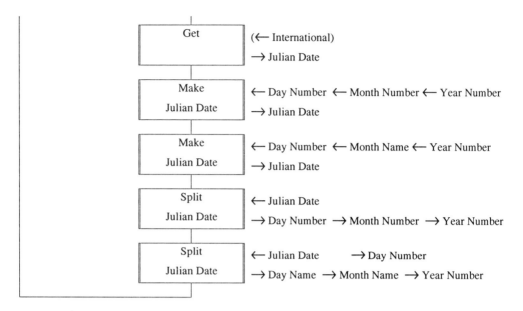

The object diagram gives an overview of the types, exceptions and operations which are provided as part of or in support of the ADT. Types are shown exported in double lined boxes, exceptions in heavy double lined boxes and subprograms in simple boxes. The object diagram should be supplemented by design documentation which describes in greater detail the data types and operations which are provided.

In order for the description of the operations to be fully understood, the nature of the supporting data types has to be made clear, so the detailed design documentation commences with data structure diagrams for the supporting types:

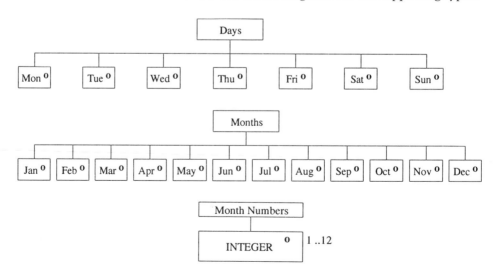

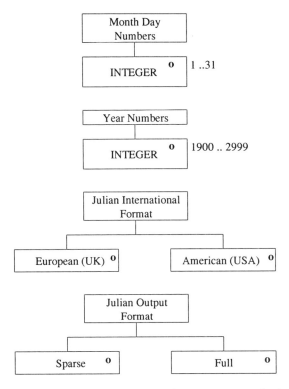

Each operation should be specified as an interface diagram which can be used to produce the declaration of an Ada subprogram. A concise yet precise description of the operation's actions should also be provided at this stage.

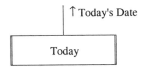

```
function Today return JulianDates;
-- Returns the current date as a JulianDates value.
```

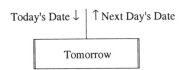

```
function Tomorrow( AnyDate : in JulianDates) return
                                        JulianDates;
-- Returns the date of the succeeding day. May raise
-- JulianDateError exception if this is after the
-- last possible date.
```

253

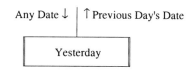

```
function Yesterday( AnyDate : in JulianDates) return
                                             JulianDates;
-- Returns the date of the preceding day. May raise
-- JulianDateError exception if this is before
-- the first possible date.
```

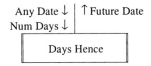

```
function DaysHence( AnyDate : in JulianDates;
             NumDays : in POSITIVE ) return JulianDates;
-- Returns the date of the number of days in the future from
-- the date supplied. May raise JulianDateError exception
-- if this is after the last possible date.
```

```
function DaysPast( AnyDate : in JulianDate;
             NumDays : in POSITIVE ) return JulianDate;
-- Returns the date of the number of days in the past from
-- the date supplied. May raise JulianDateError exception
-- if this is before the first possible date.
```

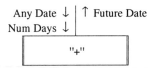

```
function "+"( AnyDate : in JulianDates;
          NumDays : in INTEGER ) return JulianDates;
-- Returns the date of the number of days in the future or
-- past from the date supplied. May raise JulianDateError
-- exception if this is before/after the first/last possible
                                                        date.
```

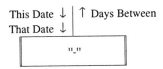

```
function "-"( ThisDate : in JulianDates;
              ThatDate : in JulianDates) return INTEGER ;
-- Returns the number of days between the two dates supplied.
```

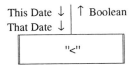

```
function "<"( ThisDate : in JulianDates;
              ThatDate : in JulianDates) return INTEGER ;
-- Returns True if ThisDate is earlier than ThatDate.
```

(Interface diagrams and subprogram declarations for "<=", ">" and ">=" omitted. The declarations of "=" and "<>" are not required, as will be explained below.)

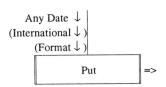

```
procedure Put( AnyDate : in JulianDates;
           International : in JulianInternationalFormat := UK;
                 Format : in JulianOutputFormat := Sparse);
-- Outputs AnyDate in the format specified, with Full output
-- format overriding any international format specified.
```

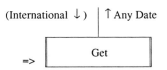

```
procedure Get( AnyDate : out JulianDates;
           International : in JulianInternationalFormat := UK);
-- Inputs a JulianDate value in the format specified.
```

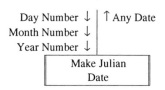

```
function MakeJulianDate( Day   : in MonthDayNumbers;
                         Month : in MonthNumbers;
                         Year  : in YearNumbers) return
                                              JulianDates;
-- Constructs a JulianDate from the values supplied. May raise
-- JulianDateError exception if the date is invalid.
```

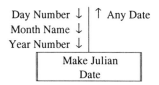

```
function MakeJulianDate( Day   : in MonthDayNumbers;
                         Month : in Months;
                         Year  : in YearNumbers) return
                                              JulianDates;
-- Constructs a JulianDate from the values supplied. May raise
-- JulianDateError exception if the date is invalid.
```

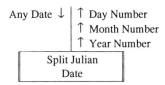

```
procedure SplitJulianDate( AnyDay : in JulianDates;
                           Day    : out MonthDayNumbers;
                           Month  : out MonthNumbers;
                           Year   : out YearNumbers);
-- Deconstructs the JulianDate supplied into its components.
```

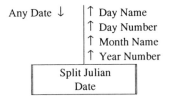

```
procedure SplitJulianDate( AnyDay    : in JulianDates;
                           DayName   : out Days;
                           Day       : out MonthDayNumbers;
                           MonthName : out Months;
                           Year      : out YearNumbers );
  -- Deconstructs the JulianDate supplied into its components.
```

Two of these subprograms, *MakeJulianDate* and *SplitJulianDate*, are **overloaded**. An overloaded subprogram is one which has more than one meaning, the meanings being determined by the number and types of the parameters. The two versions of the *MakeJulianDate* procedure differ in requiring either a month number or a month name to specify the month of the date to be made. Ada is able to determine which of the subprograms is intended by the developer by examining the data type of the month parameter supplied. The *Put* and *Get* subprograms are also overloaded by this package adding additional meanings to these subprogram names.

The relational and arithmetic operators are also overloaded by this package specification. Ada can recognize that the declaration of functions, with names such as " $-$ ", indicates that they can be used either in **prefix** notation or **infix** notation. **Prefix** notation is the usual format for subprograms and requires the actual parameters to follow the name of the subprogram in brackets. For example:

```
DaysElapsed := "-"( EndDate, StartDate);
```

Infix notation allows a more natural, and clearly preferable, expression:

```
DaysElapsed := EndDate - StartDate;
```

The Ada *JulianDate* package specification file

The next stage in the production of the *JulianDate* data type is the implementation of the package design in the form of an Ada package specification source code file. Before this can be accomplished a decision concerning the implementation of the *JulianDate* ADT will have to be made. No consideration has yet been given to the precise declaration of the *JulianDate* data type. This is deliberate in this example, and very advisable for any ADT. All the design considerations so far have concentrated upon *what* operations the data type is to supply; it is only at this stage that a decision concerning *how* the data type is to be implemented should be made. The reason for this is to allow the data type to supply operations which are required from its real world based analysis, and not to be influenced by the operations which are implied from the data type's representation.

There are three possible forms of declaration that determine which operations will be available for objects of the type being specified. The data type can be declared *public*, in which case client programs of the package will have full knowledge of the nature of the ADT's implementation and will be able to use any appropriate operations. The data type can be declared **private**, in which case client programs of the package will have no knowledge of the nature of the ADT's implementation and the only operations available are those which are exported from the package, together with assignment (:=), equality (=) and inequality (/=) operations. Finally the data type can be declared **limited private**, which is equivalent to a **private** declaration, but the assignment, equality and inequality operations are not supplied. These considerations can be summarized in the following table:

Declaration	Operations available to clients
limited private	Only those exported from the package
private	As for **limited private** plus assignment (:=), equality (=) and inequality (/=)
public	As for **private** plus any operations appropriate from the type's declaration

The principle of *information hiding* suggests keeping as much information as possible hidden from client programs and implies that a **limited private** declaration should be considered first. Only if there are reasons for allowing the assignment, equality and inequality operations should a **private** declaration should be made. A *public* declaration should only be made in exceptional circumstances if there are compelling reasons to do so.

In this example the implementation of the *JulianDates* type will be as a new INTEGER type with a limited range, but this information will be hidden from clients of the package. If a **private** declaration is made, the assignment of one *JulianDates* value to a *JulianDates* object and the equality and inequality comparisons of two *JulianDates* values will be implemented as the corresponding operations of the *JulianDates* base type INTEGER. These are acceptable implementations of these operations and the decision to implement the data type with a **private** declaration is appropriate. This decision was anticipated in the detailed design of the package given above when the omission of the assignment, 'is equal' and 'is not equal' operations was commented upon. The implementation of the Ada *JulianDate* package specification file might be

```
0001    -- Filename JulianDate_.pkg (k8 julianda.ads).
0002    -- Non-extendible ADT package to implement JulianDates data
                                                              type.
0003    -- developed for the Ada book Section II Chapter 12.
```

```
0004    --
0005    -- Fintan Culwin, v0.1, Jan 1997.
0006
0007    package JulianDate is
0008
0009       type JulianDates is private;
0011
0012       type Days   is ( Mon, Tue, Wed, Thu, Fri, Sat, Sun);
0013       type Months is ( Jan, Feb, Mar, Apr, May, Jun,
0014                        Jul, Aug, Sep, Oct, Nov, Dec);
0015
0016       type MonthNumbers    is INTEGER range 1 .. 12;
0017       type MonthDayNumbers is INTEGER range 1 .. 31;
0018       type YearNumbers     is INTEGER range 1900 .. 2999;
0019
0020       type JulianOutputFormat is ( Sparse, Full);
0021       -- Sparse format is 01/01/1996.
0022       -- Full   format is Mon 01 Jan 1996.
0023
0024       type JulianInternationalFormat is ( UK, USA);
0025       -- UK  format is dd/mm/yyyy
0026       -- USA format is mm/dd/yyyy
0027
0028       JulianDateError : exception;
0029
0030
0031       function Today return JulianDates;
0032       -- Returns today's date as a Julian value.
0033
0034       function Tomorrow( AnyDate : in JulianDates)
0035                                          return JulianDates;
0036       -- Returns the date of the succeeding day.
0037
        -- declaration of other subprograms omitted from the design
0096
0097       procedure SplitJulianDate( AnyDay    : in JulianDates;
0098                                  DayName   : out Days;
0099                                  Day       : out MonthDayNumbers;
0100                                  MonthName : out Months;
0101                                  Year      : out YearNumbers);
0102       -- Deconstructs the Julian date supplied into its
                                                  components.
0103
0104    private
0105
0106       MinJulianDate : constant := 0;
0107       -- There are 401766 days between 1/1/1900 and 31/12/2999.
0108       MaxJulianDate : constant := 401766;
```

```
0109
0110      type JulianDate is INTEGER
0111                          range MinJulianDate .. MaxJulianDate;
0112
0113   end JulianDate;
```

The package specification file starts, as should all Ada source code files, with comments. The first comment states the name of the source code file; the suggested name for an ADT package specification file is to use the singular name of the data type followed by an underscore, with the extension "*.pkg*". Applying these rules to the *JulianDate* type gives the name "*JulianDate_.pkg*". An underscore is added to indicate in derived files, such as a listing file "*JulianDateADT_.lis*", that the file contains a package specification listing. Finally the extension "*pkg*" indicates a package specification file, as opposed to a package definition file. The eight character 'krunched' (k8) name, *julianda.ads*, is also given in the comment.

The package may have a context clause bringing into use other packages from the library. This option is not present in this example and the first non-comment line indicates the declaration of a package called "*JulianDate*". The declarative part of the package specification follows and is divided into a public part and possibly a private part.

The first declaration in the public part is the declaration of the ADT itself, which in accord with the decision above is declared as a **private** type. This **private** declaration in the public part of the specification makes the private part of the package specification non-optional.

The public part of the package specification continues with the *public* declaration of the supporting types, using the data structure diagrams from the ADT's design and the techniques explained in the previous chapters. Before the subprograms are declared the *JulianDateError* **exception** is declared in line 0029. The public part of the specification concludes with the declaration of the subprograms which are taken directly from the design.

The package specification concludes with a private part, indicated by the **private** reserved word on line 0104. Because of the declaration of a **private** type on line 0009, a private part of the package specification must be included. The contents of the private part of a package specification are not visible to clients of the package and must contain the full specification of any **private** or **limited private** types which are declared in the public part. In this example the *JulianDates* data type is declared as being a new INTEGER type with a restricted range. Comments are used to indicate the meanings of the bounds of the range, without which the comments would make very little sense. Finally, on line 0113, the end of the package specification is marked.

If a decision had been made to declare the ADT as **limited private**, then the declaration of the *JulianDate* type on line 0009 would have to be changed to

```
0009   type JulianDate is limited private
```

With this change in place no changes would be required to the private part of the package specification, but consideration would have to be given to declaring assignment (":=") and equality ("=") subprograms in the public part of the package specification. It would not be necessary to declare an inequality operation explicitly as Ada would be able to recognize that an inequality relation ("/=") is a Boolean negation (**not**) of the equality operation.

If a decision had been made to declare the ADT as a *public* type then the declaration of the *JulianDate* type in the private part of the package specification, and the supporting **constant** declarations, would have to be moved into the public part of the specification replacing the existing **private** declaration. If this were done then the private part of the package specification would become optional and could be omitted from the specification.

With a *public* declaration a client program of the package would have full knowledge of the nature of the representation of the *JulianDates* data type and could make use of any integer operations. This would allow client programs to multiply two *JuilanDates* together, or divide two together or even use the exponentiation operator to find the cube of a *JulianDates* value. As discussed above, none of these operations make any sense in terms of the nature of a calendar date and making the *JulianDates* data type **private** prevents a client program from using such operations.

When the package specification file has been entered as a text file, it can be submitted to the Ada compiler which would report any syntax errors in the specification. Once the syntax errors, if any, have been removed the specification can be compiled into the Ada program library. When the package specification is in the library any client programs which make use of the package can be compiled, even before the package definition file has been produced.

The Ada *JulianDate* package definition file

The discussion in this chapter could continue with either how clients can make use of the *JulianDates* type or how the definition of the *JulianDates* type is implemented. The decision to continue with the package definition is arbitrary. The package definition file commences with the usual comments, a context clause and some declarations:

```
0001    -- filename JulianDate.pkb (K8 julainda.adb).
0002    -- Non extendible JulianDates data type package definition,
0003    -- developed for the Ada book Section II Chapter 12.
0004    --
0005    -- Fintan Culwin, v0.1, Jan 1997.
0006
0007    with ADA.TEXT_IO, ADA.CALENDAR, ADA.CHARACTERS.LATIN_1;
```

```
0008    use ADA.TEXT_IO, ADA.CHARACTERS.LATIN_1;
0009
0010    package body JulianDate is
0011
0012       -- various i-o packages
0013       package IntegerIO is new ADA.TEXT_IO.INTEGER_IO( INTEGER );
0014       package DaysIO   is new ADA.TEXT_IO.ENUMERATION_IO( Days );
0015       package MonthsIO  is new ADA.TEXT_IO.ENUMERATION_IO( Months );
0016       use IntegerIO, DaysIO, MonthsIO;
0017
0018
0019       -- various constants used for calculations
0020       DaysPerYear     : constant INTEGER := 365;
0021       DaysPer4Years   : constant INTEGER := 1461;
0022       DaysPer100Years : constant INTEGER := 36524;
0023       DaysPer400Years : constant INTEGER := 146097;
0024
0025       -- declaration of two local subprograms
0026       function IsLeapYear( AnyYear : in YearNumbers )
0027                                              return BOOLEAN;
0028       -- Returns true if AnyYear is a leap year, false otherwise.
0029
0030       function DaysInMonth( Month : in MonthNumbers;
0031                             Year  : in YearNumbers )
0032                                         return MonthDayNumbers;
0033       -- Returns the number of days in the Month supplied,
0034       -- allowing for leap years as appropriate.
```

It is suggested that the names of package definition files are constructed using rules similar to the rules for the naming of package specification files. The name of this file is the SINGULAR name of the ADT, "*JulianDate*", with the package extension ".*pkb*" for package body. These rules give the name of this package as "*JulianDate.pkb*". The context clause brings three ADA standard packages, ADA.TEXT_IO, ADA.CALENDAR and ADA.CHARACTERS.LATIN_1, into use. ADA.TEXT_IO is brought into use in order that its input–output packages can be used. ADA.CALENDAR is brought into use in order that its facility to obtain the date from the computer's system clock can be used in the definition of the subprogram *Today*, as will be explained below. ADA.CHARACTERS.-LATIN_1 is brought into use to allow the manifest name of the space character to be used.

The start of the **package** declaration, also known as the package **body**, is marked on line 0010. The package starts with the instantiation and bringing into use of various input–output packages for the data types declared publicly in the package specification. The instantiation of these input–output packages in the body of the package makes them private to the package and their facilities are not available to clients of the package.

The package body continues with the declaration of various constants which will be used in various subprogram definitions; the meaning of their values will be explained below. The declarations at the start of the package body conclude with the declaration of two subprograms which are private to the body of the package. Subprograms declared in the package body are only available for use within the package body; they are not visible to the clients of the package. The definition and use of these subprograms will be explained below.

The package body continues with the definition of the subprograms which were declared in the package specification file. These definitions will be presented in an arbitrary sequence.

The relational and arithmetic *JulianDate* operations

The definition of the *JulianDate* relational and arithmetic operations can make use of the underlying INTEGER *JulianDates* representation. The design and definition of the addition operation is

p1: Assume addition successful.   **q1**: Implicit CONSTRAINT_ERROR.
a1: If CONSTRAINT_ERROR.   **q2** Explicit *JulianDateError*.

```
0001    function "+"( AnyDate : in JulianDates;
0002                  NumDays : in INTEGER) return JulianDates is
0003    begin -- "+"
0004       return JulianDates( INTEGER(AnyDate) + NumDays);
0005    exception
0006       when CONSTRAINT_ERROR =>
0007          raise JulianDateError;
0008    end "+";
```

The implementation of the addition operation makes use of the INTEGER addition operation. In order to do this the *JulianDates* parameter *AnyDate* is type converted into an INTEGER value, added to the INTEGER *NumDays* parameter and the resulting value type converted back into a *JulianDates* value. If the

resulting value is outside the bounds of the *JulianDates* type a CONSTRAINT_
ERROR will be implicitly raised. An exception handler traps the implicit
CONSTRAINT_ERROR and explicitly raises a *JulianDateError* in order to
propagate the error.

The implementation of the subtraction operation is considerably simpler as
there is no possibility of any exception being raised:

```
0001    function "-"( Left, Right : in JulianDates)
0002                                        return INTEGER is
0003    begin -- "-"
0004       return INTEGER( Left) - INTEGER( Right);
0005    end "-";
```

Several other subprograms make use of the addition operation in their
implementation:

```
0001    function Tomorrow( AnyDate : in JulianDates)
0002                                        return JulianDates is
0003    begin -- Tomorrow
0004       return AnyDate + 1;
0005    end Tomorrow;
0006
0007
0008    function Yesterday( AnyDate : in JulianDates)
0009                                        return JulianDates is
0010    begin -- Yesterday
0011       return AnyDate + (-1);
0012    end Yesterday;
0013
0014
0015    function DaysHence( AnyDate : in JulianDates;
0016                        NumDays : in POSITIVE)
0017                                        return JulianDates is
0018    begin -- DaysHence
0019       return AnyDate + NumDays;
0020    end DaysHence;
0021
0022
0023    function DaysPast( AnyDate : in JulianDates;
0024                       NumDays : in POSITIVE)
0025                                        return JulianDates is
0026    begin -- DaysPast
0027       return AnyDate + (-INTEGER( NumDays));
0028    end DaysPast;
```

All of these operations use the already declared addition operation. The *Yesterday*
and *DaysPast* operations ensure that the addition operation, not the subtraction

operation, is used by explicitly adding a negated value. These implementations rely upon the addition implementation raising any required exception, and do not have to concern themselves with exceptions. The implementation of the various relational operations also makes use of the *JulianDates* INTEGER representation:

```
0001    function "<" ( Left, Right : in JulianDates)
0002                                          return BOOLEAN is
0003    begin -- "<"
0004       return INTEGER( Left) < INTEGER( Right);
0005    end "<";
0006
0007
0008    function ">" ( Left, Right : in JulianDates)
0009                                          return BOOLEAN is
0010    begin -- ">"
0011       return INTEGER( Left) > INTEGER( Right);
0012    end ">";
0013
0014
0015    function "<="( Left, Right : in JulianDates)
0016                                          return BOOLEAN is
0017    begin -- "<="
0018       return not( Left > Right);
0019    end "<=";
0020
0021
0022    function ">="( Left, Right : in JulianDates)
0023                                          return BOOLEAN is
0024    begin -- ">="
0025       return not( Left < Right);
0026    end ">=";
```

The implementation of the two functions "<=" and ">=" makes use of the fact that "<=" is equivalent to **not** ">", and that ">=" is equivalent to **not** "<".

The *JulianDate* constructors

There are two *JulianDate* constructors, differing in passing either the *Month-Number* (e.g. 5) or the *MonthName* (e.g. May) as the month parameter. The design of the constructor using the *MonthNumber* is

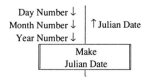

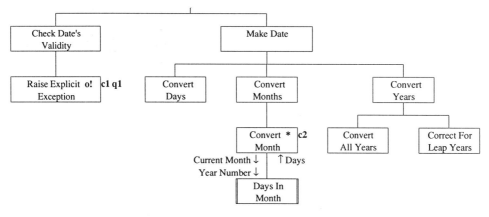

c1: If date is not valid.
c2: For all complete months.

q1: Raise explicit *JulianDateError*.

The basis of the algorithm is to convert the parameters supplied into a count of the number of days which have elapsed since 1 Jan 1900. This is accomplished by first allowing for the number of days which have elapsed in the month, adding the number of days in each complete month in the year, and then adding all the days in all the years since year 1900. This last action first assumes that all years have 365 days and then allows for leap years using the rule that every fourth year is a leap year, apart from every hundredth year which is not, unless it is a four-hundredth year in which case it is a leap year.

Before the conversion is attempted the validity of the date supplied in the parameters is ensured. The number of days in the month supplied is compared with the value returned from the private function *DaysInMonth*, and a *Julian-DateError* is raised if this indicates that the date is invalid (e.g. 29/2/1995). A situation where the execution of a subprogram is abandoned if the parameters are shown to be invalid is known as ***defensive programming*** and the structure where the subprogram is ***ab***andoned is known as an ***abend***. The implementation of the design might be

```
0001    function MakeJulianDate( Day   : in MonthDayNumbers;
0002                             Month : in MonthNumber;
0003                             Year  : in YearNumbers )
0004                                       return JulianDates is
0005
0006        LocalDay : JulianDates := 0;
0007        LocalYear : INTEGER :=
0008                INTEGER( Year) - INTEGER( YearNumbers'FIRST);
0009
0010    begin -- MakeJulianDate
0011        -- Abend if date is impossible.
0012        if (INTEGER(Day) >
```

```
0013              INTEGER(DaysInMonth( Month, Year))) then
0014          raise JulianDateError;
0015      end if;
0016
0017      -- Start with the number of days in the month.
0018      LocalDay := INTEGER( Day);
0019
0020      -- Add the number of days in each complete month passed.
0021      for ThisMonth in MonthNumber range 2 .. Month loop
0022          LocalDay := LocalDay +
0023                  INTEGER(DaysInMonth( ThisMonth-1,Year));
0024      end loop;
0025
0026      -- Then the number of years, ignoring leap years.
0027      LocalDay := LocalDay + LocalYear * DaysPerYear;
0028      -- Correct for the number of leap years.
0029      LocalDay := LocalDay + (Year / 4) -
0030                            (Year / 100) +
0031                            (Year / 400)) ;
0032      -- Correct for counting from day 0 not 1.
0033      LocalDay := LocalDay -1;
0034      return JulianDates( LocalDay);
0035  end MakeJulianDate;
```

This implementation will operate correctly for dates in January as the number of days in January (range 1 .. 31) will be added first, following which the loop control expression is effectively range 1 .. 0 which will iterate zero times, before the number of days in the years component are calculated and added. This function relies upon the implementation of the private *DaysInMonth* function, whose design can be summarized in the rhyme:

> 30 days hath September, April, June and November.
> All the rest have thirty one.
> Save February, which has 28 in each clear year,
> and 29 in each leap year.

The design, based upon this rhyme, is

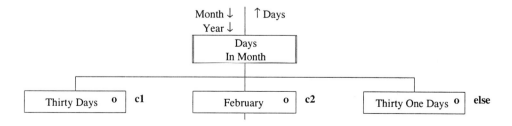

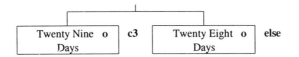

c1: If September, April, June or November.
c2: If February.
c3: If leap year.

and the implementation might be

```
0001    function DaysInMonth( Month : in MonthNumber;
0002                          Year  : in YearNumbers )
0003                                     return MonthDayNumbers is
0004
0005       LocalDays : MonthDayNumbers;
0006
0007    begin -- DaysInMonth
0008       case Month is
0009          -- 30 days have Sept ...
0010          when 4 | 6 | 9 | 11 =>
0011             LocalDays := 30;
0012          -- save Feb ....
0013          when 2 =>
0014             if IsLeapYear( Year) then
0015                LocalDays := 29;
0016             else
0017                LocalDays := 28;
0018             end if;
0019          -- all the rest have 31.
0020          when others =>
0021             LocalDays := 31;
0022       end case;
0023       return LocalDays;
0024    end DaysInMonth;
```

The implementation of this function in turn relies upon the implementation of the private function *IsLeapYear*. The rules for deciding if a given year is or is not a leap year were given above. Using these rules, the implementation of the function is

```
0001    function IsLeapYear( Year : in YearNumbers)
0002                                     return BOOLEAN is
0003
0004    begin -- IsLeapYear
0005       return ( ((Year mod 400)  = 0) or
0006                 ((Year mod 4  )  = 0) and
```

268

```
0007                    ((Year mod 100) /= 0)) );
0008    end IsLeapYear;
```

Finally the alternative constructor function, which takes a *MonthName* instead of a *MonthNumber* to identify which month, can be implemented as a call to the existing constructor after the *MonthName* has been converted to a *MonthNumber*.

```
0001    function MakeJulianDate( Day   : in MonthDayNumbers;
0002                             Month : in Months;
0003                             Year  : in YearNumbers )
0004                                        return JulianDates is
0005
0006        LocalMonthNumber : MonthNumbers := (Months'POS(Month) +1)
0007
0008    begin -- MakeJulianDate
0009        return MakeJulianDate( Day, LocalMonthNumber, Year);
0010    end MakeJulianDate;
```

This constructor relies upon the alternative constructor to determine if the date is invalid, and to raise a *JulianDateError* exception if the construction of an invalid date is attempted. When the POS attribute is applied to the *Months* value in line 0006 an ordinal value in the range 0 to 11 is obtained. However, *MonthNumbers* are in the range 1 to 12 and thus to obtain the correct *MonthNumbers* value 1 is added to the ordinal value.

The *JulianDate* deconstructors

Although not technically destructors in the sense that they destroy an existing *JulianDates*, the two *SplitJulianDate* procedures are in a sense the inverse functions to the constructors and as such can be described as deconstructors. The design of the function can also be thought of as the inverse of the constructor function:

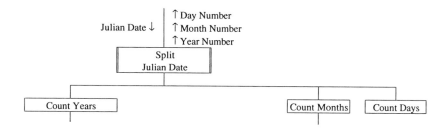

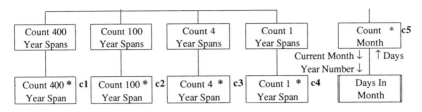

c1: For all remaining 400 year spans.
c2: For all remaining 100 year spans.
c3: For all remaining 4 year spans.

c4: For all remaining 4 year spans.
c5: For all remaining month spans.

The basis of the design is to start by subtracting from the *JulianDates* value the number of days in 400 years, adding 400 to the number of years in the year field of the split date. This continues until the number of days remaining is less than the number of days in 400 years. This process is then repeated for the number of days in 100 years, then four years, then each (non-leap) year. The *JulianDate* constant values with names such as *DaysPer400Years* which were declared at the start of the package body are used to facilitate this part of the procedure.

Once the number of years has been determined the remaining *JulianDate* value indicates the number of days in the identified year. A similar loop subtracts the number of days in each month, allowing for the possibility of a leap year, from the days remaining, and at the same time counts the number of months, until the number of days remaining is less than the number of days in the next possible month. The remaining *JulianDate* value now indicates the number of days in the identified month. The implementation of this procedure might be

```
0001    procedure SplitJulianDate( AnyDay : in JulianDates;
0002                                Day    : out MonthDayNumbers;
0003                                Month  : out MonthNumbers;
0004                                Year   : out YearNumbers ) is
0005
0006        DaysRemaining        : INTEGER := INTEGER( AnyDay);
0007        LocalYears           : INTEGER := 1900;
0008        LocalMonths          : INTEGER := 0;
0009        LocalDays            : INTEGER := 0;
0010
0011    begin -- SplitJulianDate
0012        -- Start with the number of 400 year periods.
0013        while DaysRemaining >= DaysPer400Years loop
0014            LocalYears    := LocalYears + 400;
0015            DaysRemaining := DaysRemaining - DaysPer400Years;
0016        end loop;
0017
0018        -- Then the number of 100 year periods.
0019        while DaysRemaining >= DaysPer100Years loop
0020            LocalYears    := LocalYears + 100;
```

```
0021            DaysRemaining := DaysRemaining - DaysPer100Years;
0022        end loop;
0023
0024        -- Then the number of 4 year periods.
0025        while DaysRemaining >= DaysPer4Years loop
0026            LocalYears    := LocalYears + 4;
0027            DaysRemaining := DaysRemaining - DaysPer4Years ;
0028        end loop;
0029
0030        -- Then the number of years.
0031        while DaysRemaining >= DaysPerYear loop
0032            LocalYears    := LocalYears + 1;
0033            DaysRemaining := DaysRemaining - DaysPerYear ;
0034        end loop;
0035
0036        -- Now the number of months.
0037        while DaysRemaining > INTEGER( DaysInMonth(
0038                                  MonthNumbers(LocalMonths +1),
0039                                YearNumbers( LocalYears))) loop
0040          DaysRemaining := DaysRemaining - INTEGER( DaysInMonth(
0041                                  MonthNumbers( LocalMonths +1),
0042                                  YearNumbers( LocalYears) ));
0043          LocalMonths := LocalMonths + 1;
0044        end loop;
0045
0046        -- Now the days.
0047        LocalDays := = DaysRemaining;
0048
0049    Day   := MonthDayNumbers( LocalDays +1);
0050    Month := MonthNumbers( LocalMonths +1);
0051    Year  := YearNumbers( LocalYears);
0052    end SplitJulianDate;
```

The implementation takes advantage of the private knowledge that the *JulianDays* type is a new INTEGER type by making all local variables INTEGER. This simplifies some of the calculations by restricting the amount of type conversion required. This results in values for *LocalDays* and *LocalMonths* which might start at zero, requiring one to be added to them before they are type converted and exported at the end of the procedure. As with the constructor functions, the alternative deconstructor procedure can be implemented by making use of the existing deconstructor procedure:

```
0001    procedure SplitJulianDate( AnyDay  : in JulianDate;
0002                               DayName : out Days;
0003                               Day     : out MonthDayNumbers;
0004                               Month   : out Months;
0005                               Year    : out YearNumbers ) is
```

```
0006
0007        LocalMonth : MonthNumbers;
0008
0009    begin -- SplitJulianDate
0010        SplitJulianDate( AnyDay, Day, LocalMonth, Year );
0011        Month    := Months'VAL( LocalMonth -1);
0012        DayName := Days'VAL( INTEGER(AnyDay));
0013    end SplitJulianDate;
```

Following the call of the existing *SplitJulianDate* procedure the returned month number is converted into a *Months* enumeration value using the VAL attribute of the *Months* type, allowing for the difference between ordinal and *MonthNumbers* values as mentioned above. The day name is obtained by taking the VAL attribute of the *Days* type. Fortunately 1 Jan 1900 was a Monday and thus no correction to obtain the correct value is required.

The output of a *JulianDate* value

The output of a *JulianDate* value, using the overloaded *Put* procedure, uses the following design:

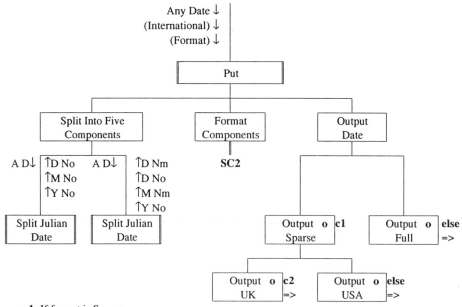

c1: If format is Sparse.
c2: If UK international format requested.

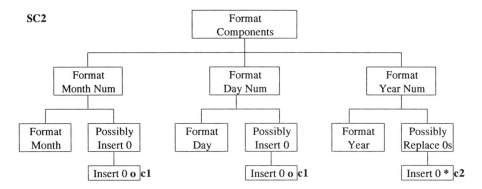

c1: If first character is a space.
c2: While current character is a space.

The implementation of this design might be:

```
0001    procedure Put( AnyDay      : in JulianDates;
0002                   International : in JulianInternationalFormat := UK;
0003                   Format        : in JulianOutputFormat := Sparse) is
0004
0005        LocalMonthNum   : MonthNumbers;
0006        LocalMonth      : Months;
0007        LocalDay        : Days;
0008        LocalDayNumber  : MonthDayNumbers;
0009        LocalYears      : YearNumbers;
0010
0011        MonthNumString    : STRING := "mm";
0012        MonthDayNumString : STRING := "dd";
0013        YearString        : STRING := "yyyy";
0014
0015        Index             : INTEGER;
0016
0017    begin -- Put
0018        -- Split the day into all five possible components.
0019        SplitJulianDate( AnyDay, LocalDayNumber
0020                                    LocalMonthNum, LocalYears );
0021        SplitJulianDate( AnyDay, LocalDay, LocalDayNumber,
0022                                    LocalMonth, LocalYears );
0023
0024        -- format numeric types into strings
0025        PUT( MonthNumString, INTEGER( LocalMonthNum));
0026        if ( MonthNumString(1) = SPACE ) then
0027            MonthNumString(1) := '0';
0028        end if;
0029
0030        PUT( MonthDayNumString, INTEGER( LocalDayNumber));
```

273

```
0031        if ( MonthDayNumString(1) = SPACE ) then
0032            MonthDayNumString(1) := '0';
0033        end if;
0034
0035        PUT( YearString, INTEGER( LocalYears));
0036        Index := 1;
0037        while( YearString( Index) = SPACE ) loop
0038            YearString( Index) := '0';
0039            Index := Index +1;
0040        end loop;
0041
0042        -- Output to default.
0043        if ( Format = Sparse ) then
0044            if( International = UK ) then
0045                PUT( MonthDayNumString & '/' &
0046                    MonthNumString & '/' & YearString);
0047            else
0048                PUT( MonthNumString & '/' &
0049                    MonthDayNumString & '/' & YearString);
0050            end if;
0051        else -- Full format.
0052            PUT( LocalDay , WIDTH => 4);
0053            PUT( Space & MonthDayNumString & Space);
0054            PUT( LocalMonth );
0055            PUT( Space & YearString );
0056        end if;
0057    end Put;
```

The *Format Component* part of the implementation makes use of the INTEGER_IO PUT procedure option which outputs the value of the INTEGER parameter into a STRING variable supplied as the first parameter. When the INTEGER parameter is a *MonthNumber* or a *DayNumber* the output will consist of a single character if the value is less than ten, and two characters otherwise. The string into which the value is output is always two characters long. If only a single character is output, it is right justified preceded by a single space character. The optional component identified on the design as *Possibly Insert 0* will replace this space character with a '0' to satisfy the formatting specification. The final formatting component formats a *YearNumber* in a similar manner, but in this situation there may be up to three spaces before the digits and to replace all leading space characters an indefinite iteration is used.

The final component of the design, *Output Date*, is implemented as a nested **if** structure to allow for all three possible output formats. The output of the *Sparse* formats uses the formatted numeric values which have already been prepared, in the sequence appropriate for the international format requested, catenating them together with slashes. The output of the *Full* format uses the instantiated ENUMERATION_IO PUT procedures to output the month and day names.

The input of a *JulianDate* value

The input of a *JulianDate* value, using the overloaded *Get* procedure, uses a design which is in some senses an inverse of the *Put* design. However, as with the constructor and deconstructor functions, the input of a value has to ensure that the value being constructed is valid, a requirement which is not necessary for a constructor or an output procedure. A possible design for the *JulianDate Get* procedure might be

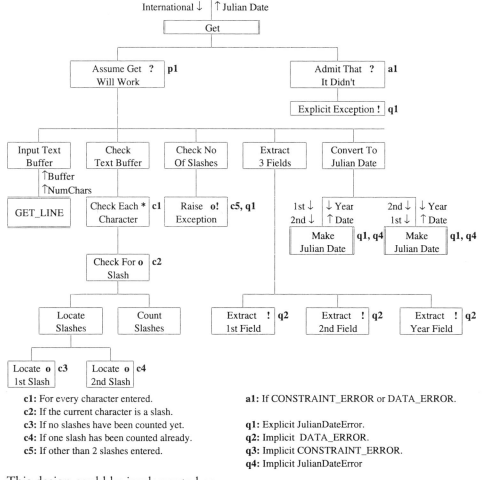

c1: For every character entered.
c2: If the current character is a slash.
c3: If no slashes have been counted yet.
c4: If one slash has been counted already.
c5: If other than 2 slashes entered.

a1: If CONSTRAINT_ERROR or DATA_ERROR.

q1: Explicit JulianDateError.
q2: Implicit DATA_ERROR.
q3: Implicit CONSTRAINT_ERROR.
q4: Implicit JulianDateError

This design could be implemented as

```
0001    procedure Get( AnyDay : out JulianDates;
0002         International : in JulianInternationalFormat := UK ) is
0003
```

275

```
0004        Buffer        : STRING := "dd/mm/yyyy";
0005        NumSlash      : NATURAL := 0;
0006        FirstSlash,
0007        SecondSlash,
0008        NumChars,
0009        Dummy         : NATURAL;
0010        FirstValue,
0011        SecondValue,
0012        YearValue     : INTEGER;
0013
0014
0015    begin -- Get
0016        GET_LINE( Buffer, NumChars );
0017
0018        -- Count and note position of the slashes.
0019        for ThisCharIndex in 1 .. NumChars loop
0020            if ( Buffer( ThisCharIndex) = SOLIDUS) then
0021                if    ( NumSlash = 0 ) then
0022                    FirstSlash := ThisCharIndex;
0023                elsif ( NumSlash = 1 ) then
0024                    SecondSlash := ThisCharIndex;
0025                end if;
0026                NumSlash := NumSlash +1;
0027            end if;
0028        end loop;
0029
0030        -- Must have exactly two slashes.
0031        if ( NumSlash /= 2 ) then
0032            raise JulianDateError;
0033        end if;
0034
0035        -- Extract the numeric fields.
0036        GET( Buffer( 1 .. (FirstSlash-1)),
0037            FirstValue, Dummy );
0038        GET( Buffer((FirstSlash+1) .. (SecondSlash-1)),
0039            SecondValue, Dummy );
0040        GET( Buffer((SecondSlash+1) .. NumChars),
0041            YearValue, Dummy );
0042
0043        if International = UK then -- UK format dd/mm/yyyy
0044            AnyDay := MakeJulianDate( MonthDayNumbers(FirstValue),
0045                                     MonthNumbers( SecondValue),
0046                                     YearNumbers( YearValue));
0047        else -- USA format mm/dd/yyyy
0048            AnyDay := MakeJulianDate( MonthDayNumbers( SecondValue),
0049                                     MonthNumbers( FirstValue),
0050                                     YearNumbers( YearValue));
0051        end if;
```

```
0052    exception
0053       when DATA_ERROR | CONSTRAINT_ERROR
0054          raise JulianDateError;
0055    end Get;
```

The entire procedure is contained within a posit/admit structure which will trap any CONSTRAINT_ERRORs or DATA_ERRORs which are raised and propagate them as *JulianDateError* exceptions. The posit part of the procedure first accepts the user's input into a buffer and then counts the number of slash characters ("/") and records the locations of the first two slashes. Should the user have entered a string which does not contain exactly two slashes the posit is abended by raising an explicit *JulianDateError*. The pre-declared term SOLIDUS on line 0020 is the name for the slash character ('/') in the package ADA.CHARACTERS.LATIN_1.

If the user has entered a string which contains two slashes, the location of the slashes is stored in the variables *FirstSlash* and *SecondSlash*. The values of these variables are used to delineate the slices of three strings within the buffer which are passed as parameters to the version of the *IntIO* GET procedure which attempts to convert the strings into integer values. If the string slices do not contain a valid integer representation an implicit DATA_ERROR exception will be raised at this point, and will be handled in the admit part of the procedure.

If three integer values are extracted from the buffer, they are passed to the *MakeJulianDate* procedure to construct a *JulianDates* value. The type conversion of the parameters may cause a CONSTRAINT_ERROR exception to be raised and the *MakeJulianDate* procedure may itself raise a *JulianDateError*, regarded by this design as the implicit raising of an exception. The sequence in which the actual parameters *FirstValue* and *SecondValue* are passed to the *MakeJulianDate* procedure's actual parameters *Day* and *Month* is decided by the value of the *International* format parameter, corresponding to a *UK* or a *USA* input format.

The *Today* function

Finally, the design and implementation of the *Today* function are considered, which relies upon facilities provided by Ada to obtain the date from the computer's hardware. These facilities are provided by a system package called ADA.CALENDAR. The CALENDAR package supplies an ADT called TIME, and a function called CLOCK which can be used to obtain the system time as a TIME value. Once a TIME value has been obtained, CALENDAR enquiry functions can be used to obtain the values for the year, month and day components. The design of the *JulianDate Today* function starts by using these subprograms and, having obtained suitable values from the CALENDAR package, uses the *MakeJulianDate* constructor function together with type conversion to obtain the date as a

JulianDate value. The design for this function might be

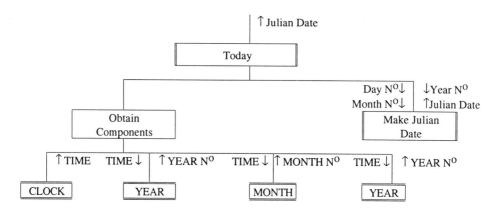

and the implementation might be

```
0001    function Today return JulianDates is
0002    -- Use the Ada CALENDAR functions to get today's date,
0003    -- and then convert it into a JulianDates value.
0004
0005        AdaNow   : ADA.CALENDAR.TIME;
0006        AdaYear  : ADA.CALENDAR.YEAR_NUMBER;
0007        AdaMonth : ADA.CALENDAR.MONTH_NUMBER;
0008        AdaDay   : ADA.CALENDAR.DAY_NUMBER;
0009        LocalDay : JulianDate;
0010
0011    begin -- Today
0012        AdaNow   := ADA.CALENDAR.CLOCK;
0013        AdaYear  := ADA.CALENDAR.YEAR( AdaNow);
0014        AdaMonth := ADA.CALENDAR.MONTH(AdaNow);
0015        AdaDay   := ADA.CALENDAR.DAY( AdaNow);
0016
0017        LocalDay := MakeJulianDate( MonthDayNumbers( AdaDay),
0018                                    MonthNumbers(    AdaMonth),
0019                                    YearNumbers(     AdaYear ));
0020        return LocalDay;
0021    end Today;
```

The inclusion of the function *Today* in the package specification was mainly intended to complete the package and to make it useful. The intricacies of the CALENDAR package should not be considered as important at this stage. If the CALENDAR facilities were not available then accessing the value of the system clock would require detailed knowledge of the actual computer's hardware and complex systems level programming. This detailed knowledge and systems programming have been included in the implementation of the CALENDAR functions by the compiler manufacturer. Because of the standardization of Ada whatever combination of compiler and computer is being used, the TIME function of the CALENDAR package can always be used to obtain the current date and time.

A client program

Only a trivial *JulianDate* client program will be presented to complete this chapter. A more complex client program will be provided in the next chapter, where the testing of software will be introduced. The *JulianDate* package will also be used in Section III of the book, where more complex data structures will be introduced. The trivial program will obtain the current date using the *Today* function and then display it using the *Put* procedure. Although it is trivial it is sufficient to indicate that parts of the package appear to be working. Improving the confidence beyond 'appear to be working' will be the subject of the next chapter. The implementation of the client program, *ShowDate*, might be

```
0001   -- Filename ShowDate.ada (k8 showdate.adb).
0002   -- Program to demonstrate that the JulianDate package
0003   -- appears to be working. Produced for Ada book Section
0004   -- II chapter 12.
0005   --
0006   -- Fintan Culwin, v0.1, Jan 1997.
0007
0008   with ADA.TEXT_IO, JulianDate;
0009   use  ADA.TEXT_IO, JulianDate;
0010
0011   procedure ShowDate is
0012
0013      TodaysDate : JulianDate := Today;
0014
0015   begin -- ShowDate
0016      PUT( "The date is ");
0017      Put( TodaysDate );
0018      NEW_LINE;
0019   end ShowDate;
```

EXERCISES

12.1 Design and implement a *JulianDate* client program which will ask users for their date of birth and then tell them how many days have elapsed since they were born.

12.2 The implementation of many of the subprograms in the package body is rather complex. To assist understanding their construction and operation produce a complete trace of the client program from Exercise 12.1.

12.3 The *JulianDate* package might be complemented by a *DayTime* package which could represent and manipulate times using a 24 hour clock format (e.g. 23:39). Design, implement and demonstrate a suitable package.

12.4 Using the *JulianDate* package from this chapter and the *DayTime* package from Exercise 12.3 construct a *DateTime* package which would combine the two data models to give a complete time representation (e.g. *1 Jan 1996 00:01*).

12.5 Reimplement the *JulianDates* package making use of development by extension. For example, the basic package may only supply arithmetic and relational operations with constructor and deconstructor actions added by a first extension and i–o facilities by a second extension. Which of the two implementations do you think is the easiest to understand and which is the easiest to reuse?

CHAPTER 13
Testing software

Having designed, implemented and demonstrated the operation of a software module, it is now necessary to test it. A demonstration that software appears to work correctly for some inputs is not the same as testing it. All that is demonstrated by putting some data through the module and obtaining the correct results is that it will perform correctly for those particular inputs; it does not give any indication that the software will perform correctly for all possible sets of inputs.

Even demonstrating that the output from the software is correct is sometimes difficult. For the programs and packages which have been developed so far the correctness of the output can be easily decided. With more complicated software it is not always as easy to determine the correct output for a given set of inputs.

To test software it is thus necessary to predict its behaviour and to determine if the outputs provided are or are not correct. This is only possible if the person performing the testing has a sufficient understanding of the specification of the software. This again illustrates the need to have a complete understanding of the specification in order to be able to develop effective software efficiently.

There are many different approaches to testing software. This chapter will introduce the most obvious testing approach, known as *black box* testing. A later chapter will introduce additional approaches such as *glass box* testing. To illustrate the approach the *JulianDate* package from the previous chapter will be tested.

Exhaustive testing

One way of ensuring that a program is totally correct is to run the program with all possible sets of inputs which it is designed to accept. If the program performs correctly for all these inputs then the program has been exhaustively tested and a complete demonstration of its correctness has been obtained.

This is rarely a practical possibility; virtually all specifications are too complex to allow exhaustive testing. A simple program specification to illustrate this might be to subtract two *JulianDate* values from each other and display the difference. There are two inputs to this program and there is a single output, the number of days between the two inputs.

The private part of the *JulianDate* package specification, given in the previous chapter, indicates that there are 401_766 different dates. To test this program exhaustively, all possible *JulianDate* values will have to be subtracted from all other possible *JulianDate* values. Thus to complete the testing every value of the first date will have to be combined with all possible values of the second date. This will involve having to test approximately 400_000 * 400_000 pairs of dates, and this will require over 160_000_000_000 test runs. Even if these inputs are set up by a computer program and the output is checked by a computer program, this is an unacceptably large number of tests to perform. If it is an impractical proposition to perform an exhaustive test on a simple program like this, it will be equally impractical to perform exhaustive testing upon more complicated software specifications.

Testing rationale

As exhaustive testing is not feasible, a module can only be demonstrated to be correct for a non-exhaustive set of test inputs. The basis of a test rationale is to assume that if the software deals with these inputs correctly, and the inputs are sufficiently representative of all possible sets of input data, then it can be assumed that the software will operate correctly for all valid sets of input data.

This does not provide a ***proof*** of the correctness of the software; the conclusion that it will operate correctly for all possible sets of input data is only an ***assumption***. The validity of the assumption depends upon the sets of input data being sufficiently representative of all possible sets of input data. Consequently a requirement of a test design is to select a set of test data which can be argued to be sufficiently representative of all possible inputs. A second requirement of the program testing processes is to test the software adequately with the minimum of effort. Testing can be a time consuming and expensive process. It is a requirement that the tester should design the minimum adequate set of test data which can be used.

The test of the software will be made with respect to its specification. If the specification is incomplete or ambiguous, or the programmer's understanding of the specification incomplete, then adequate testing will not be possible. Testing can only be used to provide evidence that the software module produced will perform according to its specification. However, if the specification is incorrect or the module is inappropriate as part of a system then the module will not fulfil its role within the system. This is a system testing consideration and will not be covered in this book.

The process of testing

Testing software is an activity which needs to be designed and planned. For a large project testing will have to be performed throughout the production of the software. Parts of the software will have to be tested as they are produced and before other parts can be constructed. These considerations will be introduced in a later section on production techniques. For small specifications, such as those which have been introduced so far, testing the complete module is an appropriate option.

The process of testing should be planned as a part of the planning of the production of the software. The production of the *test rationale* and *test plans* can, and should, take place before, or as, the design of the software is produced. Documentation of testing is an important part of the program documentation. The testing section of the documentation can be divided into three parts: the *test rationale*, the *test plan* and the *test log*.

A *test rationale* is a method of determining from the specification, or for *glass box* testing from the source code, the minimal set of test data required to test the module adequately. The *black box* considerations which will be introduced in this section are an example of a particular rationale. A rationale is complemented with *methods* which can be used with the basic rationale to implement the tests. The test rationale and method chosen will produce a list of *cases* which have to be tested.

Using the list of cases to be tested a number of *test runs* can be constructed. The test runs should ensure that each case identified by the rationale is tested at least once. The list of test runs will form the second part of the test report known as the *test plan*. The test plan should list the test runs giving each test run a test number, starting with the simplest possible test and progressing towards the most complex. The information for each test run should include the cases which will be tested, the input data to be supplied and an indication of how the output from the program can be shown to be correct. The precise layout of the test plan will depend upon the actual method of testing chosen. The necessary layouts will be explained below as the different test methods are introduced.

The third part of the test report is the *test log*. This contains details of how testing was applied to the development of the software. It should consist of a space for the test run number, the date on which this particular test run was performed and a space for a comment on the success, or otherwise, of the test.

The physical evidence of testing should be included in the report as an appendix. For simple interactive programs like the ones which have been used so far, the test evidence could consist of a printed log of the final session when all the tests were successfully passed. Most operating systems provide a facility whereby a copy of everything which happens on the screen will also be copied to a text file which can be later printed. If such a facility is not available, then it is usually possible for screen dumps to be obtained. A *screen dump* is a facility which will copy the image on the screen to the printer. A series of screen dumps can be used to illustrate the success of each test run.

For more complicated specifications, involving the use of files, the physical evidence of testing may also consist of printed copies of the contents of the files, indicating how the contents of the files have changed during the testing process. Whatever method of producing test evidence is used the test evidence should be cross referenced to the test plan in order that a verification of the testing can be shown.

Once the code has been produced the tests can be applied. Testing proceeds by applying each test from the test plan in sequence. If the module passes a test in the test plan testing can continue with the next test from the plan. If a module fails a test then the reasons why the failure occurred will have to be found and the fault corrected. This process of finding and correcting the faults in a partially working program is known as *debugging*.

For a simple module, after it has been debugged, possibly redesigned and recoded to correct a fault, testing should recommence from the first test in the test plan. It is possible that having introduced a change to remove a fault, the change has also caused it now to fail a test which it had previously passed.

Each test run, successful or unsuccessful, should be recorded in the test log. If the module passes the test, all that is required is the date on which the test was applied and the fact that the module successfully passed the test. If the module fails the test, the date should be recorded, together with an indication of how the output indicates that the test failed. After the fault has been found a note of why the module failed the test should be made on the test log. The test log will then continue starting with the first test run again.

When the last test in the test plan has been successfully completed the testing process is complete and the software can be assumed to be performing according to specification. It may be necessary to repeat the final test runs in order to produce permanent physical evidence that the module has passed all the planned tests.

In the development of a large software system by a team of programmers, it is usual and advisable for arrangements to be made for components to be tested by people other than those who produced them. It is possible for programmers to become 'blind' to the faults in their products and consequently fail to design adequate tests. As black box test planning can proceed from the specification, one group of programmers can design the tests while another group is designing and implementing the component which will be tested. This ensures that the testing is not influenced by the experience of developing the software.

These processes can be summarized in a diagram:

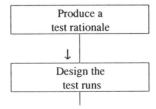

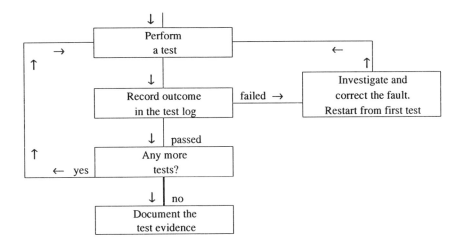

The documentation of the testing processes is required in order that the module can be maintained; if any changes are subsequently made to the module it will be necessary for all existing tests to be performed again. It may also be necessary for new test cases to be added to the test plan in order to test any maintenance changes which have been made to the module. These additional tests will then be included in the module's test plan for future maintenance.

The test log is also required for the process of producing the module to be controlled. It will indicate the amount of time which has been spent testing and the number of faults which were discovered during testing. This may give an indication of either the thoroughness of the testing process and/or the adequacy of the original design. Testing and debugging can take a large proportion of the effort involved in a development project and ideally a module should pass all the tests on the first attempt.

Although it is unrealistic to expect a module to pass all tests on the first attempt, the chances of a module passing its tests can be improved if it is properly designed and implemented. A second method of attempting to ensure that a module passes its tests on the first attempt is to design an inadequate set of tests. Although the module will pass these tests any faults in it will become apparent at a later stage, possibly when the software has been released to the users, and will then have to be corrected.

It is possible to test a module design with the test cases before the program is produced. This is done by tracing the behaviour of the module when the design is available. This is known either as a ***desk check*** or a ***walk through***; these techniques will be introduced in the chapter on production.

If testing a module reveals a fault it has to be investigated and corrected. The fault can be relatively minor, perhaps the consequence of a typing error. In this case the design of the module does not need to be altered and the error can be easily corrected. The test may also reveal a design error which is much more serious. It will involve the design of the module having to be changed and may involve extensive rewriting of the source code.

Thus the sooner in the production process a fault can be found, the easier it is to correct the fault. The production of an adequate design for a module, and the testing of the design, before expressing it as program code will reveal faults at an early stage allowing them to be easily rectified.

The *black box* rationale in practice

The *black box* rationale will be introduced by the development of a test plan for the *JulianDate* package. The plan will be applied by an automated *test harness* program. A *test harness* is a client program whose purpose is to apply and record the outcome of the tests from the test plan to the package. This automates the testing process allowing the tests to be applied, and reapplied, with the minimum of effort.

Once the *JulianDate* package has passed all the tests from the test plan it can be assumed to be correct and can be released for use in client modules which require *JulianDate* facilities. Testing of these components in turn need not be concerned with testing the *JulianDate* facilities, which can be assumed to be correct. Of course it is only an assumption that the *JulianDate* module is correct and a fault in the client may eventually be traced back to a fault in the *JulianDate* module. This would require the fault in the *JulianDate* module to be corrected before production of the client can continue, causing additional disruption and expense. This again emphasizes that thorough testing of program components, as a part of the production process, is essential to the efficient and economic construction of software. This might also suggest that the more a component is used, the more faults will be discovered and subsequently corrected. Thus a component obtained from a repository will not only reduce the development effort required for a project but also, as the component is publicly available and used, be likely to contain fewer errors.

Testing of *Put* and *Today*

Testing of the *JulianDate* package will rely upon the output of dates on the terminal; consequently the first test to be applied is a test of the output procedure *Put*. In order to output a value a date has to be obtained and the easiest date to obtain is that returned from the *Today* function. There are two initial problems here. First, a fault in the output value may be caused by a fault in the *Today* function or a fault in the *Put* procedure. There would be no simple method to determine which *JulianDate* facility is at fault. The second initial problem is that the implementation of the *Today* function makes use of the *MakeJulianDate* function. However, this is not a *black box* consideration; testing of a facility relies upon the specification and its interface and not upon its implementation. Thus testing of the *Today* function cannot be regarded as an implicit test of the *MakeJulianDate* function, which would have to be tested separately.

The first stage in producing a test plan for the *Put* procedure is the construction of a **black box diagram**. A **black box diagram** shows all inputs and outputs to and from a program module. The black box diagram for the *Put* procedure is

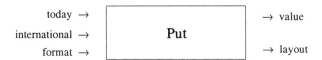

The next stage is to produce **range diagrams** for all inputs and outputs. A range diagram illustrates the range of possible values of the input or output and indicates the points in the range which will be tested. All of the inputs and outputs for this procedure have discrete ranges and the range diagrams will reflect this. The range diagrams for the *today* input and the *value* output are

```
                   system date
     today              o
                        ^

                        a

                   today's date        any other date
     value              o                   o
                        ^                   ^

                        b                   c
```

This diagram indicates that the *today* input is the system date as obtained by the *Today* function from the operating system and is not amenable to manipulation by the tester. The *value* output can be categorized as either today's date or any other date. These diagrams produce the first three **test cases**, labelled **a**, **b** and **c** on the diagrams. The remaining range diagrams for the other inputs and output are

```
                     default (UK)          UK              USA
   international          o                 o               o
                         ^                 ^               ^

                         d                 e               f
                   default (sparse)       sparse          full
   format                o                 o               o
                         ^                 ^               ^

                         g                 h               i
                       full             sparse UK       sparse USA
   layout                o                 o               o
                         ^                 ^               ^

                         j                 k               l
```

These diagrams indicate the possible values of the inputs and the possible layouts of the date output, as indicated in the specification of the procedure. Each possible value on each range diagram has been identified as a ***test case***. The test cases can now be listed to summarize them conveniently, and to add additional information:

Case	Value	Notes
a	system date	Not manipulable
b	today's date	Correct
c	not today's date	Incorrect
d	international default	Default is UK (dd/mm/yyyy)
e	international UK	UK is dd/mm/yyyy
f	international USA	USA is mm/dd/yyyy
g	format default	Default is sparse, either UK or USA
h	format sparse	Either UK or USA format
i	format full	Format is day dd mon yyyy
j	full format	Format is day dd mon yyyy
k	sparse UK	Format is dd/mm/yyyy
l	sparse USA	Format is mm/dd/yyyy

The final stage of test design is to combine the test cases into a minimum set of ***test runs***, of increasing complexity, which will be known as the ***test plan***:

Julian Date test plan 1 – test of procedures *Put* and function *Today*

Run no.	International	Format	Predicted outcome	Cases
1	–	–	dd/mm/yyyy	a, (b/c), d, g, k
2	UK	–	dd/mm/yyyy	a, (b/c), e, g, k
3	USA	–	mm/dd/yyyy	a, (b/c), f, g, l
4	–	sparse	dd/mm/yyyy	a, (b/c), d, h, k
5	UK	sparse	dd/mm/yyyy	a, (b/c), e, h, k
6	USA	sparse	mm/dd/yyyy	a, (b/c), f, h, l
7	–	full	day dd mon yyyy	a, (b/c), d, i, j
8	UK	full	day dd mon yyyy	a, (b/c), e, i, j
9	USA	full	day dd mon yyyy	a, (b/c), f, i, j

The basis of producing the test plan is to note that the *international* input can have one of three values and that the *international* input can have one of three values and that these inputs are independent of each other. This gives a total of nine possible input combinations, each of which will have to be tested. The output of each input combination is predicted at this stage from the specification of the procedure and noted in the predicted output column. Finally the cases covered in each test run are listed in order that a final check can ensure that each case is considered at least once during testing. The actual output value cannot be predicted and this is noted as (b/c) indicating that either could occur. An additional note on the test plan would indicate that case c occurring in the output would indicate a test failure, probably caused by a fault in the *Today* function.

Once a test plan is completed a test harness procedure to test the *Put* procedure can be produced:

```
0001    -- Filename JulianTest.ada (K8 juliante.adb).
0002    -- Automated test harness client program for the JulianDate ADT.
0003    -- Produced for Ada book, Section II Chapter 13.
0004    --
0005    -- Fintan Culwin, v0.1, Jan 1997.
0006
0007    with ADA.TEXT_IO, JulianDate;
0008    use  ADA.TEXT_IO, JulianDate;
0009
0010    procedure JulianTest is
0011
0012       procedure TestPutJulianDate is
0013
0014          TodaysDate : JulianDates := Today;
0015
0016    begin -- TestPutJulianDate
0017       NEW_LINE(2);
0018       PUT_LINE(" Test of Put for JulianDate");
0019       NEW_LINE(2);
0020
0021       PUT_LINE("Date displayed should be current system date,");
0022       PUT_LINE("otherwise function Today is suspect.");
0023       NEW_LINE(2);
0024       PUT("Test 1, format should be dd/mm/yyyy       ");
0025       Put( TodaysDate ); NEW_LINE;
0026       PUT("Test 2, format should be dd/mm/yyyy       ");
0027          Put( TodaysDate, International => UK ); NEW_LINE;
0028
0029          -- other tests omitted
0030
0031       PUT("Test 9, format should be day dd mon yyyy  ");
0032       Put( TodaysDate, International => USA,
0033                        Format       => Full ); NEW_LINE;
0034       NEW_LINE(2);
0035    end TestPutJulianDate;
0036
0037    begin -- JulianTest
0038       TestPutJulianDate;
0039    end JulianTest;
```

Execution of this program would automatically apply all nine tests from the test plan to the *JulianDate Put* procedure and produce an output on the terminal which could be rapidly and conveniently checked to ensure that all tests had been passed. If any of the tests had failed then this would indicate a fault in the *Put* procedure within the package, which would have to be investigated and corrected before testing could continue. Assuming that all tests were passed on the first attempt, a note could be made on the test log, and a printed copy of the output of the harness program obtained for the test evidence. If the initial test had failed, the fault corrected and the tests successfully reapplied, the test log at this stage might look like

Date	Test no.	Comments or signature
8/6/95	1	Failed tests 1.8 & 1.9, owing to non-implementation of the format override
9/6/95	1	Passed **Fintan Culwin** Evidence in test log appendix part 1

This test log is for purposes of illustration only; the implementation of the *Put* procedure in the previous chapter is known to be correct.

The production of this test plan and test harness client is derived from the package specification and does not rely upon the implementation. It can be produced by the testers as soon as the specification is finalized, while the developers are producing the package implementation. Thus the developers can hand the implementation over to the testers for testing as soon as it is produced and should the module fail the test it would be handed back to the developers for correction.

Testing the *MakeJulianDate* procedure

The black box diagram for the month number version of the *MakeJulianDate* function is

Day Number →   **Make Julian Date**   → JulianDate
Month Number →
Year Number →   → JulianDateError

and the range diagrams are

```
DayNumber        1 - - - - - - - - - - - - - - - - - 28- - -29- - -30- -31
                 ^                                    ^     ^     ^    ^
                 a                                    b     c     d    e
```

```
MonthNumber        1--2--3--4--5--6--7--8--9--10--11--12
                   ^  ^  ^  ^  ^  ^  ^  ^  ^   ^   ^   ^
                   f  g  f  h  f  h  f  f  h   f   h   h


YearNumber         1900------------------------------2999
                    ^         ^       ^    ^          ^
                    i         j       k    l          m


JulianDate         01/01/1900-----------------31/12/2999
                       ^                ^            ^
                       n                o            p


                        not raised           raised
JulianDateError            o                   o
                           ^                   ^
                           q                   r
```

The first four of these diagrams indicate that the *value* input or output is continuous and the cases are used to indicate the ranges of values which are treated differently. The first range diagram, for *DayNumber*, indicates that the full range of the value is between 1 and 31 and that all values between 1 and 28 are considered identical; however, the values 28, 29, 30 and 31 are considered different. The reasoning for the other test cases on the range diagrams can be deduced from the list of test cases:

Case	Value	Notes
a	day value 1	Smallest day value
b	day value 28	Largest value valid for any month number
c	day value 29	Valid for Feb only on leap years, otherwise valid for all other months
d	day value 30	Valid for all months other than Feb
e	day value 31	Invalid for April, June, Sept, Nov & Feb
f	months 1, 3, 5, 7, 8, 10, 11, 12	Months which have 31 days
g	months 4, 6, 9, 11	Months which have 30 days
h	month 2	February
i	year 1900	Smallest possible year value
j	year mod 4 = 0	Common leap years (1904)
k	year mod 100 = 0	Centuries are not leap years .. (2100)
l	year mon 400 = 0	.. apart from every 400 years (2000)
m	year 2999	Largest possible year value
n	01/01/0000	Smallest possible JulianDate value
o	(e.g. 30/03/1995)	Other possible JulianDate values
p	31/12/2999	Largest possible JulianDate value
q	not raised	JulianDateError not raised
r	raised	JulianDateError raised

These cases can be combined to produce a test plan:

JulianDate Test Plan 2. *MakeJulianDate*, numeric month parameter version.

Run no.	Day value	Month value	Year value	Outcome (UK format)	Cases
1	1	1	1900	01/01/1900	a, f, i, o, q
2	31	12	2999	31/12/2999	e, h, n, q, q
3	28	2	1904	28/02/1904	b, g, k, p, q
4	29	2	1904	29/02/1904	c, g, k, p, q
5	28	2	1905	28/02/1905	b, g, j, p, q
6	29	2	1905	exception	c, g, j, r
7	30	3	1995	30/03/1995	d, f, j, p, q
8	31	3	1995	exception	e, f, j, r
9	29	2	2100	exception	c, g, l, r
10	29	2	2000	29/02/2000	c, h, m, p, q

This is clearly not an exhaustive set of tests. The set of tests has to be evaluated to decide if they are sufficiently representative of all possible sets of input values to decide that if the function passes all these tests then there is a high possibility that the function will deal correctly with all possible input values. Assuming that they are, then a test harness procedure for the *MakeJulianDate* test plan can be produced and added to the test harness program:

```
0001    procedure TestMakeJulianDateNumeric is
0002
0003        TestDate : JulianDates;
0004
0005    begin -- TestMakeJulianDateNumeric
0006        NEW_LINE(2);
0007        PUT_LINE(" Test of MakeJulianDate, numeric version.");
0008        NEW_LINE(2);
0009
0010        begin -- explicit exception block
0011            PUT("Test 1, output should be 01/01/1900: ");
0012            TestDate := MakeJulianDate( 01, 01, 1900 );
0013            Put( TestDate ); NEW_LINE;
0014        exception
0015            when others =>
0016                PUT_LINE(" an exception was raised, test failed!");
0017        end; -- explicit exception block
0018
0019        -- other tests omitted
0020
0021        begin -- explicit exception block
0022            PUT("Test 6, exception should be raised: ");
0023            TestDate := MakeJulianDate( 29, 02, 1905 );
```

```
0024              PUT_LINE(" no exception raised, test failed!");
0025         exception
0026            when others =>
0027                PUT_LINE(" an exception was raised, test passed!");
0028         end; -- explicit exception block
0029
0030         -- other tests omitted
0031
0032    end TestMakeJulianDateNumeric;
```

The implementation of this test harness procedure makes use of the *MakeJulian-Date Put* procedure which has already been tested. If *Put* had not been tested and one of these tests appeared to fail by the output of an incorrect value it could not be easily decided if the fault is caused by the *MakeJulianDate* procedure making an incorrect date or by the *Put* procedure outputting a correct date incorrectly. As *Put* is assumed to be correct from the first test plan then any faults detected in this test plan can be assumed to be caused by *MakeJulianDate*.

Testing the relational operators

The testing of the relational operators relies upon the range diagram for the *JulianDate* data type and the understanding that one date is considered greater than another date if it occurred later in time. The range diagram and list of test cases are

```
JulianDate      01/01/1900----------------------31/12/2999
                      ^         ^        ^ ^ ^        ^       ^
                      a         b        c d e        f       g
```

JulianDate test case values for relational tests

Case	Value	Notes
a	First Date	Lowest possible JulianDate value
b	Second Date	Result of Tomorrow(First Date)
c	Yesterday	Result of Yesterday(Today)
d	Today	Result of the Today function
e	Tomorrow	Result of Tomorrow(Today)
f	Penultimate Date	Result of Yesterday(Last Date)
g	Last Date	Highest possible JulianDate value

This diagram indicates that the first and last values are in some way special and lists some other convenient cases to be used. The first test to consider is the equality operator, which will rely upon ensuring that any two *JulianDate* values

293

known to be equal are shown to be equal and that values known to be higher or lower are shown to be unequal. The inequality operator can be tested by reversing the Boolean outcomes of the equivalent equality tests. A failure at this stage might be caused by a failure of the *Tomorrow* or *Yesterday* functions used to obtain the different values or a failure of the relational operators themselves. A failure will indicate a fault in one of these components, but will not indicate which one.

The results of the *Today*, *Tomorrow* and *Yesterday* functions can be used to test partially the *greater than* and the *greater than or equal to* relational operators. By applying the *Tomorrow* function to the minimum *JulianDate* value and testing the resulting value to be greater than the minimum value, the testing can be completed. The test rationale would argue that if the day after the first day is greater than the first day then all succeeding days must also be greater. Similar considerations would have to be applied to the *less than* and the *less than or equal to* relational operators, which have been omitted from the following test plan:

JulianDate test plan 3 – test of relational operators

Test no.	Operation	Left	Right	Predicted outcome
1	equality	Today	Today	True
2	equality	Today	Tomorrow	False
3	equality	Today	Yesterday	False
4	inequality	Today	Today	False
5	inequality	Today	Tomorrow	True
6	inequality	Today	Yesterday	True
7	greater than	Tomorrow	Today	True
8	greater than	Today	Today	False
9	greater than	Yesterday	Today	False
10	greater than	Second date	First date	True
11	greater than or equal to	Tomorrow	Today	True
12	greater than or equal to	Today	Today	True
13	greater than or equal to	Yesterday	Today	False

Other required tests omitted

The coverage of test cases is not particularly relevant to the testing of these relational operators and has been omitted from this table. Using the test plan an automated procedure for the test harness program can be produced:

```
0001    procedure TestRelationalJulianDate is
0002
0003        TodaysDate        : constant JulianDates := Today;
0004        TomorrowsDate     : constant JulianDates
0005                                    := Tomorrow( TodaysDate);
```

```
0006        YesterdaysDate  : constant JulianDates
0007                                 := Yesterday( TodaysDate);
0008        FirstDate       : constant JulianDates :=
0009                                 MakeJulianDate( 01, 01, 1900);
0010        LastDate        : constant JulianDates :=
0011                                 MakeJulianDate( 31, 12, 2999);
0012        SecondDate      : constant JulianDates
0013                                 := Tomorrow( FirstDate);
0014        PenultimateDate : constant JulianDates
0015                                 := Yesterday( LastDate);
0016
0017    begin -- TestRelationalJulianDate
0018        NEW_LINE( 2);
0019        PUT_LINE("   Test of JulianDate relational operators ");
0020        NEW_LINE(2);
0021
0022        PUT_LINE("Test of equality operator ");
0023        PUT( "Test 1 ");
0024        if TodaysDate = TodaysDate then
0025           PUT_LINE(" passed.");
0026        else
0027           PUT_LINE(" failed!");
0028        end if;
0029
0030        -- other tests omitted
0031
0032        PUT( "Test 10 ");
0033        if SecondDate > FirstDate then
0034           PUT_LINE(" passed.");
0035        else
0036           PUT_LINE(" failed!");
0037        end if;
0038
0039        -- other tests omitted
0040
0041    end TestRelationalJulianDate;
```

Testing the arithmetic operations

The testing method in the examples above relied upon a ***parallel*** predictive method. This method relies upon the tester being able to predict the actual output of the program and this is indicated in the predicted behaviour and/or the predicted output column of the test plan. There are two possible problems with parallel methods, the first being that for a complex specification predicting the actual output may rely upon a long and complicated computation, which may itself only be feasible by the use of a computer program. The second possible problem is that the software developer and the test designer, who may be the same person, may share the same misconception regarding how the specification is to be interpreted and thus how the result is to be computed. In this case both the results produced by the program and the results predicted by the test designer will be identical, but incorrect. Consequently the program will appear to pass a test which it should have failed.

As it is not always advisable, easy or convenient to predict the actual output there are other possible methods which can be used in the design of a black box test plan. The first of these is *inverse* testing, which is suitable where a software component can be 'driven in reverse' causing it to negate the effects of 'driving it forwards'. The second is *relational* testing, where the effects of using a software component are constant over a range of inputs. Thus if the effect can be measured, it should be equal whatever value is used. Finally there is *composite* testing which involves breaking the output of a software module into its component parts and testing each component individually. These alternative testing methods will be demonstrated in the remaining tests of the *JulianDate* package.

The arithmetic operations to be tested in this section are *Tomorrow*, *Yesterday*, *DaysHence*, *DaysPast*, "+" and "–". It is possible to test these operations using a combination of relational and inverse testing.

Inverse testing can be used to test *Tomorrow* and *Yesterday* by noting that 'tomorrow's yesterday is today' and that 'yesterday's tomorrow is today'. This test by itself will not produce a high confidence that these functions are correct. But by adding combinations of equivalent operations, such as 'one day hence from yesterday is today' and that 'one day added to one day past is today' an acceptable level of confidence can be achieved. A test plan based upon these considerations might be

JulianDate test plan 4 – inverse testing of arithmetic operations

Test no.	Assertion
1	Tomorrow(Yesterday(Today)) = Today
2	DaysPast(DaysHence(Today, 1), 1) = Today
3	Tomorrow(DaysPast(Today, 1)) = Today
4	Yesterday(DaysHence(Today, 1)) = Today
5	DaysPast((Today + 1), 1) = Today
6	DaysPast((FirstDate + 401766), 401766) = FirstDate
7	DaysPast(LastDate, 401766) + 401766 = LastDate
8	Yesterday(FirstDate) = JulianDateError
9	Tomorrow(LastDate) = JulianDateError

Inverse testing in a test plan can be indicated by the use of an assertion. For example, test 3 can be read as 'if the value of applying the yesterday operator to the result of computing one day hence from today is today, then the test has been passed'. An assertion in this context is defined as 'a statement which must be shown to be true in order for the test to be passed'.

Tests 6 and 7, which compute values across the entire duration of the *JulianDate* implementation, have been included to increase confidence further. They provide the rationale that if the arithmetic operations will deal correctly with the minimum and maximum duration, then they will deal correctly with any duration. Tests 8 and 9 are strictly parallel, not inverse, tests, and have been added to complete the testing of the *Yesterday* and *Tomorrow* functions. A more complete test plan would include equivalent tests which raise exceptions for the *DaysHence*, *DaysPast* and " + " functions. Using the inverse test plan a suitable harness procedure can be produced:

```
0000    procedure TestJulianDateArithmeticInverse is
0001
0002       -- there are 401766 days between 01/01/1900 and 31/12/2999
0003       MaximumDuration : constant := 401766;
0004       TodaysDate       : constant JulianDates := Today;
0005       LastDate         : constant JulianDates :=
0006                                 MakeJulianDate( 31, 12, 2999);
0007       ResultingDate    : JulianDates;
0008
0009       -- other declarations omitted
0010
0011    begin -- TestJulianDateArithmeticInverse
0012       NEW_LINE( 2);
0013       PUT_LINE("Inverse testing of JulianDate "
0014                & " arithmetic operations.");
0015       NEW_LINE(2);
0016
0017       PUT( "Test 1 ");
0018       ResultingDate := Yesterday( Tomorrow( TodaysDate));
0019       if ResultingDate = TodaysDate then
0020          PUT_LINE(" passed.");
0021       else
0022          PUT_LINE(" failed!");
0023       end if;
0024
0025       PUT( "Test 2 ");
0026       ResultingDate := DaysPast( DaysHence( Today, 1), 1);
0027       if ResultingDate = TodaysDate then
0028          PUT_LINE(" passed.");
0029       else
0030          PUT_LINE(" failed!");
0031       end if;
0032
0033       -- other tests omitted
0034
```

```
0035        PUT( "Test 7 ");
0036        ResultingDate := DaysPast( LastDate, MaximumDuration)
0037                                        + MaximumDuration;
0038        if ResultingDate = LastDate then
0039            PUT_LINE(" passed.");
0040        else
0041            PUT_LINE(" failed!");
0042        end if;
0043    end TestJulianDateArithmeticInverse ;
```

Confidence in the arithmetic operations can be improved further by including relational tests in the test plan. One example of relational testing should suffice: the difference between the second day and the first day should be equal to the difference between the last day and the penultimate day. The relational test plan would express this as

JulianDate test plan 5 – relational testing of arithmetic operations

Test no.	Assertion
1	(SecondDate – FirstDate) = (LastDate – PenultimateDate)

The value of the dates in this test are those given in the relational operators test above, and this single test could be included in the relational tests' harness procedure *TestJulianDateArithmetic*. In this example it would also be possible, and necessary, to test the " – " operator explicitly using parallel testing. In the example in test plan 5, it could be predicted that the value of both expressions in the assertion would be 1, and this should be checked.

A more realistic relational example might be to consider a program which converts centigrade temperature values to Fahrenheit equivalents. A relational test in this circumstance would predict that the differences in Fahrenheit between any two successive integer centigrade values should be approximately equal allowing for floating point approximations as explained in Chapter 9. The test could then take any two pairs of successive centigrade values, calculate their Fahrenheit equivalents, find the two differences between the resulting pairs of values and ensure that they were acceptably equal. This could be extended to a partial parallel test by predicting that the difference should be 1.80 in both cases. The point behind relational testing is that the actual calculation, which might be cumbersome and error prone, need not be done. Only the equality of two differences in the outcomes needs to be predicted, which in some cases is much more convenient.

Testing the *SplitJulianDate* procedure

The testing of the *SplitJulianDate* procedure can be performed using composite testing. The basis of this method is to split a value into its composite parts, and then to use some technique to ensure that the values of the composite parts are correct. To implement this for a *JulianDate* value the *MakeJulianDate* procedure, which has already passed its tests, has to be used. The prediction made in this case is that the values of the components returned from *SplitJulianDate* will be equal to the values of the components which are used to make the *JulianDate* which is to be split. This can also be considered to be a joint inverse test of *MakeJulianDate* and *SplitJulianDate*, but as *MakeJulianDate* has by this stage already passed its tests, the concentration of testing is on the composite testing of *SplitJulianDate*.

JulianDate test plan 6 – composite testing of *SplitJulianDate*

Test no.	Composite value	Day value	Month value	Year value
1	19/05/1995	19	05	1995

The implementation of this plan as a harness procedure might be

```
0001    procedure TestSplitJulianDate is
0002
0003        InDay   : constant MonthDayNumbers := 19;
0004        InMonth : constant MonthNumbers    := 05;
0005        InYear  : constant YearNumbers     := 1995;
0006
0007        JulianValue : JulianDates;
0008        OutDay      : MonthDayNumbers;
0009        OutMonth    : MonthNumbers;
0010        OutYear     : YearNumbers;
0011
0012    begin -- TestSplitJulianDate
0013        NEW_LINE( 2);
0014        PUT_LINE("Testing of SplitJulianDate "
0015        NEW_LINE(2);
0016
0017        JulianValue := MakeJulianDate( InDay, InMonth, InYear);
0018        SplitJulianDate( JulianValue, OutDay, OutMonth, OutYear);
0019
0020        if ( InDay   = OutDay   ) and
0021             InMonth = OutMonth ) and
0022             InYear  = OutYear  ) then
0023            PUT_LINE("Test has been passed.");
0024        else
0025            PUT_LINE("Test has failed!");
0026        end if;
0027    end TestSplitJulianDate;
```

Testing the remaining facilities

There remain three subprograms to be tested: the two overloaded versions of *MakeJulianDate* and *SplitJulianDate*, and the input procedure *Get*. The testing of *MakeJulianDate* and *SplitJulianDate* can be accomplished using the same test rationale which has already been derived for the alternative versions of these procedures, and could be included in the same test harness procedures.

The testing of the *Get* procedure is a little more problematic. The testing method which seems the most appropriate is parallel testing, using *Put* to output the value which has been input and predicting that the value output should be equal to the value input. The contents of the test plan can be based upon the contents of the *MakeJulianDate* test plan, with additional cases included to consider the input of single digit month and day numbers and year numbers consisting of less than four digits.

All tests so far have been conducted automatically, requiring no input from the user. Testing of the *Get* procedure would seem to require the user to have to type in the values requested by the test plan, as this fragment from a possible test harness program suggests:

```
0000   begin -- exception block for test 5
0001      PUT_LINE( "Test Number 5 ");
0002      PUT( "Please input 28/2/05 ");
0003      Get( TestDate); SKIP_LINE; NEW_LINE;
0004      PUT( "Your input should be output as 28/02/0005 : ");
0005      Put( TestDate); NEW_LINE;
0006   exception
0007      when others =>
0008         SKIP_LINE; NEW_LINE;
0009         PUT_LINE("An exception was raised, " &
0010                  "the test has failed!");
0011   end; -- exception block for test 5
```

This is not particularly difficult but could become tedious, and also error prone, if the test plan had to be followed a large number of times. Many operating systems allow input which the program expects to come from the keyboard to be **redirected** to the program from a text file. If this facility is available it would allow this part of the testing to be automated. For example, with most versions of the Unix operating system, the following command line could be used:

```
%JulianGetTest < JulianGetData > JulianGetResults
```

This would execute the program called *JulianGetTest*, taking its input from the text file *JulianGetData* and sending the output of the program to a text file called *JulianGetResults*. The *JulianGetData* file could be created with a text editor and each line in the file would contain the input which the program expects. So in this example line 5 of the file for the fragment above would contain 28/2/05. The output from the program would be in the file *JulianGetResults* and could be examined to determine the results of the tests or printed for permanent physical evidence of the testing.

If this facility is available then testing of the *JulianDate Get* procedure could also be performed automatically, or if required the program *JulianGetTest* could be used interactively. As suggested above, in order to facilitate this the interactive tests should be contained in a separate program from the non-interactive testing. This allows them to be used in an interactive or non-interactive manner separate from the non-interactive tests.

Comparison of methods and techniques

The contents of this chapter provide a partial test rationale and test plan for the testing of the *JulianDate* package. It should be clear from this that the testing of a software component is every bit as complex as its production. What is perhaps not as clear from this chapter is that processes of designing tests are not as clear cut as the processes of software design and testing. A good test is one which has a high probability of detecting a fault and a good test designer is one who can produce such tests. The techniques introduced in this chapter, and additional techniques which will be introduced later, should be regarded as the starting points for the production of test plans; additional tests will be required in almost all cases.

The validity of the testing process is determined by the quality of the rationale. The rationale includes the black box diagrams, range diagrams, test cases and test plans, but should also contain a written commentary justifying why the successful passing of the tests provides sufficient confidence in the correctness of the software. A mechanistic application of the rationales is unlikely to produce sufficient confidence in the software and the imaginative application of testing principles is required in all cases.

The extent of the confidence required will depend upon the purpose of the software and upon the consequences of software failure. For a trivial program implementing a small, possibly temporary, part of a much larger software system, where the consequences of failure are fairly negligible, then the test rationale may be minimal. For a program which performs a 'mission critical' task for the organization using it the rationale must be sufficiently thorough. Some software systems are so critical, particularly those involving a risk to human life, that testing of the program should consist of a validation process which attempts to use mathematical reasoning to provide an almost absolute proof of the program's correctness. Such proofs, known as *formal methods*, are at the moment not very well known and require such extensive, and thus expensive, skills that they are considered beyond the scope of this book.

Testing is essential to ensure the quality of the software product, but in itself cannot introduce quality into the product. To ensure that the product has quality attributes, and thus has a high possibility of passing its tests with minimal effort, all stages of the production process are rigorously carried out. This implies that the developer must have a good understanding of the specification, produce a validated design and implement the design rigorously. Although testing is a time consuming and expensive process, the resulting quality assurance will pay off in the life span of the product. In the case of the *JulianDate* ADT, if the design, production and testing are carried out rigorously, then the ADT can subsequently be used by a large number of client programs with a high probability that no further development or maintenance will be required.

Of the four methods, *parallel*, *inverse*, *relational* and *composite*, the only certainty is that the parallel method can always be applied to all programs. However, if there is a choice of methods, then the methods should be considered in the sequence

$$
\begin{aligned}
\text{most favoured} &\rightarrow \text{inverse} \\
& \text{composite} \\
& \text{relational} \\
\text{least favoured} &\rightarrow \text{parallel}
\end{aligned}
$$

The consideration should include not only the applicability of the method but also the ease and possibility of performing the composite or relational comparisons which will validate the outputs. Usually a combination of the methods will be used, as illustrated above.

Finally the possibility of automated testing should always be considered, even in the case of interactive programs as described above. The advantages of automated testing are that a larger number of tests can be applied in a shorter period of time with greater accuracy. It also allows the tests to be repeated either after the program has been amended when it has failed one of the tests, or when the program has been changed during maintenance. The disadvantage of automated testing is that a computer program to test the program under test has to be designed and implemented. This program itself will require testing before its result, which is the proof of the program under test, can be relied upon. This in itself is not an overwhelming problem as the effort of testing the test harness program will be repaid in the greater number of tests and the greater ease of testing the original program and can be used to retest the module after maintenance.

Software development or software assembly

Once the ADT has been produced, tested and validated in use it can be placed in a *software repository* for use by other developers, possibly working on projects which have little or no relationship with the project which developed the ADT originally. The repository may be private to the organization which originally developed the ADT, in which case it will form part of the capital assets of the organization and may even be sold to other organizations. Alternatively there are a number of public repositories mostly accessible via the Internet where ADTs, and other software components, can be deposited and obtained free of charge.

This availability of already developed tested software components presents an opportunity and a major problem. The opportunity is to move from **software construction**, where the entire product is developed from scratch, to **software assembly**, where the majority of the product consists of previously developed components and the developer's role is to provide a small amount of 'glue' to stick them together. The major problem with this technique is knowing which components exist, where they are deposited and if they are totally suitable for their intended use. These problems cause many developers to reject the idea of software assembly and spend much of their time reinventing the wheel for every new project.

Ada, and other modular languages such as Modula and to an extent C++, make software assembly more attractive by separating a software component into a specification which expresses *what* the component does and an implementation which expresses *how* it does it. The reuse of software components should largely be concerned with what facilities the components offer and should not be unduly concerned with how they achieve their purpose. The Ada '95 standard starts to make software assembly a more attractive option by specifying a large number of packages, such as CHARACTER.LATIN_1, CALENDAR, DECIMAL, etc., which all compiler manufacturers are required to supply. One intention is that developers will become more used to using reusable components and will start to consider assembly instead of development.

EXERCISES

13.1 Obtain and apply the complete test rationale to the *JulianDates* package making a record of the outcome.

13.2 Devise and apply a complete test rationale to the *DayTime* package from Exercise 4.3. The process should result in a test rationale, test plans, test harness clients and a test log.

13.3 Devise and apply a complete test rationale to the *CashRegisters* type from Section I Chapter 5, producing deliverables as in Exercise 13.2 above.

13.4 Devise a complete test rationale to the *MultipleCashRegisters* type from Section I Chapter 8.

13.5 Compare the outcomes of Exercises 13.4 and 13.3. What parts of the test rationale for the *MultipleCashRegisters* type simply reproduce the test rationale for the *CashRegisters* type? Use this information to produce a revised rationale for the *MultipleCashRegisters* type and apply it.

CHAPTER 14

Production and debugging

The processes of producing even the small software components which have been introduced so far are so complex that it is unlikely that they could be completed in a single session. For programs which are of a more realistic length and are produced by a team of software developers it is clear that the production of the program will be a complex task. This production task will have to be planned and managed. This chapter introduces the considerations of production planning and suitable techniques by which it can be managed.

A single programmer working on a small project will have to plan the sequence of tasks which will lead to the completion of the project within some timescale. For a team of programmers working on a large project, the team leader will have to allocate independent sections of the project between the different members of the team. For a large project subteams may have to be organized and managed. Each team will have to produce a production plan for their part of the project. The team leader will have to co-ordinate the production plans of each team to ensure that the project can be completed within the time constraints and other resources available for the project.

Some parts of the production plan, particularly those which are concerned with the correction of faults which are discovered during testing, are very difficult to allow for. The most effective way by which these problems can be minimized is to use production techniques which minimize the number of errors which are present and which localize the effects of those errors. However, recognizing that even the most scrupulous design and implementation techniques are unlikely to remove all possible errors, there is a need for techniques for the detection and correction of known errors. This process is known as *debugging*.

Production planning

A production plan lists the stages which are required for the production of a particular program, identifies dependencies between the stages, schedules the stages and allocates resources to each stage. Each stage in the plan should be small enough for an accurate estimate to be made of the amount of time it will take to complete. An estimate of the amount of time required for the complete project can then be obtained by adding together the time estimated for each of the individual stages.

It is usually essential that certain parts of the project are completed before subsequent parts can be implemented. These relationships are known as ***dependencies*** and can be used to help organize the sequence of stages and group sets of tasks together. Completion of a group of tasks will mark a significant point in the production of the program; such a point is known as a ***milestone***.

Where a program is being implemented by a team of programmers, the team leader has a responsibility to try to make sure that the parts produced by each of the teams are completed on time. As the stages are being completed the programmers involved will maintain a log of the actual time taken to complete each task. This log will be available to the team leader and can be used to determine the progress towards the production milestones, and thus towards production of the independent program parts, and thus towards completion of the whole project.

At any stage during the production process it is possible, but unlikely, that all parts are on or ahead of schedule. It is also possible, and less unlikely, that all parts are behind schedule and are behind by a consistent factor. In this case the overall production of the project is delayed but as all parts are equally delayed the implementation considerations will not be affected, beyond extending the completion date.

What is most likely is that some parts of the process are ahead of schedule, some parts are on schedule and some parts are behind schedule. In this situation it may be possible for the team leader to reallocate resources from the parts which are ahead of schedule to the parts which are behind schedule. If this is possible the overall production of the project can be better managed, and possibly completed on time. This form of project control is only possible if an overall production plan has been constructed at the outset of the project and if the developers maintain open, accurate and honest records of progress.

For a novice developer the idea of a production plan for a programming project can seem impossible. During the early stages in learning to develop software it is very difficult to estimate in advance how long to allocate to each task, or even to decide what are appropriate tasks and milestones. For skilled programmers such an estimation is easier to make but is always made with the consideration that unforeseen difficulties may arise, leading to an extension of the actual time taken on a particular stage.

Learning how to produce accurate production plans is an essential part of learning how to develop software and, like all other aspects of learning to develop software, is best achieved by practice. For every programming project which is more complex than a simple exercise, a production plan should be made at the outset and reviewed after completion of the project. Although the initial plans are likely to be wildly inaccurate, over a period of time and practice the skill of producing accurate plans should develop.

Most novice programmers are in a comparable position to a programming team leader in that they will be working to a deadline, a date upon which the programming project has to be complete, and are also working with limited resources, the amount of time which they can spend upon the project. The novice programmer is in the position of the team leader, having to assess the progress being made against the amount of time and resources already used and the amount of time and resources remaining.

If the production plan contains implementation considerations and the project starts to run behind schedule, then it may be possible for a restricted but working version of the program to be produced within the limits of the project. Such a submission by a novice programmer is likely to be better received than an incomplete and non-working program which would probably have been produced if a production plan had not been used.

An initial production plan

In order to illustrate a production plan a programming project based upon the following outline program specification will be considered:

The program is concerned with weekly diaries. A weekly diary consists of five daily diaries each of which has six appointment slots. An appointment slot either is blank if the appointment has not been booked, or contains the name and time of the appointment which has been booked.

The main menu will offer the user the following options:

```
                   Weekly Diary

    A. Load diary from file.
    B. Make an appointment.
    C. Cancel an appointment.
    D. Print diary.
    E. Save diary to file.
    F. Exit program.
```

The first stage in the construction of a production plan is to identify the resources which are available. It is assumed that this project has a four week deadline and about 25 hours per week are available, giving a total of about 100 hours for completion. The *JulianDate* package from the previous chapter and the *DayTime* package from the previous chapter's exercises are also identified as resources which will be used in the production of this program. All other parts of the program will be developed from scratch.

This production plan is given only as an example; an actual production plan for a real project would differ significantly in its stages and allocations. In particular this version of the production plan contains no dependency considerations which determine which parts of the project have to be complete before other parts of the project can commence. The basic plan is to divide the project into four major milestones:

Milestone	Activities
1	Project planning and implementation of the main menu
2	Design and test plans for the menu options
3	Implementation, testing and debugging of the menu options
4	Collation of documentation and project review

A production plan for the stages to the first milestone of the project might be

Stage	Activity	Allocation	Actual
1-1	Clarify specification	2 (2)	
1-2	Produce production plan	4 (6)	
1-3	Design user interface	3 (9)	
1-4	Document user interface	2 (11)	
1-5	Main menu design	2 (13)	
1-6	Main menu test plan	2 (15)	
	Total to first milestone	15 (16)	

Each of the six stages in this part of the plan has been given an allocation of hours; the total number of hours to completion of that stage is also shown in brackets. The final line shows that an allocation of 15 hours has been made to complete all these stages. One extra hour has been added, as an overrun, to allow for any delays in reaching this milestone.

This first part of the production plan includes within itself an allocation of time for the production of the plan, and also for the inclusion of any dependency considerations which would be required for planning the succeeding stages of production.

There is space on the production plan for the actual number of hours taken to complete the stage to be recorded. When the milestone is reached the number of hours actually taken can be compared with the number of hours allocated, and progress towards completion of the project can be determined.

The user interfaces for both the high level menu and the options controlled by the menu are designed and documented completely at this stage. These describe how the program will interact with the user, and together with the specification will be required for the design and implementation of the program. They define *what* the program will look like to the user; they do not attempt to define *how* it will be implemented by the developer.

The production of the high level menu design and the high level test plan are also completed in this stage and have been given a total allocation of four hours. This may seem a very tight allocation but a standard design for this component, and a test plan for it, are readily available and will be given shortly. Some modification of the design and/or the test plan may be required, but the basis of the design is complete, correct, available, and suitable for reuse. As a verified design is available there is little point in reinventing it by developing an alternative design from scratch. The use of standard designs for standard activities will allow a program to be completed faster, easier and with fewer errors. The reuse of designs will, however, only be successful if the programmer has an adequate understanding of the program components which are being included.

The plan for production as far as the second milestone might be as follows:

Stage	Activity	Allocation	Actual
2-1	Design option A	3 (19)	
2-2	Test plan for option A	2 (21)	
2-3	Design option B	3 (24)	
2-4	Test plan for option B	2 (26)	
2-5	Design option C	3 (29)	
2-6	Test plan for option C	2 (31)	
2-7	Design option D	3 (34)	
2-8	Test plan for option D	2 (36)	
2-9	Design option E	3 (39)	
2-10	Test plan for option E	2 (41)	
2-11	Design review	4 (45)	
	Total to second milestone	45 (50)	

This shows the second milestone in the project. When this stage is reached the design of the entire project has been completed and it is estimated that about half the time available to the project will be required to reach this point. It has been assumed that each of the five modules is of equal complexity, and that each will take a total of five hours to design and to produce a test plan. An overrun of five hours has been allowed for in the production plan for this milestone.

In a real project it is possible that operations concerned with some or all of the four options are standard and can be incorporated into the designs and the test plans directly. This would allow them to be completed faster, thus reducing the time allocation. Other options may be more complex and require more time to be allocated. If this could be determined at the planning stage from the specification, and from the project designer's experience, it would allow a more accurate production plan to be constructed.

This milestone also includes a design review, stage 2-11. The quality of the product and the completion of the remaining production stages are dependent upon the quality of the design. The allocation of time to the preceding design stages (1-5, 2-1, 2-3, 2-5, 2-7 and 2-9) included some time for the designs of the individual components to be reviewed. At this stage, the design in its entirety should be checked, preferably by the use of a *peer reviewed walk through*.

A *peer reviewed walk through* is where the designer of a software module presents the design of the module to a group of other developers. The presentation consists of the design documentation and a commentary upon the reasons why this design was decided upon and which other possible designs were rejected. Once the overall design of the module has been presented, assuming that there are no significant objections, the effectiveness of the design is demonstrated by tracing its operation with test data from the test plan.

The intention of the *walk through* is to validate the design before it is committed to production. There are several intentions for the use of *peer reviews*. First, they allow developers, other than those who developed the design, to examine it critically for possible faults. It is possible for a developer to work too closely with a design and become blind to its faults; a peer review allows other developers to agree its design.

The second reason for a peer review is to distribute responsibility for all parts of the design through the development team. Following a peer review, responsibility for the correctness of the design lies with the group of reviewers, not with the individual designer. One consequence of this is to promote an *egoless programming* ethos within the team. An individual member of the team feeling he or she either has that sole responsibility for, or even owns, a part of a project can cause problems. The developer may resist the idea that a fault is localized in that part of the program and may become offended when the fault is proved. Alternatively the programmer may have to be redeployed on to another project, or may become unavailable through illness, resignation, jury service or dismissal, etc. Without a distributed responsibility and some familiarity with the design distributed through the team, such non-availability of a team member may cause problems.

Other advantages of peer reviews are to disseminate good design practice through the team, to ensure that a consistent design style is used and to ensure that similar parts of the program are implemented with similar designs. The final advantage is the attempt to ensure that all components of the system will operate correctly when brought together. As the peer reviewers are simultaneously designing the other parts of the project it is hoped that any incompatibilities would be spotted at the design reviews.

The plan for the third milestone would be

Stage	Activity	Allocation	Actual
3-1	Implement high level	3 (53)	
3-2	Test high level	4 (57)	
3-3	Implement option A	3 (60)	

3-4	Test option A	4 (64)
3-5	Implement option B	3 (67)
3-6	Test option B	4 (71)
3-7	Implement option C	3 (74)
3-8	Test option C	4 (78)
3-9	Implement option D	3 (81)
3-10	Test option E	4 (85)
3-11	Implement option F	3 (88)
3-12	Test option F	4 (92)
	Total to third milestone	92 (97)

This milestone implements and tests first the high level control and then each of the four options in turn. The allowance of time for testing in this section is deliberately generous; it is unlikely that three hours of testing would be required to test any of the options. The allowance recognizes that testing may fail and that debugging of the option will be required. The overrun allowance of five hours allocated to the milestone also recognizes this possibility.

These stages are probably the most difficult to control: the testing, debugging, redesigning and reimplementation cycle can, and frequently does, consume vast amounts of time. The best way of controlling the amount of time which could be spent at this stage is to ensure that the preceding stages concerned with design are adequately completed. A well designed component is more likely to complete testing with fewer problems, causing production to be easier and allowing more control over the production processes. However, in recognition of the fact that debugging can rarely be avoided completely, an example of debugging a faulty program component will be given later in this chapter.

The final milestone could be

Stage	Activity	Allocation	Actual
4-1	Collate documentation	5 (102)	
4-2	Project review	3 (105)	
	Total to complete project	105 (107)	

This final milestone completes the project. Stage 4-1 is concerned with the collation of the project documentation; this is not the same as the production of the documentation. Each of the stages in the project would have produced a part of the documentation, which has now to be collected together and indexed. The final stage is an allowance of time to review the project and evaluate the experience.

An estimate of between 105 and 107 hours is required for a project which was originally allocated 100 hours. It would have been more comfortable if the estimated production time including overheads had required less than 100 hours, allowing it to be completed according to the plan within the initial allocation. A requirement of 107 hours is close enough to the limit of 100 hours to be acceptable, as it is possible that not all the overheads will be required.

It should be remembered that at this stage this is only a plan; the actual hours taken to complete each stage will most probably differ from those allocated within the plan. There is little point in reviewing the plan to change an estimated allocation of 107 hours to an estimated allocation of 100. When the project has been completed it is likely that the actual number of hours taken will differ by more than seven hours from the planned allocation.

If the production plan had indicated that the estimated allocation of time would overrun the actual allowance by a significant amount, then a review of the plan would have been appropriate. If the review does not reduce the estimated requirement significantly, then additional resources would be needed for completion of the project. If this is not possible then the resources available could be used to complete only a part of the specification. In a real programming project, this would indicate to the project manager that additional resources should be allocated to ensure that this part of the project could be completed on time.

The production plan becomes a production log when the actual times taken for each stage are filled in as the project is completed. An analysis of the production log after completion of the project will provide feedback concerning the accuracy of the original estimates. This feedback can be used to plan the allocation of hours to future projects more accurately and can be used to measure any increase in efficiency from one project to the next.

A production plan with dependency considerations

A production plan with dependency considerations for the specification above would include consideration of the sequence in which the menu options are best implemented. This is achieved by establishing dependencies between the options. In the example specification above it is not possible to load a file from disk until a file exists on the disk which can be loaded. This implies that option E (save) will have to be completed before option A (load) can be started. In order to test that option E is working correctly an inverse test using option A would be most appropriate; likewise in order to test option A an inverse test involving option E would be most appropriate.

The saving and loading of a blank file would not be a convincing or useful test. Consequently option B (book) would be required to be implemented, before options E and A could be tested. This would allow the saving and loading of non-empty data files which would be a better indication that the save and load options were working correctly.

In order to establish that option B was working correctly option D (print) would be required. A parallel test method would predict that if an appointment was booked for a certain day at a certain time in a certain name, then the print of the diary would confirm it. Following this the remaining option D (cancel) could be implemented and subsequently tested in the same manner.

This gives the dependency considerations as follows:

> high level control
> option B (make appointment)
> option D (print diary)
> option E (save diary)
> option A (load diary)
> option C (cancel appointment)

A dependency plan is concerned with implementing the functions of a program in a manner which allows incremental development and testing to be performed. For this program it would make sense to redesign the production plan to separate menu options B and D from menu options E and A and from option C. The revised production plan will include a larger number of milestones:

1. High level design and desk testing, user interface and production plans.

2. Design of options B and D.

3. Design of options E and A.

4. Design of options C.

5. Implementation and testing of high level control.

6. Implementation and testing of B and D.

7. Implementation and testing of E and A.

8. Implementation and testing of C.

9. Documentation and review.

The incorporation of dependency considerations within the production plan will not extend the total allocation of time for the project. It will, however, produce more milestones in the project which will allow a greater degree of project control.

Although options E and A have been separated from options B and D and from option C, the design of the complete program is finalized before the implementation of any parts of it is started. It would not be correct to plan the design, and then implement options B and D, before the design of options E and A was produced. The reason for this is that it is possible that the design of options E and A will reveal considerations which have an effect upon the design of options B and D. If options B and D have already been implemented then they may have to be reimplemented, which is a more time consuming task than redesigning them before implementation.

The completion of milestone 5 when the high level menu was implemented and shown to be working correctly, using program *stubs* for all options, produces a working but very restricted version of the program. A stub is an empty subprogram, which allows a program to be compiled and linked, but does nothing more than announce that it has been called when it is called. Examples of the use of stubs will be given later in this chapter.

The completion of milestone 6 when options B and D have been implemented and tested produces a less restricted, working version of the program. At this stage it would be possible to make appointments and to print a diary. The data entered could not, however, be saved and loaded between sessions, nor can appointments be cancelled. The completion of milestone 8 when options E, A and C have been implemented and tested completes the implementation of the program, and produces a complete version of the program.

If the production schedule became untenable during the production of options B and D, the production of the remaining options could be reviewed. The project could be completed on time but restricted to the implementation of milestone 6. The design of the missing modules and a test plan for them would have been produced, and could be included in the report. Although much of the planned functionality is missing, the process has resulted in a product which can be partly used. Without a production or implementation plan it would have been much more difficult to control the process and it is unlikely that a useful working subset of the functions of the program could have been produced.

An implementation plan for a more complex specification would itself be more complex. It may involve a first implementation of only a part of each option. In the example above option B – make appointment – may be initially implemented to book an appointment without checking to ensure that an appointment is not already booked. This restricted implementation could then be used to allow implementation and testing of the remaining options. The implementation plan would allocate time for the further development of the option, involving checking that an appointment was not already booked, at a later stage.

If the production plan was not adhered to and the project ran behind schedule, the preliminary version of option B would be available. If the production plan had been held to then it would have been replaced by the fully working version. Thus a restricted but still useful version of the specification would be available on time, which is a better product than a non-working partial version.

These partial versions of the program have other uses. If a program is required urgently then the partial version could be released for use, while the final version was being produced. If a program is not required urgently then the partial version could be demonstrated to the sponsor, allowing confirmation from the sponsor that the implementation is congruent to what was expected.

Where production of a project was divided between teams of programmers, the production of an initial version of part of the project a team is working on can be planned. This restricted version could then be used by the other teams to test their components and would at a later stage be replaced by the fully working version. This incremental approach to implementation of programs is only possible if all the options have been considered at the design stage. The enhancement of the options should not necessitate a redesign of an option; it should only be the implementation of an already designed option.

Tracing and debugging

The previous chapter showed how testing can be used to reveal faults in a program, and the previous part of this chapter showed how production planning can make some allowance for the detection and correction of such faults. When a program fails a test it indicates that a fault is present; it does not necessarily give any indication of what caused the fault. Diagnosing and locating the cause of a known fault, and its subsequent correction, is known as *debugging*, and the main technique for finding faults is *tracing*. The action of tracing a program is similar to walking through a design, or walking through a program listing. The simplest method of tracing a program is to desk-trace it.

Desk-tracing a program, or a section of a program, involves following the path of execution through the program listing by hand, while recording the values of various program objects. At some stage in execution, the path of control will diverge from the expected path of control, and/or the value of some object will diverge from its expected state. This will reveal the fault in the program.

The fault can only be recognized if the expected path of control and the expected values of objects can be predicted by the person tracing the program. This again emphasizes the need to understand the specification and to produce and understand a detailed design, before coding a program. Without this knowledge the expected behaviour of a program cannot be predicted and thus the divergent behaviour of a program fault cannot be recognized.

A faulty program to demonstrate debugging

To demonstrate the processes of debugging and testing, the specification from the first part of this chapter will be implemented as far as milestone 2. At this milestone the main menu is fully implemented, dispatching to menu options present only as stubs. In order for debugging to be demonstrated a minor fault will be introduced into the implementation. Although the nature of this fault is so straightforward that it could, and should, be detected and corrected at the listing review stage, the testing, test failure and debugging will be demonstrated. If these processes are understood in the context of a simple specification such as this, they will be available for use on faults which are not as obvious.

The detailed user interface for this program option might be:

```
                      Weekly Diary

          A. Load diary from file.
          B. Make an appointment.
          C. Cancel an appointment.
          D. Print diary.
          E. Save diary to file.
          F. Exit program.

          Please enter choice z
          Sorry you must enter 'A' to 'F'
          (or 'a' to 'f') only. Please try again.
          Please enter choice a

          This is option A

          Press <enter> to continue.

                      Weekly Diary

          A. Load diary from file.
          B. Make an appointment.
          C. Cancel an appointment.
          D. Print diary.
          E. Save diary to file.
          F. Exit program.

          Please enter choice
   {Any number of valid or invalid choices here.}
          Please enter choice f
          Have a nice day!
   {Program terminates.}
```

This detailed implicit specification is in part similar to the specifications in the previous section for obtaining a yes/no input from the user. As the problem is similar the solution may also be similar and the design from Section I can be used as a basis of this design. This may sound like cheating but having produced and verified a design for one program, there is no reason why a part of that design cannot be included in or adapted for another program.

This idea of taking verified designs from one program and including them in another program can be taken a stage further. There are standard designs available for common program operations. These designs can be found in introductory programming texts and in manuals on algorithms. Several standard algorithms will be introduced later in this book. If a design for a program component has been produced, documented and described in a text there is no reason for programmers not to use that design within programs which are being developed. This is only likely to be successful if the programmer understands the design and implementation of the component to be included or reused. If the programmer does not have such an understanding then the component may be used inappropriately.

The design for this specification, based upon a design given previously, might be

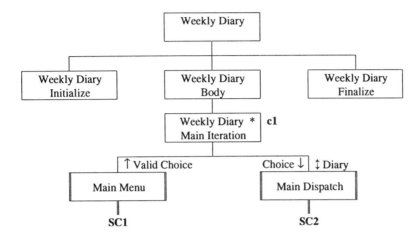

c1: While exit not chosen by the user.

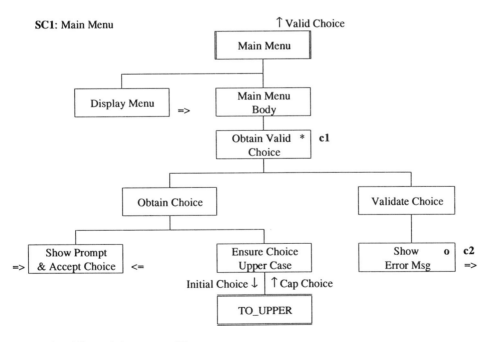

c1: While user's input not valid.
c2: If users input not valid.

SC2 Main Dispatch   Choice ↓ | ↕ Diary

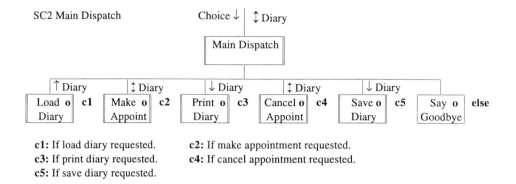

c1: If load diary requested.   **c2:** If make appointment requested.
c3: If print diary requested.   **c4:** If cancel appointment requested.
c5: If save diary requested.

The implementation of this design follows. This version contains a deliberate error which will be used to illustrate the processes of debugging. The program header might be

```
0001    -- Filename WeeklyDiary.ada (k8 weeklydi.adb).
0002    -- The faulty program from SII C14, used for explaining
0003    -- debugging operations.
0004    --
0005    -- Fintan Culwin, v0.1, Jan 1996.
0006
0007    with ADA.TEXT_IO, ADA.CHARACTERS.HANDLING;
0008    use  ADA.TEXT_IO, ADA.CHARACTERS.HANDLING;
0009
0010    procedure WeeklyDiary is
0011
0012       package IntegerIO is new ADA.TEXT_IO.INTEGER_IO( INTEGER);
0013       use IntegerIO;
0014       MinimumMenuChoice : constant CHARACTER := 'A';
0015       MaximumMenuChoice : constant CHARACTER := 'F';
0016       ExitChoice        : constant CHARACTER := 'F';
0017            -- Initial value must be an invalid menu choice.
0018       UsersChoice : CHARACTER := CHARACTER'PRED
                                              ( MinimumMenuChoice);
0019
0020       type Diaries is -- details omitted
0021
0022       TheDiary : Diaries;
0023
```

The techniques for the declaration of the data type *Diaries* will be introduced in the next section. All that is required to understand and follow this example is that such a data type can be declared and that the operations to manipulate a variable object of type *Diaries* will be implemented within the subprograms when they are developed from the stubs which will be presented here. The main part of the program procedure might be as follows:

```
0126   begin -- WeeklyDiary
0127      WeeklyDiaryInitialize( TheDiary);
0128      while UsersChoice /= ExitChoice loop
0129         MainMenu( UsersChoice);
0130         MainDispatch( UsersChoice, TheDiary);
0131      end loop;
0132      WeeklyDiaryFinalize( TheDiary);
0133   end WeeklyDiary;
```

The two components from the design, *WeeklyDiaryInitialize* and *Weekly-DiaryFinalize*, do not require any explicit implementation in this fragment. The initialization requires the value of *UsersChoice* to be set so that the loop test will fail on the first evaluation causing the loop to be entered. This requirement has been taken care of in the variable's declaration. There are no required finalization actions so this component does not require implementation; it has been left on the design in order to facilitate any maintenance changes. The main part of the program procedure implements the main iteration of the program calling the two procedures *MainMenu* and *MainDispatch* as indicated on the design. The implementation of the procedure *MainMenu* might be

```
0024   procedure MainMenu( TheChoice : out CHARACTER) is
0025
0026      LocalChoice : CHARACTER;
0027
0028      procedure DisplayMenu is
0029
0030      begin -- DisplayMenu
0031         NEW_LINE;
0032         PUT_LINE("      Weekly Diary ");
0033         NEW_LINE;
0034         PUT_LINE("A. Load diary from file.");
0035         PUT_LINE("B. Make an appointment.");
0036         PUT_LINE("C. Cancel an appointment.");
0037         PUT_LINE("D. Print diary.");
0038         PUT_LINE("E. Save diary to file.");
0039         PUT_LINE("F. Exit program.");
0040      end DisplayMenu;
0041
0042   begin -- MainMenu
0043      DisplayMenu;
```

```
0044        while LocalChoice <= MinimumMenuChoice and
0045             LocalChoice >= MaximumMenuChoice loop
0046          PUT("Please enter choice ");
0047          GET( LocalChoice); SKIP_LINE;
0048          LocalChoice := TO_UPPER( LocalChoice);
0049          if LocalChoice <= MinimumMenuChoice or
0050             LocalChoice >= MaximumMenuChoice then
0051             PUT_LINE("Sorry you must enter '"
0052                        & MinimumMenuChoice
0053                        & "' to '"
0054                        & MaximumMenuChoice & "'");
0055             PUT_LINE( "(or '" & TO_LOWER( MinimumMenuChoice)
0056                        & "' to '" & TO_LOWER
0057                                       ( MaximumMenuChoice)
0058                        & "' only). Please try again.");
0058          end if;
0059        end loop;
0060        TheChoice := LocalChoice;
0061     end MainMenu;
0062
```

A decision has been made to implement the component *DisplayMenu* as a subprocedure of the procedure *MainMenu* in order to simplify the procedure *MainMenu*. As this is a simple implementation decision, there is no need for the design to be revised. The body of *MainMenu* is implemented directly from the design and uses the facilities for the manipulation of characters and strings, introduced in Chapter 10, to format the error message. This has been done with regard to maintainability; should the number of menu options change in a future release of the program, a change to the value of the constant *MaximumMenu-Choice* will automatically reconfigure both the loop control and the issuing and format of the error message.

The implementation of the procedure *MainDispatch* might be

```
0063   procedure MainDispatch( ChoiceMade : in      CHARACTER;
0064                            TheDiary   : in out Diaries) is
0065
0066      procedure LoadDiary( TheDiary : out Diaries) is
0067      begin -- LoadDiary
0068         PUT_LINE("This is the load diary option.");
0069         PUT("Press <enter> to continue ");
0070         SKIP_LINE;
0071      end LoadDiary;
0072
0073      procedure MakeAppointment( TheDiary : in out Diaries) is
0074      begin -- MakeAppointment
0075         PUT_LINE("This is the make an appointment option.");
```

```
0076              PUT("Press <enter> to continue ");
0077              SKIP_LINE;
0078        end MakeAppointment;
0079
0080        procedure CancelAppointment
                                  ( TheDiary : in out Diaries) is
0081        begin -- CancelAppointment
0082              PUT_LINE("This is the cancel an appointment option.");
0083              PUT("Press <enter> to continue ");
0084              SKIP_LINE;
0085        end CancelAppointment;
0086
0087        procedure PrintDiary( TheDiary : in Diaries) is
0088        begin -- PrintDiary
0089              PUT_LINE("This is the print diary option.");
0090              PUT("Press <enter> to continue ");
0091              SKIP_LINE;
0092        end PrintDiary;
0093
0094        procedure SaveDiary( TheDiary : in Diaries) is
0095        begin -- SaveDiary
0096              PUT_LINE("This is the save diary option.");
0097              PUT("Press <enter> to continue ");
0098              SKIP_LINE;
0099        end SaveDiary;
0100
0101        procedure SayGoodbye is
0102        begin -- SayGoodbye
0103              PUT_LINE("Have a nice day!.");
0104              SKIP_LINE;
0105        end SayGoodbye;
0106
0107    begin -- MainDispatch
0108        case ChoiceMade is
0109           when 'A' => LoadDiary( TheDiary);
0110           when 'B' => MakeAppointment( TheDiary);
0111           when 'C' => CancelAppointment( TheDiary);
0112           when 'D' => PrintDiary( TheDiary);
0113           when 'E' => SaveDiary( TheDiary);
0114           when 'F' => SayGoodbye;
0115           when others => null;
0116        end case;
0117    end MainDispatch;
0118
```

With a program as complex as this containing a number of procedures with various levels of nesting, it is useful to produce a **subprogram map** to illustrate the overall structure of the program. A subprogram map for this implementation might be

```
procedure WeeklyDiary is

    procedure MainMenu() is

        procedure DisplayMenu is
        begin -- DisplayMenu
        end DisplayMenu;

    begin -- MainMenu
        DisplayMenu;
    end MainMenu;


    procedure MainDispatch() is

        procedure LoadDiary() is
        begin -- LoadDiary
        end LoadDiary;

        procedure MakeAppointment() is
        begin -- LoadDiary
        end LoadDiary;

        procedure CancelAppointment() is
        begin -- CancelAppointment
        end CancelAppointment;

        procedure PrintDiary () is
        begin -- PrintDiary
        end PrintDiary;
```

```
        procedure SaveDiary() is
        begin -- SaveDiary
        end SaveDiary;


        procedure SayGoodbye is
        begin -- SayGoodbye
        end SayGoodbye;


begin -- MainDispatch
    LoadDiary ();
    MakeAppointment ();
    CancelAppointment ();
    PrintDiary ();
    SaveDiary ();
    SayGoodbye;
end MainDispatch;

begin -- WeeklyDiary
    MainMenu ();
    MainDispatch ();
end WeeklyDiary;
```

A subprogram map shows which subprograms are nested within other subprograms, and from this which areas of the program the subprogram can be seen from and thus can be called from. In the example above, the *WeeklyDiary* procedure can see the *MainDispatch* procedure and thus can call it, but it cannot see any of the procedures contained within *MainDispatch* and thus cannot call them. The procedure map is also used to indicate where in the program subprograms are called. As with other maps, for example a town street map, a subprogram map shows the relationship between the various components at a high level of detail and does not attempt to illustrate all aspects of the program.

The overall design of this *menu dispatch* system separates the actions of obtaining a validated response from the user from the action of dispatching to a subprogram on the value of the response. A common design error would be to include the dispatching operation within the menu component:

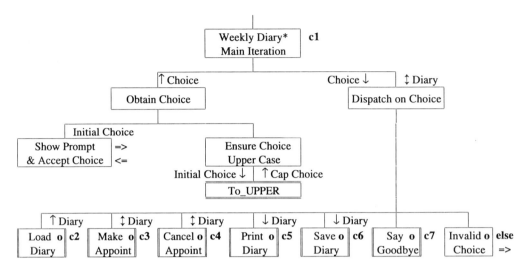

c1: While exit not chosen.   **c2:** If load diary requested.
c3: If make appointment requested.   **c4:** If cancel appointment requested.
c5: If print diary requested.   **c6:** If save diary requested.
c7: If exit program requested.

This is considered an error for two reasons. First, the implemented design has clearly divided the dispatch operation from the menu operation, operations which the alternative design confuses. Second, a consequence of this design fault would be revealed if, during maintenance, the program had to be given an alternative interface style, possibly involving a pointer operated pull-down menu. In the implemented design the menu component would have to be replaced and the dispatch operation could be left unchanged. In the alternative version there is not such a clear distinction between the menu and dispatch operations, which would cause undue problems for the reimplementation.

The *Weekly Diary* test plan

A black box test rationale for the entire program, including those parts which are present only as stubs in this version, would commence with a test plan to ensure that the menu dispatch system was operating correctly. The full test rationale would continue with a number of other test plans which would test the options offered by the menu. The black box diagram and partitioned range diagrams for testing the menu dispatch system might be:

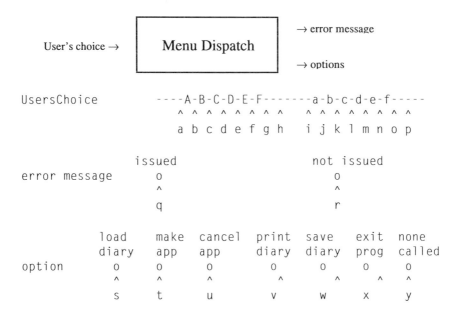

The list of test cases from these diagrams is

Case	Value	Notes
a	User's Choice '@'	First value less than 'A'
b	User's Choice 'A'	Load diary option, upper case
c	User's Choice 'B'	Make appointment option, upper case
d	User's Choice 'C'	Cancel appointment option, upper case
e	User's Choice 'D'	Print diary option, upper case
f	User's Choice 'E'	Save diary option, upper case
g	User's Choice 'F'	Exit program option, upper case
h	User's Choice 'G'	First value greater than 'F'
i	User's Choice " ' "	First value less than 'a'
j	User's Choice 'a'	Load diary option, lower case
k	User's Choice 'b'	Make appointment option, lower case
l	User's Choice 'c'	Cancel appointment option, lower case
m	User's Choice 'd'	Print diary option, lower case
n	User's Choice 'e'	Save diary option, lower case
o	User's Choice 'f'	Exit program option, lower case
p	User's Choice 'g'	First value greater than 'f'
q	Error message	Error message issued
r	No error message	No error message issued
s	Option Load Diary	Load diary message shown
t	Option Make app	Make appointment message shown
u	Option cancel app	Cancel appointment message shown

v	Option Print Diary	Print diary option message shown
w	Option Save Diary	Save diary option message shown
x	Exit program	Have a nice day message shown, and program terminates
y	No option	No option message shown

A test plan derived from these test cases might be

Weekly Diary test plan 1 – menu dispatch

Test run no.	User's choice	Program action	Cases
1	'@'	Error message	a, q, y
	'A'	Load diary message	b, r, s
	'B'	Make appointment message	c, r, t
	'C'	Cancel appointment message	d, r, u
	'D'	Print diary message	e, r, v
	'E'	Save diary message	f, r, w
	'G'	Error message	h, q, y
	'F'	Goodbye message and exit	g, r, x
2	' '	Error message	i, q, y
	'a'	Load diary message	j, r, s
	'b'	Make appointment message	k, r, t
	'c'	Cancel appointment message	l, r, u
	'd'	Print diary message	m, r, v
	'e'	Save diary message	n, r, w
	'g'	Error message	p, q, y
	'f'	Goodbye message and exit	o, r, x

When this test plan was applied to the program it failed at the start of the first test. The observed behaviour of the program was

```
                Weekly Diary

A. Load diary from file.
B. Make an appointment.
C. Cancel an appointment.
D. Print diary.
E. Save diary to file.
F. Exit program.


                Weekly Diary

A. Load diary from file.
B. Make an appointment.
C. Cancel an appointment.
```

```
D. Print diary.
E. Save diary to file.
F. Exit program.
```

{program execution continues indefinitely}

The behaviour of the program is clearly incorrect without having to check the behaviour against that predicted in the test plan or required by the specification.

Debugging the program

Debugging should take place in the knowledge of a known fault, or faults, and should commence with a theory of what the fault might be. Where there are multiple faults then only one fault should be debugged at a time. If more than one fault is debugged at a time then the attention of the programmer will be diverted between the two faults and it is likely that neither will be effectively fixed.

There is only one place in the program where the procedure *DisplayMenu* is called from: within the procedure *MainMenu*, outside the scope of the input loop. The theory to be investigated in this debugging session is that the loop in *MainMenu* is iterating indefinitely and that the menu is being redisplayed when the procedure *DisplayMenu* is called as a part of the re-execution of *MainMenu*. To investigate this theory only the procedure *MainMenu* needs to be traced, using the following trace table:

Line	LocalChoice	TheChoice	Notes
0042	?	?	Initial values

Each line of the table indicates the location in the program, the values of various variables and a column for any appropriate notes. In this table there are two objects to be considered, the parameter variable *TheChoice* and the local variable *LocalChoice*. The first line to be traced is line 0042 where the executable part of the procedure starts with a **begin;** this is commented in the notes column as showing the initial values of the variables. At this stage the variables have no known value; the parameter variable is *out only* and as such it is assumed to have no known value on entry to the procedure and can only be given a value within the procedure. The no known value is indicated by a question mark (?) in the value columns, and should not be confused with a CHARACTER variable which has the value of the question mark character ('?'). The trace table continues by indicating in turn each line which is executed, updating the values which the variables will have when the line has been executed:

0043   ?   ?   execution of DisplayMenu assumed

The next line to be executed is line 0043 which calls the procedure *DisplayMenu*. The execution of this procedure is assumed rather than traced as it is known only to output the menu and does not change the value of any variables. Execution will continue with

---

0044/45   ?   ?   **while** loop test cannot be evaluated!

This indicates a fault. The **while** loop test on lines 0044 and 0045 relies upon the value of the variable *LocalChoice*. The trace table indicates that this variable does not have a value and thus the loop control test cannot be evaluated. When the program is executed, as opposed to traced, Ada will be able to evaluate the loop control test using whatever value happens to be present in the variable *Local-Choice*. For some values the loop control test will evaluate false causing the loop to iterate, on others it will evaluate true causing the loop to terminate without executing the loop body.

This style of fault, where the behaviour changes from run to run, is one of the most difficult to detect and debug. In this example, if the loop control is true then the program appears to be working correctly at this stage; if it is false a faulty behaviour is shown. If the random values of *LocalChoice* cause the loop control to evaluate true 99% of the time and false 1% of the time, then it is likely that the fault would not be discovered during formal testing and would be discovered by the user after the program has been released. However, it would be very difficult to replicate the fault once it had shown itself, giving the situation where the user had reported a fault but is unable to replicate the fault for further investigation. A fault such as this is known as an ***intermittent fault*** and is very difficult to detect, which is a prerequisite for correction. Such faults can only be avoided by the techniques of rigorous design and production processes.

This particular fault can be corrected by assigning the variable *LocalChoice* an appropriate initial value when it is declared on line 0026:

```
0026    LocalChoice : CHARACTER := CHARACTER'PRED( MinimumMenuChoice);
```

The character value which precedes the *MinimumMenuChoice* cannot be an acceptable menu choice value and should ensure that the loop iterates at least once on all occasions. However, when this change was made, the program rebuilt and testing restarted, exactly the same fault manifested itself. With the change assumed the start of the trace table would be

Line	LocalChoice	TheChoice	Notes
0042	'@'	?	Initial values
0043	'@'	?	Execution of *DisplayMenu* assumed
0044–45	'@'	?	while loop test false, loop terminates

The loop control expression can be evaluated by substituting the actual values of the variables and constants, giving

```
while '@' <= 'A' and '@' >= 'F' loop
```

The left term '@' < 'A' is true, the right term '@' > 'F' is false and the combined expression true **and** false is false. In order for the program to behave correctly this test must evaluate true and this can be ensured by replacing the **and** operator with an **or** operator. When this change was made, the program rebuilt and testing restarted, the following behaviour was produced:

```
            Weekly Diary

A. Load diary from file.
B. Make an appointment.
C. Cancel an appointment.
D. Print diary.
E. Save diary to file.
F. Exit program.
Please enter choice @
Sorry you must enter 'A' to 'F'
(or 'a' to 'f') only. Please try again.
Please enter choice A
Sorry you must enter 'A' to 'F'
(or 'a' to 'f') only. Please try again.

This is option A.
Press <enter> to continue.

            Weekly Diary

A. Load diary from file.
B. Make an appointment.
C. Cancel an appointment.
D. Print diary.
```

```
E. Save diary to file.
F. Exit program.

{program execution continues}
```

The first test is now successful, informing the user that the input is unacceptable and requesting another input. The second value from the test plan 'A', which should be accepted, is also reported to the user as an error although option A was correctly called. A trace of the program's execution up to the point where the fault was detected would be

Line	LocalChoice	TheChoice	Notes
0042	'@'	?	Initial values
0043	'@'	?	Execution of *DisplayMenu* assumed
0044–45	'@'	?	While loop test true, loop iterates
0046	'@'	?	Input prompt displayed
0047	'@'	?	User's choice input
0048	'@'	?	TO_UPPER does not change value
0049	'@'	?	If test evaluates true
0051–57	'@'	?	Error message output
0044–45	'@'	?	**while** loop test true, loop iterates
0046	'@'	?	Input prompt displayed
0047	'A'	?	User's choice input
0048	'A'	?	TO_UPPER does not change value
0049	'A'	?	**if** test evaluates True

The first time line 0047 is executed the user inputs the value '@' which replaces the existing value '@' in *LocalChoice*. The second time line 0047 is executed, the user inputs the value 'A' clearly replacing the existing value. The fault appears on line 0049, where the **if** test should evaluate false causing the error message not to be displayed. The evaluation of this expression can be shown as

```
if 'A' <= 'A' or 'A' >= 'F' then
```

The left term is true and the right term is false, and the combined expression is true **or** false which is true. The fault is the use of the <= and >= operators instead of the < and > operators

```
if 'A' < 'A' or 'A' > 'F' then
```

This would evaluate false, causing the message not to be displayed. If the correction was made, the program rebuilt and retested, test 2 would still fail. The behaviour would now be that although no error message was output, option A was not called, the menu was not redisplayed and the user was asked again to input a choice. Tracing of the program would indicate that the loop control expression on lines 0044 and 0045 would require a similar amendment.

Debugging

The faults which are present in this version of the program are so simple that they should have been spotted and corrected during a structured walk through of the code as it is produced. However, the technique of tracing a program's execution can be used for more subtle faults which are more difficult to detect by a walk through.

The fault in this program is one of the commonest, a failure to design and implement a Boolean expression correctly, and reinforces the advice given in the previous section to construct, and desk-test, all such expressions with extreme care. Although the fault was simple, tracing the program's execution to discover it consumed a large amount of time and effort. The person performing the debugging requires two things. First this person will have to have a detailed knowledge of the program specification and design in order to be able to determine where the behaviour of the program being debugged deviates from the expected behaviour. The other thing is a detailed knowledge of the programming language so that the person can determine the effects of the program statements and determine from the code the next statement which would be executed.

The best debugging method is known as *anti-bugging*, that is attempting to design and implement programs correctly in the first instance. As has already been noted it is unlikely that this is ever achieved but on the basis that small programs are easier to debug than large ones, incremental development of software, using a production plan and subprogram stubs, will make debugging easier. The version of the program above can be considered as the high level menu driver of a more complex program. The successful completion of the test plan achieves the second milestone where the menu dispatch system is known to be working correctly. Program production can continue by replacing subprogram stubs with functional versions of the subprograms according to the production plan. The further development should have no effect upon the menu/dispatch system, but the tests of the menu dispatch system should be repeated when the complete program has been assembled to ensure that this is the case. This process of retesting a component *in situ* after it has been tested in isolation is known as *integration testing*.

Debugging a program can be made more effective by using debugging techniques very thoughtfully. A debugging trace on a program can generate a vast amount of information, most of which is irrelevant to the fault being sought. When a program fails a test, the person debugging the program should be able to produce a theory which would explain the fault. The theory can then be confirmed or refuted by using the program design, the program listing and careful reasoning. Only if this approach is impossible should a debugging trace be attempted.

The theory will indicate which parts of the program and which data objects to concentrate upon. This will restrict the amount of information produced from the trace. If the theory is confirmed by either of these methods then the fault has been detected. If the theory is not confirmed then the debugging process has removed one theory from consideration, and the process can continue with a different theory.

Debugging can also be assisted by using an ***interactive debugger***, sometimes known as a ***program animator***. This allows the program to be executed from the terminal under the control of the animator. At any point in the program, execution can be interrupted and the contents of any variables examined or changed. Execution can then continue either one line at a time or until a defined point in the program has been reached. Using an interactive debugger avoids one of the problems with hand tracing. An assumption made about the behaviour of the program by the person performing the debugging may be incorrect, and the faulty behaviour of the program may be missed owing to this incorrect assumption. This problem is most likely if the person debugging the program is also the designer and/or the implementor of the program. An interactive debugger will not make the incorrect assumption but will display exactly what has happened during the program's execution.

The only problem with using a program animator to assist in the debugging of a program is its ease of use. The debugging process as explained above is most effective if it is performed thoughtfully and a debugging trace is only used as a last resort, to confirm or refute a theory which attempts to explain the program's aberrant behaviour. Many novice programmers use an animator without first attempting to think through the possible causes of the fault. The effect of this is that they are not able to restrict the debugger to a small part of the program and not always able to recognize the point at which the program's behaviour becomes aberrant. The most effective debugging tool is the intelligence of the person performing the debugging and this should be fully deployed before an animator is used.

EXERCISES

14.1 For your next development project very carefully record the amount of time taken in a production log. When the project is finished examine the production log to determine where you under- or overestimated the amount of time required.

14.2 Repeat Exercise 14.1 for all future development projects until your estimates become sufficiently accurate. Then determine which parts of the process are taking the most time and devise strategies to reduce the amount of time taken in those stages. Use future logs to determine if the strategy is effective.

CHAPTER 15
Software documentation

The products of a software project are the program itself and the project documentation which supports it. Of these two products the documentation is the more important. If, for any reason, the program is lost, it should be possible to recreate it with minimal effort from the documentation. If the program documentation were to be lost it would be much more difficult to recreate it from the program listing. The first part of this chapter will introduce the reasons for, and the contents of, the documentation which should accompany a software product.

Program documentation can be divided into two parts, the *technical documentation* and the *user documentation*. The technical documentation is intended for use by engineers who have the responsibility for maintaining the software during its life cycle. The user documentation attempts to provide instructions on how to operate the software and its major component is a description of the *user interface*. The user interface is the only part of a program which the user will directly experience and thus is the basis for the the user's evaluation of the program. The design of the user interface should be made with regard to usability, and there are a number of guidelines which can be employed in an attempt to ensure that an acceptable interface is produced.

This chapter will only consider the technical documentation; user interface design and user documentation have already been considered in Chapter 11.

The technical documentation

One purpose of technical documentation is to provide a description of the production processes, for the designs and design decisions made and details of the testing of the initial version of the software. Although this initial use of technical documentation, to validate the initial production process, is sufficiently useful in itself, the major use of technical documentation is to support the software during the maintenance phase of its life cycle.

During the life span of a program maintenance changes will be required. These maintenance changes will have to be designed and the starting point for their design will be the original designs which should be included within the original project documentation. After the changes have been designed and implemented, testing of the changes and retesting of the unchanged components will be required. The original test rationale, the test plans and the test logs would be available from the original program documentation. Having these available will allow the maintenance changes to be tested with minimal difficulty.

Attempting to make maintenance changes without the documentation, using only the program source code, is a very difficult task. In order to design the changes the original design will have to be recreated from the listing; this *reverse engineering* of the design is difficult, time consuming and error prone. In a commercial environment the time taken will be an unnecessary expense which can be obviated by having available the original program documentation.

When maintenance changes have been made, the program documentation will have to be updated to reflect these changes. At any stage in the lifetime of a program the program documentation should reflect the state of the program at that point in time. Thus not only will the program itself change over time but the documentation associated with it will also change.

Novice developers do not always understand the importance of documentation and neglect the task. If the program being produced by the novice is being produced following the guidelines in this book, most of the documentation will be generated as the stages in producing the program are completed. For example, the program design stages will produce program and data structure charts. The test planning stages will produce test rationales and test plans. The production of the documentation at the end of the project will then become a matter of collating all the documents which have already been used in the production of the program.

Where programs are attempted without planning or design, the production of program documentation is a more difficult task. It is usually omitted until the end of the project and then becomes a description of the program, rather than documents which directly support the project. The difference between the two types of documentation is readily apparent to a reader. It is also a chore to produce the documentation after the project has 'finished' and is usually skimped by novice developers leading to poor quality documentation.

The technical documentation can be divided into six parts: the introduction, the production log, the data design, the program design, the program testing and the program evaluation. In addition a number of appendices will be required.

Technical documentation, introduction

The introduction to the project documentation should include a general introduction giving the name of the project, the name of the programmer or programming team which produced the program, the name of the sponsor of the program, the date when the program was produced, the machine(s) the program is intended to run on and the language (or languages) the project is written in.

The introduction should also contain a brief summary of the function of the software component. Where the component is a part of the system, reference should be made to the system documentation which can be used to establish the context of this program.

The agreed specification and any interpretations, assumptions, extensions or deletions from the specification will be included in the introductory documentation. It would also be useful for a copy of the user guide to be included in this introduction.

Finally the introduction should include reference to any non-standard reusable components, for example ADTs, which will be used in the implementation of this artefact. This should include any components which have been initially produced as a part of this project, but which have been identified as having a high potential for reuse and have been developed as such.

Technical documentation, production plans

The production plan, together with any implementation considerations, should be included at this point in the technical documentation. The production plan should be accompanied by a production log, completed at the end of the production process, which records the actual as opposed to planned progress. The reasons why parts of the production process took significantly longer, or shorter, than was planned for should be included as a commentary.

The production plan, and log, may not seem initially to be useful for maintenance purposes. However, a program module which was difficult to produce may well turn out to be a module which requires an undue amount of maintenance. The production log, like the rest of the technical documentation, is a live document which needs to be updated throughout the life cycle of the component. Thus the amount of resources which have been devoted to a particular part of the program can be audited throughout the life cycle. This may be useful if, for example, a particular module is shown to be continually troublesome requiring almost continuous maintenance; the cumulative production log may provide evidence that it might be cost effective to redesign and reimplement the module from scratch.

Technical documentation, data design

The data design for simple programs will be straightforward, consisting of a list of the major data objects which are used by the program. The data tables which have been used as a design tool and produced during the design phase can be used to form this part of the documentation.

A complex program operating on simple data will have a large number of data objects, but only the most important of these need to be described in the documentation. In most cases there is little point in describing the name, type and use of minor variables such as a loop parameter. There is a requirement to describe the name, type and use of major variables or constants which represent important objects within the program, such as the user's choice from the main menu.

When a program becomes more complex it will contain a large number of subprograms and in such circumstances it would be appropriate to integrate the majority of this aspect of data design within the program design section which follows. Each subprogram design in the design section would be accompanied by a data table indicating the names, types, initial values and use of the formal parameters and any local variables which are required. The overall data table in this section of the documentation would then consist only of the major data objects which have a scope of all, or a large part of, the entire program.

The complete data tables will also be implicit in the program listings. The types and names of data objects used by a program are explicitly included in the listing as they are declared. The intended usage of the objects declared should either be obvious from the name chosen for them, or be made obvious by a comment accompanying the declaration.

When the structure of the data which is being processed by a program is more complex, requiring the developer to implement new types or subtypes, the design of these data structures and the reasons for selecting between alternate possible designs should be included in the data design section of the technical documentation. This data design section precedes the program design section as the nature of the actions to be performed is determined by the nature of the objects which the actions will be applied to.

Where a program makes use of external files the types and format of the files should also be described in this section. The use of external files will be introduced in the next section.

Technical documentation, program design

The major part of the program design documentation will be the program structure charts. A set of structure charts describing the program should be included and they should be cross referenced to each other, allowing the complete design to be followed. Each chart should be small comprising of at most ten or 12 component boxes and should attempt to describe a single logical facility of the program, or a complete subprogram.

It should not be assumed that the structure chart by itself is always a complete intelligible description of the design. It may be necessary for comments to be included on a chart to explain why a particular design was chosen from alternative possible designs, or to explain the structure of the design if it is not clear from the structure chart. In most cases these comments should be minimal and straightforward. If they are becoming complex then a commentary on the design of the program may have to be provided separately. This commentary would give an overview of the program design and explain the design decisions which had been taken to choose between alternative designs.

Most of this documentation would have been produced as the program was designed in the design stage. Only the commentary may have to be produced at the final stage after the program has been produced.

Technical documentation, program testing

The program testing section of the documentation should contain the test rationales and the test plans only; the test logs would be included in the report as an appendix. These documents would have been produced when the testing was designed in the design phase of the project and when the program was tested following construction. Details of the format of the testing documentation for black box testing can be found in the Chapter 13.

Details of any test files used to test the program, or test harnesses used for automatic testing of the program, should also be included. These files should be preserved when the project is completed as they will be required by maintenance programmers when the program is maintained. They can be used when retesting the program to ensure that the changes made to the program have not affected any existing parts of the program. The testing of an updated version of a program to ensure that it complies, where appropriate, with the previous version of the program is known as *regression testing*, and is an essential part of program maintenance.

The test harnesses and test files will require updating to allow them to be used effectively to test the maintained version of the program. These updated test files will have to be stored, together with the original test files, so that they can be used when further maintenance is required. This implies that effective techniques for the storage, identification and retrieval of a large number of test harness and test data files will have to be employed.

Testing programs, program evaluation

The evaluation section of a project report is the only part of the project documentation which is appropriate for a novice developer, but not for a professional project. It provides an opportunity for novice programmers to include in their project report a critical appraisal of the work they have done. The appraisal should include comments on both the production process and the product itself.

The evaluation provides an opportunity to reflect upon the lessons learned from the experience of producing the program. If the project has not been completed, the adequacy, or otherwise, of the production plan can be analyzed and the parts of the plan which were overambitious can be identified.

If any parts of the program which have been implemented do not perform according to specification, the shortcomings can be commented on. Likewise if any late changes had to be made to the specification, or any limitations of the program were discovered in testing, a report on them can be presented. The processes of software development can only be effectively learned by the actual experience of developing software. The evaluation provides an opportunity for novice developers to reflect upon the experiences which they have had and the mistakes which they have made. An honest and thorough evaluation will reduce the chances that future projects will repeat the same mistakes which were made in the current project.

Technical documentation, the program listing

The program listing will be included in the report as a major appendix. A well produced program listing is to an extent self-documenting as the correct use of comments, layout and sensibly named identifiers in the listing will make it readable.

The listing should commence with the opening comments identifying what, why, who, when and where. For a program listing which is in the maintenance phase the opening comments should also include a summary of the maintenance history, each entry indicating which maintenance changes were made, why they were made, who made them and when they were made. The ***version number*** should precede these comments to allow earlier or later versions of the component to be easily identified. Pre-release versions should be numbered less than 1.0, with version 1.0 being used for the initial release version. The version number should be incremented in some way for each subsequent release. A very minor modification may only require a small increment, for example 1.01. A more substantive modification, or an accumulation of minor modifications, may require a more substantive increment, for example 1.1. A version 2.0 revision would indicate either a substantive revision, incorporating significant new facilities, or an accumulation of less substantive modifications.

Comments should be included within the program listing to delineate explicitly the scope of any control structures used, to explain the usage of all variables declared and at the start of every procedure and function to explain the purpose of the procedure and function (possibly cross referenced to the program structure charts). A comment should also be included in the program listing where the meaning of an action performed by the program statements may be unclear to someone reading the program.

The program listing will be produced from the implementation phase of the project. The comments should be included within the listing as it is produced. If this is done they can then be used to assist the production of the source code. They should not be added to the program listing after it has been completed in order to satisfy style requirements.

The program listing should be presented in a readable format. It is possible to load the final program listing into a word processor in order to include page headers, footers and page numbers. An attempt should be made to make sure that page breaks occur at convenient points in the listing. This can be accomplished by including a **pragma** direction in the listing. A **pragma** (pragmatic) is a direction to the compiler to take some optional action. The direction 'pragma PAGE;' can appear anywhere in a program listing. It has no effect upon the program's compilation or execution but will ensure that a new page is started at that point when a program listing is produced. If the compiler can produce a paginated listing file then this should be used for the listing included in the report. The pages should be separated (burst) and bound in sequence to allow them to be easily read.

Technical documentation, other appendices

Other appendices which should be included in the project report are the test logs which should be cross referenced to the test plans, and should have evidence highlighted and possibly annotated that indicates that the test has been passed. A separate appendix should list all the files which have been used in the production of the program or used in the testing of the program. A further appendix should identify the location of any non-standard reusable components which were used in the production of the program. This should include any components which were initially produced for this particular project, but which have been identified as having a high potential for reuse.

Technical documentation for reusable components

The discussion of the technical documentation above has concentrated upon those software components which are used for the production of a single program. The processes of producing a program for a particular specification may identify an ADT, or other type of component, which has a high potential for reuse in other projects. The technical documentation for these components should be presented separately from the technical documentation of the program produced.

Although the initial production of a reusable software component is itself a complex task, the major problem with successful reuse has been shown to be the location and identification of suitable components. The production of technical documentation for a reusable component should commence from this perspective. In order for a component to be reused it will have to be placed into a software repository. An established software repository will have some cataloguing system to which a component being placed in the repository will have to adhere. A catalogue entry for the *JulianDateADT* developed in Chapter 12 might be

Component Name	*JulianDateADT*
Component Type	*ADT*
Keywords	*dates, time, calendar, Julian dates*
Brief Description	*A Julian Date ADT, offering relational, pseudo-arithmetic and internationalized input–output facilities.*
Location	*http://www.scism.sbu.ac.uk/Law*
Maintainer	*Fintan Culwin (fintan@sbu.ac.uk)*
Other Comments	*Full design and design rationale contained in associated book.*

The catalogue entry will be maintained in an electronic catalogue allowing the repository to be searched according to the required fields. Perhaps the most useful of these might be the keywords field: once a requirement had been identified from a program specification to record and manipulate dates a keyword search of the repository would locate the above record, possibly amongst other components which have something to do with dates. The contact information in the record, possibly indicating the component's location in the repository being searched, would allow more complete details of the component to be retrieved for further consideration. If no repository is currently in use then the catalogue entry above could be used as the basis of establishing a repository.

For an Ada reusable component the next most important and convenient document would be the component's package specification file. This should indicate clearly in the opening comments more details of what facilities the component offers to clients. The header should also clearly indicate which other standard or non-standard components the package which is being specified is dependent upon. Each subprogram, data type, subtype, exception, or other object which is exported from the package should be clearly commented with a description of what this offers to a client. There should be little or no indication of how the package implements the facilities which it offers.

The remaining parts of the documentation of a reusable component are comparable with those required for a program and consist of an introduction, production and maintenance logs, a data design, program designs consisting of an object diagram for the entire package and program structure charts for each public or private subprogram of the package. Finally, details of the test regime which was used, and which can be reused to validate the implementation, can and should be included, together with the source code for the package body.

EXERCISES

15.1 If you have not already discovered it, investigate your Ada environment to find out how to produce paginated program listings with line numbers.

15.2 Investigate your environment to find out if there is a technique by which JSP or object diagrams can be produced automatically from your source code listings. If you have such a facility learn how to use it and determine if it assists in the documentation of your development projects.

15.3 Obtain a copy of a catalogue from one of the repositories listed in Appendix A. Search the catalogue to locate a component for the manipulation of dates. Compare the facilities of the component from the repository with those of the *JulianDate* package from Chapter 12.

15.4 Produce a catalogue entry for the *MultipleCashRegisters* and *Maximum-RoomMonitors* types from Section I, using the format of the catalogue entries from Exercise 15.3.

CHAPTER 16
Standard packages

The Ada '95 language is defined in a document called the Ada '95 *language reference manual* (LRM). The LRM not only defines the meaning and use of all the reserved words which define the language, but also defines the contents of various packages. Many of these packages, such as ADA.TEXT_IO, have to be provided in order for the compiler to be described as Ada '95. There are other packages, such as ADA.NUMERICS.GENERIC_COMPLEX_TYPES, which are optional but in practice all compiler manufacturers will provide all the packages described in the LRM. These packages are known as **standard packages**. The LRM is freely available in electronic format via the Internet, and details of its location can be found in Appendix A.

Some compiler manufacturers will supply other packages in addition to those described in the LRM. For example, the VAX Ada compiler supplies a package called INDEXED_IO which provides facilities for the use of indexed files, which is not required or described in the LRM. Indexed and other methods of file organization, and use, will be described in Section III.

In addition to packages provided by compiler manufacturers, packages for specific purposes can be purchased, or obtained free of charge from software repositories. Examples of packages in these categories might include packages to provide Ada programs with facilities to create graphical user interfaces (GUIs). There are several commercial packages which will allow Ada programs to create GUIs for Microsoft Windows and several free packages which will allow Ada programs to create GUIs for X Windows. Details of several Ada software repositories available on the Internet are given in Appendix A.

The use of pre-supplied packages allows an Ada program to be developed faster and thus cheaper. Rather than having to develop the Ada program code which will implement the required functionality, a package supplying the functionality can simply be used. Additionally it can be expected that a commercial package, and supposed that a free package, will have had any bugs within them either removed or documented, improving the quality of the developed program. This is producing applications by **software assembly**, that is using pre-supplied components, rather than **software construction**, that is building the code from scratch.

There is one potential problem with using packages which are not described as required in the LRM. A program relying upon the facilities supplied by a non-standard package will not be portable between environments unless an identical package is available in the environment which the program is being ported to.

This chapter will introduce the contents of a selection of the Ada '95 standard packages. A knowledge of the contents of the standard packages is essential for novice Ada developers, as it may prevent them from attempting to implement facilities which are already provided and encourages software assembly rather than software construction.

The standard packages

There are three libraries of packages described in the LRM: ADA, INTERFACES and SYSTEM. The packages in INTERFACES provide facilities to interface Ada programs with other programming languages such as C, COBOL or Fortran. The packages in SYSTEM provide facilities for system programming. The contents of these two libraries are considered to be inappropriate for novice programmers and will not be described further in this book. The library ADA contains a large number of packages, many of which are also considered to be too specialized or complex for an introductory book. The packages within ADA which have already been described in previous chapters, or which will be described in this chapter, or which will be described in succeeding chapters, are as follows:

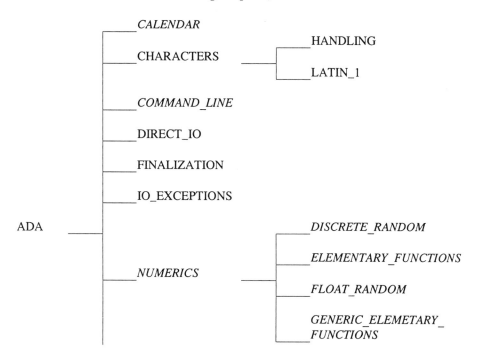

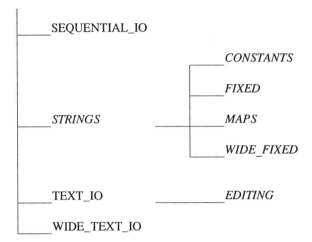

The packages shown in italics will be described in this chapter. The diagram illustrates the parent/child relationship of packages within the library. Thus the package HANDLING is a child package of CHARACTERS which is itself a child package of ADA.

The packages INTEGER_IO, FLOAT_IO and ENUMERATION_IO are not shown on this diagram as they are not child packages of TEXT_IO, but are contained within it. These packages, and some of the packages which will be described in this chapter, are examples of *generic packages* which have to be *instantiated* before instances of them can be used. Before describing the selection of standard packages the meaning and mechanism of instantiation will be described.

Instantiation and generic packages

Instantiations of the ADA.TEXT_IO generic packages have been used extensively since the earliest chapters of this book. An instantiation of ADA.-TEXT_IO.INTEGER_IO was first given in Section I Chapter 2 as

```
package IntegerIo is new ADA.TEXT_IO.INTEGER_IO( INTEGER);
use IntegerIo;
```

These statements were described at the time as being required in order for the program being developed to have access to the facilities for the input and output of INTEGER values. The discussion of Ada numeric types in Chapter 9 indicated that it was possible for new Ada integer types to be declared:

```
type NewIntegerType is INTEGER range MinNewValue ..
                                      MaxNewValue;
```

The new type could not share the already instantiated *IntegerIO* package as the two types were not assignment compatible. A separate instantiation is required for the input and output of *NewIntegerType* values:

```
package NewIntegerIO is new ADA.TEXT_IO.INTEGER_IO
                                    ( NewIntegerType);
use NewIntegerIO;
```

The generic package ADA.TEXT_IO.INTEGER_IO, which as a generic package cannot be brought into direct **use**, can be thought of as a *factory package*, capable of manufacturing usable packages tailored for a particular integer type. The generic package is capable of creating *instances* of itself, and thus the name of this process is *instantiation*. The specification of this package within ADA.TEXT_IO is as follows:

```
generic
    type NUM is range <>;
package INTEGER_IO is
-- Declaration of DEFAULT_WIDTH and DEFAULT_BASE omitted.
-- The declaration of the types FIELD and NUMBER_BASE are
-- in ADA.TEXT_IO.

    procedure GET( ITEM  : out NUM;
                   WIDTH : in  FIELD);

    procedure PUT( ITEM  : in NUM;
                   WIDTH : in FIELD := DEFAULT_WIDTH;
                   BASE  : in NUMBER_BASE := DEFAULT_BASE );

    -- Other subprogram declarations omitted.

end INTEGER_IO;
```

The reserved word **generic** indicates that this is the declaration of a generic unit, in this case a generic package. Between the terms **generic** and **package** is the declaration of the *generic parameters*. In this example there is a single generic parameter with the formal name NUM; the remaining part of its declaration indicates that it is an INTEGER type parameter. A fuller explanation of the specification of the types of generic parameters will be given later in the book, when the design and construction of generic units will be described.

Within the specification of the generic package, and within the corresponding body, variables of type NUM, constants of type NUM, functions of type NUM and parameters of type NUM can be declared and operated upon as if they were objects of an INTEGER type.

The process of instantiation can be thought of as the systematic replacement of the name of the *generic formal parameter* with the name of the *generic actual parameter* throughout the package specification and body, and the subsequent compilation of the text produced. In the second example above the instantiation of the package *NewIntIO* can be thought of as the compilation of a package which has the following specification:

```
            Supposed specification of the instantiated package
                                               NewIntegerIO.

        package NewIntegerIO is

            procedure GET( ITEM  : out NewInteger;
                           WIDTH : in FIELD);

            procedure PUT( ITEM  : in NewInteger;
                           WIDTH : in FIELD := DEFAULT_WIDTH;
                           BASE  : in NUMBER_BASE := DEFAULT_BASE);

        end NewIntegerIO;
```

The instantiation of the package *IntegerIO* can be thought of as the compilation of an equivalent package with all references to NUM replaced by INTEGER. The rules for the association of *generic actual parameters* and *generic formal parameters* are comparable with the rules for the association of subprogram parameters. In the example above only an integer type, including the pre-declared type INTEGER, is compatible with the formal parameter NUM. Any attempt to use an inappropriate parameter will be detected as a compilation error.

The package ADA.CALENDAR

The required package CALENDAR implements an ADT whose data type is called TIME and whose object diagram and package specification are as follows:

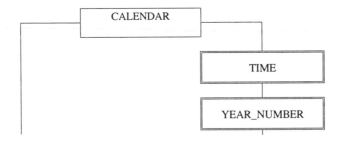

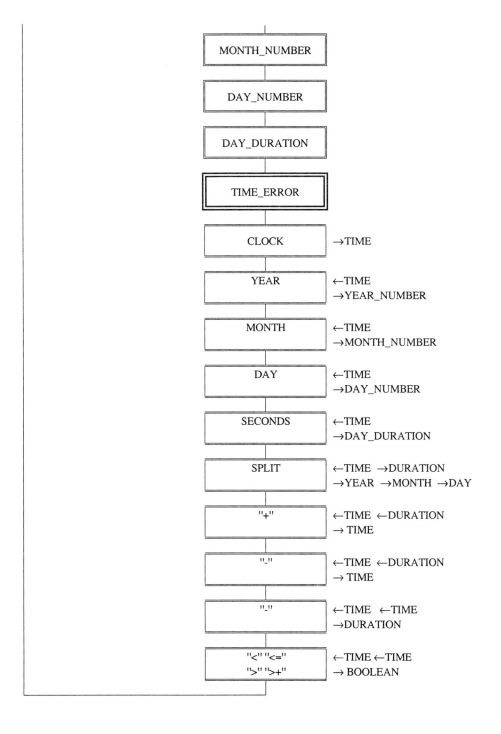

MONTH_NUMBER	
DAY_NUMBER	
DAY_DURATION	
TIME_ERROR	
CLOCK	→TIME
YEAR	←TIME →YEAR_NUMBER
MONTH	←TIME →MONTH_NUMBER
DAY	←TIME →DAY_NUMBER
SECONDS	←TIME →DAY_DURATION
SPLIT	←TIME →DURATION →YEAR →MONTH →DAY
"+"	←TIME ←DURATION → TIME
"-"	←TIME ←DURATION → TIME
"-"	←TIME ←TIME →DURATION
"<" "<=" ">" ">+"	←TIME ←TIME → BOOLEAN

```
0001    -- Filename ADA.Calendar_.pkg.
0002    -- Ada 95 standard package.
0003
0004    package ADA.CALENDARis
0005
0006       type TIME is private;
0007
0008
0009       subtype YEAR_NUMBER  is INTEGER range 1901 .. 2099;
0010       subtype MONTH_NUMBER is INTEGER range 1 .. 12;
0011       subtype DAY_NUMBER   is INTEGER range 1 .. 31;
0012
0013       subtype DAY_DURATION is DURATION range 0.0 .. 86_400.0
0014
0015       function CLOCK return TIME;
0016
0017       function YEAR    (Date : in TIME) return YEAR_NUMBER;
0018       function MONTH   (Date : in TIME) return MONTH_NUMBER;
0019       function DAY     (Date : in TIME) return DAY_NUMBER;
0020       function SECONDS (Date : in TIME) return DAY_DURATION;
0021
0022       procedure SPLIT
0023          (DATE    : in TIME;
0024           YEAR    : out YEAR_NUMBER;
0025           MONTH   : out MONTH_NUMBER;
0026           DAY     : out DAY_NUMBER;
0027           SECONDS : out DAY_DURATION);
0028
0029       function TIME_OF
0030          (YEAR    : in YEAR_NUMBER;
0031           MONTH   : in MONTH_NUMBER;
0032           DAY     : in DAY_NUMBER;
0033           SECONDS : in DAY_DURATION := 0.0)
0034                        return TIME;
0035
0036       function "+" (LEFT  : in TIME;
0037                     RIGHT : in DURATION) return TIME;
0038       function "+" (LEFT  : in DURATION;
0039                     RIGHT : in TIME) return TIME;
0040       function "-" (LEFT  : in TIME;
0041                     RIGHT : in DURATION) return TIME;
0042       function "-" (LEFT  : in TIME;
0043                     RIGHT : in TIME) return DURATION;
0044
0045       function "<"  (LEFT, RIGHT : in TIME) return BOOLEAN;
0046       function "<=" (LEFT, RIGHT : in TIME) return BOOLEAN;
0047       function ">"  (LEFT, RIGHT : in TIME) return BOOLEAN;
0048       function ">=" (LEFT, RIGHT : in TIME) return BOOLEAN;
```

```
0049
0050      TIME_ERROR : exception;
0051
0052    private
0053
0054      -- Private details are environment specific.
0055
0056    end ADA.CALENDAR;
```

The package CALENDAR has already been used in Chapter 12 where it was used by the *JulianDate* ADT to obtain the current date. This is one of the major intended uses of this package and to support it, it supplies the function TIME which will return the current date and time. The functions YEAR, MONTH, YEAR and SECONDS will return the indicated component of a TIME value, with SECONDS indicating the number of seconds past midnight. The TIME_OF and SPLIT subprograms supply a constructor and deconstructor facility respectively. The remaining arithmetic and relational operators have the expected uses.

The package CALENDAR is also intended to be used with the Ada **delay** statement. This statement suspends program execution, either for a specified period or until a particular time is reached. The **delay** statement by itself, followed by a numeric value, will suspend program execution for the number of seconds specified. For example:

```
delay 2.5; -- Suspend execution for 2.5 seconds.
```

The alternative is to use a **delay until** statement which has to be followed by a value of type TIME and suspends program execution until the time specified. For example:

```
NewMillenium : TIME := TIME_OF( YEAR => 2000,
                                MONTH => 1,
                                DAY   => 1,
                                SECONDS => 0.0);

delay until NewMillenium;
PUT_LINE( "Happy new millennium!!" );
```

The package COMMAND_LINE

The package COMMAND_LINE may or may not be supplied depending upon the operating system which the compiler is intended for, although the vast majority of operating systems support its functionality and it can be expected to be supplied. It is intended to allow Ada programs access to command line arguments. A

command line argument is used in a command line driven operating system interface to supply information to a program as it is launched. For example, a program called ***more*** exists in most operating systems, and can be readily constructed if it does not. It is used in the form ***more filename***, and will display the contents of the file identified on the terminal one screenful at a time. The *filename* is a command line argument to the program ***more***, which should terminate with a helpful message if no argument is supplied.

The object diagram and package specification of COMMAND_LINE are as follows:

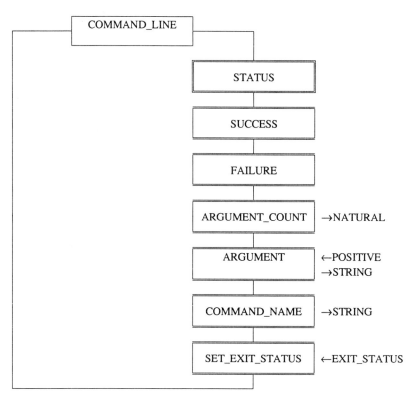

```
0001    -- Filename COMMAND_LINE_.PKG.
0002    -- Ada 95 standard package.
0003
0004
0005    package ADA.COMMAND_LINE is
0006
0007        function ARGUMENT_COUNT return NATURAL;
0008
0009        function ARGUMENT (NUMBER : in POSITIVE) return STRING;
0010
```

```
0011        function ARGUMENT (NUMBER : in POSITIVE)
0012        return STRING;
0013
0014        function COMMAND_NAME return STRING;
0015
0016        type EXIT_STATUS is new INTEGER;
0017
0018        SUCCESS : constant EXIT_STATUS;
0019        FAILURE : constant EXIT_STATUS;
0020        -- Other EXIT_STATUS codes may be defined for a
0021        -- particular environment.
0022
0023        procedure SET_EXIT_STATUS(CODE : in EXIT_STATUS);
0024
0025    private
0026
0027        -- Private details are environment specific.
0028
0029    end ADA.COMMAND_LINE;
```

The function ARGUMENT_COUNT will return the number of arguments which are supplied to the program, the name of which can be obtained by using the function COMMAND_NAME. The individual command line parameters to the program can be obtained using the function ARGUMENT. A trivial example of using these facilities is as follows:

```
0001    -- Filename CommandLineDemo.adb (k8 commandd.adb).
0002    -- Demonstration of the COMMAND_LINE standard package.
0003    -- Developed for Ada book Section II Chapter 16.
0004    --
0005    -- Fintan Culwin, v0.1, Jan 1997.
0006
0007    with ADA.TEXT_IO, ADA.COMMAND_LINE;
0008    use  ADA.TEXT_IO, ADA.COMMAND_LINE;
0009
0010    procedure CommandLineDemo is
0011
0012        package IntegerIO is new ADA.TEXT_IO.INTEGER_IO
                                                    ( INTEGER);
0013        use IntegerIO;
0014
0015        NumberOfArguments : NATURAL;
0016
0017    begin -- CommandLineDemo
0018        SET_COL( 10);PUT_LINE( "Command line demonstration
                                                    program");
0019        NEW_LINE( 2);
0020
```

```
0021      NumberOfArguments := ARGUMENT_COUNT;
0022
0023      if NumberOfArguments = 0 then
0024          PUT( "No command line arguments for ");
0025          PUT_LINE( COMMAND_NAME );
0026          SET_EXIT_STATUS( FAILURE );
0027      else
0028          PUT( "The arguments for "); PUT( COMMAND_NAME );
0029          PUT_LINE( " are:");
0030          for ThisArgument in 1 .. NumberOfArguments loop
0031              PUT( "Argument number ");
0032              PUT( ThisArgument);
0033              PUT( " is ");
0034              PUT_LINE( ARGUMENT( ThisArgument), WIDTH => 3);
0035          end loop;
0036          SET_EXIT_STATUS( SUCCESS );
0037      end if;
0038  end CommandLineDemo;
```

A more realistic example would have to examine the contents of the command line arguments looking for the occurrence of a particular string or pattern. This process can be facilitated by use of the ADA.STRINGS.FIXED package which follows.

The remaining subprogram in ADA.COMMAND_LINE is SET_EXIT_STATUS which can be used to communicate the success or failure of the program back to the environment which executed it. The package mandates two EXIT_STATUS codes, although additional codes can also be supplied for a particular environment. This facility is intended for use in non-interactive (*batch*) programs which are called from an operating system *script*. The script can then take alternative actions depending upon the exit code returned.

The packages ADA.NUMERICS.FLOAT_RANDOM and ADA.NUMERICS.DISCRETE_RANDOM

The packages ADA.NUMERICS.DISCRETE_RANDOM and ADA.NUMERICS.-FLOAT_RANDOM are intended for the generation of random values. The FLOAT_RANDOM package is a non-generic package for the generation of random floating point values in the range 0.0 to 1.0. The DISCRETE_RANDOM package is a generic package which will be described following the simpler FLOAT_RANDOM package.

An abbreviated object diagram and package specification for ADA.-NUMERICS.FLOAT_RANDOM are as follows:

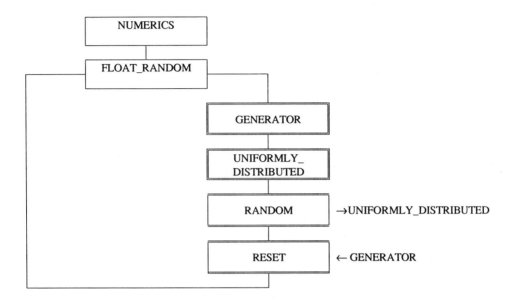

The function RANDOM will return a random floating point number in the range 0.0 to 1.0. A naïve implementation might use this facility as follows:

```
0001    -- Filename NaiveRandomNumberDemo.adb (k8 randomde.adb).
0002    -- Naive demonstration of the
0003    -- ADA.NUMERICS.FLOAT_RANDOM standard package.
0004    -- Developed for Ada book Section II Chapter 16.
0005    --
0006    -- Fintan Culwin, v0.1, Jan 1997.
0007
0008    with ADA.TEXT_IO, ADA.NUMERICS.FLOAT_RANDOM;
0009    use  ADA.TEXT_IO, ADA.NUMERICS.FLOAT_RANDOM;
0010
0011    procedure NaiveRandomNumberDemo is
0012
0013       package FloatIO is new ADA.TEXT_IO.FLOAT_IO( FLOAT);
0014       use FloatIO;
0015
0016       RandomNumber : UNIFORMLY_DISTRIBUTED;
0017       Seed         : GENERATOR;
0018
0019    begin -- NaiveRandomNumberDemo
0020       SET_COL( 10);
0021       PUT_LINE( "Naive random number demonstration program");
```

```
0022        NEW_LINE( 2);
0023
0024        for ThisNumber in INTEGER range 1 .. 12 loop
0025            RandomNumber := RANDOM( Seed);
0026            PUT( RandomNumber, FORE =>2, AFT =>8, EXP =>0);
0027        end loop;
0028        NEW_LINE;
0028    end NaiveRandomNumberDemo;
```

When this program was executed it produced the following sequence of random values:

0.38284349	0.19592047	0.82367277	0.61172348
0.07315630	0.63775766	0.87761402	0.78996736
0.51105821	0.03533179	0.35762187	0.98233021

If the upper limit of the definite loop in line 0024 were changed to a large value, it would be seen that the sequence of values was truly random. However, if the program were executed for a second time, exactly the same sequence would be obtained. Indeed, every time the program was executed the same sequence would be produced. The reason for this is that the sequence of random values is determined by the value of the generator which has a fixed default value. The generator can be reset by a call of the procedure RESET:

```
RESET( Seed);
```

If this is included before the start of the loop, a random sequence of random values would be obtained. The process is known as **seeding** the random number generator, and the identifier for the GENERATOR variable has been named to reflect this.

The object diagram and package specification given above were described as abbreviated as there are additional, more complex, facilities in the package for the creation and manipulation of generators. Details of these additional facilities will not be given in this book.

The package ADA.NUMERICS.DISCRETE_RANDOM is a generic package which can be instantiated with any **discrete** type, or subtype. An example of its instantiation with an enumeration type follows.

```
0001    -- Filename DiscreteRandomDemo.adb (k8 disrndde.adb).
0002    -- Demonstration of the generic
0003    -- ADA.NUMERICS.DISCRETE_RANDOM standard package,
0004    -- instantiated with an enumeration type.
0005    -- Developed for Ada book Section II Chapter 16.
0006    --
```

```
0007    -- Fintan Culwin, v0.1, Jan 1997.
0008
0009    with ADA.TEXT_IO, ADA.NUMERICS.DISCRETE_RANDOM;
0010    use  ADA.TEXT_IO;
0011
0012    procedure DiscreteRandomDemo is
0013
0014       type Days is ( Mon, Tue, Wed, Thu, Fri, Sat, Sun);
0015
0016       package RandomDays is new
0017                        ADA.NUMERICS.DISCRETE_RANDOM( Days);
0018
0019       package DaysIO is new ADA.TEXT_IO.ENUMERATION_IO( Days);
0020       use RandomDays, DaysIO;
0021
0022       RandomDay : Days;
0023       Seed      : GENERATOR;
0024
0025    begin -- DiscreteRandomDemo
0026       SET_COL( 10);
0027       PUT_LINE( "Discrete random demonstration program");
0028       NEW_LINE( 2);
0029
0030       RESET( Seed);
0031       for ThisDay in INTEGER range 1 .. 12 loop
0032          RandomDay := RANDOM( Seed);
0033          PUT( RandomDay);
0034          NEW_LINE;
0035       end loop;
0036    end DiscreteRandomDemo;
```

A more usual instantiation of the package would be to configure it to produce random integer values within a defined range. For example, the British National Lottery requires a player to choose a series of different integer values in the range 1 to 49. A suitable instantiation of the ADA.NUMERICS.DISCRETE_RANDOM package for this requirement might be as follows:

```
MinimumLotteryChoice := 1;
MaximumLotteryChoice := 49;
subtype LotteryNumbers is INTEGER
        range MinimumLotteryChoice .. MaximumLotteryChoice;
package RandomLotteryNumbers is new
            ADA.NUMERICS.DISCRETE_RANDOM( LotteryNumbers);
```

The packages ADA.NUMERICS.ELEMENTARY_FUNCTIONS and ADA.NUMERICS.GENERIC_ELEMENTARY_FUNCTIONS

The package ADA.NUMERICS.ELEMENTARY_FUNCTIONS supplies a set of mathematical and trigonometric functions for the pre-declared FLOAT type. The specification of this package will be given without an object diagram as this is an example of a package supplying a related set of subprograms and not an ADT.

```
0001   -- Filename ADA.NUMERICS.ELEMENTARY_FUNCTIONS.
0002   -- Ada 95 standard package supplying mathematical and
0003   -- trigonometric functions for the pre-declared FLOAT type.
0004
0005   package ADA.NUMERICS.ELEMENTARY_FUNCTIONS is
0006
0007      -- Square root.
0008      function SQRT    (X            : in FLOAT) return FLOAT;
0009
0010      -- Natural Logarithm and Logarithm to given base.
0011      function LOG     (X            : in FLOAT) return FLOAT;
0012      function LOG     (X, BASE      : in FLOAT) return FLOAT;
0013
0014      -- Exponent to base e and exponentiation.
0015      function EXP     (X            : in FLOAT) return FLOAT;
0016      function "**"    (LEFT, RIGHT  : in FLOAT) return FLOAT;
0017
0018      -- Trigonometric functions.
0019      function SIN     (X            : in FLOAT) return FLOAT;
0020      function SIN     (X, CYCLE     : in FLOAT) return FLOAT;
0021      function COS     (X            : in FLOAT) return FLOAT;
0022      function COS     (X, CYCLE     : in FLOAT) return FLOAT;
0023      function TAN     (X            : in FLOAT) return FLOAT;
0024      function TAN     (X, CYCLE     : in FLOAT) return FLOAT;
0025      function COT     (X            : in FLOAT) return FLOAT;
0026      function COT     (X, CYCLE     : in FLOAT) return FLOAT;
0027      function ARCSIN  (X            : in FLOAT) return FLOAT;
0028      function ARCSIN  (X, CYCLE     : in FLOAT) return FLOAT;
0029      function ARCCOS  (X            : in FLOAT) return FLOAT;
0030      function ARCCOS  (X, CYCLE     : in FLOAT) return FLOAT;
0031
0032      function ARCTAN(Y : in FLOAT; X : in FLOAT := 1.0)
0033                                          return FLOAT;
0034      function ARCTAN(Y : in FLOAT; X : in FLOAT := 1.0;
0035                  CYCLE : in FLOAT) return FLOAT;
```

```
0036
0037        function ARCCOT (X : in FLOAT; Y : in FLOAT := 1.0)
0038                                          return FLOAT;
0039        function ARCCOT (X : in FLOAT; Y : in FLOAT := 1.0;
0040                     CYCLE : in FLOAT) return FLOAT;
0041
0042        function SINH    (X : in FLOAT) return FLOAT;
0043        function COSH    (X : in FLOAT) return FLOAT;
0044        function TANH    (X : in FLOAT) return FLOAT;
0045        function COTH    (X : in FLOAT) return FLOAT;
0046        function ARCSINH (X : in FLOAT) return FLOAT;
0047        function ARCCOSH (X : in FLOAT) return FLOAT;
0048        function ARCTANH (X : in FLOAT) return FLOAT;
0049        function ARCCOTH (X : in FLOAT) return FLOAT;
0050
0051    end ADA.NUMERICS.ELEMENTARY_FUNCTIONS;
```

The functions have their usual mathematical meanings and may raise a NUMERICS.ARGUMENT_ERROR or a CONSTRAINT_ERROR exception if the value of a parameter, or of a result, is unacceptable. Details of the precise reasons why these exceptions may be raised can be found in the LRM. The trigonometric functions which do not have a CYCLE parameter expect their argument(s), and return a value, in radians. Otherwise the CYCLE parameter can be used to indicate the required bounding of the values; the most obvious value might be 360, indicating that the values are in degrees.

The package ADA.NUMERICS.GENERIC_ELEMENTARY_FUNCTIONS provides an equivalent generic package which can be instantiated with any floating point type. Indeed the provision of the ELEMENTARY_FUNCTIONS package will most probably be a pre-supplied instantiation of this package for the type FLOAT. The parent package, ADA.NUMERICS, exports the ARGUMENT_ERROR exception and constant values for PI and E.

The package ADA.STRINGS and its child packages

The package ADA.STRINGS and its child packages provide a large number of facilities for the manipulation of the pre-declared types STRING and WIDE_STRING. They also supply other implementations of the string type, such as UNBOUNDED_STRINGS, instances of which, in comparison with the pre-declared STRING types, have an indeterminate length. The contents of these packages are varied and complex and only a sample of the available facilities can be presented here. Full details of the contents of the various packages can be found in the LRM.

357

The parent package, ADA.STRINGS, exports a number of constants, exceptions and enumeration types which are used by its children. The object diagram and package specification are as follows:

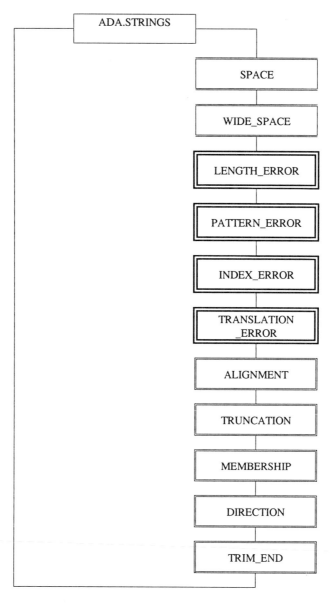

```
0001    -- Filename ADA.STRINGS_.PKG.
0002    -- Ada 95 standard package.
0003
```

```
0004    package ADA.STRINGS is
0005
0006        SPACE       : constant CHARACTER      := ' ';
0007        WIDE_SPACE : constant WIDE_CHARACTER := ' ';
0008
0009        LENGTH_ERROR, PATTERN_ERROR,
0010        INDEX_ERROR, TRANSLATION_ERROR : exception;
0011
0012        type ALIGNMENT  is (LEFT, RIGHT, CENTRE);
0013        type TRUNCATION is (LEFT, RIGHT, ERROR);
0014        type MEMBERSHIP is (INSIDE, OUTSIDE);
0015        type DIRECTION  is (FORWARD, BACKWARD);
0016        type TRIM_END   is (LEFT, RIGHT, BOTH);
0017
0018    end ADA.STRINGS;
```

The packages ADA.STRINGS.MAPS and ADA.STRINGS.CONSTANTS

The package ADA.STRINGS.MAPS supplies two ADTs called CHARACTER_ SET and CHARACTER_MAPPING together with appropriate operations. CHARACTER_SET operations are provided to construct sets of characters from ranges of characters, to perform Boolean operations on these sets and set-specific operations such as membership and subset.

A CHARACTER_MAPPING object is a value which relates characters in one sequence to characters in another sequence. It is intended to be used to translate character and string values from one mapping to another. Operations are supplied for the construction of mappings and for the conversion of CHARAC- TER values.

The package ADA.STRINGS.CONSTANTS supplies pre-declared CHARACTER_SETS and CHARACTER_MAPPINGS. These include sets for: control characters, graphic characters, letter characters, lower case characters, upper case characters, basic characters, decimal digit characters, hexadecimal digit characters, alphanumeric characters and ISO 646 characters. The pre-declared mappings include mappings to lower case characters, to upper case characters and to basic characters. Full details of the members of these sets and mappings can be found in the LRM.

The package ADA.STRINGS.FIXED

The package ADA.STRINGS.FIXED supplies a large number of subprograms for the manipulation of the pre-declared type STRING. These operations include operations to:

- copy strings when the lengths of the two strings differ.

- search for the occurrence of one string within a second string.

- count the number of characters in a string which are members of a set.

- map one string onto another string, using a character mapping.

- replace a slice of a string with another string.

- insert one string into another string.

- overwrite a slice of a string with another string.

- delete a slice of a string.

- trim a string by removing characters from the start and/or end.

- trim and centre a string.

- obtain the start or end of a string.

- produce a string by repeatedly catenating a string or a character.

The full details of these subprograms can be located in the LRM.

An example program using ADA.STRINGS and ADA.COMMAND_LINE

The following program gives some indication of the possible uses of the facilities provided by the ADA.STRINGS packages. For reasons of space only a small selection of the available facilities and a limited description of the facilities which are used can be given.

The program to be developed is called *CodeList* and is intended to process a source code file to produce a listing file which includes line numbers, like the listings in this book. The program requires the name of the source code file to be processed as a required command line parameter and also has three optional parameters. These parameters are /*w* indicating the width in characters of the listing, /*p* indicating the number of lines on a page and /*s* indicating the line number to start with. All of these parameters can be expressed in upper or lower case and have to be followed by an integer value. The command line parameters can be given in any sequence. An example of the use of the subprogram might be as follows:

```
CodeList /w 60 /p 50 /s 100 CodeList.ada
```

This would process the file *CodeList.ada*, producing a file called *CodeList.lis*, with line numbers starting at 0100, 60 characters per line and 50 lines per page. If the command line parameters are not acceptable the following advice will be given:

```
Usage : CodeList {/w nn /p nn /s nn} filename
        /w page width, number of characters per line.
        /p page length, number of lines per page.
        /s start line number.
```

The program which will be developed in this chapter will be limited to processing the command line arguments. The remaining parts of the program will be used as an end of chapter exercise in the next section, after the facilities for manipulating external files have been introduced.

The processing of the command line arguments relies upon a data structure called *ControlRecords* whose data structure declaration and definition is as follows:

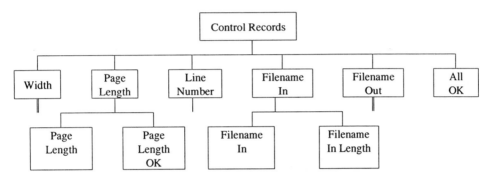

The components *Width* and *LineNumber* will be refined into two components comparable with the refinement of *PageLength* which is shown; likewise *FilenameOut* will be refined as *FilenameIn*. The implementation of this data structure might be as follows:

```
0020    DefaultLineWidth  : constant := 80;
0021    DefaultPageLength : constant := 50;
0022    DefaultLineNumber : constant := 01;
0023    MaxFilenameLength : constant := 60;
0024
0025    subtype FilenameStrings is STRING( 1 .. MaxFilenameLength);
0026
0027    type ControlRecords is
0028    record
0029        WidthOK         : BOOLEAN := TRUE;
0030        Width           : NATURAL := DefaultLineWidth;
0031        PageLengthOK    : BOOLEAN := TRUE;
0032        PageLength      : NATURAL := DefaultPageLength;
0033        LineNumberOK    : BOOLEAN := TRUE;
0034        LineNumber      : NATURAL := DefaultLineNumber;
```

361

```
0035      FilenameIn         : FilenameStrings := ( others =>
                                                         SPACE );
0036      FilenameInLength   : NATURAL;
0037      FilenameOut        : FilenameStrings := ( others =>
                                                         SPACE );
0038      FilenameOutLength  : NATURAL;
0039      AllOK              : BOOLEAN := TRUE;
0040   end record;
```

The high level design of the program is as follows:

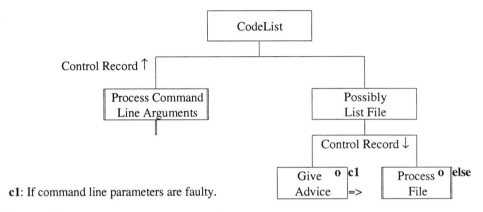

c1: If command line parameters are faulty.

The subprogram *ProcessCommandLineArguments* has the responsibility of ensuring that the command line parameters are, or are not, faulty, and if they are not faulty extracting the information from them into the *ControlRecord*. The design of this subprogram is as follows:

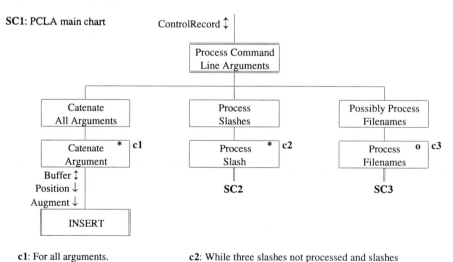

c1: For all arguments.
c3: If error not detected.

c2: While three slashes not processed and slashes remain to be processed and error not detected.

362

The data tables for the entire procedure and the implementation as far as *CatenateAllArguments* are as follows:

Constants for *ProcessCommandLineArguments*

Name	Type	Value	Notes
Slash	STRING	"/"	Slash introducing parameter
DotString	STRING	"."	Filename extension character
ListExtension	STRING	".lis"	List filename extension
BigBufferSize	NATURAL	256	Max no. of chars on command line.

Variables for *ProcessCommandLineArguments*

Name	Type	Notes
Control	ControlRecords	Parameter variable to communicate results
Buffer	STRING	Holds catenated arguments, default spaces
BufferPosition	NATURAL	Current end of data in buffer
NumberOfArguments	NATURAL	Number of command line arguments
NumberFound	NATURAL	Number of arguments located
SlashPosition	NATURAL	Location of slash in buffer
SlashFound	BOOLEAN	Flag to indicate if slash is found
NumberEnd	NATURAL	End of slash and number in buffer
DotPosition	NATURAL	Location of dot in buffer

```
0001    procedure ProcessCommandLineArguments(
0002                        Control : in out ControlRecords) is
0003
0004        Buffer              : STRING( 1.. BigBufferSize)
0005                                       := ( others => SPACE);
0006        BufferPosition      : NATURAL := 1;
0007        NumberOfArguments   : NATURAL := ARGUMENT_COUNT;
0008        NumberFound         : NATURAL := 0;
0009        SlashPosition       : NATURAL;
0010        SlashFound          : BOOLEAN := TRUE;
0011        NumberEnd           : NATURAL;
0012        DotPosition         : NATURAL;
0013
0014    begin -- ProcessCommandLineArguments
0015        -- Catenate all arguments together in the Buffer.
0016        for ThisArgument in 1 .. NumberOfArguments loop
0017            Buffer := REPLACE_SLICE( Buffer, BufferPosition,
0018                BufferPosition + ARGUMENT
0019                                    ( ThisArgument)'LENGTH,
                    ARGUMENT( ThisArgument));
```

```
0020                BufferPosition := BufferPosition +
0021                              ARGUMENT( ThisArgument)'LENGTH +1;
0022          end loop;
```

This part of the procedure collects all the command line arguments into a single buffer to simplify the processing which follows. It does this by iterating through every argument and using the ADA.STRINGS.FIXED REPLACE_SLICE function, whose declaration in the package is as follows:

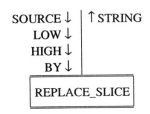

```
function REPLACE_SLICE( SOURCE : in STRING;
                        LOW    : in POSITIVE;
                        HIGH   : in NATURAL;
                        BY     : in STRING) return STRING;
    -- Insert BY into SOURCE at location LOW .. HIGH.
```

In the program fragment above this function is used to replace a slice of the buffer, which is known to contain spaces initially, with an argument from the command line. It starts at the location *BufferPosition* and ends at a location determined by the length of the string being inserted. Within the loop the value of *BufferPosition* is incremented by the length of the inserted string plus one, to allow the next argument from the command line to be correctly inserted. The effect of this fragment is to collect all the arguments from the command line in *Buffer*, each separated by a single space.

The design and implementation of the *ProcessSlashes* component are as follows:

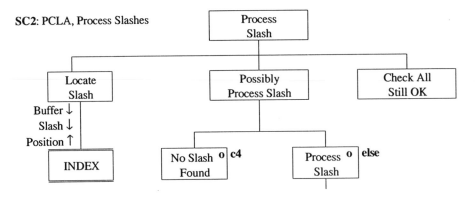

364

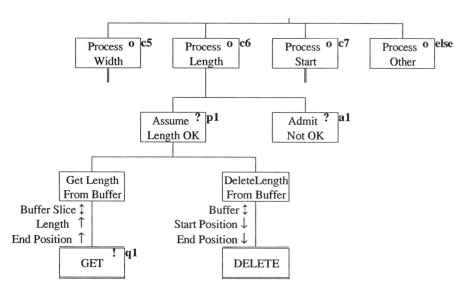

c4: If slash character located.
c5: If width indicator located.
c6: If length indicator located.
c7: If start indicator located.

p1: Assume integer will be extracted from the buffer.
a1: Admit integer was not extracted, DATA_ERROR.
q1: Raise DATA_ERROR if not an integer value.

```
0023            -- Process slashes.
0024            while Control.AllOK and
0025                  NumberFound < 3 and
0026                  SlashFound loop
0027              SlashPosition := INDEX( Buffer, Slash);
0028              if SlashPosition = 0 then
0029                  SlashFound := FALSE;
0030              else
0031                  case Buffer( SlashPosition +1) is
0032                  when 'w' | 'W' =>
0033                      begin -- Exception block
0034                          GET( Buffer( SlashPosition +2 ..
0035                                        Buffer'LENGTH),
0036                              Control.Width, NumberEnd);
0037                          DELETE( Buffer, SlashPosition, NumberEnd);
0038                          Control.WidthOK := TRUE;
0039                      exception
0040                      when DATA_ERROR =>
0041                          Control.WidthOK := FALSE;
0042                      end; -- Exception block.
0043
0044                  when 'p' | 'P' =>
0045                      begin -- Exception block
                            --Omitted, essentially same as above.
```

365

```
0054                    end; -- Exception block.
0055
0056            when 's' | 'S' =>
0057              begin -- Exception block
                    --Omitted, essentially same as above.
0066              end; -- Exception block.
0067
0068            when others =>
0069              Control.AllOK := FALSE;
0070            end case;
0071
0072            Control.AllOK := Control.AllOK      and
0073                             Control.WidthOK    and
0074                             Control.PageLengthOK and
0075                             Control.LineNumberOK;
0076         end if;
0077      end loop;
```

The implementation of this part of the procedure makes use of the ADA.-
STRINGS.FIXED subprograms, INDEX and DELETE. The interface diagrams and
declarations for these subprograms are as follows:

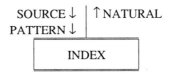

```
function INDEX( SOURCE  : in STRING
                PATTERN : in STRING) return NATURAL;
-- Search SOURCE for PATTERN, returning the start of
-- its location if found or 0 if it cannot be found.
```

```
procedure DELETE( SOURCE  : in out STRING;
                  FROM    : in     POSITIVE;
                  THROUGH : in     NATURAL);
-- Delete the characters in the slice from FROM to
-- FROM + THROUGH, moving the rest of the string to the
-- left and filling from right with spaces.
```

The control of the loop in the fragment is controlled by a loop which iterates while everything is known to be OK in the control record, and there are still slash characters in the string and less than three slash characters have been located. Within the loop, if a slash character is located using INDEX, the following character is used to control a **case** statement which has three non-default options, corresponding to the three recognized slash possibilities. The default option is used to process characters which are not recognized. If no slash character is found when INDEX is called the *SlashFound* flag is set to terminate the loop.

Each non-default option in the **case** structure is essentially identical and only the processing of one option is shown in the design and code. The processing is implemented as an explicit **exception** processing block. The posit part uses the *IntIO* GET procedure to attempt to extract an integer value from the *Buffer* string, starting at the location following the *slash character* combination. If this is not possible the **exception** handler is invoked and the appropriate flag is set in the control record. If an integer value is extracted into the control record, the final parameter from the GET call indicates the last numeric character in the buffer which was used. This value is used, together with the value returned from INDEX indicating the location of the slash, to DELETE the entire *slash character value* sequence from the *Buffer* string.

Following the **case** structure within the loop the final action is to the set the *AllOK* flag in the control record to the **and**ed value of all four flags in the control record. This will have the effect of terminating the loop if a non-recognized *slash character* combination was used on the command line, or if an integer value could not be found following any valid *slash character* combination.

The final part of the procedure *ProcessCommandLineArguments* will process the filename command line argument, providing no error has already been detected. The design and implementation of this part of the procedure are as follows:

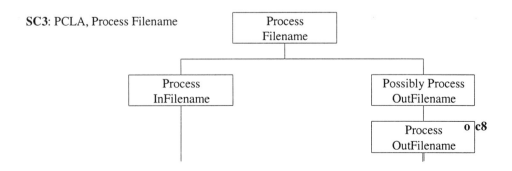

SC3: PCLA, Process Filename

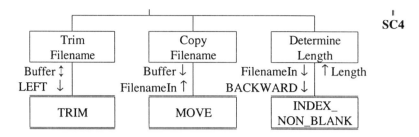

c8: If filename exists.

This design makes use of three STRINGS.FIXED subprograms, TRIM, MOVE and INDEX_NON_BLANK. The interface diagrams and declarations of these subprograms are as follows:

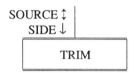

```
procedure TRIM( SOURCE : in out STRING;
                SIDE   : in     TRIM_END );
-- Trim the string by removing all leading or trailing
-- spaces, moving the remaining contents to the LEFT or
-- RIGHT respectively and filling any remaining characters
-- with spaces.
```

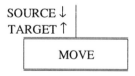

```
procedure MOVE( SOURCE : in  STRING;
                TARGET : out STRING);
-- Move SOURCE to TARGET, which need not be the same
-- length, dropping characters or inserting spaces as
-- appropriate.
```

SOURCE ↓ | ↑NATURAL
(GOING ↓) |

```
┌─────────────┐
│   INDEX_     │
│  NON_BLANK   │
└─────────────┘
```

```
function INDEX_NON_BLANK( SOURCE : in STRING;
                         GOING  : in DIRECTION := FORWARD);
-- Returns the location of the first non-space character by
-- default, or the last non-space if GOING is BACKWARD.
```

The data types SIDE and DIRECTION are supplied by the parent package STRINGS for use in subprograms such as these. The implementation of this fragment is as follows:

```
0079        -- Possibly Process the filenames.
0080        if Control.AllOk then
0081            TRIM( Buffer, LEFT);
0082            MOVE( Buffer, Control.FilenameIn);
0083            Control.FilenameInLength :=
0084                    INDEX_NON_BLANK( Control.FilenameIn,
0085                                     BACKWARD);
0086            Control.AllOK := Control.FilenameInLength > 0;
0087
```

The removal of the slash arguments in the previous part of the procedure would leave the *Buffer* containing only the filename, if any was supplied on the command line. The effect of this fragment is to move what is left in the *Buffer* into the *FilenameIn* field of the control record and record its length in the *FilenameInLength* field. Should the length of the filename be 0, the *AllOk* flag in the record is set to indicate an error. The design of the *ProcessFilenameOut* component is as follows:

SC4: PCLA, Process FilenameOut

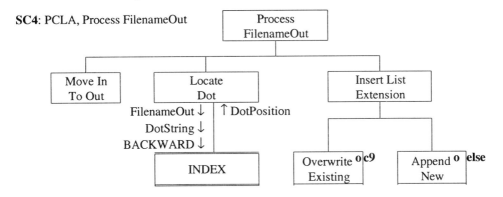

c9: If three character extension located.

The basis of the design is to establish if a three letter extension, for example '.*ada*', terminates the filename. If so the existing three letter extension is replaced with '.*lis*', otherwise the '.*lis*' extension is added to the output filename. To facilitate this part of the procedure two STRING constants, *DotString* ('.') and *List-*

Extension (".lis") are provided. The implementation of this design is as follows:

```
0088            -- Possibly process the output filename.
0089          if Control.AllOK then
0090            Control.FilenameOut := Control.FilenameIn;
0091            Control.FilenameOutLength :=
0092                            Control.FilenameInLength;
0093            DotPosition := INDEX( Control.FilenameOut,
0094                            DotString, BACKWARD);
0095            if DotPosition = Control.FilenameOutLength
0096                        - ListExtension'LENGTH +1 then
0097              REPLACE_SLICE( Control.FilenameOut,
                                    DotPosition,
0098              DotPosition + ListExtension'LENGTH,
0099                                ListExtension);
0100            else
0101              REPLACE_SLICE( Control.FilenameOut,
0102                        Control.FilenameOutLength,
0103            Control.FilenameOutLength +
                                ListExtension'LENGTH,
0104                                ListExtension);
0105            Control.FilenameOutLength :=
0106            Control.FilenameOutLength +
                                ListExtension'LENGTH);
0107          end if;
0108        end if; -- Of Possibly process filenames.
```

This completes the procedure with the *ControlRecord AllOk* flag set to indicate the success or otherwise of the parsing of the command line arguments. If the parsing was successful the values of the *Width*, *Length* and *Start* fields may have been changed from their default values; additionally the *FilenameIn* and *FilenameOut* fields will indicate the files to be processed.

It was mentioned at the start of the chapter on the STRING data type that the processing of text information is probably more prevalent than the processing of numeric information. The example in this section of the chapter has been included to show how involved such processing can become. There is no string manipulation facility in the ADA.STRINGS packages which could not be implemented by the developer using the pre-declared STRING facilities. However, the use of the facilities in the standard package allows the developer to concentrate upon the logical processing of the text information without having to reinvent the wheel by developing standard string manipulation operations.

The package ADA.TEXT_IO.EDITING

The package ADA.TEXT_IO.EDITING provides facilities for the output formatting

of decimal data types. The package exports: an ADT called PICTURES which is used
to define the manner in which decimal information is to be presented, a public **record**
type called LOCALE which can be used to configure the output for international use
and a generic package called EDITED_OUPUT. The generic package exports a PUT
subprogram for the output of decimal values. Only a brief overview of the
capabilities of this package will be given; further details can be found in the LRM.

One common use of the decimal edited output facilities is for the printing of
values on computer generated cheques. In an attempt to prevent the cheque being
illegally amended the values are presented in a format such as "£***,*12.45", the
asterisk character being used in the place of space characters. To produce such
output a PICTURE value is used to represent the pattern of the value to be
presented. The PICTURE value is constructed from a string containing a sequence
of characters which can include

Picture character	Effect
$	Blank or CURRENCY string from LOCALE
B	Digit or blank
*	Digit or FILL from LOCALE
_	SEPARATOR from LOCALE
.	RADIX_MARK from LOCALE

An example of a possible string might be "$$_$**_*99.99" which can be
interpreted from right to left as follows. The last two characters are always digits
indicating the decimal part of the number, and are always preceded by a radix
symbol (.99). To the left of the radix symbol there is always at least two digit
characters (99). If the integer part of the value is less than 100 000 up to three fill
characters are used to guarantee five characters (* * _ *). If the integer part of the
value is greater than 99 999 the currency symbol string will appear without a space
immediately to the left of the value ($$_$). All digit and fill characters to the left
of the radix are grouped in threes, separated by separator characters.

Using the pattern and rules above, assuming the currency string is "$", the
radix is '.', the separator is ',' and the fill character is ' * ', the following values will
give the output indicated:

Value	Display
0.12	$ * * * , * 00.12
1.23	$ * * * , * 01.23
1234.56	$ * * 1 , 234.56
123456.78	$123 , 456.78
1234567.89	$1 , 234 , 567.89

The formatting information has to be supplied to the output procedure as a value of a data type called PICTURE. To construct a PICTURE value from a string the constructor function TO_PICTURE can be used. For example:

```
DemoPicture := TO_PICTURE( "$$_$**_*99.99" );
```

With this picture clause, and assuming a suitably instantiated EDITED_OUPUT package, output can be directed to the terminal using a PUT procedure call such as

```
PUT( DemoValue, PIC => DemoPicture);
```

The internationalization facilities can be made use of by preparing a LOCALE record and using it as an optional third parameter of the PUT procedure. For example:

```
LocaleForMars : LOCALE := ( CURRENCY   => "Ω",
                            FILL       => '&',
                            SEPARATOR  => '#',
                            RADIX_MARK => '@' );
PUT( DemoValue, PIC     => DemoPicture,
                SYMBOLS => LocaleForMars );
```

Which would produce output such as "Ω&&1#234@56" corresponding to the third line of the table above. The facilities of the TEXT_IO.PICTURES package and the rules for the construction and use of PICTURE strings have only been touched on in this section. For some applications concerned with commercial data processing, the facilities of this package are essential. Full details of the facilities can be found in the LRM.

EXERCISES

16.1 Implement a lottery number generator client for the British National Lottery which requires seven numbers between 1 and 49 to be chosen. This version of the program may generate the same number twice, in which case this program can be run again until no duplicate numbers are produced. A version of this program which guarantees not to produce duplicate numbers will be introduced in the next sections.

16.2 Use the facilities of the ADA.CALENDAR package and the **delay until** statement to implement a rudimentary clock which displays the time every second.

16.3 Adapt the program from Exercise 16.2 and make use of the ADA.-COMMAND_LINE package to implement an alarm clock client. The program will expect the user to specify a time on the command line and will give advice if it is not a valid time, or if it is not in the future. Otherwise the program should do nothing until the time specified, when it should alert the user.

16.4 Revisit the string programs from Chapter 10 and make suitable use of the facilities of ADA.STRINGS where appropriate.

16.5 Revisit the interest generation programs from Section I Chapter 7 making use of a fixed decimal type and of the ADA.TEXT_IO.EDITING facilities for the manipulation and output of financial information.

16.6 Is the random number generator truly random? For example, if it is instantiated to simulate the tossing of a coin by randomly choosing between the two enumerated values *Heads* and *Tails*, then over a large number of trials it should choose *Heads* as often as *Tails*.

SECTION III

Arrays, Recursion, Access Types and Files

CHAPTER 17
Iteration in structure: arrays

The data objects which have been introduced so far have been treated as single objects. Even records, which consist of a number of components, are treated for most purposes as a single object. Most programs have requirements which can best be met by using a collection of objects all of the same type. *Iterative data structures* are capable of holding a number of objects, all of which are of the same type. The term *array* is the name given to these data structures. A data structure diagram of a general array has the form

This diagram indicates that an array is an iteration of single items, each of which is known as a component *element* of the array. Simple arrays of this form are sometimes known as *vectors*. Within the array an individual element can be identified by its position. The data type which is used to determine the position of elements within the array is known as the array's *index type*. Each element in the array can be referred to by using its index value.

When designing arrays for particular requirements the nature of the elements which comprise the arrays must always be known. The data type which will be used to index the array must also be known. The number of items which will comprise the array may or may not be known. If the number of items which will comprise the array can be decided in advance then a *constrained* array type can be declared. The alternative possibility is to declare an array type without explicitly declaring the number of items which will comprise the array until an object of the array type is declared; such an array is known as an *unconstrained* array.

Declaring constrained arrays

In order to declare a constrained array the type of the items which comprise the elements of the array has first to be decided. Elements of an array can be of any Ada data type, including programmer declared types. Once the type of the elements of the array has been decided, the type and the range of the index which will determine the number of elements in the array have to be decided. The index type of an array must be a ***discrete*** type. This, as previously explained, is an Ada data type where each value of the type can be listed. Discrete types include the pre-declared types INTEGER, BOOLEAN, CHARACTER and any developer declared enumerated type.

Having decided upon the two data types which are required to declare the array, it can then be designed using a data structure diagram and implemented as an Ada type. For example, a program may require an array of eight INTEGERS indexed from 1 to 8. This identifies the type of the elements of the array as INTEGER and the index type of the array as INTEGER with the range 1 to 8. The data structure diagram of this array and its subsequent implementation in Ada might be

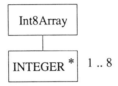

```
MaxArraySize : constant INTEGER := 8;
subtype Index8Ranges is INTEGER range 1 ... MaxArraySize;

type Int8Arrays is array( Index8Ranges) of INTEGER;

Int8Array : Int8Arrays;
```

The declaration of an array type specifies first the range of the index and, as indicated above, it is suggested as good style to use an explicit subtype for this term. The type declaration finishes with the element type, in this example INTEGER. As with other data type declarations it is suggested that plural noun phrase should be used for the type name allowing the singular form to be used as a variable identifier. The structure of the variable object *Int8Array* can be visualized as

Int8Array

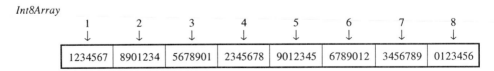

The array itself is called *Int8Array* and is of type *Int8Arrays*. Each component element of the array is of type INTEGER and is shown as having an arbitrary integer value. The index to the array is of subtype *Index8Ranges* with values from

1 to 8. When an array object is declared the elements of the array have no particular value, unless an explicit aggregate set of values is supplied. It is not possible to specify a default value for an array type.

When an INTEGER range is used to index an array, the lower bound of the index range does not have to be 1. Both of the following are valid array declarations:

```
MinFloatArrayIndex : constant INTEGER := 0;
MaxFloatArrayIndex : constant INTEGER := 7;

subtype FloatArrayRanges is INTEGER
         range MinFloatArrayIndex .. MaxFloatArrayIndex;

type FloatArrays is array ( FloatArrayRanges) of FLOAT;
FloatArray : FloatArrays;

MinIntegerArrayIndex : constant INTEGER := 25;
MaxIntegerArrayIndex : constant INTEGER := 32;

subtype IntegerArrayRanges is INTEGER
         range MinIntegerArrayIndex .. MaxIntegerArrayIndex;

type IntegerArrays is array ( IntegerArrayRanges) of
                                                  INTEGER;

IntegerArray : IntegerArrays;
```

The variable objects *FloatArray* and *IntegerArray* can be visualized as follows:

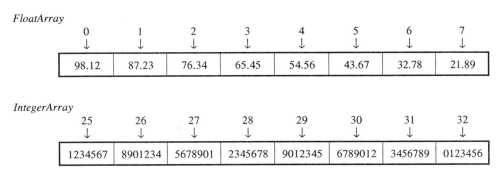

Each element of *FloatArray* is of type FLOAT and is shown in the diagram as having an arbitrary floating point value. Each element of *IntegerArray* is of type INTEGER and is shown in the diagram as having an arbitrary integer value. The indexes to both arrays are of type *INTEGER*. In the case of *FloatArray* the range of the index is from 0 to 7, giving eight elements in total. In the case of *Integer-Array* the range of the index is from 25 to 32, also giving eight elements in total.

There is no indication here of why the indexes should have such bounds. The index to an array need not be of type INTEGER, nor need the components of the array be simple numeric objects:

```
MaxStringSize          : constant INTEGER := 8;
MinStringArrayIndex : constant CHARACTER := 'a';
MaxStringArrayIndex : constant CHARACTER := 'e';

subtype String8s is STRING( 1 .. MaxStringSize );
subtype StringArrayRanges is CHARACTER
        range MinStringArrayIndex .. MaxStringArrayIndex;

type StringArrays is array ( StringArrayRanges) of String8s;
StringArray : StringArrays;
```

The array *StringArray* can be visualized as follows:

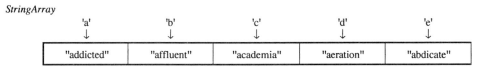

StringArray

'a'	'b'	'c'	'd'	'e'
↓	↓	↓	↓	↓
"addicted"	"affluent"	"academia"	"aeration"	"abdicate"

This array is of type *StringArrays*, and each element of the array is of type *String8s* and shown in this diagram as containing an arbitrary word. The index type of this array is the CHARACTER subtype *StringArrayRanges* with a range from '*a*' to '*e*', giving a total of five elements. The final example is an array whose index type is an enumeration range and whose element type is a record:

```
with DayTime; use DayTime;

MaxAppointmentStringSize : constant INTEGER := 12;
subtype AppointmentStrings is
                STRING( 1 .. MaxAppointmentStringSize);

type AppointmentIndices is ( Morning, Lunch, Afternoon,
                                                    Tea);

type Appointments is
record
    Appointee : AppointmentStrings;
    Start     : DayTimes;
    End       : DayTimes;
end record;

type DayAppointments is array ( AppointmentIndices)
                            of    Appointments;
TodaysAppointments : DayAppointments;
```

The *DayTime* package supplies a data type called *DayTimes* capable of representing a time of day (e.g. *17:45*), which was a suggested end of chapter exercise in Section II Chapter 12. A data structure diagram for the type *DayAppointments* might be

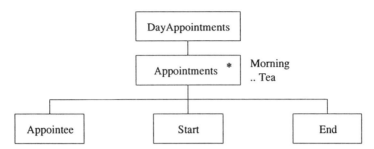

This data structure diagram combines the iteration notation of arrays with the sequence notation of records. This is congruent to the declaration of the type *DayAppointments* as an iteration of records. A visualization of the array *TodaysAppointments*, with illustrative values, would be

TodaysAppointments

	Morning ↓		Lunch ↓		Afternoon ↓		Tea ↓	
	Chaplin		Bunter		Decker		Abrahams	
	08:30	09:00	09:30	11:00	13:00	13:45	16:00	17:00

Array aggregate values

It is not possible to specify a default value for an array type or subtype. It is, however, possible for instances of an array to be explicitly given a value expressed in an **array aggregate** as they are declared. As with record aggregates or subprogram calls, an array aggregate can use **named** or **positional** notation to specify which components of the array are being given which values. The following array declaration will be used to illustrate the form and use of array aggregates:

```
SmallArrayMinimum : constant INTEGER := 3;
SmallArrayMaximum : constant INTEGER := 5;

subtype SmallArrayRanges : is INTEGER
          range SmallArrayMinimum .. SmallArrayMaximum;

type SmallArrays is array ( SmallArrayRanges) of FLOAT;
```

It is not possible for an array aggregate value to be specified in the declaration of the array type. It is optional for array variables to be given an initial value using an array aggregate value. It is required that array constants be given a value using an aggregate when they are declared.

```
-- Explicit initialization of a variable array using
-- positional notation.
FirstSmallArray : SmallArrays := ( 1.2, 2.4, 2.6 );
-- Explicit initialization of a variable array using
-- named notation.
SecondSmallArray : SmallArrays
                := ( 4 => 2.4, 5 => 3.6, 3 => 1.2 );
```

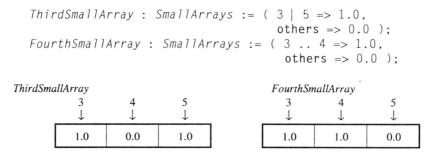

The positional notation supplies a list of values which are associated with elements in the array, starting with the first element of the array, and not all values need to be stated. Named notation uses the index value of the element to be initialized to associate an element of the array with a value. Named array aggregates can use the range (..), selector (|) and **others** constructs to specify which values are to be associated with which elements:

```
ThirdSmallArray : SmallArrays := ( 3 | 5 => 1.0,
                                   others => 0.0 );
FourthSmallArray : SmallArrays := ( 3 .. 4 => 1.0,
                                    others => 0.0 );
```

These examples indicate that the '|' symbol can be used to indicate disjoint elements which are to have the same value, and that the range construct (*value .. value*) can be used to specify a range of elements to be given the same value. Any elements which are not explicitly identified can be identified using the **others** phrase.

Declaring unconstrained arrays

When the declaration of a constrained array type is made, the type of the index and the bounds of the index have to be declared. There are some applications where this is not desirable: for example, in some situations the required bounds of an array cannot be ascertained until the program is executing. Ada allows for these situations by the provision of unconstrained array type declarations. With an unconstrained array type declaration only the type of the array index has to be declared; the actual bounds of the array for a particular object are deferred until an array object is declared. The type of the element of the array cannot be deferred and has to be declared when the constrained array type is declared. Examples of unconstrained array type declarations, which are comparable with the constrained array type declarations which have been used so far, would be as follows:

```
type IntegerUarrays    is array ( INTEGER    range <> )
                            of   INTEGER;
type FloatUarrays      is array ( INTEGER    range <> )
                            of   FLOAT;
type StringUarrays     is array ( CHARACTER range <> )
                            of   String8;
type DayUappointments is array ( AppointmentIndices
                                            range <> )
                            of   Appointments;
```

These declarations declare the type of the elements of the array and the type of the index, but do not specify a particular range. The term '<>', which is used to indicate that the array is unconstrained, is known as a ***box***. When an object of an unconstrained array type is declared the actual bounds have to be specified. For example:

```
SmallIntArray      : IntegerUarrays( 10 .. 17);   -- 8   elements
LargeIntArray      : IntegerUarrays( 0  .. 99);   -- 100 elements
SmallFloatArray    : FloatUarrays(   0  .. 5);    -- 6   elements
LargeStringArray : StringUarrays( 'A' .. 'Z'); -- 26  elements

HalfDayAppointments : DayUappointments( Afternoon .. Tea);
                                            -- 2 elements
```

It is also possible for a constrained array subtype of an unconstrained array type to be declared. For example:

```
subtype ConstrainedArraySubtypes is IntegerUarray( 1 .. 7);
```

Unconstrained arrays are most useful as the formal parameters of subprograms giving them a greater generality than equivalent subprograms declared with constrained array parameters. This use of constrained arrays will be explained later in this chapter.

Attributes of arrays

Attributes which can be used with arrays can be applied to an array type or can be applied to an array object. When applied to an array type, the attribute determines the nature of all objects of that type. When applied to an array object, the attribute determines the nature of the object only.

The attributes which can be applied to arrays include FIRST, LAST, RANGE and LENGTH. The attribute FIRST will evaluate to the value of the lower bound of the array's index range and will be of the base type of the type of the array's index. Likewise LAST will evaluate to the value of the upper bound of the array's index range and will be of the base type of the array's index. The attribute RANGE when applied to an array will evaluate to a range expression whose effective declaration is *ArrayType*'FIRST .. *ArrayType*'LAST. The final attribute LENGTH will evaluate to an integer value equal to the number of elements in the array. Examples of the use of these attributes, using array types and array objects which have been declared earlier in this chapter, include

Expression	Type	Value
Int8Arrays'FIRST	INTEGER	1
Int8Arrays'LAST	INTEGER	8
Int8Array'RANGE	implicit INTEGER subtype	1 .. 8
Int8Array'LENGTH	UNIVERSAL INTEGER	8
StringArrays'FIRST	CHARACTER	'a'
StringArrays'LAST	CHARACTER	'e'
StringArray'RANGE	implicit CHARACTER subtype	'a' .. 'e'
StringArray'LENGTH	UNIVERSAL INTEGER	5
LargeStringArray'FIRST	CHARACTER	'A'
LargeStringArray'LAST	CHARACTER	'Z'
LargeStringArray'RANGE	implicit CHARACTER subtype	'A' .. 'Z'
LargeStringArray'LENGTH	UNIVERSAL INTEGER	26
TodaysAppointments'FIRST	*AppointmentIndex*	*Morning*
TodaysAppointments'LAST	*AppointmentIndex*	*Tea*
HalfDayAppointments'RANGE	implicit *AppointmentIndex* subtype	*Afternoon .. Tea*
HalfDayAppointments'LENGTH	UNIVERSAL INTEGER	2
IntegerUarrays'FIRST	is not allowed	
FloatUarrays'LAST	is not allowed	
StringUarrays'RANGE	is not allowed	
DayUappointments'LENGTH	is not allowed	

Some range attributes when applied to unconstrained array types are meaningless, and will be detected by the Ada compiler as an error. For example, the attribute determining the number of elements in an array cannot be applied to an unconstrained array type as the number of elements is indeterminate. The attribute can, however, be applied to an array object declared from an unconstrained array type as the declaration of the object requires the number of elements to be specified.

Using arrays

The most common requirement when using an array is to reference an element at a particular position in the array. This is done by using an index expression of the appropriate type and within the appropriate range. The value of the index identifies which of the elements in the array is being referenced. For example, using the arrays shown in the visualizations at the start of this chapter, the following references can be made:

Expression	Type	Value
AnInt8Array(2)	INTEGER	8901234
DemoFloatArray(4)	FLOAT	54.56
DemoStringArray('d')	*String8*	"aeration"
TodaysAppointments(*Tea*)	*Appointment*	Abrahams
		16:00 | 17:00

If an attempt is made to access an element using an index whose type is incorrect, or whose type is correct but whose value is outside the appropriate range, a CONSTRAINT_ERROR exception will be raised.

It is possible to access each element of an array sequentially, from the lower to the upper bound, by iterating through the range of the array's index. For example, to print out the contents of the variable *StringArray* the following program fragment could be used:

```
for ThisString in StringArray'RANGE loop
   PUT_LINE( StringArray( ThisString));
end loop;
```

The RANGE attribute of the *StringArray* variable is used to control the bounds of the definite iteration, ensuring that all valid indexes of the array from FIRST to LAST are generated. On each iteration the array element indexed by the loop parameter is displayed on the terminal using the PUT_LINE procedure. When an array object declared from an unconstrained array is used with this facility the bounds of the iteration will be automatically matched to the bounds of the array object, as in

```
for ThisString in LargeStringArray'RANGE loop
    PUT_LINE( LargeStringArray( ThisString));
end loop;
```

This program fragment does not need to know of the actual declared bounds of the array *LargeStringArray*; whatever actual bounds were specified when the object was declared will be determined by the use of the array RANGE attribute.

Two complete arrays can be assigned to each other. This can most easily be accomplished if the arrays are of identical constrained types. If the arrays are of different types but are compatible in the type of their elements and the types of their indexes, then the assignment can be accomplished by the use of type conversion. Thus the type *Int8Array* whose index range was 1 .. 8 and the *IntegerArrays* type whose index range was 25 .. 32 are assignment compatible. They are compatible as they are both arrays whose element type is INTEGER, whose index type is INTEGER and both arrays contain eight elements. The effect of the statement

```
Int8Array := Int8Arrays( IntegerArray);
```

is to type-convert the variable *IntegerArray* into type *Int8Arrays* and subsequently to assign the value of *IntegerArray* (25) to *Int8Array* (1), *IntegerArray* (26) to *Int8Array* (2), and so on up to the assignment of *IntegerArray* (32) to *Int8Array* (8). Slices of arrays can be assigned in a similar manner:

```
FirstSmallArray := SmallArrays( SmallFloatArray( 2 ..4));
```

The right hand side of this assignment statement is a three element slice of the array *SmallFloatArray* declared from the unconstrained type *FloatUarrays*. The slice is converted to the constrained type *SmallArrays* by the use of type conversion. This type conversion is possible as the elements of *FirstSmallArray* and *SmallFloatArray* are both FLOAT, the indexes are both INTEGER and the length of both arrays is 3. The effect of the statement is to transfer the value of *SmallFloatArray* (2) to *FirstSmallArray* (3), and correspondingly (3) to (4), and (4) to (5).

Two arrays can be catenated together to provide a single array. For example:

```
SecondSmallArray( 4 .. 5) :=
        SmallArrays( SmallFloatArray( 5) & SmallFloatArray( 1))
```

The effect of this statement is to catenate together element 5 and 1 of the array *SmallFloatArray* and then assign it, via type conversion, to a two element slice of the array *SecondSmallArray*.

The relational operators can be applied to arrays if the arrays are compatible, or can be made compatible with slicing and/or type conversion and if a suitable relational operator exists for the elements of the array. Thus the expression

```
Int8Array < Int8Arrays( SmallIntArray);
```

will be true if every INTEGER element of *Int8Array* is less than the corresponding INTEGER element of *SmallIntArray*.

It is possible for entire arrays, or slices of arrays, to be passed as the actual parameters of subprograms or to be the return type of functions. It is in these situations where unconstrained arrays can be the most valuable. For example, a function may be required which calculates the sum of the integers contained within an integer indexed array. The data flow diagram for this function would be

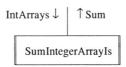

Using a constrained array type as the type of the formal parameter of this function, the declaration would be

```
function SumIntegerArrayIs( AnArray : in Int8Arrays)
                                  return INTEGER;
```

This declaration declares the type of the array which can be used as the formal parameter of the function to be of the constrained array type *Int8Arrays*. The only array objects which can be made compatible with this declaration are arrays whose element type is INTEGER, whose index type is INTEGER and whose length is 8. The alternative declaration of the function using the unconstrained array type as the formal parameter would be

```
function SumIntegerArrayIs( AnArray : in IntegerUarrays)
                                  return INTEGER;
```

The arrays which can be made compatible with this formal parameter are those whose element type is INTEGER, whose index type is INTEGER and whose length is indeterminate. This class of arrays include arrays of the unconstrained array type *IntegerUarrays* which is the type of the formal parameter. The constrained array variable *Int8Array* of the type *Int8Arrays* has the correct structure but is of the wrong type: it can be converted to the appropriate type by using the type conversion facility (as in *IntegerUarrays(Int8Array)*). Suitable calls of this second version of the function would therefore include the following:

```
TheTotal := SumIntegerArrayIs( SmallIntArray);
-- SmallIntArray is of type IntegerUarrays, length 8.

TheTotal := SumIntegerArrayIs( LargeIntArray);
-- LargeIntArray is of type IntegerUarrays, length 100.

TheTotal := SumIntegerArrayIs( IntegerUarrays( Int8Array));
-- Int8Array is of type Int8Arrays, it is converted
-- to type IntegerUarrays to make it type compatible with
-- the type of the formal parameter, length 8.
```

The declaration of the formal parameter as an unconstrained array type allows the function to take as an actual parameter either an unconstrained array or a constrained array. The declaration of the formal parameter as a constrained type only allows it to take as actual parameters arrays of the constrained type or restricted slices of unconstrained arrays.

The second declaration of the function is able to accommodate all the possible actual parameters which the first declaration can take, plus other actual parameters which the first declaration cannot accept. The second declaration is thus more general in its possible application, thus reducing the need for maintenence changes. It is therefore regarded as better design style to make functions and procedures as general as possible and consequently the second declaration is regarded as a 'better' implementation of the requirement. The design and definition of the function *SumIntegerArrayIs*, taking an unconstrained formal argument, would be

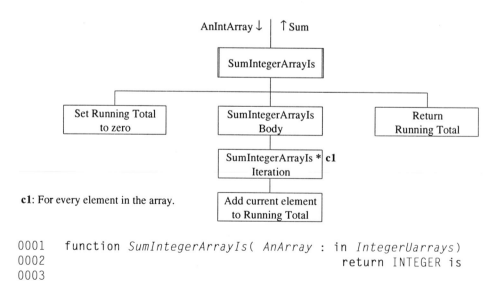

```
0001    function SumIntegerArrayIs( AnArray : in IntegerUarrays)
0002                                          return INTEGER is
0003
```

```
0004         RunningTotal : INTEGER := 0;
0005
0006    begin -- SumIntegerArrayIs
0007       for ThisElement in AnArray'RANGE loop
0008          RunningTotal := RunningTotal + AnArray( ThisElement);
0009       end for;
0010       return RunningTotal
0011    end SumIntegerArrayIs;
```

The use of the RANGE attribute in the implementation of this function allows it to accept as a formal parameter an instance of the unconstrained array type *IntegerUarrays* with arbitrary bounds. This is the technique by which the increased generality of unconstrained array parameters, mentioned above, is accomplished.

An example array program

A newsagent stocks the following newspapers:

Sun, Star, Mirror, Express, Mail, Times, Observer

Of these the *Sun* and the *Star* are not published on Sunday and the *Observer* is only published on Sunday. The newsagent requires a system which will record details of the number of papers required on a particular day. Initially the system is to deal with Sunday papers only, but is to be designed to be easily expanded to deal with the daily papers. The following functions are required of the system:

- To input the number of copies of each paper required.

- To display a table of all papers and copies required.

The data will be stored in an array of natural integers indexed by an enumeration type called newspapers. The data structure diagram of the array is

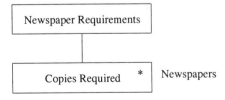

As the number of copies required is an integer value with a minimum of zero, the *CopiesRequired* element of the array will be implemented as the integer subtype NATURAL. The array *NewspaperRequirement* will be implemented as an

unconstrained array, of index type *Newspapers* whose bounds are the entire range of newspapers specified.

The *Sunday Newspapers* will be a constrained instance of this array whose bounds are those newspapers which are printed on a Sunday only. This allows a second instance of the array, *Daily Newspapers*, to be implemented whose bounds are those newspapers which are printed on a weekday.

The specification indicates that there are only two actions which are to be performed upon an instance of this array: to set the value of all elements of the array from the terminal and to display the contents of the array on the terminal. The data flow diagrams of these two actions, and their subprogram declarations, might be

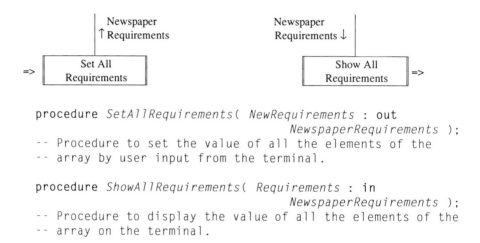

```
procedure SetAllRequirements( NewRequirements : out
                                 NewspaperRequirements );
-- Procedure to set the value of all the elements of the
-- array by user input from the terminal.

procedure ShowAllRequirements( Requirements : in
                                 NewspaperRequirements );
-- Procedure to display the value of all the elements of the
-- array on the terminal.
```

The data structures required for this application and the procedure declarations would be best implemented as a package, whose specification might be

```
0001   -- Filename NewspaperRequirement_.pkg (k8 newspape.adb).
0002   -- Initial version for Ada '95 book, Section III, Chapter
                                                              17.
0003   --
0004   -- Fintan Culwin, v0.1, Jan 1997.
0005
0006   package NewspaperRequirement is
0007
0008      type Newspapers is ( Sun, Star, Mirror,
0009                           Express, Times, Observer);
0010
0011      subtype SundayNewspapers is Newspapers
0012                           range Mirror .. Observer;
0013
```

```
0014        subtype DailyNewspapers is Newspapers
0015                                    range Sun .. Times;
0016
0017        type NewspaperRequirements is array ( Newspapers
                                                    range <>)
0018                                    of   NATURAL;
0019
0020        procedure SetAllRequirements( NewRequirements : out
0021                                    NewspaperRequirements );
0022        -- Procedure to set the value of all the elements of the
0023        -- array by user input from the terminal.
0024
0025        procedure ShowAllRequirements( Requirements : in
0026                                    NewspaperRequirements );
0027        -- Procedure to display the value of all the elements of
0028        -- the array on the terminal.
0029
0030    end NewspaperRequirement;
```

The body of this package would implement the two procedures. The design of these procedures might be

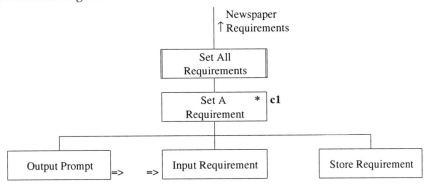

c1: For each Newspaper stocked.

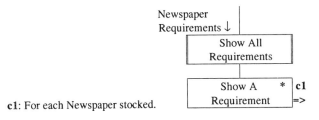

c1: For each Newspaper stocked.

The program structure diagrams for these procedures are very similar to the data structure diagrams which describe the array structure. This is not a coincidence: if a procedure has to set or show all the elements which are contained in the

391

array then it will have to iterate through each element of the array to do so. Thus the design of a procedure to process a data object has to reflect the structure of the data object. The *NewspaperRequirement* package body might be as follows:

```
0001    -- Filename NewspaperRequirement.pkb (k8 newspape.adb).
0002    -- Initial version for Ada book, Section III, Chapter 17.
0003    --
0004    -- Fintan Culwin, v0.1, Jan 1997.
0005
0006    with ADA.TEXT_IO;
0007    use  ADA.TEXT_IO;
0008
0009    package body NewspaperRequirement is
0010
0011       package IntegerIO is new ADA.TEXT_IO.INTEGER_IO
0012                                                  ( INTEGER);
0012       package NewspapersIO is new
0013                      ADA.TEXT_IO.ENUMERATION_IO( Newspapers);
0014       use IntegerIO, NewspapersIO;
0015
0016       procedure SetAllRequirements( NewRequirements : out
0017                                     NewspaperRequirements ) is
0018       begin -- SetAllRequirements
0019          for ThisPaper in NewRequirements'RANGE loop
0020             PUT("Please enter requirements for the ");
0021             PUT( ThisPaper, SET => LOWER_CASE, WIDTH => 10);
0022             GET( NewRequirements( ThisPaper)); SKIP_LINE;
0023          end loop;
0024       end SetAllRequirements;
0025
0026
0027       procedure ShowAllRequirements( Requirements : in
0028                                      NewspaperRequirements ) is
0029       begin -- ShowAllRequirements
0030          for ThisPaper in Requirements'RANGE loop
0031             PUT("Requirements for the ");
0032             PUT( ThisPaper, SET => LOWER_CASE, WIDTH => 10);
0033             PUT(" are ");
0034             PUT( Requirements( ThisPaper)); NEW_LINE;
0035          end loop;
0036       end ShowAllRequirements;
0037
0038    end NewspaperRequirement;
```

These two procedures would be required to be called from a client program which would offer a menu to the newsagent offering the choice of setting or displaying the Sunday newspaper requirements. For the purpose of testing the procedures they can be called from a test harness which will first call the *SetAllRequirements* procedure and then call the *ShowAllRequirements* procedure. A suitable test harness might be as follows:

```
0001    -- Filename NewspaperTestHarness.ada (k8 newstest.adb).
0002    -- Test harness program for the initial version of the
0003    -- NewspaperRequirement from Ada book,
0004    -- Section III, Chapter 17.
0005    --
0006    -- Fintan Culwin, v0.1, Jan 1997.
0007
0008    with ADA.TEXT_IO, NewspaperRequirement;
0009    use  ADA.TEXT_IO, NewspaperRequirement;
0010
0011    procedure NewspaperTestHarness is
0012
0013       subtype SundayRequirementsArray is
0014             NewspaperRequirements( SundayNewspapers);
0015
0016       SundayRequirements :
0017                 SundayRequirementsArray := ( others =>0);
0018
0019    begin -- NewspaperTestHarness
0020       SetAllRequirements( SundayRequirements);
0021       ShowAllRequirements( SundayRequirements);
0022    end NewspaperTestHarness;
```

The effect of the harness is to create a constrained array subtype and a variable object of that type which is indexed by only those newspapers which are published on a Sunday. This variable is then passed to the two procedures, first to have all its values set from the terminal and then to have its contents displayed on the terminal. The inclusion of a menu procedure to call either of the two procedures as indicated by the user of the program would complete the specification.

The program can be adapted for a single weekday operation by the declaration of a constrained array subtype whose index range would be of the enumeration subtype *DailyNewspapers*. The expansion of this specification to accommodate weekly newspaper requirements will be presented in the next chapter.

EXERCISES

17.1 Implement a second test harness demonstration program for the *NewspaperRequirement* package which will illustrate the use of the package for *DailyNewspapers*.

17.2 The *SumIntegerArrayIs* subprogram could be complemented by other subprograms such as *AverageIntegerArrayIs* which returned the average value of the integers stored in the array, *MinimumIntegerArrayIs* which returns the minimum and *MaximumIntegerArrayIs* which returns the maximum. Design the interfaces for these subprograms and implement them as an *IntegerArrayUtility* package then provide a demonstration test harness for them.

17.3 Design an appropriate data structure for holding details of monthly rainfall totals for one year. Implement this as an ADT package providing facilities to input values into the structure, determine the total rainfall, the average rainfall, the wettest month, the driest month, and output, with appropriate formatting, the values in the structure. Reuse the menu dispatch design from Section II Chapter 14 to provide a demonstration test harness.

17.4 Revisit the lottery number program from Exercise 16.1 and store the numbers in a suitable array before outputting them.

CHAPTER 18

Two (and more) dimensional arrays

When the array declaration was formally defined in the previous section, it was stated that the elements of an array can be of any Ada type. This includes the possibility of an array being declared whose component elements are themselves an array. A general data structure diagram for an array of this form is as follows:

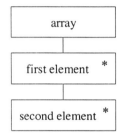

This diagram indicates that this array type consists of an iteration of *first element* and each of these elements is itself an iteration of *second element*. The simple arrays which were introduced in the previous chapter, containing a single iteration, are known as *one dimensional* arrays; the addition of a second iteration forms a *two dimensional* array. Many of the operations which were introduced for one dimensional arrays are inherited by two dimensional arrays, or have corresponding operations which can be applied to two dimensional arrays.

This expansion of a simple array into a two dimensional array can be continued: if each *second element* is itself an iteration of *third element* a *three dimensional* array will be defined. Additional iterations can be added giving rise to higher dimensional arrays. This chapter will introduce two dimensional arrays in detail before considering arrays of higher dimensions.

Declaring two dimensional constrained arrays

To introduce the declaration of two dimensional arrays, a two dimensional array of floating point values, indexed by an INTEGER in the range 1 to 5 and by a

CHARACTER in the range 'a' to 'e', will be used. The data structure diagram for this array would be as follows:

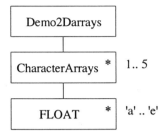

There are two possible methods which can be used to declare two dimensional arrays. The first, as suggested by the diagram above, is to declare a one dimensional array type called *CharacterArrays*, which is then used as the element type of a second one dimensional array called *Demo2Darrays*. The interpretation of this data structure diagram might be

```
MinimumCharacterIndex : constant CHARACTER := 'a';
MaximumCharacterIndex : constant CHARACTER := 'e';

subtype CharacterIndices is CHARACTER range
            MinimumCharacterIndex .. MaximumCharacterIndex;

type CharacterArrays is array     CharacterIndices of FLOAT;

MinimumIntegerIndex : constant INTEGER := 1;
MaximumIntegerIndex : constant INTEGER := 5;

subtype IntegerIndices is INTEGER range
            MinimumIntegerIndex .. MaximumIntegerIndex;

type Demo2Darrays is array IntegerIndices of
                                        CharacterArrays;

First2Darray : Demo2Darrays;
```

A visualization of the structure *First2Darray*, with arbitrary floating point values, would be

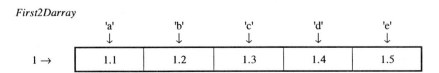

	'a' ↓	'b' ↓	'c' ↓	'd' ↓	'e' ↓
2 →	2.1	2.2	3.1	2.4	2.5

	'a' ↓	'b' ↓	'c' ↓	'd' ↓	'e' ↓
3 →	3.1	3.2	3.3	3.4	3.5

	'a' ↓	'b' ↓	'c' ↓	'd' ↓	'e' ↓
4 →	4.1	4.2	4.3	4.4	4.5

	'a' ↓	'b' ↓	'c' ↓	'd' ↓	'e' ↓
5 →	5.1	5.2	5.3	5.4	5.5

The variable object *First2Darray* is of type *Demo2Darrays*; each element of this array can be referenced by a single INTEGER subscript in the range 1 to 5 (e.g. *First2Darray*(3)) and is of type *CharacterArrays*. A second CHARACTER subscript in the range 'a' to 'e' can be added to this expression (e.g. *First2Darray*(3)('c')) to identify a particular floating point value from the array. In the visualization above the floating point value referenced by the subscript values (3)('c') has the value 3.3.

The alternative design and definition of a two dimensional array does not require the intermediate one dimensional array; instead the array type is constructed directly as a double iteration. The appropriate data structure diagram, implementation and visualization of this form of two dimensional array would be as follows:

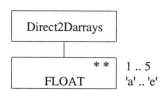

```
MinimumCharacterIndex : constant CHARACTER := 'a';
MaximumCharacterIndex : constant CHARACTER := 'e';

subtype CharacterIndices is CHARACTER range
            MinimumCharacterIndex .. MaximumCharacterIndex;

MinimumIntegerIndex : constant INTEGER := 1;
MaximumIntegerIndex : constant INTEGER := 5;
subtype IntegerIndices is INTEGER range
            MinimumIntegerIndex .. MaximumIntegerIndex;
```

```
type Direct2Darrays is array (IntegerIndices,
                              CharacterIndices)
                        of FLOAT;

Second2Darray : Direct2Darrays;
```

Second2Darray

	'a' ↓	'b' ↓	'c' ↓	'd' ↓	'e' ↓
1 →	1.1	1.2	1.3	1.4	1.5
2 →	2.1	2.2	3.1	2.4	2.5
3 →	3.1	3.2	3.3	3.4	3.5
4 →	4.1	4.2	4.3	4.4	4.5
5 →	5.1	5.2	5.3	5.4	5.5

This structure is more restricted in its possibilities when compared with structures of type *First2Darray*. It is possible to refer to the entire structure as *Second2Darray* which is a reference of type *Direct2Darrays*. It is also possible to refer to an individual element of the array by use of two subscripts with appropriate values: for example, *Second2Darray*(3, 'c') which identifies the element with the value 3.3. However, it is not possible to reference a part of the array by use of a single subscript (*Second2Darray(3)*) as was possible with the first form of declaration above.

As the first form of declaring a two dimensional array is more congruent with the concept of a two dimensional array and as it has more possibilities it should be favoured. The second method of declaring a two dimensional array should only be used if it is certain that it will never be necessary or advantageous to reference a component array.

The one dimensional array of *Appointment* which was introduced in the previous section to hold details of a day's appointments can be expanded to a two dimensional array of appointments which can be used to hold details for a week. The design and declaration of a suitable structure might be as follows:

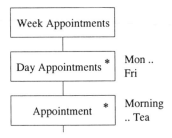

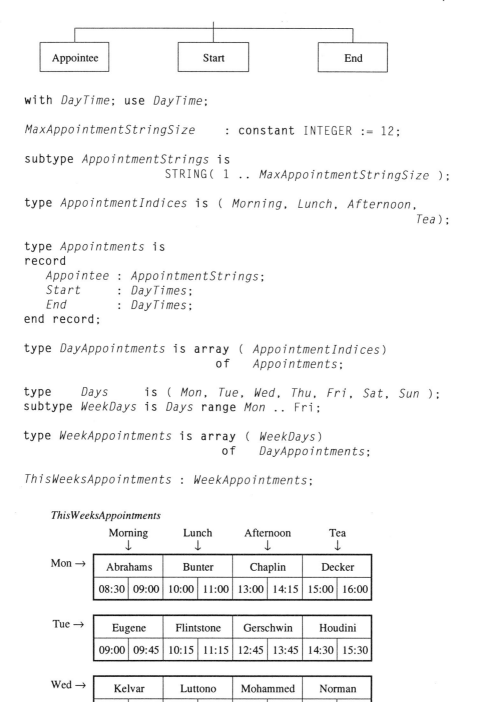

```
with DayTime; use DayTime;

MaxAppointmentStringSize    : constant INTEGER := 12;

subtype AppointmentStrings is
              STRING( 1 .. MaxAppointmentStringSize );

type AppointmentIndices is ( Morning, Lunch, Afternoon,
                                             Tea );

type Appointments is
record
   Appointee : AppointmentStrings;
   Start     : DayTimes;
   End       : DayTimes;
end record;

type DayAppointments is array ( AppointmentIndices )
                    of    Appointments;

type   Days    is ( Mon, Tue, Wed, Thu, Fri, Sat, Sun );
subtype WeekDays is Days range Mon .. Fri;

type WeekAppointments is array ( WeekDays )
                    of    DayAppointments;

ThisWeeksAppointments : WeekAppointments;
```

ThisWeeksAppointments

	Morning ↓		Lunch ↓		Afternoon ↓		Tea ↓	
Mon →	Abrahams		Bunter		Chaplin		Decker	
	08:30	09:00	10:00	11:00	13:00	14:15	15:00	16:00

Tue →	Eugene		Flintstone		Gerschwin		Houdini	
	09:00	09:45	10:15	11:15	12:45	13:45	14:30	15:30

Wed →	Kelvar		Luttono		Mohammed		Norman	
	09:15	10:00	10:30	10:45	12:30	13:45	14:45	15:45

Thu →	O'Reilly		Pinter		Sharma		Turner	
	08:15	09:00	09:45	10:30	13:15	14:15	15:00	15:30

Fri →	Undress		VanGough		Wimpole		Zacharia	
	09:00	09:30	10:00	11:30	12:00	14:00	15:30	17:00

The entire object, *ThisWeeksAppointments*, is of type *WeekAppointments*; each element of this array can be referenced with a single subscript of the subtype *WeekDays*. For example, for *ThisWeeksAppointments(Fri)*, the type of such a reference is *DayAppointments*. As this is itself an array type, an individual element of this array can be referenced by using a second subscript of type *Appointment-Indices*. This two subscript reference can be expressed as *ThisWeeksAppointments(Fri)(Tea)* which is of type *Appointments* and identifies the appointment with Zacharia at 15:30 to 17:00.

The type *Appointments* is a record type. Consequently a dot selector can be used to reference one of the components of the record. Thus *ThisWeeksAppointments(Fri)(Tea).Appointee* is of type *AppointmentStrings* and has the value "Zacharia", *ThisWeeksAppointments(Fri)(Tea).Start* is of type *DayTimes* and has the value 16:30 and *ThisWeeksAppointments(Fri)(Tea).Finish* is of type *DayTimes* and has the value 17:00.

Declaring two dimensional unconstrained arrays

The advantages of declaring unconstrained two dimensional arrays are comparable with those which exist for the declaration of one dimensional unconstrained arrays. Unfortunately it is only possible to declare a two dimensional unconstrained array directly by specifying that both subscripts are unconstrained. It is not possible to declare a two dimensional array as an unconstrained array of unconstrained arrays. An example of the declaration of an unconstrained two dimensional array type and a constrained subtype of this type which is comparable with the declaration of the *Direct2Darrays* type above might be as follows:

```
MinimumCharacterIndex : constant CHARACTER := 'a';
MaximumCharacterIndex : constant CHARACTER := 'e';
```

```
subtype CharacterIndices is CHARACTER range
            MinimumCharacterIndex .. MaximumCharacterIndex;
MinimumIntegerIndex : constant INTEGER := 1;
MaximumIntegerIndex : constant INTEGER := 5;

subtype IntegerIndices is INTEGER range
            MinimumIntegerIndex .. MaximumIntegerIndex;

type Unconstrained2Darrays is array ( INTEGER   range <>,
                                      CHARACTER range <>)
                                            of FLOAT;

subtype SecondDirect2DArrays is
            Unconstrained2Darrays( IntegerIndices,
                                   CharacterIndices);

Third2Darray : SecondDirect2Darrays;
```

A visualization of the variable object *Third2Darray* would be identical to the visualization of *Second2Darray* above.

Two dimensional array aggregates

Instances of two dimensional arrays can be given values using named or positional array aggregates, whose forms are expressed in a comparable manner with those used for one dimensional arrays introduced in the last chapter. Examples using the array variables declared above include

```
-- Example using positional notation
Second2Darray := ( ( 1.1, 1.2, 1.3, 1.4, 1.5),
                   ( 2.1, 2.2, 2.3, 2.4, 2.5),
                   ( 3.1, 3.2, 3.3, 3.4, 3.5),
                   ( 4.1, 4.2, 4.3, 4.4, 4.5),
                   ( 5.1, 5.2, 5.3, 5.4, 5.5));

-- Example using named notation
Third2Darray := ( 1 => ( 1.1, 3.1, 4.5, 6.7, 8.9),
                  4 .. 5 => ( 'b' .. 'd' => 3.3,
                              'a'        => 2.2,
                              'e'        => 4.4),
                  others => ( 'a' | 'c' => 0.0,
                              others    => 2.1));
```

The values assigned by this second aggregate are

Third2Darray

	'a' ↓	'b' ↓	'c' ↓	'd' ↓	'e' ↓
1 →	1.1	3.1	4.5	6.7	8.9
2 →	2.1	0.0	0.0	2.1	2.1
3 →	2.1	0.0	0.0	2.1	2.1
4 →	2.2	3.3	3.3	3.3	4.4
5 →	2.2	3.3	3.3	3.3	4.4

Two dimensional array attributes

The attributes which are applicable to one dimensional arrays are also applicable in a modified form to two dimensional arrays. Each attribute has to be indexed with an integer value to indicate which dimension of the array is being referenced. Attribute expressions with an index value of 1 are used to ascertain the attribute value of the first dimension; attribute expressions with an index value of 2 are used to ascertain the attribute value of the second dimension. Some examples using the array types and objects which have been declared in this section will make this clear:

Expression	Type	Value
First2Darray'FIRST(1)	INTEGER	1
First2Darray'LAST(1)	INTEGER	5
First2Darray'RANGE(1)	implicit INTEGER subtype	1 .. 5
First2Darray'LENGTH(1)	INTEGER	5
First2Darray'FIRST(2)	CHARACTER	'a'
First2Darray'LAST(2)	CHARACTER	'e'
First2Darray'RANGE(2)	implicit CHARACTER subtype	'a' .. 'e'
First2Darray'LENGTH(2)	INTEGER	5
ThisWeeksAppointments'FIRST(1)	*Days*	*Mon*
ThisWeeksAppointments'FIRST(2)	*AppointmentIndex*	*Morning*
ThisWeeksAppointments'LAST(1)	*Days*	*Fri*
ThisWeeksAppointments'LAST(2)	*AppointmentIndex*	*Tea*
WeekAppointments'RANGE(1)	implicit *Days* subtype	*Mon .. Fri*

*WeekAppointments'*RANGE(2)	implicit *AppointmentIndex* subtype	*Morning .. Tea*
*WeekAppointments'*LENGTH(1)	INTEGER	*5*
*WeekAppointments'*LENGTH(2)	INTEGER	*4*
*Unconstrained2Darray'*FIRST(1)	is not allowed	
*Unconstrained2Darray'*RANGE(1)	is not allowed	

Higher dimensional arrays

The concept of an array of arrays can be taken a stage further to the concept of an array of arrays of arrays. This structure would be known as a three dimensional array. For example, the two dimensional *WeekAppointments* structure declared earlier in this chapter could be used as the basis of a yearly diary by using it as the element type of an array type called *YearAppointments*. The additional parts of the declaration to accommodate this would be as follows:

```
WeeksInYear : constant INTEGER := 52;
subtype WeekIndices is INTEGER range 1 .. WeeksInYear;

type YearAppointments is array ( WeeksIndices)
                  of   WeekAppointments;

ThisYearsAppointments : YearAppointments;
```

The references which can be made with this structure include the following:

Expression	Type
ThisYearsAppointments	*YearAppointments*
ThisYearsAppointments(14)	*WeekAppointments*
ThisYearsAppointments(14)(Wed)	*DayAppointments*
ThisYearsAppointments(14)(Wed)(Lunch)	*Appointments*
ThisYearsAppointments(14)(Wed)(Lunch).Appointee	*AppointmentStrings*
ThisYearsAppointments(14)(Wed)(Lunch).Start	*DayTimes*
ThisYearsAppointments(14)(Wed)(Lunch).End	*DayTimes*

As the declaration of *YearAppointments* requires three indexes to be specified, the referencing of a single appointment requires the value of three indexes to be expressed. A visualization of a three dimensional array is possible, as an iteration of two dimensional arrays:

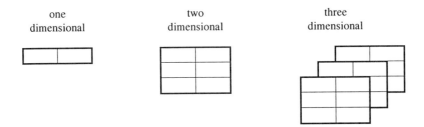

one	two	three
dimensional	dimensional	dimensional

It is possible to declare arrays of more than three dimensions. Ada does not place any restrictions upon the number of dimensions which can be used in the declaration of an array data type. However, there are reasons for never going beyond three or at most four dimensions. The first reason is cognitive: our brains are capable of holding a mental image of a three dimensional structure as we live in a three dimensional world. Producing a mental image of a structure having four or more dimensions is beyond most people's capacity and without a clear cognitive image the meaning of each dimension becomes unclear.

The remaining reasons are more practical. As the number of dimensions in a structure increases the number of subscripts required to reference a fundamental element increases and the chances of an error creeping in increase. The other practical reason is the usage of space: as the number of dimensions increases the chance of a fundamental element actually being used decreases. In the example above, the chance of having an appointment booked today is very high, the chance of having an appointment booked in the next week is not quite so high, but the chance of having an appointment booked in a year's time is low. A different method of representing the information which is not as wasteful of storage space would be a better solution.

Using two dimensional arrays

To illustrate the use of two dimensional arrays the newsagent specification from the last chapter will be expanded. The newsagent, having approved the Sunday newspaper implementation, commissions an expansion of the system to deal with weekday (Monday to Saturday) requirements. The program is to be menu driven and is to offer the following options:

- To input from the terminal all requirements for all papers on all weekdays.

- To input from the terminal all requirements for all papers on a particular day, including Sundays.

- To input from the terminal the requirement for a particular paper on a particular day, including Sunday.

- To output on the terminal all requirements for all papers on all weekdays.

- To output all requirements for a particular day, including Sunday.

- To output requirements for a particular paper on all weekdays.

These options will be offered to the user in the form of a menu, which will include an option to exit from the system. As with the newspaper example from the previous section, the newspaper data structure and the operations which can be performed upon it will be encapsulated within a package, which will be made use of by the client program which implements the system.

The data structure required by the system will be an unconstrained two dimensional array of NATURAL integers, with indexes of the enumerated types *Days* and *Newspapers*. The name of this type will be *WeeklyNewspaperRequirements* and its data structure diagram would be as follows:

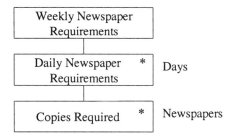

Two instances of this array will be required, one with a daily range from Monday to Saturday and a newspaper range encompassing all newspapers published on a weekday. The other instance of the array will have a daily range from Sunday to Sunday (i.e. a range of one day); its newspaper range will encompass all newspapers published on a Sunday. The data structure part of the package specification which implements the general array and suitable subtypes might be as follows:

```
0001    -- Filename NewspaperRequirement_.pkg (k8 newspape.ads).
0002    -- Second version for Ada book, Section III, Chapter 18.
0003    --
0004    -- Fintan Culwin, v0.1, Jan 1997.
0005
0006    package NewspaperRequirement is
0007
0008       type Newspapers is ( Sun, Star, Mirror,
0009                            Express, Times, Observer);
0010
```

```
0011          subtype SundayNewspapers is Newspapers
0012                                    range Mirror .. Observer;
0013
0014          subtype DailyNewspapers is Newspapers
0015                                    range Sun .. Times;
0016
0017          type Days is ( Mon, Tue, Wed, Thu, Fri, Sat, Sun );
0018
0019          subtype WeekDays is Days range Mon .. Sat;
0020
0021          subtype SunDays is Days range Sun .. Sun;
0022
0023          type NewspaperRequirements
                               is array ( Days       range <>,
0024                                      Newspapers range <>)
0025                               of    NATURAL;
0026
```

Notice that these declarations overload the enumeration literal *Sun*: it is used once as the name of a newspaper and once as the name of a day. In the use of this package it must be clear from the context which meaning of *Sun* is intended. If the meaning is not clear from the context then the type has to be explicitly stated with a **type mark**, as in *Newspapers'(Sun)* or *Days'(Sun)*. With these declarations in use, a particular instance of the array suitable for the storage of weekday requirements would be the following:

```
subtype WeekdayRequirements is
        NewspaperRequirements( WeekDays, DailyNewspapers );

WeekDayOrders : WeekdayRequirements;
```

A visualization of the structure of the variable object *WeekDayOrders* is:

WeekDayOrders	*Sun* ↓	*Star* ↓	*Mirror* ↓	*Express* ↓	*Times* ↓
Mon →					
Tue →					
Wed →					
Thu →					
Fri →					
Sat →					

where each element of the two dimensional array is a NATURAL integer. The second instance of the array can be declared as follows:

```
subtype SundayRequirements is
        NewspaperRequirements( SunDays, SundayNewspapers);

SundayOrders : SundayRequirements;
```

The structure of the variable object *SundayOrders* can be visualized as follows:

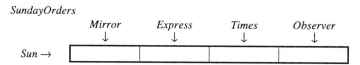

The first option from the menu can be satisfied by a procedure called *GetAll-Requirements*, with the following data flow diagram:

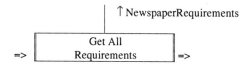

The data flow diagram indicates that the procedure requires a single ***out only*** parameter of type *NewspaperRequirements*. The effect of the procedure will be to set all elements of the array from the terminal. The second option from the menu can be satisfied by a procedure called *GetDayRequirements*, with the following data flow diagram:

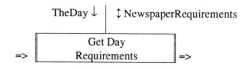

This diagram indicates that this procedure requires an ***in out*** parameter of type *NewspaperRequirements* and an ***in only*** parameter of type *Days*. The requirements parameter is ***in out*** as only a part of the structure is being given a value and the values of the other parts of the structure need to be preserved. This is in contrast to *GetAllRequirements* where the entire structure is being given a value and thus an ***out only*** mode is appropriate. The effect of the procedure is to set all newspaper requirements indicated by the value of *TheDay*. The procedure can be called with the actual parameter *WeekdayOrders* and a *Days* value of the subtype *WeekDays*, when it is required to get a weekday newspaper requirement. Alternatively the procedure can be called with the actual parameter *Sunday-Requirements* and the value *Sun* for *TheDay*, when it is required to get Sunday's newspaper requirements.

The third option from the menu can be satisfied by a procedure called *GetARequirement*, with the following data flow diagram:

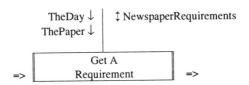

The interpretation of this diagram is similar to the interpretation of the *GetDay-Requirement* above. By varying the actual parameters which are supplied to the procedure it can be used to obtain a weekday or a Sunday newspaper requirement. The three remaining options from the menu can be implemented from three corresponding procedures with the following data flow diagrams:

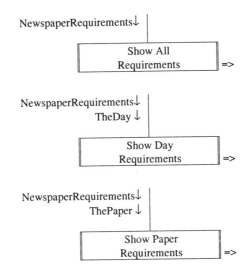

As with the procedures *GetDayRequirements* and *GetARequirement*, the procedure *ShowDayRequirements* can be used to show a weekday or a Sunday requirement by appropriate use of different actual parameters. The procedure declarations can be derived from the data flow diagrams, and the package specification can be completed as follows:

```
0027    -- Completion of NewspaperRequirement ADT package
0028    -- specification file.
0029
0030    procedure GetAllRequirements( TheRequirements : out
0031                                      NewspaperRequirements);
0032    -- Procedure to set all paper requirements for
0033    -- all days specified in parameter, from the terminal.
```

```
0034
0035     procedure GetDayRequirements( TheRequirements : in out
0036                                   NewspaperRequirements;
0037                                   TheDay : in Days);
0038     -- Procedure to set requirements for all papers
0039     -- for day specified only, from the terminal.
0040
0041     procedure GetARequirement( TheRequirements : in out
0042                                NewspaperRequirements;
0043                                TheDay    : in Days;
0044                                ThePaper  : in Newspapers);
0045     -- Procedure to set requirements for paper specified
0046     -- for day specified, from the terminal.
0047
0048     procedure ShowAllRequirements( TheRequirements : in
0049                                    NewspaperRequirements);
0050     -- Procedure to display all requirements in the array
0051     -- specified, upon the terminal.
0052
0053     procedure ShowDayRequirements( TheRequirements : in
0054                                    NewspaperRequirements;
0055                                    TheDay   : in Days);
0056     -- Procedure to display a particular day's paper
0057     -- requirements on the terminal
0058
0059     procedure ShowPaperRequirements( TheRequirements : in
0060                                      NewspaperRequirements;
0061                                      ThePaper : in Newspapers);
0062     -- Procedure to display a particular paper's requirements
0063     -- over all days, on the terminal
0064
0065     end NewspaperRequirement;
```

Once the package specification has been finalized the design of the subprograms which constitute the package can commence. The processes which were used to design the subprogram declarations were based upon the newsagent's requirements, and are an expression of *what* is to be done. The completion of the package in the package body expresses *how* these actions are to be done and should not be influenced by considerations of what has to be done. The package specification should be designed before the package body as what is to be done should not influence how it is to be done.

The design for the procedure *GetAllRequirements* has the following rationale. In order to get all requirements, each day's requirements have to be got. This can best be accomplished by repeatedly using the procedure *GetDayRequirements*. In order to get a day's requirements, each paper's requirement has to be got. This can best be accomplished by repeatedly using the procedure *GetARequirement*. These considerations produce the following designs:

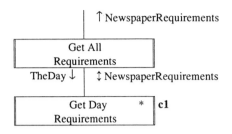

c1: For all required days.

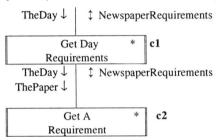

c2: For all required papers.

Thus the design of the procedure *GetAllRequirements* which has to process the entire array is effectively implemented as a double iteration. This is required as the data structure diagram of the structure to be processed consists of a double iteration and the nature of the data structure determines the nature of the processing required. The implementation of these two procedures within the package body might be as follows:

```
0001    -- Filename NewspaperRequirement.pkb (k8 newspape.adb).
0002    -- Second version for Ada book, Section III, Chapter 18.
0003    --
0004    -- Fintan Culwin, v0.1, Jan 1997.
0005
0006    with ADA.TEXT_IO;
0007    use ADA.TEXT_IO;
0008
0009    package body NewspaperRequirement is
0010
0011       package IntegerIO    is new INTEGER_IO( INTEGER);
0012       package NewspapersIO is new ENUMERATION_IO( Newspapers);
0013       package DaysIO       is new ENUMERATION_IO( Days);
0014       use IntegerIO, NewspapersIO, DaysIO;
0015
0016
```

```
0017    procedure GetAllRequirements( TheRequirements : out
0018                                  NewspaperRequirements) is
0019    begin -- GetAllRequirements
0020      for ThisDay in TheRequirements'RANGE( 1) loop
0021        GetDayRequirements( TheRequirements, ThisDay);
0022      end loop;
0023    end GetAllRequirements;
0024
0025
0026    procedure GetDayRequirements( TheRequirements : in out
0027                                  NewspaperRequirements;
0028                                  TheDay        : in Days) is
0029    begin -- GetDayRequirements
0030      for ThisPaper in TheRequirements'RANGE( 2) loop
0031        GetARequirement( TheRequirements, TheDay,
0032                                                  ThisPaper);
0032      end loop;
0033    end GetDayRequirements;
0034
```

Both of these procedures rely directly or indirectly upon the use of the procedure *GetARequirement* whose design and implementation might be:

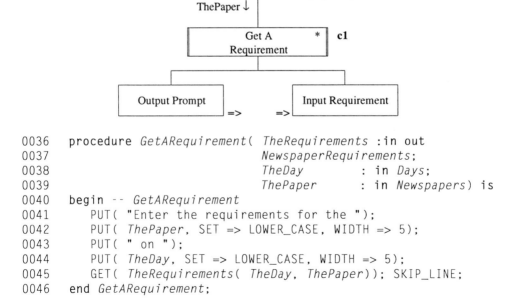

```
0036    procedure GetARequirement( TheRequirements :in out
0037                               NewspaperRequirements;
0038                               TheDay      : in Days;
0039                               ThePaper    : in Newspapers) is
0040    begin -- GetARequirement
0041      PUT( "Enter the requirements for the ");
0042      PUT( ThePaper, SET => LOWER_CASE, WIDTH => 5);
0043      PUT( " on ");
0044      PUT( TheDay, SET => LOWER_CASE, WIDTH => 5);
0045      GET( TheRequirements( TheDay, ThePaper)); SKIP_LINE;
0046    end GetARequirement;
```

The design for the procedure *ShowAllRequirements* is more complex as the output is to be in the form of a table. The user interface design of the weekday table which has to be produced by the program, with illustrative data, might be as follows:

```
            Newsagents Weekly Paper Requirements

            Sun     Star     Mirror    Express    Times

    Mon     1111    1112     1113      1114       1115

    Tue     1121    1122     1123      1124       1125

    Wed     1131    1132     1133      1134       1135

    Thu     1141    1142     1143      1144       1145

    Fri     1151    1152     1153      1154       1155

    Sat     1161    1162     1163      1164       1165
```

A data structure diagram for this table might be as follows:

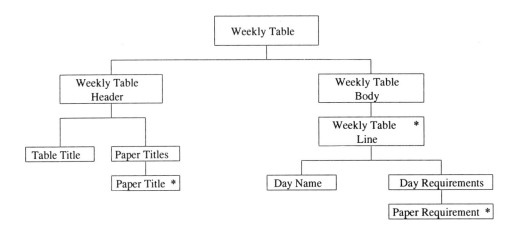

The design of a procedure which will produce this table will have to take account of the structure of the table which has to be produced and the structure of the two dimensional array from which the data in the table will be obtained. The design of the procedure *ShowAllRequirements* is based upon the data structure of the table shown above. The essence of the description of the table body is an iteration of paper requirements, within an iteration of daily requirements. This description of the essence of the production of the table is congruent with the description of the two dimensional array which contains the information from which the table is composed, allowing both requirements to be met with a relatively simple procedure:

```
0049   procedure ShowAllRequirements( TheRequirements : in
0050                                      NewspaperRequirements) is
0051   begin -- ShowAllRequirements
0052      -- Output the table header, starting with the table
                                                          title.
0053      SET_COL( 20);
0054      PUT_LINE( "Newsagents Weekly Paper Requirements);
0055      -- .. followed by the paper titles.
0056      SET_COL( 10);
0057      for ThisPaper in TheRequirements'RANGE( 2) loop
0058         PUT( ThisPaper, SET => LOWER_CASE, WIDTH => 10);
0059      end loop;
0060      NEW_LINE( 2);
0061
0062      -- Output the table body, one day at a time.
0063      for ThisDay in TheRequirements'RANGE( 1) loop
0064         -- First the day name.
0065         PUT( ThisDay, SET => LOWER_CASE, WIDTH => 10);
0066         -- Then the requirements
0067         for ThisPaper in TheRequirements'RANGE( 2) loop
0068            PUT( TheRequirements( ThisDay,
                                   ThisPaper),WIDTH=>10);
0069         end loop;
0070         NEW_LINE;
0071      end loop;
0072   end ShowAllRequirements;
```

The remaining procedures *ShowDayRequirements* and *ShowARequirement* can be implemented as follows:

```
0074   procedure ShowARequirement( Requirement : in NATURAL;
0075                                   TheDay      : in Days;
0076                                   ThePaper    : in Newspapers) is
0077   -- Subsidiary procedure to output a single requirement.
0078   -- Used by both ShowDayRequirements and
                                      ShowPaperRequirements.
0079   begin -- ShowARequirement
0080      PUT( "Requirements for the ");
0081      PUT( ThePaper, SET => LOWER_CASE, WIDTH => 10);
0082      PUT( " on ");
0083      PUT( TheDay, SET => LOWER_CASE, WIDTH => 10);
0084      PUT( Requirement, WIDTH => 10); NEW_LINE;
0085   end ShowARequirement;
0086
0087
```

```
0088    procedure ShowDayRequirements( TheRequirements : in
0089                                   NewspaperRequirements;
0090                                   TheDay          : in Days) is
0091    begin -- ShowDayRequirements
0092       for ThisPaper in TheRequirements'RANGE( 2) loop
0093          ShowARequirement( TheRequirements( TheDay, ThisPaper),
0094                                             TheDay, ThisPaper);
0095       end loop;
0096    end ShowDayRequirements;
0097
0098
0099    procedure ShowPaperRequirements( TheRequirements : in
0100                                     NewspaperRequirements;
0101                                     ThePaper        : in Newspapers) is
0102    begin -- ShowPaperRequirements
0103       for ThisDay in TheRequirements'RANGE( 1) loop
0104          ShowARequirement( TheRequirements( ThisDay, ThePaper),
0105                                             ThisDay, ThePaper);
0106       end loop;
0107    end ShowPaperRequirements;
```

The implementation of these procedures employs a subsidiary procedure called *ShowARequirement* which will display an individual requirement from the array. As this is a common operation of both procedures it has been factored out into a separate procedure which is private to the package body. This procedure is then called from each of the two procedures when it is required.

Finally the package has to be contained within a client program which will call the appropriate procedures from the package with the appropriate actual parameters to implement the action requested by the user. A possible main dispatch routine from this program might be as follows:

```
-- UsersChoice is the user's choice from the menu,
-- WeekdayOrders and SundayOrders are as declared above.
-- GetDay and GetPaper are safe enumeration input
-- procedures. MainMenu is a procedure to show the menu to
-- the user and input a valid lower case choice.

MainMenu( UsersChoice);
while UsersChoice /= ExitChoice loop
   case UsersChoice is
      -- Get all weekday requirements
      when 'A' => GetAllRequirements( WeekdayOrders);
      -- Get requirements for a single Day
      when 'B' =>
         GetDay( AnyDay);
         if AnyDay /= Sun then
            GetDayRequirements( WeekdayOrders, AnyDay);
```

```
          else
              GetDayRequirements( SundayOrders, AnyDay );
          end if;

   -- Get requirements for a particular paper
   -- on a particular day.
   when 'C' =>
       GetDay( AnyDay );
       GetPaper( AnyPaper );
       if AnyDay /= Sun then
           GetARequirement( WeekdayOrders, AnyDay,
                                              AnyPaper);
       else
           GetARequirement( SundayOrders, AnyDay,
                                              AnyPaper);

       end if;

   -- Show all weekday requirements.
   when 'D' =>
       ShowAllRequirements( WeekdayOrders);

   -- Show a single day's requirements.
   when 'E' =>
       GetDay( AnyDay);
       if AnyDay /= Sun then
           ShowDayRequirements( WeekdayOrders, AnyDay);
       else
           ShowDayRequirements( SundayOrders, AnyDay);
       end if;

    -- Show a single, weekday, paper's requirements.
    when 'F' =>
        GetPaper( AnyPaper);
        ShowPaperRequirements( WeekdayOrders, AnyPaper);

    when others => null;
  end case;
  MainMenu( UsersChoice);
end loop;
```

This program fragment can be considered the dispatch construct of the *MainMenu/dispatch* design presented in the previous section. The fragment commences by obtaining a menu choice from the user by calling the *MainMenu* procedure and, within a loop, which iterates until the user indicates that he or she wishes to exit the program, dispatches control to a suitable routine using a **case** statement. Each branch of the **case** statement calls a suitable procedure from the package with suitable parameters. For some options it is necessary to obtain a *Days* or a *Newspaper* value from the user before the package procedure is called. For options B), C) and E) a selection is made on the basis of the day specified by the user's input between a call of a procedure with parameters suitable for a weekday, or parameters suitable for a Sunday.

EXERCISES

18.1 What changes would be required to the newspaper system if a new Sunday newspaper called the *Sport* were published?

18.2 A page of text can be represented as a two dimensional array of characters. Revisit Exercise 10.3 to count the number of words on a page. A chapter of text can be regarded as an unconstrained array of pages. Extend the program further to count the number of words in a chapter.

18.3 A sentence can be regarded as an iteration of characters which is terminated by a punctuation character ('.', '?', '!'). A paragraph can be regarded as an iteration of characters terminated by two occurrences of an end of line marker (ASCII code 10 and/or 13). Design and produce a subprogram which will count the number of sentences or the number of paragraphs in a chapter, as described in Exercise 18.2.

18.4 Design and implement a package suitable for theatre bookings. The theatre has 26 rows of seats labelled 'A' to 'Z', each row having 30 seats. Devise suitable requirements, implement these requirements in a package, and provide a menu harness program to allow these facilities to be used for the booking of a single performance. Expand the system to be able to deal with a week's bookings.

18.5 Revisit the annual rainfall problem in Exercise 17.3 and extend it to record details of a decade's rainfall. Then revisit it again to record details of a century's rainfall.

CHAPTER 19
Recursion

There is one further iterative program control technique, known as *recursion*. A recursive iteration involves a subprogram calling itself, directly or indirectly. If a subprogram simply called itself as a part of its execution, then the called execution would itself call a further execution, which would itself call itself and there would be no end to the number of calls made. This situation is known as *infinite recursion* and is similar to the fault in indefinite loops where a faulty loop control condition causes the loop to iterate infinitely. To avoid an infinite loop the loop control condition has to be very carefully constructed in order to ensure that at some stage it can be guaranteed that it will cause the loop to terminate. To avoid infinite recursion, the recursive subprogram has to be carefully constructed to ensure that at some stage the subprogram terminates without calling itself.

Data structures, as well as program structures, can be described and constructed recursively. A recursive description of a data structure contains a smaller, possibly simpler, version of itself in its description. Where the recursive component is simpler there comes a stage in the recursion where the description is trivial and the possibility of an infinitely recursive description can be avoided.

Recursion in everyday life

Recursion is rarely met in everyday life and when it is met can cause some surprise. One commonly experienced recursive situation is where two mirrors are placed almost parallel to each other and as someone walks between them they see a reflection in one mirror, which includes the reflection of themselves in the other mirror. This reflection in the other mirror contains a reflection of themselves in the first mirror, which contains a reflection of themselves in the second mirror, and so on. The resulting image seen in the mirror is of an infinite sequence of reflections each a little smaller than the previous one, disappearing into the distance. When this is experienced unexpectedly, or when it is experienced by a child, the effect is to stop and wonder at it.

A second, less common, experience of recursion occurs occasionally on the covers of magazines. The cover of a recent Christmas edition of a popular magazine contained an image of Father Christmas reading a copy of the self-same edition of the magazine. The copy of the magazine clearly showed the cover, which contained an image of the cover of the magazine, which itself contained an image of the cover. Although the resolution of the printing quickly became such that even the representation of the cover was only a small area of solid colour, in the imagination of the viewer the sequence continued to infinity. The cover of this book is similarly recursive.

The recent interest in fractal images has made images of recursion more popularly available. Figure 19.1 contains a fractal image known as the Seaprinski triangle which can be constructed recursively. If the lower left quarter triangle, or the lower right or upper centre quarter triangle, of the image is imagined as expanded and moved to cover the extent of the original triangle, the resulting image would be identical with the original image. This process could be continued indefinitely indicating the recursive nature of the fractal image, and the infinite amount of detail which it contains. Recursive fractal images are not only a mathematician's curiosity: some commercial image compression software relies upon their characteristics and the structures of some medically important biochemical molecules have been shown to be recursive.

The problem with recursion for novice software developers, and even for many experienced software developers, is that human cognition is based upon human

Figure 19.1 The Seaprinski triangle.

experience and recursion is rarely experienced in real life. The concept of a sequence, as in a sequence of actions to make a cup of tea, is readily assimilated from experience into software. Likewise the concept of selection, as in Indian or Chinese tea, and the concept of iteration, as in pour out cups of tea until everyone has one, are also readily assimilated. As the examples above illustrate recursive experiences are much rarer, and almost always to some degree artificial, which implies that the developer's concept of recursion cannot readily be assimilated from the real world experience.

There are some data structures, and associated algorithms, whose structure is best described recursively. Although any recursive structure, or algorithm, can be replaced with an equivalent iterative structure or algorithm, there are many situations where the recursive version is much simpler, and thus easier to build and maintain, than the iterative version. For these reasons a knowledge of, and experience of developing, recursive data structures and algorithms is an essential part of learning to develop software. The recursion examples which will be introduced in this chapter could all be better constructed using iterative techniques, but there are some data structures which are best described recursively. These structures will be introduced later in the book. It is hoped that by experiencing recursion at an early stage in learning to develop software, the assimilation of these recursive structures will be eased.

Recursive subprograms

Tracing an example of a recursive process is the only way to provide an easy explanation of recursion. To do this a procedure called *CountDown* will be implemented. The procedure *CountDown* requires a single *in only* integer parameter greater than zero and on execution the procedure will output all the integers from the value of the parameter down to 1. For example, if the procedure *CountDown* was called with a parameter having the value 5, the output would be '5 4 3 2 1'. This requirement could best be implemented using a definite iterative loop of the form

```
for Number in reverse 1 .. CountFrom loop
   PUT( Number);
end loop;
```

A first recursive procedure

The procedure will be implemented using recursion for illustration only. The first stage of implementation is to describe the output of the procedure recursively.

Using the example above the output of *CountDown*(5) can be defined as the output of the integer value 5 followed by the output from *CountDown*(4). The output of *CountDown*(4) can be defined as the output of the integer value 4 followed by the output from *CountDown*(3), and so on.

In general terms the execution of *CountDown*(n) can be defined recursively as the output of the integer value n, followed by the output produced by the execution of *CountDown*($n-1$). This description of the output can be expressed in the following design and Ada procedure:

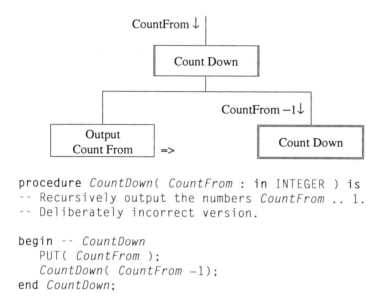

```
procedure CountDown( CountFrom : in INTEGER ) is
-- Recursively output the numbers CountFrom .. 1.
-- Deliberately incorrect version.

begin -- CountDown
   PUT( CountFrom );
   CountDown( CountFrom -1);
end CountDown;
```

In a program structure chart, or a data structure chart, a double edged component box is used to indicate a recursive component. In this design the indication is that the implementation of *CountDown* will recursively call the subprogram *CountDown*.

The feature of the implementation which makes it recursive is the procedure call to *CountDown* which occurs within the executable statements of the procedure. This implies that in order to perform the procedure *CountDown* the procedure *CountDown* will have to be performed, but in order to do so the procedure *CountDown* will have to be performed and so on.

This version of the procedure contains a deliberate error. As the procedure is always called recursively from within the procedure there is no limit to the number of calls which could be made. For example, if it were initially called as *CountDown*(3) the execution would be to output the value of the parameter, 3, and then call the procedure with the parameter '*CountFrom* – 1', which is equivalent to '3 – 1', which is the call of *CountDown* with the value 2.

The execution of this call of the procedure will output the number 2 and then call the procedure with the value '2 – 1', which is a call of *CountDown* with the value 1. The execution of this invocation of the procedure will output the number 1 and then call the procedure with the value '1 – 1', which is a call of *CountDown* with the value 0. This call will output the value 0. According to the specification the value 0 should not have been output, but the process will continue with the call of *CountDown* with the value '0 – 1'. This call will output the value –1 and then invoke the procedure with the value '–1 – 1', which will output the value –2 and so on. The process would continue indefinitely continuing to output negative integers until an attempt was made to evaluate INTEGER'FIRST – 1, at which point an exception would be raised. A more likely termination of the program would be for the user to interrupt it before the exception was raised.

The error in this design of the procedure is that it contains no terminating condition and enters a process of infinite recursion. With a recursive process it is necessary to define a terminating condition which will prevent further recursive calls of the process and it is also necessary to ensure that this condition will at some stage be satisfied.

The general definition of the *CountDown* process has to be expanded to indicate the terminating condition before the procedure can be correctly implemented. In this example the terminating condition can be defined as a call of *CountDown*(0). The output of *CountDown*(0) can be defined as nothing, and the attempted execution of *CountDown*(0) will not cause any further calls of the *CountDown* procedure. The expanded definition of the *CountDown* process would be as follows: *CountDown*(n) can be defined as the output of the integer value n followed by the call of *CountDown*(n – 1), unless the value of n is zero, in which case nothing is output. The revised design and implementation might be

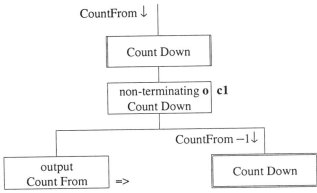

c1: If CountFrom is greater than zero.

```
procedure CountDown( CountFrom : in INTEGER ) is
-- Recursively output the numbers CountFrom .. 1,
-- correct version.
```

```
begin -- CountDown
   if CountFrom > 0 then
      PUT( CountFrom );
      CountDown( CountFrom -1);
   end if;
end CountDown;
```

This version of the procedure will only invoke itself recursively if the value of the parameter is greater than 0. If the value of the parameter is 0 the procedure will terminate without the output of 0 and without calling the procedure recursively. This version can be traced as the first version was with the value 3. The effects of the execution would be to output the value 3, followed by a call of the procedure with the value 2. This invocation would output the value 2 and call the procedure with the value 1. This invocation would output the value 1, followed by a call of the procedure with the value 0. This invocation of the procedure would, as explained above, do nothing, *terminating all invocations of the procedure* and completing the specified output of the initial call correctly.

A second recursive procedure

The key phrase in the last paragraph was 'terminating all invocations of the procedure'. The recursive procedure call in *CountDown* is the last executable statement; thus when execution of *CountDown*(0) terminates, control returns to *CountDown*(1). As there are no further executable statements, *Count-Down*(1) terminates immediately passing control to *CountDown*(2) and subsequently to *CountDown*(3) where the initial procedure call terminates. This aspect of the invocation of a recursive procedure can be better explained with a procedure which has actions to be performed following the recursive call of the procedure.

A complementary specification to *CountDown* would be a procedure called *CountUp* which has a single integer parameter greater than zero. The output of the procedure will be all the integers from one up to the value of the parameter. So if the procedure were called with the value 5 the output would be '*1 2 3 4 5*'.

Once again this procedure could best be implemented as a definite loop, but will be implemented recursively to illustrate the processes and use of recursion. The key to implementing the procedure recursively is again to define its output recursively. The output of *CountUp*(5) can be defined as the output produced by *CountUp*(4) followed by the output of the value 5. In general terms the output of *CountUp*(n) can be defined as the output produced by the execution of *CountUp*(n − 1) followed by the output of n, unless the value of n is zero in which case nothing is to be output.

The design and implementation of this procedure might be

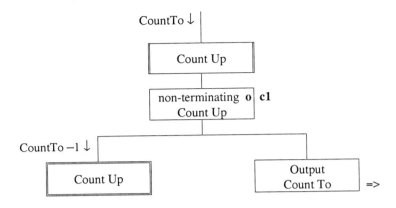

c1: If CountTo is greater than zero.

```
procedure CountUp( CountTo : in INTEGER ) is
-- Recursively output the numbers 1 .. CountTo.

begin -- CountUp
    if CountTo > 0 then
        CountUp( CountTo -1);
        PUT( CountTo );
    end if;
end CountTo;
```

In this procedure there is an executable statement following the recursive call. When this procedure is called with the value 3, the sequence of actions will be first to call the procedure with the value '*CountTo* – 1', which is equivalent to a call of the procedure with the value 2. The first action of this invocation of the procedure will be to call the procedure with the value '2 – 1', which is a call of the procedure with the value 1. The first action of this invocation of the procedure will be to call the procedure with the value '1 – 1', which is the invocation of the procedure with the value 0. This invocation of the procedure with the value 0 will have no actions, as the condition at the start of the procedure will evaluate false, and the invocation of the procedure will terminate.

Upon termination of any subprogram program control is returned to the place in the program where control was passed to it. In this example this is the point in the execution of the procedure when the value of the parameter was 1 and the procedure was called recursively with the value 0. The next statement to be executed is the PUT(*CountTo*) procedure call which will output the value of *CountTo* which is 1. There are no further actions to be taken by this invocation of the procedure so it terminates and passes control back to where it was called from. This place is the point in the execution of the procedure when the value of the parameter was 2 and the procedure was called recursively with the value 1. The next statement to be executed is the PUT procedure call which will output the value 2 and as there are no further actions to be performed the procedure will terminate. Control will be passed back to the point in the procedure where it was called with *CountTo* equal to 3 which will be output by this invocation of the procedure before it terminates.

This sequence of events can be visualized in a diagram of the recursive transfer of program control to and from invocations of the procedure:

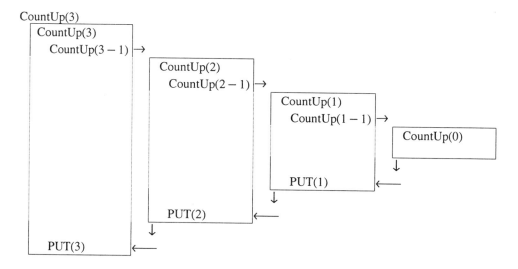

The diagram shows that the initial invocation of *CountUp*(3) calls the first recursive invocation of *CountUp* with the value of the parameter set to 2. This calls a second recursive invocation with the value 1, which calls a third recursive invocation with the value 0. When the fourth invocation is being executed the other three invocations are suspended, waiting for the current invocation to terminate. When the current invocation terminates, without any output, the remaining parts of the third invocation are executed. Following this the remaining parts of the second and then the first are executed, before control is passed back to the place in the program where the first invocation was called from.

Each invocation of the procedure is separate from all other invocations of the procedure. The diagram shows that at the maximum recursive level of the execution of *CountUp*(3) there are four separate invocations of the procedure. The parameter variable *CountTo* is a separate parameter variable in all four invocations, having different values in each.

At any point in the execution only one invocation of the procedure is active; the other invocations are inactive but the information required to reactivate them is held on the return stack. The information stored in any **stack frame** would be the name of the subprogram, the position within the subprogram where control is to be returned to and the value of any local objects. When the currently executing subprogram terminates this information is used to allow execution to continue from the same point and with the same values reinstated to any local variables. The stack frame when the fourth invocation of the *CountUp* procedure was executing can be visualized as follows:

	Subprogram	Position	Variables
Top of stack →	CountUp	line 4	CountTo → 1
	CountUp	line 4	CountTo → 3
	CountUp	line 4	CountTo → 3
	Program	line ?	vars → ?
	Procedure		

As control returns from the recursive invocations when they terminate, frames are removed from the top of the stack and used to reinstate the execution of the calling procedure at the point where the procedure was called. The final frame is popped when *CountUp*(3) terminates passing control back to the program procedure, assuming this is where *CountUp*(3) was called from.

The passing of control from the procedure to another invocation of the procedure is known as a ***recursive descent***; the consequential passing of control back from the recursively invoked procedure is known as a ***recursive ascent***. There is no limit in Ada to the number of frames which can be placed on the stack and thus no limit to the number of levels of recursion which can be invoked. This can lead to the situation of infinite recursion, where a recursive process continues to descend without ever reaching a terminating condition which would cause a recursive ascent.

A recursive function

Recursion is not limited to procedures: it is also possible for functions to be designed and implemented recursively. To illustrate this a function called *SumToN* will be implemented. The function is of type POSITIVE and requires a single POSITIVE parameter. The effect when this function is called is to compute and return the sum of all the integers between 1 and the value of the parameter. For example, if the function were invoked with the value 5 it would return the value 15 $(1 + 2 + 3 + 4 + 5 = 15)$.

The best method of designing and implementing this function would be to use a definite iteration; a recursive implementation will be used only to illustrate the use of recursive functions.

The method of designing a recursive function is to define the actions of the function recursively. For this function the definition would be that the value of

SumToN(n) is *n* plus the value of *SumToN(n − 1)*. This is a partial definition; it correctly expresses the recursive method of computing *SumToN* but does not define a terminating condition. As has been emphasized for recursive procedures, the terminating condition for a recursive process must be identified before it can be safely implemented. The terminating condition of *SumToN* is the case where it is invoked to compute the *SumToN* value of 1. The recursive definition given above would define this as 1 plus *SumToN(0)* but it can be better defined simply as the value 1. The full recursive definition of this function is thus that the value of *SumToN(n)* is *n +* the value of *SumToN(n − 1)*, unless the value of *n* is 1 in which case the value of *SumToN(1)* is 1. Using this definition the design and implementation of the function might be

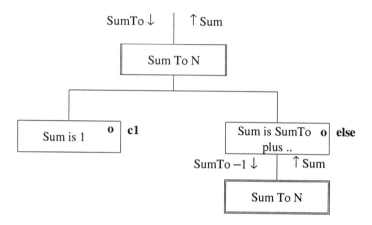

c1: If SumTo is greater than zero.

```
function SumToN( SumTo : in POSITIVE) return POSITIVE is
-- Recursive function to compute the sum of all integers
-- from 1 to SumTo.

begin -- SumToN
   if SumTo = 1 then
      return 1;
   else
      return SumTo + SumToN( SumTo -1);
   end if;
end SumToN;
```

The behaviour of this function can be explained by using a diagram of its recursive descent, similar to the diagram used to illustrate the recursive descent of the *CountUp* procedure:

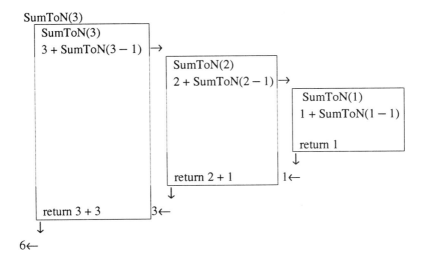

The diagram differs from the *CountUp* diagram by indicating the value which is returned from the function when its execution terminates. The execution commences with the request to compute the value of *SumToN*(3); this is computed as '3 + *SumToN*(3 – 1)' which recursively calls *SumToN*(2). This invocation computes this as '2 + *SumToN*(2 – 1)' which recursively calls *SumToN*(1). This invocation terminates the recursion returning the value 1 to the place where it was invoked from. This value is used to evaluate the value of *SumToN*(2) as 2 + 1, completing the execution of *SumToN*(2) and returning the value 3 as the result of *SumToN*(2). This value is used to evaluate *SumToN*(3) as 3 + 3, which is returned as the result of the original call *SumToN*(3).

Recursion and data structures

Recursion is a particularly appropriate process to be used to manipulate certain data structures. In order to illustrate this, a recursive process to manipulate a simple structure will be designed, implemented and traced. The structure which will be used to illustrate recursive processing of a structure is a STRING. In order to allow recursive string processing to be designed, a recursive description of a string will have to be produced.

The recursive description of a STRING commences by describing a STRING as an empty or a non-empty string. An empty string needs no further elaboration; a non-empty string can be described as a character, followed by the rest of the string, which is known as a substring. The substring is itself a string and can be described as an empty string or a non-empty string. If it is non-empty then it can be described as the character at the start of the substring followed by the

427

substring of the substring. The recursive data structure diagram of a string would thus be

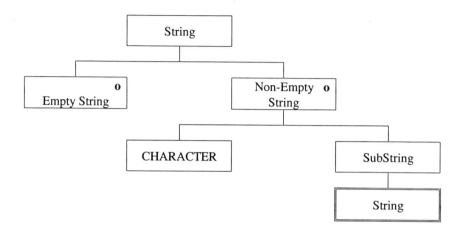

The data structure diagram of the string includes as a part of its description a component which is itself a string; it is thus a recursive description of a string. The recursive part of the data structure is indicated by the double lined component box.

This diagram identifies the terminating condition which will be required when recursive processes to manipulate strings are designed. Many of these processes will have to traverse the string, terminating when the end of the string is encountered. The end of a string is indicated on the diagram as an empty string. When during the recursive traversal of a string an empty string is encountered, it indicates that all characters in the string have been processed.

One use of this recursive description is to use it to implement a procedure which will display the string in reverse order. A recursive process to do this would display the last character of the string, following which the contents of the string apart from the last character should be displayed. However, if the string to be displayed is an empty string, then nothing should be displayed. A program structure chart for this subprogram would be

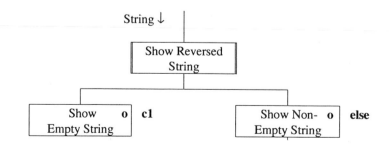

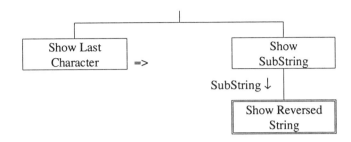

c1: If empty string.

```
procedure ShowReversedString( AnyString : in STRING) is
-- Show a string in reverse order, recursively.

begin ShowReversedString
    if AnyString'LENGTH > 0 then
        PUT( AnyString( AnyString'LAST));
        ShowReversedString( AnyString( AnyString'FIRST ..
                                    (AnyString'LAST-1)))
    end if;
end ShowReversedString;
```

If this procedure is initially called with the string "*A test*", upon the first invocation the length of the string will be 6 and the **if** condition will be TRUE. The body of the **if** statement will first output the last character of the string, '*t*', and then the *ShowReversedString* procedure is called recursively. The string passed as a parameter would be the string which extends from the first character to the last character but one of the original string, that is the string "*A tes*". This string will be processed by the second invocation of *ShowReversedString* in the same manner as the first. The last character, '*s*', will be output and the string excluding this character, "*A te*", will be passed on to the third invocation of the procedure.

The third invocation will output the last character, '*e*', and call a fourth invocation with the string "*A t*". The fourth invocation will output '*t*' and call a fifth with the string "*A*". This fifth invocation will output the last character, ' ', a space, and call a sixth invocation with the string "*A*".

This sixth invocation will output the last character of this string, "*A*", and cause a seventh invocation with a string which excludes this character. This string is "", which is a null string with a length of 0. This string will cause the **if** condition to evaluate FALSE, and the procedure will terminate without any output. Upon termination of the seventh invocation control is passed back to the sixth invocation, which has no further actions before it terminates. The remaining invocations of the procedure are likewise ascended without any actions.

The effect of all these actions is to output the sequence of characters "*tset A*", which is the original string in reverse order. A small change in the original procedure will display the string in its normal sequence:

```
procedure ShowForwardString( AnyString : in STRING) is
-- Show a string in reverse order, recursively.

begin ShowForwardString
   if AnyString'LENGTH > 0 then
      ShowForwardString( AnyString( AnyString'FIRST ..
                                    (AnyString'LAST-1)));
      PUT( AnyString( AnyString'LAST));
   end if;
end ShowForwardString;
```

The only difference between the two versions of the procedure is in the position of the PUT procedure call which outputs a single character, relative to the recursive call of the procedure. The positioning of the PUT before the recursive call of *ShowReversedString* causes the string to be output in reverse order during the recursive descent. The positioning of the PUT after the recursive call of *ShowForwardString* causes the string to be output in normal order during the recursive ascent.

The positioning of the PUTs in *ShowReversedString* and *ShowForwardString* is comparable with the positioning of the PUTs in the procedures *CountDown* and *CountUp* presented earlier in this chapter. *CountDown* and *CountUp* differed only in the positioning of the PUT relative to the recursive call of the procedure. The effect of the different positions was to display the list of numbers in ascending or descending order, depending upon whether they were output during the recursive descent or during the recursive ascent.

The two procedures *ShowReversedString* and *CountDown* are described as **head recursive**, while the two procedures *ShowForwardString* and *CountUp* are described as **tail recursive**. The phrases head recursive and tail recursive refer to the positioning of executable statements before or after the recursive call of the subprogram of which they themselves are a part. It is possible for a subprogram to be both head and tail recursive, having executable statements before and after the recursive subprogram call. An example of such a subprogram will be given in the next part of this chapter.

Mutual recursion

It is possible for a process to be invoked recursively indirectly. If a process calls a second process non-recursively and this process calls the first process, then the first process has been called by a process which it itself called. The original process which has been called by indirect recursion now has the possibility of recalling the second process recursively. Such a pair of processes is said to be ***mutually recursive***.

To illustrate this possibility a subprogram will be presented which will count down and then count up. If this subprogram, called *Bounce*, were invoked as *Bounce*(3) then the output of the program would be '3, 2, 1, 2, 3'. The implementation of this procedure will make use of two mutually recursive procedures: one called *BounceOdd* which will process an odd number and then call the second procedure, *BounceEven*, which will process an even number before calling *BounceOdd*. As this program is purely illustrative no design will be presented. The implementation of this program is

```
0001    -- Filename MutualDemo.ada, (k8 mutualde.adb).
0002    -- Program to illustrate mutual recursion of two subprograms.
0003    --
0004    -- Fintan Culwin, v0.1, Jan 1997.
0005
0006    with ADA.TEXT_IO; use ADA.TEXT_IO;
0007
0008    procedure MutualDemo is
0009
0010       package IntegerIO is new INTEGER_IO( INTEGER);
0011       use IntegerIO;
0012
0013       -- subprogram declarations
0014       procedure BounceOdd(  OddNum : in POSITIVE );
0015       procedure BounceEven( EvenNum : in POSITIVE );
0016
0017       -- subprogram definitions
0018       procedure BounceOdd(  OddNum : in POSITIVE ) is
0019
0020       begin -- BounceOdd
0021          if OddNum = 1 then
0022             PUT( 1, WIDTH => 4);
0023          else
0024             PUT( OddNum, WIDTH => 4);
0025             BounceEven( OddNum -1);
0026             PUT( OddNum, WIDTH => 4);
0027          end if;
0028       end BounceOdd;
0029
0030
0031       procedure BounceEven( EvenNum : in POSITIVE ) is
0032
0033       begin -- BounceEven
0034          PUT( EvenNum, WIDTH => 4);
0035          BounceOdd( EvenNum -1);
0036          PUT( EvenNum, WIDTH => 4);
```

```
0037       end BounceEven;
0038
0039
0040   begin -- MutualDemo
0041       BounceOdd( 9);
0042   end MutualDemo;
```

This implementation requires the procedures to be declared before they are defined as the definition of *BounceOdd* requires knowledge of the declaration of *BounceEven*. This can only be accomplished by declaring *BounceEven* before *BounceOdd* is defined. The recursive mechanics of the execution of this program will be left as an end of chapter exercise. The only points to note are that the terminating condition is expressed in one procedure, *BounceOdd*, only and that both procedures are both head and tail recursive. This implementation is not totally secure as a call of *BounceOdd* with an even parameter will cause an exception to be raised. The reasons for this will be left as an end of chapter exercise.

Recursion and iteration

A recursive design can always be replaced by an iterative design and an iterative design can always be replaced by a recursive design. The rationale for deciding between recursion and iteration would almost always favour iteration for two overriding reasons. The first reason for favouring iteration is that it is, for reasons explained above, simpler for humans to understand. This would seem to imply that an iterative algorithm would be easier to implement and maintain.

The second reason for favouring iteration is that it is less demanding of machine resources. As has been explained above, every level of recursion requires the initialization of a stack frame as the recursive subprogram is called and the restoration from the stack frame when the recursive invocation terminates. This requires large amounts of memory to be used and can slow down program execution dramatically.

There is one overriding reason for favouring recursion over iteration in some circumstances. Once the cognitive hurdle of recursion as a concept has been overcome some recursive designs are extremely simple and elegant compared with equivalent iterative designs. In particular some dynamic data structures, which will be introduced later in this book, have very simple recursive algorithms which can be used to manipulate them compared with very complex iterative algorithms. Where a recursive process is much more elegant than an equivalent iterative design it is to be favoured for these reasons.

EXERCISES

19.1 Produce a recursive descent/ascent diagram based upon the diagrams used in this chapter to illustrate the execution of *BounceOdd*(3).

19.2 Produce a recursive descent/ascent diagram based upon the diagrams used in this chapter to illustrate the execution of *BounceOdd*(2). Take care, as this will result in an infinite recursion!

19.3 If the PUT statement in *ShowReversedString* and *ShowForwardString* were changed to PUT(AnyString(AnyString'FIRST)), what other changes would be required to the procedures so that they fulfil their specifications?

19.4 Design, implement and demonstrate a recursive *Factorial* function. The factorial of a number *n* is defined as $n * n-1 * n-2 * .. * 1$.

19.5 Design, implement and demonstrate a recursive procedure called *Reverse-String*. This function will take a STRING value as a parameter and return a string whose contents are the reversed contents of the original string.

CHAPTER 20
Access types

Access data types allow a variable to be referenced indirectly. All references to the values of variables used so far in this book have been *direct references*, which have used the name of the variable to refer directly to its value. An *indirect reference* would obtain the value of an object by a direct reference to an access value which points (indirectly) to the value being referenced. This can be illustrated in the following diagram:

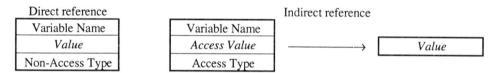

The value stored in an access type variable is the memory address of an object which stores a value of the type which the access type is declared to access. As shown on the diagram above, this can be thought of as a *pointer* which points from the access variable to the value being accessed.

The situations where the use of access variables to store indirectly and retrieve values is advantageous are not immediately obvious. Some of these situations will be indicated throughout this chapter as the facilities are introduced, but the major advantages of access types will not become apparent until later in the book when the topics of *class wide programming* and *dynamic structures* are explored in detail.

This chapter will introduce access types by considering the dynamic allocation of accessed variables, and then the use of access types to access static **aliased** variables. Finally, the use of class wide access types and the indirect calling of subprograms will be considered.

Dynamically allocated access variables

An access data type is declared as a type which can be used to reference indirectly some other data type. A variable declared as being of an access type does not itself contain the data but is capable of indicating where in the computer's memory the data are located; this process is known as ***designating***. An example may make this clearer. Assuming that the following record data type is declared

```
type People is
record
    PersonalName : NameStrings    := ( others => SPACE );
    FamilyName   : NameStrings    := ( others => SPACE );
    Weight       : PersonWeights  := 0.0;
    Height       : PersonHeights  := 0;
end record;
```

an access data type capable of designating instances of a record of the type *People* can then be declared:

```
type PeoplePointers is access People;
```

Having declared the access type it is then possible to declare a variable instance of the type:

```
APersonPointer : PeoplePointers;
```

The variable *APersonPointer* is of type *PeoplePointers* and is capable of holding an **access value** which points to an area of the computer's memory which can be treated as being an anonymous ***dynamically allocated*** variable of type *People*. The variable is said to be ***anonymous*** as it does not have an identifier by which it can be referenced; it can only be referenced indirectly via its access value. It is said to be dynamically allocated as it comes into existence under the control of the program logic, which is under the control of the developer. The alternative, normal, creation of variables is known as ***static*** and is under the control of the computer and run time system. In order to make the access value point to a suitable area of memory, sufficient memory for the storage of the information will have to be reserved and the access variable initialized to designate this area. This can be accomplished using the reserved term **new**, for example:

```
APersonPointer := new People;
```

The effect of this statement, known as an ***allocator statement***, is to reserve an area of memory sufficient for the storage of a *People* record, initialize the components of the *People* record as required by the record's declaration and then to return the address of the allocated record to be assigned to the access variable. This can be visualized as:

Before   **After**

The left hand diagram shows the state of the access variable before execution of the allocator statement. An access variable which is not given a suitable value upon declaration is automatically given a safe value. This safe value is a **null** pointer value and is indicated as such on the diagram. The right hand diagram illustrates the situation following the execution of the allocator statement. An area of memory capable of holding all the information in a *People* record has been allocated and the access variable has been initialized to designate it. The record declaration indicates that there are default values for all the fields of the record and these values are shown on the diagram.

It would also be possible for the contents of the newly allocated record to be initialized from a record aggregate value, using either positional or named notation, specified as part of the allocator statement. For example:

```
-- Initialization from a positional aggregate.
APersonPointer := new People ' ( "George      ",
                                 "Gerschwin  ",
                                 57.6, 182 );

-- The same initialization from a named aggregate.
APersonPointer := new People ' (
                Height       => 182,
                FamilyName   => "Gerschwin  ",
                Weight       => 57.6,
                PersonalName => "George      ");
```

Having declared a pointer and initialized it to designate a record which contains data, there needs to be some way by which the data can be referenced. This facility uses the dot notation and the reserved word **all** as follows:

APersonPointer	is of type	*PeoplePointers*
APersonPointer.**all**	is of type	*People*
APersonPointer.**all**.*PersonalName*	is of type	*NameStrings*
APersonPointer.**all**.*FamilyName*	is of type	*NameStrings*
APersonPointer.**all**.*Weight*	is of type	*PersonWeights*
APersonPointer.**all**.*Height*	is of type	*PersonHeights*

For the latter four of these references the term **all** can be omitted; for example, the term *APersonPointer*.**all**.*FamilyName* is equivalent to *APersonPointer*.*Family-Name*. The last facility which Ada provides for access variables is to allow them to be given a safe value which indicates that the access value does not designate anything. It was mentioned above that this value is **null** and is automatically given to all access variables which are declared without having any other suitable value. Where there are situations in a program where an access variable is not currently being used to point to anything then it should be explicitly given the safe value **null**. For example:

```
APersonPointer := null;
```

Any attempt made to reference the values designated by an access variable which has a **null** value will result in a CONSTRAINT_ERROR exception being raised.

A first example program

In order to demonstrate the facilities for the use of access variables which have been introduced so far, an example program for the following specification will be developed:

> The program will input from the user details of two people, using the *People* record structure as previously declared. Having input the two records it will then output them in alphabetical order.

It is assumed that a package called *Person*, whose object diagram and specification are as follows, is available.

```
0001    -- Filename Person_.pkg (k8 person.adb).
0002    -- Specification of the People ADT, first used in
```

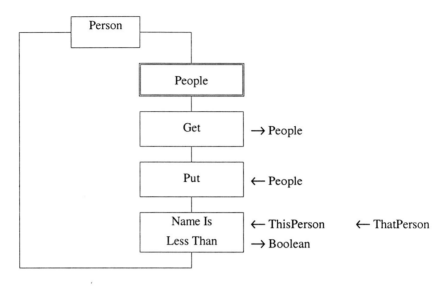

```
0003    -- Section III Chapter 20.
0004    --
0005    -- Fintan Culwin, v0.1, Jan 1997.
0006
0007    with ADA.CHARACTERS.LATIN_1;
0008    use  ADA.CHARACTERS.LATIN_1;
0009
0010    package Person is
0011
0012       type People is private;
0013
0014       procedure Get( AnyPerson : out People);
0015       -- Procedure to obtain details of a person from the
                                                    terminal.
0016
0017       procedure Put( AnyPerson : in People);
0018       -- Procedure to display details of a person on the
                                                    terminal.
0019
0020       function NameIsLessThan( ThisPerson : in People;
0021                                ThatPerson : in People)
0022                                        return BOOLEAN;
0023       -- Function returns true if ThisPerson's name is
0024       -- alphabetically less than ThatPerson's name and
0025       -- false otherwise.
0026
0027    private
0028
0029       MinimumPersonWeight : constant INTEGER := 0.0;
```

```
0030        MaximumPersonWeight : constant INTEGER := 250.00;
0031
0032        MinimumPersonHeight : constant INTEGER := 0;
0033        MaximumPersonHeight : constant INTEGER := 300;
0034
0035        MaximumNameLength   : constant INTEGER := 15;
0036
0037     subtype PersonWeights is FLOAT
0038            range MinimumPersonWeight .. MaximumPersonWeight;
0039
0040     subtype PersonHeights is INTEGER
0041            range MinimumPersonHeight .. MaximumPersonHeight;
0042
0043     subtype NameStrings is STRING( 1 .. MaximumNameLength);
0044
0045     type People is
0046     record
0047        PersonalName : NameStrings   := ( others => SPACE);
0048        FamilyName   : NameStrings   := ( others => SPACE);
0049        Weight       : PersonWeights := 0.0;
0050        Height       : PersonHeights := 0;
0051     end record;
0052  end Person;
```

The design of the client program to satisfy the specification above might be as follows:

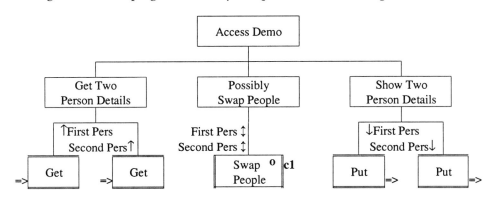

c1: If first person is alphabetically greater than second person.

On this design the parameters labelled *First Pers* and *Second Pers* are all of type *People*. The implementation of this design might be as follows:

```
0001    -- Filename AccessDemo1.ada (k8 accessd1.adb).
0002    -- Demonstration of dynamically accessed data objects,
0003    -- Section III Chapter 20.
0004    --
```

```
0005    -- Fintan Culwin, v0.1, Jan 1997.
0006
0007    with ADA.TEXT_IO, Person;
0008    use  ADA.TEXT_IO, Person;
0009
0010    procedure AccessDemo1 is
0011
0012       type PersonPointers is access People;
0013
0014       FirstPerson  : PersonPointers := new People;
0015       SecondPerson : PersonPointers := new People;
0016
0017
0018       procedure SwapPeople( OnePerson   : in out People;
0019                             OtherPerson : in out People ) is
0020
0021          LocalPerson : People;
0022
0023       begin -- SwapPeople
0024          LocalPerson := OnePerson;
0025          OnePerson   := OtherPerson;
0026          OtherPerson := LocalPerson;
0027       end SwapPeople;
0028
0029
0030    begin -- AccessDemo1
0031       SET_COL( 10);
0032       PUT_LINE( "Dynamic access variable demonstration");
0033       NEW_LINE( 2);
0034
0035       PUT_LINE( "Please enter first person details ");
0036       Get( FirstPerson.all);
0037       NEW_LINE;
0038
0039       PUT_LINE( "Please enter second person details ");
0040       Get( SecondPerson.all);
0041       NEW_LINE;
0042
0043       if NameIsLessThan( SecondPerson.all, FirstPerson.all)
                                                              then
0044          SwapPeople( FirstPerson.all, SecondPerson.all);
0045       end if;
0046
0047       PUT_LINE( "In alphabetical order they are ... ");
0048       Put( FirstPerson.all);
0049       NEW_LINE;
0050       Put( SecondPerson.all);
0051    end AccessDemo1;
```

The subprograms exported from the *Person* package, *Put*, *Get* and *NameIsLessThan*, all have formal parameters of type *People*. The calls of the subprograms in the client program supply as actual parameters the indirectly referenced, dynamically allocated *People* records. The package is totally unaware of this, as the declaration of the type *PersonPointers* is made outside the scope of the package and the dereferenced access variables are of the required type. This is possible as the indirectly referenced records are of a **private** type and the only operations which can be performed upon them are those appropriate for a **private** type and those supplied by the *Person* package.

The subprogram within the client program, *SwapPeople*, is called to swap the contents of the two records if the second record is alphabetically less than the first record. A visualization of this subprogram being called might be as follows:

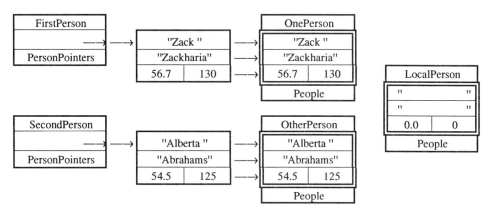

The left hand side of the diagram indicates the dereferenced pointers passing the records which they are designating as actual parameters to the formal parameters *OnePerson* and *OtherPerson*. The local variable *LocalPerson* is also shown on the *SwapPeople* side of the diagram. Following the execution of the first line of the subprogram, '*LocalPerson* := *OnePerson*', the state of the three objects in *SwapPeople* would be as follows:

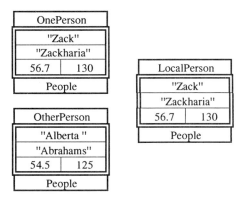

After execution of the second line, '*OnePerson* := *OtherPerson*', the visualization would be as follows:

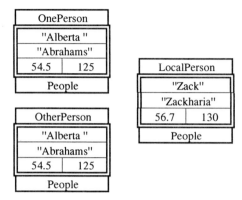

The final line of the subprogram is '*OtherPerson* := *LocalPerson*', which will have the following effect:

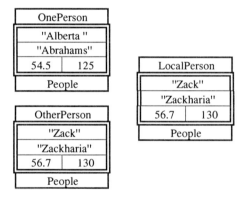

At the end of the subprogram, as both parameters are **in out** mode, the contents of the formal parameters are copied back into the actual variables:

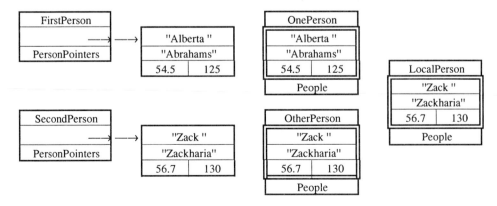

The effect of the subprogram has been that the *FirstPointer*, which was designating the Zack record, is now designating the Alberta record, and the *SecondPointer*, which was designating the Alberta record, is now designating the Zack record. As the records which the access variables are designating have been swapped, the dereferenced pointers passed to the *Put* procedures will output the two records in alphabetical order.

The same effect could have been obtained by redeclaring the *SwapPeople* subprogram to take parameters of type *PeoplePointers*. The changed declaration and subsequent implementation would now be

```
0018    procedure SwapPeople
                            ( OnePerson   : in out PeoplePointers;
0019                          OtherPerson : in out PeoplePointers) is
0020
0021       LocalPerson : PeoplePointers;
0022
0023    begin -- SwapPeople
0024       LocalPerson := OnePerson;
0025       OnePerson   := OtherPerson;
0026       OtherPerson := LocalPerson;
0027    end SwapPeople;
```

With this subprogram declaration in the client program, the call of the subprogram *SwapPeople* would have to be changed to pass the pointer rather than the record to which the pointer is pointing to:

```
0043    if NameIsLessThan( SecondPerson.all, FirstPerson.all) then
0044       SwapPeople( FirstPerson, SecondPerson);
0045    end if;
```

The diagram of this call, corresponding to the first diagram above, would be as follows:

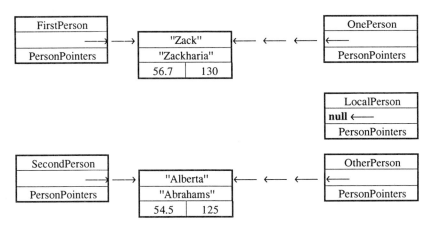

443

In this implementation it is the values of the pointers which are passed from the actual to the formal parameters. The formal parameters following this transfer of value have the same value as the actual parameters, and thus they both designate the same dynamically allocated record. The local access variable is shown with a safe **null** value which is the default value for any access variable declaration. The effect of the first statement, '*LocalPerson := OnePerson*', can be visualized as

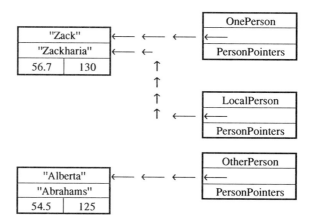

As the access variables *OnePerson* and *LocalPerson* both have the same value, they must both designate the same dynamic record, as shown. Following the execution of the second line for the subprogram, '*OnePerson := OtherPerson*', the situation can be visualized as

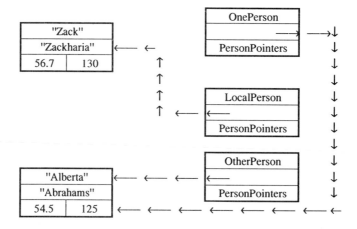

And following the final line of the subprogram, '*OtherPerson := LocalPerson*':

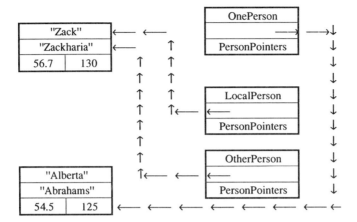

As the subprogram terminates the values of the pointers in the formal parameters are passed back in to the values of the actual parameters. This situation can be visualized as follows:

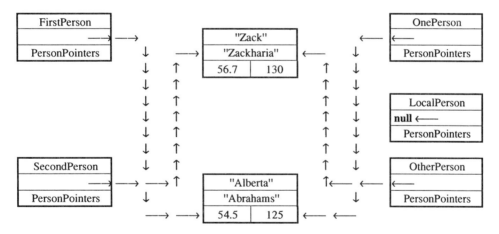

The effect again is that the *FirstPointer* which was pointing to the Zack record is now pointing to the Alberta record, and the *SecondPointer* which was pointing to the Alberta record is now pointing to the Zack record. This is exactly the same statement as was made following the trace of the first version of *SwapPeople* and demonstrates the equivalence of the two implementations.

Access values and static variables

In addition to using access variables indirectly to reference dynamically allocated anonymous variables it is also possible to use access variables to point to normal

445

statically allocated variables. For reasons which will be explained below this is a potentially dangerous practice and accordingly Ada requires that the static variable be specially declared if the facility is to be used. The following demonstration program illustrates the use of access values to reference indirectly static variables.

```
0001    -- Filename StaticDemo.ada (k8 staticde.adb).
0002    -- Program to illustrate the additional requirements to
0003    -- declare access types to access static variables.
0004
0005    with ADA.TEXT_IO;
0006    use ADA.TEXT_IO;
0007
0008    procedure StaticDemo is
0009
0010        package IntegerIO is new ADA.TEXT_IO.INTEGER_IO
                                                    ( INTEGER);
0011        use IntegerIO;
0012
0013        type IntegerPointers is access all INTEGER;
0014
0015        AnIntegerPointer : IntegerPointers;
0016        AnInteger        : aliased INTEGER := 42;
0017
0018    begin -- StaticDemo
0019        SET_COL( 10); PUT_LINE( "Static access types demo
                                                    program." );
0020        NEW_LINE( 2);
0021
0022        AnIntegerPointer := AnInteger'ACCESS;
0023
0024        PUT( "The value referenced directly is " );
0025        PUT( AnInteger); NEW_LINE( 2);
0026
0027        PUT( "The value referenced indirectly is");
0028        PUT( AnIntegerPointer.all ); NEW_LINE( 2);
0029
0030        AnIntegerPointer.all := AnIntegerPointer.all * 2;
0031
0032        PUT( "The value changed by indirect reference is");
0033        PUT( AnInteger); NEW_LINE( 2);
0034
0035    end StaticDemo;
```

Upon execution the output of this program was

```
          Static access types demo program.

The value referenced   directly is 42

The value referenced indirectly is 42

The value changed by indirect reference is 84
```

The type declared on line 0013 is an **access** type which can be used to designate INTEGER values. The keyword **all** indicates that it can be used for dynamically allocated INTEGER values and also for static variables. The declaration of the INTEGER variable *AnInteger* on line 0016 warns Ada, and the developer, by use of the keyword **aliased** that it may be referenced indirectly.

The access variable *AnIntegerPointer* is initialized to point to the INTEGER variable *AnInteger* by use of the ACCESS attribute on line 0022. The ACCESS attribute can only be applied to a variable which has been declared as **aliased**, and evaluates to an access value which designates that variable. The relationship between the access variable and the static variable following execution of line 0022 can be visualized as

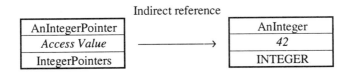

Having established this relationship, line 0028 indicates how the value of the *AnInteger* variable can be indirectly referenced via the access variable *AnInteger-Pointer*. Line 0030 indicates that not only can the value of the variable be referenced indirectly, it can also be changed indirectly, as confirmed on line 0033.

This program also illustrates one of the potential dangers of using indirect references to static variables. Between lines 0016 where the variable *AnInteger* is given a value and line 0033 where the value is output and shown to have changed, there is no reference to the variable either on the left hand side of an assignment statement or as an actual *in out* or *out only* parameter. Thus the value of the variable has changed by indirect reference. Although in a program of this length it is not particularly difficult for the developer to remember that the value of a variable can change directly or indirectly, this is not the case for programs of a more realistic length. It has been demonstrated that indirect modifications of variable values are a very common cause of program bugs, and that such bugs are very difficult to locate and correct.

This is the reason why Ada requires that a variable which may have to be referenced indirectly has to be declared as an **aliased** variable. Greater protection against such errors can be provided by declaring that the access type can only indirectly reference the value of a variable object and cannot modify its value. The corresponding definition would be as follows:

```
0013   type IntegerPointers is access constant INTEGER;
```

With this **type** declaration, variables of the access type can point to INTEGER variables or INTEGER constants, but can only indirectly reference the value of the INTEGER object and cannot change the value if the object is a variable.

The other major problem with the use of access to variables can be illustrated by the following subprogram:

```
0001   procedure Dangerous( APointer : out IntegerPointers ) is
0002
0003      LocalVariable : aliased INTEGER;
0004
0005   begin --
0006      APointer := LocalVariable'ACCESS;
0007   end Dangerous;
```

The subprogram exports via the *out only* formal parameter, *APointer*, an access value which designates the *LocalVariable*. The problem with this subprogram is that by the time a call of the subprogram comes to an end the variable object which is being referenced by the exported value does not exist. Local variables of subprograms are created when the subprogram is called and are destroyed when the call terminates. Thus for a call of the subprogram above, the calling environment has obtained an access value to an object which no longer exists. There is no sensible reason why this should have been attempted, but the causes of program bugs are rarely very sensible. This particular problem would be detected by Ada using a rule which prevents the access value being obtained in the first place.

The dangers of using access values to reference variables have been stressed in this chapter. For these, and for other, reasons the use of such facilities within Ada programs is rare and is usually limited to systems level programming or interfacing Ada programs to subprograms which have been written in other languages. The use of the keyword **aliased** should always have to be very carefully justified in, if not banned from, Ada programs.

Class wide access types

Section I Chapter 8 briefly introduced the concept of a *class wide* type. The *class hierarchy diagram* of the types *TransactionCounters*, and *MultipleCashRegisters* which were developed by extension in that chapter was as follows:

The class wide type rooted at *TransactionCounters* would encompass all three types shown in the hierarchy diagram. This type could be expressed in an Ada program as *TransactionCounters*'CLASS; however, no variable instance of this type could be declared. As the class hierarchy is extendible it cannot be known at compile time what the largest type in the hierarchy would be and thus space for it in memory cannot be allocated. At a particular instant in time, when the program is compiled, the largest of the types in the class hierarchy could be decided and this maximal amount of space allocated. However, it is possible that at some stage in the future the hierarchy is further extended and a new extended type is larger than the previous largest type. The client program would then be obsolete and require recompilation. Avoiding recompilation when a type is extended is one of the features of extendible types and thus such a solution is not possible.

The hierarchy which will be considered in this chapter differs from the hierarchy presented in Section I Chapter 8, in that the *CashRegisters* and the *MutipleCashRegisters* types have an additional, *Put*, action declared. The interface diagrams and procedure declarations for these actions are as follows:

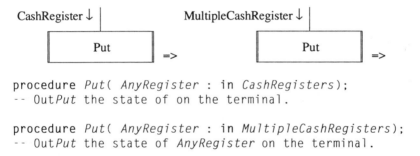

```
procedure Put( AnyRegister : in CashRegisters);
-- OutPut the state of on the terminal.

procedure Put( AnyRegister : in MultipleCashRegisters);
-- OutPut the state of AnyRegister on the terminal.
```

Although it is not possible to declare variables of the class wide type, it is possible to declare formal parameters of the class wide type and to declare an access type which designates an instance of the class wide type. When a formal parameter of a class wide type is declared, an actual parameter of any of the types in the class hierarchy is acceptable. This feature of class wide programming will be introduced in detail in the next section, and this part of this chapter will merely provide an introduction. Where a variable of an access to a class wide type is being used it is possible to allocate dynamically an instance of any of the types in the hierarchy, and cause the access variable to designate it.

This feature can be illustrated by considering a requirement of a program for a supermarket which has a number of *CheckOuts*. Some of these checkouts may be restricted to cash only purchases and some may accept cash, cheques and credit cards. To model this accurately within a program an iterative structure which is capable of containing instances of both the *CashRegisters* type and the *Multiple-CashRegisters* type is required. An array of *CashRegisters* is not appropriate as it cannot contain elements of the *MultipleCashRegisters* type, and likewise an array of *MultipleCashRegisters* cannot contain elements of the *CashRegisters* type.

449

The appropriate type of array is one whose elemental type is an access type which designates instances of the *CashRegisters'*CLASS of types. The elements of an instance of this array can then be initialized to dynamically allocated instances of the *CashRegisters'*CLASS type, which can include instances of the *Cash-Registers* type and instances of the *MultipleCashRegisters* type. The elements could also be used to designate dynamic instances of any other types which are added to the hierarchy by extension, for example the *ChangeGivingCashRegister* as suggested in Exercise 5.6.

The declaration of an appropriate array type might be as follows:

```
-- Assuming that CashRegister, MultipleCashRegister are
                                        withed and used.
type CashRegisterPointers is access CashRegisters'CLASS;

type CheckOutArrays is array ( CHARACTER range <> )
                of    CashRegisterPointers;
```

An instance of the unconstrained array type *CheckOutArrays* might be declared as follows:

```
CheckOuts : CheckOutArrays( 'a' .. 'c' );
```

And for a particular configuration of checkouts at a small supermarket, initialized as follows:

```
CheckOuts( 'a' ) := new MultipleCashRegisters;
CheckOuts( 'b' ) := new CashRegisters;
CheckOuts( 'c' ) := new MultipleCashRegisters;
```

Checkouts '*a*' and '*c*' are now of the *MultipleCashRegisters* type and checkout '*b*' is of the *CashRegisters* type. A subprogram of the supermarket control program may be required which outputs details of all the registers. The implementation of this subprogram might be as follows:

```
0001   procedure Put( TheCheckOuts: in CheckOutArrays) is
0002   begin -- Put
0003      for ThisCheckOut in TheCheckouts'RANGE loop
0004         Put( TheCheckOuts( ThisCheckOut).all);
0005      end loop;
0006   end Put;
```

The bounds of the definite loop on line 0003 are limited to the range of the constrained instance, *TheCheckOuts*, of the unconstrained array parameter. If the example array *CheckOuts*, as declared and initialized above, were passed as a formal parameter the loop would iterate three times, with the loop parameter, *ThisCheckOut*, taking the successive values '*a*', '*b*' and '*c*'.

On the first iteration of the loop the value which is passed to the *Put* procedure is thus effectively CheckOuts('a').all which is a value of the type *Mutiple-CashRegisters*, and thus the *Put* procedure provided by the *MultipleCashRegister* package will be used. On the second iteration the value on line 0004 will be CheckOuts('b').all which of the type *CashRegisters* type and thus the *Put* procedure provided by the *CashRegister* package will be used. On the final iteration the value is again of the *MutipleCashRegisters* type.

What is significant in this example is that Ada cannot decide which version of the *Put* procedure to call until the program is executing. Each pointer in the array could designate a value of any of the types rooted in the class hierarchy at the *CashRegisters* type, including any of the types which may be added by extension at some future stage.

This decision on precisely what version of an overloaded procedure to call differs from all previous decisions, which were made at the time of compilation, and is a very useful feature of development by extension. When a reference is of a **definite**, as opposed to a **class wide**, type a subprogram call can be **bound** to an implementation at compile time. When a reference is of a **class wide**, as opposed to a **definite**, type a subprogram call can only be **dynamically bound** to an implementation at run time, a process known as **dynamic dispatching**.

There are some program construction issues which have to be considered when dynamic dispatching is used. These are related to guaranteeing that a suitable subprogram can be found to dispatch to when the program is executing. In the example here both the *CashRegisters* type and the *MutipleCashRegisters* type declare a *Put* procedure in their package specifications, and so Ada was assured that one or other of them could be used. The use of class wide pointer types to maintain and process heterogeneous data structures will be considered in more detail in the next section.

Pointers to subprograms

In addition to using access types indirectly to reference variables and constants it is also possible to use access types indirectly to call subprograms. Again the reasons for doing this and the consequential advantages are not immediately obvious. The commonest realistic use of this facility is the provision of a **callback** mechanism in graphical user interfaces (GUIs). A graphical user interface object (known technically as a **widget**), for example a **push button**, has a behaviour installed into it as it is created. The push button knows that when it is pressed it is to activate a behaviour, but it has no direct knowledge of precisely what behaviour. Instead the behaviour is supplied as an access to the subprogram type parameter of the push button's creation mechanism and is called indirectly when the push button is pressed.

A contrived example of this facility might be to supply a different actual *ThankYou* procedure as a parameter of a *SayGoodbye* procedure. The precise actual parameter to be passed may depend upon the value of the purchases made, or the status of the customer, or some other criterion.

```
0001    -- Filename DynamicProcedureDemo.ada (k8 dynamicpr.adb).
0002    -- Contrived example of passing a procedure as an
0003    -- actual parameter of another procedure to illustrate
0004    -- indirect calling of subprograms.
0005
0006    -- Produced for Section III Chapter 20.
0007    -- Fintan Culwin, v0.1, Jan 1997.
0008
0009    with ADA.TEXT_IO;
0010    use  ADA.TEXT_IO;
0011
0012    procedure DynamicProcedureDemo is
0013
0014       package FloatIO is new ADA.TEXT_IO.FLOAT_IO( FLOAT);
0015       use FloatIO;
0016
0017       type ThankYouProcedures is access procedure( Name : in
0018                                                            STRING);
0019       procedure SmallThankYou( Customer : in STRING) is
0020       begin -- SmallThankYou
0021          null;
0022       end SmallThankYou;
0023
0024
0025       procedure MediumThankYou( Customer : in STRING) is
0026       begin -- MediumThankYou
0027          PUT_LINE( "Thank you for your custom " &
0028                    Customer & ".");
0029       end MediumThankYou;
0030
0031
0032       procedure BigThankYou( Customer : in STRING) is
0033       begin -- BigThankYou
0034         PUT_LINE( "Thank you for your esteemed custom " &
0035                   Customer & ".");
0036         PUT_LINE( "Have a nice day!");
0037       end BigThankYou;
0038
0039
```

```
0040      procedure SayGoodbye
                        ( AmountSpent       : in FLOAT;
0041                      CustomerName      : in STRING;
0042                      ThankYouProcedure : ThankYouProcedures) is
0043      begin -- SayGoodbye
0044         PUT( "The total cost of purchases is " );
0045         PUT( AmountSpent, Fore=>5, AFT=>2, EXP=>0);
0046         NEW_LINE;
0047         ThankYouProcedure( CustomerName);
0048      end SayGoodbye;
0049
0050
0051   begin -- DynamicProcedureDemo
0052      PUT_LINE( "Dynamic procedure demonstration program");
0053      NEW_LINE( 2);
0054
0055      PUT_LINE( "Passing a small thank you as a parameter.");
0056      SayGoodbye( 1.00, "Mr. Fred Flintstone",
0057                        SmallThankYou'ACCESS);
0058      NEW_LINE( 2);
0059
0060      PUT_LINE( "Passing a middle thank you as a parameter.");
0061      SayGoodbye( 1.00, "Mr. Barney Rubble",
0062                        MediumThankYou'ACCESS);
0063      NEW_LINE( 2);
0064
0065      PUT_LINE( "Passing a big thank you as a parameter.");
0066      SayGoodbye( 10.00, "Ms. Thelma Flintstone",
0067                        BigThankYou'ACCESS);
0068      NEW_LINE( 2);
0069
0070   end DynamicProcedureDemo;
```

The output from this program when executed was as follows:

```
Dynamic procedure demonstration program

Passing a small thank you as a parameter.
The total cost of purchases is     1.00

Passing a middle thank you as a parameter.
The total cost of purchases is     1.00
Thank you for your custom Mr. Barney Rubble.

Passing a big thank you as a parameter.
The total cost of purchases is    10.00
Thank you for your esteemed custom Ms. Thelma Flintstone.
Have a nice day!
```

Line 0017 of the listing declares an access type, called *ThankYouProcedures*, which designates a **procedure** which requires a single parameter of type STRING. The only program objects which are compatible with this type are the access values of procedures which are declared to have a single parameter of type STRING. Three procedures, *SmallThankYou*, *MediumThankYou* and *BigThankYou*, whose interfaces are compatible with this type are then declared.

The procedure *SayGoodbye* declares its third formal parameter as type *ThankYouProcedures* whose formal parameter name is *ThankYouProcedure*. Line 0047 within the procedure *SayGoodbye* is an indirect call of this procedure parameter, passing *CustomerName* as the required STRING parameter of the call.

As it is not possible for the subprogram to change the value of an access subprogram parameter it must be passed as an *in only* parameter. This is the default mode of parameter passing for all parameters, and will be used in all situations if no explicit declaration of a mode is made. The style guide suggested in this book is always to state the parameter mode of formal parameters, apart from those which designate subprograms. The intention is that the absence of a mode in the parameter declaration will alert the maintenance developer that this is a subprogram procedure being passed.

The design of a subprogram which makes use of an indirect call of a subprogram procedure uses a bold box to indicate the indirect call. Using this convention the design of the *SayGoodbye* procedure above would be

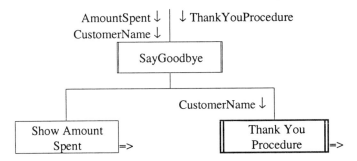

The program procedure calls the *SayGoodbye* procedure three times, passing as a third actual parameter each of the three procedures *SmallThankYou*, *Medium-ThankYou* and *BigThankYou* in turn. The ACCESS attribute is used with the name of the procedure to obtain its access value, which is then passed as the actual parameter to the third formal parameter. Thus, within a call of the *SayGoodbye* procedure, the call of the parameter procedure *ThankYouProcedure* will indirectly call one of the three example procedures. As shown in the program output above for Fred Flintstone this is a small thank you, for Barney Rubble a medium thank you and for Thelma Flintstone a big thank you.

As with the use of access values indirectly to reference static variables, the use of access variables indirectly to call subprograms is not very common in general Ada programs. When the facility is used Ada is very strict concerning the compatibility of formal and actual parameters. A formal subprogram access parameter is only compatible with an actual subprogram access parameter if it matches in the number and types of parameters, and in the case of functions the type returned.

EXERCISES

20.1 Extend the *AccessDemo1* program so that it will accept and sort three *Peoples* values, and provide a trace of the operation of the program.

20.2 One possible advantage of swapping access values which designate records rather than swapping the records themselves, is that the swapping of access values will take less time. Adapt the *AccessDemo1* program so that it swaps the records a large number of times and attempt to determine if this advantage is significant.

20.3 Choose one of the exercises from previous chapters which involves the manipulation of a **private** data type and reimplement it making use of indirect rather than direct references.

20.4 Implement the supermarket program as described in the chapter. Extend the implementation to make use of the *ChangeGivingCashRegister* from Exercise 5.6.

20.5 Extend the *DynamicProcedureDemo* program to issue a *NoThankYou* for very small purchases and a *GrovellingThankYou* for very large purchases.

20.6 Revisit the annual monthly rainfall program in Exercise 17.3 and make use of a dynamically called function to determine the minimum and maximum rainfall values.

CHAPTER 21
Text files

All the programs which have been presented so far have made no attempt to store any data which has been input or computed. Any information which has been present in the program has been lost as soon as the program terminates. Many, if not most, program specifications require that once information has been input into a system it is retained and made available to either the same program when it is executed again or another program which forms part of the system. This is made possible by storing information in external structures called *files*.

Ada supports several types of external file, the most obvious of which is the text file. A *text file* is composed of ASCII characters, and can have a structure composed of lines and pages. This type of file is cognitively comparable with pages of a report or a book, or the files which are produced by a text editor and are used as source code files for a compiler. As the file is composed of ASCII characters it can be loaded into a text editor or word processor and read by a human on the screen, or sent to a printer for a permanent readable copy.

The other types of external structure are *structured files*, *direct files* and *streams* which are not usually readable by humans. These files are intended to store information from a program in a format which is related to the format used to store the information within the computer. This format is usually more compact that the ASCII format and will thus take up less disk space and will load and save faster than the same information stored in ASCII format. However, such compact formats have the disadvantage that they are not usually readable by humans.

Also, as the format used for non-text files is possibly particular to the compiler being used, it cannot be guaranteed that information written by an Ada program can be easily read by a program which is written in another programming language. Indeed it cannot be guaranteed that the file could be read by a program which was compiled with a different Ada compiler from the one which was used to compile the program which wrote the file.

This gives a second important usage for text files. As the format of text files is standardized they can be used to transfer information between different programs, with fewer potential problems than if an internal format were used.

The use of text files will be introduced in this chapter, structured files will be introduced in the next chapter and streams in the next section. Direct files will not be introduced in detail, but some indication of how they differ from structured files will be given when structured files are considered. In addition to the standard package ADA.TEXT_IO which will be described in this chapter, a package called ADA.WIDE_TEXT_IO is also supplied for use with WIDE_CHARACTER based input–output. The facilities of this package are identical to those of ADA.TEXT_IO and, as with the description of CHARACTER and STRING data types, no detailed consideration will be included.

The structure of text files

Two special text files have already been extensively used by the programs in this book. Input to the program, normally from the keyboard, is assumed to arrive from a special text file called STANDARD_INPUT. Output from the program, normally sent to the screen, is assumed to go to a special text file called STANDARD_OUTPUT. As was explained in the chapter on testing, it is possible for most operating systems to *redirect* output to places other than the screen, and to redirect input from places other than the keyboard. However, the program would be unaware of this and does not require any changes, or special processing to be included, for these situations. There is also a second special output text file called STANDARD_ERROR where error messages from the Ada run time system are sent. This allows error messages to be sent to the terminal even if other, non-error, output is being redirected to a file.

These files are special as they are assumed to be *open* when the program starts and do not have to be *closed* before the program terminates. All other text files have to be *open*ed before they are used and should be *closed* after the program has finished with them, before it terminates. The structure of these files can be regarded simply as a sequence of ASCII characters, followed by a marker known as the *end of file*. The end of file marker is not normally visible when the file is viewed or printed. This understanding of the structure can be expressed as on the following data structure diagram:

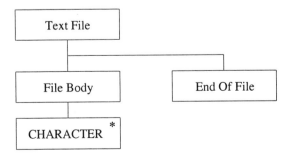

This is the simplest data structure diagram for a text file, but it is not the only possible diagram. In some situations it may make more sense to think of the file as an iteration of lines, the end of each line being indicated by an ***end of line*** marker and each line composed of an iteration of characters. This understanding would produce the following data structure diagram:

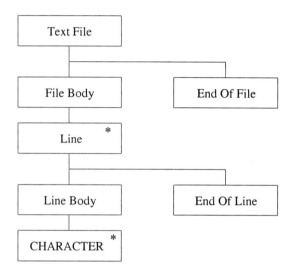

In other situations the nature of the file as an iteration of pages may be important, in which case the following data structure diagram would be appropriate:

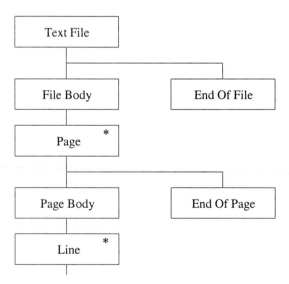

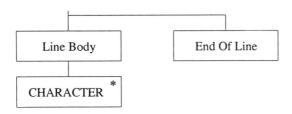

These are not the only three possible data structure diagrams for a text file and none of them, nor any of the other possible diagrams, can be said to be the best diagram of text files in general. For example, if a data structure diagram were required to illustrate the structure of this book two further levels of structure, to describe the book as an iteration of section and to describe each section as an iteration of chapter together with end of section and end of chapter markers, would have to be inserted between the *File Body* and *Page* levels. There is very rarely a single, totally correct data structure diagram for any concept; the best that can be achieved is to produce the most appropriate data structure diagram for a particular specification.

Text file management and use

Having described the general structure of text files in the previous part of this chapter, this part will introduce the facilities which Ada provides for the management and use of text files. The standard package ADA.TEXT_IO contains facilities for the declaration and manipulation of text files, and also procedures suitable for the input and output of CHARACTER and STRING values. The instantiable packages contained within TEXT_IO: INTEGER_IO, FLOAT_IO and ENUMERATION_IO contain the versions of the subprograms required for the input–output of additional data types in a text format.

The use of text files within a program can be divided into several sections: first the internal file object has to be declared, then the file has to be opened or created, following which the file can be used for input (reading) or output (writing) before it is closed when it is no longer required. Each of these stages will be introduced in turn below.

Declaring file objects

A file existing, or being created, on an external storage medium such as a disk, requires two names in order to be manipulated by an Ada program. The most obvious name is the ***external name*** by which the file is stored on the disk, but it is not a good idea to use this as the ***internal name*** by which the file will be known within the program. The reason for this is that the same program often needs to operate with many different external files. For example, a text editor being used to prepare source code files for compilation would be expected to be able to open and edit any text file on the disk and not be restricted to one particular file. Consequently the file is referenced within the program as a variable of a type supplied by ADA.TEXT_IO and a connection is made between this variable and the file on the disk when the file is opened or created.

The ADA.TEXT_IO package supplies a type called FILE_TYPE to its clients. Programs which have a requirement to manipulate external text files have first to declare variables of this type. For example:

```
-- Assuming ADA.TEXT_IO is withed and used.
FileIn  : FILE_TYPE;
FileOut : FILE_TYPE;
```

The type identifier FILE_TYPE is not very indicative of the type of file which is being declared and it is also used as a type identifier for structured and direct files. Thus a program which has a requirement to manipulate text files and either structured files or direct files, or both, would have several different possible meanings for FILE_TYPE. This is one of the situations where explicit qualification of the meaning of a package facility is advocated, even in situations where the only type of files being used are text files. The appropriate version of the declarations above would therefore be

```
-- Even though TEXT_IO is withed and used,
-- explicit qualification is advised.
FileIn  : ADA.TEXT_IO.FILE_TYPE;
FileOut : ADA.TEXT_IO.FILE_TYPE;
```

While a file is open the position within the file where information will next be written to, or next read from, is known as the position of the ***file pointer***. For a newly created empty output file the file pointer is at the start of the file and advances as information is written to the file, always remaining at the end of the file. For a file opened in append mode, the file pointer is initially positioned at the end of the existing file and remains at the end of the file as information is added to the file.

For a file opened in input mode, the file pointer is initially positioned at the start of the file and advances towards the end of the file as information is transferred into the program. When the file pointer reaches the end of an input file no more information can be input into the program, and an exception will be raised if any attempt is made to read beyond the end of file. To assist with the processing of information from an input file a Boolean function can be used to determine if the file pointer is at the end of file position.

Opening, creating and closing files

An individual text file object within a program can be used either to input information from the file to the program or to output information from the program to the file, but not both at the same time. The direction of information flow is always thought of from the program's point of view, not from the file's point of view. Thus a program inputs information from a file, but information is input into the file when the program outputs, and vice versa.

The **mode** of a file refers to this direction of information flow and for text files can take one of the values IN_FILE for files open for input, and OUT_FILE or APPEND_FILE for files open for output. The difference between an output file opened in OUT_FILE mode and APPEND_FILE mode is that OUT_FILE will create a new empty file whereas APPEND_FILE will add information to the end of an existing file, or create a new empty file if one does not exist. The mode is specified as a parameter to the TEXT_IO procedure OPEN when it is called to open a connection between the program and an external file. The interface diagram and effective declaration of this procedure are:

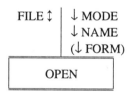

```
procedure OPEN( FILE : in out FILE_TYPE;
                MODE : in     FILE_MODE;
                NAME : in     STRING;
                FORM : in     STRING := "" );
```

Where FILE is the file variable object declared as above, NAME is the external filename of the file to be opened or created and FORM (*form*at) is supplied for operating-system-specific purposes. The second parameter, MODE, is of the TEXT_IO pre-declared enumerated type FILE_MODE:

```
type FILE_MODE is ( IN_FILE, OUT_FILE, APPEND_FILE);
```

The effect of the procedure, when it is called, is to attempt to make a connection between the internal program object and the external file identified by the filename. If the connection cannot be made, one of the following TEXT_IO exceptions will be raised:

Exception	Reason
STATUS_ERROR	File is already open
NAME_ERROR	File does not exist or name is invalid
USE_ERROR	Mode is not supported

TEXT_IO also supplies a procedure called CREATE which is effectively identical to OPEN, but has the default value OUT_FILE for the MODE parameter. It can be used in preference to the OPEN procedure when a new output file is required.

As soon as an open file, being used for either input or output, has been finished with it should be closed. This is accomplished by calling the CLOSE procedure:

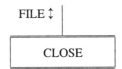

```
procedure CLOSE( FILE : in out FILE_TYPE );
```

The only exception which might be raised is STATUS_ERROR, if the file is not currently open. Although all files should be explicitly closed before a program terminates, a program is not erroneous if they are not. Any open files would be closed by the operating system after the program has terminated, but this facility should not be relied upon and all files which are opened should always be explicitly closed by the program, as soon as they are no longer required.

Writing to and reading from text files

The procedures used for the output of text information from the program to text files are overloaded versions of the PUT procedures which have already been introduced in previous chapters. For every version of the PUT procedure – the version in TEXT_IO which is used to output CHARACTER and STRING values, the instantiated INTEGER_IO versions used to output INTEGER values, the instantiated FLOAT_IO versions used to output floating point values and the instantiated ENUMERATION_IO versions used to output enumerated values – there is an additional version which can be used to output information to a named file rather than to STANDARD_OUTPUT. These versions have an additional parameter which is always the first parameter, has the formal name FILE, and is of the type ADA.TEXT_IO.FILE_TYPE. All other aspects of the PUT procedures are

462

identical to the versions which have already been introduced. For example, the two versions of a call to output a formatted floating point value to the terminal screen and to an open output file would be

```
PUT( FloatVariable, EXP =>0, FORE =>3, AFT => 2);
PUT( FileOut, FloatVariable, EXP =>0, FORE =>3, AFT => 2);
```

There is also a version of the PUT_LINE procedure for CHARACTER and STRING values which can be used to output to files. The exceptions which may be raised when these procedures are called are

Exception	Reason
MODE_ERROR	File is not open for output
USE_ERROR	File is open for output but item could not be written

Corresponding to the overloaded PUT procedures for the output of information to text files, there are overloaded versions of the GET procedures for the input of information from text files. As with PUT, these versions differ by having an additional initial parameter of type ADA.TEXT_IO.FILE_TYPE, with the formal name FILE, which identifies the file to input values from. For example:

```
GET( EnumerationVariable);
GET( FileIn, EnumerationVariable);
```

There is also a version of the GET_LINE procedure for CHARACTER and STRING values which can be used to input from files. The exceptions which may be raised when these procedures are called are

Exception	Reason
DATA_ERROR	The sequence of characters in the file does not represent a value of the required type
CONSTRAINT_ERROR	A valid value has been input, but it is outside the possible range of the subtype expected
MODE_ERROR	File is not open for input
END_ERROR	There is no more information in the file

In the design of ADTs, as introduced in Section II Chapter 12, the overloading of the GET and PUT procedures for the output and input of values of the ADT was recommended. In addition to supplying versions of *Get* and *Put* for input and output from and to the standard input and standard output files, additional overloadings which allow values to be input from and output to a text file should be included. In the interface design of these subprograms, the first parameter should always be the file parameter and have the formal name *File*. The implementation of these subprograms for the *JulianDate* package will be left as an end of chapter exercise.

Control of page layout

There are a large number of subprograms for the formatting of page layout. Each page consists of a number of lines, and each line of a number of characters. For a newly created output file the page length and the line length are **unbounded**, that is the file consists of an iteration of simple characters with no end of line or end of page markers. Following the specification of a line length or a page length, the output of characters to the file will automatically include end of line or end of page markers when the limits of a line or page have been reached. The interface diagrams for these subprograms are

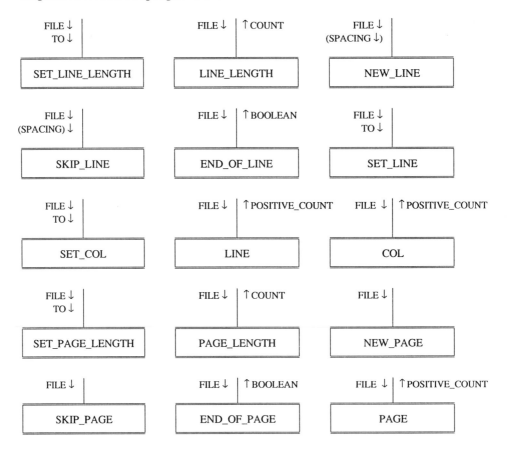

The declarations for these subprograms, and the relevant type and subtype declarations, in ADA.TEXT_IO are:

```
type FILE_TYPE is limited private;

type COUNT is range 0 .. implementation-defined;
type POSITIVE_COUNT is COUNT range 1 .. COUNT'LAST;
UNBOUNDED : constant COUNT := 0;

procedure SET_LINE_LENGTH( FILE : in FILE_TYPE;
                           TO   : in COUNT );
-- Sets the line length of the file specified to the value
-- specified.

function LINE_LENGTH( FILE : in FILE_TYPE) return COUNT;
-- Returns the line length of the file specified, 0 if
-- unbounded.

procedure NEW_LINE( FILE    : in FILE_TYPE;
                    SPACING : in POSITIVE_COUNT := 1 );
-- Outputs the number of new lines specified to
-- the file specified.

procedure SKIP_LINE( FILE    : in FILE_TYPE;
                     SPACING : in POSITIVE_COUNT := 1 );
-- Reads and discards characters from the file until the
-- specified number of end of lines has been read.

function END_OF_LINE( FILE: in FILE_TYPE) return BOOLEAN;
-- Returns True if the next character is an end of line.

procedure SET_LINE( FILE : in FILE_TYPE;
                    TO   : in POSITIVE_COUNT );
-- Outputs (possibly 0) new lines until the line specified
-- is reached, possibly throwing a new page first.

procedure SET_COL( FILE : in FILE_TYPE;
                   TO   : in POSITIVE_COUNT );
-- Outputs (possibly 0) spaces until the column specified is
-- reached, possibly throwing a new line first.

function LINE( FILE : in FILE_TYPE) return POSITIVE_COUNT;
-- Returns the current line position.

function COL( FILE : in FILE_TYPE) return POSITIVE_COUNT;
-- returns the current column position.
```

```
procedure SET_PAGE_LENGTH( FILE : in FILE_TYPE;
                           TO   : in COUNT);
-- Sets the page length of the file specified to the value
-- specified.

function PAGE_LENGTH( FILE  : in FILE_TYPE) return COUNT;
-- Returns the page length of the file specified, 0 if
                                                unbounded.

procedure NEW_PAGE( FILE    : in FILE_TYPE);
-- Outputs a single end of page marker to the file
                                              specified.

procedure SKIP_PAGE( FILE   : in FILE_TYPE;
-- Reads and discards characters from the file until an
-- end of page marker has been read.

function END_OF_PAGE( FILE : in FILE_TYPE) return BOOLEAN;
-- Returns True if the next character is an end of line.

function PAGE( FILE : in FILE_TYPE) return POSITIVE_COUNT;
-- Returns the current page position.
```

The following exceptions may be raised by these subprograms for the reasons indicated:

Exception	Reason
END_ERROR	The end of the file was reached
LAYOUT_ERROR	An attempt to set the column position or line position beyond the limits of the page
MODE_ERROR	The file is not open with the appropriate mode
USE_ERROR	Line or page length is not acceptable
STATUS_ERROR	The file is not open

Other ADA.TEXT_IO subprograms

The other, miscellaneous, subprograms contained within ADA.TEXT_IO are

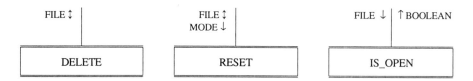

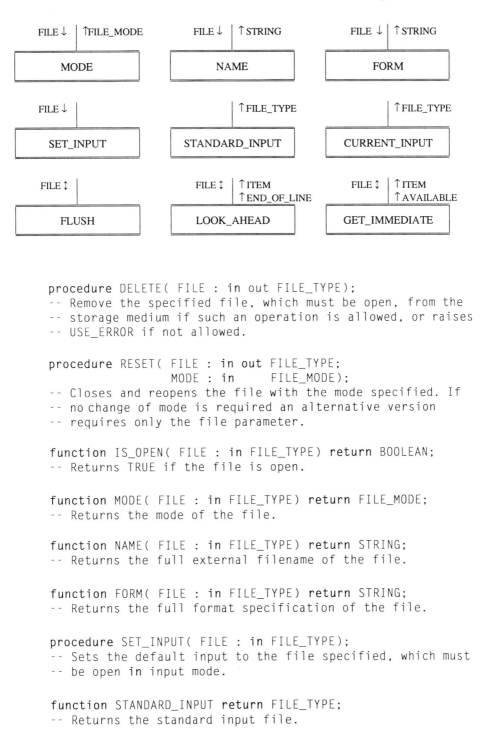

```
procedure DELETE( FILE : in out FILE_TYPE);
-- Remove the specified file, which must be open, from the
-- storage medium if such an operation is allowed, or raises
-- USE_ERROR if not allowed.

procedure RESET( FILE : in out FILE_TYPE;
                 MODE : in     FILE_MODE);
-- Closes and reopens the file with the mode specified. If
-- no change of mode is required an alternative version
-- requires only the file parameter.

function IS_OPEN( FILE : in FILE_TYPE) return BOOLEAN;
-- Returns TRUE if the file is open.

function MODE( FILE : in FILE_TYPE) return FILE_MODE;
-- Returns the mode of the file.

function NAME( FILE : in FILE_TYPE) return STRING;
-- Returns the full external filename of the file.

function FORM( FILE : in FILE_TYPE) return STRING;
-- Returns the full format specification of the file.

procedure SET_INPUT( FILE : in FILE_TYPE);
-- Sets the default input to the file specified, which must
-- be open in input mode.

function STANDARD_INPUT return FILE_TYPE;
-- Returns the standard input file.
```

```
function CURRENT_INPUT return FILE_TYPE;
-- Returns the current default input file.


procedure FLUSH( FILE : in out FILE_TYPE);
-- Ensures that the internal and external output files are
-- synchronized. i.e. all output has been sent to the
                                                  screen.
procedure LOOK_AHEAD( FILE        : in out FILE_TYPE;
                      ITEM        : out    CHARACTER;
                      END_OF_LINE : out    BOOLEAN);
-- Obtains the next character from the file, if not at end
-- of line, without getting it.


procedure GET_IMMEDIATE( FILE      : in out FILE_TYPE;
                         ITEM      : out    CHARACTER;
                         AVAILABLE : out    BOOLEAN);
-- Obtains the next character from the file, if available,
-- without getting it.
```

The exceptions which may be raised by these subprograms are comparable with the exceptions which may be raised for the subprograms described above. The three subprograms SET_INPUT, STANDARD_INPUT and CURRENT_INPUT all have equivalent versions for the STANDARD_OUPUT and STANDARD_ERROR files. The GET_IMMEDIATE subprogram can be used to test the keyboard to see if there is a character waiting, which might indicate that the user has responded to a prompt. If there are no characters waiting then the program can be designed to perform a small amount of useful processing before testing the keyboard again. Only when the user had responded to the prompt would the program give its full attention to the user's input.

Example text file programs

In order to reinforce the technical reference description of the ADA.TEXT_IO package described above, two example programs for the manipulation of text files will be designed, implemented and traced in this part of the chapter.

The *TextFileCounter* program

The first program which will be developed is intended to count the number of characters, the number of lines and the number of pages contained in a file, whose name is supplied by the user. A suitable error dialog will be included when the

filename is requested, and an option will be offered to abandon the entire
operation. A possible user interface for the program might be as follows:

```
Text File Counter


Please enter the filename
(or press <enter> to finish) > DoesNotExist.Doc

The file DoesNotExist.Doc could not be opened.
Please try again.


Please enter the filename
(or press <enter> to finish) > SecIIIChap21.Doc


The file /AdaBook/SectionIII/SecIIIChap21.Doc contains:
        28  pages,
      1345  lines,
     60672  characters.
```

The high level design for this program might be based upon two processes: one
which interacts with the user to obtain a validated filename and opens the file, or
returns an indication that the user abandoned the operations: and a second process
which actually processes the file. This design, and the subprogram declarations
derived from it, might be as follows:

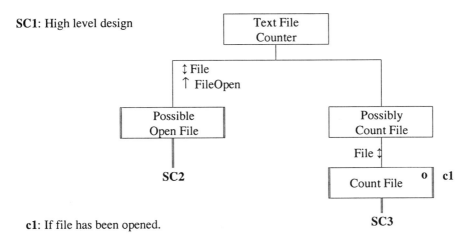

SC1: High level design

c1: If file has been opened.

```
procedure PossibleOpenFile
            ( File       : in out ADA.TEXT_IO.FILE_TYPE;
              FileIsOpen : out     BOOLEAN );
```

```
                    -- Obtain from the user the name of a file and attempt to
                                                                  open it.
                    -- On exit if FileIsOpen is True then File has been
                    -- successfully opened, otherwise FileIsOpen is False and
                    -- the user has abandoned the process.

                    procedure CountFile( File : in out ADA.TEXT_IO.FILE_TYPE);
                    -- Process the open file passed, counting and displaying
                    -- the number of pages, lines and characters within it.
```

The implementation of this part of the program, and the context clause, might be

```
0001    -- Filename TextFileCounter.ada (k8 textfile.adb).
0002    -- Program to count the number of pages, lines and
0003    -- characters in a file specified by the user.
0004    -- Written for Section III Chapter 21.
0005    --
0006    -- Fintan Culwin, v0.1, Jan 1997.
0007
0008    with ADA.TEXT_IO;
0009    use  ADA.TEXT_IO;
0010
0011    procedure TextFileCounter is
0012
0013        package IntegerIO is new ADA.TEXT_IO.INTEGER_IO
                                                        ( INTEGER);
0014        use IntegerIO;
0015
0016        MaximumFilenameLength : constant := 40;
0017        subtype FilenameString is STRING( 1 ..
                                         MaximumFilenameLength);
0018
0019        FileIn     : ADA.TEXT_IO.FILE_TYPE;
0020        FileIsOpen : BOOLEAN;
0021
0022        procedure PossibleOpenFile(FileToOpen : in out
0023                                           ADA.TEXT_IO.FILE_TYPE;
0024                     FileHasBeenOpened : out BOOLEAN) is
            -- Definition of PossibleOpenFile assumed.

0057        procedure ProcessFile(FileToProcess : in out
0058                                       ADA.TEXT_IO.FILE_TYPE) is
            -- Definition of ProcessFile assumed

0090    begin -- TextFileCounter
0091        PossibleOpenFile( FileIn, FileIsOpen);
0092        if FileIsOpen then
```

```
0093            ProcessFile( FileIn);
0094        end if;
0095    end TextFileCounter;
```

The design and implementation of the *PossibleOpenFile* component might be as follows:

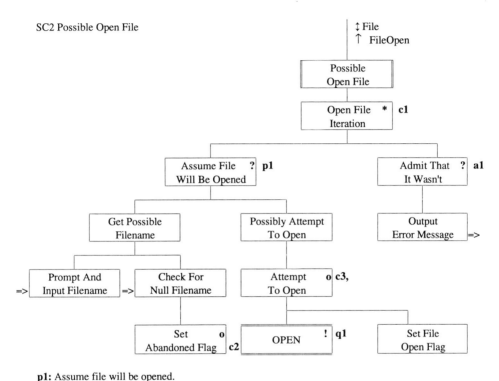

p1: Assume file will be opened.
a1: If file opening raised an exception.
c1: While file not opened and operation
     not abandoned.

q1: If file cannot be opened.
c2: If user entered a null filename.
c3: If abandoned flag not set.

```
0022    procedure PossibleOpenFile( FileToOpen : in out
0023                                    ADA.TEXT_IO.FILE_TYPE;
0024                    FileHasBeenOpened : out BOOLEAN ) is
0025
0026    Filename              : FilenameString;
0027    FilenameLength        : NATURAL;
0028
0029    FileIsOpen            : BOOLEAN := FALSE;
0030    OperationIsAbandoned  : BOOLEAN := FALSE;
0031
```

```
0032    begin -- PossibleOpenFile
0033       while ( not FileIsOpen) and ( not OperationIsAbandoned)
                                                                    loop
0034          begin -- explicit exception block
0035             PUT_LINE("Please enter the filename.");
0036             PUT("(or press <enter> to finish) >");
0037             GET_LINE( Filename, FilenameLength );
0038             if FilenameLength = 0 then
0039                OperationIsAbandoned := TRUE;
0040             end if;
0041             if not OperationIsAbandoned then
0042                OPEN( FileToOpen, MODE => IN_FILE,
0043                   NAME => Filename( 1 .. FilenameLength));
0044                FileIsOpen := TRUE;
0045             end if;
0046          exception
0047             when USE_ERROR | STATUS_ERROR | NAME_ERROR =>
0048                NEW_LINE; PUT("The file ");
0049                PUT( Filename( 1 .. FilenameLength));
0050                PUT_LINE(" could not be opened.");
0051                PUT_LINE("Please try again.");
0052          end; -- explicit exception block
0053       end loop;
0054    end PossibleOpenFile;
```

The basis of the design is that of an interactive exception handler which was first presented in Section II Chapter 11. This design, and even the procedure, is sufficiently general for it to be capable of being reused whenever the user is required to input a filename. The design and implementation of the *CountFile* component might be as follows:

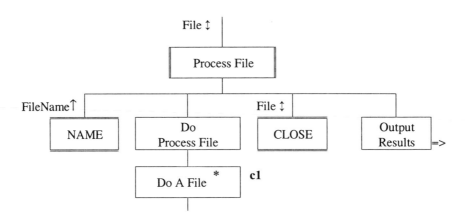

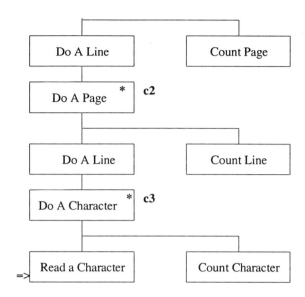

c1: While not end of file.
c2: While not end of page.
c3: While not end of line.

```
0057    procedure ProcessFile(FileToProcess : in out
0058                                   ADA.TEXT_IO.FILE_TYPE) is
0059
0060    NumberOfPages       : NATURAL := 0;
0061    NumberOfLines       : NATURAL := 0;
0062    NumberOfCharacters  : NATURAL := 0;
0063
0064    DummyCharacter      : CHARACTER;
0065    Filename            : STRING := NAME( FileToProcess);
0066
0067    begin -- ProcessFile
0068       while ( not( END_OF_FILE( FileToProcess))) loop
0069          while ( not( END_OF_PAGE( FileToProcess))) loop
0070             while ( not( END_OF_LINE( FileToProcess ))) loop
0071                GET( FileToProcess, DummyCharacter);
0072                NumberOfCharacters := NumberOfCharacters +1;
0073             end loop;
0074             NumberOfLines := NumberOfLines +1;
0075          end loop;
0076          NumberOfPages := NumberOfPages +1;
0077       end loop;
0078
0079       CLOSE( FileToProcess );
0080
```

```
0081        NEW_LINE(2);
0082        PUT_LINE("The file " & Filename & " contains");
0083        PUT( NumberOfPages); PUT_LINE(" pages,");
0084        PUT( NumberOfLines); PUT_LINE(" lines,");
0085        PUT( NumberOfCharacters); PUT_LINE( " characters.");
0086        NEW_LINE( 2);
0087    end ProcessFile;
```

The basis of this design is the data structure diagram which was used to illustrate the structure of a text file as an iteration of pages, lines and characters. This is not a coincidence; the design of the actions which are used to process a data structure must take into account the structure of the data being processed. Thus, as the text file is thought of as an iteration of pages, and each page is an iteration of lines, and each line is an iteration of characters, the action which processes the entire file must process each page, and in order to do so it must process each line, and in order to do so it must process each character. This technique of designing a program structure chart from a consideration of data structure charts will be expanded upon throughout the rest of this book.

The *StudentReport* program

The second program which will be used to illustrate the use of text files involves the reading of formatted information from an input text file and producing a formatted report of the information in a second text file. A text file of student records, which may have been produced by another Ada program, or by a program written in another programming language, or even produced by a word processor, is to be used as the input file. The format of this file is as follows:

```
Student Name        Assignments     Exam

Ade Abrahams        85              90
Bessie Bunter       32              40

....                ..              ..
Zac Zacharia        68              55
```

The external name of this file is '*oldstu.dat*'. It contains a line for each student on a course, starting at line 3 of the file. Each line contains three pieces of information: the student's name which starts at column 3 of the line and is at most 20 characters in length; then an integer assignment score in the range 0 to 100 and an integer exam score in the same range.

It is required to process the file to produce a new output file called '*newstu.dat*' which contains the same information in a similar format, with the addition of the student's aggregate score at the end of each line. The aggregate score is determined by a 60/40 weighing of assignment and exam score and is to be displayed to one decimal place of accuracy. Using the input file shown above the corresponding output file would be as follows:

```
            STUDENT RESULTS REPORT

    Student Name      Assignments   Exam    Average

    Ade Abrahams      85            90      87.0
    Bessie Bunter     32            40      36.8

    ....              ..            ..
    Zac Zacharia      68            55      60.2
```

A suitable design for this program might be as follows:

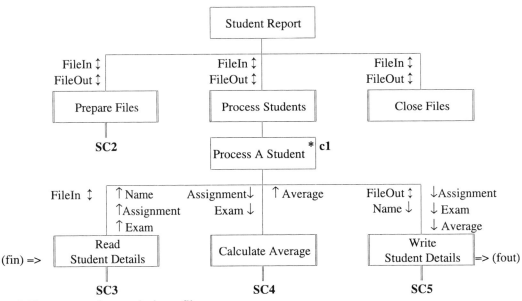

c1: For every student on the input file.
   (fin is input file, fout is output file.)

The details of the components *PrepareFiles*, *ReadStudentDetails*, *Calculate-Average* and *WriteStudentDetails* have been omitted from this design for the sake of simplicity and will be given implicitly in the implementation which follows. The essential part of the design is the *ProcessStudents* component where the file is not thought of as an iteration of characters, or lines or pages, but as an iteration of details concerning an individual student. This conceptualization of the structure of the file in terms of the information which it contains and the processing which has to be performed upon it, instead of its physical structure, assists with the design of the program which is more concerned with the information the file contains than that it is composed of characters.

The design indicates that the program procedure consists of three components, each of which has as parameters the input file and the output file. Thus the construction of the program procedure and the program's context clause might be as follows:

```
0001    -- Filename StudentReport.ada (k8 studentre.adb).
0002    -- Contains student report text file processing example
0003    -- from Ada book Section III Chapter 21.
0004    --
0005    -- Fintan Culwin, v0.1, May 1997.
0006
0007    with ADA.TEXT_IO;
0008    use  ADA.TEXT_IO;
0009
0010    procedure StudentReport is
0011
0012        package IntegerIO is new ADA.TEXT_IO.INTEGER_IO
                                                     ( INTEGER);
0013        package FloatIO is new ADA.TEXT_IO.FLOAT_IO( FLOAT);
0014        use IntegerIO, FloatIO;
0015
0016        MaxStudentNameLength : constant INTEGER := 20;
0017        MaximumScore         : constant INTEGER := 100;
0018        AssignmentWeighting  : constant FLOAT   := 0.4;
0019        ExamWeighting        : constant FLOAT   := 0.6;
0020
0021        FileIn  : ADA.TEXT_IO.FILE_TYPE;
0022        FileOut : ADA.TEXT_IO.FILE_TYPE;
0023
0024        procedure PrepareFiles( InputFile  : in out
0025                                    ADA.TEXT_IO.FILE_TYPE;
0026                                OutputFile : in out
0027                                    ADA.TEXT_IO.FILE_TYPE) is
            -- Definition of PrepareFiles assumed.

0077        procedure ProcessStudents( InputFile  : in out
0078                                    ADA.TEXT_IO.FILE_TYPE;
0079                                OutputFile : in out
0080                                    ADA.TEXT_IO.FILE_TYPE) is
            -- Definition of ProcessStudents assumed.

0137        procedure CloseFiles( InputFile  : in out
0138                                    ADA.TEXT_IO.FILE_TYPE;
```

```
0139                           OutputFile : in out
0140                                   ADA.TEXT_IO.FILE_TYPE) is
          -- Definition of CloseFiles assumed.

0144      begin -- StudentReport
0145          PrepareFiles( FileIn, FileOut);
0146          ProcessStudents( FileIn, FileOut);
0147          CloseFiles( FileIn, FileOut);
0148      end StudentReport;
```

The detailed design of the procedure *PrepareFiles* divides it into two subsidiary
procedures *PrepareInputFile* and *PrepareOutputFile*. The *PrepareInputFile* has the
responsibility for opening the input file and positioning the file ready to read the
first student's record. The procedure *PrepareOutputFile* has the responsibility for
opening the output file and getting it ready for the first line of student details to be
output. The implementation of this part of the program might be

```
0024      procedure PrepareFiles( InputFile  : in out
0025                                  ADA.TEXT_IO.FILE_TYPE;
0026                          OutputFile : in out
0027                                  ADA.TEXT_IO.FILE_TYPE) is
0028
0029
0030          procedure PrepareInputFile( InputFile : in out
0031                                  ADA.TEXT_IO.FILE_TYPE) is
0032          -- Procedure to prepare file for input by opening file
0033          -- and positioning at start of line 3.
0034
0035          begin -- PrepareInputFile
0036             OPEN( FILE => InputFile,
0037                   MODE => IN_FILE,
0038                   NAME => "oldstu.dat");
0039             SET_LINE( InputFile, 3);
0040          end PrepareInputFile;
0041
0042
0043          procedure PrepareOutfile( OutputFile : in out
0044                                  ADA.TEXT_IO.FILE_TYPE) is
0045          -- Procedure to create new file for output and output
0046          -- headings to the file.
0047
0048          begin -- PrepareOutputFile
0049             CREATE( FILE => OutputFile,
0050                   NAME => "newstu.dat");
0051
0052             -- do report heading on line 2
```

477

```
0053          SET_LINE( OutputFile, 2); SET_COL( OutputFile, 30);
0054          PUT( OutputFile , "STUDENT RESULTS REPORT ");
0055
0056          -- do line heading on line 4
0057          SET_LINE( OutputFile, 4);
0058          SET_COL( OutputFile, 5);
0059          PUT( OutputFile, "Student Name");
0060          SET_COL( OutputFile, 35);
0061          PUT( OutputFile, "Assignments ");
0062          SET_COL( OutputFile, 50);
0063          PUT( OutputFile, "Exams ");
0064          SET_COL( OutputFile, 65);
0065          PUT( OutputFile , "Average");
0066
0067          -- move to line 6 for first student line
0068          SET_LINE( OutputFile, 6);
0069       end PrepareOutputFile;
0070
0071
0072    begin --
0073       PrepareInputFile( InputFile );
0074       PrepareOutputFile( OutputFile);
0075    end PrepareFiles;
```

The procedure *PrepareInputFile* which receives the input file as an ***in out*** parameter, opens the external text file '*oldstu.dat*' and then uses SET_LINE to move the file pointer to the start of line 3, where the first student data line can be found. The procedure *PrepareOutputFile* which receives the output file as an ***in out*** parameter, creates the external text file '*newstu.dat*' and then uses the procedures SET_LINE, SET_COL and the STRING version of the PUT procedure to output the headings to the file, leaving the file pointer positioned at the start of line 6 ready for the output of the first student detail line.

The procedure *CloseFiles* has the straightforward task of closing both files and can be implemented as follows:

```
0137    procedure CloseFiles( InputFile  : in out TextFiles;
0138                          OutputFile : in out TextFiles) is
0139    begin -- CloseFiles
0140       CLOSE( InputFile);
0141       CLOSE( OutputFile);
0142    end CloseFiles;
```

The iterative procedure *ProcessStudents* can be implemented using a **while** loop which terminates when the end of the input file is detected. On each iteration of the loop the three subprograms *ReadStudentDetails*, *CalculateStudentAverage* and *WriteStudentDetails* are called. The implementation of *ProcessStudents* might be as follows:

```
0077    procedure ProcessStudents( InputFile  : in out TextFiles;
0078                               OutputFile : in out TextFiles) is
0079
0080        subtype Scores       is INTEGER range 0 .. MaximumScore;
0081        subtype StudentNames is STRING( 1 ..
                                                MaxStudentNameLength);
0082
0083        TheName            : StudentNames;
0084        TheAssignmentScore : Scores;
0085        TheExamScore       : Scores;
0086        TheAverage         : FLOAT;
0087
0088
0089        procedure ReadStudentDetails
                              ( ReadFrom : in out
0090                                       ADA.TEXT_IO.FILE_TYPE;
0091                            ReadName   : out    StudentNames;
0092                            ReadAssign : out    Scores;
0093                            ReadExam   : out    Scores) is
           -- Definition of procedure ReadStudentDetails assumed
                                                            here.

0101        function CalculateAverageScore( AnAssignment  : Scores;
0102                                        AnExamination : Scores)
0103                                                return FLOAT is
           -- Definition of function CalculateAverageScore assumed
                                                            here.

0110        procedure WriteStudentDetails
                              ( WriteTo       : in out
0111                                       ADA.TEXT_IO.FILE_TYPE;
0112                            WriteName    : in StudentNames;
0113                            WriteAssign  : in Scores;
0114                            WriteExam    : in Scores;
0115                            WriteAverage : in FLOAT) is
           -- Definition of procedure WriteStudentDetails assumed
                                                            here.

0127    begin -- ProcessStudents
0128       while not( END_OF_FILE( InputFile)) loop
0129          ReadStudentDetails( InputFile, TheName,
0130                              TheAssignmentScore, TheExamScore);
0131          TheAverage := CalculateAverageScore
                                          ( TheAssignmentScore,
0132                                        TheExamScore);
```

```
0133           WriteStudentDetails( OutputFile, TheName,
0134                                TheAssignmentScore,
0135                                TheExamScore, TheAverage);
0136      end loop;
0137   end ProcessStudents;
```

The types which are required to represent an individual student's details within the program are declared at this level of the program, as it is only at this level and the levels below it that the precise details are required to be known. This is an example of using scope to implement information hiding: the only parts of the program which should know about how a student is represented are those which have a need to know. Just as the program objects which are used to represent objects in the real world are declared at the lowest possible level in a program in order to make them as local as possible, so data types should also be declared to be as local as possible.

The only exception to this rule is the declarations of constants which should always be made at the start of a program text so that they can be easily located and changed should their values have to be modified during maintenance. The procedure *ReadStudentDetails* could be implemented as:

```
0089   procedure ReadStudentDetails
                          ( ReadFrom    : in out
0090                                       ADA.TEXT_IO.FILE_TYPE;
0091                ReadName   : out    StudentNames;
0092                ReadAssign : out    Scores;
0093                ReadExam   : out    Scores) is
0094   begin -- ReadStudentDetails
0095      SET_COL( ReadFrom, 3);
0096      GET( ReadFrom, ReadName);
0097      GET( ReadFrom, ReadAssign);
0098      GET( ReadFrom, ReadExam);
0099      SKIP_LINE( ReadFrom);
0100   end ReadStudentDetails;
```

The procedure commences by positioning the file pointer at column 3 of a line where the start of the student's name can be found. The string version of the GET procedure is then used to input the student's name. The effect of this procedure is to input from the text file as many characters as the string is capable of holding. The string being used to contain a student's name is 20 characters long and as the specification states that the maximum length of a student's name is 20 characters, it is long enough to guarantee that the student's name will be input into it. The use of GET to input a STRING value from a text file is safe in circumstances such as these, where the number of characters in the information being input can be guaranteed.

The procedure continues by inputting the student's assignment score and the student's exam score, using the integer version of the GET procedure. There is no need to position the file pointer at the precise column where these fields can be found on the line using SET_COL, as the effect of the procedure is to skip over any leading spaces until an integer value is found. Should a non-integer value be found on the file then a DATA_EXCEPTION will be raised. The procedure terminates by advancing the file pointer on to the start of the next line, using SKIP_LINE, ready for the next student line to be input or the end of file to be detected.

The function *CalculateAverageScore* can be implemented in a straightforward manner as follows:

```
0101    function CalculateAverageScore
                            ( AnAssignment  : Scores;
0102                          AnExamination : Scores)
0103                                        return FLOAT is
0104    begin -- CalculateAverageScore
0105       return( FLOAT( AnAssignment) * AssignmentWeighting +
0106            ( FLOAT( AnExamination) * ExamWeighting);
0107    end CalculateAverageScore;
```

The calculation of a student's average score is implemented as a distinct function rather than including the calculations within *ReadStudentDetails* or *WriteStudentDetails*, as the calculation is not logically connected with either of those operations. It is possible that in a future version of the program the rules for calculating an average score may differ from those of the current version. By isolating the calculations into a distinct location, such maintenance is ensured.

Finally the implementation of *WriteStudentDetails* might be as follows:

```
0110    procedure WriteStudentDetails
                            ( WriteTo       : in out
0111                                          ADA.TEXT_IO.TextFiles;
0112                          WriteName    : in StudentNames;
0113                          WriteAssign  : in Scores;
0114                          WriteExam    : in Scores;
0115                          WriteAverage : in FLOAT ) is
0116    begin -- WriteStudentDetails
0117       SET_COL( WriteTo, 5);
0118       PUT( WriteTo, WriteName);
0119       SET_COL( WriteTo, 35);
0120       PUT( WriteTo, WriteAssign, WIDTH =>4);
0121       SET_COL( WriteTo, 50);
0122       PUT( WriteTo, WriteExam, WIDTH =>4);
0123       SET_COL( WriteTo, 65);
0124       PUT( WriteTo, WriteAverage, FORE =>4, AFT =>1, EXP=>0);
0125       NEW_LINE( WriteTo);
0126    end WriteStudentDetails;
```

The procedure commences by advancing to column 5 and outputting the student's name using the STRING version of the PUT procedure. The file pointer is then advanced to the relevant columns and the assignment and exam scores are output using the INTEGER version of the PUT procedure. Likewise the file pointer is advanced to the required column before the student's average score is output using the FLOAT version of the PUT procedure. The procedure terminates after calling NEW_LINE to advance the file pointer to the next line, ready for the next line of student details to be output. A subprogram map of the entire program concludes this chapter:

```
procedure StudentReport is

    procedure PrepareFiles() is

        procedure PrepeareInputFile() is
        begin -- PrepareInputFile
        end PrepareInputFile;

        procedure PrepareOutputFile() is
        begin -- PrepareOutputFile
        end PrepareOutputFile;

    begin -- PrepareFiles
    end PrepareFiles

    procedure ProcessStudents() is

        procedure ReadStudentDetails() is
        begin -- ReadStudentDetails
        end ReadStudentDetails;

        function CalculateAverageScore() is
        begin -- CalculateAverageScore
        end CalculateAverageScore;
```

```
                    procedure WriteStudentDetails() is
                    begin -- WriteStudentDetails
                    end WriteStudentDetails;


              begin -- ProcessStudents
                ReadStudentDetails();
                CalculateAverageScore();
                WriteStudentDetails();
              end ProcessStudents;


                    procedure CloseFiles() is
                    begin -- CloseFiles
                    end CloseFiles;


        begin -- StudentReport
          PrepareFiles();
          ProcessStudents();
          CloseFiles();
        end StudentReport;
```

EXERCISES

21.1 The designs of the subprograms in the *StudentReport* program have been omitted from this chapter for the sake of brevity. Reverse engineer the designs from the code presented.

21.2 Produce a trace table for the execution of the *StudentReport* program using the example data given in the chapter.

21.3 Extend the *StudentReport* program so that it calculates the number of students, average assignment score, average examination score and average overall score. These details should be output, with suitable formatting, at the end of the report.

21.4 Reimplement the *JulianDate* package to include overloaded *Get* and *Put* procedures which will output and input to and from an external text file. Extend the demonstration harness client to test these facilities.

21.5 Design, build and demonstrate a program which will process an input file to produce an output file with four digit line numbers preceding each line. The line numbers should be zero filled, as with the listings in this book. The name of the input file should be supplied on the command line, with suitable advice given if it cannot be opened. The name of the output file should be derived from the input file, replacing any trailing dot extension (e.g. '*.adb*') with '*.lis*'.

21.6 Extend the program from Exercise 21.4 to produce a paginated listing, with a page heading showing the filename and a page footer showing the page number, the date and time at which the file was produced.

CHAPTER 22
Sequential files and direct files

Sequential files and *direct files*, collectively known as *structured files*, store information outside the program in a non-text format. The major advantage of a non-text format, compared with a text format, is that the information is stored in a compressed manner, which implies that the amount of space taken to store the information and the amount of time it takes to load and save it are reduced. This advantage is also a major disadvantage. The text format is both readable by humans and easily understandable by different programs, even when the programs are running on different computers using different operating systems and have been written in different programming languages. In comparison, the format used by structured files is possibly unique to the combination of compiler, language and operating system which creates the file. As such it is much more difficult, but not impossible, to transfer information in structured files between different programs and different machines.

A text file can store any information which can be represented as a sequence of characters; effectively it can store any information. The information stored in a text file can change from location to location within the file. For example, a sales report file may contain pages of information where each line of the majority of the pages gives details of the sales of a particular item. However, the first page may be special, containing a title for the report, and the last page may be special, containing totals for the report. On each page not all lines will contain details of sales; some lines would be reserved for page number and/or date information and some lines for summary totals. The information contained within text files is *heterogeneous*.

In contrast, the information contained in structured files is *homogeneous*. A structured file consists of an iteration of records all of which must be of the same type. Thus the information contained in a structured file cannot easily change from location to location within the file. This disadvantage also leads to a major advantage which is provided for with direct files. As all the records in a structured file are of the same type, they are of a fixed length. This allows the file pointer to be moved within the file from record to record, and provides the facility whereby the records need not be processed sequentially. With text files and sequential files the file pointer starts at the beginning of a file when it is opened or created, and can only move towards the end of the file. In a direct file the file pointer can be moved to any location in the file allowing the records to be read, or written, or rewritten, in any sequence.

There is an external structure which combines the advantages of the compact representation of information provided by structured files with the ability to store heterogeneous information. This facility is known as *streams*, rather than files, and will be introduced in the next section. However, streams do not provide the advantages of direct access to the records contained within a stream and can only be processed sequentially. This chapter will first introduce sequential files, following which direct files will be introduced.

Sequential files

A general structure diagram of a sequential file is as follows:

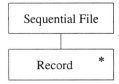

This data structure diagram is essentially identical with the general data structure diagram for a one dimensional array, which was given in Chapter 17. An array was defined as an iteration of elements, where all the elements had to be of the same type. The data structure diagram above indicates that a sequential file consists of an iteration of records, and the records all have to be of the same type. One immediate difference between arrays and sequential files is that it is not possible for the records to be of a file type. However, any other Ada type is allowed. Thus it is possible to have an array of files, but not a file of files.

Instances of arrays are constrained; the number of elements in an array has to be known at the time that the array is declared. Instances of files are unconstrained; the number of records in a file is unknown at the time that the file object is declared. Information can be stored in or retrieved from an array at any time and in any sequence. The information in a sequential file can only be read from or written to at any particular instant in time, and can only be read or written in sequence from the start of file to the end of file. The information in an array is volatile and will be lost when the program finishes. The information in a file is permanent and can exist between different runs of the same program or be used to transfer information between programs.

Instantiation of sequential file packages

Files are places where information is transferred out of a program, or places from which information is transferred into the program; thus they are concerned with *input–output* (*i–o*) operations. As with input and output from the terminal, Ada does not supply any general facilities for i–o to structured files but supplies a general facility which can be configured for the i–o of a specific data type.

The name of the generic package for structured sequential i–o is ADA.SEQUENTIAL_IO, and can be used to instantiate a new package configured for use with a specific data type in a comparable manner with the instantiation of the packages contained within TEXT_IO. Examples of the creation of suitable packages might be as follows:

```
-- Assuming that the package ADA.SEQUENTIAL_IO is at
-- least withed in the context clause.

package IntegerSIO is new ADA.SEQUENTIAL_IO( INTEGER);
-- Instantiation of a package called IntegerSIO suitable
-- for the i-o of INTEGER values.

package FloatSIO is new ADA.SEQUENTIAL_IO( FLOAT);
-- Instantiation of a package called FloatSIO suitable
-- for the i-o of FLOAT values.

-- Assuming that the JulianDate package is at least withed.
package JulianDateSIO is new
                ADA.SEQUENTIAL_IO( JulianDate.JulianDates);
-- Instantiation of a package called JulianDateSIO suitable
-- for the i-o of JulianDates values.

-- Assuming that the CashRegister package is at least
                                                   withed.
package CashRegisterSIO is new
          ADA.SEQUENTIAL_IO( CashRegister.CashRegisters);
-- Instantiation of a package called CashRegisterSIO
-- suitable for the i-o of values CashRegisters.
```

Each of these new packages, *IntegerSIO*, *FloatSIO*, *JulianDateSIO* and *Cash-RegisterSIO*, created by each of these declarations, is capable of being used for the creation and use of files which are suitable for the input and output of the types specified. Thus the facilities of the package *IntegerSIO* can only be used for the input and output of INTEGER values and for no other types. The instantiation of the package *JulianDateSIO*, see Section II Chapter 12, does not require any private knowledge of the structure of a *JulianDates* object and thus can be accomplished by a client of the package and is not restricted to the private part of the *JulianDates* package. Likewise the package *CashRegisterSIO*, see Section I Chapter 8, has been instantiated for the i–o of *CashRegisters* values and cannot be used for the i–o of any its extended type *MultipleCashRegisters*.

As suggested in the examples above a naming convention for instantiated

SEQUENTIAL_IO packages should be adopted. The suggested convention is to use the singular name of the data type which the file can store with '*SIO*', for SEQUENTIAL_*IO*, appended to it. Having instantiated an *SIO* package within the scope of a compilation unit it is automatically **with**ed and can be brought into use in a manner comparable with TEXT_IO instantiated packages such as *FloatIO*.

The individual *SIO* packages provide a file data type, whose name is FILE_TYPE, which can be used to declare file objects. The packages also provide a set of subprograms which are appropriate for use on these file objects.

Declaring SEQUENTIAL_IO file objects

The declaration of a SEQUENTIAL_IO file object of type FILE_TYPE can be accomplished in a similar manner to the declaration of TEXT_IO files introduced in the previous chapter. However, there is an implicit ambiguity which can be demonstrated in the following program fragment:

```
-- Assuming that IntegerSIO and JulianDateSIO are both in
-- use.
IntegerFile  : FILE_TYPE;
BirthdayFile : FILE_TYPE;
```

If only one file i–o package were in **use**, then these declarations would be unambiguous as there would only be one possible FILE_TYPE. However, both *IntegerSIO* and *JulianDateSIO* export a type called FILE_TYPE, as does TEXT_IO if it also is in use. As there is no other information concerning the intended FILE_TYPE in the declarations above they are ambiguous and will be reported as compilation errors. When more than one file i–o package is in use the declarations must be made unambiguous by stating the full name of the intended type, as follows:

```
-- Assuming that IntegerSIO and JulianDateSIO are both in
-- use.
IntegerFile  : IntegerSIO.FILE_TYPE;
BirthdayFile : JulianDateSIO.FILE_TYPE;
```

Even in situations where there is only one possible meaning of FILE_TYPE, the full name of the type identifying which package it comes from should be used. This advice was given in the previous chapter for text files and is intended to allow easier maintenance of programs. Even though an initial version of a program may only be dealing with a single type of external file, it cannot be guaranteed that other file types will not be required in future versions. The other reason for the advice is that the term FILE_TYPE by itself is inherently ambiguous to a developer and should always be qualified to assist with the understanding of a program when it is read.

Opening, creating, closing and maintaining files

As with text files in the previous chapter a sequential file has to be OPENed before it can be used to input information into the program or CREATEd before it can be used to transfer information from the program to the file. All files have to be CLOSEd when they are no longer required. These three subprograms are conceptually identical to the OPEN, CREATE and CLOSE subprograms for text files which were described in the previous chapter. Additionally there is a set of subprograms for file maintenance:

DELETE	RESET	IS_OPEN
MODE	NAME	FORM

These subprograms are also conceptually identical to the subprograms which were introduced for text files in the previous chapter. The set of operations concerned with control of page layout introduced in the previous chapter have no comparable operations in *SIO* packages.

Reading from and writing to sequential files

Information can be transferred from the program to the file by use of the WRITE procedure. The data flow diagram and effective declaration of this procedure in SEQUENTIAL_IO are as follows:

```
procedure WRITE( FILE : in FILE_TYPE;
                 ITEM : in ELEMENT_TYPE );
```

where FILE is the internal name of the file being written to and ITEM is a value of the declared type of the items in the file. The effect of the procedure, when it is executed, is to transfer the contents of ITEM to a new record which is appended to the end of the file. This will be explained further in the example program later in this chapter. There are a number of problems which may occur which will prevent the procedure from executing successfully and will raise the following exceptions:

Exception	Reason
MODE_ERROR	will be raised if the file is not in OUT_FILE or APPEND_FILE mode
USE_ERROR	will be raised if the capacity of the file is exceeded

Information can be transferred from the file to the program by use of the READ procedure. The data flow diagram and effective declaration of this procedure in SEQUENTIAL_IO are as follows:

```
procedure READ( FILE : in  FILE_TYPE;
                ITEM : out ELEMENT_TYPE);
```

where FILE is the internal name of the file being read from and ITEM is a variable of the declared type of the file. The effect of the procedure, when it is executed, is to transfer the contents of the next record in the file, if any, into ITEM. This will be explained further in the example program later in this chapter. There are a number of problems which may occur which will prevent the procedure from executing successfully and will raise the following exceptions:

Exception	Reason
MODE_ERROR	will be raised if the file is not in IN_FILE mode
END_ERROR	will be raised if no more elements exist in the file
DATA_ERROR	will be raised if the data read is not a value of type ITEM

Example SEQUENTIAL_IO programs

To illustrate the use of sequential files two programs will be developed, implemented and traced. The first program will obtain a series of records from the terminal and write them to an external file. The second program will read the records back from the file and display them upon the terminal. The records which are to be used in these examples are of a type which will be known as *Birthdays*, whose structure is as follows:

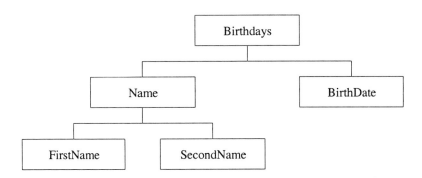

This type will be supplied by a package called *Birthday* whose object diagram and package specification are as follows:

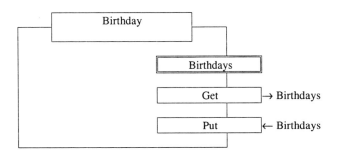

```
0001    -- Filename Birthday_.pkg (k8 birthday.ads).
0002    -- ADT specification for a Birthday record type.
0003    -- Produced for Section III Chapter 22.
0004    --
0005    -- Fintan Culwin, v0.1, Jan 1997.
0006
0007    with JulianDate, ADA.CHARACTERS.LATIN_1;
0008    use  JulianDate, ADA.CHARACTERS.LATIN_1;
0009
0010    package Birthday is
0011
0012        type Birthdays is private;
0013
0014        procedure Put( AnyBirthday : in Birthdays);
0015        -- Procedure to show a birthday on the terminal.
0016
0017        procedure Get( AnyBirthday : out Birthdays);
0018        -- Procedure to obtain a birthday from the terminal.
0019
0020    private
```

```
0021
0022        MaxNameLength : constant INTEGER := 20;
0023        subtype NameStrings is STRING( 1 .. MaxNameLength);
0024
0025        type Names is
0026        record
0027           FirstName   : NameStrings := ( others => SPACE );
0028           SecondName  : NameStrings := ( others => SPACE );
0029        end record;
0030
0031        type Birthdays is
0032        record
0033           Name       : Names;
0034           BirthDate  : JulianDates;
0035        end record;
0036
0037    end Birthday;
```

This package specification is dependent upon the package *JulianDate* which was developed in Section II Chapter 12. The body of this package will not be presented as it contributes nothing to the understanding of the use of sequential files. Details of how to obtain the source code for the body are located in Appendix A.

One extension of an already introduced **record** facility is introduced in the *Birthdays* **record** type in the **private** part of the package. The record type *Birthdays* contains a field called *Name* which is itself a **record**. This is in accord with the data structure diagram given above, but implies that two dot '*field of record*' operators will be required to reference either the *FirstName* or *SecondName* of the record. Assuming that a variable instance of the type *Birthdays* called *Birthday* has been declared, the following references could be made:

`Birthday`	is of type	`Birthdays`
`Birthday.BirthDate`	is of type	`JulianDates`
`Birthday.Name`	is of type	`Names`
`Birthday.Name.FirstName`	is of type	`NameStrings`
`Birthday.Name.SecondName`	is of type	`NameStrings`

Using the type *Birthdays* exported from this package a sequential file of birthdays would have the following data structure diagram:

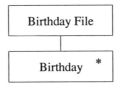

The design of the program to create a file of *Birthday* records might be as follows:

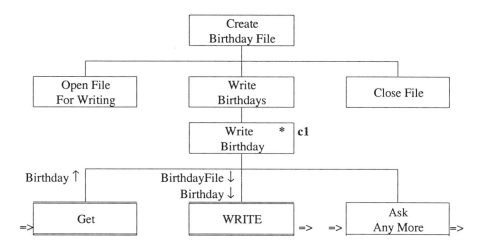

c1: While user wants to write more birthdays.

The implementation of this design might be as follows:

```
0001    -- Filename CreateBirthdayFile.ada (k8 createbi.adb).
0002    -- Program to demonstrate writing records to an
0003    -- instantiated sequential file.
0004    -- Developed for Ada book Section III Chapter 22.
0005    --
0006    -- Fintan Culwin, v0.1, Jan 1997.
0007
0008    with ADA.TEXT_IO, ADA.SEQUENTIAL_IO, Birthday;
0009    use  ADA.TEXT_IO, Birthday;
0010
0011    procedure CreateBirthdayFile is
0012
0013       package BirthdaySIO is new ADA.SEQUENTIAL_IO( Birthdays);
0014       use BirthdaySIO;
0015
0016       BirthdayFile : BirthdaySIO.FILE_TYPE;
0017       Birthday     : Birthdays;
0018       Response     : CHARACTER;
0019       MoreToWrite  : BOOLEAN := True;
0020
0021    begin -- CreateBirthdayFile
0022       PUT_LINE( "Create New Birthday File demonstration
                                                      program." );
0023       NEW_LINE( 2);
0024
```

```
0025      CREATE( BirthdayFile, MODE => OUT_FILE,
0026                                 NAME => "Reminder.dat");
0027
0028      while MoreToWrite loop
0029         Get( Birthday);
0030         WRITE( BirthdayFile, Birthday);
0031
0032         PUT( "Any more (y/n) ");
0033         GET( Response); SKIP_LINE;
0034         MoreToWrite := Response = 'y';
0035      end loop;
0036
0037      CLOSE( BirthdayFile);
0038   end CreateBirthdayFile;
```

The design of the program to read a file of *Birthday* records might be as follows:

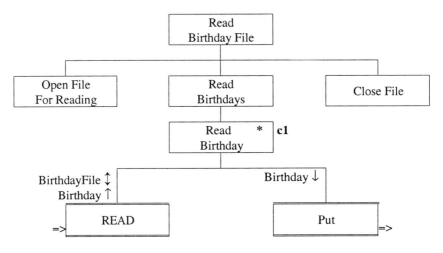

c1: While not end of file.

The implementation of this design might be as follows:

```
0001   -- Filename ReadBirthdayFile.ada (k8 readbirt.adb).
0002   -- Program to demonstrate reading records from an
0003   -- instantiated sequential file.
0004   -- Developed for Ada book Section III Chapter 22.
0005   --
0006   -- Fintan Culwin, v0.1, Jan 1997.
0007
0008   with ADA.TEXT_IO, ADA.SEQUENTIAL_IO, Birthday;
0009   use  ADA.TEXT_IO, Birthday;
0010
```

```
0011    procedure ReadBirthdayFile is
0012
0013        package BirthdaySIO is new ADA.SEQUENTIAL_IO( Birthdays);
0014        use BirthdaySIO;
0015
0016        BirthdayFile : BirthdaySIO.FILE_TYPE;
0017        Birthday     : Birthdays;
0018
0019    begin -- ReadBirthdayFile
0020        PUT_LINE( "Read New Birthday File demonstration
                                                    program." );
0021        NEW_LINE( 2 );
0022
0023        OPEN( BirthdayFile, MODE => IN_FILE,
0024                            NAME => "Reminder.dat" );
0025
0026        while not END_OF_FILE( BirthdayFile) loop
0027            READ( BirthdayFile, Birthday);
0028            Put( Birthday);
0029            NEW_LINE;
0030        end loop;
0031
0032        CLOSE( BirthdayFile);
0033    end ReadBirthdayFile;
```

A trace of the sequential demonstration programs

The program commences with the call of the SIO procedure CREATE to make a
new external file called '*Reminder.dat*'. The state of the system at the point in the
program when the CREATE procedure has just been executed can be visualized as
follows:

Reminder.dat   *Create Birthday File*

← file pointer

| Birthday |
| ?? |
| Birthdays |

The diagram shows an empty birthday file, with its file pointer pointing to the
start of the file. For a file which is opened in OUT_MODE or APPEND_MODE
the file pointer indicates the location in the file where the next record will be
written to. The right hand side of the diagram shows the program containing a

variable of type *Birthdays* which has its default value. Following the execution of the *Birthday Get* procedure on line 0029 the state of the system may change to that shown in the following diagram:

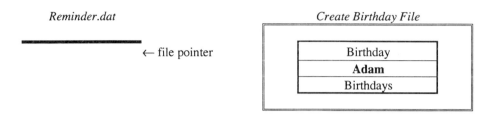

It is assumed that the user has input the birthday details of a person called Adam, and to simplify the diagrams only the first name has been shown. The next line, line 0030, is a call of the *BirthdaySIO* WRITE procedure specifying the *Birthday* variable as the value to be written to the file. Following the execution of this procedure call the state of the system will change as follows:

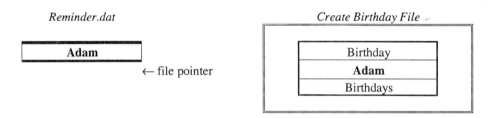

The file now contains a single record containing Adam's birthday details; the file pointer is still at the and of the file ready for another record to be appended. The state of the *Birthday* variable has not changed as only its value has been copied to the file. If it is assumed that the user indicates that more birthday details are to be added to the file and that when asked the user will input details of a person called Beth, the state of the program following the second execution of the *Get* procedure on line 0029 would be as follows:

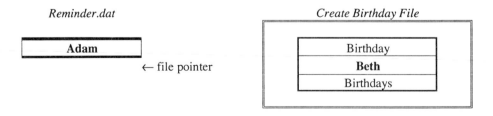

which, after the second execution of the WRITE procedure on line 0030, becomes

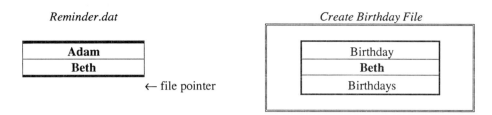

This process will continue within the iterative program structure, transferring a sequence of birthday details from the terminal to the file via the *Birthdays* record. The only limit to the number of records which can be stored on the file is the amount of backing storage space available. For the purposes of this trace, the process will be assumed to continue with an indefinite number of records, finishing with Zack's record. The state of the system when the file is CLOSEd, on line 0037, is shown as follows:

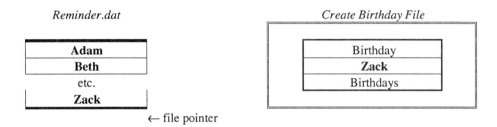

A similar diagram can be constructed for execution of the second program *ReadBirthdayFile*. The state of this program after the file has been OPENed, on line 0023, can be visualized as follows:

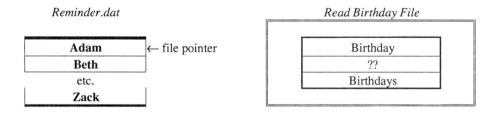

The diagram shows that the file pointer is at the start of the file ready to read the first record from the file, while the *Birthdays* record within the program has a default value. The condition controlling the loop on line 0026, '**while not** END_OF_FILE(*BirthdayFile*)', will evaluate true causing the body of the loop to be executed. The first action of the loop is to READ the file, transferring the contents of the record pointed to by the file pointer into the *Birthday* variable. The state of the system following execution of this procedure is as follows:

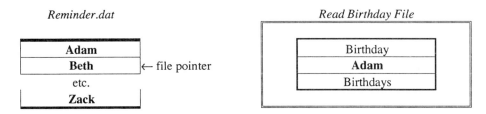

Adam's details have been transferred from the file to the program and the file pointer has moved towards the end of the file. Execution continues with line 0028 where a call to the *Birthday Put* procedure outputs details of Adam's birthday to the terminal. Following the NEW_LINE on line 0029 the body of the loop comes to an end and the loop control condition is evaluated for a second time. The condition will still evaluate true, causing the loop body to be executed for a second time. The state of the system following the READ on line 0027 is as follows:

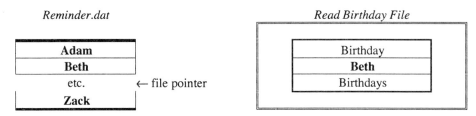

The contents of the *Birthday* variable have been overwritten with the details which have been transferred from the file. The second *Put* call on line 0028 will output Beth's details and at the end of the loop the third evaluation of the loop control condition will evaluate true causing the loop body to be executed for a third time. Program execution continues iteratively with records being read from the file and output to the terminal, until Zack's details have been output. The state of the system at this stage is as follows:

Reminder.dat   *Read Birthday File*

| Adam |
| Beth |
| etc. |
| Zack |

← file pointer

| Birthday |
| Zack |
| Birthdays |

The last record of the file, Zack, has already been transferred from the file to the program and subsequently displayed. The file pointer is now at the end of file position. If the READ procedure were attempted at this stage an exception will be raised as there is no next record to transfer. This will not happen as the END_OF_FILE function controlling the loop will now evaluate true, preventing another iteration of the loop. The termination of the loop after all records have been read from the file and displayed on the terminal causes the CLOSE procedure to be executed, closing the file. Following this action the program itself terminates.

The designs and implementations which have been presented here can be used as a basis for other designs which have a requirement to create or process sequential files.

Direct files

Direct files offer an alternative method of file organization and record access, compared with sequential files. With direct file organization it is possible to access any record in the file, one at a time, in any sequence. When sequential organization is in use it is only possible to access the records in the file in the order in which they exist, or are being created, on the file. Direct files also differ from sequential files in that they can be opened in a mode which allows records to be read from or written to. This form of access to records in a file is known as *random access*.

Although it is possible to access a dynamic file in a random manner it is also possible for a dynamic file to be accessed in a sequential manner, commencing at the current position of the file pointer. How the file is accessed depends upon the requirements of the specification.

Random file access is implemented by use of a *key* value which uniquely identifies a particular record in the file. For random access the key value of the required record has to be specified when the read or write operation is attempted. The key which is used for direct files is the record's *ordinal* position in the file. The ordinal position of a record is the position of the record relative to the start of the file. Thus the first record in a dynamic file has an ordinal position of 1 and a key value of 1, the second record has the key value 2, the fifth record the key value 5, the 100th record the key value 100, etc. If it is required to read the fifth record from a dynamic file then the read operation has to specify that the key of the record which is to be read from the file is 5. If it is required to write the tenth record to a dynamic file then the write operation has to specify that the key of the record to be written to the file is 10.

Files having a dynamic organization have many advantages over files which have a sequential organization. A dynamic file has all the properties of a sequential file, plus those which are concerned with random access. It does, however, have one major disadvantage: it is not possible for a direct file to have 'holes' in it. If a direct file contains a single stored record whose key value is 100 then all records with key values 1 to 99 are also physically present in the file, although they may not have defined values.

Direct files become most useful when the values of the keys which are used by the file are in a strict ordinal sequence, that is i.e. 1, 2, 3, 4 ..., or can be mapped onto this sequence. Key sequences which are strictly ordinal are not very common in real world applications. A third method of file organization, known as **indexed** file organization, exists, where the key values do not have to be strictly ordinal. Indexed files are not defined in the Ada standard, although many environments include non-standard indexed file facilities.

A second, and minor, disadvantage of direct files is that they require more system resources to implement them. A sequential file can be stored on a sequential storage medium, such as magnetic tape, or can be stored upon a dynamic medium, such as magnetic disk. Direct files can only be stored upon a dynamic medium. Although direct files are more expensive to implement than sequential files, for many applications the advantages of direct files outweigh their disadvantages.

Creating and maintaining direct files

The generic package for the instantiation of direct file i–o packages is ADA.DIRECT_IO and is used to create new direct i–o packages for use with a particular record type in a manner which is directly comparable with the creation of a new SEQUENTIAL_IO package.

```
-- Assuming that the package ADA.DIRECT_IO is at
-- least withed in the context clause.

package IntegerDIO is new ADA.DIRECT_IO( INTEGER);
-- Instantiation of a package called IntegerDIO suitable
-- for the i-o of INTEGER values.

package FloatDIO is new ADA.DIRECT_IO( FLOAT);
-- Instantiation of a package called FloatDIO suitable
-- for the i-o of FLOAT values.

-- Assuming that the JulianDate package is at least withed.
package JulianDateDIO is new
           ADA.SEQUENTIAL_IO( JulianDate.JulianDates);
-- Instantiation of a package called JulianDateDIO suitable
-- for the i-o of JulianDate values.

-- Assuming that the CashRegister package is at least
                                              withed.
package CashRegisterDIO is new
           ADA.SEQUENTIAL_IO( CashRegister.CashRegisters);
-- Instantiation of a package called DIO suitable
-- for the i-o of CashRegisters values.
```

As was suggested for instantiated SEQUENTIAL_IO packages a naming convention should be adopted for instantiated DIRECT_IO packages. The suggested convention is to use the singular name of the data type which the file can store with '*DIO*', for DIRECT_IO, appended to it. Having instantiated a *DIO* package within the scope of a compilation unit it is automatically **with**ed and can be brought into use in a manner comparable with TEXT_IO instantiated packages such as *FloatIO*.

These *DIO* packages contain a collection of subprograms for the creation and maintenance of direct files whose records are of the types specified. Many of these subprograms are directly comparable with the subprograms provided for sequential and text files. The following subprograms are unchanged from those provided for sequential or text files:

> FORM NAME IS_OPEN

The following procedures and functions differ from those provided for sequential files, primarily by the addition of a third possible access mode, known as INOUT_FILE:

> CREATE MODE OPEN RESET

A direct file open in INOUT_FILE mode can be used at the same point in a program either for input or for output. Direct files can also be opened in one of the modes IN_FILE or OUT_FILE, in which case they can only be read from or written to respectively. The DIRECT_IO version of the CREATE procedure has the default mode INOUT_FILE, but the DIRECT_IO version of the OPEN procedure has no default mode specified.

Using direct files

The direct file packages supply modified READ and WRITE procedures for random reading from and writing to direct files. They also supply unchanged READ and WRITE procedures for sequential reading from and writing to direct files.

The packages also supply a data type for representing the ordinal position of a record in the file and a set of procedures and functions for directly manipulating the file pointer using this type. The data type supplied for representing ordinal positions is a new INTEGER type called COUNT, with a range of values from 0 to a maximum value which differs from compiler to compiler. The package also supplies a subtype of count called POSITIVE_COUNT, whose range of values includes all the values of COUNT apart from 0. The effective declaration of these types in DIRECT_IO is as follows:

```
type COUNT          is 0 .. {implementation defined};
type POSITIVE_COUNT is 1 .. COUNT'LAST;
```

The data flow diagram and effective declaration of the new random READ procedure, using the subtype POSITIVE_COUNT to indicate which record is to be read from the file, are as follows:

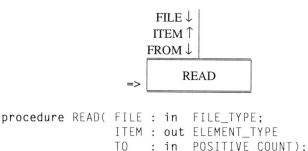

```
procedure READ( FILE : in  FILE_TYPE;
                ITEM : out ELEMENT_TYPE
                TO   : in  POSITIVE_COUNT );
```

The additional parameter FROM indicates the ordinal position in the file from which the record is to be read. The effect of this procedure, when it is executed, is to position the file pointer at the position specified, to transfer the record from that position into ITEM and then to advance the file pointer to the next record in the file. There are a number of problems which may occur which will prevent the procedure from executing successfully and will raise the following exceptions:

Exception	Reason
MODE_ERROR	will be raised if the file is in OUT_FILE mode
DATA_ERROR	will be raised if the data read is not a value of type ITEM
END_ERROR	will be raised if the pointer is beyond the end of file

The data flow diagram and effective declaration of the new random WRITE procedure, using the subtype POSITIVE_COUNT to indicate which record is to be written to the file is as follows:

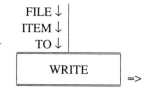

```
procedure WRITE( FILE : in FILE_TYPE;
                 ITEM : in ELEMENT_TYPE
                 TO   : in POSITIVE_COUNT );
```

The additional parameter TO indicates the ordinal position in the file at which the record is to be written. The effect of this procedure, when it is executed, is to position the file pointer at the position specified and then to transfer the contents of ITEM to the record at that position. If the position specified is beyond the current end of the file then sufficient new uninitialized records are appended to the end of the file to increase its size to that required. The file pointer is then advanced to beyond the end of the record which has just been written. There are a number of problems which may occur which will prevent the procedure from executing successfully and will raise the following exceptions:

Exception	Reason
MODE_ERROR	will be raised if the file is in IN_FILE mode
USE_ERROR	will be raised if the capacity of the file is exceeded

An additional procedure is provided which can be used to position the file pointer without reading or writing a record. The data flow diagram and effective declaration of this procedure in DIRECT_IO are as follows:

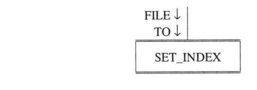

```
procedure SET_INDEX( FILE : in FILE_TYPE;
                     TO   : in POSITIVE_COUNT );
```

When it is executed, the effect of the procedure is to move the file pointer to the position specified. This point may be beyond the physical end of the file in which case no exception is raised and no records are appended to the file.

Two additional functions are also provided: the first of these can be used to determine the current position of the file pointer. The data flow diagram and effective declaration of this procedure in DIRECT_IO are as follows:

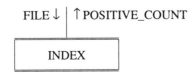

```
function INDEX( FILE : in FILE_TYPE)
                      return POSITIVE_COUNT;
```

The effect of this function is to return the current position of the file pointer. This position may be beyond the physical end of the file. No exceptions are associated with this function. The remaining function can be used to determine the size of a file. The data flow diagram and effective declaration of this procedure in DIRECT_IO are as follows:

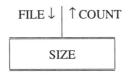

```
function SIZE( FILE : in FILE_TYPE)
                     return COUNT;
```

The effect of this function is to return the size of the file in records; if the file is empty the size returned will be zero. There are no exceptions associated with this function.

An example program specification

To illustrate the use of direct files a program will be developed, implemented and have its execution described. The program is concerned with car servicing where the information of the date on which a car is serviced and the mileage at the time of the service is to be stored. The records which are to be used in this example are of a type which will be known as *CarServiceRecords*, whose structure is as follows:

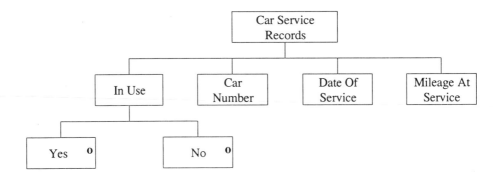

This type will be supplied by a package called *CarServiceRecord* whose object diagram is as follows:

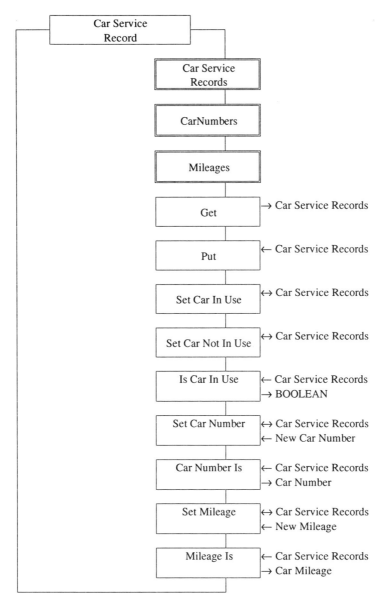

The details of the implementation of this package are not given in this book as they contribute little to the understanding of direct files. However, in order to comprehend fully the client program which follows there are several aspects of the design and implementation which require consideration. The *InUse* field of the *CarServiceRecords* is a BOOLEAN field which is used to indicate if the record on the file currently holds details of a car. The *SetMileage* subprogram will not only update the value of the *MileageAtService* field to the value of the *NewMileage* parameter, but also update the value of the *DateOfService* field to the current date.

A client program, called *CarDemo*, which makes use of this ADT and of ADA.DIRECT_IO, is based upon a *main menu/main dispatch* design as presented in Section II Chapter 14. The main menu from this client program offers the following options:

```
                Car Service Demo

        A. Create Car Record.
        B. Update Car Record.
        C. Delete Car Record.
        D. Show all Records.
        E. Exit program.
```

Before the menu is offered to the user for the first time an initialize subprogram called *CheckFile* is called. The purpose of this procedure is to determine if a *DIO* file with the filename supplied exists on the backing store. If no such file exists then the subprogram creates a new file, initializing all the records on the file as being not in use. The design and implementation of this subprogram are as follows:

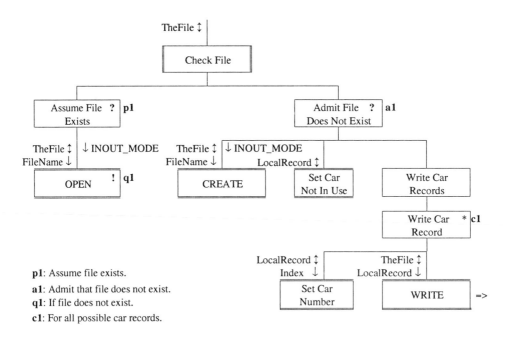

pl: Assume file exists.

a1: Admit that file does not exist.

q1: If file does not exist.

c1: For all possible car records.

```
0001   procedure CheckFile( TheFile : in out
0002                               CarServiceRecordDIO.FILE_TYPE) is
0003   -- Test for the existence of the file, creating and
0004   -- initializing it if it does not exist. Returns under all
0005   -- conditions with the file open.
0006   -- Uses global STRING constant FileName.
0007
0008      LocalRecord : CarServiceRecords;
0009
0010   begin -- CheckFile
0011      begin -- exception handler
0012         OPEN( TheFile, NAME => FileName,
0013                        MODE => INOUT_FILE );
0014      exception
0015         when CarServiceRecordDIO.NAME_ERROR =>
0016         -- The file does not exist - so create it.
0017         CREATE( TheFile, NAME => FileName,
0018                          MODE => INOUT_FILE );
0019         SetCarNotInUse( LocalRecord);
0020         for ThisCar in CarNumbers loop
0021            SetCarNumber( LocalRecord, ThisCar);
0022            WRITE( TheFile, LocalRecord);
0023         end loop;
0024      end; -- exception block
0025   end CheckFile;
```

In this design, and the designs which follow, the subprograms supplied by the *CarServiceRecord* package are shown with double horizontal lines as, so far as this client program is concerned, they are pre-declared.

The declarative region of the program procedure, *CarDemo*, instantiates a DIRECT_IO package called *CarServiceRecordDIO*, using the instantiation techniques described above, and subsequently brings the package into direct visibility.

The *FileName* actual parameter of the OPEN and CREATE subprogram calls is a global string constant. This implementation decision was taken to simplify the construction of the client and is not a realistic implementation. If a file with the name specified, and direct organization, exists then the OPEN subprogram call will execute without raising an exception and the subprogram will terminate, leaving the file open.

If the file cannot be opened a NAME_ERROR exception will be raised by the *CarServiceRecordDIO* version of the OPEN procedure. As this program also brings into direct visibility the i–o packages TEXT_IO and *IntegerIO*, there are three packages defining an exception called NAME_ERROR. Accordingly the exception handler on line 0014 has to indicate explicitly which of the possible NAME_ERROR exceptions it is intended to handle.

Within the exception handler a new *CarServiceRecordDIO* file is created and then, within a definite loop whose range is defined by the range of the subtype

CarNumbers, uses the *CarServiceRecordDIO* sequential WRITE procedure to write a sequence of records to the file. Each record written to the file has the *InUse* field set to false indicating that the record does not contain details of a car's servicing and has the *CarNumber* field set to the ordinal location of the record within the file. As with the alternative path of execution the subprogram terminates without closing the file. Thus whichever path of execution is taken through the subprogram it can be guaranteed that the file identified by *FileName* exists and is open, before the main menu is offered to the user.

Writing a record to a direct file

The first of the options offered by the menu is to create a new car record. The design and implementation of the subprogram which implements this option are as follows:

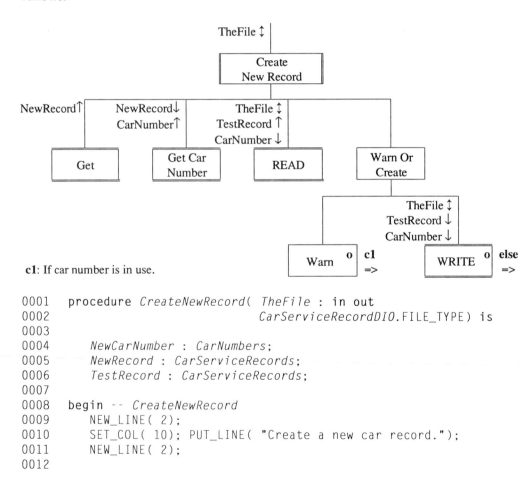

```
0001    procedure CreateNewRecord( TheFile : in out
0002                               CarServiceRecordDIO.FILE_TYPE) is
0003
0004       NewCarNumber : CarNumbers;
0005       NewRecord : CarServiceRecords;
0006       TestRecord : CarServiceRecords;
0007
0008    begin -- CreateNewRecord
0009       NEW_LINE( 2);
0010       SET_COL( 10); PUT_LINE( "Create a new car record.");
0011       NEW_LINE( 2);
0012
```

```
0013        Get( NewRecord);
0014        NewCarNumber := GetCarNumber( NewRecord);
0015        READ( TheFile, TestRecord,
0016             CarServiceRecordDIO.POSITIVE_COUNT( NewCarNumber));
0017
0018        if IsCarInUse( TestRecord) then
0019           PUT_LINE( "This car number is in use. If you want");
0020           PUT_LINE( "to reuse it, it must be deleted first.");
0021        else
0022           WRITE( TheFile, NewRecord,
0023              CarServiceRecordDIO.POSITIVE_COUNT
                                              ( NewCarNumber));
0024        end if;
0025    end CreateNewRecord;
```

The basis of this design and implementation is to obtain details of a new car record from the user and subsequently to obtain from the *NewRecord* the value of the *CarNumber* field. This *CarNumbers* value is then used as the third parameter of a direct READ subprogram call. The use of the third parameter identifies this call as a direct read, as opposed to a sequential read which requires only two parameters. The value of the third parameter, which identifies the ordinal position of the record to be read, has to be of type POSITIVE_COUNT and is type converted from the subtype *CarNumbers* as a part of the call.

The record read from the file is then tested to determine if it is currently in use. A record which is currently in use cannot be created, and if so the user is warned that the operation has not succeeded. Otherwise the details which were obtained from the user are written to the file in the position indicated by the user, by use of a direct READ call.

Updating a record on a direct file

The second menu option is to update the mileage details of an existing record. The design and implementation of the subprogram to implement this option are as follows:

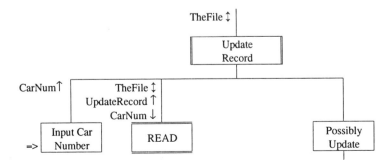

509

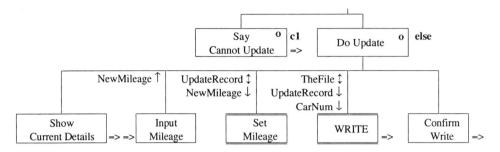

c1: If record not in use.

```
0001    procedure UpdateRecord( TheFile : in out
0002                             CarServiceRecordDIO.FILE_TYPE) is
0003
0004        UpdateCarNumber : CarNumbers;
0005        UpdateRecord    : CarServiceRecords;
0006        NewMileage      : Mileages;
0007
0008    begin -- UpdateRecord
0009        NEW_LINE( 2);
0010        SET_COL( 10); PUT_LINE( "Update a car record.");
0011        NEW_LINE( 2);
0012
0013        PUT( "Please enter the car number ");
0014        GET( UpdateCarNumber); SKIP_LINE;
0015        READ( TheFile, UpdateRecord,
0016             CarServiceRecordDIO.POSITIVE_COUNT
0017                                      ( UpdateCarNumber));
0017
0018        if not IsCarInUse( UpdateRecord) then
0019            PUT_LINE( "This car number is not in use.");
0020        else
0021            PUT_LINE( "The current details are");
0022            Put( UpdateRecord); NEW_LINE( 2);
0023            PUT( "Please enter the new mileage ");
0024            GET( NewMileage);
0025            SetMileage( UpdateRecord, NewMileage);
0026            WRITE( TheFile, UpdateRecord,
0027                 CarServiceRecordDIO.POSITIVE_COUNT
                                           ( UpdateCarNumber));
0028            PUT_LINE( "OK record mileage updated.");
0029        end if;
0030    end UpdateRecord;
```

The essential basis of this design is similar to the design of *CreateNewRecord* above. The car number is obtained from the user and then used to specify which record is to be read from the file. If this record is not currently in use then it cannot be updated and the user is informed of this. Otherwise the details of the record are displayed to the user and the new mileage obtained and stored in the record before the record is (re)written to the file.

Deleting a record on a direct file

The design and implementation of the delete record subprogram are as follows:

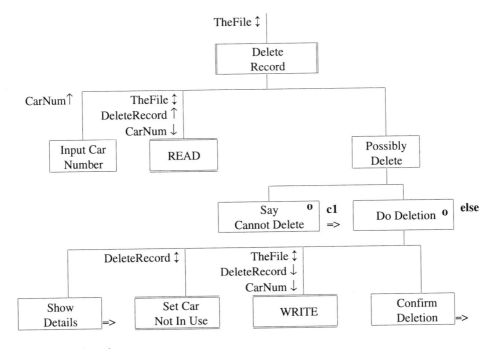

c1: If record not in use.

```
0001    procedure DeleteRecord( TheFile : in out
0002                                CarServiceRecordDIO.FILE_TYPE) is
0003
0004        DeleteCarNumber : CarNumbers;
0005        DeleteRecord : CarServiceRecords;
0006
0007    begin -- DeleteRecord
0008        NEW_LINE( 2);
0009        SET_COL( 10); PUT_LINE( "Delete a car record.");
0010        NEW_LINE( 2);
0011
```

```
0012       PUT( "Please enter the car number " );
0013       GET( DeleteCarNumber ); SKIP_LINE;
0014       READ( TheFile, DeleteRecord,
0015            CarServiceRecordDIO.POSITIVE_COUNT
                                        ( DeleteCarNumber ));
0016
0017       if not IsCarInUse( DeleteRecord) then
0018          PUT_LINE( "This car number is not in use.");
0019       else
0020          PUT_LINE( "The current details are");
0021          Put( DeleteRecord); NEW_LINE( 2);
0022          SetCarNotInUse( DeleteRecord);
0023          WRITE( TheFile, DeleteRecord,
0024             CarServiceRecordDIO.POSITIVE_COUNT
                                        ( DeleteCarNumber ));
0025          PUT_LINE( "OK record deleted.");
0026       end if;
0027    end DeleteRecord;
```

Processing a direct file sequentially

The final menu option is to list all the records which are currently in use. The design and implementation of a subprogram to satisfy this requirement are as follows:

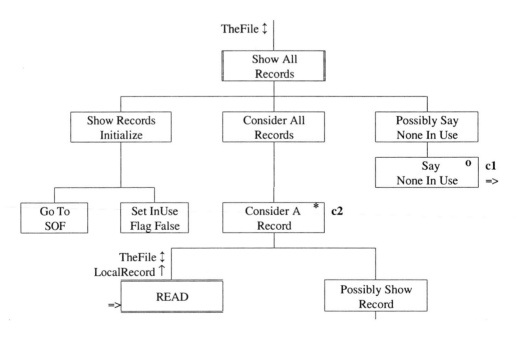

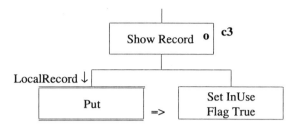

c1: If no records are in use.

c2: While not end of file.

c3: If record in use.

```
0001    procedure ShowAllRecords( TheFile : in out
0002                              CarServiceRecordDIO.FILE_TYPE) is
0003
0004        LocalRecord : CarServiceRecords;
0005        AtLeastOneInUse : BOOLEAN := FALSE;
0006
0007    begin -- ShowAllRecords
0008        SET_COL( 10); PUT_LINE( "All car service records");
0009        NEW_LINE( 2);
0010
0011        SET_INDEX( TheFile, 1);
0012        while not END_OF_FILE( TheFile) loop
0013            READ( TheFile, LocalRecord);
0014            if IsCarInUse( LocalRecord) then
0015                Put( LocalRecord);
0016                NEW_LINE;
0017                AtLeastOneInUse := True;
0018            end if;
0019        end loop;
0020
0021        if not AtLeastOneInUse then
0022            PUT_LINE( "No cars are currently in use.");
0023            NEW_LINE( 2);
0024        end if;
0025    end ShowAllRecords;
```

The basis of this design and implementation is to position the file pointer at the start of the file (SOF) using the SET_INDEX procedure. An indefinite loop then iterates through the file using the sequential READ procedure, terminating when it reaches the end of the file. Each record is tested to determine if it is in use and if so is displayed on the terminal. During this process a flag is maintained and if it indicates that no records have been output it informs the user, before the subprogram terminates.

As with the design and implementation of the SEQUENTIAL_IO demonstration programs presented previously in this chapter, the designs and implementations presented in this part of the chapter can be used as the basis of programs which have a requirement to process direct files.

EXERCISES

22.1   Reimplement the sequential file demonstration programs so that the user can input the name of the file to be created or read. When creating the filename supplied should not identify a file which already exists. When reading the filename supplied should identify a file which already exists. The processes should iterate until a suitable filename is given or the user indicates, by not entering anything at the filename prompt, the wish to abandon the program.

22.2   Extend the creation filename dialog given above so that if the user supplies a filename that already exists the user is given the opportunity to re-enter the filename, to overwrite the existing contents of the file or to append details to the file.

22.3   Review the designs and implementations of the two processes from Exercises 22.1 and 22.2 so that they can be easily reused in different programs. Then prove that this is so by extending the program from Exercise 21.4 to make use of the file opening process.

22.4   The user interface of *CreateNewRecord* requires that the user inputs an entire car record before, possibly, informing the user that that *CarNumber* cannot be used. Improve the interface so that this problem is avoided and reimplement the procedure.

22.5   A warehouse consists of a number of storage locations called *Bins*. Each bin is identified by a letter in the range A to Z and a number in the range 1 to 120. Each bin has a description of its contents, which contains at most 25 characters, and an integer value in the range 0 to 500 for the number of things which it currently contains.

Design, implement and test a program to model the operation of the warehouse. It should allow for the contents of a particular bin to be examined, for items to be stored in and moved from the warehouse, to find an empty bin, etc.

SECTION IV

Object Oriented Programming

CHAPTER 23
Encapsulated static variables

Packages were first introduced in Section I as a convenient means by which a set of related subprograms could be collected together. The use of packages was subsequently extended to include *extendible data types* (EDT) and *abstract data type* (ADT) facilities. The package construct can also be used to implement other design approaches one of which, known as the ***encapsulated static variable*** (ESV) design, will be the major focus of this chapter.

With EDT and ADT designs the package exported to its client programs a data type and a set of operations which could be applied to values of that type. The intentions were that within a client program a programmer declared data type should be indistinguishable from a pre-declared type. It was also hoped that as the package had been designed from real world considerations, it would be more useful within the client than pre-declared types and would have a high degree of potential reusability.

However, the values of the ADT were external to the package, even when the precise representation and nature of the type was hidden within the private part of the package. For most applications this is acceptable, but for some applications it introduces a potential insecurity as objects of the type could be manipulated in some manner outside the package.

An ESV design, in contrast, only exports operations. The object, or objects, which these operations will act upon are hidden, hence ***encapsulated***, within the body of the package where it can be absolutely guaranteed that they will only be manipulated by the ESV's operations. An ESV implementation is thus more secure than an ADT implementation. The encapsulated variable exists outside the scope of any subprograms within the package and its value is unchanged between calls of package subprograms; hence ***static***. The major disadvantage of an ESV is that only a single instance, or a very small number of instances, of the real world concept being modelled can be used within the program.

One of the design requirements for the Ada language was that it should be a suitable environment for the development of programs concerned with ***real time control***, such as the control of factory robots, washing machines or even canned drink dispensers. In such situations a model of the machine being controlled is encapsulated within the package body, and the design intention is that the state of the model at all times reflects the physical state of the machine. As the package is able in some sense to remember the state of the machine, such packages are sometimes known as ***memory packages***.

An example ESV specification

To introduce the design and implementation of an ESV part of a canned drink dispenser will be modelled. A schematic diagram of a canned drink dispenser is given in Figure 23.1. The parts of the machine visible to the user consist of a message display, a slot where coins can be entered, a reject button, drink select buttons, a coin return tray and a can dispensing tray. The hidden parts of the machine consist of a coin classifier, coin hoppers where coins are stored and a drink hopper where cans are stored prior to being dispensed.

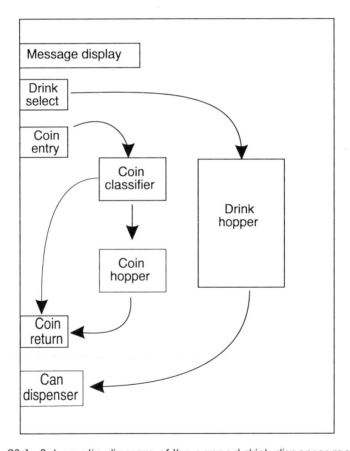

Figure 23.1 Schematic diagram of the canned drink dispenser machine.

A simplified specification of the entire machine might be:

The machine will be operated by the user entering coins into the slot. Any coins which are not accepted by the coin classifier will be returned directly to the user. After the first coin has been deposited the value of all coins deposited will be displayed. When a sufficient value has been entered no more coins will be accepted.

At any stage after the first coin has been deposited, the user can press the reject button and have the coins which have been entered returned. Once a sufficient value of coins has been input the drink select buttons will become active and a can of drink and appropriate change dispensed to the user when any button is pressed.

If the drink hopper ever becomes empty, or the coin hopper becomes full, or any other fault occurs in the machine, the coins deposited by the user should be returned and the machine should shut down with a suitable message on the display.

It is intended that the machine will be used in different countries and the software should be engineered accordingly.

For the purposes of this example only the *coin hopper* will be implemented in detail as an ESV; the other parts will be implemented in a simplified manner within the test harness client program. The implementation of the other parts of the drink dispenser as ESVs will be left as an end of chapter exercise.

The design of the coin hopper

The design of the coin hopper proceeds in the same manner as the design of an ADT or an EDT. The required operations of the coin hopper are determined from a consideration of the real world operations which can be performed upon a coin hopper, prior to any decisions concerning how the operations or the data structure are to be implemented.

The design and implementation of the *Coins* ADT

As it is a requirement that the machine be implemented in a manner which allows it to be re-engineered for use in different countries, the package will require a supporting package to implement the concept of *Coins* as an ADT. In addition to representing a single coin the package also exports a type which can be used to represent a set of coins. This type, known as *CoinSets*, is an array of individual *coin stacks* indexed by the *Coins* type. Each stack is implemented as a NATURAL integer and thus the hopper is able to contain zero or more coins of each denomination. A data design, package design and implementation as a package specification tailored for British coins might be as follows:

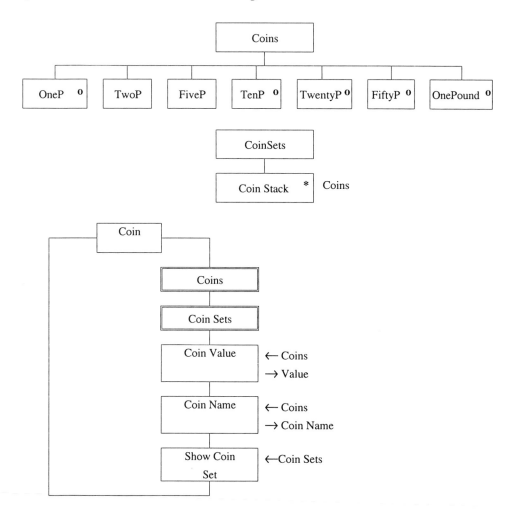

```
0001    -- Filename Coin_.pkg (k8 coin.ads).
0002    -- ADT package to implement Coins data type,
0003    -- developed for the Ada book Section IV Chapter 23.
0004.   --
0005    -- Fintan Culwin, v0.1, Jan 1997.
0006
```

```
0007    package Coin is
0008
0009       type Coins is ( OneP, TwoP, FiveP, TenP,
0010                                       TwentyP, FiftyP, OnePound);
0011
0012       type CoinSets is array ( Coins) of NATURAL;
0013
0014       MaximumCoinNameString : constant INTEGER := 13;
0015       subtype CoinNameStrings is
0016                            STRING ( 1 .. MaximumCoinNameString);
0017
0018       function CoinValue( AnyCoin : in Coins) return POSITIVE;
0019       -- Function to return the value of the coin supplied.
0020
0021       function CoinName( AnyCoin : in Coins)
0022                                       return CoinNameStrings;
0023       -- Function to return the name of the coin supplied.
0024
0025       procedure ShowCoinSet( AnySet : in CoinSets);
0026       -- Procedure to display on the terminal screen a
0027       -- representation of the coins in the coin set.
0028
0029    end Coin;
```

The procedure *ShowCoinSet* is included only for purposes of interactive testing of the ESV; for a real machine the coins would be dispensed from the machine rather than displayed on the terminal screen. The body of this ADT package might be implemented as follows:

```
0001    -- Filename Coin.pkb.
0002    -- ADT package body to implement the Coins data type,
0003    -- developed for the Ada book Section IV Chapter 23.
0004    --
0005    -- Fintan Culwin v0.1 May 1995.
0006
0007    with ADA.TEXT_IO;
0008    use  ADA.TEXT_IO;
0009
0010    package body Coin is
0011
0012       package CoinsIO   is new ADA.TEXT_IO.ENUMERATION_IO( Coins);
0013       package IntegerIO is new ADA.TEXT_IO.INTEGER_IO( INTEGER);
0014       use CoinsIO, IntegerIO;
0015
0016       CoinValues : constant array ( Coins) of POSITIVE
0017                        := ( 1, 2, 5, 10, 20, 50, 100 );
0018
```

```
0019        CoinNames : constant array ( Coins) of CoinNameStrings
0020                    := ( ("One Pence "), ("Two Pence "),
0021                         ("Five Pence "), ("Ten Pence "),
0022                         ("Twenty Pence "), ("Fifty Pence "),
0023                         ("One Pound " ));
0024
0025
0026        function CoinValue( AnyCoin : in Coins)
0027                                            return POSITIVE is
0028        begin -- CoinValue
0029           return CoinValues( AnyCoin);
0030        end CoinValue;
0031
0032
0033        function CoinName( AnyCoin : in Coins)
0034                                         return CoinNameStrings is
0035        begin -- CoinName
0036           return CoinNames( AnyCoin);
0037        end CoinName;
0038
0039
0040         procedure ShowCoinSet( AnySet : in CoinSets) is
0041         begin -- ShowCoinSet
0042            for ThisCoin in Coins loop
0043               if AnySet( ThisCoin) > 0 then
0044                  PUT( AnySet( ThisCoin), WIDTH => 3);
0045                  PUT( " " & CoinNames( ThisCoin));
0046                  PUT_LINE( " coin(s)." );
0047               end if;
0048            end loop;
0049         end ShowCoinSet;
0050
0051    end Coin;
```

As this package contains within it all the details of which coins are available, their names and their values, the re-engineering of the coin hopper for a different country would require only that this package is changed and its clients are recompiled.

The design of the *CoinHopper* ESV

The actions required of a real world coin hopper are to accept, store and dispense coins. A more detailed investigation of these actions might produce the following object diagram:

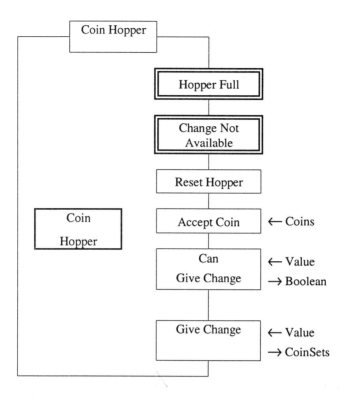

The inclusion of a representation of the *CoinHopper* within the scope of this object diagram indicates that the object contains an encapsulated variable object and thus is best implemented as an ESV. As it is totally contained within the limits of the object diagram its value can only be manipulated by the subprograms exported from the diagram. The encapsulated variables of an ESV are also known as the *data attributes* of the ESV. The implementation of this design as an Ada package specification might be as follows:

```
0001    -- Filename CoinHopper_.pkg (k8 coinhopp.ads).
0002    -- Package to implement a CoinHopper ESV,
0003    -- developed for the Ada book, Section IV Chapter 23.
0004    --
0005    -- Fintan Culwin, v0.1, Jan 1997.
0006
0007    with Coin;
0008    use  Coin;
0009
0010    package CoinHopper is
0011
```

```
0012        HopperFull            : exception;
0013        ChangeNotAvailable : exception;
0014
0015        procedure ResetHopper;
0016        -- Parameterless procedure to reset the hopper to an initial
0017        -- state by putting some coins into all coin stacks apart
0018        -- from the one with the highest value.
0019
0020        procedure AcceptCoin( AnyCoin : in Coins);
0021        -- Procedure to accept a coin storing it in the appropriate
0022        -- stack. If the stack is full a HopperFull exception will
0023        -- be raised.
0024
0025        function CanGiveChange( Value : in NATURAL)
0026                                                 return BOOLEAN;
0027        -- Function will return True if the hopper can dispense
0028        -- coins to the Value requested and False otherwise.
0029
0030        function GiveChange( Value : in NATURAL)
0031                                                 return CoinSets;
0032        -- Returns a set of coins which represent the value
0033        -- required. The procedure should only be called after the
0034        -- function CanGiveChange has indicated that change can be
0035        -- given. However, if change should not be available a
0036        -- ChangeNotAvailable exception will be raised.
0037
0038    end CoinHopper;
```

The *CoinHopper* ESV implementation

The implementation of an ESV requires the declaration within the package body of a variable outside the scope of any subprogram. A variable declared in this manner has its scope and visibility limited to the package body, including any subprograms within the package body. It is created, and possibly initialized, when the package is brought into use and destroyed when the package goes out of scope. The lifetime of the variable is effectively that of the program, being created when the program starts running and being destroyed when it terminates. References to the variable within the subprograms within the package body are *global* references and as the variable has an existence outside the subprogram any changes to its value are permanent. References to an encapsulated static variable are one of the circumstances where global variable references are acceptable as this is the only mechanism by which the package can be given a memory.

For the *CoinHopper* package body the encapsulated static variable is of the type *CoinSets* and within the package body a limit on the number of coins which can be held in each stack is enforced. The implementation of the package body might be as follows:

```
0001    -- Filename CoinHopper.pkb (k8 coinhopp.adb).
0002    -- Package body to implement CoinHopper ESV,
0003    -- developed for the Ada book, Section IV Chapter 23.
0004    --
0005    -- Fintan Culwin, v0.1, Jan 1997.
0006
0007
0008    package body CoinHopper is
0009
0010
0011        ResetCoinLevel   : constant := 9;
0012        MaximumCoinLevel : constant := 50;
0013
0014        TheCoinHopper : CoinSets := ( others => 0);
0015
0016
0017        procedure ResetHopper is
0018        begin -- ResetHopper
0019          for ThisCoin in Coins'FIRST .. Coins'PRED(Coins'LAST)
                                                                     loop
0020              TheCoinHopper( ThisCoin) := ResetCoinLevel;
0021          end loop;
0022        end ResetHopper;
0023
0024
0025        procedure AcceptCoin( AnyCoin : in Coins) is
0026        begin -- AcceptCoin
0027          if TheCoinHopper( AnyCoin) = MaximumCoinLevel then
0028              raise HopperFull;
0029          else
0030              TheCoinHopper( AnyCoin) := TheCoinHopper( AnyCoin)
                                                                      +1;
0031          end if;
0032        end AcceptCoin;
0033
0034
0035        function CanGiveChange( Value : in NATURAL)
0036                                        return BOOLEAN is
0037
0038            LocalHopper    : CoinSets := TheCoinHopper;
0039            RemainingValue : NATURAL := Value;
0040
0041        begin -- CanGiveChange
0042          for ThisCoin in reverse Coins'FIRST .. Coins'LAST loop
```

```
0043              while RemainingValue >= CoinValue( ThisCoin) and
0044                    LocalHopper( ThisCoin) > 0              loop
0045                 RemainingValue := RemainingValue -
0046                                     CoinValue( ThisCoin);
0047                 LocalHopper( ThisCoin) :=
0048                                     LocalHopper( ThisCoin) -1;
0049            end loop;
0050        end loop;
0051
0052        if RemainingValue > 0 then
0053            return FALSE;
0054        else
0055            return TRUE;
0056        end if;
0057    end CanGiveChange;
0058
0059
0060    function GiveChange( Value : in NATURAL)
0061                            return CoinSets is
0062
0063        TempHopper      : CoinSets := TheCoinHopper;
0064        LocalHopper     : CoinSets := ( others => 0);
0065        RemainingValue : NATURAL := Value;
0066
0067    begin -- GiveChange
0068        for ThisCoin in reverse Coins'FIRST .. Coins'LAST loop
0069            while RemainingValue >= CoinValue( ThisCoin) and
0070                  TempHopper( ThisCoin) > 0              loop
0071                RemainingValue := RemainingValue -
0072                                    CoinValue( ThisCoin);
0073                TempHopper( ThisCoin) :=
0074                                    TempHopper( ThisCoin) -1;
0075                LocalHopper( ThisCoin) :=
0076                                    LocalHopper( ThisCoin) +1;
0077            end loop;
0078        end loop;
0079
0080        if RemainingValue = 0 then
0081            TheCoinHopper := TempHopper;
0082            return LocalHopper;
0083        else
0084            raise ChangeNotAvailable;
0085        end if;
0086    end GiveChange;
0087
0088  end CoinHopper;
```

The first two of the subprograms in the package are relatively straightforward and their designs will not be presented. The first subprogram, *ResetHopper*, fills all stacks in the hopper, apart from that which holds coins of the highest denomination, with an initial number of coins. This subprogram is intended to be called before the *CoinHopper* is used and represents the state of the hopper in the machine after it has been serviced, containing sufficient coins to give change to the first few users. The second subprogram, *AcceptCoin*, will store the coin in the appropriate stack unless that stack is already full in which case a *HopperFull* exception will be raised.

The remaining two subprograms, *CanGiveChange* and *GiveChange*, are very similar and a design and description of *GiveChange* will suffice for both. The design of *GiveChange* might be as follows:

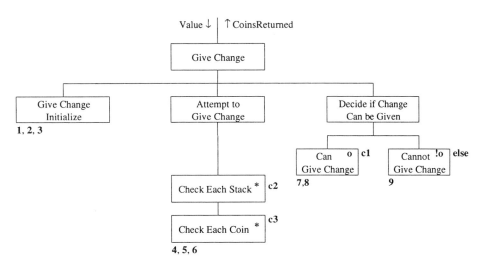

c1: If change can be made.
c2: For every stack.
c3: While change has not been made and stack is not empty.

1: Set TempHopper to The Hopper.
2: Empty LocalHopper.
3: Set RemainingValue to Value.
4: Decrement RemainingValue by value of coin.
5: Remove coin from TempHopper.

6: Add coin to LocalHopper.
7: Copy Temp Hopper to The Hopper.
8: Return LocalHopper.
9: Raise ChangeNotAvailable exception.

Data table for procedure GiveChange

Name	Type	Notes
TheHopper	*CoinSets*	The ESV variable
Value	POSITIVE	The value to dispense
LocalHopper	*CoinSets*	The coins to be dispensed
TempHopper	*CoinSets*	Working copy of TheHopper
RemainingValue	NATURAL	The value remaining to dispense

Perhaps the most significant part of the design is that a copy of the ESV, *TheHopper*, is taken and manipulated in order to preserve the state of the encapsulated variable until it is known if change can or cannot be given. If change cannot be given the state of the encapsulated variable is unchanged, otherwise the changed value of the copy is copied back to the encapsulated variable.

The basis of the main part of the procedure, *AttemptToGiveChange*, iterates through each coin stack starting with coins of the highest value. A second iteration for each coin stack moves coins from the temporary hopper into the local hopper and decrements the remaining value to be dispensed by the value of the coin moved. This iteration is terminated when the remaining value is zero, indicating that change has been made or when the remaining value is less than the value of the coin being dispensed. At the end of this process a remaining value of zero indicates that change has been made; any other value indicates that the correct change is not available. The function *CanGiveChange* differs from *GiveChange* by establishing if change can be given from the coin hopper without actually altering its value.

The *CanDispenser* client

In order to demonstrate the use of the *CoinHopper* ESV a simple client implementing a simulation of a canned drink dispenser will be developed. To simplify the simulation it will be assumed that an inexhaustible drink can hopper containing only a single type of drink is in the machine. The basis of the design of the machine is to offer the user a menu containing four possible options: the input of a coin, or the pressing of the reject button, or the pressing of the dispense button, or exiting from the program. Not all of these options will be available every time the menu is offered, for example the reject button will only be available if the value already entered by the user is greater than zero. The high level design of the simulation might be as follows:

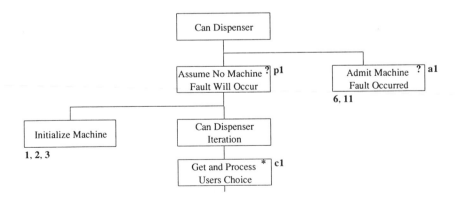

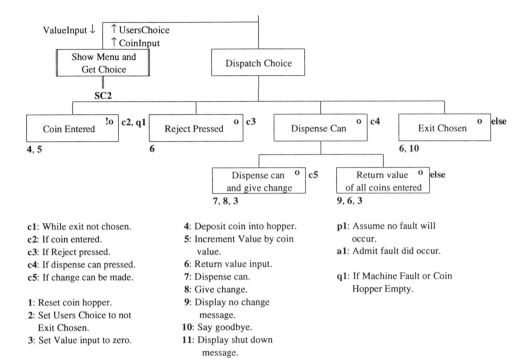

c1: While exit not chosen.
c2: If coin entered.
c3: If Reject pressed.
c4: If dispense can pressed.
c5: If change can be made.

1: Reset coin hopper.
2: Set Users Choice to not
   Exit Chosen.
3: Set Value input to zero.

4: Deposit coin into hopper.
5: Increment Value by coin
   value.
6: Return value input.
7: Dispense can.
8: Give change.
9: Display no change
   message.
10: Say goodbye.
11: Display shut down
    message.

p1: Assume no fault will
    occur.
a1: Admit fault did occur.

q1: If Machine Fault or Coin
    Hopper Empty.

Assuming the existence of the procedure *ShowMenuAndGetChoice*, this design could be implemented as follows:

```
0001    -- Filename CanDispenser.ada (k8 candispe.adb).
0002    -- Demonstration client program for the CoinHopper ESV,
0003    -- developed for the Ada book, Section IV Chapter 23.
0004    --
0005    -- Fintan Culwin v0.1 Jan 1997.
0006
0007    with ADA.TEXT_IO, ADA.CHARACTERS.HANDLING, Coin, CoinHopper;
0008    use  ADA.TEXT_IO, ADA.CHARACTERS.HANDLING, Coin, CoinHopper;
0009
0010    procedure CanDispenser is
0011
0012       package IntegerIO is new ADA.TEXT_IO.INTEGER_IO( INTEGER);
0013       package CoinsIO   is new ADA.TEXT_IO.ENUMERATION_IO(
                                                          Coins);
0014       use CoinsIO,IntegerIO;
0015
0016       type UsersChoices is ( CoinEntry,   RejectPress,
0017                               DispenseCan, ExitChosen );
0018       UsersChoice  : UsersChoices := CoinEntry;
0019       CanCost      : constant INTEGER := 45;
```

529

```
0020       ValueInput     : NATURAL := 0;
0021       CoinInput      : Coins;
0022       ChangeGiven    : CoinSets;
0023       CoinInputValue : POSITIVE;
0024
0025   procedure ShowMenuAndGetChoice( CurrentValue : in NATURAL;
0026                                      TheChoice    : out
                                                        UsersChoices;
0027                                      TheCoin      : out Coins) is
0101
0102
0103   begin -- CanDispenser
0104      ResetHopper;
0105      while UsersChoice /= ExitChosen loop
0106         ShowMenuAndGetChoice( ValueInput, UsersChoice,
                                                       CoinInput);
0107
0108         case UsersChoice is
0109            when CoinEntry =>
0110                  AcceptCoin( CoinInput);
0111                  ValueInput := ValueInput + CoinValue(
                                                        CoinInput);
0112            when RejectPress =>
0113                  ChangeGiven := GiveChange( ValueInput);
0114                  ShowCoinSet( ChangeGiven);
0115                  ValueInput := 0;
0116            when DispenseCan =>
0117                  if CanGiveChange( ValueInput - CanCost) then
0118                     ChangeGiven := GiveChange(ValueInput -
                                                          CanCost);
0119                     PUT_LINE( "The machine just dispensed a " &
0120                                 "can of drink.");
0121                     ShowCoinSet( ChangeGiven);
0122                     ValueInput := 0;
0123                  else
0124                     PUT_LINE("Cannot give change ");
0125                     ChangeGiven := GiveChange( ValueInput);
0126                     ShowCoinSet( ChangeGiven);
0127                     ValueInput := 0;
0128                  end if;
0129            when ExitChosen =>
0130                  PUT_LINE( "Have a nice day!");
0131         end case;
0132      end loop;
0133   exception
0134      when HopperFull =>
0135         ChangeGiven := GiveChange( ValueInput);
0136         ShowCoinSet( ChangeGiven);
```

530

```
0137              PUT_LINE("This machine is no longer in use.");
0138    end CanDispenser;
```

The subsidiary procedure *ShowMenuAndGetChoice* has to offer a different menu to the user depending upon the state of the machine and upon the number of coins exported by the *Coin* package. The possible menus which might be displayed, assuming British coins, are

```
Canned drink dispenser simulation   Canned drink dispenser simulation
0 currently entered                 10 currently entered

A. One Pence    coin.               A. One Pence    coin.
B. Two Pence    coin                B. Two Pence    coin
C. Five Pence   coin                C. Five Pence   coin
D. Ten Pence    coin                D. Ten Pence    coin
E. Twenty Pence coin                E. Twenty Pence coin
F. Fifty Pence  coin                F. Fifty Pence  coin
G. One Pound    coin                G. One Pound    coin
H. Exit program.                    H. Refund the coins.

Please enter choice                 Please enter choice


              Canned drink dispenser simulation
              50 currently entered

              A. Dispense can.
              B. Refund the coins.

              Please enter choice
```

The design and implementation of this procedure will be presented here as they provide a practical example of the use of enumeration types and as this is an example of an ***adaptive user interface***:

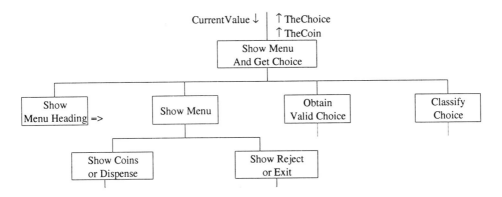

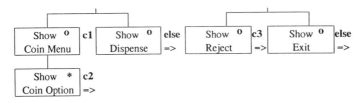

c1: If Current Value less than cost of a can.
c2: For each coin.

c3: If Current Value greater than zero.
c4: If Current Value is zero.
c4: If the Users Choice is invalid.

The components *ObtainValidChoice* and *ClassifyChoice* have been omitted from this design in the interests of clarity. The *ObtainValidChoice* component is a standard fragment to conduct a dialog with the user, offering a menu, obtaining a response and issuing an error message, until an acceptable choice is provided. The *ClassifyChoice* component consists of the four way selection which classifies the response made from the menu into tone of the *UsersChoices* enumerated options. The implementation of the complete procedure might be as follows:

Constant for *ShowMenuAndGetChoice*

Name	Type	Value	Notes
MinMenuChar	CHARACTER	'A'	Minimum choice on menu

Variables for *ShowMenuAndGetChoice*

Name	Type	Value	Notes
MaxMenuChar	CHARACTER	*MinMenuChar*	Maximum choice offered on menu
CurrentChar	CHARACTER	Undefined	Current max choice on menu
ChoiceMade	CHARACTER	*Invalid Choice*	User's response to the menu prompt
DispenseChar	CHARACTER	*ChoiceMade*	Character indicating Dispense option
RejectChar	CHARACTER	*ChoiceMade*	Character indicating Reject option
ExitChar	CHARACTER	*ChoiceMade*	Character indicating Exit option
ChoiceIsValid	BOOLEAN	FALSE	Flag to control validation loop
ThisCoinName	*CoinName Strings*	Undefined	Coin name for menu options

```
0025    procedure ShowMenuAndGetChoice( CurrentValue : in NATURAL;
0026                                    TheChoice    : out
                                                       UsersChoices;
0027                                    TheCoin      : out Coins) is
0028
0029         MinMenuChar : constant CHARACTER := 'A';
0030         MaxMenuChar : CHARACTER;
```

```
0031          CurrentChar  : CHARACTER := MinMenuChar;
0032          ChoiceMade   : CHARACTER
0033                                 := CHARACTER'PRED( MinMenuChar);
0034          DispenseChar : CHARACTER := ChoiceMade;
0035          RejectChar   : CHARACTER := ChoiceMade;
0036          ExitChar     : CHARACTER := ChoiceMade;
0037          ChoiceIsValid  : BOOLEAN := FALSE;
0038          ThisCoinName    : CoinNameStrings;
0039
0040
0041    begin -- ShowMenuAndGetChoice
0042       -- Output the heading.
0043       NEW_LINE( 5);
0044       SET_COL( 15); PUT_LINE( "Canned drink dispenser
                                                    simulation");
0045       SET_COL( 15); PUT( CurrentValue, WIDTH => 3);
0046       PUT_LINE( " currently in machine.");
0047       NEW_LINE( 2);
0048
0049       -- Possibly output a menu for the coins.
0050       if CurrentValue < CanCost then
0051          for ThisCoin in Coins loop
0052              ThisCoinName := CoinName( ThisCoin);
0053              PUT( CurrentChar);
0054              PUT_LINE( " " & ThisCoinName & " coin.");
0055              CurrentChar := CHARACTER'SUCC( CurrentChar);
0056          end loop;
0057       else -- Or a choice to dispense a can.
0058          PUT( CurrentChar );
0059          PUT_LINE( " dispense a can.");
0060          DispenseChar := CurrentChar;
0061          CurrentChar  := CHARACTER'SUCC( CurrentChar);
0062       end if;
0063
0064       -- Output Reject or exit option.
0065       if CurrentValue > 0 then
0066          PUT_LINE( CurrentChar & " refund the coins");
0067          RejectChar := CurrentChar;
0068       else
0069          PUT( CurrentChar & " exit program ");
0070          ExitChar := CurrentChar;
0071       end if;
0072       MaxMenuChar := CurrentChar;
0073
0074       -- Get a valid user choice.
0075       while not ChoiceIsValid loop
0076          NEW_LINE;
0077          PUT("Please enter choice ");
```

```
0078          GET( ChoiceMade ); SKIP_LINE;
0079          ChoiceMade    := TO_UPPER( ChoiceMade);
0080          ChoiceIsValid := ChoiceMade in
0081                                     MinMenuChar .. MaxMenuChar;
0082       if not ChoiceIsValid then
0083          PUT_LINE("Please enter a choice between " &
0084          MinMenuChar & " and " & MaxMenuChar & ".");
0085       end if;
0086    end loop;
0087
0088       -- classify the choice
0089    if    ChoiceMade = ExitChar then
0090       TheChoice := ExitChosen;
0091    elsif ChoiceMade = RejectChar then
0092       TheChoice := RejectPress;
0093    elsif ChoiceMade = DispenseChar then
0094       TheChoice := DispenseCan;
0095    else
0096       TheChoice := CoinEntry;
0097       TheCoin := Coins'VAL( CHARACTER'POS( ChoiceMade) -
0098                             CHARACTER'POS( MinMenuChar));
0099    end if;
0100  end ShowMenuAndGetChoice;
```

This completes the simulation of the canned drink dispenser. The parallels between the physical machine and the model presented in this package should be clear. The ESV package implements the model of the coin hopper and it maintains the state of the hopper throughout execution of the client program. The high-level control of the machine is implemented in the client program, which, in a more realistic simulation, would require other ESVs such as a can hopper.

If a real machine were being engineered, then only the package body file would require changes. The model of the coin hopper, which, in this simulation is implemented in software, would be replaced by low-level program code which interfaced to the physical machine when it was constructed. The provision of a logical interface to the machine in the package specification and constraining the actual details to the body allow the high-level software controlling the machine to be developed and tested before the physical machine has actually been constructed.

EXERCISES

23.1 Re-implement the *CoinHopper* ESV to use American denomination coins (5c, 10c, 25c and 50c); the cost of a can of drink for an American machine should be 80c.

534

23.2 Design and implement a *CanHopper* ESV which will be stocked with a number of cans at the start of the program, will dispense a can every time requested to do so by a client program and will raise a *CanHopperEmpty* exception if it is asked to dispense when its hopper is empty.

23.3 Re-implement the *CoinHopper* ESV to raise a *HopperFull* exception if more than a specified number of one denomination of coin are ever entered.

23.4 Re-implement the system so that the user has a choice of drinks from the machine. At what point would it be sensible to implement the *CanHopper* as an ADT or EDT, and what changes would this require in the client program?

CHAPTER 24
Programming by extension revisited

The remainder of this section will extend the introduction to extendible data types (EDTs) which was given in Section I, and briefly extended in Section III in Chapter 20 on access types. The introduction included details of the facilities for:

- a **tagged** type to have additional *actions* and/or *data attributes* added to it producing a new *extended type*;

- the extended type to be further extended creating a *hierarchy* of types;

- a *class* of types to be defined, encompassing all types which were rooted at a particular *parent* type;

- *class wide* actions to be declared as subprograms which require a formal parameter of the class wide type;

- *static* and *dynamic dispatching* on the class wide type to occur depending upon the moment in time when Ada could determine the precise type of the actual parameter.

If the determination of the precise type could be made at the time of compilation then the subprogram to be used could be *statically bound*. Otherwise the decision would have to be deferred until the program was executing and *dynamic dispatching* to the subprogram has to be used.

All of these concepts will be revisited and revised in this and the following chapters. Additional concepts concerned with programming by extension making use of the facilities which have been introduced in Sections II and III will be developed. Initially the differences between abstract data types, encapsulated static variables and extendible data types may not seem clear: a summary of the most important differences between the design approaches is included later in this chapter.

This chapter will concentrate upon the techniques by which a program specification can be analyzed and from the analysis a class hierarchy of data types designed and constructed. The emphasis of this book is on the practical construction of software in Ada and consequently the introduction to analysis will necessarily be perfunctory. Appendix A contains details of other books which develop the concepts of specification analysis with a view to extendible data types in much greater detail.

Specification analysis and class design

The basis of an analysis technique to extract the design of a class hierarchy is to extract from the program specification all significant verb and noun phrases, refining the list to exclude synonyms. Each noun is then considered a *candidate type* and each verb a *candidate action*. The candidate types are then further divided into those which are part of the software model to be built and those which are in the software's environment. This part of the analysis process defines the boundary between the software and the surroundings within which it will be used. The analysis continues by concentrating only upon those parts of the specification which are part of the software model.

The list of candidate types is then organized into a hierarchical tree of relationships which are labelled either *has a* or *is a*. The *has a* relationship defines the possession of a *data attribute* by a type and the *is a* relationship defines the extension of a type. The tree is then iteratively refined with a view to moving the *is a* relations as high up the tree as possible. Each node on the tree connected by an *is a* relation is now considered promoted from a candidate type to a *possible extended type*, and each *has a* relation is a *possible data attribute* of the type. Each candidate action is then associated with either a *possible extended type* or a *possible data attribute*. It is possible, and likely, that an action may be allocated to more than one possible type, each of which would implement a part of the required functionality. It is also possible, though unlikely, that a data attribute has to be allocated to more than one type in the hierarchy. Should this happen the decision should be carefully reviewed to ensure that a redesign of the hierarchy would not allow the data attribute to be allocated to a single type.

Finally the tree is further refined to produce *appropriate granularity*. It is suggested that each extended type in the tree should add as little as possible to its parent type; this defines the meaning of appropriate granularity. There are several reasons for this advice, the most obvious being that this will make each extended type simple and thus straightforward to implement. A less obvious reason is to avoid the *fragile base class* problem, which arises when a future extension of the class hierarchy turns out to be impossible to implement as there is no appropriate base class to extend from. By producing an initial hierarchy which has a large number of small refinements, and thus a large number of types in the hierarchy, it is hoped that a suitable place for all future extensions can be located. One consequence of this process is that a number of types in the hierarchy will never be intended to have instances of them declared. Such types are known as *abstract types*, not to be confused with abstract data types, and are implemented as such.

The analysis and design of the library hierarchy

To provide an example of the analysis and design techniques outlined above a specification concerned with the administration of the contents of a library will be considered. The initial outline specification is concerned only with the modelling of individual library items; the extension of this specification to modelling a collection of items will be considered in succeeding chapters. The specification with noun phrases in **bold italics** and verb phrases in ***bold underlined italics*** is as follows:

The library contains a large number of ***items***, each uniquely identified by an ***acquisition number***. Not all items are ***available for loan*** but those that are have a ***date issued*** and ***date due back*** ***recorded***. Any item on loan also has the ***membership number*** of the ***person borrowing*** the item ***recorded***.

The commonest ***items*** in the library are ***books***, which have the ***ISBN number***, ***author***, ***title*** and ***binding*** (either ***hardback*** or ***softback***) ***recorded***. ***Periodicals*** include ***magazines***, ***newspapers*** and ***journals*** which have the ***title*** and the ***date of publication*** ***recorded***. Additionally ***journals*** and ***magazines*** may have the ***volume number*** and ***issue number*** ***recorded***.

The ***audio visual items*** include ***audio cassettes***, ***video cassettes*** and ***computer disks***. ***Audio cassettes*** and ***video cassettes*** have the ***title***, ***author*** or ***director*** and the ***duration*** of the contents ***recorded***. Computer disks may be ***floppy disks*** or ***CD Roms***, and both have a ***title***: floppy disks also have the ***format***, either ***pc*** or ***mac***, ***recorded***.

The initial requirements are to ***add*** an item to the libraries ***stock***, to ***display*** details of an ***item*** and to ***issue*** an ***item on loan***.

The process of analysis outlined above may produce the following class hierarchy:

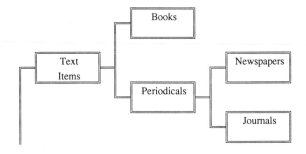

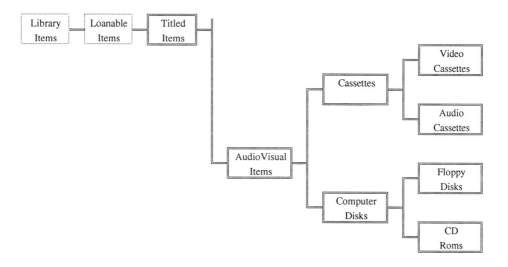

The decisions which were made and the association of actions with types will be explained in the sections which follow. An initial analysis might suggest that for this specification only the types at the end of the hierarchy should be non-abstract, as these are the only instances which will be available to a user of the hierarchy's clients. For example, it would be possible for a library member to borrow a *Book* or a *CDRom*, but not an *AudioVisualItem* or a *TitledItem*. However, for reasons which will be introduced in the next chapters, this simple analysis has to be refined and a non-abstract data type does not fully correspond with the concept of a real world object. Thus the *TitledItem* data type, and all types derived from it, are considered non-abstract.

The design and implementation of the common base of the hierarchy

The description of the implementation of the hierarchy will commence with the three common types, *LibraryItems*, *LoanableItems* and *TitledItems*, at the base of the hierarchy. The first two types are shown in the class hierarchy diagram in dotted boxes as it is never intended that they will ever have variable objects of the type explicitly declared. Their function in the hierarchy is to provide the structure through which the types shown in double lined boxes will be constructed through extension. Types such as those at the base of the hierarchy, which will never have variable instances declared, are known as **abstract types** and the mechanisms by which this can be indicated in an Ada program will be described below.

The *LibraryItems* type

The base of the entire hierarchy is the *LibraryItems* type; this type has a single data attribute which is the most fundamental component of a library item, its *AcquisitionNumber*. It implements three **public actions**, one to *Get* an acquisition number from the terminal and one to *Put* an acquisition number to the terminal. These two public actions are intended to allow a user to construct or examine a library item by terminal interaction. The remaining action is an enquiry function, called *AcquisitionNumberIs*, which will return the *AcquisitionNumber* of a *LibraryItem*. The object diagram for this package is as follows:

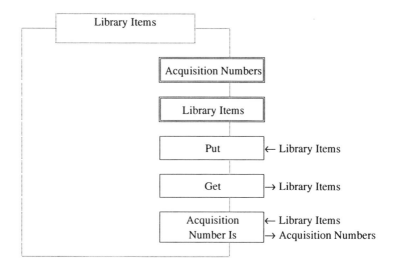

The dotted lines around the outside of the object indicate that this an abstract object, although the solid lines around the actions indicate that none of its actions are abstract. Abstract actions will be introduced later in this section. The implementation of this design as an Ada package specification is as follows:

```
0001    -- Filename LibraryItem_.pkg (k8 libraryi.ads).
0002    -- Base type for the library hierarchy.
0003    -- Developed for the Ada book Section IV Chapter 24.
0004    --
0005    -- Fintan Culwin, v0.1, Jan 1997.
0006
0007    package LibraryItem is
0008
0009        subtype AcquisitionNumbers is new INTEGER
0010                                 range 0 .. INTEGER'LAST;
0011
```

```
0012        type LibraryItems is abstract tagged private;
0013
0014        -- Subprograms to get or put the acquisition number
0015        -- by interaction with the terminal.
0016        procedure Get( Item : out LibraryItems);
0017        procedure Put( Item : in LibraryItems);
0018
0019        function AcquisitionNumberIs( Item : in
                                                 LibraryItems'CLASS)
0020                                     return AcquisitionNumber;
0021
0022    private
0023
0024        type LibraryItems is tagged
0025        record
0026            AcquisitionNumber : AcquisitionNumbers := 0;
0027        end record;
0028
0029    end LibraryItem;
```

The implementation of *AcquisitionNumbers* as an INTEGER subtype is for the purpose of this example only. In a more realistic implementation it is likely that an acquisition number would be a much more complex entity, including date and sequence information, and would be implemented as an ADT. The type *LibraryItems* is declared as an **abstract tagged private** type. It is **private** for the reasons which have already been repeatedly emphasized and **tagged** as it is intended to be extended in its child packages. It is declared as an **abstract** type as it is not intended that any actual instances of the type will ever be required, and Ada will not allow a variable object of an **abstract** type to be declared.

The declaration of the *Get* and *Put* subprograms indicates that they require a parameter of the *LibraryItems* type, whereas the declaration of the *AcquisitionNumberIs* subprogram indicates that it requires a parameter of the *LibraryItems*'CLASS type. The difference between these two parameter declarations is that the *Get* and *Put* subprograms will only accept an actual parameter of the *definite LibraryItems* type. However, the *AcquisitionNumberIs* subprogram will accept a *class wide LibraryItems* parameter; this includes parameters of the definite *LibraryItems* type and also any types which are derived from it by extension.

A *class wide* action is one which takes a *class wide* parameter, and this indicates that this subprogram cannot be overridden in any derived types. Thus the declaration of the *AcquisitionNumberIs* subprogram is indicating that this is the only place in the hierarchy where this action is provided. In contrast the *non-class-wide* declaration of the *Get* and *Put* actions indicates that these actions can be overridden as the type is extended. A class wide action can thus be statically bound and a non-class-wide action will require dynamic dispatching. If there is ever any doubt between a class wide and a non-class-wide subprogram declaration, a non-class-wide declaration should be made in order to allow for the action to be overridden in the future, even if the need for this cannot be seen from the current specification.

The full declaration of the *LibraryItems* data type as a **tagged record**, containing the encapsulated *AcquisitionNumber* data attribute in the **private** part, completes the package specification file. The package body file is omitted from this chapter as it is simple to implement, accessing the *Acquisition-Number* component of the *Item* formal parameter *LibraryItems* record type. Details of how to obtain a copy of the package body file are contained in Appendix A.

The *LoanableItems* type

This child type of *LibraryItems* adds data attributes and actions which are concerned with loaning an item. It could have been possible to divide the hierarchy at this point into loanable and non-loanable classes. However, if this division was made then all of the hierarchy below this point would have to be duplicated, for example there would have to be a type to represent loanable books and a separate type to represent non-loanable books. This needless duplication can be avoided by regarding loanable as a *has a* data attribute, rather than loanable and non-loanable items being *is a* extensions of *LibraryItems*. The *Loanable* attribute will be added as a BOOLEAN flag together with three other data attributes, two of type *JulianDates*, indicating the date on which the item was loaned and the date on which it is due to be returned. The third attribute is the *MemberNumber* which indicates the identity of the person who has borrowed the item.

The value of the *DateOut* field is used to indicate the loan status of a loanable item. If the item is not on loan this field will contain the default value *NullDate* and the value of the fields *DateDue* and *MemberNumber* will be undefined. If the value of the *DateOut* field is not null, it indicates the date on which the item was loaned; the *DateDue* field indicates the date on which the item is due to be returned and the *MemberNumber* the identity of the person who has borrowed the item.

In addition to these data attributes, *Put* and *Get* actions comparable with those provided for the *LibraryItems* type will have to be supplied. Additionally the actions which are specifically concerned with loaning an item are also introduced at this point in the hierarchy: issuing the loan, returning the loan, enquiring if an item is loanable and enquiring if a loanable item is overdue. The object diagram of the *LoanableItems* type is as follows:

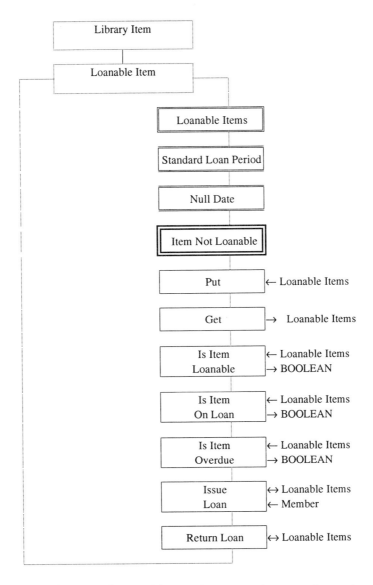

This is also an abstract object with no abstract actions as shown by the dotted lines; the implementation of this design as an Ada package specification is as follows:

```
0001    -- Filename LibraryItem.Loanable_.pkg (k8 librloan.ads).
0002    -- Adds loanable fields and date out/in to library items.
0003    -- Requires JulianDate ADT see Section II Chapter 14.
0004    -- Developed for the Ada book Section IV Chapter 24.
0005    --
```

```
0006   -- Fintan Culwin, v0.1, Jan 1997.
0007
0008   with LibraryItem, JulianDate;
0009   use  LibraryItem, JulianDate;
0010
0011   package LibraryItem.Loanable is
0012
0013      StandardLoanPeriod : constant   := 14;
0014      NullDate : constant JulianDates := MakeJulianDate( 1, 1,
                                                                  0);
0015
0016      ItemNotLoanable : exception;
0017
0018      subtype MemberNumbers is INTEGER range 0 .. INTEGER'LAST;
0019      type LoanableItems is abstract new LibraryItems with
                                                           private;
0020
0021      procedure Get( Item : out LoanableItems);
0022      procedure Put( Item : in LoanableItems);
0023
0024      -- Enquiry functions for loanable data attributes.
0025      function IsItemLoanable(Item : in LoanableItems'CLASS)
0026                                               return BOOLEAN;
0027
0028      function IsItemOnLoan( Item : in LoanableItems'CLASS)
0029                                               return BOOLEAN;
0030
0031      function IsItemOverdue( Item : in LoanableItems'CLASS)
0032                                               return BOOLEAN;
0033
0034      -- Subprograms to issue and return a Loanable Item, will
0035      -- raise ItemNotLoanable exception for non-loanable items.
0036      procedure IssueLoan( Item : in out LoanableItems'CLASS;
0037                           OnLoanTo : in MemberNumbers);
0038      procedure ReturnLoan( Item : in out LoanableItems'CLASS);
0039
0040   private
0041
0042      type LoanableItems is new LibraryItems with
0043      record
0044         Loanable : BOOLEAN        := FALSE;
0045         DateOut  : JulianDates    := NullDate;
0046         DateDue  : JulianDates    := NullDate;
0047         LoanedTo : MemberNumbers  := 0;
0048      end record;
0049
0050   end LibraryItem.Loanable;
```

The declaration of *MemberNumbers* as an INTEGER subtype in this package is for purposes of illustration only. A more realistic implementation would import the *MemberNumbers* type as an ADT from an external package. The data type *LoanableItems* is declared as **abstract** for the same reasons as its parent type *LibraryItems* was declared **abstract**. The remaining part of its public declaration indicates that it is derived by extension from its parent type and that the extensions are **private**. It is not necessary to state explicitly that it is a **tagged** type as all extended types are themselves extendible.

The declaration of the *Get* and *Put* subprograms is comparable with previous declarations. The declaration of the remaining subprograms declares the type of their *Item* formal parameter as *LoanableItems*'CLASS, the class wide *LoanableItems* type as opposed to the definite *LoanableItems* type used in *Get* and *Put*. The distinction is that the *Get* and *Put* subprograms will only accept a parameter of the specific type whereas the remaining subprograms will accept an actual parameter either of the specific type or of any type which is derived from it by extension. As all non-abstract types in the class hierarchy are derived from this type this is the only place in the hierarchy where these actions need to be explicitly declared. All types which are derived from the *LoanableItems* type, including those which are not presently shown in the class hierarchy diagram, will be able to be issued, returned, determined to be loanable or not and determined to be overdue or not, without type conversion being necessary.

The design of the *Get* subprogram is as follows:

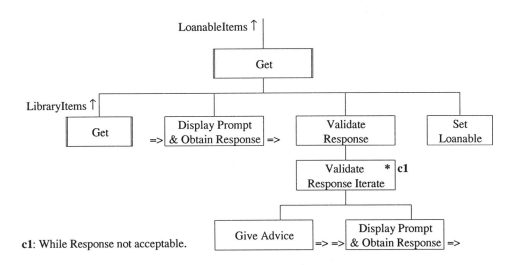

c1: While Response not acceptable.

The implementation of the *LoanableItems Get* subprogram commences by calling the *LibraryItems Get* subprogram in order to obtain the *AcquisitionNumber* of the loanable item which is being input. It then conducts a standard dialog with the user to obtain a validated **yes**/**no** response, indicating if the item is or is not loanable, before setting the *Loanable* attribute from the response. The implementation of this design is as follows:

```
0014    procedure Get( Item : out LoanableItems) is
0015
0016        Response : CHARACTER := SPACE;
0017
0018    begin -- Get
0019        Get( LibraryItems( Item));
0020        PUT( "Is the item loanable (y/n) ");
0021        GET( Response); SKIP_LINE;
0022        Response := TO_UPPER( Response);
0023        while Response /= 'Y' and Response /= 'N' loop
0024            PUT_LINE( "Please enter 'Y', 'y', 'N' or 'n' only.");
0025            GET( Response); SKIP_LINE;
0026            Response := TO_UPPER( Response);
0027        end loop;
0028        Item.Loanable := Response = 'Y';
0029    end Get;
```

Line 0019 implements the call to the *LibraryItems Get* procedure by type converting the formal parameter variable *Item* of the explicit type *LoanableItems* to the type *LibraryItems* as the *LibraryItem Get* subprogram was declared as requiring a parameter of the explicit type *LibraryItem*. Technically this type conversion is only a **view conversion** as within the body of the *LibraryItems Get* subprogram the parameter is viewed as being of type *LibraryItems* and the data attributes added by extension are not visible. The extended data attributes still exist and become visible again after the call of the *LibraryItem Get* procedure has completed. If this part of the subprogram were implemented as follows

```
0014    procedure Get( Item : out LoanableItems) is
0015
0016        Response : CHARACTER := SPACE;
0017        LibraryPart : LibraryItems := LibraryItems( Item);
0018
0019    begin -- Get
0020        Get( LibraryPart);
0021        -- This is not possible.
0022        Item := LoanableItems( LibraryPart)
```

then an **actual type conversion**, not a **view conversion**, will take place at line 0017 and the additional data attributes added by extension will be discarded. The call of *Get* on line 0020 does not need to be qualified and will obtain an acquisition number. However, as the additional parts have been discarded a simple type conversion, such as that on line 0022, is not possible. A more complex type conversion from a parent type to a child type is possible, if values for the additional data components are provided. The type conversion on line 0022 could be successfully implemented as follows, assuming that the variables *Loanable-Value*, *DateOutValue*, *DateDueValue* and *MemberValue* have been declared and have suitable values.

```
0022    Item := LoanableItems( LibraryPart with
0023                           Loanable => LoanableValue,
0024                           DateOut => DateOutValue,
0025                           DateDue => DateDueValue,
0026                           LoanedTo => MemberValue);
```

This is an example of an ***extension aggregate*** where aggregated values of the parts of the record which are added by extension are specified using the usual aggregate notation, following the name of the parent value and the reserved word **with**.

The remainder of the full *LibraryItems Get* procedure concludes with a standard implementation of a get *yes/no* user dialog, following which the value of the data attribute *Loanable* in the extended record is set according to the response provided by the user. The remaining data attributes, *DateOut*, *DateDue* and *LoanedTo*, have suitable default values and are not given a value from the terminal when LoanableItems is obtained.

The design of the *LibraryItems Put* procedure is as follows:

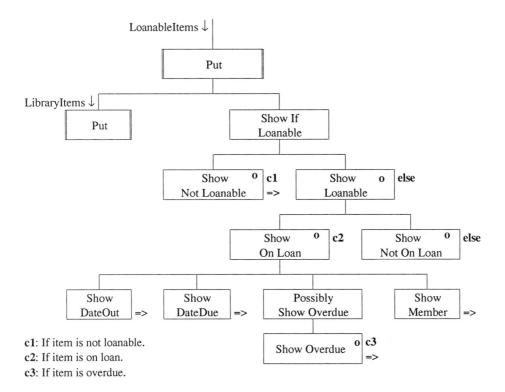

c1: If item is not loanable.
c2: If item is on loan.
c3: If item is overdue.

The design indicates that the first action is to output the *LibraryItem* part of the *LoanableItem*, following which the attributes added by extension are considered. If the item is not loanable, a not-loanable message is output; otherwise the item must be loanable and if it is not currently on loan a not-on-loan message is output; otherwise the item must be on loan and the *DateOut* and *DateDue* fields are displayed. A check is made following the output of the *DateDue* and an overdue message is output if the item is overdue, before the member number is output. The implementation of this design is as follows:

```
0031    procedure Put( Item : in LoanableItems) is
0032    begin -- Put
0033       LibraryItem.Put( LibraryItems(Item));
0034       if not Item.Loanable then
0035          PUT_LINE( "Item is not loanable.");
0036       else
0037          if Item.DateOut = NullDate then
0038             PUT_LINE( "Item not on loan.");
0039          else
0040             PUT( "Loaned on "); SET_COL( 25);
0041             PUT( Item.DateOut, Format => Full);
0042             NEW_LINE;
0043             PUT( "Due back "); SET_COL( 25);
0044             PUT( Item.DateDue, Format => Full);
0045             if IsItemOverdue( Item) then
0046                PUT(" ** OVERDUE **");
0047             end if;
0048             NEW_LINE;
0049             PUT( "On loan to "); SET_COL( 25);
0050             PUT( Item.LoanedTo); NEW_LINE;
0051          end if;
0052       end if;
0053    end Put;
```

A *LoanableItem* which is loanable but not on loan is indicated by the default *NullDate* value in the *DateOut* field; in this case the value of *DateDue* and *LoanedTo* are undefined. A *LoanableItem* which is loanable and on loan has a non-default value in its *DateOut*, *DateDue* and *LoanedTo* fields. This consideration is the basis of the three remaining subprograms, the first of which, the function *IsItemOverdue*, is used in the implementation of *Put* above. The function is too simple to require a design and is implemented as follows:

```
0056    function IsItemOverdue( Item : in LoanableItems'CLASS)
0057                                              return BOOLEAN is
0058    begin -- IsItemOverdue
0059       return Item.Loanable and then
0060                   Today > Item.DateDue;
0061    end IsItemOverdue;
```

548

The implementation of this function makes use of the ***short circuit* and then** BOOLEAN operator. This version of the **and** operator will only evaluate the second term '*Today > Item.DateDue*' if the first term (*Item.Loanable*) evaluates true. The **and** rule can only be true if both terms are true, so if the first term is false the result of the entire expression must be false. The **and then** operator *short circuits* the evaluation by only evaluating the second term if it is required. The detailed consideration of the meaning of this subprogram has indicated that a non-loanable item can never be overdue, so the first term (*Item.Loanable*) will be false for a non-loanable item and the second term will be short circuited.

The remaining subprograms are very straightforward and they can be implemented and presented without requiring a design.

```
0064    function IsItemLoanable(Item : in LoanableItems'CLASS)
0065                                         return BOOLEAN is
0066    begin -- IsItemLoanable
0067       return Item.Loanable;
0068    end IsItemLoanable;
0069
0070    function IsItemOnLoan(Item : in LoanableItems'CLASS)
0071                                         return BOOLEAN is
0072    begin -- IsItemOnLoan
0073       return Item.Loanable and then
0074              Item.DateOut /= NullDate;
0075    end IsItemOnLoan;
0076
0077
0078    procedure IssueLoan( Item     : in out LoanableItems'CLASS;
0079                         OnLoanTo : in     MemberNumbers);
0080    begin -- IssueLoan
0081       if not Item.Loanable then
0082          raise ItemNotLoanable;
0083       else
0084          Item.DateOut  := Today;
0085          Item.DateDue  := DaysHence( Today, StandardLoanPeriod);
0086          Item.LoanedTo := OnLoanTo;
0087       end if;
0088    end IssueLoan;
0089
0090
0091    procedure ReturnLoan( Item : in out LoanableItems'CLASS) is
0092    begin -- ReturnLoan
0093       if not Item.Loanable then
0094          raise ItemNotLoanable;
0095       else
0096          Item.DateOut := NullDate;
0097       end if;
0098    end ReturnLoan;
```

These latter two procedures should only be called if the *Item* is loanable and both will raise the *ItemNotLoanable* exception if they are called with an *Item* which is not loanable. Otherwise they are both implemented by setting or resetting the *DateOut* field to the current date or to the *NullDate*. Additionally the *IssueLoan* procedure sets the *DateDue* field to a date in the future determined by the value of the constant *StandardLoanPeriod*, and the *LoanedTo* field to the *MemberNumber* supplied as a parameter.

The simplicity of the implementation of the last four subprograms, which implement the class wide loanable behaviour, illustrates one of the major advantages of development by extension. With a large number of small types in the class hierarchy each extension will add a small amount of functionality to its parent type, and the implementation of the actions related to this functionality will generally be straightforward. This improves application development as it is easier and faster to develop a number of small simple subprograms than one large complex subprogram. Because each subprogram is less complex it is more likely to be implemented correctly and, should it be faulty, easier to debug. However, this advantage comes at the price of a complex class hierarchy.

The *TitledItems* type

The remaining type at the common base of the hierarchy is the non-abstract *TitledItems* type. This type adds a *Title* data attribute to the *LoanableItems* type, as the specification indicates that all items in the library have a title. Only the object diagram and package specification of this type will be presented because, as discussed above, the implementation of an extended type which adds only a simple data attribute to an existing type is straightforward.

It would have been possible to redesign this part of the hierarchy to include the *Titled* data attributes and actions within the base type, or within the *Loanable-Items* type, or even to collapse all three types into one type. The decision to use three distinct types was taken in order to illustrate the construction of a hierarchy by a large number of small extensions, and to resist the temptation to make large types which contain attributes which are not logically related. The object diagram for the *TitledItems* data type is as follows:

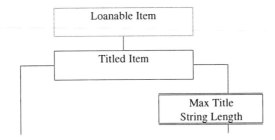

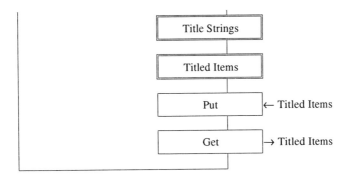

Only the *Put* and *Get* subprograms are required for this type and their implementation is straightforward, each calling the appropriate parent *LoanableItems Put* or *Get* before outputting or inputting the *Title* field.

```
0001    -- Filename LibraryItem.Loanable.Titled_.pkg (k8
                                              liloatit.ads).
0002    -- Adds a title to the LoanableItems type.
0003    -- Developed for the Ada book Section IV Chapter 24.
0004    --
0005    -- Fintan Culwin, v0.1, Jan 1997.
0006
0007    with LibraryItem.Loanable, ADA.CHARACTERS.LATIN_1;
0008    use  LibraryItem.Loanable, ADA.CHARACTERS.LATIN_1;
0009
0010    package LibraryItem.Loanable.Titled is
0011
0012       MaxTitleStringLength : constant := 30;
0013       subtype TitleStrings is STRING( 1 ..
                                      MaxTitleStringLength);
0014
0015       type TitledItems is new LoanableItems with private;
0016
0017       procedure Get( Item : out TitledItems);
0018
0019       procedure Put( Item : in  TitledItems);
0020
0021    private
0022
0023       type TitledItems is new LoanableItems with
0024       record
0025          Title : TitleStrings := ( others => SPACE);
0026       end record;
0027
0028    end LibraryItem.Loanable.Titled;
```

Testing the common base classes

Development of the class hierarchy could continue with the design and implementation of either the *TextItems* or *AudioVisualItems* type, both of which are children of the *TitledItems* type. However, this would defer any testing of the types implemented so far. In keeping with a **build test build test** development philosophy it would be sensible to test the implementation of the class hierarchy at this stage, before it splits into two major subclasses. A client program which demonstrates the use of the *TitledItems* type and which could be extended from a formal test plan into an interactive test harness might be as follows:

```
0001    -- Filename TitledItemsTest.ada (k8 titledit.adb).
0002    -- Client program to demonstrate the correct operation
0003    -- of the Library common base hierarchy.
0004    -- Developed for Ada book section IV chapter 24.
0005    --
0006    -- Fintan Culwin, v0.1, Jan 1997.
0007
0008    with ADA.TEXT_IO, LibraryItem.Loanable.Titled;
0009    use  ADA.TEXT_IO, LibraryItem.Loanable,
0010                      LibraryItem.Loanable.Titled;
0011
0012    procedure TitledItemsTest is
0013
0014        TestItem : TitledItems;
0015
0016    begin -- LibraryTest
0017        PUT_LINE( "Demonstration of the initial library
                                                hierarchy");
0018        NEW_LINE(2);
0019
0020        PUT_LINE( "Test of interactive input and output.");
0021        Get( TestItem);
0022
0023        NEW_LINE( 2);
0024        Put( TestItem);
0025
0026        NEW_LINE( 2);
0027        PUT_LINE( "Test of is loanable enquiry function.");
0028        if IsItemLoanable( TestItem) then
0029           PUT_LINE("Item is loanable.");
0030        else
0031           PUT_LINE("Item is not loanable.");
0032        end if;
0033
0034        NEW_LINE( 2);
```

```
0035        PUT_LINE( "Test of issue loan enquiry function.");
0036        begin -- explicit exception block
0037            IssueLoan( TestItem, 42);
0038            PUT_LINE( "If item is loanable,
0039                            & " this message should appear.");
0040            Put( TestItem);
0041        exception
0042          when ItemNotLoanable =>
0043              PUT_LINE( "If item is not loanable,"
0044                            & " this message should appear.");
0045        end; -- explicit exception block
0046
0047        NEW_LINE( 2);
0048        if IsItemLoanable( TestItem) then
0049            PUT_LINE( "Test of return loan for loanable items.");
0050            ReturnLoan( TestItem);
0051            Put( TestItem);
0052        else
0053            PUT_LINE( "No test of return loan for non-loanable
                                                          item");
0054        end if;
0055
0056        NEW_LINE( 2);
0057        PUT_LINE( "Test of the acquisition number enquiry
                                                    function.");
0058        PUT( "The acquisition number is ");
0059        PUT( AcquisitionNumberIs( TestItem)); NEW_LINE;
0060    end TitledItemsTest;
```

When executed the program produced the following sample interaction:

```
Demonstration of the base of the library hierarchy

Test of interactive input and output.

Please enter the acquisition number 123456
Is the item loanable (y/n) h
Please enter 'Y', 'y', 'N' or 'n' only.
Is the item loanable (y/n) y
Please enter the title   Ada: A Developmental Approach

Acquisition number        123456
Item not on loan.
Title              Ada: A Developmental Approach

Test of is loanable enquiry function.
Item is loanable.
```

```
Test of issue loan enquiry function.
If item is loanable this message should appear.
Acquisition number      123456
Loaned on               FRI 17 JUL 1995
Due back                FRI 03 AUG 1995
On loan to              42
Title                   Ada: A Developmental Approach

Test of return loan for loanable items.
Acquisition number      123456
Item not on loan.
Title                   Ada: A Developmental Approach
```

The interaction illustrates details of a *TitledItem* being obtained from the user and then being output in its default, non-loaned, state. Subsequently the enquiry functions and exceptions are partly demonstrated whilst the item is loaned and returned.

The context clause of the client program **with**s and **use**s the *TitledItem* package in order to have direct visibility (**use**) of the *TitledItems* type. It also has to bring into direct visibility the *LoanableItem* package in order to obtain direct visibility of the *IssueLoan* and *ReturnLoan* procedures. However, it does not have to **with** the *LoanableItem* package as the **with**ing of a child package automatically **with**s all its ancestor packages. The calls of the two *LoanableItem* procedures do not have to view-convert the actual parameter, of type *TitledItems*, to the type *LoanableItems*, as the declared type of the formal parameter is of the class wide *Loanable-Items*'CLASS type and as a child type of *LoanableItems* the actual parameter is of this class wide type.

The *TextItems* and *BookItems* types

The type hierarchy splits at this point into the *TextItems* class and the *AudioVisualItems* class. This chapter will continue with a detailed discussion of the implementation of the *TextItems* class and conclude with an overview of the *AudioVisualItems* class.

The implementation of the *TextItems* data type adds no additional data attributes to its parent type *TitledItems*, and its two actions, *Put* and *Get*, are implemented simply as calls to the parent *Put* and *Get* actions. Although the *TextItems* type adds no data attributes or actions to the class hierarchy, it is logically required from the analysis. The purpose of including the *TextItems* type in the class hierarchy is to provide a point in the hierarchy where the *BookItems* and *PeriodicalItems* types can be introduced, and also in recognition of the possibility that additional categories of *TextItems* may have to be added in the future. The object diagram and package specification of the *TextItem* package are as follows:

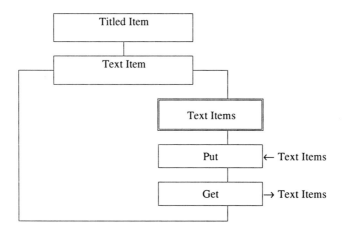

```
0001    -- Filename LibraryItem.Loanable.Titled.Text_.
0002    -- pkg (k8 lilotite.ads). Provides a purely abstract child
0003    -- type class of the LoanableItems type in the library
0004    -- hierarchy. Used to provide a location for the
0005    -- derivation of the Book and Periodical types.
0006    -- Developed for the Ada book Section IV Chapter 24.
0007    --
0008    -- Fintan Culwin, v0.1, Jan 1997.
0009
0010    with LibraryItem.Loanable.Titled;
0011    use  LibraryItem.Loanable.Titled;
0012
0013    package LibraryItem.Loanable.Titled.Text is
0014
0015        type TextItems is new TitledItems
0016                                 with private;
0017
0018        procedure Get( Item : out TextItems);
0019
0020        procedure Put( Item : in TextItems);
0021
0022    private
0023
0024        type TextItems is new TitledItems
0025                             with null record;
0026
0027    end LibraryItem.Loanable.Titled.Text;
```

The declaration of the *TextItems* type, in line 0024, declares the type as an extension of the *TitledItems* type adding a **null record**. The declaration is an acceptable shorthand for the following full declaration:

```
0024   type TextItems is new TitledItems with
0025   record
0026       null;
0027   end record;
```

The implementation of the *TextItems Put* and *Get* procedures in the package body file is as single line procedures which call the *TitledItems Get* and *Put* procedures using **view conversion**. The implementation of the *TextItems Get* procedure is as follows:

```
0001   procedure Get( Item : out TextItems) is
0002   begin -- Get
0003       Get( TitledItems( Item));
0004   end Get;
```

The *BookItem* package extends the *TextItems* type by the addition of the data attributes *Author*, *ISBN* and *Binding*, either *hard* or *soft*. The package also declares actions to *Get* and *Put* values of the *BookItems* type and an enquiry function to determine the type of binding. The ISBN attribute is an *International Standard Book Number* which is used to identify uniquely every book published, and is usually displayed on the back cover of every book, including this one. As with other data attributes already introduced in the hierarchy, the declaration of the *ISBNNumbers* data type by the *BookItem* package is for purposes of illustration only; a more realistic implementation would implement this as a separate ADT package. The object diagram for the *BookItem* package, and its implementation as a package specification file, are as follows:

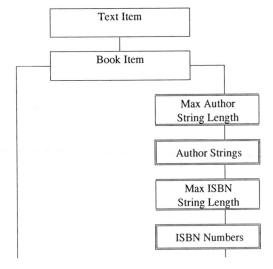

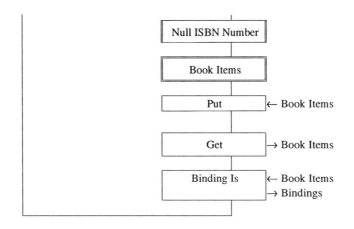

```
0001    -- Filename LibraryItem.Loanable.Titled.Text.Book_.pkg
0002    -- (k8 lltitebo.ads).Provides a non-abstract class in the
0003    -- Library hierarchy.
0004    -- Developed for the Ada book Section IV Chapter 24.
0005    -- Fintan Culwin, v0.1, July 1997.
0006
0007    with LibraryItem.Loanable.Titled.Text, ADA.CHARACTERS.LATIN_1;
0008    use  LibraryItem.Loanable.Titled.Text, ADA.CHARACTERS.LATIN_1;
0009
0010    package LibraryItem.Loanable.Titled.Text.Book is
0011
0012        MaxAuthorStringLength : constant INTEGER := 30;
0013        subtype AuthorStrings is
0014                        STRING( 1 .. MaxAuthorStringLength);
0015
0016        MaxISBNStringLength : constant := 10;
0017        subtype ISBNNumbers is
0018                STRING( 1 .. MaxISBNStringLength);
0019
0020        NullISBNNumber : constant ISBNNumbers := ( others =>
0021                                                        SPACE);
0021
0022        type Bindings is ( Hard, Soft);
0023
0024        type BookItems is new TextItems with private;
0025
0026        procedure Get( Item : out BookItems);
0027
0028        procedure Put( Item : in  BookItems);
0029
0030        function BindingIs( Item : in BookItems) return Bindings;
0031
0032    private
```

```
0033
0034        type BookItems is new TextItems with
0035        record
0036           Author  : AuthorStrings := ( others => SPACE );
0037           ISBN    : ISBNNumbers := NullISBNNumber;
0038           Binding : Bindings;
0039        end record;
0040
0041    end LibraryItem.Loanable.Titled.Text.Book;
```

The implementation of the *Get* and *Put* procedures in the package body is as
expected. They start by calling the parent type, *TextItems*, *Get* or *Put* procedures, before *Get*ting or *Put*ting the additional attributes. In the *Get* procedure,
when the *Binding* is being input, this involves an interactive dialog with the user,
who enters a character code '*b*' or '*s*' to indicate the type of binding. The design
and implementation of this part of the procedure are directly comparable with
the part of the *LoanableItem Get* procedure which obtains the *Loanable* status of
an *Item* and is presented above. The body of the package will not be presented
here.

A client demonstration program for the *BookItems* data type can be adapted
from the *TitledItemsTest* program presented above. The major change is in the
context clause and the declaration of the test variable which now has to be of the
BookItems type. The appropriate part of the *BookItemTest* client program is as
follows:

```
0001    -- Filename BookItemsTest.ada (k8 bookitem.adb).
0002    -- Client program to demonstrate the correct operation
0003    -- of the BookItems data type.
0004    -- Developed for Ada book Section IV Chapter 24.
0005    --
0006    -- Fintan Culwin, v0.1, Jan 1997.
0007
0008    with ADA.TEXT_IO, LibraryItem.Loanable.Titled.Text.Book;
0009    use  ADA.TEXT_IO, LibraryItem.Loanable,
0010                      LibraryItem.Loanable.Titled.Text.Book;
0011
0012    procedure BookItemsTest is
0013
0014        TestItem : BookItems;
```

The only other change would be to add a test of the enquiry function *BindingIs*.
Technically the test of the *LibraryItems AcquisitionNumberIs* and of the
LoanableItems subprograms *IsItemOverdue*, *IsItemLoanable*, *IssueLoan* and
ReturnLoan need not be included as the actions are inherited in the class
hierarchy, and as they have been shown to be correct in the *TitledItemsTest*
program their retesting here is redundant. However, the costs involved in retesting

are not very high and the additional confidence might be advantageous. The output of the *BookItems Put* procedure might be as follows:

```
Acquisition number   123456
Loaned on            SAT 18 JUL 1995
Due back             SAT 04 AUG 1995
On loan to           007
Title                Ada: A Developmental Approach
Author               Fintan Culwin
ISBN                 0123456789
```

The *PeriodicalItems, NewspaperItems* and *JournalItems* types

The remaining types in the *TextItems* class are the *PeriodicalItems* type, which adds one additional data attribute called *DateOfIssue* to the *TextItems* type. *DateOfIssue* is of the *JulianDates* type and is required by both child types: *NewspaperItems* and *JournalItems*. The *NewspaperItem* package implements a non-abstract *NewspaperItems* type without adding any data attributes to the *PeriodicalItem* type. The *JournalItem* package implements a non-abstract *JournalItems* type by adding data attributes of type NATURAL for the *VolumeNumber* and *IssueNumber* of the journal. The analysis of the initial specification decided that the nouns **magazines** and **journals** were sufficiently synonymous for a single type to subsume both concepts. All three packages also declare *Get* and *Put* subprograms for the output and input of their values.

The *TitledItemsTest* client program can be easily adapted to demonstrate the implementation of the non-abstract *NewspaperItems* and *JournalItems* types, in a similar manner to the way it was adapted for the *BookItems* class above. The output of the *Put* procedures for the two types might be as follows:

```
Output of a NewspaperItems value

Acquisition number   123456
Item is not loanable.
Title                The Times.
Date of Publication  MON 01 JAN 1995


Output of a JournalItems value

Acquisition number   123456
Item is not loanable.
Title                Byte.
Date of Publication  TUE 01 FEB 1996
Volume 26 Issue 1.
```

The *AudioVisualItems* class types

The implementation of the other part of the hierarchy below *TitledItems* will not be presented in detail. All of these packages provide *Get* and *Put* subprograms for the types which they provide. The implementation of these subprograms is, as expected, a call to the parent's *Get* or *Put* procedure, followed by the input or output of the additional data attributes, if any, which they introduce into the hierarchy. Additionally the *FloppyDiskItem* package provides an enquiry function called *FormatIs* which returns a value of the *DiskFormats* type, in this implementation either *PC* or *MAC*.

An overview of the packages, giving details of the data attributes and actions which are provided, follows:

Audio visual items

Package name:	LibraryItem.Loanable.Titled.AudioVisual
Data type name:	AudioVisualItems
Data attributes:	None
Actions	Put, Get

Cassette items

Package name:	LibraryItem.Loanable.Titled.AudioVisual.Cassette
Data type name:	CassetteItems
Data attributes:	PlayingTime of type NATURAL, playing time in minutes
Actions	Put, Get, PlayingTimeIs

Audio cassette items

Package name:	LibraryItem.Loanable.Titled.AudioVisual.Cassette.Audio
Data type name:	AudioCassetteItems
Data attributes:	None
Actions	Put, Get

Video cassette items

Package name:	LibraryItem.Loanable.Titled.AudioVisual.Cassette.Video
Data type name:	VideoCassetteItems
Data attributes:	VideoFormat of type VideoFormats: Beta, VHS or NTSC
Actions	Put, Get, FormatIs

Computer disk items

Package name:	LibraryItem.Loanable.Titled.AudioVisual.ComputerDisk
Data type name:	ComputerDiskItems
Data attributes:	None
Actions	Put, Get.

Floppy disk items

Package name:	LibraryItem.Loanable.Titled.AudioVisual.ComputerDisk.FloppyDisk
Data type name:	ComputerDiskItems
Data attributes:	DiskFormat of type DiskFormats: PC or Mac
Actions	Put, Get, FormatIs

CD Rom items

Package name:	LibraryItem.Loanable.Titled.AudioVisual.ComputerDisk.CDRom
Data type name:	CDRomItems
Data attributes:	NONE
Actions	Put, Get

The implementation of these data types would follow the implementation of the other part of the hierarchy described above. The full implementation of these types is available, see Appendix A for details.

The hierarchy in retrospect

The complete hierarchy implements seven distinct non-abstract types which represent the different loanable items which the library offers. A review of the class hierarchy at this stage, comparing it with the brief specification given at the start of the chapter, will indicate the allocation of *has a* and *is a* relations to the types and data attributes in the hierarchy which implement the nouns in the specification. The allocation of the verbs from the hierarchy to the different types can also be validated.

The hierarchy itself may be complex, but the individual types within it are themselves relatively simple. The comparison which should be made is to the alternative possible implementations of the library's requirements. One possibility is for all of the loanable items to be implemented in a single massive type. This type would quickly become extremely complex and thus difficult to maintain. Should an additional loanable category be added by the library the entire type would have to be considered. After changes had been made to the type, both it and any clients which were dependent upon it would require retesting.

The other alternative possible design is to implement each loanable category as a distinct type, independent of any other types. This would involve massive duplication of the class wide and other inherited actions from the hierarchy. For example, each of the distinct types would require the implementation of the *Loanable* behaviours, which are introduced into the hierarchy by the *Loanable-Items* type. Thus each distinct type would have to encompass the complexity of a large proportion of the hierarchy and there would be massive duplication of essential attributes and operations.

One consequence of this would be a massive increase in the costs of maintenance. A change in the rules for the loaning of an item would require maintenance of a single type in the class hierarchy and subsequent retesting of a single extended non-abstract type. For the alternative approach each distinct type would require the changes to be effected and each would require retesting.

If a new category of loanable item were introduced by the library this would require the development of an entirely new type, which would be as complex as any of the types which had already been developed.

Thus although the hierarchy is complex, the alternative possible implementations are more complex and more difficult to maintain or to extend. The hierarchy provides a class which models a single item from the libraries stock, but the library contains a large number of stock items. The next chapter will introduce another hierarchy, which uses the class wide facilities of the existing hierarchy, to provide a list of library items which can be used to provide a primitive model of a library's operations.

EXERCISES

24.1 Add some additional categories of items to the hierarchy described here. For example, a third *TextItems* called *OperaLibrettos* which requires a *Composer* data attribute, or a third *AudioVisualItem* called *Paintings* which requires a *Painter* and *DatePainted* data attributes.

24.2 The ISBN data attribute of the Books type should be implemented as an ADT. Find out the rules which govern the construction of a valid ISBN and design and implement a suitable package.

24.3 The *MemberNumber* attribute of *LoanableItems* is itself suitable for implementation as an extended hierarchy which contains a fundamental *MemberNumber* data attribute. The other data attributes which might be required include *Name*, *Address*, *MembershipType* (*Visitor*, *Student* or *Staff*). Different types of members will have a different *MaximumNumber* of books which they can borrow. Actions which will have to be considered include *Put* and *Get*, *IssueLoan*, *ReturnLoan*, *NumberOfBooksOnLoan* and *AnyBooksOverdue*. Design, implement and test this hierarchy.

24.4 A petrol pump can be switched on or switched off, it can be dispensing in gallons or in litres, it can be dispensing at a price or dispensing free of charge (e.g. in a private garage). It can also be dispensing unleaded, leaded or diesel fuels, and at all stages maintains a record of the total amount of fuel which it has dispensed since it was last turned on. The essential action of the pump is to dispense a requested amount of fuel and return the cost, if any, of the fuel dispensed.

Using this description identify the significant noun phrases and verb phrases, and then design, implement and test a hierarchy which implements a *PetrolPumps* type.

24.5 Extend the hierarchy from Exercise 24.4 to include a *WaterPumps* type which is only concerned if it is on or off and will dispense any amount of water at a time.

24.6 Extend the hierarchy again to include a *SoftDrinksPump* which will dispense *coke*, *orange* or *lemonade* in *small*, *medium* or *large* sizes, with or without crushed ice.

CHAPTER 25

Heterogeneous data structures

The previous chapter introduced a class hierarchy, the most extended types of which are able to represent single instances of the items which are available for loan from a library. This chapter will introduce a class of data types which provide an iterative data structure, whose base type is called *LibraryLists*, and which is capable of holding a collection of many instances of the *LibraryItems* class of types. As the precise data types of the items held in the library vary, the list must be constructed to be able to hold items of a class wide type. A data structure containing items of different types is known as a **heterogeneous structure**. The array types which were introduced in Section II could only hold items of a specific stated type, and are known as **homogeneous** structures.

A simple client program to manipulate the list will be developed in this chapter to provide a harness from which the implementation of the list can be demonstrated. One major aspect of a realistic client's functionality, the ability to store and load heterogeneous lists to and from a backing store, will be omitted from the implementations in this chapter. This omission will be rectified in the following chapter, where the problem of maintaining the list in a defined sequence will also be considered.

The class hierarchy overview

An overview of the hierarchy which will be developed in this chapter is presented in the following class hierarchy diagram:

The **abstract** base type for the hierarchy is the *LibraryLists* type which provides a fundamental data attribute and associated actions concerned with the number of items in the list. The first child type, *EditableLists*, adds actions to add and remove items, to and from the list. The *ListableLists* type adds actions which allow the list to be displayed, and *SearchableLists* adds actions which allow a list to be searched. The final type in this version of the hierarchy, *IssueableLists*, adds actions to issue and return an item from the list.

The *LibraryLists* type

The base of the *LibraryList* hierarchy is the **abstract** *LibraryLists* type. The *LibraryList* package maintains a fundamental data attribute which counts the number of items in the list, together with associated public actions and exceptions. The object diagram for this package is as follows:

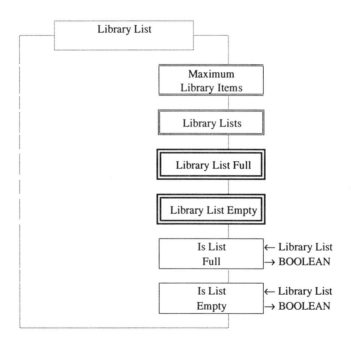

The package exports a constant called *MaximumLibraryItems* which defines the maximum number of items which the list can hold. Techniques for the construction of lists which do not have a limit upon the number of items that they can hold are too complex to be introduced at this stage. Such lists are known as unconstrained lists and will be introduced later in this section.

The base class data type itself is called *LibraryLists* and is exported as an **abstract private tagged** type. The package exports two public enquiry functions, one to determine if the list is full and one to determine if the list is empty. The

565

implementation of this design is as follows:

```
0001   -- Filename LibraryList_.pkg (k8 library1.ads).
0002   -- Base class for the library list hierarchy.
0003   -- Developed for the Ada book Section IV Chapter 25.
0004   --
0005   -- Fintan Culwin, v0.1, Jan 1996.
0006
0007
0008   package LibraryList is
0009
0010      MaximumLibraryItems : constant INTEGER := 4;
0011
0012      type LibraryLists is abstract tagged private;
0013
0014      LibraryListFull  : exception;
0015      LibraryListEmpty : exception;
0016
0017      function IsListFull( TheList : in LibraryLists'CLASS)
0018                                            return BOOLEAN;
0019
0020      function IsListEmpty( TheList : in LibraryLists'CLASS)
0021                                            return BOOLEAN;
0022
0023   private
0024
0025      type StockItemsIndex is new INTEGER
0026                            range 0 .. MaximumLibraryItems;
0027
0028      type LibraryLists is tagged
0029      record
0030         NumberOfItems : StockItemsIndex := 0;
0031      end record;
0032   end LibraryList;
```

The implementation of the public part of the package is taken directly from the object diagram. The value of the constant *MaximumLibraryItems* is for purposes of demonstration only; a realistic client would require a much larger value.

The **private** part of the package declares a new INTEGER type, called *StockItemsIndex*, which is used to count the number of items in the list. The lower bound of this type is zero, which would indicate that the list is empty. The upper bound is the value of the constant *MaximumLibraryItems*, which would indicate that the list is full. The *LibraryLists* record contains a single component, called *NumberOfItems*, which will be maintained always to indicate the number of items in the list.

The implementation of the two functions in the package body is straightforward:

```
0009    function IsListFull( TheList : in LibraryLists'CLASS)
0010                                          return BOOLEAN is
0011    begin -- IsListFull
0012       return TheList.NumberOfItems = StockItemsIndex'LAST;
0013    end IsListFull;
0014
0015
0016    function IsListEmpty( TheList : in LibraryLists'CLASS)
0017                                          return BOOLEAN is
0018    begin -- IsListEmpty
0019       return TheList.NumberOfItems = StockItemsIndex'FIRST;
0020    end IsListEmpty;
```

The two exceptions are not actually used in this package. They are introduced into the hierarchy at this stage as they will be required by the child packages, and this is the logical place for them to be defined.

The *EditableLists* type

This extension of the **LibraryLists** type adds two public actions: one to add an item to the list and one to remove an item from the list. The object diagram of this package is as follows:

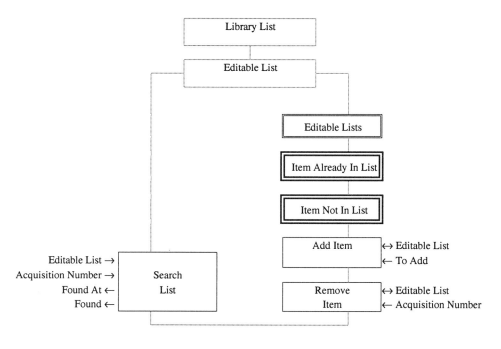

A particular *AcquisitionNumber* uniquely identifies a library item, and thus adding an item with an *AcquisitionNumber* which is already in the list indicates an attempt to add an item to the list for a second time. Accordingly the *AddItem* action will raise an *ItemAlreadyInList* **exception** under these circumstances. It is intended that a client program will use the enquiry function *IsListFull* to ensure that a list has space before calling the *AddItem* action. However, should an attempt be made to add an item to a list which is full the *LibraryListFull* **exception** will be raised.

The *RemoveItem* action identifies the item to be removed by its *Acquisition-Number*. As with the *AddItem* action it is anticipated that the client will ensure that the list is not empty and that an item with the required *AcquisitionNumber* is within the list. However, should an attempt be made to remove an item from an empty list a *LibraryListEmpty* exception will be raised and if an attempt is made to remove an item which is not in the list an *ItemNotInList* exception will be raised.

The package also exports a private action called *Search List* to its children. This procedure will search the list for an item which has the *AcquisitionNumber* specified. If the specified item can be found in the list the *Found* parameter is returned TRUE and the *FoundAt* parameter indicates the location in the list where it was found. If the specified item cannot be found in the list the *Found* parameter is returned FALSE and the *FoundAt* parameter contains an undefined value. The implementation of this design as a package specification file is as follows:

```
0001    -- Filename LibraryList.Editable_.pkg (k8 libredit.ads).
0002    -- Adds editability to the LibraryList hierarchy.
0003    -- Developed for the Ada book Section IV Chapter 25.
0004    --
0005    -- Fintan Culwin, v0.1, Jan 1997.
0006
0007    with LibraryList, LibraryItem;
0008    use  LibraryList, LibraryItem;
0009
0010    package LibraryList.Editable is
0011
0012        type EditableLists is abstract new LibraryLists with
                                                        private;
0013
0014        ItemAlreadyInList : exception;
0015        ItemNotInList     : exception;
0016
0017        procedure AddItem( TheList : in out EditableLists'CLASS;
0018                           ToAdd   : in        TitledItems'CLASS);
0019
0020        procedure RemoveItem( TheList   : in out
                                              EditableLists'CLASS;
0021                              ToRemove : in  AcquisitionNumbers);
```

```
0022
0023    private
0024
0025       procedure SearchList( TheList : in   EditableLists'CLASS;
0026                             ToFind  : in   AcquisitionNumbers;
0027                             FoundAt : out  StockItemsIndex;
0028                             Found   : out  BOOLEAN );
0029
0030
0031       subtype StockItemsRange is StockItemsIndex range
0032                                   1 .. StockItemsIndex'LAST;
0033
0034       type LibraryItemPointers is access TitledItems'CLASS;
0035
0036
0037       type LibraryStockLists is array ( StockItemsRange)
0038                                   of   LibraryItemPointers;
0039
0040       type EditableLists is abstract new LibraryLists with
0041       record
0042          Stock  : LibraryStockLists;
0043       end record;
0044
0045   end LibraryList.Editable;
```

The **private** part of the package declares a type called *LibraryItemsPointers*, implemented as a ***class wide access type*** which has the capability of designating any of the types in the *LibraryItems* hierarchy below the *TitledItems* type. The *TitledItems* type is the lowest type in the hierarchy which is a parent to all types which will actually be used to store details of a library item. It was for this reason that the *TitledItems* type was declared non-abstract in the previous chapter, as it is not possible to create a dynamic instance of an **abstract** type. As this is in the **private** part of this specification a client of the package does not have to be concerned with *how* the items are stored and can simply add an item to the list by passing it to the *AddItem* procedure, without having to be concerned with pointer manipulation.

An access type is required as it is the basis of implementing a heterogeneous list. It is not possible to declare an array of class wide instances, as the precise size of the elements of the array cannot be known until they are actually stored. In order to implement a list which can contain items of differing types an array of pointers is first declared. Each pointer in the array can then be used to designate a different type of item. The array of pointers is declared in the **private** part of the specification as the *LibraryStockLists* type, and forms the extension to the *LibraryLists* data type when the *EditableLists* type is declared. A data structure diagram for the *EditableLists* follows; this structure will be explored in detail below.

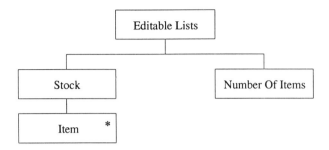

The *NumberOfItems* component is inherited from the *LibraryLists* type. A subtype of the *StockItemsIndex* type, called *StockItemsRange*, whose lower bound is 1 and upper bound is the same as *StockItemsIndex*, is declared and used as the index type of an array type called *LibraryStockLists*. The element type of this array is the *LibraryItemsPointers*. The declaration of the *EditableLists* type then adds a component of this array type, called *Stock*, to the *LibraryLists* type.

The intention of this data structure is that all array elements in the range 1 to the value of the *NumberOfItems* component contain pointers to the *TitledItems'*-CLASS instances which are stored in the list. Any other elements in the array do not point to valid data. This implies that if the value of *NumberOfItems* is zero then the range of valid pointers is null (0 .. 0) and thus none of the elements in the array point to valid data. It is an essential requirement of the private actions of the hierarchy that this intention is always honoured, in order to maintain the integrity of the data structure.

A client of this package can only determine if a list is empty or full, add an item to the list and remove an item from the list. This is not a sufficient set of actions to construct a realistic client from and the additional actions will be added by extension. This design decision was taken to ensure that each type in the class hierarchy is not overcomplex. The design and implementation of the *AddItem* subprogram are as follows:

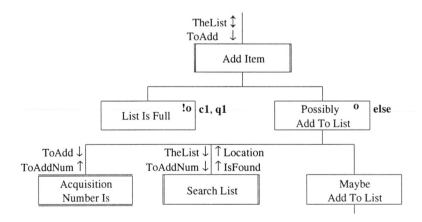

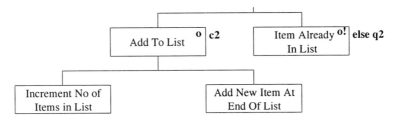

c1: If the list is full.   **q1**: Explicit *ListFull.*
c2: If item is not located   **q2**: Explicit *ItemAlreadyInList.*

```
0013    procedure AddItem( TheList : in out EditableLists;
0014                       ToAdd   : in       TitledItems'CLASS) is
0015
0016    Location                : StockItemsIndex;
0017    IsFound                 : BOOLEAN;
0018    NewAcquisitionNumber    : AcquisitionNumbers;
0019    ToAddPointer            : LibraryItemPointers :=
0020                                    new TitledItems'CLASS'(ToAdd);
0021
0022    begin -- AddItem
0023       if IsListFull( TheList) then
0024          raise LibraryListFull;
0025       else
0026          NewAcquisitionNumber := AcquisitionNumberIs( ToAdd);
0027          SearchList( TheList, NewAcquisitionNumber,
0028                      Location, IsFound);
0029          if IsFound then
0030             raise ItemAlreadyInList;
0031          else
0032             TheList.NumberOfItems := TheList.NumberOfItems + 1;
0033             TheList.Stock(TheList.NumberOfItems) :=
0034                                                  ToAddPointer;
0034          end if;
0035       end if;
0036    end AddItem;
```

In anticipation of the possibility of a new item being added to the list a pointer designating a copy of the item *ToAdd* is prepared in the declarative region of the subprogram. The type of the object being designated is specified as *TitledItems*'CLASS and the value of the object as the value of the *ToAdd* formal parameter. When this declaration is evaluated the type of the actual parameter will be known and Ada can decide at run time how much space is to be allocated for the information.

In the executable part of the subprogram, if the list is not full it is first searched to ensure that an item with the same acquisition number of the item *ToAdd* is not already present in the list. The acquisition number of the item *ToAdd* is obtained by using the enquiry function *AcquisitionNumberIs*, which is supplied by *LibraryItem*. The design indicates that the subprogram *AcquisitionNumberIs* is pre-supplied, as it is provided by the *LibraryItem* package which is not under development. The type of the formal parameter of this function is *LibraryItems'*-CLASS, the actual parameter supplied is of the type *TitledItems'*CLASS which is an extended *LibraryItems* type and is thus compatible. If an item with the same acquisition number is already present the *ItemAlreadyInList* **exception** is raised, otherwise the item is actually added to the list.

The implementation of the design component *AddToList*, on lines 0032 to 0033, adds the new item to the list, or more accurately a pointer to the new item, by first incrementing the value of the component *NumberOfItems*, and then assigning the value of the pointer which designates the item *ToAdd* to the end of the list.

The effect is to add the item *ToAdd* to the end of the list as a dynamically allocated instance which is designated by an element of the array. This will allow the information in *ToAdd* to be retrieved by dereferencing the pointer. The state of a list, called *AnyList*, containing two elements, identified as *This* and *That*, can be visualized as follows:

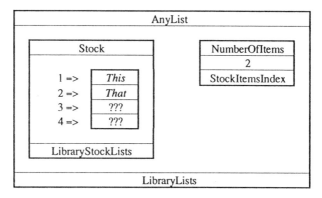

If a third item, identified as *TheOther*, is added the state of the list will change to the following:

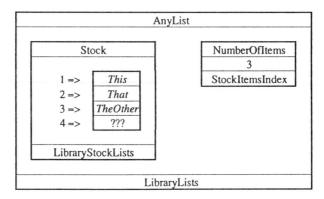

The implementation of the *AddItem* action depends upon the implementation of the *SearchList* private action. The design and implementation of this procedure are as follows:

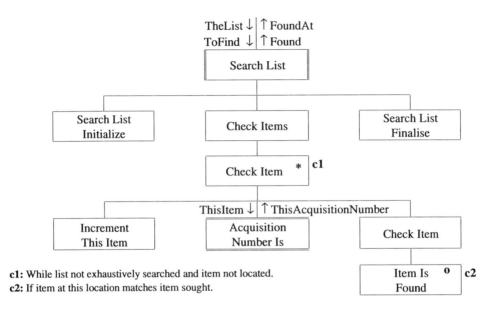

c1: While list not exhaustively searched and item not located.
c2: If item at this location matches item sought.

```
0059    procedure SearchList( TheList : in  EditableLists'CLASS;
0060                          ToFind  : in  AcquisitionNumbers;
0061                          FoundAt : out StockItemsIndex;
0062                          Found   : out BOOLEAN) is
0063
0064       ThisItem              : StockItemsIndex
0065                                     := StockItemsIndex'FIRST;
0066       Located               : BOOLEAN := FALSE;
0067       ThisAcquisitionNumber : AcquisitionNumbers;
0068
0069    begin -- SearchList
0070       while not Located and then
0071                TheList.NumberOfItems > ThisItem loop
0072          ThisItem := ThisItem +1;
0073          ThisAcquisitionNumber := AcquisitionNumberIs(
0074                          TheList.Stock( ThisItem).all);
0075          if ThisAcquisitionNumber = ToFind then
0076             Located := TRUE;
0077          end if;
0078       end loop;
0079       FoundAt := ThisItem;
0080       Found   := Located;
0081    end SearchList;
```

The basis of the design is to iterate through the list stopping when the list has been exhaustively searched, or when the *AcquisitionNumber* of the current item is equal to the *AcquisitionNumber* being sought. Line 0074 can be interpreted as follows: the first term, *TheList*, is the identifier of the formal parameter of the *Editable-Lists*'CLASS. The second term, *.Stock*, identifies the array component of the record which is of the *LibraryStockLists* type. The term (*ThisItem*), uses the local variable *ThisItem* of the *StockItemsIndex* type to select one of the elements from the array, which is of the *LibraryItemPointers* type. The final term, *.all*, dereferences the pointer and designates a dynamic instance of the *TitledItems*'-CLASS, which is compatible with the type of the formal parameter of the *AcquisitionNumberIs* function.

This search algorithm design can be regarded as a **standard design** and will be discussed in detail in the next section. The *RemoveItem* subprogram also makes use of the *SearchList* function. The design and implementation of this action are as follows:

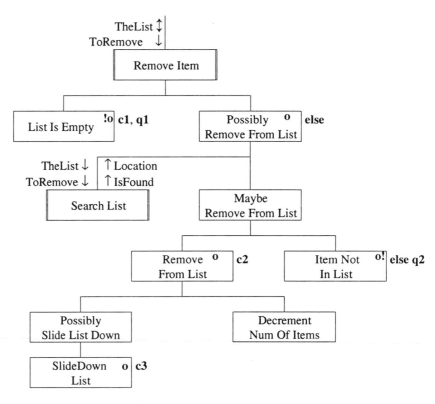

c1: If the list is empty.   **q1**: Explicit *ListEmpty*.
c2: If item is located.   **q2**: Explicit *ItemNotInList*.
c3: If item not at end.

```
0029    procedure RemoveItem( TheList  : in out EditableLists'CLASS;
0030                          ToRemove : in      AcquisitionNumbers)
                                                                   is
0031
0032        Location : StockItemsRange;
0033        IsFound  : BOOLEAN;
0034
0035    begin -- RemoveItem
0036        if IsListEmpty( TheList) then
0037            raise LibraryListEmpty;
0038        else
0039            SearchList( TheList, ToRemove, Location, IsFound);
0040            if not IsFound then
0041                raise ItemNotInList;
0042            else
0043                if Location /= TheList.Stock'LAST then
0044                    TheList.Stock( Location ..
0045                                         TheList.NumberOfItems-1) :=
0046                    TheList.Stock( Location+1 ..
0047                                         TheList.NumberOfItems);
0048                end if;
0049                TheList.NumberOfItems := TheList.NumberOfItems -1;
0050            end if;
0051        end if;
0052    end RemoveItem;
```

Assuming that the list is not empty, and that the item to be removed can be located, the action of removing an item from the list is implemented by possibly moving a slice of the array and subsequently decrementing the *NumberOfItems* component. If the item to be removed is at the end of the part of the list in use which, depending upon the value of *NumberOfItems*, is not always the same as the end of the array, the sliding action is not required. Otherwise the slice of the array which is moved starts at one position past the location of the item being removed, and extends to the end of the list. This slice is moved down one position to start at the location of the item being removed. Using the second visualization above, a request to delete the item identified as *That*, would cause the slice of the array from index position 3 to index position 3 to be moved to the slice from index position 2 to index position 2. The resulting state of the array would be as follows:

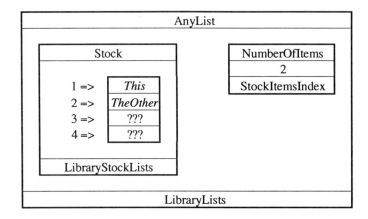

The *ListableLists* type

This type provides the operations which allow the list to be completely or partially listed. The object diagram for this type is as follows:

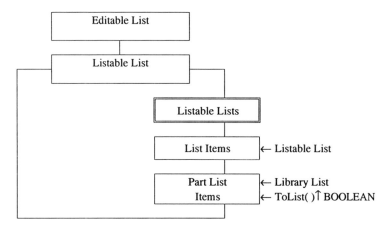

The first action *ListItems* will display the contents of the entire list on the terminal. The second action requires a BOOLEAN subprogram function parameter, with the formal name *ToList*, which will be called to determine if each particular element in the list should, or should not, be displayed. The use of subprograms as parameters was introduced in Section II, and examples of the use of subprogram parameters to the *PartListItems* action will be given below. The package specification derived from this object diagram is as follows:

```
0001    -- Filename LibraryList.Editable.Listable_.pkg (k8
                                          liedilis.ads).
0002    -- Adds Listability to the library list hierarchy.
```

576

```
0003    -- Developed for the Ada book Section IV Chapter 25.
0004    --
0005    -- Fintan Culwin, v0.1, Jan 1996.
0006
0007    with LibraryList.Editable, LibraryItem.Loanable;
0008    use  LibraryList.Editable, LibraryItem.Loanable;
0009
0010    package LibraryList.Editable.Listable is
0011
0012        type ListableLists is new EditableLists with private;
0013
0014        type ToListFunctions is access
0015                function( AnyItem : in LoanableItems'CLASS)
                                                    return BOOLEAN;
0016
0017        procedure ListItems( TheList : in ListableLists'CLASS);
0018
0019        procedure PartListItems( TheList : in ListableLists'CLASS;
0020                                 ToList   : ToListFunctions);
0021
0022    private
0023
0024        type ListableLists is new EditableLists
0025                                 with null record;
0026
0027    end LibraryList.Editable.Listable;
```

The declaration of the data type *ToListFunctions* on lines 0014 and 0015 declares a
subprogram access type which is able to designate a BOOLEAN function which takes
a single parameter of type *LoanableItems*'CLASS. This type is then specified as the
type of the function parameter of the *PartListItems* procedure. Examples of the use of
this procedure and suitable functions which can be supplied will be given below. The
ListableLists type adds no additional data attributes to its parent type *EditableLists*
and is declared in the **private** part of the package specification as a **null record**.

The design and implementation of the procedure *ListItems* are as follows:

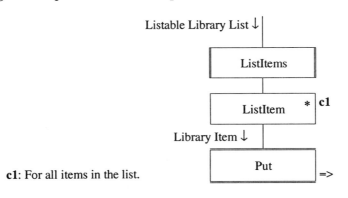

c1: For all items in the list.

577

```
0022   procedure ListItems( TheList
0023                          : in ListableLibraryLists'CLASS) is
0024   begin -- ListItems
0025     for ThisItem in StockItemsRange'FIRST ..
0026                      TheList.NumberOfItems loop
0027        Put( TheList.Stock( ThisItem).all );
0028     end loop;
0029   end ListItems;
```

The basis of the design is to iterate through the list, passing each item on the list a pre-supplied *Put* procedure for it to be output. The call of the *Put* procedure is an example of **dynamic dispatching**. The actual parameter passed to the procedure is the value designated by the access variable in the *Stock* component of *TheList*. This is a value of one of the *TitledItems*'CLASS of types, but the precise type cannot be known until the pointer is dereferenced. Thus Ada is not able to determine which possible *Put* procedure should be called until the program is executing. This requires all possible *Put* procedures to be brought into direct visibility, producing a complex context clause for the package body, whose **use** subclause is as follows:

```
0013   use ADA.TEXT_IO,
0014       LibraryList,
0015       LibraryList.Editable,
0016       LibraryItem.Loanable.Titled.Text.Book,
0017       LibraryItem.Loanable.Titled.Text.Periodical.Newspaper,
0018       LibraryItem.Loanable.Titled.Text.Periodical.Journal,
0019       LibraryItem.Loanable.Titled.AudioVisual.Cassette.Audio,
0020       LibraryItem.Loanable.Titled.AudioVisual.Cassette.Video,
0021       LibraryItem.Loanable.Titled.AudioVisual.ComputerDisk.
                                                   FloppyDisk,
0022       LibraryItem.Loanable.Titled.AudioVisual.ComputerDisk.
                                                   CDRom;
```

The design and implementation of the *PartList* procedure are as follows:

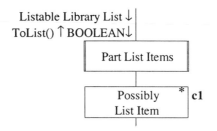

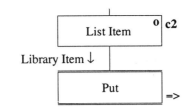

c1: For all items in the list.
c2: If item is to be listed.

```
0031   procedure PartListItems( TheList
0032                              : in ListableLibraryLists'CLASS;
0033                            ToList : ToListFunctions) is
0034   begin -- PartListItems
0035      for ThisItem in StockItemsRange'FIRST ..
0036                              TheList.NumberOfItems loop
0037         if ToList( TheList.Stock( ThisItem).all) then
0038            Put( TheList.Stock( ThisItem).all);
0039         end if;
0040      end loop;
0041   end PartListItems;
```

The design indicates that an actual subprogram **function** parameter, of type *ToListFunctions*, is required when the procedure is called. This function will be called indirectly passing each item from the list in turn. The BOOLEAN value returned from the function call is used to decide if the current item in the list is to be output. Examples of the use of this facility will be given below.

A client program

It is now possible to implement a client program which will offer minimal functionality to the user. The main menu of the complete application might be as follows:

```
Library list demonstration

A. Add    item to list.
B. Remove item from list.
C. List   items.
D. Search for item.
E. Issue  item.
F. Return item.
G. Exit.

Please enter choice >
```

The hierarchy developed so far is able to supply actions which allow the first three options to be implemented. The remaining options will be implemented when additional extensions are introduced. The high level design and implementation of a *menu/dispatch* system have already been given in Section I, and its adaptation to this specification will be assumed.

The *add item to list* main menu option

The first main menu option, *add item to list,* will offer a second menu to the user to indicate which type of item is to be added, assuming that the list is not yet full.

```
          Library demonstration, add item.

A.    Add a  book.
B.    Add a  newspaper.
C.    Add a  journal.
D.    Add an audio cassette.
E.    Add a  video cassette.
F.    Add a  computer disk.
G.    Add a  CD Rom.
H.    Exit without adding anything.

      Please enter choice >
```

This submenu is a second *menu/dispatch* system based upon the same design as the first, and possibly sharing some of its components. The dispatch part of this system, simplified to offer options only to add a book or a newspaper, might be designed and implemented as follows:

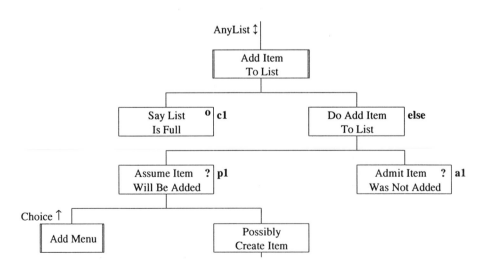

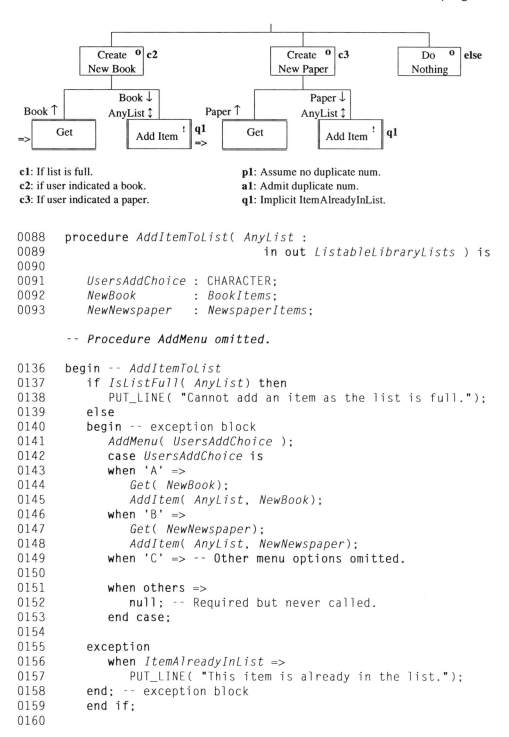

c1: If list is full.

c2: if user indicated a book.

c3: If user indicated a paper.

p1: Assume no duplicate num.

a1: Admit duplicate num.

q1: Implicit ItemAlreadyInList.

```
0088    procedure AddItemToList( AnyList :
0089                                    in out ListableLibraryLists ) is
0090
0091        UsersAddChoice : CHARACTER;
0092        NewBook        : BookItems;
0093        NewNewspaper   : NewspaperItems;

        -- Procedure AddMenu omitted.

0136    begin -- AddItemToList
0137        if IsListFull( AnyList) then
0138            PUT_LINE( "Cannot add an item as the list is full.");
0139        else
0140        begin -- exception block
0141            AddMenu( UsersAddChoice );
0142            case UsersAddChoice is
0143            when 'A' =>
0144                Get( NewBook);
0145                AddItem( AnyList, NewBook);
0146            when 'B' =>
0147                Get( NewNewspaper);
0148                AddItem( AnyList, NewNewspaper);
0149            when 'C' => -- Other menu options omitted.
0150
0151            when others =>
0152                null; -- Required but never called.
0153            end case;
0154
0155        exception
0156            when ItemAlreadyInList =>
0157                PUT_LINE( "This item is already in the list.");
0158        end; -- exception block
0159        end if;
0160
```

```
0161      NEW_LINE( 2);
0162      PUT( "Press enter to continue " ); SKIP_LINE;
0163   end AddItemToList;
```

The basis of the implementation is, within the options of the **case** statement, to obtain and store an instance of the precise *TitledItems*'CLASS indicated by the user in response to the menu *AddMenu*. The procedure *AddMenu* will only return a validated user's choice, currently in the range 'A' to 'H'. This implies that the **others** option in the **case** structure can never be taken and a comment to this effect has been included.

The effect for the users is that they will be presented with an interaction which requires them to supply the information which is appropriate for the type of item which they have selected. Should an additional non-abstract type be added to the library hierarchy at some time in the future then a small change will be required in the **case** statement and to the menu, but no other changes will be required.

Once an item has been obtained from the user, it is added to the list by a call of the *LibraryList* action *AddItem*. This call will raise the *ItemAlreadyInList* exception if the acquisition number entered by the user is already in the list. This exception is handled within the scope of the *AddItemToList* subprogram, by informing the user that the item had not been added.

The *remove item from list* main menu option

The *remove item from list* option has the following design and implementation:

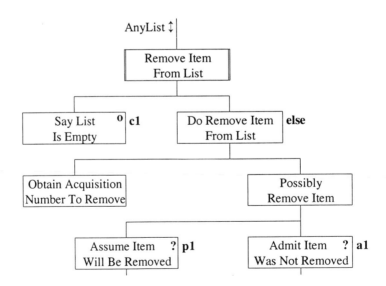

```
AnyList ↕┐
ToRemove ↓│
         │
    ┌────────────┐    ┌────────────┐    ┌────────────┐
    │ Remove  ! q1│    │   Say      │    │  Say Not   │
    │  Item      │    │  Removed  =>│    │  In List  =>│
    └────────────┘    └────────────┘    └────────────┘
```

c1: If list is empty.   **a1**: Admit item not in list.
p1: Assume item in list.   **q1**: Implicit ItemNotInList.

```
0059    procedure RemoveItemFromList( AnyList :
0060                                        in out IssueableLists) is
0061
0062        AcquisitionNumberToRemove : AcquisitionNumbers;
0063
0064    begin -- RemoveItemFromList
0065        if IsListEmpty( AnyList) then
0066          PUT_LINE( "The list is empty.");
0067        else
0068          NEW_LINE( 2);
0069          PUT( "Please enter the acquisition number"
0070              & " of the item to remove");
0071          GET( AcquisitionNumberToRemove); SKIP_LINE;
0072          begin -- explicit exception block
0073            RemoveItem( AnyList,
0074                    AcquisitionNumberToRemove);
0075            PUT_LINE( "OK. Item has been removed.");
0076          exception
0077            when ItemNotInList =>
0078              PUT_LINE( "The item is not in the list!");
0079          end; -- explicit exception block
0080        end if;
0081    end RemoveItemFromList;
```

The basis of this implementation is, if the list is not empty, to obtain from the user an acquisition number indicating the identity of the item to be removed. The *LibraryList RemoveItem* procedure is then called and should the *ItemNotInList* exception be raised the user is informed the item is not in the list, otherwise the user is informed that the item has been removed.

The *list items* main menu option

The *list items* main menu option leads to a list items submenu offering the following example options:

```
                List items menu

    A.      List all items.
    B.      List loanable items.
    C.      List items on loan.
    D.      List all overdue items.
    E.      Exit without listing

    Please enter choice >
```

This submenu is only called if the list is not empty and its implementation uses the standard *menu/dispatch* design. The **case** structure in the dispatch part of the design is implemented as follows:

```
0245    case UsersListChoice is
0246    when 'A' =>
0247         ListItems( AnyList);
0248    when 'B' =>
0249         PartListItems( AnyList,
0250                 IsItemLoanable'ACCESS);
0248    when 'C' =>
0249         PartListItems( AnyList,
0250                 IsItemOnLoan'ACCESS);
0248    when 'D' =>
0249         PartListItems( AnyList,
0250                 IsItemOverdue'ACCESS);
0251    when 'E' =>
0252         null;
0253    when others =>
0254         null;
0255    end case;
```

The first option, to list all items in the list, calls the *LibraryList.ListableList ListItems* procedure which will display all of the items in the list. The remaining options make use of the *PartListItems* procedure from the same package. This procedure requires a function parameter to be supplied as the second actual parameter of the call. Functions with the required declaration are provided by the *LoanableItem* package and these are specified as the actual parameter to the calls. Thus if the user asks for a list of all loanable items, each item on the list will be supplied as a parameter to the *IsItemLoanable* function and only those which cause the value TRUE to be returned will be output.

It would be advantageous for an arbitrary class wide BOOLEAN function to be supplied to the *PartList* procedure: for example, a function called *IsItemA-Newspaper* which would cause only the newspapers stored in the list to be output.

Unfortunately for very technical reasons Ada does not allow an arbitrary function to be used. The only functions which can be supplied as the actual subprogram parameter are BOOLEAN functions with a *LoanableItems*'CLASS parameter and which are declared in the class hierarchy above the *LibraryList.Editable.Listable* package.

It is possible to achieve the required effect of using a more arbitrary function by the use of **generic** facilities. This problem will be explored further in Chapter 27 when *generic program units* are introduced.

The *SearchableLists* type

The *SearchableLists* type adds no data attributes to the *ListableLists* type and provides two public actions to search a list for an item which has the acquisition number specified. The first action is a function which searches a supplied list for the given acquisition number and returns a BOOLEAN value if an item with the acquisition number is present. The second action is also a function which searches a list for an acquisition number, but it will either raise the *ItemNotInList* exception or return the item being sought. The intention is that a client program should use the BOOLEAN function first to ensure that an item with the required acquisition number is present in the list before attempting to retrieve it. However, the retrieval function is implemented defensively and will raise the exception as noted if the item is not present in the list.

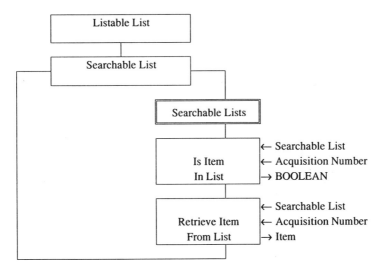

```
0001    -- Filename LibraryList.Editable.Listable.Searchable_.pkg
0002    -- (k8 liedilis.ads). Adds Searchability to the library list
```

```
0003     -- hierarchy. Developed for the Ada book Section IV Chapter
                                                                   25.
0004     --
0005     -- Fintan Culwin, v0.1, Jan 1996.
0006
0007     with LibraryList.Editable.Listable;
0008     use  LibraryList.Editable, LibraryList.Editable.Listable;
0009
0010     package LibraryList.Editable.Listable.Searchable is
0011
0012        type SearchableLists is new ListableLists with private;
0013
0014        function IsItemInList(
0015                            TheList : in SearchableLists'CLASS;
0016                            ToFind  : in AcquisitionNumbers)
0017                                                return BOOLEAN;
0018
0019        function RetrieveItemFromList(
0020                            TheList : in SearchableLists'CLASS;
0021                            ToFind  : in AcquisitionNumbers)
0022                                       return TitledItems'CLASS;
0023
0024     private
0025
0026        type SearchableLists is new ListableLists
0027                                          with null record;
0028
0029     end LibraryList.Editable.Listable.Searchable;
```

The design and implementation of *IsItemInList* are as follows:

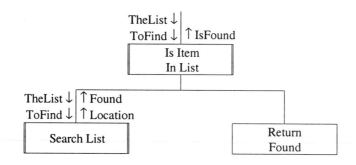

```
0012     function IsItemInList(
0013                            TheList : in SearchableLists'CLASS;
0014                            ToFind  : in AcquisitionNumbers)
0015                                            return BOOLEAN;
0016
```

```
0017        Location   : StockItemsIndex;
0018        LocalFound : BOOLEAN;
0019
0020    begin -- SearchListForItem
0021        SearchList( TheList, ToFind, Location, LocalFound);
0022        return LocalFound
0023    end SearchListForItem;
```

The implementation of this procedure makes use of the private *SearchList* procedure which was introduced into the hierarchy by the *EditableLists* type. This procedure was declared in the **private** part of the package specification and as such is visible to the descendants of the *EditableLists* type. The BOOLEAN value returned from the call of this procedure is returned as the result of the function.

The design and implementation of *RetrieveItemFromList* are very similar:

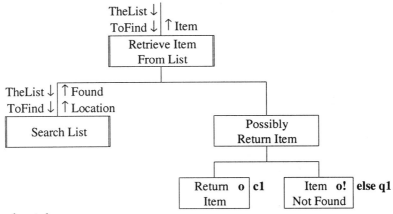

c1: If item located.
q1: Explicit ItemNotInList exception.

```
0027    function RetrieveItemFromList(
0028                           TheList : in SearchableLists'CLASS;
0029                           ToFind  : in AcquisitionNumbers)
0030                                   return TitledItems'CLASS is
0031
0032    Location   : StockItemsIndex;
0033    LocalFound : BOOLEAN;
0034
0035    begin -- RetrieveItemFromList
0036        SearchList( TheList, ToFind, Location, LocalFound);
0037        if LocalFound then
0038            return (TheList.Stock( Location).all);
0039        else
0040            raise ItemNotInList;
```

```
0041        end if;
0042    end RetrieveItemFromList;
```

The value returned from the function is the value of the object designated by the access value in the position indicated by the *Location* value obtained from *SearchList*. This may be of any of the *TitledItems*'CLASS types and thus has an indeterminate size, which makes the use of this function a little complicated. One technique is to pass the value returned directly to another subprogram which requires an *in only* parameter. An example of this usage will be given when the client program is revisited below.

The other possible use is to use the returned value to assign a value to a *TitledItems*'CLASS instance. However, it is not possible to declare an instance of the *TitledItems*'CLASS type without also giving it an initial value. Thus the only way in which this function can be used to give a value to an object is within a declarative region. For example:

```
NewItem : TitledItems'CLASS :=
            RetrieveItemFromList( AnyList,
                                   AcquisitionNumber);
```

This use of functions of this type will be explored further in the last chapter of this section.

The *IssueableLists* type

The *IssueableLists* type adds no data attributes to the *SearchableLists* type and provides two public actions, one to issue an item stored in the list and one to return an item stored in the list. It is anticipated that a client program will only call these procedures if the item indicated is stored in the list and is loanable. Should the item not be loanable the *ItemNotLoanable* exception, provided by the *LoanableItems* package, will be raised. If the item indicated is not stored in the list the *ItemNotInList* exception provided by the *EditableList* package will be raised. The object diagram and package specification for the *IssueableLists* type are as follows:

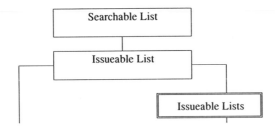

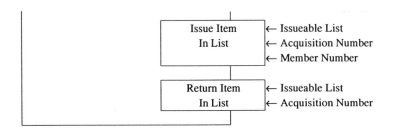

```
0001    -- Filename LibraryList.Editable.Listable.Searchable.
0002    -- Issuable_.pkg (k8 leliseis.ads).
0003    -- Adds Issueability to the library list hierarchy.
0004    -- Developed for the Ada book Section IV Chapter 25.
0005    --
0006    -- Fintan Culwin, v0.1, Jan 1996.
0007
0008    with LibraryList.Editable.Listable.Searchable,
0009         LibraryItem.Loanable;
0010    use  LibraryList.Editable.Listable.Searchable,
0011         LibraryItem.Loanable;
0012
0013    package LibraryList.Editable.Listable.Searchable.Issueable is
0014
0015       type IssueableLists is new SearchableLists with private;
0016
0017       procedure IssueItemInList(
0018                        TheList : in IssueableLists'CLASS;
0019                        ToIssue : in AcquisitionNumbers;
0020                        IssueTo : in MemberNumbers);
0021
0022       procedure ReturnItemInList(
0023                        TheList  : in IssueableLists'CLASS;
0024                        ToReturn : in AcquisitionNumbers);
0025
0026    private
0027
0028       type IssueableLists is new SearchableLists
0029                                           with null record;
0030
0031    end LibraryList.Editable.Listable.Searchable.Issueable;
```

The design and implementation of the *IssueItemFromList* procedure are as follows:

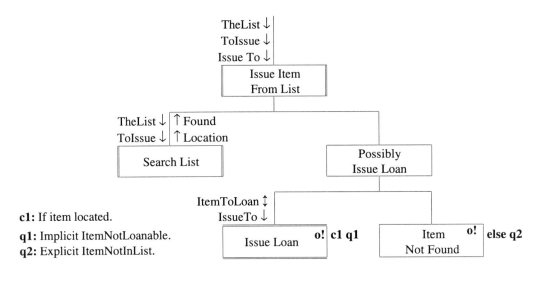

c1: If item located.

q1: Implicit ItemNotLoanable.

q2: Explicit ItemNotInList.

```
0017    procedure IssueItemInList(
0018                               TheList : in IssueableLists'CLASS;
0019                               ToIssue : in AcquisitionNumbers;
0020                               IssueTo : in MemberNumbers) is
0021
0022       Location : StockItemsIndex;
0023       IsFound : BOOLEAN;
0024
0025    begin -- IssueItemInList
0026       SearchList( TheList, ToIssue, Location, IsFound);
0027       if IsFound then
0028          IssueLoan(
0029              LoanableItems'CLASS(
0030                               TheList.Stock( Location).all),
0031              IssueTo);
0032       else
0033          raise ItemNotInList;
0034       end if;
0035    end IssueItemInList;
```

The basis of the design is to use the private *SearchList* procedure and, if the item is not located, to raise the *ItemNotInList* exception. Otherwise the *LoanableItems IssueLoan* procedure is called, passing the view converted item which was located within the list and the member number. The required type of the item parameter for the *IssueLoan* procedure is *LoanableItems*'CLASS. The type of the items designated by the pointers in the list is *TitledItems*'CLASS so type qualification is required to ensure the actual parameter is compatible with the formal parameter. If the item is not loanable then the *IssueLoan* procedure will raise an *ItemNot-*

Loanable exception, otherwise if the item could not be located during the search an explicit *ItemNotInList* exception will be raised.

The mode of the parameter *TheList* is specified as *in only*, despite the fact that the contents of the list may change as a result of the action. The reason for this is that although the values of the items designated by the pointers in the list may change the value of the pointers themselves will not change. The pointer will still designate the same items; it is only the state of an item which has changed. It might be preferable for the mode of the list to be specified as *in out*, but this raises the possibility of the pointers being inadvertently changed during maintenance. The specification as *in only* is an implementation decision which might not always be valid. It was specified *in only* in this example in order to reinforce the nature of the implementation of the list.

The other procedure in the *IssueableItems* package, *ReturnItemInList*, is very similar to, and a little simpler than, *IssueItemFromList* and will not be presented.

The client program revisited

The extension of the library hierarchy allows the main menu options which were omitted from the previous version of the demonstration program to be completed. Option D from the main menu, *search a list*, is realized within the program as a procedure called *SearchTheList* whose design and implementation are as follows:

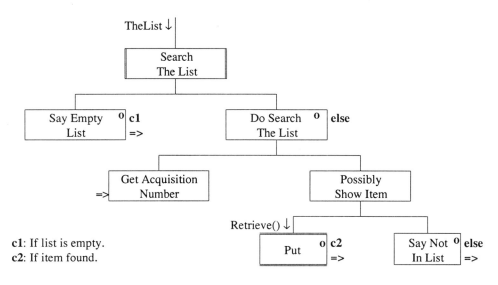

```
0273    procedure SearchTheList( AnyList :in IssueableLists ) is
0274
```

```
0275        ItemToFind : AcquisitionNumbers;
0276        ItemIsFound : BOOLEAN;
0277
0278     begin -- SearchTheList
0279        NEW_LINE( 2); PUT_LINE( "Search the list.");
0280
0281        if IsListEmpty( AnyList) then
0282           PUT_LINE( "The list is empty.");
0283        else
0284           PUT( "Please enter the acquisition number ");
0285           GET( ItemToFind); SKIP_LINE;
0286           if IsItemInList( AnyList, ItemToFind) then
0287              Put( RetrieveItemFromList( AnyList, ItemToFind));
0288           else
0289              PUT_LINE( "That item is not in the list.");
0290           end if;
0291        end if;
0292
0293        NEW_LINE( 2);
0294        PUT( "Press enter to continue "); SKIP_LINE;
0295     end SearchTheList;
```

The basis of the design is, assuming the list is not empty, to use the *SearchableLists IsItemInList* to decide if the item is in the list. If so, the *RetrieveItemFromList* function is called to provide a value for the dispatching *Put* call, which will output details of the retrieved item for the user. Otherwise the user is informed that the item sought is not in the list.

The design and implementation of main menu option E, *issue item from list*, as a procedure called *IssueAnItem*, are as follows:

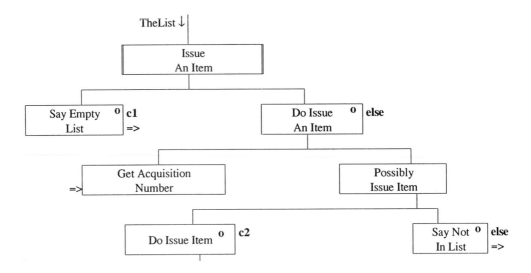

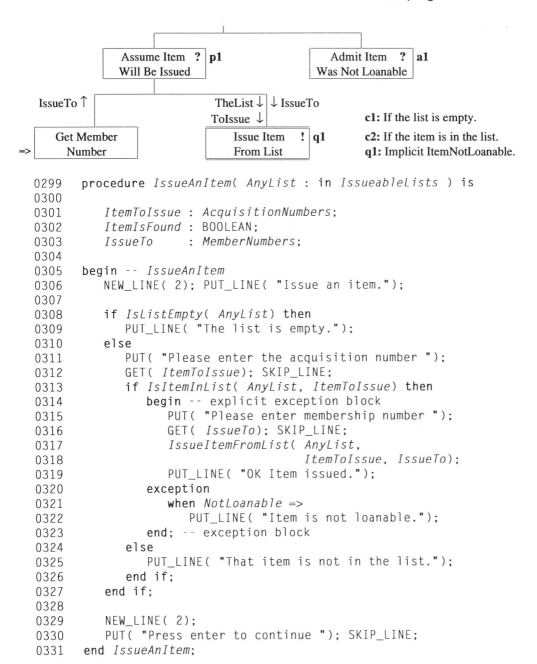

```
0299      procedure IssueAnItem( AnyList : in IssueableLists ) is
0300
0301          ItemToIssue : AcquisitionNumbers;
0302          ItemIsFound : BOOLEAN;
0303          IssueTo     : MemberNumbers;
0304
0305      begin -- IssueAnItem
0306          NEW_LINE( 2); PUT_LINE( "Issue an item.");
0307
0308          if IsListEmpty( AnyList) then
0309              PUT_LINE( "The list is empty.");
0310          else
0311              PUT( "Please enter the acquisition number ");
0312              GET( ItemToIssue); SKIP_LINE;
0313              if IsItemInList( AnyList, ItemToIssue) then
0314                  begin -- explicit exception block
0315                      PUT( "Please enter membership number ");
0316                      GET( IssueTo); SKIP_LINE;
0317                      IssueItemFromList( AnyList,
0318                                         ItemToIssue, IssueTo);
0319                      PUT_LINE( "OK Item issued.");
0320                  exception
0321                      when NotLoanable =>
0322                          PUT_LINE( "Item is not loanable.");
0323                  end; -- exception block
0324              else
0325                  PUT_LINE( "That item is not in the list.");
0326              end if;
0327          end if;
0328
0329          NEW_LINE( 2);
0330          PUT( "Press enter to continue "); SKIP_LINE;
0331      end IssueAnItem;
```

The basis of the design, assuming that the list is not empty, is to obtain from the user the acquisition number of the item being sought. If a call of *IsItemInList* indicates that this item is stored in the list the membership number of the person borrowing the item is obtained and the *IssueItemFromList* procedure is called. This procedure may cause an *ItemNotLoanable* exception to be raised, which is handled within the procedure by displaying a suitable message for the user.

The implementation of the final main menu option, *return an item*, is very similar to, and a little simpler than, the *IssueAnItem procedure*. The design and implementation of the procedure *ReturnAnItem* will not be presented.

EXERCISES

25.1 Extend the example client program developed in this chapter to allow for the other item types developed in Exercise 24.1 to be stored and issued.

25.2 The *LibraryMember* hierarchy developed in Exercise 24.3 will require an administration system to store details of the membership. Adapt the *LibraryList* hierarchy developed in this chapter to store a list of the library members.

25.3 Review the implementation of the *LibraryList* hierarchy from this chapter and the *LibraryMember* hierarchy from Exercise 25.2. What proportion of the two hierarchies is essentially identical, and thus concerned with lists in general rather than the particular lists being implemented?

CHAPTER 26

Ordering and storing heterogeneous structures

This chapter will complete the implementation of the *LibraryLists* hierarchy by the addition of a further extended class which, by the replacement of a single action, will cause the list to be transformed from an unordered to an ordered list. This transformation will be emphasized as illustrating the power of development by extension. All the actions which have already been introduced into the hierarchy will be available unchanged to clients of the extended type. The replacement of a single action in the child package will cause the nature of the list, and its usefulness to the users of the client programs, to change dramatically.

One further essential requirement will still be missing from the *LibraryList* hierarchy: the ability to transfer the information in the list to and from external storage. For reasons which will be explained later in the chapter, this requirement is not as straightforward as the facilities for the writing and reading of non-extendible types which were introduced in Section II. A final extension to the *LibraryLists* hierarchy will enable these facilities.

Finally, after the completion of the example client, *LibraryDemonstration*, the processes of constructing software by extension, which have been introduced by example in the previous two chapters, will be formally reviewed.

The *OrderedLists* type

The *OrderedLists* type is a child of the *IssueableLists* type which adds no additional data components and exports a single action. The action is called *AddItem* and **overrides** the *AddItem* action which was introduced into the hierarchy by the *EditableLists* type.

Whereas the original *AddItem* action from the *LibraryList.Editable* package always added the new item at the end of the list, the new *AddItem* action will add the new item into the list at a position determined by the value of the *Aquisition-Number* of the new item. The item with the smallest acquisition number will always be placed at the start of the list and the item with the largest acquisition number will always be placed at the end of the list. Thus every item in the list either is at the end of the list, or has an acquisition number which is smaller than that of the next item in the list. The acquisition number is known as the **key** of the list, as it determines the sequence in which items are maintained in the list.

The object diagram and package specification of the *OrderedLists* type are as follows:

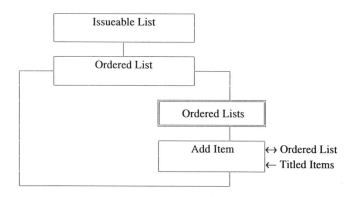

```
0001    -- Filename LibraryList.Editable.Listable.
0002    -- Searchable.Issuable.Ordered_.pkg (k8 lelsisor.ads).
0003    -- Adds Orderability to the library list hierarchy.
0004    -- Developed for the Ada book Section IV Chapter 26.
0005    --
0006    -- Fintan Culwin, v0.1, July 1997.
0007
0008    with LibraryList.Editable.Listable.Searchable.Issueable;
0009
0010    package LibraryList.Editable.Listable.
0011           Searchable.Issueable.Orderable is
0012
0013       type OrderedLists is new IssueableLists with private;
0014
0015       procedure AddItem( TheList : in out OrderedLists'CLASS;
0016                          ToAdd   : in      TitledItems'CLASS);
0017
0018    private
0019
0020       type OrderedLists is new IssueableLists
0021                             with null record;
0022
0023    end LibraryList.Editable.Listable.
0024        Searchable.Issueable.Orderable;
```

The design of the *OrderedLists AddItem* procedure is as follows:

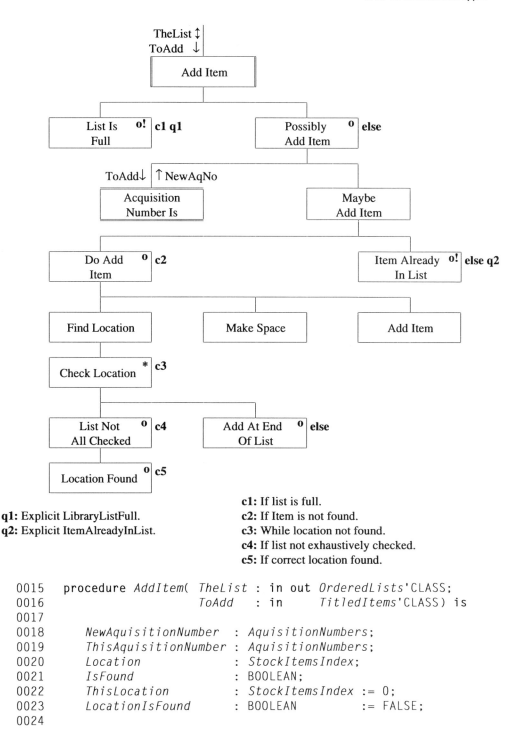

TheList ↕
ToAdd ↓

Add Item

List Is **o!** **c1 q1**
Full

Possibly **o** **else**
Add Item

ToAdd↓ | ↑NewAqNo

Acquisition
Number Is

Maybe
Add Item

Do Add **o** **c2**
Item

Item Already **o!** **else q2**
In List

Find Location

Make Space

Add Item

Check Location ***** **c3**

List Not **o** **c4**
All Checked

Add At End **o** **else**
Of List

Location Found **o** **c5**

q1: Explicit LibraryListFull.
q2: Explicit ItemAlreadyInList.

c1: If list is full.
c2: If Item is not found.
c3: While location not found.
c4: If list not exhaustively checked.
c5: If correct location found.

```
0015    procedure AddItem( TheList : in out OrderedLists'CLASS;
0016                       ToAdd   : in        TitledItems'CLASS) is
0017
0018        NewAquisitionNumber  : AquisitionNumbers;
0019        ThisAquisitionNumber : AquisitionNumbers;
0020        Location             : StockItemsIndex;
0021        IsFound              : BOOLEAN;
0022        ThisLocation         : StockItemsIndex := 0;
0023        LocationIsFound      : BOOLEAN         := FALSE;
0024
```

```
0025    begin -- AddItem
0026       if IsListFull( TheList) then
0027          raise LibraryListFull;
0028       else
0029          NewAquisitionNumber := AquisitionNumberIs( ToAdd);
0030          SearchList( TheList, NewAquisitionNumber,
0031                                       Location, IsFound);
0032          if IsFound then
0033             raise ItemAlreadyInList;
0034          else
0035             while not LocationIsFound loop
0036                ThisLocation := ThisLocation +1;
0037                if ThisLocation <= TheList.NumberOfItems then
0038                   ThisAquisitionNumber   :=
0039                      AquisitionNumberIs(
0040                        TheList.Stock( ThisLocation).all);
0041                   if NewAquisitionNumber < ThisAquisitionNumber
                                                               then
0042                      LocationIsFound := TRUE;
0043                   end if;
0044                else
0045                   LocationIsFound := TRUE;
0046                end if;
0047             end loop;
0048             TheList.Stock( ThisLocation +1 ..
0049                            TheList.NumberOfItems +1) :=
0050             TheList.Stock( ThisLocation ..
0051                            TheList.NumberOfItems);
0052             TheList.Stock( ThisLocation) :=
0053                       new TitledItems'CLASS'(ToAdd);
0054             TheList.NumberOfItems := TheList.NumberOfItems +1;
0055          end if;
0056       end if;
0057    end AddItem;
```

The basis of the design is first to make sure that the list is not full, and subsequently that an item with the same acquisition number as the item being added is not already in the list. If so the item can be added and the first task is to find the correct location for it to be inserted. This proceeds by an indefinite iteration which continues until the correct location for the new item is determined or until all items in the list have been considered, in which case the new item must be added at the end of the list. The correct location for the insertion of the new item is the location of the first item in the list whose acquisition number is greater than the acquisition number of the item being added.

Once the correct location has been found the item can be inserted into the list by moving all subsequent items one position up the list and then inserting the new item into the space which has just been vacated, before incrementing the count of the number of items in the list. Using a visualization of a list which is similar to the visualizations used in the previous chapter, the state of the list containing two items called *This* and *That* with acquisition numbers 12 and 16 respectively can be visualized as follows:

```
┌─────────────────────────────────────────────────────────────┐
│                          AnyList                             │
│  ┌──────────────────────────────┐   ┌─────────────────────┐  │
│  │            Stock             │   │    NumberOfItems    │  │
│  │                              │   │          2          │  │
│  │   1 =>  ┌────┬──────┐        │   │   StockItemsIndex   │  │
│  │   2 =>  │ 12 │ This │        │   └─────────────────────┘  │
│  │   3 =>  │ 16 │ That │        │                            │
│  │   4 =>  │    │  ??? │        │                            │
│  │         │    │  ??? │        │                            │
│  │         └────┴──────┘        │                            │
│  │                              │                            │
│  │       LibraryStockLists      │                            │
│  └──────────────────────────────┘                            │
│                      OrderedLists                            │
└─────────────────────────────────────────────────────────────┘
```

If an item with the title *TheOther* and the acquisition number 14 is added to the list, it should be inserted between the two existing items. The program component *FindLocation* will terminate with the value of *ThisLocation* set to 2, indicating that the new item, *ToAdd*, should be placed at this position within the list. To accomplish this the implementation first makes space, on lines 0048 and 0049, by moving the slice *ThisLocation* to *NumberOfItems* (2 .. 2) to the position *ThisLocation* +1 to *NumberOfItems* +1 (3 .. 3), before inserting the new item into *Location* (2) at line 0050. The state of the list after the procedure has concluded can be visualized as follows:

```
┌─────────────────────────────────────────────────────────────┐
│                          AnyList                             │
│  ┌──────────────────────────────┐   ┌─────────────────────┐  │
│  │            Stock             │   │    NumberOfItems    │  │
│  │                              │   │          3          │  │
│  │   1 =>  ┌────┬──────────┐    │   │   StockItemsIndex   │  │
│  │   2 =>  │ 12 │ This     │    │   └─────────────────────┘  │
│  │   3 =>  │ 14 │ TheOther │    │                            │
│  │   4 =>  │ 16 │ That     │    │                            │
│  │         │    │  ???     │    │                            │
│  │         └────┴──────────┘    │                            │
│  │                              │                            │
│  │       LibraryStockLists      │                            │
│  └──────────────────────────────┘                            │
│                      OrderedLists                            │
└─────────────────────────────────────────────────────────────┘
```

Within the client program, *LibraryDemonstration*, all that is required is to change all references to the data type *IssueableLists* to references to *OrderedLists* and to ensure that the *AddItem* subprogram call is unambiguous. The *LibraryDemonstration* program has two versions of the *AddItem* subprogram visible, one from *EditableLists* whose declaration is

```
procedure AddItem( TheList : in out EditableLists'CLASS;
                   ToAdd   : in     TitledItems'CLASS);
```

and one from *OrderedLists* whose declaration is

```
procedure AddItem( TheList : in out OrderedLists'CLASS;
                   ToAdd   : in     TitledItems'CLASS);
```

If the procedure is called without qualification, with an actual parameter of the *OrderedLists* type, then the call is ambiguous. The formal parameter is a member of the *EditableLists* class of types and also a member of the *OrderedLists* class of types. As Ada has a choice of possible subprograms which could be called, explicit qualification of the subprogram name is required as in

```
LibraryList.Editable.Listable.
Searchable.Issueable.Ordered.AddItem( TheList, ItemToAdd);
```

The effect when running the *LibraryDemonstration* program is that the options which list the items will now list the items in ascending acquisition number sequence, indicating that the items are stored in an ordered manner. No other changes have been made to the program by the developer and all other actions continue to operate exactly as before. For the user an ordered list may be much more useful than an unordered list and the developer has been able to deliver this benefit with minimal effort.

For the developer the full advantage of this development technique becomes obvious when the alternative development possibilities are considered. With development by extension an existing type has been replaced by an extended type which has had one action totally replaced. As no other changes have been made to the source code no retesting of any established client functionality is required as there can be no units which are dependent upon the new module.

If development by extension were not being used then the existing *AddItem* action would first have to be located and its implementation understood by the maintenance developer. This might be the same person who developed the original *AddItem* action, but if a period of time has elapsed since it was originally developed this person may have lost all familiarity with the implementation. Once understood the changes to *AddItem* would have to be designed, possibly requiring a complete redesign, and subsequently built. After implementation the new *AddItem* action would have to be tested, and so would many other aspects of the client's functionality which were dependent upon the module which has been changed.

Writing heterogeneous lists to, and reading from, backing store

The external iterative structures supplied by ADA.TEXT_IO, ADA.-SEQUENTIAL_IO and ADA.DIRECT_IO which were introduced in Section II are not suitable for the writing and reading of **tagged** types. The reasons for this are mostly concerned with the extendible nature of such types. As the types are extendible, the size of each record to be written or read is indeterminate.

It would be possible, but very complex, to write **tagged** types to a text file. However, in order to read the items back from the file some information must be prepended to the information written in order for the reading program to decide which precise type is about to be input. This would then be handled within the reading program by a multiple selection structure, containing a branch for each possible distinct type. This would imply that the extension of the hierarchy by the addition of types would require the parts of the source code concerned with reading and writing to external files to be maintained. This compromises the major advantage of programming by extension, which allows the vast majority of source code to remain unchanged when the hierarchy is extended.

It would also be possible to instantiate an ADA.SEQUENTIAL_IO package, or even with some operating systems an ADA.DIRECT_IO package, for the input and output of class wide **tagged** types. However, this again would require complex reading and writing subprograms to be produced, which would require extensive maintenance when the class hierarchy was extended.

Files and streams

Ada provides an input–output package which can readily be used for the input and output of **tagged** types, and which supports the philosophy that a client program of a class wide type should require no modification when the hierarchy is extended. The name of this package is ADA.STREAMS.STREAM_IO and a partial object diagram for it is as follows:

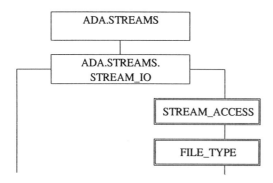

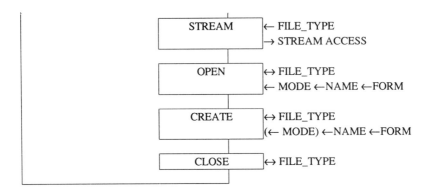

The parent class of ADA.STREAMS.STREAM_IO, ADA.STREAMS provides the basic operations for the input and output of information to and from general streams. A **stream**, as opposed to a file, is capable of implementing a communications link, for example an interprocess communication link or a network communication link, as well as a link to an external file. The STREAM_IO package provides the specific resources which allow the connection of streams to external files. The additional possible packages for stream communication with other entities are not defined by the standard and will not be considered further.

In addition to the overloaded subprograms, CREATE, OPEN and CLOSE shown in the object diagram above, there are subprograms called DELETE, RESET, MODE, NAME, FORM, IS_OPEN, END_OF_FILE, and various supporting types and exceptions, whose use and effects are very similar to the corresponding operations supplied by ADA.SEQUENTIAL_IO. The remaining subprogram, the function STREAM, has the following declaration:

```
function STREAM( FILE : in FILE_TYPE) return STREAM_ACCESS;
```

The function will take a parameter of an open ADA.STREAMS.STREAM_IO FILE_TYPE file and return a STREAM_ACCESS value, which can subsequently be used for the stream oriented subprograms which will be introduced below.

All **tagged** types have a class wide subprogram attribute called OUTPUT, whose effective data flow diagram and declaration are as follows:

```
procedure OUTPUT( STREAM : in STREAM_ACCESS;
                  ITEM   : in AnyTaggedType'CLASS);
```

The first parameter identifies the stream on which the information is to be written and the second the **tagged** value which is to be written. The effect of the procedure when it is called is to write a representation of the ITEM to the stream, raising the usual exceptions if this is not possible. The corresponding INPUT attribute subprogram is

STREAM_ACCESS ↓ | ↑ ITEM

INPUT

```
function INPUT( STREAM : in STREAM_ACCESS )
                            return AnyTaggedType'CLASS;
```

The effect of this function when it is called is to read the next item from the stream, returning its value via the function mechanism. The usual exceptions will be raised if this is not possible. There are additional attribute subprograms which can be used to write and read values of non-tagged types to and from streams.

Writing and reading heterogeneous lists

The stream facilities which were introduced above can be used to write and read the contents of a heterogeneous list of *LibraryItems* to and from a stream which is connected with an external file. To accomplish this a final extension to the *LibraryItems* hierarchy will be introduced. This final type, called *StoreableLists*, will extend the *OrderedLists* type by the addition of two actions called *WriteList* and *ReadList*. The object diagram and package specification for this type are as follows:

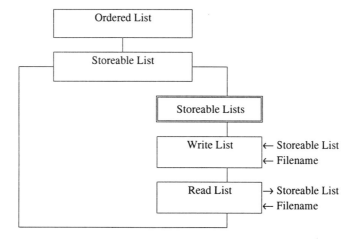

```
0001    -- Filename LibraryList.Editable.Listable.
0002    -- Searchable.Issuable.Ordered.Storeable_.pkg (k8
                                                lelsiost.ads).
0003    -- Adds Stream i-o to the library list hierarchy.
0004    -- Developed for the Ada book Section IV Chapter 26.
0005    --
0006    -- Fintan Culwin, v0.1, July 1997.
0007
0008    with LibraryList.Editable.Listable.
0009         Searchable.Issueable.Orderable;
0010
0011    package LibraryList.Editable.Listable.
0012            Searchable.Issueable.Orderable.Storeable is
0013
0014       type StoreableLists is new OrderedLists with private;
0015
0016       procedure WriteList( TheList  : in StoreableLists'CLASS;
0017                            Filename : in STRING);
0018
0019       procedure ReadList( TheList  : out StoreableLists'CLASS;
0020                           Filename : in  STRING);
0021
0022    private
0023
0024       type StoreableLists is new OrderedLists
0025                            with null record;
0026
0027    end LibraryList.Editable.Listable.
0028        Searchable.Issueable.Orderable.Storeable;
```

The design and implementation of the *WriteList* procedure are as follows:

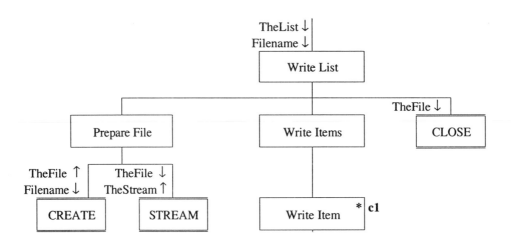

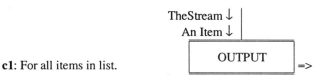

c1: For all items in list.

```
0015     procedure WriteList( TheList  : in StoreableLists'CLASS;
0016                          Filename : in STRING) is
0017
0018        TheFile   : ADA.STREAMS.STREAM_IO.FILE_TYPE;
0019        TheStream : STREAM_ACCESS;
0020
0021     begin -- WriteList
0022        CREATE( TheFile, NAME => Filename);
0023        TheStream := STREAM( TheFile);
0024        for ThisItem in 1 .. TheList.NumberOfItems loop
0025            LibraryItems'CLASS'OUTPUT( TheStream,
0026                                   TheList.Stock( ThisItem).all);
0027        end loop;
0028        CLOSE( TheFile);
0029     end WriteList;
```

This basis of this design and implementation is comparable with that which was used when the items from an array were being written to a sequential file in Section II. It differs in only two respects. First, the STREAM function is used to obtain a STREAM_ACCESS value by which the file can be manipulated. Second, the actual transfer of information from the program to the file is accomplished by a call of the class wide OUTPUT **procedure**.

The call on line 0025 specifies the OUTPUT **procedure** attribute of the *Library-Items*'CLASS type, which allows values of any of the types which are derived from the *LibraryItems* type by extension to be written to the stream. The actual values which are written are the *LibraryItems*'CLASS values which are designated by the slice of the *Stock* array delineated by the *NumberOfItems* component. As the items being written are of the *LibraryItems* class wide type, any future extensions to the *LibraryItem* hierarchy will not require any changes to be made to this subprogram.

The design and implementation of the *ReadList* procedure are as follows:

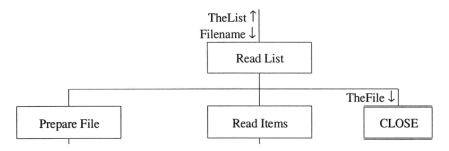

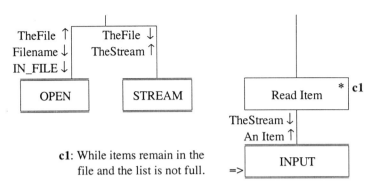

c1: While items remain in the
file and the list is not full.   =>

```
0032    procedure ReadList( TheList  : out StoreableLists'CLASS;
0033                        Filename : in  STRING) is
0034
0035       TheFile    : ADA.STREAMS.STREAM_IO.FILE_TYPE;
0036       TheStream  : STREAM_ACCESS;
0037       ItemsRead  : StockItemsIndex := TheList.Stock'FIRST;
0038
0039    begin -- ReadList
0040       OPEN( TheFile, NAME => Filename,
0041                      MODE => IN_FILE );
0042       TheStream := STREAM( TheFile);
0043
0044       while not END_OF_FILE( TheFile )       and
0045             ItemsRead < TheList.Stock'LAST loop
0046          ItemsRead := ItemsRead +1;
0047          TheList.Stock( ItemsRead) :=
0048             new LibraryItems'CLASS'
0049                  (LibraryItems'CLASS'INPUT( TheStream));
0005       end loop;
0051       CLOSE( TheFile);
0052    end ReadList;
```

The basis of this design and implementation is comparable with the design and implementation of a subprogram which was inputting information from a sequential file to an array given in Section II. The differences are concerned with obtaining a STREAM_ACCESS value to manipulate an open file, and use of the *LibraryItems*'CLASS INPUT procedure to read **tagged** values from the stream.

Having obtained a **tagged** value from the stream, in lines 0047 to 0049, it is used to initialize a **new** dynamically allocated *LibraryItems*'CLASS record whose access value is assigned to one of the pointers in the *Stock* array. Ada is able to determine from the tag of the value read the precise type of the value which has been read and thus is able to allocate a dynamic area sufficiently large to accommodate it. Again, any future extension to the *LibraryItem* hierarchy of types will not require any changes to this procedure.

This package can be incorporated into the *LibraryDemonstration* program by changing all references of the type *OrderedLists* to the type *StoreableLists*. Two options need to be added to the main menu, one to write the list to the file and one to read the list from the file. The subprograms which are called from these menu options would obtain a filename from the user and pass it, and the *StoreableList*, to the *WriteList* or *ReadList* procedure.

An overview of the hierarchies and *LibraryDemonstration* client

The previous two and a half chapters have provided an extended example of the processes of development of hierarchies of types by extension, and the provision of an example client which makes use of the hierarchies. The example can be thought of as a case study of the development process and has been deliberately introduced at this stage in the book to illustrate the complexity of a (semi-)realistic client program. The environment of the client program can be visualized as shown in Figure 26.1.

The diagram indicates that the *LibraryDemonstration* client is dependent upon many packages from the standard library, including two which are instantiated from ADA.TEXT_IO. It also indicates that it is dependent upon the *LibraryItems* hierarchy and the *LibraryLists* hierarchy. The *LibraryLists* hierarchy itself is also dependent upon the *LibraryItems* hierarchy. This is a complex environment which contains a total of 23 programmer developed packages, which are listed in Table 26.1. Only one of these packages, *JulianDate*, is being reused, although it is intended that some parts of the hierarchy would be used by more than one client within a library administration suite of programs. The complexity of this environment has to be contrasted with the simplicity of the individual packages. Each package has been designed to be as simple and as straightforward as possible.

Some indications of the complexity of the packages are given in the table. The column headed *lines* is the number of lines of source code in the package body. Where this value is shown as *NDY*, it indicates that the unit is *not developed yet*. The number of lines in a unit should be interpreted by remembering that each file contains header comments, two blank lines between subprograms and spare lines within subprograms. The actual number of lines of effective source code is smaller than the value given here.

The column headed *subs* is the number of subprograms which are declared in the public part of the package, *usubs* is the number of unique subprograms in the public part of the package, and *tsubs* is the total number of subprograms with which a type supplied by the package is associated. A unique subprogram is one whose name and/or parameter list differs from all other existing subprograms, with the exception that the declaration of a subprogram which differs only in the

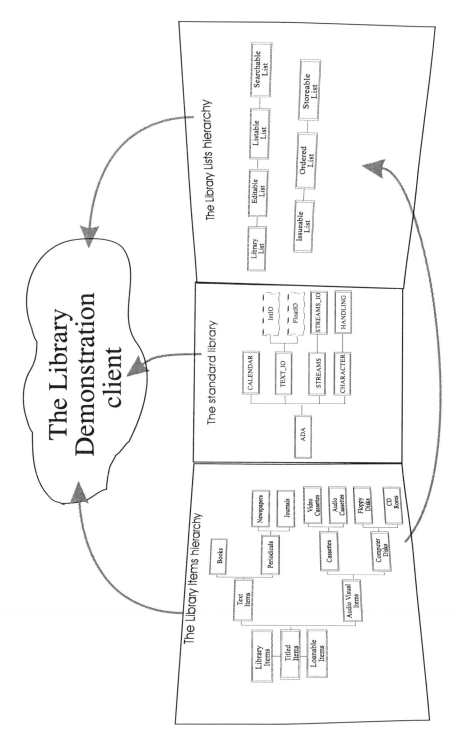

Figure 26.1   The LibraryDemonstration client environment.

Table 26.1 The packages used by the *LibraryDemonstration* client.

Package	lines	subs	usubs	tsubs	types	exec
JulianDate	367	16	16	16	7	1
LibraryItems	35	1	1	1	2	0
LibraryItems.Loanable	102	6	6	7	2	1
LibraryItems.Loanable.Titled	33	2	0	7	2	0
LibraryItems.Loanable.Titled.Text	22	2	0	7	1	0
LibraryItems.Loanable.Titled.Text.Book	56	2	0	7	4	0
LibraryItems.Loanable.Titled.Text.Periodical	40	2	0	7	1	0
LibraryItems.Loanable.Titled.Text.Periodical.Newspaper	23	2	0	7	1	0
LibraryItems.Loanable.Titled.Text.Periodical.Journal	33	2	0	7	1	0
LibraryItems.Loanable.Titled.AudioVisual	NDY	2	0	7	8	0
LibraryItems.Loanable.Titled.AudioVisual.Cassette	NDY	3	1	8	2	0
LibraryItems.Loanable.Titled.AudioVisual.Cassette.Video	NDY	3	1	9	2	0
LibraryItems.Loanable.Titled.AudioVisual.Cassette.Audio	NDY	2	1	8	1	0
LibraryItems.Loanable.Titled.AudioVisual.ComputerDisk	NDY	2	0	7	1	0
LibraryItems.Loanable.Titled.AudioVisual.ComputerDisk.FloppyDisk	NDY	3	1	8	2	0
LibraryItems.Loanable.Titled.AudioVisual.ComputerDisk.CDRom	NDY	2	0	7	1	0
LibraryList	22	2	2	2	1	2
LibraryList.Editable	87	2	2	4	2	2
LibraryList.Editable.Listable	51	2	2	6	2	0
LibraryList.Editable.Listable.Searchable	48	2	2	8	1	0
LibraryList.Editable.Listable.Searchable.Issueable	54	2	2	10	1	0
LibraryList.Editable.Listable.Searchable.Issueable.Ordered	59	1	0	10	1	0
LibraryList.Editable.Listable.Searchable.Issueable.Ordered.Storable	55	2	2	12	1	0

change of a formal type to an extended type of the same class is not considered unique. The total number of subprograms is the number of unique subprograms, both in the package itself and any class wide subprograms in the hierarchy above, in which the extended type being declared can participate. This set of subprograms are also known as the ***primitive subprograms*** for the type.

The column headed *types* indicates the number of types and subtypes which are declared in the public part of the package and the column headed *exce* the number of exceptions.

Although the units shown as NDY have not yet been developed, the object diagram designs for the units have been produced and some of the measurements are available from the design. This information would allow the development team manager to estimate, from the degree of complexity of the completed modules and the resources used to produce them, the amount of resources which would be required to develop these units. This production management information is one of the benefits which can be obtained from measuring software attributes.

These are not the only possible measurements which could have been made. For example, the number of data attributes which a package adds to the data type and the total number of data attributes could also have been indicated. The types of measurements which can be made on source code and the difficulties of interpreting them will be explored in detail in the next section. For the time being all that will be asserted is that the values given above, in some undefined way, indicate the complexity of the packages.

The most complex package is, undoubtedly, the *JulianDate* package which is implemented as an ADT. Excluding this the most complex package is, arguably, the *LibraryItems.Loanable* package. Taking this as an example the six subprograms which it provides are implemented in approximately 90 lines of source code, indicating that each subprogram takes an average of 15 lines of source code. Thus, on average, each subprogram is not particularly complex; the complexity arises from the number of different packages and their interactions with each other.

The two hierarchies indicate two different patterns of complexity. The *LibraryItems* hierarchy introduces most of its complexity in the first extension, the *LibraryItems.Loanable* package, with a total of six subprograms. Thereafter most packages are implemented by the addition of a single data attribute and the overloading of the two fundamental programs, *Put* and *Get*. Some of the data types in the *AudioVisual* class add additional specialized attributes, for example the type of format of a *FloppyDisk*. In these cases an additional data type is exported and an enquiry function is supplied. The pattern is one of increasing data attribute complexity with a fairly constant behavioural complexity.

The *LibraryList* hierarchy reaches its maximal data attribute complexity after its first extension, the *LibraryList.Editable* package. Thereafter no additional data attributes are added, each extended package declaring a **null** extension in its private part. However, the behavioural complexity of the hierarchy increases as packages are extended. Thus the pattern here is of a hierarchy which has a fairly constant data attribute complexity and an increasing behavioural complexity.

This can be summarized by stating that the *LibraryItems* hierarchy is primarily concerned with the modelling of an object's data and only secondarily concerned with the modelling of the object's actions. However, the *LibraryLists* package is primarily concerned with the modelling of actions and only secondarily concerned with the modelling of the object's data. This again indicates a division of concerns at the design stage. The alternative design possibility might have been to attempt to design a single hierarchy which implemented both the individual library items and also a list of such items. Such an attempt is a common novice's error and generally leads to a difficult implementation which is difficult to maintain and impossible to reuse.

The complexity of this client program is thus in the design of the hierarchies, not in the complexity of the client, nor in the individual packages which comprise the hierarchies. Thus the analysis of a specification into noun clauses connected by *is a* and *has a* relations, with verb clauses from the specification associated with each noun phrase, and the subsequent design refinement into a hierarchy, is the essence of producing an elegant and effective design for a realistic client.

The subsequent stages of deciding if each identified noun phrase would be best implemented as an ADT, ESV or EDT, producing an object diagram and implementation as a package, are dependent upon the initial design. If the initial analysis and design were performed correctly then these subsequent stages should, in general, produce package designs which are relatively straightforward to implement.

The final stage, the production of an actual client program, now consists of providing a 'glue' to stick the various objects together. This glue also encompasses the user interface which, as indicated in the *LibraryDemonstration* client, can make use of standard designs.

Several other considerations should also be included in the design and production of a client from a collection of packages. The first is that the possibility of using, or adapting, existing packages should never be overlooked. Indeed this consideration should be emphasized much more positively; it should be expected that existing packages should always be reused and the production of a complete package, or hierarchy, should commence from an existing package or hierarchy. This design philosophy will shortly be made much more powerful when *generic program units* are introduced.

The considerations of maintainability and reusability are largely taken care of by these design and implementation techniques. By insisting that each package in an extendible type adds only a minimal set of data attributes and/or actions, a location in the hierarchy for any future extensions can hopefully be guaranteed. As each package, and each action within a package, is minimally complex the process of correcting an identified fault should be greatly simplified. Likewise as each extension adds a defined functionality to the hierarchy the location of an identified fault can be found from the functional nature of the fault.

The development of software by extension also assists in the production process as it can take place in small *build/test* stages. A production plan can be devised which would identify milestones as places within the hierarchy where a significant class of types had been produced. A test harness client can then be used to establish the correct implementation of the class so far. Once this milestone had been passed, the next class of types could be added to the hierarchy and the test harness extended to add additional tests for the extensions.

All of the arguments presented above suggest that the use of EDTs is to be favoured above the use of ADTs or ESVs. This is the general advice given with two possible exceptions. If the data item being modelled is conceptually simple and unlikely ever to be extended then an ADT might be appropriate. An example is the *JulianDates* data type. It seems unlikely that this type will ever be extended by the *is a* relation and is overwhelmingly likely that it will only ever be used in a *has a* relation. In such cases implementation as an ADT would seem appropriate, although such an implementation, as indicated in the table above, is likely to be complex. Once constructed the ADT is likely to have a great deal of potential reuse, as it must be a fundamental data type to appear only in *has a* relations.

The other indication that an EDT might not be the most appropriate design is where there is only a single instance of the object being modelled in the real world. The *canned drink dispenser* introduced earlier in this section is an example of a situation where only a single instance of the real world concept will ever exist within the domain of the software product. There may be a large number of dispensing machines but each has its own control system, and thus each control system is associated with a single machine. These conditions suggest that the real world concept is best implemented as an ESV design. As discussed in the chapter on ESVs, such situations tend to be concerned with real time control and as such are specialized.

If an incorrect decision is taken and a concept which should have been implemented as an EDT is implemented as an ADT or as an ESV, the re-engineering of an ADT or ESV implementation into an EDT is not especially complex. This also leads to the advice that if there is ever any doubt in the design decision concerning which style of package should be built, then an EDT package should be constructed.

Object oriented programming

The development of an application by the design and production of a hierarchy of EDTs is known as *object oriented programming* (OOP). This style of programming has become prevalent in recent years and in the conclusion to this chapter a tentative definition of OOP will be presented. Following this, examples of the use of these defining aspects of OOP within Ada will be presented.

The paragraph above promised to present only a tentative definition of OOP as there is still considerable debate concerning what actually constitutes OOP. The definition of OOP which will be explored in this part of the chapter is as follows:

Object oriented programming	involves	*encapsulation*
	and	*inheritance*
	and	*classes*
	and	*overloading*
	and	*polymorphism.*

Encapsulation has been repeatedly and strongly emphasized since the first chapters of this book. Within Ada the clearest example of encapsulation is the division of a package into *public* and *private* parts. Any encapsulated information is known only in the **private** part of the package and can be safely changed without any effects of the changes causing any clients of the package to require subsequent modification. Without encapsulation a change within a package may require modifications throughout the entire software system. Should this happen it cannot be guaranteed that all required changes have been made. In the best case situation this will be expensive and inconvenient; in the worst case the system may become insecure.

Two other forms of encapsulation are also provided. Declarations of data attributes and/or actions in the **private** part of Ada packages are visible to its child packages but not to its clients. This can be considered an intermediate form of visibility which allows a restricted visibility between public and private. In addition, and examples of this have not yet been introduced, it is possible for *private child packages* to be declared. These packages can be thought of as having the same visibility as the package body. Private child packages have full visibility of the parent's public and private parts, but clients have no knowledge of their existence. The major use of this facility is to allow a type to be derived by extension without allowing the extensions to become visible.

Inheritance allows new types to be incrementally built from existing types by the retention, modification and addition, but not the removal, of data attributes and actions. The simplest form of inheritance is the derivation of a **new** type from an existing type. In the Ada declaration

```
type Lengths is new INTEGER;
```

the derived type *Lengths* inherits all the operations which are supplied for the pre-declared INTEGER type. Thus the pre-declared addition function ("+") which would have the declaration

```
function "+"( Left  : in INTEGER,
              Right : in INTEGER) return INTEGER;
```

is inherited by the type *Lengths* which has a corresponding function which would

613

have the following declaration:

```
function "+"( Left  : in Lengths,
              Right : in Lengths) return Lengths;
```

For a pre-declared data type the set of operations whose signatures contain parameters of a particular data type, and are thus inherited by a **new** data type declaration, are known as the ***primitive operations*** of the data type. For a programmer declared data type, either an ADT or an EDT, the primitive operations are only those which are declared within the ADT package declaration or, for an EDT, the extended type hierarchy.

It is also possible for the derived type to modify the data attributes and actions of the parent type. Modification of the data attributes, in this form of inheritance, takes the form of specifying a restricted range for values of the new type. Modification of actions takes the form of explicitly declaring, and subsequently defining, any operations which would otherwise be inherited. For example, for the following declarations

```
type Angles is new INTEGER range 0 .. 359;
function "+"( Left  : in Angles,
              Right : in Angles) return Angles;
```

the range of values for the type *Angles* is a restricted subset of the range of values of its parent type. The addition operation will presumably modify the pre-declared INTEGER addition operation by ensuring that the rules for adding angles are enforced (e.g. *Angles* value 340 plus *Angles* value 50 would result in an *Angles* value of 30). The replacement of an operation which would otherwise have been inherited is known as ***overriding***.

A more powerful mechanism for the provision of inheritance is provided by the use of **tagged** types. In these types additional data attributes and actions are explicitly added to the parent type. The extensions can continue through many levels, adding data attributes and adding and/or modifying actions to produce a hierarchy of extended types. A *class* is defined as the set of EDTs which are derived from a particular location within the hierarchy, and *class wide actions* can be declared for such *class wide types*. Such actions can be subsequently applied to an instance which belongs to any of the specific types in the class hierarchy.

The **tagged type** facilities provided by Ada are the most powerful and elegant technique available for the provision of inheritance. As has been demonstrated in the last three chapters this technique allows an application to be developed in a large number of small stages and promises a high potential of reuse. The technique can be empowered further by the use of **generic** mechanisms which allow an algorithm to be applied to a number of distinct data types. Ada's support for *genericity* will be introduced in the remainder of this section.

Overloading is where the name of an operation can be used by different data types. The use of overloading implies that many standard operations can be supplied using an expected name. Perhaps the commonest example of overloading is the expected declaration of a PUT procedure for every data type. In Ada a developer can expect that a newly encountered data type will have a PUT action defined which, when called, will output a representation of the value supplied as an *in only* parameter to the terminal. This should be contrasted with some other environments which require every operation to have a unique name. In this situation a developer will have to locate and remember the specific name of the output action for every data type.

A more powerful form of overloading is the provision of function overloading which allows certain common function operators to be overloaded. Once an overloaded function operator has been declared a developer can then use the more natural infix notation for the specification of actions as opposed to the less natural prefix notation. The addition operation for *Angles* declared above is an example of operator overloading allowing two angles to be added as follows:

```
ResultingAngle := ThisAngle + ThatAngle;
```

Polymorphism is the utilization of overloading with class wide types. The explanation of overloading above implied that each overloaded subprogram had a unique *signature* which allowed Ada to decide upon the actual overloaded subprogram to call at compile time. With **tagged** types it is possible for a subprogram call to include a parameter of a class wide type, which may prevent Ada from deciding which actual subprogram to call until the program is executing. Overloading implies *static* (compile time) *dispatching* to subprograms, polymorphism implies *dynamic* (run time) *dispatching* to subprograms.

Polymorphism is only allowed if it can be guaranteed that for every existing specific type, and for any specific types which might be declared in the future, there is a corresponding subprogram with which it can be matched. There are two forms of guarantee: either the declaration of an actual subprogram with a matching formal parameter of the class wide type, or the declaration of an **abstract** subprogram with a matching formal parameter of the class wide type. Where an **abstract** subprogram is declared it forms a promise that an actual subprogram will be provided at some place in the hierarchy, and as instances of abstract data types cannot actually be provided, the guarantee will be honoured.

Finally there are some differences in the use of OOP terminology between Ada and other environments which may cause some confusion if the terms are misinterpreted. The term *object* itself is unfortunately capable of multiple meanings. Within Ada the term is used in the general sense of *program object*, a very wide ranging concept which includes anything which forms part of an Ada program. For example, constants, comments, variables, subprograms, exceptions, packages, type declarations, etc., can all be regarded as objects. This requires qualification of the term to be necessary in some circumstances and phrases such as 'variable object' or 'constant object' have to be used.

For most other OOP environments the term *object* has a more specific meaning and relates to extendible program entities which encapsulate state data and have a defined set of, possibly polymorphic, actions. Within Ada this concept is more accurately contained within the term *tagged object*, allowing the term *object* to be used for its general, more commonsensical, meaning.

The other common OOP term which has a different meaning in Ada from other environments is *class*. In Ada a *class* is a set of specific types, including the parent type, which are derived from any given parent type. The usage of *class* in most other OOP environments refers to all possible instances of a specific extendible type, and the declaration of the type itself. The term *class* is inherently plural and its usage for a set of specific types seems more appropriate than a usage which limits it to a single type. The general OOP meaning of *class* in Ada would be a specific extendible type.

EXERCISES

26.1 What changes are required to the *OrderedList* and *StoreableList* packages to accommodate the additional types developed in Exercise 25.1? What does this imply for future extensions of the *LibraryItem* hierarchy?

26.2 Extend the *LibraryMember* hierarchy from Exercises 24.3 and 25.2 to allow an ordered list of members to be stored and for the lists to be written to and read from external files. What proportion of these extensions is essentially identical to the extensions presented in this chapter, and thus concerned with lists in general and not the particular lists being constructed?

26.3 A fundamental facility, such as storing information, should be placed near the head of a hierarchy. Is the *StoreableLists* extension in the correct place in the hierarchy? If you decide that the extension is in the wrong place, where should it be placed and what effects will this have upon the other existing packages?

26.4 The measurements which were presented in this chapter are not the only ones which could have been made on the hierarchies. Decide upon other measurements which could be made, and comment upon the meaning and validity of the metrics produced.

CHAPTER 27
Generic program units

A generic program unit, that is a **package, procedure** or **function**, allows an algorithm to be expressed independently of the precise data type upon which it operates. This allows a greater degree of potential reusability as the generic unit, once developed and tested, can easily be configured for use with different data types. The process of configuring a generic unit for use with a particular data type, or set of data types, is known as *instantiation.*

Generic packages have been used extensively since the start of this book. The instantiation of the packages *IntergerIO* and *FloatIO* are examples of package instantiations. The generic package ADA.TEXT_IO.INTEGER_IO provides the essential algorithms for the input and output of integer data types without actually being configured for a particular integer data type. The instantiation of the package as in

```
package IntegerIO is new ADA.TEXT_IO.INTEGER_IO( INTEGER);
```

creates a particular instance, hence *instantiation*, of the package called *IntegerIO*, suitable for the input and output of values of the pre-declared INTEGER data type. The instantiation of some other standard generic packages and a more detailed description of instantiation in general was included in Section II Chapter 26 on standard packages.

A first example

To introduce the concept of generic subprograms and the techniques which can be used to design and implement a generic unit, a very simple subprogram to swap the values of two objects will be developed. A design for swapping the values of two objects is as follows:

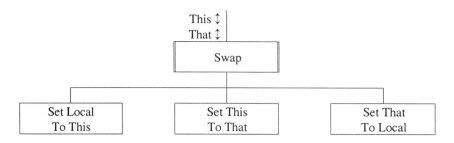

An implementation of this design which can be used to swap two INTEGER values might be as follows:

```
0001    procedure SwapIntegers( ThisInteger : in out INTEGER;
0002                            ThatInteger : in out INTEGER ) is
0003
0004        LocalInteger : INTEGER;
0005
0006    begin -- SwapIntegers
0007        LocalInteger := ThisInteger;
0008        ThisInteger  := ThatInteger;
0009        ThatInteger  := LocalInteger;
0010    end SwapIntegers;
```

The effectiveness of the implementation could be demonstrated by mounting it within a test harness and exercising it, or more conveniently by tracing the action of the subprogram with suitable test data. A second implementation of the design suitable for swapping two CHARACTER values might be as follows:

```
0001    procedure SwapCharacters
                             ( ThisCharacter : in out CHARACTER;
0002                           ThatCharacter : in out CHARACTER) is
0003
0004        LocalCharacter : CHARACTER;
0005
0006    begin -- SwapCharacters
0007        LocalCharacter := ThisCharacter;
0008        ThisCharacter  := ThatCharacter;
0009        ThatCharacter  := LocalCharacter;
0010    end SwapCharacters;
```

The effectiveness of this implementation could be demonstrated using the same techniques as were suggested above. The two implementations share the same algorithm and design. They differ only in the names of the identifiers, which is a trivial difference, and in the types of the formal parameters and of the local variable. The essence of a generic unit is to remove these data-type-specific references from the code and express them as a *generic formal parameter*. The swap design could be implemented as a *generic procedure* whose data flow design and implementation might be as follows:

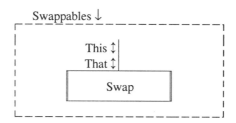

The data flow design of the subprogram is surrounded by a dashed box which indicates that this is a generic subprogram; any generic parameters are indicated as parameters to the generic box and not to the subprogram box.

```
0001    generic
0002       type Swappables is private;
0003    procedure Swap( This : in out Swappables;
0004                    That : in out Swappables) is
0005
0006       Local : Swappables;
0007
0008    begin -- Swap
0009       Local := This;
0010       This  := That;
0011       That  := Local;
0012    end Swap;
```

The implementation of the generic procedure on lines 0003 to 0012 is essentially identical to the two implementations given above. All references to the data type INTEGER or CHARACTER have been changed to references to the type *Swappables*, and the names of the identifiers have been changed to make them data neutral. The data type *Swappables* is now a *generic formal parameter* of the generic procedure *Swap*, as indicated on lines 0001 and 0002.

The reserved word **generic**, on line 0001, indicates that the declaration of a generic unit is commencing and that all declarations of types between the term **generic** and the start of the unit are declarations of *generic formal parameters*. In this example there is a single such declaration of a type called *Swappables*. The **is private** clause indicates that the only operations which can be assumed for this type are assignment and equality testing. Should an attempt be made within the definition of the generic unit to perform any other operations on objects of type *Swappables* a compilation error will be reported.

Having declared the generic *Swap* procedure, and possibly before it has been defined, it has to be instantiated before it can be used. The instantiation of the procedure for the swapping of INTEGER values might be as follows:

```
procedure SwapIntegers is new Swap( INTEGER );
```

This creates a new instance of the *Swap* procedure which is configured to swap INTEGER values. The specification of INTEGER in the instantiation is the provision of an ***actual generic parameter*** to match the ***formal generic parameter***. It is almost as if all references to the type *Swappables* in the source code of the generic procedure had been replaced with references to the type INTEGER and the resulting source code compiled. This would produce a subprogram which was identical, apart from the names of the identifiers, with the *SwapIntegers* procedure given in full above.

The generic *Swap* procedure can be instantiated with any data type which has assignment and equality operations defined for it. Examples include the following, which also illustrate the association of actual and formal generic parameters using positional and named association:

```
procedure SwapCharacters is new Swap( Swappables =>
                                                  CHARACTER );
procedure SwapDates      is new Swap( JulianDates );
procedure SwapBooleans   is new Swap( Swappables =>
                                                  BOOLEAN );
procedure SwapBooks      is new Swap( LoanableItems'CLASS );
```

The choice of different names for the four instantiated procedures is for the sake of clarity in the example. It is possible, and much more useful, usual and convenient, for all four of the instantiated procedures to be named *Swap*. Ada will be able to decide which version of the overloaded *Swap* procedure to call from the types of the actual parameters.

Generic searching

A more complex example of a generic procedure will allow more options for the specification of generic formal parameters and for the processes of designing and implementing generic procedures to be introduced. The basic algorithm for searching a list was introduced earlier in this section when a list of *Library Items* was searched. A general design for searching a list is as follows:

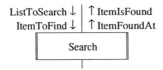

ListToSearch ↓ | ↑ ItemIsFound
ItemToFind ↓ | ↑ ItemFoundAt
Search

620

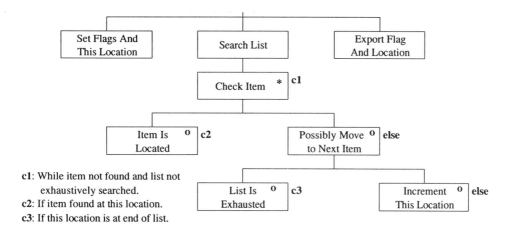

c1: While item not found and list not exhaustively searched.
c2: If item found at this location.
c3: If this location is at end of list.

To illustrate the implementation of this algorithm an array consisting of a list of integers indexed by characters will be used. The declaration of this data type and an initialized instance of it is as follows:

```
0023    type CharacterIndexes is new CHARACTER range 'A' .. 'E';
0024    type ListOfIntegersIndexedByCharacters is
0025        array ( CHARACTER range <> ) of INTEGER;
0026    ListOfIntegers :
0027        ListOfIntegersIndexedByCharacters ( CharacterIndexes ) :=
0028                                    ( 64, 78, 12, 91, 34);
```

The type *ListOfIntegersIndexedByCharacters* is an unconstrained array type whose element type is INTEGER and whose index type is CHARACTER. The variable *ListOfIntegers* is a constrained instance of this type whose index ranges from 'A' to 'E' and which has the initial value shown. The implementation of a procedure called *SearchForInteger*, based upon the design above, and suitable for searching a list of type *ListOfIntegersIndexedByCharacters*, is as follows:

```
0041    procedure SearchForInteger(
0042            ListToSearch : in ListOfIntegersIndexedByCharacters;
0043            IntegerToFind    : in  INTEGER;
0044            IntegerIsFound   : out BOOLEAN;
0045            LocationOfInteger : out CHARACTER) is
0046
0047        ThisLocation     : CHARACTER := ListToSearch'FIRST;
0048        FoundAt          : CHARACTER := ThisLocation;
0049        HasBeenFound     : BOOLEAN   := FALSE;
0050        ListIsExhausted  : BOOLEAN   := FALSE;
0051
0052    begin -- SearchForInteger
```

```
0053       while (not HasBeenFound) and (not ListIsExhausted) loop
0054         if ListToSearch( ThisLocation) = IntegerToFind then
0055           HasBeenFound := TRUE;
0056           FoundAt      := ThisLocation;
0057         else
0058           if ThisLocation = ListToSearch'LAST then
0059             ListIsExhausted := TRUE;
0060           else
0061             ThisLocation := CHARACTER'SUCC( ThisLocation);
0062           end if;
0063         end if;
0064       end loop;
0065       IntegerIsFound     := HasBeenFound;
0066       LocationOfInteger := FoundAt;
0067     end SearchForInteger;
```

The effectiveness of this implementation for searching a list of integers can be demonstrated by either tracing its operation or mounting it within a test harness. A call of the procedure to search the list, *ListOfIntegers*, declared above might be as follows:

```
SearchForInteger( ListOfIntegers, IntegerSought,
                  HasBeenFound,   IntegerFoundAt);
```

An alternative list, a list of characters indexed by integers, and an appropriate implementation of the same design might be as follows:

```
0015   type IntegerIndexes is new INTEGER range 1 .. 6;
0016   type ListOfCharactersIndexedByIntegers is
0017       array ( INTEGER range <> ) of CHARACTER;
0018   ListOfCharacters :
0019       ListOfCharactersIndexedByIntegers ( IntegerIndexes ) :=
0020                          ( 's', 'l', 'e', 'd', 'p', 'b');

0070   procedure SearchForCharacter(
0071         ListToSearch : in ListOfCharactersIndexedByIntegers;
0072         CharacterToFind     : in  CHARACTER;
0073         CharacterIsFound    : out BOOLEAN;
0074         LocationOfCharacter : out INTEGER) is
0075
0076   ThisLocation    : INTEGER := ListToSearch'FIRST;
0077   FoundAt         : INTEGER := ThisLocation;
0078   HasBeenFound    : BOOLEAN := FALSE;
0079   ListIsExhausted : BOOLEAN := FALSE;
0080
0081   begin -- SearchForCharacter
0082     while (not HasBeenFound) and (not ListIsExhausted) loop
```

```
0083        if ListToSearch( ThisLocation) = CharacterToFind then
0084           HasBeenFound := TRUE;
0085           FoundAt      := ThisLocation;
0086        else
0087           if ThisLocation = ListToSearch'LAST then
0088              ListIsExhausted := TRUE;
0089           else
0090              ThisLocation := ThisLocation +1;
0091           end if;
0092        end if;
0093     end loop;
0094     CharacterIsFound     := HasBeenFound;
0095     LocationOfCharacter := FoundAt;
0096  end SearchForCharacter;
```

The effectiveness of this alternative implementation of the design can be demonstrated using the same techniques suggested above. A call of the procedure to search the list, *ListOfCharacters*, declared above might be as follows:

```
SearchForCharacter( ListOfCharacters, CharacterSought,
                    HasBeenFound,     CharacterFoundAt);
```

The basis of the implementation of a generic version of this procedure is to identify the similarities and differences between the two versions. The differences in data types between the two versions will become generic parameters. The similarities between the implementations will become the generic body. Any remaining differences between the implementations will have to be resolved either by a reimplementation or redesign of the body or by the provision of generic subprograms. These two techniques will be illustrated below.

In the two versions above the differences in data types are the element type of the array, the index type of the array and the array type itself. This identifies three generic formal parameters of the procedure. The only other difference is in the technique used to increment the index value. In the character indexed version this is

```
ThisLocation := CHARACTER'SUCC( ThisLocation);
```

In the integer indexed version this is

```
ThisLocation := ThisLocation +1;
```

Before the generic version of this procedure can be built, this difference will have to be reconciled. Fortunately the integer version can be rewritten as follows:

```
ThisLocation := INTEGER'SUCC( ThisLocation);
```

This has exactly the same effect and is an example of reconciling differences by a reimplementation. The final decision to be made before implementing the generic version is to decide upon the types of the formal parameters. An analysis of the use of the three data types identified as generic parameters will indicate that for the element type the only operations which are performed upon it are assignment and equality testing. This identifies the formal element type as **private**, for the same reasons as a **private** formal type was declared in the *Swap* example above. The index type requires assignment, equality testing and incrementation using the SUCC attribute. This identifies the formal index type as being of a *discrete* type; the operations available for all discrete types were introduced in Section II. The array type formal parameter only requires actions which are appropriate for an array, the attributes FIRST and LAST and subscripting. Once these decisions are made the data flow interface diagram and declaration of the **generic** *Search* procedure might be as follows:

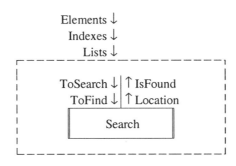

```
0042    generic
0043       type Elements is private;
0044       type Indexes is ( <> );
0045       type Lists is array ( Indexes range <>) of Elements;
0046    procedure Search( ListToSearch      : in  Lists;
0047                      ElementToFind     : in  Elements;
0048                      ElementIsFound    : out BOOLEAN;
0049                      LocationOfElement : out Indexes);
```

The declaration of the *Elements* formal generic parameter is comparable with the declaration of the *Swappables* generic parameter above. The declaration of the type *Indexes* as **is** (<>), pronounced *is box*, indicates that it is a generic discrete type. The declaration of the type *Lists* indicates that it is an unconstrained array type, whose element type is the generic formal *Elements* type and whose index is the generic formal *Indexes* type. The declaration of the procedure itself states that three of its parameters are of the generic formal types, the remaining parameter being of the pre-declared BOOLEAN type. The implementation of the procedure body is based upon the two implementations given above.

```
0064    procedure Search( ListToSearch        : in  Lists;
0065                       ElementToFind       : in  Elements;
0066                       ElementIsFound      : out BOOLEAN;
0067                       LocationOfElement   : out Indexes) is
0068
0069     ThisLocation    : Indexes := ListToSearch'FIRST;
0070     FoundAt         : Indexes := ThisLocation;
0071     HasBeenFound    : BOOLEAN := FALSE;
0072     ListIsExhausted : BOOLEAN := FALSE;
0073
0074    begin -- Search
0075      while (not HasBeenFound) and (not ListIsExhausted) loop
0076        if ListToSearch( ThisLocation) = ElementToFind then
0077          HasBeenFound := TRUE;
0078          FoundAt      := ThisLocation;
0079        else
0080          if ThisLocation = ListToSearch'LAST then
0081             ListIsExhausted := TRUE;
0082          else
0083             ThisLocation := Indexes'SUCC( ThisLocation);
0084          end if;
0085        end if;
0086      end loop;
0087      ElementIsFound    := HasBeenFound;
0088      LocationOfElement := FoundAt;
0089    end Search;
```

Before the generic procedure can be called to search a list, an appropriate version of it will have to be instantiated. Two instantiations of the generic *Search* procedure using the data types declared in the non-generic examples above might be as follows:

```
0052    procedure SearchForInteger is new
0053      Search( Elements => INTEGER,
0054              Indexes  => CHARACTER,
0055              Lists    => ListOfIntegersIndexedByCharacters);
0056
0057
0058    procedure SearchForCharacter is new
0059      Search( Elements => CHARACTER,
0060              Indexes  => INTEGER,
0061              Lists    => ListOfCharactersIndexedByIntegers);
```

Calls of these two procedures will be identical to the calls of the two non-generic versions given above. The equivalence can be demonstrated by the mounting of the generic instantiations within a test harness. The naming of the non-generic and generic procedures as *SearchForInteger* and *SearchForCharacter* is for convenience in the explanation. It would be more convenient and usual for them both to be named *Search*. Ada would be able to determine which version was intended in the call from the types of the actual parameters.

Generic packages

The use of generic facilities can be extended to the declaration of generic packages which implement a collection of related subprograms. Continuing the theme of the examples above an object diagram for a package which exports three useful generic subprograms for the manipulation of lists which are implemented as simple arrays might be as follows:

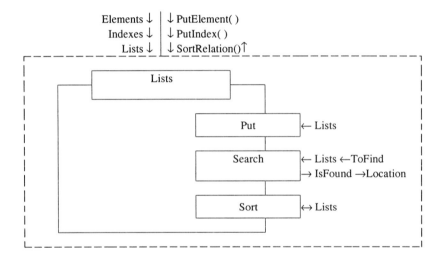

The object diagram is enclosed within a dashed box to indicate that it is a generic package and cannot be used until it has been instantiated. The formal generic parameters of the package are shown as parameters at the top of the package. The three parameters on the left hand side of the diagram are comparable with the three parameters which were used with the *Search* generic procedure described above, and define the nature of the array.

The three parameters shown on the right hand side are generic formal subprogram parameters. The first two of these, *PutElement* and *PutIndex*, are required by the generic *Put* subprogram. In order for instantiations of this subprogram to output the list they have to have a method to output values of the index type and to output values of the element type. As these are declared as being of the formal generic **private** and *discrete* types, there are no assumed output operations available for them within the package. Consequently in order for these operations to be made available to the *GenericList Put* subprogram they have to be supplied as generic formal subprogram parameters to the generic package.

The third subprogram is a BOOLEAN function called *SortRelation*. As will be explained shortly, a sorting algorithm has to have some technique to decide the relative ordering of two elements of the list which it is sorting. The elements of the list are of the formal generic type *Elements* which is declared as a generic **private** type. The only assumed operations for this type are assignment and equality testing. Consequently an explicit ordering function has to be supplied to the package for it to decide upon the ordering. The provision of these three parameters is an example of reconciling differences between two alternative implementations by the use of a subprogram parameter. The use of these three subprograms will be described in greater detail below.

The generic package specification

The generic package specification derived from the object diagram above might be as follows:

```
0001    -- Filename GenericList_.pkg (k8 genericl.ads).
0002    -- Demonstration of a generic package including the generic
0003    -- subprograms which have already been developed.
0004    --
0005    -- Written for Ada book Section IV Chapter 27.
0006    -- Fintan Culwin, v0.1, Jan 1997.
0007
0008    generic
0009       type Elements is private;
0010       type Indexes  is ( <> );
0011       type Lists    is array ( Indexes range <>) of Elements;
0012       with procedure PutElement(AnElement : in Elements);
0013       with procedure PutIndex(AnIndex    : in Indexes);
0014       with function  SortRelation( Left   : in Elements;
0015                                    Right  : in Elements)
0016                                          return BOOLEAN;
0017    package GenericList is
0018
0019       procedure Put( ListToPut : in Lists);
0020
0021       procedure Search( ListToSearch     : in Lists;
0022                         ElementToFind     : in Elements;
0023                         ElementIsFound    : out BOOLEAN;
0024                         LocationOfElement : out Indexes );
0025
0026       procedure Sort( ListToSort : in out Lists);
0027
0028    end GenericList;
```

The keyword *generic* on line 0008 indicates the declaration of a generic unit which is confirmed as a generic package on line 0017. The **generic formal parameters** are listed between these two terms. The first three parameters are **type parameters** which are comparable with the three type parameters declared for the **generic** *Search* procedure above. The last three parameters are **subprogram parameters** with the formal names as indicated. Upon instantiation they must be matched by an **actual generic parameter** whose signature exactly matches that stated in their declaration. Examples of suitable instantiations will be given below.

The remainder of the package specification declares the three procedures exported by the generic package. The declaration of the *Search* subprogram is identical to the declaration of the generic *Search* subprogram described above. The other two subprogram declarations are derived from the data flow on the object diagram above.

The generic package body

The generic package body contains the definition of three subprograms exported by the package specification above. The definition of the *Search* procedure is identical to the declaration of the generic *Search* procedure given above. The definition of the *Put* procedure is based upon the following design:

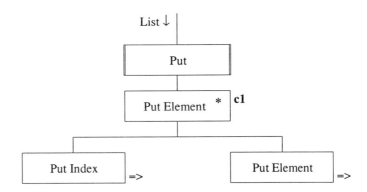

c1: For all elements in the list.

The implementation of this design is as follows:

```
0013    procedure Put( ListToPut : in Lists) is
0014
0015    begin -- Put
0016       for ThisIndex in ListToPut'RANGE loop
0017          PUT( "Element at location "); PutIndex( ThisIndex);
0018          PUT( " contains "); PutElement( ListToPut( ThisIndex));
```

```
0019          NEW_LINE;
0020       end loop;
0021    end Put;
```

The iteration through the extent of the list using the RANGE attribute ensures that each element in the list is output. Within the body of the loop first the value of the index and then the value of the element at that index location is output. This is accomplished by a call of the appropriate *PutIndex* or *PutElement* generic subprogram parameter. It is not possible for these values to be output with a simple call of a *Put* procedure as it cannot be guaranteed that under all possible instantiations a suitable *Put* procedure can be located. The only way that it can be guaranteed is for the instantiation of the package to supply an output procedure which can be called.

The remaining subprogram, *Sort*, is based upon the following design of a general sort subprogram which uses an algorithm known as an *insertion sort*. The design assumes that the list is to be sorted with the lowest value at the start, an assumption which, as will be demonstrated, is easy to reverse.

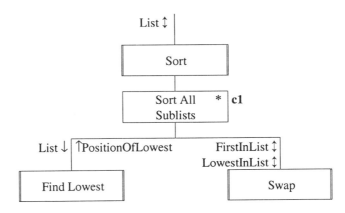

c1: For all possible sublists.

The basis of the design is to consider the list to be sorted as a sequence of sublists. The first sublist is the entire list and the second sublist is the entire list excluding the first element in the list. The third sublist is the second sublist excluding the first element of the list, or alternatively the third sublist is the entire list excluding the first two elements. The last sublist, as far as this algorithm is concerned, is a list which contains at most two elements. For an entire list which contains zero, one or two elements the first sublist is also the last sublist.

Each sublist is processed in an identical manner: the lowest element in the list is located and then swapped with the first element of the list. After the first sublist is processed in this way it can be argued that the lowest element in the entire list has been moved to the first location in the list.

After the second sublist has been processed it can be argued that the second lowest element in the entire list has been moved to the second location in the entire list. The basis of this argument is that the lowest element of the entire list is already in the first location and so is not contained within the first sublist. The lowest valued element in the first sublist is moved to the start of the sublist, which is the second location in the entire list. The value of this element must be greater than the value of the element at the start of the entire list, otherwise it would have been moved to the start of the list during the first iteration. It also must be lower than all remaining elements in the list, otherwise a lower valued element would have been moved into its location during the second iteration. As it is higher than the first element and lower than all remaining elements, it must be the second lowest valued item.

The iteration continues with all remaining sublists and the same argument can be used to prove that the third highest element in the entire list is in the third location after the third iteration, the fourth in the fourth after the fourth iteration, and so on. The iteration terminates when a list consisting of two elements has been processed. The remaining sublist consists of one element at the end of the entire list which, continuing the argument above, must be higher in value than all preceding elements. Thus as the highest valued element in the entire list it is in its correct location.

The process can be better illustrated by tracing the operation of the algorithm using a sequence of diagrams. A list of five integers, whose initial value is as given for the searching demonstration above, can be illustrated as follows:

64   78   12   91   34

The first sublist to be processed is the entire list and will result in the lowest item, at the third location, being swapped with the item at the start of the list. This produces the following list:

12   78   64   91   34

The second sublist is shown to the right of the double lines and consists of four items. The lowest element in this list is located and swapped with the item at the start of the sublist, producing the following list:

12   34   64   91   78

Following the processing of the third sublist the list is as follows:

12   34   64   91   78

In the iteration which produced this list the lowest element was already at the start of the list, but the algorithm given above would still have located it and swapped it with itself. The next sublist is the last sublist to be processed and produces the following list:

$$12 \quad 34 \quad 64 \quad 78 \quad 91$$

The algorithm will now stop, as the remaining sublist contains a single item and thus can be considered to be a sorted list containing a single item. The design of the *Sort* algorithm given above relies upon a subprogram called *FindLowest* whose design is as follows:

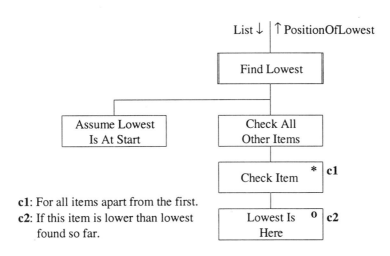

c1: For all items apart from the first.
c2: If this item is lower than lowest found so far.

The implementation of this subprogram within the body of the *GenericList* package is as follows:

```
0060    function FindLowest( ListToCheck : in Lists)
0061                                    return Indexes is
0062
0063        LowestValueSoFar : Elements :=
0064                            ListToCheck( ListToCheck'FIRST);
0065        LowestLocation  : Indexes  := ListToCheck'FIRST;
0066
0067    begin -- FindLowest
0068       for ThisIndex in Indexes'SUCC( ListToCheck'FIRST) ..
0069                                ListToCheck'LAST loop
0070         if SortRelation( ListToCheck( ThisIndex),
0071                                LowestValueSoFar) then
0072             LowestValueSofar := ListToCheck( ThisIndex);
0073             LowestLocation  := ThisIndex;
0074          end if;
0075       end loop;
0076       return LowestLocation;
0077    end FindLowest;
```

The function takes a parameter of the generic *Lists* type and returns a value of the generic *Indexes* type indicating where within the list the lowest valued element can be found. Within the implementation of the function only the operations which are appropriate to their generic types can be applied to them. The design component *AssumeLowestIsAtStart* is implemented as the assignment of values to the local variables. The variable *LowestLocation* is set to the index value of the first element in the list and *LowestValueSoFar* is set to the value of the first element of the list.

The definite loop is then constructed to iterate through all remaining elements. The lower bound of the loop is expressed on line 0068 as *Indexes*'SUCC-(*ListToCheck*'FIRST). This can be interpreted as follows: the term *ListToCheck*'FIRST is the value of the first index of the list and is of type *Indexes*. The term *Indexes*'SUCC increments this value to cause the loop iteration to start with the second index value of the list. The upper bound of the loop is the index value of the last item in the list.

The body of the loop checks the value of the currently indexed element against the value of *LowestValueSoFar* using the *SortRelation* function. If it is assumed, for the moment, that this function will return TRUE if the value of the first actual parameter is lower in value than the value of the second actual parameter, then the body of the if will be executed when an element is located in the array whose value is lower than *LowestValueSoFar*. When this occurs the value of the two local variables is set to indicate the location and value of the lowest item located so far in the list.

As the loop iteration considers all elements in the list, when the loop terminates the two local variables will indicate the lowest valued element in the entire list. The location of this value is then returned as the value of the function.

The *Sort* algorithm also relies upon the existence of a *Swap* procedure whose implementation, contained within the package body, is identical to the implementation of the generic *Swap* procedure given above.

With the *FindLowest* and *Swap* procedures implemented the *Sort* procedure can be implemented as follows:

```
0082    procedure Sort( ListToSort : in out Lists) is
0083
0084       LowestLocation : Indexes;
0085
0086    begin -- Sort
0087       for ThisIndex in ListToSort'FIRST ..
0088                        Indexes'PRED( ListToSort'LAST) loop
0089          LowestLocation :=
0090             FindLowest( ListToSort(
0091                                ThisIndex .. ListToSort'LAST));
0092          Swap( ListToSort( ThisIndex),
0093                ListToSort( LowestLocation));
0094       end loop;
0095    end Sort;
```

The implementation follows the design closely, consisting of an iteration whose body contains a call to *FindLowest* and *Swap*. The lower bound of the loop is the start of the array and the upper bound is the penultimate index value in the array, the expression for which is implemented in a manner comparable with the expression which identified the second element of a list in *FindLowest*.

The call to *FindLowest* in the body of the loop passes a slice of the array starting at the current index value and ending at the end of the array. For the first iteration this will be the entire array, for the second iteration it will be the entire array excluding the first element, and so on. The last slice passed will consist of the last two elements in the array. This is in accord with the description of the insertion sort algorithm given above.

The *FindLowest* function returns the index value of the lowest element in the slice of the array which was passed to it. This index value is used to identify the element passed to the *Swap* procedure to be swapped with the element at the head of the list.

The execution of this subprogram thus implements the insertion sort algorithm by iteratively processing all possible sublists, placing the lowest element in the sublist at the start of the sublist. This accords with the description and example of the algorithm given above. The completion of this procedure completes the package body.

A client program

To illustrate the use of the *GenericList* package a test harness client program will be described. This client program will use the same data type, *ListOfIntegers-IndexedByCharacters*, which was declared for the generic and non-generic *Search* procedures above. If the declaration of this data structure is assumed a suitable instantiation of the *GenericList* package to supply subprograms to process this array type might be as follows:

```
0030    package IntegerList is new GenericList(
0031           Elements     => INTEGER,
0032           Indexes      => CHARACTER,
0033           Lists        => ListOfIntegersIndexedByCharacters,
0034           PutElement   => PutInteger,
0035           PutIndex     => ADA.TEXT_IO.PUT,
0036           SortRelation => "<");
0037    use IntegerList;
```

The instantiation is comparable with the instantiations of generic packages such as ADA.TEXT_IO.INTEGER_IO, which have been presented throughout the book. This instantiation requires six parameters. The three data type parameters with the formal names *Elements*, *Indexes* and *Lists* are matched with the types INTEGER,

CHARACTER and *ListOfIntegersIndexedByCharacters* in the same way as these types were used to instantiate the generic *Search* procedure above.

The three subprogram formal parameters with the names *PutElement*, *PutIndex* and *SortRelation* also have to be matched as part of the instantiation. For *PutIndex* a procedure with a single *in only* parameter of the *Indexes* type is required. The *Indexes* type in this instantiation is CHARACTER and the standard package ADA.TEXT_IO provides a PUT procedure which requires a single *in only* parameter of type CHARACTER. Consequently this subprogram can be supplied as the actual parameter to match the *PutIndex* formal parameter.

Unfortunately it is not possible to use the *IntegerIO* PUT procedure as the actual parameter to match the *PutElement* subprogram. The element type in this instantiation is INTEGER and the actual parameter to match the formal *PutElement* procedure is a procedure which requires a single parameter of the INTEGER type. Although the *IntegerIO* PUT procedure takes an *in only* INTEGER parameter it also takes a second, optional, parameter called WIDTH. This disparity between the required signature of the formal subprogram parameter and the *IntegerIO* PUT procedure is sufficient to prevent it being used in the instantiation.

Instead a locally declared procedure called *PutInteger*, whose definition follows, is used. This procedure is implemented solely to provide a procedure to output an INTEGER whose signature exactly matches that required. A subprogram such as this, whose only role is to change the signature of an existing subprogram, is known as a ***skin subprogram***.

```
0024    procedure PutInteger( AnyInteger : in INTEGER ) is
0025    begin -- PutInteger
0026       IntegerIO.PUT( AnyInteger);
0027    end PutInteger;
```

The final subprogram parameter with the formal name *SortRelation* is used to determine the ordering of two elements when the list is sorted. The formal parameter is declared as a BOOLEAN function which requires two parameters of the *Elements* type. The *Elements* type in this instantiation is the pre-declared INTEGER type and the pre-declared INTEGER *less than* relational operator ("<") can be thought of as a BOOLEAN function, and is specified here as the actual parameter.

Having instantiated a new package, called *IntegerList*, it is brought into **use**. The program procedure of the test harness includes several calls to the instantiated *Put*, *Sort* and *Search* subprograms. The first part of the test harness, using the variable instance of *ListOfIntegersIndexedByCharacters* called *ListOfIntegers* declared as above, might be as follows:

```
0051    PUT_LINE( "Showing the list in its initial state");
0052    NEW_LINE;
```

634

```
0053    Put( ListOfIntegers );
0054    NEW_LINE( 2 );
0055    PUT( "Press enter to continue " );
0056    SKIP_LINE;
0057
0058    PUT_LINE( "Sorting and showing the list again" );
0059    NEW_LINE;
0060    Sort( ListOfIntegers );
0061    Put( ListOfIntegers );
0062    NEW_LINE( 2 );
0063    PUT( "Press enter to continue " );
0064    SKIP_LINE;
```

Assuming that the list has the same values as shown in the trace of the sort algorithm given above, the first call of the *IntegerList Put* procedure will produce the following output:

```
Showing the list in its initial state

Element at location A contains        64
Element at location B contains        78
Element at location C contains        12
Element at location D contains        91
Element at location E contains        34
```

After the list has been sorted the second showing of the list demonstrates that the list has been reordered into an ascending sequence:

```
Sorting and showing the list again

Element at location A contains        12
Element at location B contains        34
Element at location C contains        64
Element at location D contains        78
Element at location E contains        91
```

A small change to the instantiation will change the nature of the sorting. If the *greater than* relational operator (">") were specified instead of the less than relational operator in the instantiation, the list would be sorted in reversed order with the highest value first.

Finally, details of a second instantiation will be given. For this example a package which implements a list of books indexed by an enumeration type and ordered by their acquisition numbers will be instantiated. Only details relevant to the instantiation will be given; the adaptation of the test harness will be left as an end of chapter exercise.

```
0001    type Orderings is (First, Second, Third, Fourth, Fifth);
0002    package OrderingsIO is new
0003                    ADA.TEXT_IO.ENUMERATION_IO( Orderings);
0004    use OrderingsIO;
0005
0006    procedure PutOrdering( AnyPosition : in Orderings) is
0007    begin -- PutOrdering
0008       OrderingsIO.PUT( AnyPosition);
0009    end PutOrdering;
0010
0011
0012    type ListOfBooksIndexedByOrderings is array
0013                          (Orderings range <>) of BookItems;
0014    TheList : ListOfBooksIndexedByOrderings( Orderings);
0015
0016
0017    function LowerAquisitionNumber( ThisBook : in BookItems;
0018                                    ThatBook : in BookItems)
0019                                       return BOOLEAN is
0020    begin -- LowerAquisitionNumber
0021       return AquisitionNumberIs( ThisBook) <
0022              AquisitionNumberIs( ThatBook);
0023    end LowerAquisitionNumber;
0024
0025
0026    package BookList is new GenericList(
0027                    Elements => BookItems;
0028                    Indexes  => Orderings;
0029                    Lists    => ListOfBooksIndexedByOrderings;
0030                    PutElement => LibraryItem. ~ .Book.Put;
0031                    PutIndex   => PutOrdering;
0032                    SortRelation => LowerAquisitionNumber);
0033
0034
0035    procedure EnterDetailsOfBooks(
0036             AnyList : out ListOfBooksIndexedByOrderings) is
0037    begin -- EnterDetailsOfBooks
0038       for ThisBook in AnyList'RANGE loop
0039          PUT( "Please enter details of the");
0040          PUT( ThisBook); PUT_LINE( "Book.");
0041          Get( AnyList( ThisBook));
0042       end loop;
0043    end EnterDetailsOfBooks;
```

The type *Orderings* declared on line 0001 will be used as the index type of the array. An enumerated type is a ***discrete*** type and thus it is compatible with the *Indexes* generic formal data type parameter. The *PutIndex* generic formal subprogram parameter is matched by the locally declared **skin procedure** *PutOrdering* which changes the signature of the *OrderingsIO* PUT procedure.

The element type of the array is the *BookItems* type whose implementation has been described earlier in this section. Its output procedure, *Put*, has a signature which consists of a single **in only** *BookItems* parameter and thus is compatible with the *PutElement* generic formal subprogram parameter. The full name of this subprogram when it is specified as an actual parameter is abbreviated in line 0030 for the sake of clarity.

The array type *ListOfBooksIndexedByOrderings* is declared on lines 0012 and 0013 and is specified as an actual generic parameter on line 0029. The *SortRelation* function actual parameter, *LowerAquisitionNumber*, is declared locally on lines 0017 to 0023, making use of the *LibraryItem* enquiry function *AquisitionNumberIs*.

The instantiation of the generic package *GenericList* to produce a new package called *BookList* is accomplished on lines 0026 to 0032 making use of the types and subprograms as described above. Although a variable instance of the array type *ListOfBooksIndexedByOrderings*, called *TheList*, is declared on line 0014, no default value is specified for it. It would not be possible for a default value to be specified as the *BookItems* type is **private** and the constructor action would have to be used. Even if the *BookItems* type were **public**, it would be very cumbersome to specify a default value for the array, as values for each field of each book in the array would have to be stated. To allow an initial value to be supplied a procedure called *EnterDetailsOfBooks* has been declared on line 0035 which can be called by the test harness program procedure before the *BookList* *Put*, *Search* or *Sort* procedures are used.

The *LibraryList* hierarchy revisited

In Chapter 25 the *PartList* procedure of the *Listable* package could be used to output only those items in the list which satisfied a certain criterion. The criterion was expressed as a BOOLEAN function, but only a very limited set of functions could be used. A generic version of the *PartList* function would be able to use a larger number of BOOLEAN functions as the criterion making the facility more useful to the client program.

The data flow interface diagram and declaration of a suitable generic function for inclusion in the *LibraryList.Editable.Listable* package specification might be as follows:

```
-- Additional generic procedure for the
-- LibraryList.Editable.Listable package.
generic
   with function ListThis( AnyItem : TitledItems'CLASS)
                                            return BOOLEAN;
procedure ListSomeItems( TheList : in ListableLists'CLASS);
```

637

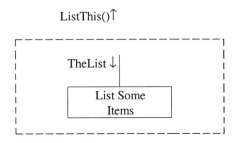

ListThis()↑

This generic procedure has been named *ListSomeItems* so that it can be included in the package with minimal confusion with the *PartList* procedure, although it would have been possible to overload *PartList* and name this procedure *PartList* as well. The formal name of the generic BOOLEAN function is *ListThis* and will be called to decide if each item in the list should be output.

The definition of the **generic** procedure is essentially identical to the definition of the *PartList* procedure and its implementation will be presented here without a design.

```
procedure ListSomeItems( TheList : in ListableLists'CLASS) is
begin -- ListSomeItems
   for ThisItem in StockItemsRange'FIRST ..
                    TheList.NumberOfItems loop
      if ListThis( TheList.Stock( ThisItem).all) then
         Put( TheList.Stock( ThisItem).all);
      end if;
   end loop;
end ListSomeItems;
```

Within a client program a suitable function will have to be declared, and subsequently defined, in order to instantiate the procedure. Assuming that the list menu of the *ListDemo* client has been extended to offer an option to list newspapers only, the additional code required to instantiate a suitable procedure called *ListNewspapers* might be as follows:

```
-- Additional code required to instantiate the ListSomeItems
-- generic procedure to list only newspapers.
function IsItemANewspaper( AnyItem : in TitledItems'CLASS)
                                            return BOOLEAN;

procedure ListNewspapers is new
            ListSomeItems( ListThis => IsItemANewspaper);

function IsItemANewspaper( AnyItem : in TitledItems'CLASS)
                                            return BOOLEAN is
```

```
begin -- IsItemANewspaper
    return AnyItem in NewspaperItems'CLASS;
end IsItemANewspaper;
```

The BOOLEAN function is called and its implementation makes use of the class membership **in** operator. The **in** operator will evaluate true if the object on the left hand side is one of the class of types specified on the right hand side. *IsItem-ANewspaper* will evaluate true if the *TitledItems'*CLASS parameter's type is of the *NewspaperItems* type, or any type derived from it by extension in the future.

Having instantiated the procedure *ListNewspapers*, it can be called from a branch of the **case** statement which forms the major part of the *ListTheItems* procedure.

```
when 'E' =>
    ListNewspapers( AnyList);
```

This instantiated procedure will be called when the user requests a list of newspapers, and it will iterate through the list calling the *IsItemANewspaper* function and only outputting those items which cause it to return true.

The use of the generic *ListSomeItems* procedure to output only some of the items stored in the list is clearly more cumbersome than using the original *PartList* procedure. However, the *ListSomeItems* procedure is capable of using a greater number of criteria than the *PartList* procedure and thus in most cases will be used.

EXERCISES

27.1 The *Sort* algorithm used in this chapter uses an *InsertionSort* algorithm. There are other possible algorithms which could have been used, for example a *BubbleSort*, *QuickSort* or *HeapSort*. Find out how these algorithms work and develop a generic subprogram for them using the development techniques suggested in this chapter.

27.2 The generic package developed in this chapter supplied the *SortRelation* as a generic parameter of the package. Reimplement this package to make the *SortRelation* a generic parameter of the *Sort* procedure. This will allow the same procedure to be used to sort into both ascending and descending sequences. This implementation will then have a generic subprogram within a generic package requiring a double instantiation; the first instantiation will instantiate a package, which contains a generic subprogram which requires a second instantiation.

27.3 Revisit the *LibraryLists* client program and extend the list menu to allow additional partial lists to be produced. This will require additional classification functions to be implemented and suitable *ListSomeItems* procedures to be instantiated.

27.4 The instantiation of the *GenericList* package as a list of books might suggest that this could be used as the basis of the list of *LibraryList* from previous chapters. Investigate this possibility: is it feasible to reimplement the entire *LibraryList* hierarchy based upon an instantiation of this package?

27.5 The production of the list of books in this chapter and Exercises 24.3, 25.2 and 26.2 have suggested that there is much more in common between the *LibraryLists* and *MemberLists* hierarchies. Review the code which implements these two hierarchies, using the techniques suggested in this chapter, and attempt to determine which generic parameters might be required.

CHAPTER 28

Homogeneous generic hierarchies

The generic facilities which were introduced in the previous chapter can be combined with the extendible data type hierarchies from the previous chapters to produce a hierarchy which can be instantiated with different data types, combining the advantages of both facilities. This chapter will provide an introduction to the design and implementation of generic hierarchies. To do so a very basic homogeneous ordered generic list will be designed and developed.

The homogeneous generic list class hierarchy

The class diagram of the hierarchy which will be developed in this chapter is as follows:

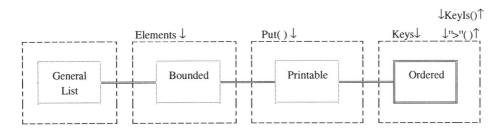

This hierarchy is somewhat similar to the *LibraryList* hierarchy which was introduced in Chapter 25. The details of the changes in the design reflect the requirement to produce a generic hierarchy, where the precise data types of the elements which will be stored in the list are not known until it is instantiated.

The base type of the hierarchy, *GeneralLists*, is shown as a generic package which does not require any generic parameters. The reasons for this will be made clear later in this chapter. The packages *Bounded*, *Printable* and *Ordered* are shown as requiring generic parameters, using the notation for generic instantiation which was introduced in the previous chapter. Details of the nature of these generic parameters will be given in the appropriate section below.

The abstract *GeneralLists* type

As with the *LibraryList* structure which was developed in Chapter 25, an abstract base type providing only minimal facilities is required. This package is generic, although it requires no generic parameters, as it will be extended to provide other generic packages. An Ada implementation rule requires that generic extensions can only be made from generic packages. The *GeneralList* package provides the basic support operations which are required for all lists, but does not provide any support for lists containing elements of any specific type. The object diagram for the *GeneralLists* type is as follows:

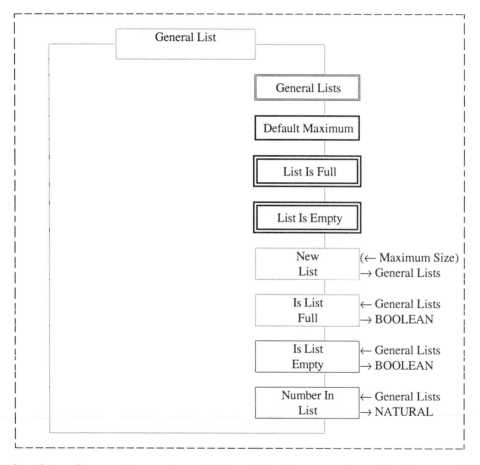

The object diagram is **generic** as indicated by the outer bounding box, and is **abstract** as indicated by the dotted outline. There are two **abstract** subprograms, *NewList* and *IsListFull*, and two non-abstract subprograms, *IsListEmpty* and *NumberInlist*.

The two abstract actions in this design do not have comparable actions in the *LibraryList* package. The *NumberInList* function returns the number of elements which are currently stored in the list, and the *NewList* function returns a new empty list which, for a bounded list only, has a limit on the number of elements which it can contain. This limitation is expressed as an optional parameter which can be omitted for an unbounded list. The package specification for this design is as follows:

```
0001    -- Filename GeneralList_.pkg (k8 general1.ads).
0002    -- Base type of a Generic list hierarchy.
0003    --
0004    -- Written for Ada book Section IV Chapter 28.
0005    -- Fintan Culwin, v0.1, Jan 1997.
0006
0007
0008    generic
0009    package GeneralList is
0010
0011        type GeneralLists is abstract tagged private;
0012
0013        DefaultMaximum := 0;
0014
0015        ListIsFull  : exception;
0016        ListIsEmpty : exception;
0017
0018        function NewList
0                (MaximumListSize : in NATURAL := DefaultMaximum)
0019                                    return GeneralLists is abstract;
0020
0021        function IsListFull( AnyList: in GeneralLists)
0022                                    return BOOLEAN is abstract;
0023
0024        function IsListEmpty( AnyList: in GeneralLists'CLASS)
0025                                        return BOOLEAN;
0026
0027        function NumberInList( AnyList : in GeneralLists'CLASS)
0028                                        return NATURAL;
0029
0030    private
0031
0032        type GeneralLists is tagged
0033        record
0034            NumberOfElements : NATURAL := 0;
0035        end record;
0036
0037    end GeneralList;
```

The *IsListFull* function is declared **abstract** as a future refinement to the hierarchy will introduce a fundamental division between bounded and unbounded lists. Bounded lists have a limit on the number of items which they can contain and thus can become full. Unbounded lists do not have such a limitation and thus can never become full. Each division will have to implement an *IsListFull* function before any non-abstract types can be declared. In the case of bounded lists this will be an actual implementation, but for unbounded lists a dummy implementation which always returns false, as an additional element can always be added, will be supplied.

The *NewList* function is declared **abstract** for a similar reason. When a bounded list is declared a limit upon the size of the list has to be specified, but an unbounded list will have no such limit. To accommodate this difference the default value of the *MaximumSize* of the list is specified as zero. An unbounded list will take no notice of this parameter and a new list can be created without supplying an actual parameter. It is also possible to create a new bounded list without specifying a *MaximumSize* although the list produced will only be able to contain zero items, and as such will not be of any practical use.

The reason why these **abstract** functions have been introduced at this place in the hierarchy is to allow a client program to be changed between a bounded and an unbounded list with minimal disruption. The declaration of an abstract subprogram provides a promise to the client that an actual subprogram conforming to the specification will be supplied for every non-abstract data type in the fully developed hierarchy. Thus a client can be constructed on the basis of these promises without being concerned with the eventual non-abstract list type which will be used.

The other two non-abstract class wide subprograms, *IsListEmpty* and *NumberInList*, are simple to implement in the package body. Both use the *NumberOfElements* component of the *GeneralLists* **record** to return an appropriate result. As class wide subprograms, this is the only place in the hierarchy where they can be declared, and no overriding declarations will be allowed in any child package. The *GeneralList* package body will not be presented; details of how it can be obtained are located in Appendix A.

The abstract *BoundedLists* type

The generic *Bounded* package introduces the abstract *BoundedLists* data type. A refinement to the hierarchy can introduce a sibling *UnBoundedLists* data type. This generic package requires instantiation with an *Elements* type which defines the specific type which will be stored in the list. The object diagram for this package is as follows:

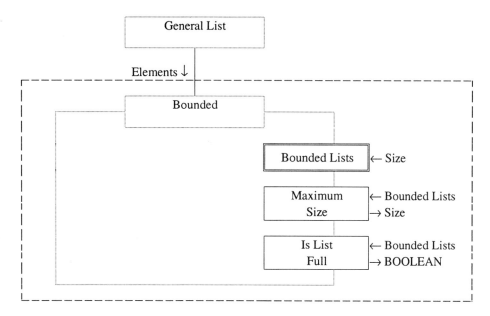

The *BoundedLists* data type exported by this package is shown on the design as requiring a parameter. This is a facility of **record** data type declarations which has not been previously introduced. Details of the technique which allows this and the reasons why it is being used here will be given below.

The two actions introduced by this package are both related to the bounded nature of the list. The function *IsListFull* can be used to determine if the list is full, and *MaximumSize* will return the number of elements which a particular list can contain. The implementation of this design as a package specification might be as follows:

```
0001    -- Filename GeneralList.Bounded_.pkg (k8 geneboun.ads).
0002    -- Extension to provide base type for bounded lists.
0003    --
0004    -- Written for Ada book Section IV Chapter 28.
0005    -- Fintan Culwin, v0.1, Jan 1997.
0006
0007    generic
0008       type Elements is private;
0009    package GeneralList.Bounded is
0010
0011       type BoundedLists( Size : in POSITIVE) is
0012                         abstract new GeneralLists with private;
0013
0014       function MaximumSize( AnyList : in BoundedLists'CLASS)
0015                                               return POSITIVE;
0016
```

```
0017        function IsListFull( AnyList : in BoundedLists)
0018                                              return BOOLEAN;
0019
0020    private
0021
0022        type ElementArrays is array (POSITIVE range <>) of
                                                          Elements;
0023
0024        type BoundedLists( Size : POSITIVE) is
0025                           abstract new GeneralLists with
0026        record
0027          Elements : ElementArrays( 1 .. Size);
0028        end record;
0029
0030    end GeneralList.Bounded;
```

The declaration of the *IsListFull* function in this package completes the promise made in the parent package specification by the declaration of the **abstract** *IsListFull* function. This function cannot be declared with a class wide parameter as this would introduce a potential ambiguity. The abstract declaration, in *GeneralList*, was declared with a class wide parameter and if this function were also declared with a class wide *BoundedLists'*CLASS parameter, then the *BoundedLists* child types would not know which of the two functions to use. By declaring this version with a specific parameter it will be inherited by all *BoundedLists* child data types and a binding to this implementation will be made at the time of compilation. The *MaximumSize* function is declared, and defined, class wide at this level in the hierarchy and thus will be available to all *Bounded-Lists* child types.

The *private* part of the package specification declares an unconstrained array type called *ElementArrays* whose index type is POSITIVE and whose element type is of the generic parameter *Elements*. The extension to the *GeneralLists* type, producing the *BoundedLists* type, adds a constrained instance of this array. The precise upper bound of this array is determined when an instance of the record is declared and is specified by the *Size* parameter of the record declaration. Thus, assuming that simple instances of this record could be declared, the following declarations would produce records, whose array components would have the following attributes:

Declaration	'FIRST	'LAST	'LENGTH
Demo1 : BoundedLists (Size => 10);	1	10	10
Demo2 : BoundedLists (100);	1	100	100
Demo3 : BoundedLists (Size => 1);	1	1	1
Demo4 : BoundedLists (Size => 0);	1	0	0

The table indicates that the declaration can specify the parameter in positional or named notation; however, it is advised that when this facility is used named notation should be favoured in the interests of clarity. A record whose structure can change, depending upon the value of a parameter supplied upon declaration, is known as a **variant record** and as its size may be unknown until it is declared it is another example of an **unconstrained data type**. The data structure diagram for this record type includes the parameter to indicate that it is a variant type; the use of noun phrases within the data structure diagram and the absence of a connecting line at the top of the diagram prevent any confusion with program structure diagrams.

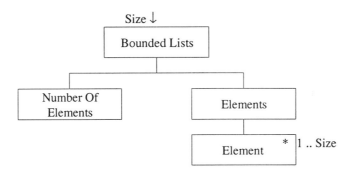

The advantage of this facility in this situation is that the size of a particular bounded list, declared from an instantiation of the generic package, can be exactly tailored to the client's requirements. This should be compared with the *Library-Lists* from Chapter 25 which placed an arbitrary, unchangeable, limit upon the size of the list.

The implementation of the *MaximumSize* function, in the package body, uses the LENGTH attribute to determine the number of elements which can be stored in the array component of the *NumberOfElements* component to determine if all locations in the array are currently in use. The implementation of these functions in the package body might be as follows:

```
0010    function MaximumSize( AnyList : in BoundedLists'CLASS)
0011                                        return POSITIVE is
0012    begin -- MaximumSize
0013       return AnyList.Elements'LENGTH;
0014    end MaximumSize;
0015
0016    function IsListFull( AnyList : in BoundedLists)
0017                                        return BOOLEAN is
0018    begin -- IsListFull
0019       return AnyList.NumberOfElements = AnyList.Elements'LENGTH;
0020    end IsListFull;
```

The instantiation of this package will be described when the generic hierarchy has been extended to include a non-abstract type.

The abstract *PrintableLists* type

This generic extension to the *BoundedLists* introduces no additional data attributes but adds a facility for the contents of the list to be output. It requires a generic subprogram parameter upon instantiation, which itself will take an ***in only*** parameter of the generic *Elements* type. The object diagram for this package is as follows:

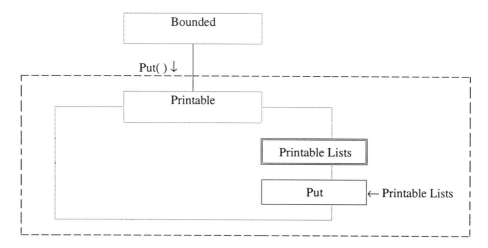

The implementation of this design as a generic package specification might be as follows:

```
0001    -- Filename GeneralList.Bounded.Printable_.pkg (k8
                                               geboupri.ads).
0002    -- Extension to provide printable bounded lists.
0003    --
0004    -- Written for Ada book Section IV Chapter 28.
0005    -- Fintan Culwin, v0.1, Jan 1997.
0006
0007    generic
0008       with procedure Put( AnElement : in Elements) is <>;
0009    package GeneralList.Bounded.Printable is
0010
0011       type PrintableLists is abstract new BoundedLists with
                                                           private;
0012
```

```
0013        procedure Put( AnyList : in PrintableLists'CLASS);
0014
0015   private
0016
0017      type PrintableLists is abstract new BoundedLists
0018                                       with null record;
0018
0019   end GeneralList.Bounded.Printable;
```

The design and implementation of the *PrintableLists Put* procedure in the package body will be presented as they consolidate the understanding of the extended data structure, prior to the introduction of the *Ordered* extension which will manipulate the structure extensively. The design and implementation of the *PrintableList Put* procedure might be as follows:

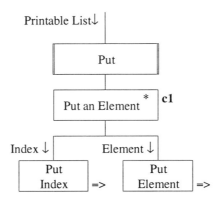

c1: For all elements in use.

```
0010   procedure Put( AnyList : in PrintableLists'CLASS) is
0011   begin -- Put
0012      for ThisElement in AnyList.Elements'FIRST ..
0013                              AnyList.NumberOfElements loop
0014         PUT( "Location "); PUT( ThisElement, WIDTH =>3);
0015         PUT( "Contains ");
0016         Put( AnyList.Elements( ThisElement));
0017         NEW_LINE;
0018      end loop;
0019   end Put;
```

The basis of the design and implementation is to iterate through all elements of the array which are indicated to be in use by the value of the component *Number-OfElements*. On each iteration the value of the index is output, using the PUT procedure supplied by an instantiation of the INTEGER_IO generic package, followed by the value of the element, using the *Put* procedure supplied as a generic parameter.

The non-abstract *OrderedLists* type

The final package in this initial version of the hierarchy introduces a generic non-abstract *OrderedLists* data type. The *Keys* data type generic parameter is used to determine the ordering of the elements within the list; it is specified as a **private** generic parameter which will only allow assignment, equality and inequality operations within the package body. In order to allow relational testing a greater than relational operator ("`>`") is specified which can be used to determine the ordering of two *Elements* values according to their keys. For this function to be used in the package it needs to have some mechanism for determining the key value of an element, and the *KeyIs* function is specified for this purpose.

The key values are used to identify uniquely an element within the list and because of this no duplicate key values are allowed. To instantiate the package the *Keys* data type, a function whose formal name is *KeyIs*, and a greater than ("`>`") relational operator function will be required as generic parameters. The object diagram for this package is as follows:

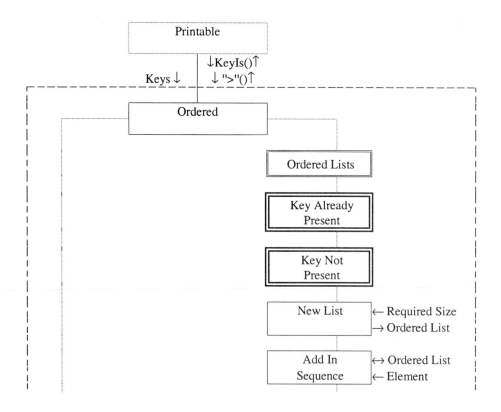

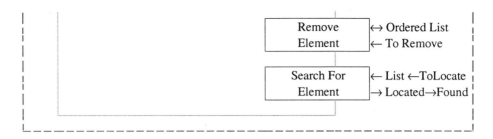

The *KeyAlreadyPresent* exception will be raised, when *AddInSequence* is called, if an attempt is made to add an element whose key is equal to the key of an element already in the list. The *KeyNotPresent* exception will be raised, when *Remove-Element* is called, if an attempt is made to remove an element whose key value is not found in the list. It is expected that the *SearchForElement* procedure will be called before either of these procedures in order to ensure that the exception will not be raised. *AddInSequence* should only be called if *SearchForElement* indicates that the element is not present and *RemoveElement* should only be called if *SearchForElement* indicates that the element is present. However, the procedures are implemented defensively and might raise the exceptions as noted above.

The final subprogram exported from the package is *NewList* which has to be present for the promise made by the **abstract** *NewList* function declaration in the base package *GeneralList* to be honoured by every non-abstract class. The implementation of this design as a package specification might be as follows:

```
0001    -- Filename GeneralList.Bounded.Printable.Ordered_pkg
0002    -- (k8 gebopror.ads). Extension to produce a unique ordered
                                                              list.
0003    --
0004    -- Written for Ada book Section IV Chapter 28.
0005    -- Fintan Culwin, v0.1, Jan 1997.
0006
0007    generic
0008       type Keys is private;
0009       with function KeyIs( AnyElement : in Elements) return
                                                              Keys;
0010       with function ">"
                         ( ThisKey : in Keys;
0011                       ThatKey : in Keys) return BOOLEAN is <>;
0012    package GeneralList.Bounded.Printable.Ordered is
0013
0014       type OrderedLists is new PrintableLists with private;
0015
0016       KeyAlreadyPresent : exception;
0017       KeyNotPresent     : exception;
0018
```

651

```
0019        function NewList
                    ( RequiredSize : in NATURAL := DefaultMaximum)
0020                                            return OrderedLists;
0021
0022        procedure AddInSequence
                        ( AnyList    : in out OrderedLists'CLASS;
0023                      NewElement : in Elements);
0024
0025        procedure RemoveElement
                        ( AnyList  : in out OrderedLists'CLASS;
0026                      ToRemove : in     Keys);
0027
0028        procedure SearchForElement
                        (AnyList      : in  OrderedLists'CLASS;
0029                     ToLocate     : in  Keys;
0030                     Located      : out BOOLEAN;
0031                     ElementFound : out Elements);
0032
0033    private
0034
0035        type OrderedLists is new PrintableLists with null record;
0036
0037    end GeneralList.Bounded.Printable.Ordered;
```

The *NewList* function, in the body of the package, creates and returns an instance of the *OrderedLists* data type. The *OrderedLists* type is a child type of the variant *BoundedLists* type and as such is itself variant; it thus requires a parameter when an instance is declared which delimits the size of the array. The parameter used in the record declaration is the *MaximumListSize* parameter of the *NewList* function. The implementation of this function might be as follows:

```
0010    function NewList
                    ( MaximumListSize : in NATURAL := DefaultMaximum)
0011                                            return OrderedLists is
0012
0013        LocalList : OrderedLists( Size => MaximumListSize);
0014
0015    begin -- NewList
0016        return LocalList;
0017    end NewList;
```

The *AddInSequence* procedure has the following design and implementation:

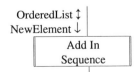

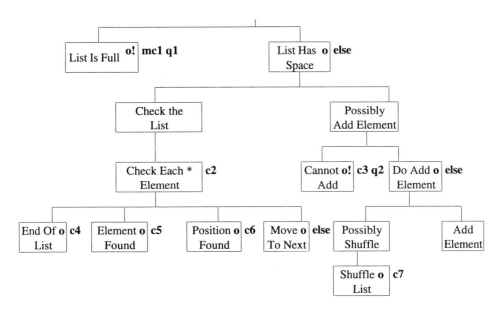

c1: If the list is already full.

c2: While position not located and list not exhausted and element not located.

c3: If element is already present.

c4: If all elements checked.

c5: If key of current element in list is equal to key of new element.

c6: If key of new element is greater than key of current element in list.

c7: If location to insert not at end of list.

q1: Raise explicit ListIsFull exception.

q2: Raise explicit KeyAlreadyPresent exception.

```
0020     procedure AddInSequence
                         ( AnyList    : in out KeyedLists'CLASS;
0021                       NewElement : in Elements) is
0022
0023         ThisElement      : POSITIVE := AnyList.TheElements'FIRST;
0024         PositionLocated  : BOOLEAN := FALSE;
0025         ListIsExhausted  : BOOLEAN := FALSE;
0026         AlreadyPresent   : BOOLEAN := FALSE;
0027
0028     begin -- AddInSequence
0029         if IsListFull( AnyList) then
0030             raise ListIsFull;
0031         else
0032             while not PositionLocated and
0033                   not ListIsExhausted and
0034                   not AlreadyPresent  loop
0035                 if ThisElement > AnyList.NumberOfElements then
0036                     ListIsExhausted := TRUE;
```

653

```
0037            elsif KeyIs( NewElement ) =
0038                   KeyIs(AnyList.TheElements( ThisElement)) then
0039                AlreadyPresent := TRUE;
0040            elsif KeyIs(AnyList.TheElements( ThisElement)) >
0041                                          KeyIs(NewElement) then
0042                PositionLocated := TRUE;
0043            else
0044                ThisElement := ThisElement +1;
0045            end if;
0046        end loop;
0047
0048        if AlreadyPresent then
0049            raise KeyAlreadyPresent;
0050        else
0051            if not ListIsExhausted then
0052                AnyList.TheElements( ThisElement +1 ..
0053                                    AnyList.NumberOfElements +1)
0054                :=  AnyList.TheElements( ThisElement ..
0055                                    AnyList.NumberOfElements);
0056            end if;
0057            AnyList.TheElements( ThisElement) := NewElement;
0058            AnyList.NumberOfElements :=
0059                                    AnyList.NumberOfElements +1;
0059        end if;
0060    end if;
0061 end AddInSequence;
```

The basis of the algorithm is, assuming that the list is not full, to examine the entire list looking for the correct location for the *NewElement* using the relational operator supplied as a generic parameter. If during this examination an element already in the list with a *KeyValue* equal to that of the *NewElement* is discovered, a flag is set which will terminate the loop and cause a *KeyAlreadyPresent* exception to be raised. Should this not happen there are two possibilities following the loop: either the *NewElement* should be added at the end of the list or part of the list has to be shuffled up to make space for the *NewElement*. Once the *NewElement* has been added to the list the *NumberOfElements* component is incremented to reflect the new size of the list.

The design and implementation of the *RemoveElement* procedure might be as follows:

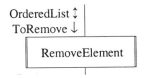

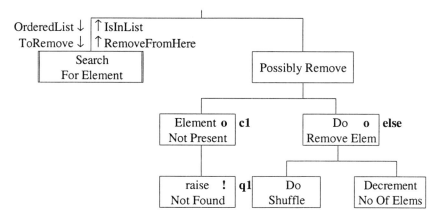

c1: If element is not located by the search.　　　　**q1**: Raise explicit KeyNotPresent exception.

```
0064    procedure RemoveElement( AnyList  : in out KeyedLists'CLASS;
0065                             ToRemove : in Keys) is
0066
0067       RemoveFromHere : POSITIVE;
0068       IsInList       : BOOLEAN := FALSE;
0069
0070    begin -- RemoveElement
0071       SearchForElement( AnyList, ToRemove, IsInList,
                                                   RemoveFromHere)
0072
0073       if not IsInList then
0074          raise KeyNotPresent;
0075       else
0076          AnyList.TheElements( RemoveFromHere ..
0077                                  AnyList.NumberOfElements -1)
0078              := AnyList.TheElements( RemoveFromHere +1 ..
0079                                  AnyList.NumberOfElements);
0080          AnyList.NumberOfElements := AnyList.NumberOfElements -1;
0081       end if;
0082    end RemoveElement;
```

The basis of this algorithm is somewhat similar to the *AddInSequence* procedure above. The list is first examined looking for an element whose key value is equal to that of the key *ToRemove*. If the element has been located the list is shuffled down one position to overwrite the element to be removed. Following this the *Number-OfElements* component is decremented to reflect the new size of the list. If an element whose key value matches the key value to be removed is not found in the list the *KeyNotPresent* exception is raised.

The final subprogram in the package body is the *SearchForElement* procedure, whose design and implementation are based closely upon other searching algorithms which have been presented in previous chapters and upon the two other subprograms in this package, which have already been explained. The design and implementation might be as follows:

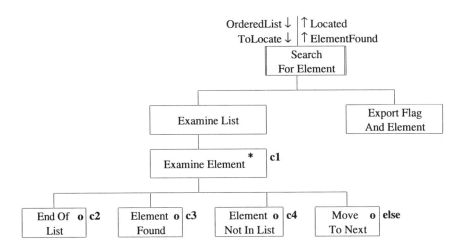

c1: While list not completely checked and element sought not found and element is not known not to be present.

c2: If all elements checked.

c2: If key value of element in list equal to key sought.

c3: If key of element in list greater than key sought.

c4: If key of current element greater than key being sought.

```
0099    procedure SearchForElement
                        ( AnyList      : in KeyedLists'CLASS;
0100                      ToLocate     : in Keys;
0101                      Located      : out BOOLEAN;
0102                      ElementFound : out Elements) is
0103
0104    ThisElement     : NATURAL := AnyList.TheElements'FIRST;
0105    HasBeenFound    : BOOLEAN := FALSE;
0106    IsNotInList     : BOOLEAN := FALSE;
0107    ListIsExhausted : BOOLEAN := FALSE;
0108
0109    begin -- SearchForElement
0110      while not HasBeenFound    and
0111            not ListIsExhausted and
0112            not IsNotInList     loop
0113        if ThisElement > AnyList.NumberOfElements then
0114          ListIsExhausted := TRUE;
0115        elsif KeyIs(AnyList.TheElements( ThisElement)) =
0116                                          ToLocate then
0117          HasBeenFound := TRUE;
```

```
0118            elsif KeyIs(AnyList.TheElements( ThisElement)) >
0119                                           ToLocate then
0120               IsNotInList := TRUE;
0121            else
0122               ThisElement := ThisElement +1;
0123            end if;
0124         end loop;
0125         Located := HasBeenFound;
0126         ElementFound := AnyList.TheElements( ThisElement);
0127      end SearchForElement;
```

Instantiating and using the hierarchy

The declaration of the non-abstract *OrderedLists* generic type allows the hierarchy to be instantiated and used by a client. This part of the chapter will give two example instantiations: the first instantiation will provide a list of integer values and a test harness to exercise it; the second instantiation will illustrate the use of a more complex *Elements* type.

The hierarchy requires five generic parameters for complete instantiation. These are the *Elements* type to be stored in the list, an output procedure for the *Elements* type, the *Keys* type, a function which returns the key value of an element and a function requiring two parameters of the *Elements* type which returns true if the key of the first element is greater than that of the second, and false otherwise. To prepare for the instantiation all of these parameters will have to be identified and/ or declared.

To instantiate the *GenericList* hierarchy for a list of INTEGER values the *Element* type is INTEGER. The output procedure will have to be a developer declared procedure, as the signature of the *IntegerIOPut* procedure contains an optional WIDTH parameter and, as it does not exactly match the required signature, cannot be used. The *Keys* generic type is also INTEGER and the *KeyIs* function will simply return the INTEGER value of the INTEGER parameter supplied. The greater than (">") function will be matched with the pre-declared INTEGER greater than function, and it need not be explicitly specified as the signature and name of the pre-declared function match those of the generic parameter.

The first part of the test harness client, *IntegerOrderedListDemo*, declares and defines the necessary subprograms prior to the instantiation of the hierarchy.

```
0001   -- Filename IntegerOrderedListDemo.ada (k8 integero.adb).
0002   -- First demonstration instantiation of the OrderedList
0003   -- generic hierarchy with INTEGER values.
0004   --
0005   -- Produced for Ada book Section IV Chapter 28.
```

```
0006    -- Fintan Culwin, v0.1, Jan 1997.
0007
0008    with ADA.TEXT_IO,
0009         GeneralList.Bounded.Printable.Ordered;
0010
0011    procedure IntegerOrderedListDemo is
0012
0013       package IntegerIO is new ADA.TEXT_IO.INTEGER_IO( INTEGER);
0014
0015       procedure PutInteger( AnyInteger : in INTEGER ) is
0016       begin -- PutInteger
0017          IntegerIO.PUT( AnyInteger);
0018       end PutInteger;
0019
0020       function IntegerKeyIs( AnyInteger : in INTEGER)
0021                                           return INTEGER is
0022       begin -- IntegerKeyIs
0023          return AnyInteger;
0024       end IntegerKeyIs;
```

Once these subprograms have been declared the instantiation of the hierarchy can commence. The base package in the hierarchy, *GeneralList*, is a generic package which requires instantiation even though it has no generic parameters. This is followed by the instantiation of the *BoundedList* package using INTEGER as the *Elements* actual parameter.

```
0026       package GeneralIntegerList is new GeneralList;
0027       use GeneralIntegerList;
0028
0029       package BoundedIntegerList is
0030          new GeneralIntegerList.Bounded( Elements => INTEGER);
0031       use BoundedIntegerList;
```

The first instantiation creates an instance of the **generic** *GeneralList* package called *GeneralIntegerList*; it is this instantiated package which is subsequently used as the package from which the bounded list will be instantiated, and not the *GeneralList* package itself.

The second instantiation creates a new instance of the *GeneralList.Bounded* package, called *BoundedIntegerList*. The *BoundedLists* data type within the new package is capable of storing INTEGER values. However, as this is an instantiation of an **abstract** data type, it is itself **abstract** and thus no variables of the *BoundedIntegerList.BoundedLists* type can be declared.

The third required instantiation is of the *Printable* package. As with the instantiation of the *Bounded* package, the *Printable* package which is to be instantiated is the child package of the already instantiated *BoundedIntegerList*, and not the child of the non-instantiated *Bounded* package. The instantiation requires the output procedure, *PutInteger*, as an actual generic subprogram procedure and can be accomplished as follows:

```
0032
0033     package PrintableIntegerList is
0034         new BoundedIntegerList.Printable( Put => PutInteger );
0035     use PrintableIntegerList
```

Likewise the final instantiation, of the *OrderedIntegerList* package, requires that the *Ordered* package, which is the child of the already instantiated *PrintableIntegerList*, be specified as the package to instantiate from. The instantiation need not explicitly specify an actual generic parameter to match the greater than ("$>$") formal function parameter, as the formal parameter was specified as accepting a default (**is** <>) and a suitable pre-declared INTEGER greater than function is visible. The instantiation can be accomplished as follows:

```
0036
0037     package OrderedIntegerList is
0038         new PrintableIntegerList( Keys => INTEGER,
0039                                   KeyIs => IntegerKeyIs );
0040     use OrderedIntegerList;
```

Once the hierarchy is instantiated an instance of the *OrderedLists* data type is declared:

```
0041
0042   IntegerList : OrderedLists := NewList( Size => 10);
```

The *OrderedLists* data type on line 0042 is from the instantiated package *OrderedIntegerList* and could have the qualified name *OrderedIntegerList.OrderedLists*. If there were more than one instantiated *OrderedList* package in **use** within a client there would be more than one possible *OrderedLists* type and the qualified name would have to be explicitly stated in order to disambiguate them.

The *OrderedLists* data type is an instantiated extended version of the *BoundedLists* data type in the *Bounded* package and as such it is a variant record and the size of the list which it contains has to be specified upon declaration. This can best be accomplished by a call to the *NewList* function which is declared **abstract** in the *GeneralList* package and actually declared in the *Bounded* package. The effect is to create a variable called *IntegerList* which is capable of containing up to ten integer values. It would have been possible to declare a list counting the default number of elements by calling *NewList* without a parameter, as in

```
   IntegerList : OrderedLists := NewList;
```

However, this list will be able to contain a maximum of zero elements, and as such will be of no practical use. Once a list has been created the program procedure can use it in a series of tests designed to demonstrate that the implementation of the subprograms in the generic hierarchy is correct. The first part of the program procedure might be as follows:

```
0044   begin -- IntegerOrderedListDemo
0045      SET_COL( 20);
0046      PUT_LINE( "Integer Ordered list demonstration program ");
0047      NEW_LINE( 2);
0048
0049      PUT_LINE( "Filling the list with ten integers");
0050      for ThisInteger in reverse 20 .. 29 loop
0051         AddInSequence( IntegerList, ThisInteger);
0052      end loop
0053
0054      NEW_LINE( 2);
0055      PUT_LINE( "The list now contains ");
0056      PUT( IntegerList);
0057
0058      NEW_LINE( 2);
0059      if IsListFull( IntegerList) then
0060         PUT_LINE( "The list is full, which is correct.");
0061      else
0062         PUT_LINE( "The list is not full, which is not correct);
0063      end if;
0064
0065      -- Other tests omitted.
0066
0067   end IntegerOrderedListDemo;
```

This part of the program procedure should first output a list containing the integer values 20 to 29 inclusive in ascending sequence, following which it should indicate that the list is full. The values are added in an inverted sequence, by use of the **reverse** option in the **for** loop, but are stored in their *KeyIs* determined sequence causing them to be stored and output in the correct sequence.

This program procedure could continue by conducting a series of automated tests on the instantiated *OrderedLists* type. Once the testing is successfully completed then the generic hierarchy can be assumed to be correct and any further instantiations would not require such extensive testing. The essential functionality of the list could be assumed to be correct on the basis of this testing and all that would be required for further instantiations would be a quick check to make sure that the *Elements* type, *Elements* output procedure, *Keys* type, *KeyIs* and greater than ("greater than ("">"") functions had been correctly specified. This could be accomplished by declaring a small list, adding at least two elements to it in the reverse of their key determined sequence and then outputting the list. If the result is as expected, that is a list of two element values in their key determined sequence, then testing of the remaining functionality of the list would not be required.

Likewise if the hierarchy is extended at any stage in the future then retesting of the existing parts of the hierarchy would not be required. However, if an automated test harness conforming to an established test rationale is available then retesting of the existing version would not be expensive, and the additional confidence which it provides might be useful.

A second instantiation

A second, more realistic, instantiation of the hierarchy will be briefly presented. This instantiation will be supported by a package called *DailyAppointment* whose extendible type, *DailyAppointments*, will allow a date and details of an appointment to be modelled. A very simplified object diagram and package specification for this requirement might be as follows:

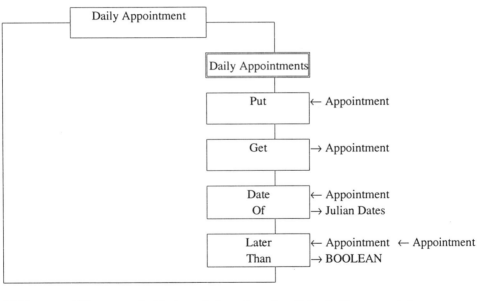

```
0001   -- Filename DailyAppointment_.pkg (k8 dailyapp.ads).
0002   -- Simple extendible EDT for a dated appointment
0003   -- to illustrate instantiation of an ordered list.
0004   --
0005   -- Produced for Ada book Section IV Chapter 28.
0006   -- Fintan Culwin, v0.1, Jan 1997.
0007
0008   with JulianDate;
```

```
0009    use  JulianDate;
0010
0011    package DailyAppointment is
0012
0013       type DailyAppointments is tagged private;
0014
0015       procedure Put( Appointment : in DailyAppointments );
0016
0017       procedure Get( Appointment : out DailyAppointments );
0018
0019       function DateOf
0020                 ( AnyAppointment : in DailyAppointments'CLASS )
                                                  return JulianDates;
0021
0022       function LaterThan(
0023                  ThisAppointment : in DailyAppointments'CLASS;
0024                  ThatAppointment : in DailyAppointments'CLASS )
0025                                              return BOOLEAN;
0026
0027    private
0028
0029       -- Private details omitted.
0030
0031    end DailyAppointment;
```

Assuming that this package is **with**ed and **use**d by a client program the instantiation of the generic *OrderedList* package for *DailyAppointments* can be accomplished as follows:

```
0024    package GeneralAppointmentList is new GeneralList;
0025
0026    package BoundedAppointmentList is
0027        new GeneralAppointmentList.Bounded(
0028                            Elements => DailyAppointments );
0029    use BoundedAppointmentList;
0030
0031    package PrintableAppointmentList is
0032        new BoundedAppointmentList.Printable(
0033                            Put => DailyAppointment.Put );
0034    use PrintableAppointmentList;
0035
0036    package OrderedAppointmentList is
0037        new PrintableAppointmentList.Ordered(
0038                            Keys  => JulianDates;
0039                            KeyIs => DateOf;
0040                            ">"   => LaterThan );
0041    use OrderedAppointmentList;
```

When the hierarchy is instantiated a demonstration test harness can be constructed using the same techniques as were used for the previous instantiation.

EXERCISES

28.1 Develop a complete test plan for the generic list and use it formally to test the integer instantiation.

28.2 Use the test plan from Exercise 28.1 to test the appointments instantiation. How much of the retesting is actually necessary given that the integer instantiation has already been tested?

28.3 Instantiate, and test, the hierarchy to store a list of *BookItems*.

28.4 The *AddInSequence* action will raise a *KeyAlreadyPresent* exception if an attempt is made to add an element which has the same key as an element already stored in the list. As this should not be regarded as an exceptional occurrence, what possible design changes could be made to allow a client of the hierarchy to avoid raising the exception?

SECTION V

Algorithms, Metrics, Testing and Production

CHAPTER 29

Algorithms and programming by contract

The previous sections of this book have largely concentrated upon *programming in the large*, the development of software by the construction of a number of independent modules which are subsequently collected together to produce an application. This section of the book will turn its attention to *programming in the small* by concentrating upon the categorization and analysis of the individual algorithms which are used within modules.

The overall quality of software is dependent upon effective design and construction techniques in both scales of construction. There are a number of techniques which can be used to ensure that at the smallest scale, effective and elegant algorithms are constructed. This chapter will commence with a formal definition of an algorithm and describe the attributes which can be used to evaluate it informally. More formal techniques which can be used to specify, and subsequently ensure, that an algorithm correctly implements its specification will then be presented. These techniques are known as *programming by contract*.

Subsequent chapters will then attempt to introduce practical measurements which can be applied to algorithms and the reasons why such measurements might be made. These considerations lead to a technique of testing called *white box testing* which complements the technique of *black box testing* which was introduced in Section II.

On returning to the larger scale of software construction, testing techniques within the larger software life cycle will be introduced, together with further considerations of different techniques for designing and controlling the production of a large software project. Finally software measurement techniques which are more appropriate to programming in the large will be introduced.

Algorithms

An algorithm can be formally defined as 'a sequence of definite instructions which when followed will achieve some purpose'. The keywords in this definition might be *purpose* and *definite*. Purpose implies that the algorithm will have a specific task to perform, which should be expressed in its specification. Definite implies that each instruction which forms part of the algorithm must be unambiguous and capable of being performed in a reasonable amount of time.

An instruction forming part of an algorithm to construct a subprogram design might be 'refine the design into an appropriate level of granularity'. This can be regarded as an indefinite instruction as the appropriate degree of granularity is not precisely defined and might be interpreted in different ways by different developers. A more precise version of the instruction might be 'refine the design until each component can be implemented in at most three instructions in the implementation language'. This can be regarded as a more acceptable instruction as there is a clear criterion which determines when the instruction has been completed.

An instruction to count all possible integer values is definite but cannot be regarded as an acceptable part of an algorithm as the instruction cannot be completed in a finite amount of time. An alternative instruction to count the number of grains of sand on a beach can be completed in a finite amount of time, but the amount of time which it would take might be unreasonable within the context of the overall purpose of the algorithm.

Algorithms exist for many purposes and are expressed in many different ways. Examples of algorithms include recipes in cookery books, servicing instructions in a computer's hardware manual or knitting patterns. All computer programs are expressions of algorithms, where the instructions are expressed in the computer language being used to develop the program. Computer programs are described as expressions of algorithms, as an algorithm is a general technique for achieving some purpose which can be expressed in a number of different ways.

In the previous section two different sorting algorithms were introduced, each of which could be used to reorder a list into some defined sequence. It would be possible to express the same algorithms as instructions to a human who had a similar requirement to reorder some list, for example to sort a list of medical record cards into a sequence determined by the date of birth on the card. These instructions could employ the *insertion sort* algorithm, or the **bubble sort** algorithm, or one of many other available algorithms. Thus an algorithm as a general technique for expressing the process of completing a defined task is independent of the precise manner in which it is expressed.

There are many possible algorithms which can be used to perform almost any particular task. As there are many standard tasks which have to be performed in many different situations, for example sorting or searching a list or formatting a surname, there are many well defined, well tested and well documented algorithms which can be used. Such algorithms are known as *standard algorithms* and a knowledge of the commonest of them is an essential part of any novice software developer's education.

There are collections of standard algorithms available in several standard textbooks, details of some of which are given in Appendix A. For modular computer languages, which include Ada, Java and C++, there are also repositories of freely available source code modules on the Internet. Locations of some of these repositories are also given in Appendix A. Where the language includes generic capabilities, as introduced in Section IV Chapter 27, these implementations of standard algorithms may be expressed in a way which allows them to be implemented with many different data structures. The first action of a competent software developer when required to produce an application in an unfamiliar domain should be to research appropriate standard algorithms.

Formal and informal algorithm analysis

There are a number of standard criteria which can be used to evaluate any algorithm and which can be divided into formal and informal techniques. A formal criterion is one which yields a result which can be expressed in a logical or arithmetic statement; an informal criterion is one which yields a less precisely stated result.

The criteria, which are about to be introduced, can be used to evaluate two or more different possible algorithms in order to choose which one should actually be implemented for a particular requirement. The techniques can also be used when a proposed optimization of an existing implementation is considered. Some of the most useful informal criteria which can be used include the following:

Effectiveness. This is the most fundamental criterion and is concerned with an algorithm fulfilling its specification. As it is sometimes difficult to determine if an algorithm is always effective for all possible sets of input data, there are formal techniques which can be used in an attempt to determine this.

Termination. This is strictly an attribute of effectiveness but is sufficiently important for it to be considered as a distinct criterion. For an algorithm to be useful it must at some stage terminate and it is again not always possible to be certain of this for all possible sets of input data.

Generality. The definition of any algorithm should specify the input data which it will require and the output data which it will produce. An algorithm which will accept a greater range of input data and/or produce a greater range of output data is more general and likely to be a more useful algorithm, as it may be usable in a wider range of situations without requiring amendments.

Efficiency. This is sometimes taken as the most important criterion and is not always adequately specified. Possible subcriteria include speed of execution, amount of main or secondary storage required or amount of complexity of maintenance. The basic rule for considering efficiency it that it is not possible to optimize an algorithm against any efficiency subcriterion until it has first been shown to be effective.

>*Elegance.* This is the most subjective aspect of informal algorithm analysis. An elegant algorithm is one which is both simple and ingenious; of these two factors simplicity is far more important than ingenuity.

Examples of the application of these criteria will be given in the remainder of this chapter and in the chapters which follow.

Formal statements of an algorithm's specification

In order to assess the effectiveness of an algorithm there has to be some statement of its purpose, known as its specification. This specification can be made either in a natural language or in some more formal manner. For example, the natural language specification of a sorting algorithm might be as follows:

>The algorithm takes a list in some undefined state and produces a list which is ordered according to some key attribute of its elements.

A more formal statement of this specification involves the introduction of a more precise notation, using the following general terms:

:	such that
η	is the set of all discrete values.
η_n^m	is the set of all discrete values between n and m inclusive.
$\iota \forall \eta_n^m:$	is the successive generation of all values in the set η_n^m.
$\Im()$	is a function returning a value.
$\Delta()$	is true if all conditions in the brackets are true (*for all*).
$\exists()$	is true if at least one of the conditions in brackets is true (*there exists*).
$\Lambda()$	is negation.
&&	is the Boolean and relation.
‖	is the Boolean or relation.

For processing a list in particular the following terms will be used:

L	is a list.
$L(\iota)$	is an element of the list.
$\Im(L(\iota))$	is the key value of the element indexed ι in the array.

A sorted list, with members indexed from n to m, can be expressed using this notation as

$$\Delta(\iota\forall\eta_n^{m-1}:(\Im(L(\iota))<=\Im(L(\iota+1))))$$

which can be read as:

> All (Δ) index values from the start of the list to the penultimate index value ($\iota\forall\eta_n^{m-1}$) are such that (:) the key value of each element ($\Im(L(\iota))$) is less than or equal to the key value of the succeeding element ($\Im(L(\iota+1))$).

This can be argued to be a very precise definition of an ordered list. The expression of this definition using the symbolic terms is less ambiguous, less verbose and more amenable to logical derivation and development than the natural language version.

The formal statement of the ordered list can be used as the condition which must be true after a sort algorithm has completed for it to be considered effective. Alternatively it can also be used as a condition which must be true before an algorithm can commence. For example, the *binary chop* search algorithm requires a list to be sorted before it can search it.

A condition which must be true within the context where it is expressed is known as an *assertion*. An assertion which has to be satisfied before an algorithm can proceed is known as a *pre-condition* and an assertion which has to be satisfied after an algorithm has completed is known as a *post-condition*. The combination of *pre-condition* and *post-condition* can be used as a formal expression of an algorithm's specification as it unambiguously defines the relationship between the input data and the output data.

The pre-condition can also be used to determine the *generality* of an algorithm. For example, considering the *binary chop* algorithm, if $\Re$ is the Boolean result of the search, $\$$ is the key value sought, L is the list being searched and $\ddot{I}$ is the index value of the located item if the key value is located, the pre-condition might be expressed as

$$\Delta(\iota\forall\eta_n^{m-1}:(\Im(L(\iota))<=\Im(L(\iota+1))))$$

which is that the list is sorted and the post-condition might be

$$(\Re\&\&(\Im(L(\ddot{I}))=\$)\,\|\,(\Lambda(\Re)\&\&\Lambda(\ni(\iota\forall\eta_n^m:(\Im(L)\iota))=\$)$$

This can be read as

> It is the case that the result ($\Re$) is true and the key value of the index being returned ($\ddot{I}$) is equal to the key value sought ($\$$). Or ($\|$) the result is false ($\Lambda(\Re)$) and there is not (Λ) any element in the list ($\ni(\iota\forall\eta_n^m)$) whose key value (($\Im(L(\iota))$)) is equal to the key value sought ($\$$).

For the *sequential search* algorithm the post-condition is unchanged but there are no pre-conditions, which can be most conveniently represented as the pre-condition true. Thus the always true pre-condition for the sequential search compared with the sometimes true sorted pre-condition for the binary chop search is an indication of the greater generality of the sequential search algorithm.

Programming by contract

The use of pre- and post-conditions allows the development of software to be thought of as an implicit, or explicit, contract between the calling environment and the called subprogram. The calling environment fulfils its part of the contract by ensuring that it only ever calls the subprogram with a set of actual parameters which comply with the pre-condition. The subprogram in its turn fulfils the contract by ensuring that if it is supplied with acceptable input parameters it will always provide results which comply with its post-condition. That is to say, it will fulfil its advertised specification to transform its input data into the output data.

To illustrate this consideration a function to calculate the square root of a floating point value to a specified degree of accuracy will be used. The data flow interface diagram and subprogram specification for this function are as follows:

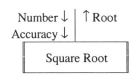

```
function SquareRoot( Number   : in FLOAT;
                     Accuracy : in FLOAT) return FLOAT;
-- Compute and return the square root of the number
-- requested, to the accuracy specified.
```

If this function is called to compute the square root of 2.0 to an accuracy of 0.1 any value returned whose square is between 1.9 and 2.1 would be acceptable. The square of 1.38 is 1.9044 and the square of 1.44 is 2.0736 and thus any value in this approximate range could be returned. If the accuracy requested were 0.01 then any value whose square lies between 1.99 and 2.01 would be acceptable and if the accuracy were 0.001 then the resulting squared value must be between 1.999 and 2.001. A design, data table and implementation of this requirement might be as follows:

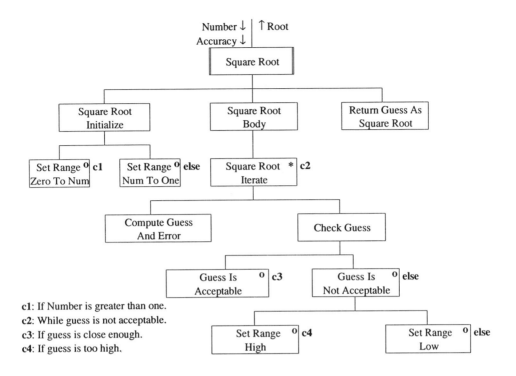

Number ↓ | ↑ Root
Accuracy ↓

Square Root

| Square Root Initialize | Square Root Body | Return Guess As Square Root |

| Set Range ⁰ **c1** Zero To Num | Set Range ⁰ **else** Num To One | Square Root * **c2** Iterate |

| Compute Guess And Error | Check Guess |

| Guess Is ⁰ **c3** Acceptable | Guess Is ⁰ **else** Not Acceptable |

| Set Range ⁰ **c4** High | Set Range ⁰ **else** Low |

c1: If Number is greater than one.
c2: While guess is not acceptable.
c3: If guess is close enough.
c4: If guess is too high.

Variables for *SquareRoot* function

Identifier	Type	Initial value	Notes
Number	FLOAT		Parameter: number to find root of
Accuracy	FLOAT		Parameter: required accuracy of result
MaximumValue	FLOAT	Number or 1.0	Top of range being considered
MinimumValue	FLOAT	0.0 or Number	Bottom of range being considered
CurrentGuess	FLOAT		Middle of range being considered
CurrentGuessSquared	FLOAT		Square of current guess
CurrentError	FLOAT		Difference between guess^2 and number
CloseEnough	BOOLEAN	FALSE	Flag to control iteration

```
0014    function SquareRoot( Number    : in FLOAT;
0015                         Accuracy : in FLOAT) return FLOAT is
0016
0017    MaximumValue        : FLOAT;
0018    MinimumValue        : FLOAT;
0019    CurrentGuess        : FLOAT;
0020    CurrentGuessSquared : FLOAT;
0021    CurrentError        : FLOAT;
```

```
0022    CloseEnough          : BOOLEAN := FALSE;
0023
0024  begin -- SquareRoot
0025     if Number > 1.0 then
0026        MaximumValue := Number;
0027        MinimumValue := 0.0;
0028     else
0029        MaximumValue := 1.0;
0030        MinimumValue := Number;
0031     end if;
0032     while not CloseEnough loop
0033        CurrentGuess := (MaximumValue + MinimumValue) / 2.0;
0034        CurrentGuessSquared := CurrentGuess * CurrentGuess;
0035        CurrentError := abs( Number - CurrentGuessSquared);
0036        if CurrentError <= Accuracy then
0037           CloseEnough := TRUE;
0038        else
0039           if CurrentGuessSquared >= Number then
0040              MaximumValue := CurrentGuess;
0041           else
0042              MinimumValue := CurrentGuess;
0043           end if;
0044        end if;
0045     end loop;
0046     return CurrentGuess;
0047  end SquareRoot;
```

The basis of the design is to maintain a current range within which the square root being sought is known to exist. The initial extent of this range is either zero to the value being sought or the value being sought to 1.0 if the number whose square root is being sought is less than 1.0. The square roots of values in the range between 0.0 and 1.0 are greater than the value itself; for example, the square root of 0.5 is approximately 0.701. Values greater than 1.0 have a square root whose value is less than the value itself; for example, the square root of 2.0 is approximately 1.41. The current guess of the square root's value is always the value in the middle of the range being considered.

To simplify reading the code the square of the current guess and the absolute difference between the square and the number whose square root is required are explicitly stored in named variables. The algorithm proceeds iteratively by computing and testing the current guess until the absolute difference between the square of the current guess and the number whose root is required is sufficiently accurate. On each iteration where the guess is shown to be insufficiently accurate the range of values being considered is adjusted to the upper or lower half of the current range, depending upon whether the square of the current guess is higher or lower than the value whose square is being sought.

It is instructive to trace this algorithm with test data in order to become familiar with its operation; this is suggested as an end of chapter exercise. However, this algorithm should not be regarded as elegant or totally effective. It is used here as it is sufficiently simple and accurate for the purposes of algorithm analysis and will be used repeatedly through this section.

The algorithm as it stands makes a number of assumptions concerning the values which are supplied to it. It assumes that the value of *Number* is always positive, as the square roots of negative numbers cannot be represented as floating point values. It also assumes that the *Accuracy* to which it is asked to compute the value is greater than zero. It is possible to compute the square root of a small subset of floating point values, for example 25.0, exactly. However, for the vast majority of floating point values, for example 2.0, the best which can be obtained is an approximation. The pre-condition for this function is therefore that the value of *Number* is greater than or equal to zero and the value of *Accuracy* is greater than zero.

The post-condition can be stated as the square of the value returned is greater than or equal to *Number* minus *Accuracy* and is also less than or equal to *Number* plus *Accuracy*. If *N* represents the number whose square root is being sought, *A* the required accuracy of the result and *R* the result, the pre-condition and post-condition can be more formally expressed as follows:

$$\text{pre-condition } N >= 0.0 \ \&\& \ A > 0.0$$
$$\text{post-condition } N - A >= R \times R <= N + A$$

Once the pre- and post-conditions of the *SquareRoot* function have been expressed more formally, they should be included in the comments which accompany the declaration of the function in the design, or in any package which exports the function:

```
function SquareRoot( Number   : in FLOAT;
                     Accuracy : in FLOAT) return FLOAT;
-- Compute and return the square root of the number
-- requested to the accuracy specified.
-- Pre  : Number >= 0.0 and Accuracy > 0.0.
-- Post : Number - Accuracy >= Result * Result
                            <= Number + Accuracy.
```

The formal expression should augment rather than replace the informal comments as the informal comments are more useful for a quick scan of the subprogram's specification to determine if it might be suitable for a particular requirement. The more formal expression of the specification can then be used to become absolutely certain that the subprogram is suitable.

Enforcing the contract

So far the pre- and post-conditions for the *SquareRoot* function have been used
formally to state its specification and to advertise the contract which it offers to
the calling environment; there is no provision for the contract to be enforced.
Enforcement of the contract can be best implemented by the explicit raising of an
exception if either the pre-condition or the post-condition is violated. One
technique to accomplish this is to design and implement a package to supply
assertion checking and exception raising facilities to any environment which
requires them. The design and specification of a suitable package might be as
follows:

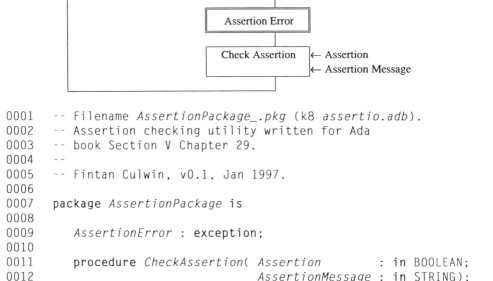

```
0001    -- Filename AssertionPackage_.pkg (k8 assertio.adb).
0002    -- Assertion checking utility written for Ada
0003    -- book Section V Chapter 29.
0004    --
0005    -- Fintan Culwin, v0.1, Jan 1997.
0006
0007    package AssertionPackage is
0008
0009       AssertionError : exception;
0010
0011       procedure CheckAssertion( Assertion        : in BOOLEAN;
0012                                 AssertionMessage : in STRING);
0013    -- Raise AssertionError if the Assertion is True
0014    -- otherwise do nothing.
0015
0016    end AssertionPackage;
```

The single procedure supplied by the package takes a BOOLEAN value and a
STRING as parameters. When it is called it will raise the *AssertionError* exception
if the BOOLEAN value is FALSE, and do nothing otherwise. The use which the
procedure makes of the STRING parameter will be described below. This
procedure can be used to enforce the contract in the *SquareRoot* function by
calling it twice, once at the start of the function to enforce the pre-assertion and

once at the end of the function to enforce the post-assertion. The call to enforce the pre-assertion might take the form

```
0024    begin -- SquareRoot
0025        CheckAssertion( (Number >= 0.0 and Accuracy > 0.0),
0026                        "Square root pre-assertion error");
```

The actual parameters to the call of *CheckAssertion* are an Ada BOOLEAN expression which states the pre-assertion and a message which identifies where and why the assertion was raised. The call of *CheckAssertion* to enforce the post-assertion might take the form

```
0047        CheckAssertion( ((CurrentGuess * CurrentGuess >=
0048                                    Number - Accuracy) and
0049                        (CurrentGuess * CurrentGuess <=
0050                                    Number + Accuracy)),
0051                        "Square root post-assertion error");
0052        return CurrentGuess;
0053    end SquareRoot;
```

The Boolean expression is complex, but correctly expresses the post-condition in Ada. The effect of these two calls is to test the pre- and post-conditions: if a condition evaluates false either the pre-condition or post-condition of the contract has been violated and an *AssertionError* exception will be raised. The design of the function will have to be changed to reflect the changes in the implementation. A revised design might be as follows:

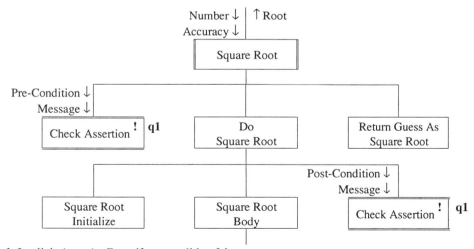

q1: Implicit *AssertionError* if pre-condition false.
q2: Implicit *AssertionError* if post-condition false.

The use of this facility to enforce the sorted post-condition of a sorting algorithm or the sorted pre-condition of the binary chop algorithm is a little more complex. It is not possible to write a simple Boolean expression to state that the list is sorted; instead a Boolean function will have to be used. The design and implementation of a suitable generic function, using the same generic parameters which were used in Section IV Chapter 27, might be as follows:

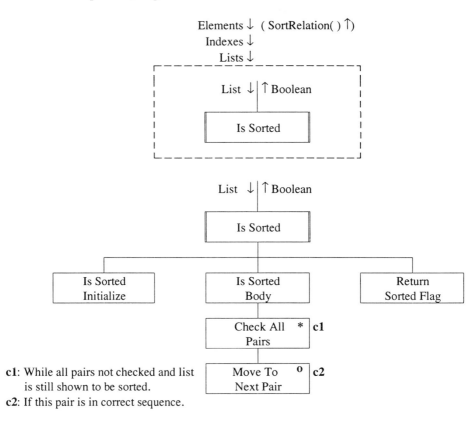

c1: While all pairs not checked and list is still shown to be sorted.

c2: If this pair is in correct sequence.

```
0040    function IsSorted( AnyList : in Lists) return BOOLEAN is
0041
0042      IsStillSorted : BOOLEAN := TRUE;
0043      ThisIndex     : Indexes := AnyList'FIRST;
0044
0045    begin -- IsSorted
0046       while IsStillSorted                  and
0047              ThisIndex < AnyList'LAST loop
0048          IsStillSorted := SortRelation( AnyList( ThisIndex),
0049                            AnyList( Indexes'SUCC( ThisIndex)));
0050          if IsStillSorted then
0051             ThisIndex := Indexes'SUCC( ThisIndex);
```

```
0052          end if;
0053        end loop;
0054        return IsStillSorted;
0055    end IsSorted;
```

Assuming that a suitable instantiation of this function is available, it can be used as the BOOLEAN expression which is passed to the *CheckAssertion* function. There is no pre-condition for a sorting algorithm which, as explained above, can simply be expressed as true. Thus the pre-condition *CheckAssertion* call might be included for the sake of consistency as follows:

```
CheckAssertion( TRUE,
             "Insertion sort pre-condition assertion error");
```

If the instantiated generic *IsSorted* function is also called *IsSorted*, the post-condition check can be expressed as follows:

```
CheckAssertion( IsSorted( ListToSort),
             "Insertion sort post-condition assertion error");
```

This will cause the *IsSorted* function to be called and the BOOLEAN value returned, indicating if the list is or is not sorted, will be passed to the *Check-Assertion* procedure. Thus if the list is shown not to be sorted the value passed will be false and the *AssertionError* exception will be raised; otherwise the list must be sorted, the value returned and passed is true and the *AssertionError* exception will not be raised. The assertion checking contract enforcement of the binary chop search procedure will be left as an end of chapter exercise.

There is one possible problem with this approach: in order to test the post-condition of the *Sort* subprogram, a separate *IsSorted* subprogram has to be called. This subprogram will also have its own pre- and post-condition contract which should be enforced. The pre-condition for the *IsSorted* function is true, and the post-condition should be that the list which has been checked has not been changed. This post-condition part of the contract can be assured by noting that the list is only passed to the *IsSorted* function in **in only** mode.

However, there is a general problem that in order to enforce a pre- or post-condition for a particular subprogram it may be required to call a subprogram, which may itself require a subprogram to be called to enforce its conditions, which in turn ... and so on. This potential problem with contract enforcement will be considered in the concluding part of this chapter.

The ADA.EXCEPTIONS standard package

The package body for the *AssertionPackage* was omitted from the previous part of this chapter because its implementation makes use of a standard package which has not yet been introduced. The name of the standard package is ADA.EXCEPTIONS and it supplies additional facilities for the raising and handling of exceptions. A partial object diagram of the package and the partial package specification are as follows:

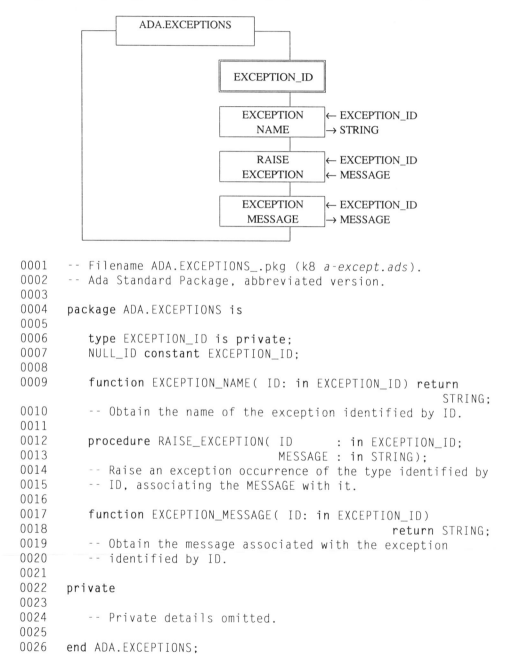

```
0001    -- Filename ADA.EXCEPTIONS_.pkg (k8 a-except.ads).
0002    -- Ada Standard Package, abbreviated version.
0003
0004    package ADA.EXCEPTIONS is
0005
0006        type EXCEPTION_ID is private;
0007        NULL_ID constant EXCEPTION_ID;
0008
0009        function EXCEPTION_NAME( ID: in EXCEPTION_ID) return
                                                                STRING;
0010        -- Obtain the name of the exception identified by ID.
0011
0012        procedure RAISE_EXCEPTION( ID      : in EXCEPTION_ID;
0013                                   MESSAGE : in STRING);
0014        -- Raise an exception occurrence of the type identified by
0015        -- ID, associating the MESSAGE with it.
0016
0017        function EXCEPTION_MESSAGE( ID: in EXCEPTION_ID)
0018                                                    return STRING;
0019        -- Obtain the message associated with the exception
0020        -- identified by ID.
0021
0022    private
0023
0024        -- Private details omitted.
0025
0026    end ADA.EXCEPTIONS;
```

The purpose of this part of the package is to allow a developer to associate some information, contained in the MESSAGE parameter, with the explicit raising of an exception, and for an exception handler to be able to retrieve this information. In order to raise an exception using the RAISE_EXCEPTION procedure a value of type EXCEPTION_ID is required. A suitable value can be used by using the IDENTITY attribute which, when applied to the name of an exception, will produce a unique value for the exception occurrence.

The implementation of the *CheckAssertion* procedure in the body of the *AssertionPackage* makes use of these facilities explicitly to raise an *AssertionError* exception passing its *AssertionMessage* parameter on as the MESSAGE parameter of the RAISE_EXCEPTION procedure call. The implementation of the package body is as follows:

```
0001    -- Filename AssertionPackage_.pkg (k8 assertio.adb)
0002    -- Assertion checking utility written for Ada book
0003    -- Section V Chapter 29, introduces ADA.EXCEPTIONS.
0004    --
0005    -- Fintan Culwin, v0.1, Jan 1997.
0006
0007    with ADA.EXCEPTIONS;
0008    use  ADA.EXCEPTIONS;
0009
0010    package body AssertionPackage is
0011
0012        procedure CheckAssertion
                                ( Assertion        : in BOOLEAN;
0013                              AssertionMessage : in STRING) is
0014        begin -- CheckAssertion
0015            -- If the Assertion fails,
0016            -- explicitly raise an AssertionError.
0017            if not Assertion then
0018                RAISE_EXCEPTION( AssertionError'IDENTITY,
0019                                                AssertionMessage);
0020            end if;
0021        end CheckAssertion;
0022
0023    end AssertionPackage;
```

The effect of calling the *CheckAssertion* procedure when the *Assertion* parameter has the value false is to raise an *AssertionError* exception. This exception could be handled at a higher level, using an exception handler based upon the following implementation:

```
when AssertionError =>
    PUT_LINE( "Assertion error detected message is");
    PUT_LINE( EXCEPTION_MESSAGE( AssertionError));
```

Within the scope of the exception handler the name of the exception, *Assertion-Error*, can be used as a value of type EXCEPTION_ID and, as shown in this example, used to retrieve any message associated with the exception occurrence. If this handler was invoked owing to a mis-implementation of the body of the *SquareRoot* function it might produce the following output:

```
Assertion error detected message is
Square root post-condition assertion error.
```

Alternatively if the handler were invoked owing to the *SquareRoot* function being called with invalid parameters it might produce the following output:

```
Assertion error detected message is
Square root pre-condition assertion error.
```

The usefulness of these facilities to a developer is that they assist with the detection of errors and also can direct the developer's attention towards the location of the fault which produced the error. A pre-condition assertion error will direct the developer's attention to the calling environment, while a post-condition error will direct attention to the subprogram itself.

Assertions and contract enforcement in practice

The techniques introduced in this chapter for the formal statement of an algorithm's specification and the enforcement of that specification by the concept of programming by contract and assertion checking will produce implementations of algorithms which are very robust. However, the techniques do not come free of charge and will add to the costs of software production, although they should also reduce the costs of software maintenance.

A novice software developer should become aware of the existence of these techniques and should practise them. However, their deployment in practice is a more open question. All that has been provided here is an initial overview of an introduction to the topic of *formal methods*. This is an approach to software development which aims to devise a notation for the formal specification of an algorithm and, using the specification as a premise, to use algebraic manipulation to derive the required source code. The intention is that if the premise is correct and if the manipulations are consistent and coherent then both an implementation and a proof of the correctness of the implementation will have been obtained.

The current state of the formal methods approach is that it is an emerging technology which has moved out of industrial and academic research labs, and is being deployed in some areas with some success. However, it has also been shown to be not without its problems; it is extremely expensive to implement and is beyond the capabilities of the vast majority of software developers.

The opinion of the author is that the concept of *fitness for purpose* should be employed to determine if formal methods, at their current state of development, are appropriate. Where the consequences of software failure are either life threatening or mission critical to the organization which is using the software, then not only are the costs of formal methods justified but the use of formal methods should be very strongly encouraged. However, the vast majority of software is not in this category and thus the costs of formal methods may not be justified.

The concept of programming by contract is implicit in all subprograms and the informal or formal specification of a pre- and post-condition for all subprograms will make the implicit contract explicit at very little cost. Thus the advice is to make a statement of the contract in the specification of all subprograms which are produced.

Enforcement of the contract is a little more problematic. As was mentioned above this can cause a situation of reduction to absurdity, where the enforcement of a contract may require a subprogram which itself requires enforcement, which in its turn requires enforcement, and so on. In practice this rarely happens because at some stage the inherent facilities of Ada can be relied upon to enforce the contract. Thus in the example discussed above the post-condition of the *IsSorted* function, that the list not be changed by the function, can be ensured by the specification of the lists' formal parameter mode as *in only* and the assurance from Ada that an *in only* parameter will not be changed by the subprogram.

Contract enforcement, where it is appropriate, should also be subject to a fitness for purpose analysis. The subprograms may be initially constructed without contract enforcement and, if the resources permit, contract enforcement can be added at a later stage. However, should the required production quality insist that contracts are enforced, then the assertion checking of the pre- and post-condition should be implemented first, before the bodies of the subprograms. The intention is that contract enforcement can then be used to ensure continually that each subprogram's specification is being correctly implemented throughout the construction phase.

In any situation the concept of programming by contract and the inclusion of pre- and post-conditions in a specification will concentrate the developer's attention on fulfilling the specification, which will hopefully cause the quality of the produced software to be improved.

EXERCISES

29.1 Produce a set of instructions which could be given to a human which would allow a deck of personal record cards to be sorted into an order decided by date of birth. Compare this set of instructions with the set of instructions which you would give to a computer to achieve the same purpose.

29.2 Trace the *SquareRoot* function when it is called to calculate the square root of 2.0 to an accuracy of 0.1.

29.3 Devise a black box test plan for the *SquareRoot* function and apply it using a test harness demonstration program. Make use of the pre-assertion and post-assertion exception handler.

29.4 Extend the generic sorting package from Section IV Chapter 27 to include pre- and post-assertion checking.

29.5 Revisit one of the programs which you have already developed from one of the previous exercises and introduce pre- and post-assertion checking where appropriate.

CHAPTER 30

Measuring software

Before a process can be controlled it has first to be measured. This chapter will introduce techniques which can be used to make a numerical measurement of some attributes of individual algorithms. The measurements which can be made are collectively referred to as **software metrics** and can be divided into two major classes, **static metrics** and **dynamic metrics**. **Static metrics** refer to the measurements which can be made with only the source code, design or specification available. **Dynamic metrics** are measurements which can only be made on the software as it is executing.

The first topic which will be explored in this chapter is a static analysis of algorithms which attempts to predict dynamic behaviour. In particular this measure attempts to predict the effects of increasing the size of the data set which the algorithm will process. The searching and sorting algorithms which were introduced in previous chapters will be analyzed with a view to predicting their behaviour as the size of the list to be searched or sorted increases. This measurable attribute of an algorithm is known as the **order of an algorithm**.

Subsequently a number of simple practical dynamic measurements will be introduced, the results of which can be used to attempt to validate the predictions made regarding the order of sorting and searching algorithms. Software metrics will be returned to later in this section when static metrics and metrics which are more appropriate to large scale software development will be introduced.

The order of an algorithm

To introduce the concept and techniques of determining the order of an algorithm an analysis of the order of the two searching algorithms, the **sequential search** and the **binary chop**, which were introduced in previous chapters, will be presented. Following this the two sorting algorithms will be analyzed in a similar manner. The **insertion sort** was first introduced in Section IV Chapter 27; an alternative sorting algorithm known as the **bubble sort** will be presented in this chapter. The first part of the chapter will conclude with a summary and consideration of the implications of the results which have been obtained.

In order to make this part of the chapter more comprehensible the source code of the generic implementations of those procedures which have already been introduced will be repeated. However, in the interests of brevity the designs will not be repeated, and can be located in Section IV Chapter 27.

The order of searching algorithms

The implementation of the generic sequential search algorithm, as designed and presented in Section IV Chapter 27, is as follows:

```
0060    generic
0061       type Elements is private;
0062       type Indexes is ( <> );
0063       type Lists is array ( Indexes range <>) of Elements;
0064    procedure Search( ListToSearch        : in Lists;
0065                      ElementToFind        : in Elements;
0066                      ElementIsFound       : out BOOLEAN;
0067                      LocationOfElement    : out Indexes) is
0068
0069       ThisLocation    : Indexes := ListToSearch'FIRST;
0070       FoundAt         : Indexes := ThisLocation;
0071       HasBeenFound    : BOOLEAN := FALSE;
0072       ListIsExhausted : BOOLEAN := FALSE;
0073
0074    begin -- Search
0075       while (not HasBeenFound) and (not ListIsExhausted) loop
0076          if ListToSearch( ThisLocation) = ElementToFind then
0077             HasBeenFound := TRUE;
0078             FoundAt      := ThisLocation;
0079          else
0080             if ThisLocation = ListToSearch'LAST then
0081                ListIsExhausted := TRUE;
0082             else
0083                ThisLocation := Indexes'SUCC( ThisLocation);
0084             end if;
0085          end if;
0086       end loop;
0087       ElementIsFound    := HasBeenFound;
0088       LocationOfElement := FoundAt;
0089    end Search;
```

The basis of determining the order of an algorithm is to consider the way in which the algorithm will behave in the best case, the worst case and the average case situation.

The best case situation for this algorithm is for it to locate the element being sought at the first location in the list. In this situation the main loop of the algorithm between lines 0075 and 0086 will iterate once. The worst case situation is where the item being sought cannot be located in the list. In this situation every element in the list will have to be checked before the algorithm can conclude that the item is not contained within the list. Thus the main loop will iterate as many times as there are elements in the list. For a list of ten items it will iterate ten times, for a list of 100 items it will iterate 100 times and for the general case of a list of n items it will iterate n times.

The average case situations can be considered as the average case given that the item will not be located, and the average case given that the item will be located. Where the item cannot be located, the average behaviour of the algorithm is the same as the worst case behaviour as every element will have to be checked in order to make the conclusion that the item being sought is not in the list. Where the item can be located it can be argued that as the list is unordered it can be assumed that there is an equal probability that the item being sought will be located at any position in the list. On average this will result in the item being located in the middle of the list; thus the average case behaviour of the sequential search algorithm given that the item being sought is in the list is $n/2$ iterations of the main loop.

In summary the behaviour of the sequential search algorithm for a list of n items is as follows. In the final line of the following table P_f indicates the proportion of times the item is located in the list and P_m the proportion of times the item is not contained with the list.

Order analysis for the sequential search algorithm

Best case	1
Worst case	n
Average case if item is not in the list	n
Average case if item is in the list	$n/2$
Average case	$P_f(n/2) + P_m(n)$

The implementation of the generic binary chop algorithm, whose design and implementation were first introduced in Section IV, Chapter 28, is as follows:

```
0055    procedure BinaryChopSearch
                          ( ListToSearch      : in   Lists;
0056                        ElementToFind     : in   Elements;
0057                        ElementIsFound    : out  BOOLEAN;
0058                        LocationOfElement : out  Indexes) is
0059
0060        ItemLocated : BOOLEAN := FALSE;
0061        Top         : Indexes := ListToSearch'LAST;
0062        Bottom      : Indexes := ListToSearch'FIRST;
0063        Middle      : Indexes;
```

```
0064
0065    begin -- BinaryChopSearch
0066       while not ItemLocated and
0067             Top >= Bottom    loop
0068          Middle := Indexes'VAL( (Indexes'POS( Top) +
0069                                     Indexes'POS( Bottom)) /2);
0070          if ElementToFind = ListToSearch( Middle) then
0071             ItemLocated := TRUE;
0072          else
0073             if SortRelation( ElementToFind,
0074                     ListToSearch( Middle)) then
0075                Bottom := Indexes'SUCC( Middle);
0076             else
0077                Top := Indexes'PRED( Middle);
0078             end if;
0079          end if;
0080       end loop;
0081
0082       if ItemLocated then
0083          ElementIsFound    := TRUE;
0084          LocationOfElement := Middle;
0085       else
0086          ElementIsFound := FALSE;
0087       end if;
0088    end BinaryChopSearch;
```

The analysis of the binary chop algorithm is a little more complex but can proceed in the same way by considering the best case, worst case and average case situations. The best case situation in this circumstance would be for the item to be located in the middle of the list, in which case it will be found on the first iteration.

The worst case situation, where the item being sought is not in the list, is a little more complex to determine and can be approached by considering lists of different lengths. For a list of one element it will take one iteration of the main loop for it to be determined that the single item in the list is not that being sought. For a structure with two elements two iterations would be required. The first iteration will decide that the item being considered is not that being sought and the second iteration will be restricted to a sublist containing the remaining element. This, as explained above, will take a further iteration making a total of two iterations.

For a list of up to four elements, three iterations will be required. After the first iteration the list will be divided in half, giving a sublist of at most two elements for the second iteration. As described above a sublist of two elements will require two further iterations making a total of three iterations. Continuing the argument a list of up to eight elements will require four iterations. After the first iteration a sublist of at most four items will be left to be searched, which will take three further iterations, making a total of four iterations.

Continuing this argument, each doubling of the length of the list will add one to the number of iterations of the main loop required for an unsuccessful search: 16 elements will require five iterations; 32, six; 64, seven; and so on. In general n iterations will be required to search a list of 2^n elements. Or expressing this in terms of the number of elements, n elements will require $\log_2 n$ iterations.

The average case given that the element is not in the list is again equal to the worst case. The average case, given that the element is in the list, is a little more difficult to determine. Each iteration of the loop halves the extent of the list within which the item must be located and thus the algorithm 'homes in' on the item being sought. It can be argued that the algorithm will find the item towards the end of the process when the area being considered is smaller rather than larger. Thus a simple analysis can conclude that the number of iterations is approximately equal to the number required to search the list when the item is not in the list.

The summary behaviour of the binary chop algorithm is thus as follows:

Order analysis for the binary chop search algorithm	
Best case	1
Worst case	$\log_2 n$
Average case if item is not in the list	$\log_2 n$
Average case if item is in the list	$\sim\log_2 n$
Average case	$P_f(\sim\log_2 n) + P_m(\log_2 n)$

The order of sorting algorithms

The implications of the differences between the two tables will be considered after an order of algorithm analysis has been made on the insertion sort and bubble sort algorithms. The generic version of the insertion sort algorithm, whose design was given in Section IV Chapter 27, is as follows:

```
0082    procedure InsertionSort( ListToSort : in out Lists) is
0083
0084        LowestLocation : Indexes;
0085
0086    begin -- InsertionSort
0087        for ThisIndex in ListToSort'FIRST ..
0088                        Indexes'PRED( ListToSort'LAST) loop
0089            LowestLocation :=
0090                FindLowest( ListToSort(
0091                                    ThisIndex .. ListToSort'LAST));
0092            Swap( ListToSort( ThisIndex),
0093                    ListToSort( LowestLocation));
0094        end loop;
0095    end InsertionSort;
```

The best case situation for a sort algorithm can be considered to be a list which is already sorted; a worst case situation might be where the elements in the list are in an exactly inverse order compared with the best case; and the average case might be where the elements are randomly distributed.

Taking the best case situation first the number of times that the main loop in the algorithm above will iterate is one less than the number of elements in the list. As a definite loop (**for**) construct is used this is a fixed number determined by the bounds of the iteration which are expressed as the first index value of the list and the penultimate index value in the list. The body of the loop contains a call to the *FindLowest* subprogram and a call to the *Swap* algorithm. The implementation of the *FindLowest* subprogram, whose design can also be located in Section IV Chapter 27, is as follows:

```
0060    function FindLowest( ListToCheck : in Lists)
0061                                        return Indexes is
0062
0063        LowestValueSoFar : Elements :=
0064                            ListToCheck( ListToCheck'FIRST);
0065        LowestLocation : Indexes    := ListToCheck'FIRST;
0066
0067    begin -- FindLowest
0068        for ThisIndex in Indexes'SUCC( ListToCheck'FIRST) ..
0069                                        ListToCheck'LAST loop
0070          if SortRelation( ListToCheck( ThisIndex),
0071                                        LowestValueSoFar) then
0072              LowestValueSofar := ListToCheck( ThisIndex);
0073              LowestLocation   := ThisIndex;
0074            end if;
0075          end loop;
0076          return LowestLocation;
0077    end FindLowest;
```

This subprogram also contains a loop, so a full analysis will have to consider the number of times which this loop iterates, within the context of the iteration of the loop in the *InsertionSort* procedure. The loop in the *FindLowest* function is also a definite loop whose bounds are the second index value and last index value of the list being examined. Thus if the *FindLowest* subprogram is asked to find the lowest item in a list of m items the number of iterations is $m - 1$. This can be approximated to m by noting that the first element in the list is also implicitly examined in the initialization of the local variables.

Returning to the *InsertionSort* implementation, if it is asked to sort a list of n items it will, as noted above, iterate $n - 1$ times. On the first iteration it will pass the entire list, n elements, to the *FindLowest* function. On the second iteration it will pass $n - 1$ elements to the *FindLowest* function; on the third $n - 2$ elements; on the fourth n-3 elements; and so on. On the last iteration it will ask *FindLowest* to find the lowest in a list of two elements; on the penultimate iteration to find the lowest of three elements; on the iteration before that four elements; and so on. Thus on average a call to *FindLowest* will be asked to find the lowest element in a list which is approximately $n/2$ elements long. As it is called $n-1$ times the total number of iterations of the *FindLowest* loop will be $(n-1)(n/2)$, which can be approximated to $n^2/2$. In addition to the number of iterations of the inner loop the number of swaps which are required also needs to be considered. An examination of the source code can show that there are as many swaps as iterations of the *InsertionSort* loop, that is $n-1$.

The behaviour of the sequential sort algorithm is independent of the state of the list which it is asked to sort. Both loops are definite and both are controlled solely by the size of the list which is being sorted. Thus the best case behaviour is also the worst case behaviour and is also the average case behaviour. The summary table is as follows, where the number of iterations of the innermost, *FindLowest*, loop is expressed as the number of comparisons:

Order analysis for the insertion sort algorithm

	Comparisons	Swaps
Best case	$n^2/2$	$n-1$
Worst case	$n^2/2$	$n-1$
Average case	$n^2/2$	$n-1$

The bubble sort algorithm

In order to make a comparison of the behaviour of the insertion sort algorithm a second algorithm, known as the bubble sort, will be introduced. The basis of this algorithm is to iterate repeatedly through the list comparing every adjacent pair of elements and swapping them if they are not in the correct relation. When an iteration takes place without any pairs of elements being swapped then the list is known to be sorted and the algorithm can terminate. The generic design of this algorithm might be as follows:

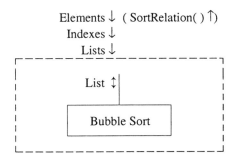

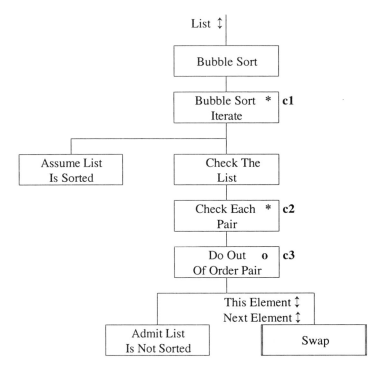

c1: While list is not known to be sorted.

c2: For all adjacent pairs.

c3: If current pair is out of sequence.

The implementation, assuming the same generic parameters as have been used before, might be as follows:

```
0037    procedure BubbleSort( ListToSort : in out Lists) is
0038
0039      ListIsSorted : BOOLEAN := FALSE;
0040
0041    begin -- BubbleSort
0042      while not( ListIsSorted) loop
0043        ListIsSorted := TRUE;
0044        for ThisIndex in ListToSort'FIRST ..
0045                    Indexes'PRED( ListToSort'LAST) loop
0046          if not SortRelation( ListToSort( ThisIndex),
0047              ListToSort( Indexes'SUCC( ThisIndex))) then
0048            Swap( ListToSort( ThisIndex),
0049                ListToSort( Indexes'SUCC( ThisIndex)) );
0050            ListIsSorted := FALSE;
0051          end if;
```

```
0052            end loop;
0053          end loop;
0054      end BubbleSort;
```

Assuming that an instantiated version of this procedure is available to a test harness client, the operation of the algorithm can be illustrated by considering the sorting of the same list of integers as was used in Section IV Chapter 27 to illustrate the operation of the insertion sort:

$$64 \quad 78 \quad 12 \quad 91 \quad 34$$

At the start of the subprogram the outermost loop, starting on line 0042, will iterate as the BOOLEAN control variable has been declared with a suitable default value. The innermost loop, starting on line 0044, is a definite loop and will iterate four times with the loop parameter indexing the first four values in the list. On the first iteration the *SortRelation* condition of the **if** statement on line 0046 will compare the values of the first and second elements, and evaluate false. This will cause the body of the **if not** to be executed and the innermost loop will iterate for a second time.

On the second iteration the second and third elements will be compared and the **if** condition will evaluate true causing the body of the **if** to be executed. This will cause the second and third elements to be swapped and the flag, *ListIsSorted*, to be set false. The state of the list at this stage is as follows:

$$64 \quad 12 \quad 78 \quad 91 \quad 34$$
$$\quad\;\; \uparrow \quad\; \uparrow$$

The arrows under the list indicate that the two values have been swapped. The innermost loop will iterate a further two times, comparing the third and fourth elements, which do not require swapping, and the fourth and fifth elements, which do. The state of the list after the innermost loop terminates can be visualized as follows:

$$64 \quad 12 \quad 78 \quad 34 \quad 91$$
$$\quad\;\; \uparrow \quad\; \uparrow \quad\; \uparrow \quad\; \uparrow$$

Upon the termination of the innermost loop the control condition of the outermost loop is evaluated. As the value of the control variable, *ListIsSorted*, was set false the loop condition will evaluate true and the outermost loop will iterate for a second time. The first action of the iteration is to reset the value of the control variable, *ListIsSorted*, to true. This is followed by a second execution of the innermost loop which will compare, and possibly swap, all adjacent pairs of elements. The state of the list after the second iteration of the outermost loop can be visualized as follows:

$$12 \quad 64 \quad 34 \quad 78 \quad 91$$
$$\uparrow \quad \uparrow \quad \uparrow \quad \uparrow$$

During this execution of the innermost loop, first the elements at the first and second locations were swapped and subsequently the elements at the third and fourth locations. As at least one swap was made the control flag was reset to false and the outermost loop will iterate for a third time. Again the control flag will be set true and the innermost loop executed, producing the list in the following state at the end of the third iteration:

$$12 \quad 34 \quad 64 \quad 78 \quad 91$$
$$\uparrow \quad \uparrow$$

As a swap was made on this iteration the control variable will be set false and a fourth iteration of the outermost loop will take place, producing the following list:

$$12 \quad 34 \quad 64 \quad 78 \quad 91$$

During this iteration none of the elements were swapped and so the control variable was not reset to false. When the outermost loop control condition is tested for the fifth time it will evaluate true causing the loop to terminate. The list is known to be sorted as no adjacent pairs of elements in the list were shown to be out of position by the *SortRelation* function. The reason why this is called a bubble sort can be deduced by considering the way in which the value 34, which was initially at the end of the list, moved one location towards its eventual location on every iteration of the outermost loop. It is as if it bubbled up the list towards the top.

The bubble sort analysis

For the bubble sort the nature of the double iteration which forms the basis of nearly all sorting algorithms is clearer as both loops are contained within the same procedure. The outer loop is an indefinite loop and the number of times which it will iterate is determined by the nature of the list which it is asked to sort. The inner loop is definite and on every execution will always iterate one fewer times than there are elements in the list being sorted. Thus the order of the inner loop is $n-1$.

For the best case situation, where the list is already sorted, the inner loop will iterate without the **if** condition evaluating true. This is because in a sorted list every succeeding element in the array must by definition comply with the *SortRelation* condition. As the **if** statement never evaluates true the BOOLEAN variable *ListIsSorted* will never be reset to false and the outer loop will terminate after one iteration. Thus in the best case situation the inner loop will iterate a total of $n - 1$ times, and as the **if** never evaluates true the swap procedure is never called and the number of swaps is zero.

For the worst case situation the analysis is a little more difficult. The basis of this analysis is to consider the element at the start of the list which has to move to the end of the list in order for the list to be sorted. On the first iteration of the outer loop it will be swapped with the second element, and on the second iteration of the loop it will be swapped with the third element. Continuing this argument, this element will move one position towards the end of the list on every iteration of the outer loop. For it to move from the start of the list to the end of the list it will have to be swapped $n - 1$ times.

Every other element in the list will also move one location towards the start or end of the loop on every iteration, and as the elements at the start or end of the list have the furthest distance to move, all other elements will be in their correct place when the element which was at the end of the loop has moved to the start of the loop. One further iteration will be required to determine that the list is now sorted. Thus the total number of iterations of the outer loop to sort an inverted list is n and the total number of iterations of the inner loop is $n(n - 1)$, which is approximately equal to n^2.

The number of exchanges can also be determined by assuming a list containing an even number of elements. For the worst case situation the element before the middle location in the list will have to be moved to the position below the middle location in the list, which can be accomplished with a single swap. The element two positions before the middle of the list will have to be moved to the location two positions below the middle of the list, which will require three swaps. This argument can be continued and will result in the conclusion that for every additional position away from the middle of the list, two additional swaps will be required.

It has already been noted that the element at the start of the list will have to be swapped $n - 1$ times to move it to the end of the list. The element at the end of the list will also require $n - 1$ swaps to move to the start of the list. The element in the second location in the list will require two fewer swaps to move it to the penultimate location in the list, that is $n - 3$ swaps. Likewise, for every additional location away from the start, or end, of the list two fewer swaps are required.

For a list containing n items, the number of swaps required for each location in the first half of the list can be shown in the following table:

Location	1	2	3	..	..	$n/2 - 2$	$n/2 - 1$	$n/2$
Swaps	$n - 1$ +	$n - 3$ +	$n - 5$ +	.. +	.. +	5 +	3 +	1

As each swap is experienced by two elements and the table above counts the number of swaps which are experienced by half the elements and as every swap always moves the elements towards their eventual location, the sum of this series will be the total number of swaps required. The sum of this series can be determined by reversing the series and adding it to itself:

$$
\begin{array}{ccccccccccccccccccc}
n-1 & + & n-3 & + & n-5 & + & .. & + & .. & + & .. & + & .. & + & 5 & + & 3 & + & 1 \\
\hline
1 & + & 3 & + & 5 & + & .. & + & .. & + & .. & + & .. & + & n-5 & + & n-3 & + & n-1 \\
\hline
n & + & n & + & n & + & n & + & n & + & n & + & n & + & n & + & n & + & n
\end{array}
$$

There are $n/2$ terms in the third row of this table so the sum of the third row is $(n/2)(n)$ which is $n^2/2$. Thus for a list which contains an even number of elements the total number of swaps required in the worst case situation is $n^2/2$. The formula for an odd number of items is a little, but not significantly, different.

The average case behaviour of the bubble sort algorithm can be shown to be approximately equal to the worst case behaviour. It can be assumed that for the worst case situation every element is approximately half the list away from its eventual location in the sorted list. This will require each element to experience a minimum of $n/2-1$ swaps. It cannot be assumed that the other element participating in the swap will benefit from the swap by being moved towards its desired location. It can be assumed that the swaps in the average case situation are only 50% as effective as the swaps in the worst case situation. This leads to the conclusion that each element has to experience approximately n swaps and as each swap moves two elements the total number of swaps is approximately $n^2/2$. This is the same number of swaps as the worst case situation required, and will need at least as many iterations of the inner loop. Thus the summary of comparisons and exchanges for the bubble sort algorithm is as follows:

Order analysis for the bubble sort algorithm

	Comparisons	Swaps
Best case	$n-1$	0
Worst case	n^2	$n^2/2$
Average case	n^2	$\sim n^2/2$

Order analysis summary

Combining the results of the analysis of all four algorithms, and for the sorting algorithms counting only the number of iterations of the innermost loop, and for the searching algorithms assuming that all average case searches are successful in locating the element sought, the following summary can be produced:

Order analysis for various algorithms

	Best case	Average case	Worst case
Sequential search	1	$n/2$	n
Binary chop search	1	$\log_2 n$	$\sim\log_2 n$
Insertion sort	$n^2/2$	$n^2/2$	$n^2/2$
Bubble sort	$n-1$	n^2	n^2

This table can be used to predict the behaviour of the various algorithms as the size of the list being searched or sorted increases. For the sequential search algorithm the time taken to search the list increases in proportion to the size of the list; doubling the size of the list will double the amount of time taken to search it. For the binary chop search algorithm the time taken to search the list increases in proportion to $\log_2$ of the size of the list; doubling the size of the list will add very little to the time taken to search it. For both sorting algorithms the time taken to sort a list is proportional to the square of the size of the list being sorted; doubling the size of the list will square the amount of time taken.

This information can be better represented graphically and is shown in Figure 30.1.

This information cannot be used to make accurate numerical predictions of the form 'if the size of the list is increased from 100 elements to 200 elements the time taken will increase from 0.5 seconds to 2 seconds'. It can only be used to make an

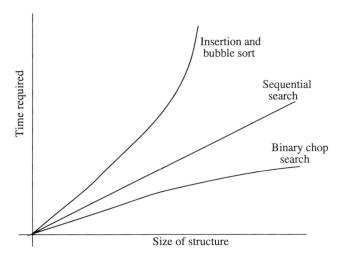

Figure 30.1 Comparison of the time taken for various algorithms to complete as the size of the structure increases.

order of magnitude prediction of the form 'if the size of the list is increased from 100 elements to 200 elements the time taken will rise exponentially'. However, even this vague statement is potentially more useful than no statement at all when the effects of using an algorithm with different sized structures are being considered.

The dramatic improvement of the binary chop algorithm over the sequential search algorithm needs to be qualified by considerations of the generality of both algorithms. The sequential search will search any list, the binary chop will only search a list which is sorted. If the costs of sorting a list are added to those of searching using the binary chop, then the selection search is the more efficient algorithm. However, if the list is being sorted for some other requirement, then the costs of searching the list can be discounted and the binary chop is a far better algorithm for all but the very smallest lists.

The detailed comparison between the insertion sort and bubble sort provides information which can be used to compare the two algorithms. The insertion sort algorithm has a constant behaviour, and its performance is independent of the state of the list. The behaviour of the bubble sort is more variable and for small lists or lists which are known to be nearly sorted the time taken may be less than that taken by the insertion algorithm.

The number of swaps required by the two sorting algorithms should also be taken into account. The insertion sort algorithm is dramatically more efficient in the number of swaps required than the bubble sort. This is a significant difference as the time taken to swap two items can be shown to be expensive in processor time. Thus the general conclusion might be that if a small list needs to be sorted or if a list is known to have only a small degree of disorder, the bubble sort algorithm should be favoured. In all other cases the insertion sort probably outperforms it.

The basic measurement which has been used in the analysis of the amount of time taken by each algorithm has been the number of iterations taken by the innermost loop. This is a very vague and imprecise measurement; it is obvious from the source code presented above that the contents of the loop vary greatly between the different algorithms. In order to become more precise about the meaning of this measurement, techniques for the practical dynamic analysis of source code will have to be introduced.

Simple dynamic measurement

This part of the chapter will introduce techniques by which the relative costs of the different fundamental operations which form the bodies of the loops can be measured. The measurement which will be made is the amount of time which is taken for an increasingly complex series of operations, the difference in time taken being indicative of the cost of the added operation. An attempt will then be made to apply these considerations to complete algorithms.

The intention of these measurements is to give an indication of the relative costs of operations, and not to become a guide regarding optimizing an algorithm with respect to the amount of time taken. Advice on optimization will be given in detail when larger scale dynamic measurements are introduced.

The fundamental program which will be used to make the measurements has the following form:

```
0001    -- Filename DynamicTimer.ada (k8 dynamict.adb).
0002    -- Program to make simple dynamic timing measurements.
0003    --
0004    -- Produced for Ada Book Section V Chapter 30.
0005    -- Fintan Culwin, v0.1, Jan 1997.
0006
0007    with ADA.TEXT_IO, ADA.CALENDAR;
0008    use  ADA.TEXT_IO, ADA.CALENDAR;
0009
0010    procedure DynamicTimer is
0011
0012       package DurationIO is new
                                  ADA.TEXT_IO.DECIMAL_IO( DURATION);
0013       use DurationIO;
0014
0015       StartTime   : TIME;
0016       EndTime     : TIME;
0017       ElapsedTime : DURATION;
0018
0019    begin -- DynamicTimer
0020       SET_COL( 10);
0021       PUT_LINE( "Simple dynamic timing");
0022       NEW_LINE( 2);
0023
0024       PUT( "The time taken for 1,000,000 iterations of " &
0025          "an empty loop is");
0026       StartTime := CLOCK;
0027       for Index in 1 .. 1_000_000 loop
0028          null;
0029       end loop;
0030       EndTime := CLOCK;
0031       ElapsedTime := EndTime - StartTime;
0032       PUT( ElapsedTime, EXP =>0); NEW_LINE(2);
0033    end DynamicTimer;
```

The data type DURATION is pre-declared by Ada for measuring time in seconds. The function CLOCK in the package ADA.CALENDAR returns a value of type TIME, also declared in ADA.CALENDAR, which indicates the time of day. A pre-declared subtraction operation will subtract one TIME value from another TIME value and return a value of type DURATION, indicating the elapsed time between the two TIME values.

The basis of the program presented above is to record the time before a null loop is iterated one million times. Following the loop the time is recorded for a second time and the elapsed time computed and displayed. The program fragment between lines 0026 and 0032 is a baseline against which the effects of additional operations can be measured.

The first thing to measure might be the cost of a swap, by adding the following lines to the initial program given above:

```
0015   -- Additional declarations for timing a swap.
0016   This : INTEGER := 42;
0017   That : INTEGER := 32;
0018   Temp : INTEGER;

0036   PUT( "The time taken for 1,000,000 non-procedural " &
0037        "integer swaps is");
0038   StartTime := CLOCK;
0039   for Index in 1 .. 1_000_000 loop
0040      Temp := This;
0041      This := That;
0042      That := Temp;
0043      Temp := This;
0044      This := That;
0045      That := Temp;
0046   end loop;
0047   EndTime := CLOCK;
0048   ElapsedTime := EndTime - StartTime;
0049   PUT( ElapsedTime, EXP =>0); NEW_LINE(2);
```

The body of the second loop actually swaps the values of the two variables *This* and *That* twice in order to restore them to their initial values, for reasons which will be made clear shortly. When this program was executed on an IBM PC clone with a 486 processor the following results were obtained:

```
The time taken for 1,000,000 iterations of an empty loop is
                                                       6.00000
The time taken for 1,000,000 non-procedural integer swaps
                                                    is 20.00000
```

This gives an arbitrary value of 14.0 for two swaps, or 7.0 for a single swap. A swap operation comprises three integer assignments, and therefore a cost of 2.33 can be associated with a single integer swap operation. By introducing a relational test around the swaps of the form if *This* > *That* then, the cost of the relational test can be deduced by the additional time which this operation takes. In order to ensure that the test controlling the if statement always evaluates true, the values have to be swapped twice in order to restore them to their initial values. In order to be able to compare this operation with the preceding operation, it too had to swap the values twice.

The process can be continued by adding more complex operations to the sequence and measuring the additional time taken. The relative costs of various operations using this method on the same machine are as follows:

Operation	Relative cost
Integer assignment	2.3
Integer swap	7.0
Relational comparison	4.0
Procedure call	11.0
Function call	13.0
Floating point assignment	3.8
Indexed loop 10 iterations	10.0
Indexed loop 100 iterations	90.0
While loop 10 iterations	12.0

These values should be treated with some reservation. The relative costs of each operation are not generalizable, the values obtained depending upon a large number of factors including: the compiler which is being used, the extent to which the compiler is being asked to optimize the code, the central processing unit of the computer on which the measurements are being made, the operating system which is running on the computer, and for multi-user or multiprocessing environments the system load. When due allowance is made for all these factors the precision of the numerical results becomes suspect. Assuming for a moment that the values are valid, the next step might be to attempt to use the results to compute the cost of a complete algorithm.

Using these measurements as a guide, an attempt to compute the costs of the various algorithms can be derived by adding the costs of the individual operations of which they are comprised. For example, the implementation of the *FindLowest* function from the insertion sort algorithm can be shown with the costs associated with each operation as follows:

```
13.0   function FindLowest( ListToCheck : in Lists)
                                    return Indexes is

04.4      LowestValueSoFar : Elements :=
                           ListToCheck( ListToCheck'FIRST);
04.1      LowestLocation   : Indexes := ListToCheck'FIRST;
       begin -- FindLowest
05.2      for ThisIndex in Indexes'SUCC( ListToCheck'FIRST) ..
                              ListToCheck'LAST loop
```

```
13.0         if SortRelation( ListToCheck( ThisIndex),
                                         LowestValueSoFar) then
04.1            LowestValueSofar := ListToCheck( ThisIndex);
04.1            LowestLocation := ThisIndex;
             end if;
          end loop;
          return LowestLocation;
       end FindLowest;
```

The difficulty of this approach may now be apparent: in order to derive a single value for the cost of the function an analysis of the dynamic behaviour of the function has to be made. The cost of the function itself is 13.0 and the cost of the once only initializations 8.9, giving a total of 21.9. The cost associated with the **for** loop is an estimation of a single iteration based upon a timed loop constructed as above. The timings within the loop indicate the cost of a single iteration, and in order to determine the average cost of a single iteration the number of times that the **if** condition within the loop evaluates true has to be estimated. Assuming that it evaluates true on 50% of all times when it is evaluated the cost of the function can be expressed as $21.9 + 5.2 + 13.0 + (0.5 * (4.1 + 4.1))n$ or approximately $40 + 4n$. Continuing this analysis with the *InsertionSort* code, as follows

```
11.0   procedure InsertionSort( ListToSort : in out Lists) is

       LowestLocation : Indexes;

       begin -- InsertionSort
05.2      for ThisIndex in ListToSort'FIRST ..
                            Indexes'PRED( ListToSort'LAST) loop
llll          LowestLocation :=
              FindLowest( ListToSort(
                                 ThisIndex .. ListToSort'LAST));
              Swap( ListToSort( ThisIndex),
14.0               ListToSort( LowestLocation));
          end loop;
       end InsertionSort;
```

the cost of the function *FindLowest* is shown as *llll* and indicates the value derived above. The total cost of this procedure is $11.0 + 19.2n + n(FindLowest(n/2))$. The call of *FindLowest* on average requires a list of length $n/2$ to be searched for reasons explained above. The total cost of the *InsertionSort* algorithm using this analysis, with integer approximations, can thus be approximated as $10 + 60n + 4n^2$.

When all the caveats regarding the manner in which the values for the cost of the individual operations were obtained, and the assumptions and simplifications which had to be made in order to compute this overall cost, the significance of the conclusion is too suspect to be reliable. This technique adds very little to the previous determination of the relative costs of algorithms using an order of algorithm analysis. Thus simplistic dynamic measurement of the costs of algorithms, by attempting to determine the cost of the individual operations and adding the individual costs together, is not a fruitful approach.

The only benefit of the approach is that the relative ordering of the costs of the different operations will give some indication of their complexity. Thus it can be assumed that the costs of swapping two values are always more expensive than comparing two values, and the costs of swapping using a procedure call are more expensive than including the relevant code in line. However, these conclusions should not be regarded as overwhelmingly important; an optimization with regard to execution time should only be attempted if the program is first working correctly and shown to be running too slowly. Then the bottlenecks within the program should be identified by a larger scale dynamic analysis, before small scale improvements are attempted upon the individual subprograms. These techniques will be explored further when more complex, larger scale dynamic analysis is introduced.

EXERCISES

30.1 Revisit the alternative sorting algorithms which were suggested in Exercise 27.1 and derive an order analysis for their performance.

30.2 Using the order analysis of various sorting algorithms from this chapter and from Exercise 30.1, and the dynamic timing approach introduced in this chapter, attempt to validate the analysis by sorting lists of different lengths with differing degrees of disorder.

30.3 One technique to mitigate the exponential increase in the resources required to sort lists as the length of the list increases is to use a *merge sort*. This approach involves splitting the list, sorting each sublist and then merging the sublists. For example, a list of 1000 elements could be divided into four lists of 250 elements, each of the four sublists then being sorted. Two of the 250 sublists could then be merged to produce a 500 element sorted list, following which the other two 250 element lists could be merged to produce a second 500 element sorted list. Finally the two 500 element lists could be merged to produce a 1000 element sorted list.

Assuming that a merge algorithm has an average case behaviour of n comparisons and $2n$ swaps, where n is the number of elements in one of the lists being merged, produce a table showing the costs of a *merge sort* for lists of various lengths compared with the costs for an insertion sort and a bubble sort.

30.4 Extend this table to show the effects of splitting the original list into 2, 4, 8 and 16 sublists. What conclusions can you make from these exercises?

30.5 Obtain a merge algorithm and produce an order analysis for it. Then implement and test the algorithm as a part of the generic sort package.

30.6 Using the package from Exercise 30.5 attempt to validate the results from Exercises 30.3 and 30.4.

CHAPTER 31

Flowgraphs and white box testing

The second part of the previous chapter indicated that techniques to attempt to relate simple dynamic measurements to a static analysis do not result in useful conclusions. A further objection to this approach is concerned with the true costs of the production of software. The most expensive part of a software development process is the costs associated with its initial production, and most particularly its maintenance, during its life cycle. The attempted measurements in the previous chapter were concerned with the speed of execution which is most closely related to the costs of the machine on which the software will run, as a faster machine can be assumed to cost more than a slower one. The construction and maintenance costs are related more to the cognitive complexity of a software component, rather than its computational complexity, although in most cases it can be expected that these two concepts are closely related.

Flowgraph analysis is a static measurement technique which produces a measurement which seems intuitively related to the cognitive complexity of an algorithm. The technique of flowgraph analysis also leads to a second approach to testing software, a technique which is known as *white box testing*. This chapter will commence with techniques of flowgraph analysis before introducing white box testing. Testing will be returned to in Chapter 34 when considerations which are not covered by the white box or black box approaches are introduced.

Flowgraph analysis

A flowgraph analysis is concerned with statically determining the number of different paths by which *flow of control* can pass through an algorithm. It can be argued that a developer or maintainer must be able to conceptualize the flow of control through an algorithm in order to understand fully its dynamic behaviour. Unless such an understanding is available the developer will not be able to predict fully the dynamic behaviour of the software and thus will not be able to ensure that all possible contingencies are allowed for in its design or implementation.

705

Producing a simple flowgraph

Although a flowgraph analysis can be made at the design stage this chapter will concentrate upon the production of flowgraphs from source code, as this is a prerequisite for the technique of white box testing. To illustrate the techniques of flowgraph analysis a flowgraph for the *SquareRoot* function introduced earlier in this section will be derived. The first implementation of the *SquareRoot* algorithm, whose design was presented in Chapter 29, is as follows:

```
0014    function SquareRoot( Number   : in FLOAT;
0015                         Accuracy : in FLOAT) return FLOAT is
0016
0017       MaximumValue        : FLOAT;
0018       MinimumValue        : FLOAT;
0019       CurrentGuess        : FLOAT;
0020       CurrentGuessSquared : FLOAT;
0021       CurrentError        : FLOAT;
0022       CloseEnough         : BOOLEAN := FALSE;
0023
0024    begin -- SquareRoot
0025       if Number > 1.0 then
0026          MaximumValue := Number;
0027          MinimumValue := 0.0;
0028       else
0029          MaximumValue := 1.0;
0030          MinimumValue := Number;
0031       end if;
0032       while not CloseEnough loop
0033          CurrentGuess := (MaximumValue + MinimumValue) / 2.0;
0034          CurrentGuessSquared := CurrentGuess * CurrentGuess;
0035          CurrentError := abs( Number - CurrentGuessSquared);
0036          if CurrentError <= Accuracy then
0037             CloseEnough := TRUE;
0038          else
0039             if CurrentGuessSquared >= Number then
0040                MaximumValue := CurrentGuess;
0041             else
0042                MinimumValue := CurrentGuess;
0043             end if;
0044          end if;
0045       end loop;
0046       return CurrentGuess;
0047    end SquareRoot;
```

The first stage in constructing a flowgraph is to note that at some stage flow of control will enter the subprogram and will at some stage leave the subprogram. This produces an initial flowgraph as shown in Figure 31.1.

A flowgraph consists of a number of *nodes*, shown as circles containing identifying letters, connected by *arcs* which have arrows indicating the direction in which flow of control will pass. The flowgraph in Figure 31.1 indicates that flow of control enters the subprogram at node *a*, flows through the arc and leaves at node *b*. The construction of the flowgraph continues by refining the flow of control within the subprogram, between points *a* and *b*.

Refinement proceeds by dividing the implementation into parts where flow of control has a single entry and exit point. In the *SquareRoot* function there is a sequence of four parts. The first part comprises the declaration and initialization of the local variables between lines 0017 and 0024, the second comprises the **if** structure between lines 0025 and 0031, the third is the **while** loop between lines 0032 and 0045 and the last is the single **return** statement on line 0046. The flowgraph can be refined to reflect these three regions of code, producing the flowgraph in Figure 31.2.

The four parts where flow of control enters and leaves are shown between nodes *a* and *c*, *c* and *d*, *d* and *e*, and between *e* and *b*. The first and last of these arcs require no further refinement as they represent regions of simple sequences of instructions, within which flow of control moves sequentially from instruction to instruction. The second arc requires further refinement which can proceed by

Figure 31.1   Initial *SquareRoot* flowgraph.

Figure 31.2   *SquareRoot* flowgraph, first refinement.

substituting the standard two way flowgraph for the arc between *c* and *d*. The standard two way flowgraph is shown in Figure 31.3.

Flow of control enters the flowgraph at node *s* and leaves at node *t*, following one of the two arcs connecting the nodes. This flowchart can be used to represent flow of control through **if** statements of the following forms:

```
-- One way if structure        -- Two way if structure
if Condition then              if Condition then
   -- Actions.                     -- First actions.
end if;                        else
                                   -- Second actions.
                               end if;
```

For the one way **if** structure flow of control can cause the *Actions* to be either performed or omitted. For the two way **if** structure flow of control can cause either *First actions* or *Second actions* to be performed. The two possible flows of control are represented by the two arcs connecting the nodes. For more complex sequential selection structures, for example an **elsif** structure or a **case** structure of the following forms, the more complex flowgraph in Figure 31.4 would be required:

```
-- Three way elseif structure      -- Three way case structure
if FirstCondition then             case SelectionValue is
   -- First actions.               when => FirstValueList
elsif SecondCondition then            -- First actions.
   -- Second actions.              when => SecondValueList
else                                  -- Second actions.
   -- Third actions.               default
end if;                               -- Third actions
                                   end case;
```

Figure 31.3 Standard flowchart for a two way selection.

Figure 31.4 Standard flowchart for a three way selection.

Additional **elsif** options or **case** options in the sequential selection structures will cause additional arcs connecting the two nodes to be added. Inserting a two way selection flowgraph into the *SquareRoot* flowchart to represent the two way **if** structure between lines 0025 and 0031, will produce the flowgraph in Figure 31.5.

Refinement continues with the arc between nodes *d* and *e* which represent the **while** loop in the implementation. The standard loop flowgraph shown in Figure 31.6.

Flow of control can pass straight from node *l* to node *m* without following the circular arc back to the node. This would be the case for a **while** loop if the first time the condition controlling the loop was tested it evaluated false. If a **for** loop was being represented then flow of control would avoid the circular route if the loop conditions were such that the body of the loop was not executed. The circular route represents the body of the loop and in circumstances where flow of control enters the loop body a representation of flow of control would indicate that node *l* was visited more than once indicating that the circular arc was followed. Inserting the standard loop flowgraph into the *SquareRoot* flowchart produces the refinement shown in Figure 31.7.

The construction of the flowgraph continues by the refinement of the body of the loop. The first refinement would divide it into a sequence of two parts: the first is the sequence of statements between lines 0026 and 0028; the second part is the nested **if** statements between lines 0029 and 0037. Substituting a flowgraph

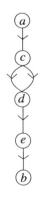

Figure 31.5   SquareRoot function, second refinement.

Figure 31.6   Standard loop flowgraph.

709

Figure 31.7   SquareRoot function, third refinement.

representing a sequence of two parts into the arc which represents the body of the loop produces the flowgraph in Figure 31.8.

The arc between *d* and *f* represents a sequence of simple instructions and requires no further refinement; the arc between *f* and *d* represents the nested **if** statement which will have to be refined in two stages. The first stage of refinement will substitute a standard two way selection flowgraph to represent the outermost **if**, producing the flowgraph in Figure 31.9.

The final refinement will replace one of the arcs between *f* and *d* with a two way flowgraph to represent the two way **if** structure on lines 0039 to 0043. The final, completely refined, flowchart for the *SquareRoot* function is shown in Figure 31.10.

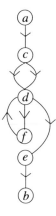

Figure 31.8   SquareRoot function, fourth refinement.

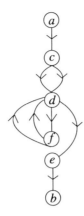

Figure 31.9   SquareRoot function, fifth refinement.

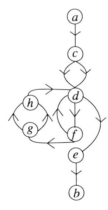

Figure 31.10   SquareRoot function, final refinement.

Flowgraph complexity analysis

The complete flowgraph which has been produced by successive refinement from the source code now indicates all the possible paths by which flow of control can pass through the *SquareRoot* function. In its current state it provides a simple pictorial representation of the dynamic complexity of the subprogram, which can be compared visually with other flowgraphs to compare the relative complexity of two or more subprograms.

A more satisfactory approach to deriving a measure of complexity from a flowgraph would require some measurement of the graph. The most obvious measurement might be to count the number of nodes and the number of arcs. In the final *SquareRoot* flowgraph above there are eight nodes and ten arcs. Each node represents a location within the software where a simple sequential flow of control joins with another simple sequential flow of control and each arc represents the flow of control through a simple sequence.

Although a count of the number of arcs and nodes gives some indication of the complexity of a flowgraph, the real indication of the software's complexity is in the *topological* relationship of the nodes and arcs. The topology of a graph is the number of non-connected areas on the graph; each non-connected area is known as a **region** and the number of regions is independent of the precise way in which the graph is laid out. The three flowcharts in Figure 31.11 have a similar number of nodes and arcs, but the two right hand flowcharts intuitively have a greater complexity than the left hand chart as they have a greater number of regions.

The left hand flowgraph has four nodes and three arcs, the middle four nodes and four arcs and the right hand flowgraph three nodes and three arcs. The relationship between the number of arcs and the number of nodes is significant. Where a flowgraph has one fewer arcs than nodes it can be argued that every arc must connect one node with another node, without any two nodes being connected by more than one arc. This will produce a flowgraph consisting of a single region, as shown on the left hand flowgraph in Figure 31.11.

Continuing the argument it can be shown that there can never be less than this number of arcs as this would result in some nodes being unconnected with the rest of the flowgraph. The situation where there are as many arcs as nodes produces flowgraphs such as the two right hand graphs in Figure 31.11 where one arc must either duplicate an existing connection between two nodes or define a loop arc connecting a node to itself. In both cases the additional arc has changed the topology of the graph by defining a region within the graph. It can be shown that for every additional arc above the number of nodes another closed region is added to the graph. The sequence of flowgraphs in Figure 31.12 illustrates that adding arcs increases the number of regions.

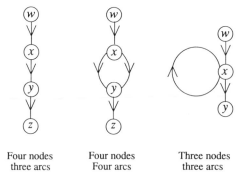

Four nodes   Four nodes   Three nodes
three arcs   Four arcs   three arcs

Figure 31.11 Nodes, arcs and complexity.

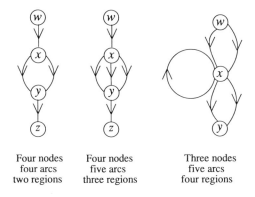

Four nodes	Four nodes	Three nodes
four arcs	five arcs	five arcs
two regions	three regions	four regions

Figure 31.12 Nodes, arcs and complexity.

Thus the number of regions in a flowgraph is the most important indicator of complexity and can be derived by counting the number of regions on the flowgraph, including the external region in the count. Alternatively the number of nodes and arcs can be counted and the number of regions decided by using the formula

$$regions = nodes - arcs + 2$$

This measure of the complexity of an algorithm, the number of regions in its flowgraph, is known as **McCabes complexity metric**. Although this technique establishes a metric for the complexity of an algorithm, it does not give any indication of the appropriate complexity which should be aimed for. Cognitive psychologists have determined that a human is only capable of maintaining and manipulating cognitive models which contain *seven plus or minus two*, that is between five and nine, *cognitive chunks* of information. Assuming that a region on a flowgraph is equivalent to a *cognitive chunk* then it can be concluded that subprograms should not be constructed which contain more than a maximum of about nine regions and preferably should be limited to less than seven.

Flowgraphs and testing

The technique of complexity measurement introduced above leads to a technique of testing known as white box testing. Before introducing this technique in detail a black box test rationale for the *SquareRoot* function will be developed in order that the two techniques can be subsequently compared.

A black box test rationale for the *SquareRoot* function

Assuming that the *SquareRoot* function will always be called with legitimate parameters the black box diagram, range diagrams, subrange diagrams, list of test cases and test plan, produced using the techniques for black box testing introduced in Section II Chapter 13, might be as follows.

Black Box Diagram

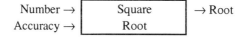

```
Number →   ┌──────────────┐   → Root
           │   Square     │
Accuracy → │   Root       │
           └──────────────┘
```

Range Diagrams

```
Number      0.0-----------------------------------------------FLOAT'LAST
Accuracy    0.0-----------------------------------------------FLOAT'LAST
Root        0.0-----------------------------------------------FLOAT'LAST
```

Subrange Diagrams

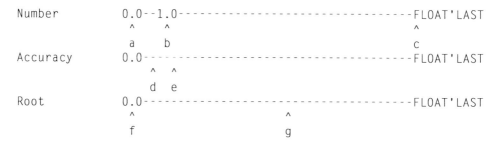

```
Number      0.0--1.0----------------------------------FLOAT'LAST
              ^    ^                                    ^
              a    b                                    c
Accuracy    0.0-------------------------------------FLOAT'LAST
                 ^  ^
                 d  e
Root        0.0-------------------------------------FLOAT'LAST
              ^                      ^
              f                      g
```

Test cases

Test cases for *SquareRoot* function

Case	Value	Notes
a	0.0	Smallest possible Number value
b	0.9	Number value below but near to 1.0
c	FLOAT'LAST	Largest possible Number value

d	0.1	Accuracy value
e	0.01	Different accuracy value
f	0.0	Smallest possible root value
g	root(F'L)	Root of FLOAT'LAST

Test plan

Run no.	Cases	Number	Accuracy	Predicted root
1	a,d,f	0.0	0.1	0.0 – 0.1
2	b,e	0.9	0.01	0.947..0.949
3	b.e.g	F'L	0.01	root(F'L) – 0.01 root(F'L) + 0.01

The *Number* range diagram has been divided into two significant subranges at the value 1.0, as values between 0.0 and 1.0 have square roots which are larger and numbers above 1.0 have square roots which are lower. This minimal black box test plan will test the *SquareRoot* function using only three test runs. This might not seem a convincing test for this function and a realistic test regime might add some additional tests as the costs of testing are not very high compared with the increased confidence which they will yield. However, as the intention in this part of the chapter is to compare black box and white box techniques only this minimal plan will be used in the comparison. In a more realistic testing environment where test plans were being produced for a large number of disparate subprograms then only a minimal plan would be used as the additional costs might not be justified.

A white box test rationale for the *SquareRoot* function

The intention in white box testing is to ensure that all possible feasible flow of control paths through a subprogram are traversed whilst the software is under test. This is not the same as saying that all statements in the subprogram will be executed as it is possible for all statements to be executed but for not all of the possible paths to be traversed. However, the converse is true: if all possible paths through a subprogram are traversed then all statements in the subprogram will necessarily be executed.

When considering the number of possible paths through a subprogram two other factors need to be remembered. The first is that some of the possible paths through a subprogram turn out upon investigation to be non-feasible paths. The second consideration is that the number of possible paths through a subprogram

715

indicated by a flowgraph analysis will indicate the minimum number of paths to ensure complete coverage. This may be less than the total number of paths which are possible when combinations of paths are allowed for. Examples of these two considerations will be given after the white box testing of the *SquareRoot* function has been presented.

The number of possible paths through a subprogram is equal to the number of regions in the subprogram's flowgraph. The final flowgraph for the *SquareRoot* function, with the regions numbered, is shown in Figure 31.13.

This indicates that there are five possible paths through the flowgraph which can be described by listing the sequence in which the nodes must be visited. The five paths in the *SquareRoot* flowgraph are as follows:

Path 1 $a\ c^1\ d\ e\ b$

Path 2 $a\ c^2\ d\ e\ b$

Path 3 $a\ c^x\ d\ f\ d\ e\ b$

Path 4 $a\ c^x\ d\ f\ g^1\ h\ d\ e\ b$

Path 5 $a\ c^x\ d\ f\ g^2\ h\ d\ e\ b$

The first two paths differ only in the arc which is followed between nodes *c* and *d*; to indicate which node is intended the nodes have been labelled 1 and 2 and the paths annotated to indicate which arc is intended. In the subsequent paths the arc traversed between *c* and *d* is shown as *x*, indicating that it does not matter which particular arc is followed.

The white box process continues by taking the black box test plan and manually determining which of the paths will be traversed by each of the test runs. It is immediately obvious that with only three test runs in the black box test plan there are not enough test runs to be certain that all five paths will be traversed.

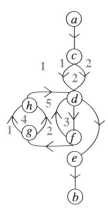

Figure 31.13   SquareRoot flowgraph with regions numbered.

A trace of the first test run from the black box test plan will indicate that the second part of the **if** statement will be followed before the loop is entered and that the value of *CurrentError* when computed on line 0028 would be 0.0, causing the **if** condition on line 0036 to be true. Consequently the value of *CloseEnough* will be set to true and the loop will terminate after the first iteration. Relating this to the flowgraph this produces the path *a c d f d e b*, which is Path 3 on the white box test plan.

The second test run will also follow the second path of the selection before entering the loop. The **if** on line 0036 will evaluate false causing the **if** on line 0039 to be evaluated. This condition will evaluate false as the current guess will be 0.95 whose square (0.9025) is greater than *Number* (0.9). Following the end of both **if** statements the loop condition will evaluate true again and the loop will iterate for a second time. The path traversed so far would be *a c d f g h d* and as the algorithm is known to terminate at some stage the path *d e b* would have to be traversed at some stage. Thus the complete path *a c d f g h d e b*, Path 4 from the white box test plan, will have been known to be traversed during test run 2.

The third black box test will differ from the second only in the arc which it traverses between nodes *g* and *h*. In this case the square will be larger than *Number* and the alternative path will be followed. The full path is *a c d f g h d e b*, which is Path 5 from the white box test plan

Paths 1 and 2 will now have to be examined to determine if they are feasible. Both of these paths will be followed only if the body of the **while** loop is never entered. An examination of the source code will indicate that this can never happen. The loop is controlled by the value of the Boolean variable *CloseEnough*, for the loop body never to execute this variable will have to have the value true when the condition is evaluated for the first time. This is not possible as the value of the variable is set to false when the variable is declared. Paths 1 and 2 are thus examples of possible paths through a flowgraph which, upon investigation, turn out to be a non-feasible path.

Unfortunately the total number of feasible possible paths is not always the same as the number of possible paths which are produced from a flowgraph. The two flowgraphs in Figure 31.14 and the example implementations both have three regions, but differ in the number of paths.

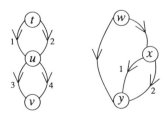

Figure 31.14 Paths and coverage.

```
if Condition1 then                    if Condition1 then
   -- First actions.                     -- First actions.
else                                  else
   -- Second actions.                    if Condition2 then
end if;                                     -- Third actions.
                                          else
                                            -- Fourth actions.
if Condition2 then                        end if;
   -- Third actions.                   end if;
elsif
   -- Fourth actions.
end if;
```

Path 1 $t^1\,u^1\,v$ Path 1 $w\,y$
Path 2 $t^2\,u^1\,v$ Path 2 $w\,x^1\,y$
Path 3 $t^1\,u^2\,v$ Path 3 $w\,x^2\,y$
Path 4 $t^2\,u^2\,v$

The reasons why the flowgraph on the left has a total of four feasible paths and the one on the right only three, despite the fact that both flowgraphs have the same degree of cyclometric complexity, are complex and are rooted in a branch of mathematics known as **graph theory**. Despite this problem the technique of flowgraph analysis and the subsequent counting of regions is still a valuable measure of cognitive complexity, and the number of **bias paths** which it indicates is the smallest number of distinct feasible paths which should be looked for. As this example indicates, there may also be more possible paths which should be checked for when the flowgraph is used as the basis of white box testing.

Black box and white box testing compared

The example above indicates that white box testing can indicate test considerations which are not produced by black box testing. The converse is also true: black box testing can produce test considerations which are not produced by white box testing.

White box testing is concerned only with testing the software product, it cannot guarantee that the complete specification has been implemented. Black box testing is concerned only with testing the specification, it cannot guarantee that all parts of the implementation have been tested. Thus black box testing is testing against the specification and will discover **faults of omission**, indicating that part of the specification has not been fulfilled. White box testing is testing against the implementation and will discover **faults of commission**, indicating that part of the implementation is faulty. In order to test fully a software product both black and white box testing are required.

White box testing is much more expensive than black box testing. It requires the source code to be produced before the tests can be planned and is much more laborious in the determination of suitable input data and in the determination of whether the software is or is not correct. The advice given is to start test planning with a black box test approach as soon as the specification is available. White box planning should commence as soon as all black box tests have been successfully passed, with the production of flowgraphs and determination of paths. The paths should then be checked against the black box test plan and any additional required test runs determined and applied.

The consequences of test failure at this stage may be very expensive. A failure of a white box test may result in a change which requires all black box testing to be repeated and the redetermination of the white box paths. The cheaper option is to regard the process of testing as one of *quality assurance* rather than *quality control*. The intention is that sufficient quality will be put into all previous design and production stages so that testing will confirm that there are very few faults present (quality assurance), rather than testing being relied upon to discover any faults in the software (quality control). A combination of black box and white box test considerations is still not a completely adequate test rationale; additional considerations will be introduced in Chapter 34.

More complex flowgraphs

In addition to the three flow of control structures whose flowgraphs were introduced at the start of this chapter there are several other flow of control considerations which may have an effect upon the flowgraph. The first consideration is the effect that calling subprograms may have.

If the subprogram is guaranteed to return without raising any exception then the subprogram call can be regarded as a simple statement in the construction of the flowgraph and can form part of an arc between nodes. This is because flow of control will enter the subprogram and will at some stage leave the subprogram with flow of control passing to the next statement in sequence.

The next consideration is the call of a subprogram which may raise an exception which will not be handled within the subprogram whose flowgraph is being constructed. There are two examples of this in the fully developed *SquareRoot* function presented previously in Chapter 29. The fully developed subprogram contained two calls to the *CheckAssertion* procedure, one to check the pre-condition at the start of the function and one to check the post-condition at the end of the function. Either of these subprogram calls might result in an *Assertion-Error* exception being raised which will not be handled within the *SquareRoot* function and will be propagated to the calling environment.

The flowgraph representation of this situation consists of regarding the call of the subprogram not as a simple sequential action, but as a conditional action which may cause flow of control to be passed to the exit point rather than to the next statement. The revised *SquareRoot* flowgraph for this version would be as shown in Figure 31.15.

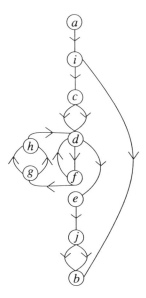

Figure 31.15   SquareRoot flowgraph with assertion checking.

Node *i* has been introduced to represent the call of *AssertionCheck* at the start of the body of the function, following the declaration and initialization of the local variables. It may result in flow of control passing onwards towards the selection at node *c* if the exception is not raised. If the exception is raised flow of control passes immediately to the point where all flow of control leaves the subprogram at node *b*. Node *j* has been introduced to represent the call of *AssertionCheck* at the end of the function immediately before the **return** statement. One of the arcs between nodes *j* and *b* represents flow of control leaving the subprogram because the *AssertionError* has been raised and the other represents flow of control leaving the subprogram when the **return** statement is executed.

Although there are three possible locations in this subprogram where flow of control can actually leave – the two places where the exception is raised and the **return** statement – all three have been collected together at node *b* in order to satisfy the requirement for a flowgraph that there is one point where control enters and one point where control leaves. A flowgraph is concerned only with the patterns of flow of control within a subprogram and not with the reasons why control leaves it. The addition of assertion checking to the *SquareRoot* function has raised its complexity from eight nodes, ten arcs and four regions to ten nodes, fourteen arcs and six regions, which is still within the recommended complexity limit.

The final consideration is a subprogram which not only may raise an exception, but will also contain an exception handler for it. To illustrate this situation a flowgraph for the *GetValidPurchasePrice* subprogram introduced to illustrate exception handling in Section II Chapter 19 will be developed. The implementation of this subprogram, whose design was given in Section II Chapter 19, is as follows:

```
0001    procedure GetValidPurchasePrice( ValidPrice : out FLOAT) is
0002
0003        IsValidPrice   : BOOLEAN := FALSE;
0004        PossiblePrice : FLOAT;
0005
0006    begin -- GetValidPurchasePrice
0007        while not IsValidPrice loop
0008            begin -- posit/admit block
0009                PUT("Please enter the purchase price ");
0010                -- implicit exception may be raised here
0011                GET( PossiblePrice); SKIP_LINE;
0012                if PossiblePrice <= MinPrice or
0013                    PossiblePrice > MaxPrice then
0014                        -- raise explicit exception
0015                        raise DATA_ERROR;
0016                end if;
0017                IsValidPrice := TRUE;
0018            exception
0019                when DATA_ERROR =>
0020                    SKIP_LINE;
0021                    PUT("This value is invalid!"); NEW_LINE;
0022                    PUT("Please enter a value ");
0023                    PUT("(including decimal parts) between ");
0024                    PUT( MinPrice, EXP=>0, FORE=>4, AFT=>2);
0025                    PUT(" and ");
0026                    PUT( MaxPrice, EXP=>0, FORE=>4, AFT=>2);
0027                    NEW_LINE;
0028            end; -- posit/admit block
0029        end loop;
0030        ValidPrice := PossiblePrice;
0031    end GetValidPurchasePrice;
```

The corresponding flowgraph for this procedure is shown in Figure 31.16.

All flow of control enters the graph at node *a* and leaves at node *h*. The arc between *a* and *b* represents the declaration and initialization of the local variables, and the arc between *b* and *h* the statement on line 0032 which exports the obtained value. The main loop is represented by the flowgraph which connects node *b* with itself.

Assuming that the user enters a valid floating point value which does not raise the exception on line 0015 flow of control will pass through nodes *c d e g* and *i* back to *b*. Node *c* represents the **begin** on line 0008 and node *i* the **end** on line

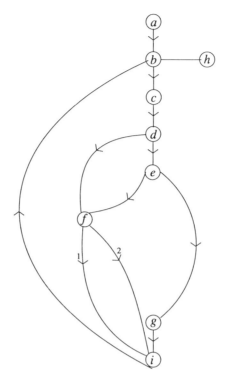

Figure 31.16 GetValidPurchasePrice flowgraph.

0028 through which all paths must pass. Node *d* represents the GET statement on line 0011, node *e* the **if** on line 0012 and the arc between *e* and *g* the flow of control which does not execute the body of the **if**. The arc between *g* and *i* represents flow of control passing through lines 0018 and 0019 before passing immediately to the end of the posit/admit block at node *i*.

If an exception is raised by the GET procedure at line 0011 then flow of control will pass from node *d* to nodes f^1 *i b*. Node *f* represents the start of the exception block and the arc labelled 1 the path to the end of the exception block which includes the DATA_ERROR exception handler. The final path passes through the body of the **if** following node *e* and caused the exception to be explicitly raised, causing flow of control to pass through the exception handler, f^1 *i b*, as before.

The techniques of flowgraph analysis, introduced in this chapter, can be used to construct white box test plans. They can also be used to derive a cognitive complexity metric but by itself this does not provide sufficient information regarding the nature of small pieces of code. Additional small scale metrics are required and a selection of these will be introduced in the next chapter.

EXERCISES

31.1 Derive flowgraphs for the various sorting algorithms *Insertion*, *Bubble*, *Quick* and *Heap*. Derive their cyclometric complexity from the flowgraphs and compare this with the order analysis from Exercise 30.1.

31.2 Derive a black box test rationale for any sorting algorithm, and then derive a white box sorting algorithm for each of the flowgraphs in Exercise 31.1. When the order analysis, the cyclometric complexity and the white box test plans are all considered, does it change your opinion of the sort algorithm which you would favour?

31.3 Revisit the black box test plan produced for the generic list package in Exercise 28.1. Construct flowgraphs for the package and produce a white box test plan. Compare the two plans and decide if additional testing is necessary.

31.4 From your recent development experience, choose two or more subprograms which caused you considerable difficulty, two or more which were hard but not difficult, and two which were easy. Derive flowgraphs for them and determine if their difficulty was related to their complexity. If not, determine what aspect of the subprograms caused them to be so difficult.

CHAPTER 32

Small scale software metrics

The two previous chapters have introduced the concepts of measurable attributes of software, a topic known as *software metrics*. This chapter will continue and consolidate the theme of measurement by first introducing the reasons why software should be measured and subsequently introducing a variety of measurements which can be made, largely on individual subprograms.

Software metrics can be divided into *specification based*, *static* and *dynamic* measurements which refer correspondingly to measurements which can be made on the specification, those which can be made on the source code and those which can only be made when the software is executing. A second division is into *small scale* and *large scale* measurements, which refer correspondingly to measurements made on an individual subprogram and measurements made on an entire software project. Between these two scales of measurement are measurements which can be made on a package and those which can be made on a class hierarchy. To distinguish these measurements they are known as *object oriented metrics*. One further set of measurements which will be introduced are directed towards the usability of software products and are known as *usability metrics*.

This chapter will introduce the processes which can be used to make measurements on individual subprograms. Larger scale metrics and usability metrics will be introduced in the next chapter.

The reasons for measurement

The two most fundamental reasons for measuring software are to control the processes of software production and to indicate the quality of the product. The act of measurement is, however, fraught with potential problems. The major problem is to define exactly what is being measured and to ensure that the metric produced reflects this attribute accurately.

There is a story concerning an early attempt to use metrics in software production which is very probably not true but is none the less very instructive. In an attempt to improve software productivity the management of a software house introduced a productivity bonus based upon the number of lines of source code which a developer completed. The first response by the developers was to start to use an excessive number of comments, as these were included in the definition of completed lines of code. The situation changed from where the management were concerned that there were too few comments in finished code to one where they were overwhelmingly concerned that it was very difficult to read the code as the comments were getting in the way.

When management excluded comments from the definition of completed lines of code, the developers then improved their measured productivity by devising techniques to increase the number of statements required to accomplish a task. For example, the following lines of Ada code will both result in the value of the variables *This* and *That* being swapped.

```
Temp := This;           TempThis := This;
This := That;           TempThat := That;
That := This;           This     := TempThat;
                        That     := TempThis
```

The right hand version requires an extra statement and would, on the measurement above, indicate that the developer using that technique was 33% more productive than the developer who used the left hand technique.

The problem in this example is that management were using an obvious metric which was simple to administer and produced a definite verifiable numeric result. However, the metric failed to measure adequately its intended attribute, productivity. Adequate measurements of productivity are more complex to define and less definite in the numbers which they produce, as will be shown shortly.

This fable also illustrates the second major problem with measurement. The act of measuring a situation can change the situation and cause the metric produced to reflect the state of the situation as it is measured, and not the situation as it would be without the measurement being made. This can cause any conclusions which are based upon the measurements not to be generalizable to situations where the measurement is not being made.

Despite these two major problems with measurement, which are properties of measurement in general and not particular to software measurement, techniques for measuring software have proved themselves to be invaluable in improving the processes of software production and the quality of produced software.

Metrics can assist with the process of software production by measuring the state of completion of a software project. Comparative measurements of productivity between two individuals or between two teams of software developers must be based upon some accurate measurement of the complexity of the development task which they are undertaking. If such a measurement can be made from the specification of a software component then the measurement process can also be used to predict the amount of resources required to complete a project.

A simple definite measurement such as the number of lines of code, or the number of subprograms, or the number of packages, which have been completed or which are yet to be completed, is not appropriate for the reasons which were explained above. A more appropriate measurement would require the complexity of each completed or required subprogram or package to be taken into account. Thus a team may have completed 50 out of 100 subprograms from a design, but might have completed less than half the project if they started with the simpler subprograms. Alternatively more than half the project might be complete if they started with the more complex subprograms. Thus a statement about the proportion of the project completed or about the amount of resources required to complete a project can only be made if there is some measurement technique which can indicate the complexity of a software unit from its specification.

Such measurements of productivity can also be used for strategic as opposed to project control. Should a new style of development, or new method of team organization, or the use of a new tool, or the use of a new programming language, be proposed, productivity metrics will be essential. The effects, either beneficial or harmful, of the proposal could be measured by predicting the productivity using established techniques and measuring the actual productivity when using the new techniques. For this to be possible the management structure of the developing organization must have available historical information concerning the complexity and productivity of the established techniques which have been gathered over a number of projects.

Metrics for the quality of software are primarily concerned with recording and tracking defects or shortcomings in the product. As with the measurement of productivity this is most useful if it can be used pro-actively to make a statement about the quality of the software when it is produced, rather than being used retro-actively to record the number of defects as they are discovered. Again the basis of an accurate prediction is to have available records of the number of defects discovered in similar products produced using similar techniques. This historical information can also be used to assess the changes in software quality which any new technique causes.

Measuring the complexity of a specification

Techniques for measuring the complexity of a specification are, for reasons discussed above, essential to the control of a software production process. This is essentially a static metric which can only be validated by first predicting the complexity of a component and subsequently measuring the effort required to develop and to maintain it.

The basis of predicting complexity from a specification is to perform a *feature point* analysis. The first stage in performing this analysis is to examine the specification and note the following factors:

Number of user inputs. A user input is where the user supplied some application oriented data to the software.

Number of user outputs. A user output is application oriented data supplied to the user. This includes printed reports, screens of information and error messages. The individual components of the reports or screens are not counted.

Number of user enquiries. A user enquiry is distinguished from a user input as it is concerned with controlling the software rather than supplying application oriented data. Thus a request to enter a record is a user enquiry, but entering the data is a user input.

Number of external files used. This excludes the standard input on which the user supplies information and the standard output on which the application displays information.

Number of external interfaces. All interfaces which transmit information to or from another part of the system are counted. These include disks, printers, modems, network links etc.

Algorithms. The algorithms required to fulfil the specification.

Each of these factors is then multiplied by a weighting as in the following table:

Function	Number	Weighting	Subtotal
Number of user inputs		4	
Number of user outputs		5	
Number of user inquiries		4	
Number of files		7	
Number of external interfaces		7	
Algorithms		3	
		function total	_____

The number of occurrences of each criterion is entered in the column headed Number and multiplied by the Weighting factor, before the weighted subtotals are summed to give a *function total* for the specification.

In addition to the measurements made above, the following questions concerning the system are answered on a five point scale, where 0 indicates that the subject of the question has no influence upon the system and 5 indicates that it is of overwhelming influence.

Feature	Response (0 to 5)
1 Does the system require backup and recovery?	
2 Are data communications required?	
3 Are any of the functions distributed between processors?	

4 Is performance time critical?
5 Will the system be installed into existing, busy, environments?
6 Does the system require on-line data entry?
7 Is data entry split over screens or sessions?
8 Are files updated on-line?
9 Are inputs, outputs or inquiries complex?
10 Is algorithmic processing complex?
11 Is the software intended to be reusable?
12 Is conversion of an existing system and installation of the new system included in the specification?
13 Is the software intended to be used in different environments?
14 Is the software user configurable?

feature total

The *function total* and the *feature total* are then combined to give a *function point value* using the following formula:

function point value = function total × [0.65 + (0.01 × feature total)]

The resulting value is intended to represent the complexity of a software project, and would require validation for a particular organization by relating the function point values to the recorded effort taken to develop the software and the number of defects recorded. The weighting values on the function total table and the numeric factors in the calculation of the final function point value are arbitrary and may need to be adapted in the light of experience.

This version of the technique is intended to be used to measure the complexity of a complete project specification rather than the complexity of an individual software component. The basic technique can be adapted for smaller scale considerations to produce feature point complexity estimates for packages and subprograms.

Static metrics

The basic technique for measuring the small scale complexity of an implementation was introduced in the previous chapter. *McCabes cyclomatic complexity* measures the number of possible paths through an algorithm by counting the number of distinct regions on a flowgraph. The measurable attribute was validated by evaluating it to the cognitive complexity of the algorithm which it was representing. However, the measurement is related to the flow of control and does not include other considerations such as the complexity of the decisions which control the flow or the operations which comprise the arcs.

The simplest and most straightforward additional measurement which could be made is to count the number of lines of source code which are required. This is a very inadequate measurement, for reasons which were explained above and because it is very dependent upon the programming language being used. Even if the measurement is accepted as valid it is still not as well defined as it might appear. For example, it is not clear how to count the following:

- Lines which consist only of comments.

- Blank lines which are included for readability.

- Lines which only contain declarations of program objects.

- Lines containing only a **begin** or **end** statement.

- Lines which contain more than an Ada statement.

- Lines which contain only part of an Ada statement.

The most straightforward measurement might be that the number of lines of code to be counted is all lines which are not blank and which are not composed entirely of comments, irrespective of the number of Ada statements or declarations which they contain. This might be better termed *effective lines of code* (ELOC). One useful measurement which can be derived from it is the ***density of comments***. This can be defined as

density of comments = number of comments/effective lines of code

The density of comments value will be between 0.0 and 1.0 and it can be used as *a quality indicator*. A quality indicator is an attribute which if present does not guarantee the quality of the product, but if absent it indicates that one aspect of quality is missing. A cut-off value for comment density might be declared by an organization and source code whose comment density fell below this value could be rejected as being undercommented.

Other aspects of the way in which source code is written are also amenable for use as quality indicators. The average length, in characters, of identifiers will give some indication of the meaningfulness of the identifiers chosen by a developer. Meaningful identifiers tend to be longer rather than shorter and a cut-off value for the average length might be decided upon.

The extent to which source code complies with indentation requirements can also be measured and a very low tolerance for deviations from the recommended use of indentation enforced. The use of capitals and lower case conventions can also be easily checked. Compliance with these factors can easily be measured by a software tool which first examines the existing source code and reformats it according to the specified conventions. It can then measure the existing source code against the reformatted code for deviations. However, if such a tool is available then it could easily be configured to output the reformatted source code ensuring that it complies with the convention. Such a tool is known as a ***pretty printer*** and if it is available a near zero tolerance for deviations from recommended style can be enforced.

All of these considerations need to be communicated to a developer and require the organization to state them explicitly in a ***source code layout style guide***, commonly known simply as a ***style guide***.

Although all of these measurements can be used as source code quality indicators they do not assist with measuring the complexity of the implementation. The basis of a cyclomatic complexity is the number of places where flow of control can divide and a refinement to the basic measurement would be to attempt to measure the complexity of these decisions. The majority of these decisions are formed from BOOLEAN expressions and an analysis of the possible forms of a BOOLEAN expression will yield a decision complexity measurement.

The simplest BOOLEAN expression is the value of a BOOLEAN variable, and this can be give an arbitrary complexity value of 1. The next simplest possible expression is a negated BOOLEAN value which can be given an increased complexity value of 1.5. Continuing this approach a complexity value can be assigned to each part of a complex BOOLEAN expression and the overall complexity derived by adding all the factors together. The following table presents a possible scale of factors for the commonest components of a BOOLEAN expression:

Expression	Value
Simple BOOLEAN variable	1.0
BOOLEAN negation (**not**)	0.5
BOOLEAN operator (**and or xor**)	1.0
Simple relation (=><)	0.5
Complex relation (/= >= <=)	1.0

Thus the BOOLEAN expression controlling a binary chop sort, which might take the following form

```
while (not Located) and (LowerBound < UpperBound) loop
```

could have its complexity calculated as: 1.5 for the **not** *Located* term, 0.5 for the less than (<) relation and 1.0 for the **and** conjunction; this gives a total of 3.0 for the overall complexity of the decision. By computing the average complexity of all the controlling expressions in the subprogram, an ***expression complexity*** metric can be obtained. This can be used in conjunction with the ***cyclometric complexity*** metric to give a better indication of a subprogram's complexity.

Many of the controlling expressions used in the source code examples in this book have been deliberately constructed so that they are controlled by a simple

Boolean variable expression. The complexity of the controlling decision is then in part determined by the supporting operations in the body of the code. An *operation complexity* metric can be determined by a similar technique to that used for computing the expression complexity above. A suitable extension to the table above for computing the complexity might be as follows:

Expression	Value
Assignment	0.5
Common arithmetic (+, −, *, /, **)	0.5
Other arithmetic (**mod, abs,** etc.)	1.0
Membership or non-membership (**in, not in**)	1.0
Implicit or explicit parenthesis	1.0
Array subscript (Array(Location))	0.5
Record component of (Record.Field)	0.5
Type conversion (e.g. INTEGER(FloatVar)	1.0
Simple attribute (e.g. 'LAST)	1.0
Function attribute (e.g. 'VAL(~))	1.5
Function **return** statement	0.5

Following the binary chop example above, the following supporting expressions might be required:

```
a) MiddleLocation := UpperLocation + LowerLocation /2;
b) Located := List( MiddleLocation) = ItemToFind;
c) UpperBound := MiddleLocation -1;
d) LowerBound := MiddleLocation +1;
```

The complexity of each of these expressions is as follows:

a) addition + implicit parenthesis + division = 2.0
b) array subscript + simple relation = 1.0
c) subtraction = 0.5
d) addition = 0.5

Thus the average *operational complexity* of these four expressions is 1.0. In addition to the **total number of expressions** and their **average operational complexity**, the **number of unique operators** used in the source code also has an influence upon its complexity. A **unique operator** is one where the name of the operator or the types of the operands is different from all other operators used in the code. For the four expressions above there are three unique operators: INTEGER addition (+), INTEGER subtraction (−) and INTEGER division (/).

This approach to determining the complexity of a software component by assigning complexity ratings to the various operations can be continued by

731

deriving a technique for the classification of subprogram calls. The complexity of a subprogram call depends upon the number and modes of its actual parameters. A complexity factor of 1.0 is allowed for an *in only* parameter, 1.5 for an *out only* parameter and 2.0 for an *in out* parameter, with a lower bound of 1.0 for parameterless subprogram calls. These values are weighted by a factor of 1.0 for subprograms declared in commonly used standard packages, 1.25 for subprograms declared in the same source code module and 1.5 for subprograms from less commonly used standard packages or from non-standard packages. Finally in recognition of the cognitive complexity of recursion a weighting of 2.0 could be allowed for a recursive call.

This approach could also be used for the computation of a complexity factor for subprogram parameters. One factor could be calculated for the subprogram parameter itself, based upon the number and modes of its parameters. A weighting factor could be used for the actual call of the subprogram in recognition of the cognitive complexity of indirectly calling a subprogram. Likewise the additional cognitive complexity of instantiating and calling a generic subprogram would also have to be allowed for. The production of complexity rules for these situations will be suggested as an end of chapter exercise.

Putting all of these complexity considerations together an overall complexity measurement of a subprogram can be made by taking the second version of the *SquareRoot* function from Chapter 29, the complexity of each operation can be shown on the source code as follows:

```
s3.0 e2.5    CheckAssertion( (Number >= 0.0 and Accuracy > 0.0),
                              "Square root pre-assertion error");
c1.5       while not CloseEnough loop
e2.0          CurrentGuess := (MaximumValue + MinimumValue) / 2.0;
e0.5          CurrentGuessSquared := CurrentGuess * CurrentGuess;
e1.0          CurrentError := abs( Number - CurrentGuessSquared);
c0.5          if CurrentError <= Accuracy then
e0.5             CloseEnough := TRUE;
              else
c0.5             if CurrentGuessSquared > Number then
e0.5                MaximumValue := CurrentGuess;
                 else
e0.5                MinimumValue := CurrentGuess;
                 end if;
              end if;
           end loop;
s3.0 e5.0    CheckAssertion( (CurrentGuess * CurrentGuess >=
                                 Number - Accuracy) and
                             (CurrentGuess * CurrentGuess <=
                                 Number + Accuracy)),
                             "Square root post-assertion error");
e0.5         return CurrentGuess;
           end SquareRoot;
```

Each complexity measure has been labelled with *e* for expression, *c* for controlling expression and *s* for subprogram call. The two subprogram calls have an *s* value recorded for the call and also an *e* value as one of the actual parameters is an expression. An *s* value of 3.0 has been computed as 2.0 for two *in only* parameters multiplied by 1.5 as the *CheckAssertion* procedure is declared in a non-standard package. Examples of the calculation of the other values have been given above. The results of the complexity analysis of this version of the *SquareRoot* function can be conveniently expressed in a table:

SquareRoot function complexity analysis

Cyclomatic complexity	6
No. of controlling expressions	3
Average complexity of controlling expressions	1.0
Maximum complexity of controlling expressions	1.5
No. of operation expressions	9
Average complexity of operation expressions	1.5
Maximum complexity of operation expressions	5.0
Number of unique operators	11
Number of subprogram calls	2
Average complexity of subprogram call	3.0
Maximal complexity of subprogram call	3.0
No. of unique subprograms called	1

In addition to the average operational and expression complexity values the maximum values have also been recorded as it is expected that it is the most complex parts of subprograms which provide the greatest potential difficulty. In addition to the number of unique operators which have been used a count of the number of unique subprograms which have been called is also recorded. The list of unique operators used is: Floating point >=, > and <, floating point assignment, floating point +, −, * and /, floating point **abs**, BOOLEAN assignment and BOOLEAN **and** conjunction.

This process of complexity analysis is so well defined that there are a number of automated tools which will perform the analysis automatically and produce such tables for inclusion in a program's technical documentation. Details of some tools which are available are given in Appendix A.

Dynamic measurements

Dynamic measurement has already been introduced in Chapter 30 where the difficulties of producing a meaningful absolute prediction of the time taken for an algorithm to complete was demonstrated. Although a precise prediction turned out not to be possible, significant information can be obtained by using *instrumented*

code and statistically analyzing the information which it furnishes. Instrumented code is source code which has been modified in order to allow dynamic measurements to be made and, as such, any results which are obtained from it may not be typical of the performance of the code when the instrumentation is removed. However, techniques of dynamic measurement have proved to be valuable both in quality control and in tuning and optimization.

The techniques are so well known and useful that many operating system and/ or compiler environments provide explicit support for the collection of, and tools for the analysis of, instrumented data. This section of this chapter will introduce some techniques which can be used without explicit support.

One dynamic measurement which is easy to collect is the number of times each subprogram is called. An initial package design and specification to support the collection of this data might be as follows:

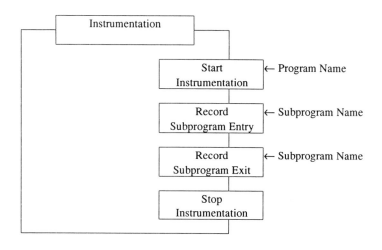

```
0001   -- Filename Instrumentation_.pkg (k8 instrume.ads).
0002   -- Simple instrumentation support package.
0003   --
0004   -- Produced for Ada book Section V Chapter 32.
0005   -- Fintan Culwin, v0.1, Jan 1997.
0006
0007   package Instrumentation is
0008
0009      procedure StartInstrumentation( ProgramName : in STRING);
0010      -- Procedure to prepare for instrumentation by opening a
0011      -- new log file with a name based upon the name
0011      -- supplied.
0012      -- pre:  Log file is not open
0013      -- post: Log file is open for writing and empty
0014
0015      procedure SubprogramEntry( SubprogramName : in STRING);
```

```
0016          -- Record details of the subprogram entry on the log file.
0017          -- pre:  Log file is open for writing.
0018          -- post: Details of entry have been written on the log
                                                                  file.
0019
0020          procedure SubprogramExit( SubprogramName : in STRING);
0021          -- Record details of a subprogram exit on the log file.
0022          -- pre:  Log file is open for writing.
0023          -- post: Details of exit have been written on the log
                                                                  file.
0024
0025          procedure StopInstrumentation;
0026          -- Close the log file and inform the user of the filename.
0027          -- pre:  Log file is open.
0028          -- post: Log file has been closed.
0029
0030      end Instrumentation;
```

To use the package the program being instrumented should call the *StartInstrumentation* subprogram as its first action and *StopInstrumentation* as its last action. When *StartInstrumentation* is called it will derive a, hopefully unique, filename from the program name supplied by appending an integer value. The value is obtained by using ADA.CALENDAR facilities and reflects the number of seconds in the current day. Once a filename has been derived a text file with that name is created and the user is informed of the filename being used. The file variable object, of type ADA.TEXT_IO.FILE_TYPE, is maintained as an encapsulated static variable and as such is available to the other subprograms in the body of the package.

The call to the *StopInstrumentation* subprogram will close the text file and inform the user once again of the filename which was used. Every subprogram in the program being instrumented is expected to call the *SubprogramEntry* procedure as its first action and the *SubprogramExit* procedure as its last action. Each of these calls will write a line to the open text file with details of the name of the subprogram and an indication if it was a subprogram entry or exit which was recorded.

If this technique was used to instrument the *WeeklyDiary* program from Section II Chapter 14, the contents of the log file after the program had been run might be as follows.

```
WeeklyDiary started
WeeklyDiaryInitialize entry
WeeklyDiaryInitialize exit
MainMenu entry
DisplayMenu entry
DisplayMenu exit
MainMenu exit
```

```
MainDispatch entry
SayGoodbye entry
SayGoodbye exit
MainDispatch exit
WeeklyDiaryFinalize entry
WeeklyDiaryFinalize exit
WeeklyDiary finished
```

There are two major pieces of information which can be obtained from an analysis of these data. The first and most obvious is a count of the number of times each subprogram was executed while the program was run under instrumentation. This information can be used to ensure that all subprograms have been executed whilst the instrumented program was under test and will also indicate which are the most commonly used subprograms. For a larger program running for a longer time it can also be used to ensure that all subprograms are actually executed during the normal operation, as opposed to the testing, of the program. If a subprogram is located which is never executed its purpose within the program might be worthy of investigation.

The second set of information which can be obtained from this file is the **call graph** and the **call depth** of the run. This will indicate which subprograms are called from which other subprograms and will also indicate the maximum depth of subprogram call nesting. A call graph derived from the log file above might be as shown in Figure 32.1.

These graphs can be used to validate the design intentions as expressed on the program structure charts and can be used to assist with the determination of a larger scale metric known as **fan-out** which will be introduced in the next chapter.

The analysis of a log file can be assisted by simple tools which can be produced to read and analyze the data which it contains, producing histograms of the number of calls and call graphs. The instrumentation can be extended in two ways. The first extension is not only to record the entry and exit into subprograms, but also to precede each line in the source code with a call to a *LogLine* subprogram. This would best be accomplished by using compiler or operating system facilities. If these facilities are not available then the same effect can be accomplished by using a program which takes as it its input the source code file and automatically

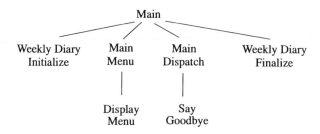

Figure 32.1 Call graph for the *WeeklyDiary* program.

inserts the required calls immediately before each line which is to be instrumented. After the instrumented program has been run a second tool can take the log file and the source code, and produce a listing file which contains the number of times each line was executed whilst the program was run under instrumentation. For example, an instrumented report of the *SquareRoot* subprogram might appear as follows:

```
0024 0003     CheckAssertion( (Number >= 0.0 and Accuracy > 0.0),
0025                          "Square root pre-assertion error");
0026 0047    while not CloseEnough loop
0027 0047        CurrentGuess := (MaximumValue + MinimumValue) /
                                                            2.0;
0028 0047        CurrentGuessSquared := CurrentGuess * CurrentGuess;
0029 0047        CurrentError := abs( Number - CurrentGuessSquared);
0030 0047        if CurrentError <= Accuracy then
0031 0003            CloseEnough := TRUE;
0032             else
0033 0044            if CurrentGuessSquared > Number then
0034 0044                MaximumValue := CurrentGuess;
0035             else
0036 0000                MinimumValue := CurrentGuess;
0037             end if;
0038         end if;
0039     end loop;
0040 0003     CheckAssertion( (CurrentGuess * CurrentGuess >=
0041                                       Number - Accuracy) and
0042                             (CurrentGuess * CurrentGuess <=
0043                                       Number + Accuracy)),
0044                          "Square root post assertion error");
0045 0003     return CurrentGuess;
0046 0003    end SquareRoot;
```

The instrumentation indicates that the subprogram was called three times, and that the main loop condition was tested a total of 0047 times. The body of the loop shows that the statement on line 0036 was never executed, which if this was an instrumented test run might indicate either that the testing was not sufficient or that for some reason it is never possible to execute it, in which case its existence in the program is suspect.

The second extension to the instrumentation is for the subprogram entry and exit actions to record the time at which they were called. This will allow the analysis of the instrumentation to indicate not only how many times the subprogram was executed, but also the total and proportional amount of time which each subprogram took. If this instrumentation is carried out over a sufficiently long period of time then any biasing effects caused by the operating system load can be assumed to have been evened out.

This information might be valuable if the response time of the software was shown to be unacceptable. Under these circumstances optimization of the software implementation might be appropriate. However, the first optimization option to be explored is to request that the compiler maximize the amount of optimization which it performs, or use a different compiler if one is available, in an attempt to meet the timing requirements. The second option might be to investigate the costs associated with obtaining a faster processor, or more main memory, or a faster hard disk. Any or all of these hardware upgrades might cause the software to meet its response time requirements, and might also turn out to be cheaper than re-engineering the implementation.

Optimization of the source code should only be attempted as a last resort and should only be attempted once the correctness of the software has been demonstrated by testing. Under these circumstances the information concerning which subprograms are taking the greatest proportion of time and which lines within the subprogram are being executed the most will be invaluable, directing the developer's attention to those parts of the program most worthy of attention. Once any possible optimization has been implemented, the entire program will require retesting to ensure that it is still a correct implementation, before establishing if it now meets its timing requirements. The precise techniques which can be used to attempt such optimization are beyond the scope of this book.

EXERCISES

32.1 Review samples of your own source code and determine a simple density of comments metric for each. To accomplish this you should design and produce an Ada program which opens your source code file as a text file and counts the number of lines and the number of lines which contain comments.

32.2 Extend the program from Exercise 32.1 to produce more sophisticated density of comment metrics. Then extend it again to derive a metric for the average length of identifier, conformance with indentation, etc.

32.3 Find out if your environment has a metrics tool, or tools, available. If not visit some of the repositories listed in Appendix A and attempt to locate suitable tools.

32.4 Find out if your environment supports the instrumentation of code as described in this chapter. If not visit some of the repositories listed in Appendix A and attempt to locate suitable facilities.

32.5 Using the tools from Exercises 32.3 and 32.4, revisit Exercise 31.4 and again attempt to find out what caused the differences in difficulty between the various subprograms.

32.6 On your next development project include a metrics report in the technical documentation.

32.7 Derive a table of complexities for all possible Ada operations and expressions which have been introduced so far. This should include generic subprograms and packages, recursive procedures and functions, overloaded subprograms and extended data types.

CHAPTER 33

Large scale metrics

The previous chapter concentrated largely upon the metrics which can be applied to individual subprograms. This chapter will continue the introduction to the uses of software metrics by considering the metrics which can be applied to larger amounts of source code.

The chapter will commence with a consideration of the use of metrics in a general development project consisting of a large number of subprograms and packages, before considering the application of metrics to individual packages and class hierarchies. Usability metrics which consider the user's interaction with the software will then be introduced before the consideration of metrics concludes with a review of the use of metrics in perspective.

General large scale metrics

Much of the general use of metrics in the larger scale follows directly from the use of smaller scale metrics. The same measurements which can be made upon individual subprograms can also be made upon a collection of subprograms. The results can then be collated and presented as a summary for each individual subprogram, for each package and for the project as a whole. There are also some additional measurements which can be made, relating to the extent to which individual subprograms or packages interact with each other. These considerations will be introduced after the use of summaries of individual subprograms has been introduced.

Summary metrics

The two major reasons for measuring software were introduced in a previous chapter as to be able to manage and to be able to predict. Software production management is concerned with the sequence and timescale in which the components of a large scale software product are produced. It was demonstrated that effective production management requires a complete design of the software to be available, in order that the number of required packages and/or subprograms can be known. As estimate of the complexity of each module is also required, in order that the resources required to produce it can be predicted.

The initial complexity estimates can be validated against the measured complexity of the components as they are produced. This will allow the techniques of complexity prediction to be continually refined and first become, and then subsequently remain, accurate. The process of refinement may influence the weighting factors used in the *feature point analysis* process, introduced in the previous chapter, to reflect accurately the actual production environment in use.

The collection of complexity metrics for each component as it is produced and the records of the amount of resources which are used to produce each component, which should also be available from the production control process, can be used to predict modules which may prove troublesome. It can be expected that there is some relationship between a subprogram's complexity and the amount of resources which are used to construct the subprogram. A scatter graph of this relationship may appear as shown in Figure 33.1.

The figure indicates that there may be a relationship between complexity and resources which applies to the subprogram labelled *A*, *B*, *C*, *D* and *E*. The subprograms *F* and *G* do not seem to be contained within this relationship and thus might require further consideration. Subprogram *F* is a complex subprogram which seems to have been completed with a smaller amount of resources than would be expected. Subprogram *G* is a simple subprogram which seems to have required more resources that would be expected. There may be good reasons for this: for example, subprogram *F* may be complex but has been constructed by the adaptation of a standard design and thus was produced more quickly than expected. Subprogram *G* may require a recursive solution, which although simple to implement is found difficult to understand by many developers. Alternatively it

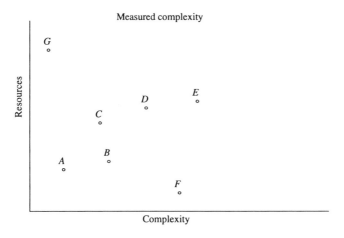

Figure 33.1 Complexity and resources.

may be the case that *F* has been shoddily implemented and *G* was given to an inexperienced developer who required additional time.

Whatever reasons caused these two subprograms to lie outside the broad relationship between complexity and resources, a scatter graph of complexity and resources has identified them as being aberrant. It can be expected that these subprograms are more likely to contain faults and thus more likely to cause problems during testing. Consequently it would be appropriate to review their implementation during the production phase as soon as their aberration was spotted, before they are submitted for testing.

The scatter graph can also be used to detect any subprograms whose absolute level of complexity is greater than some pre-determined maximum. These subprograms might also turn out to be troublesome and a production review of their construction would be appropriate.

Subprogram coupling

The major metrics which can be derived from collections of subprograms, as opposed to individual subprograms, relate to the interconnections between subprograms. This is generally referred to as *coupling* and can be divided into *fan-in* and *fan-out*. *Fan-in* is a count of the number of subprograms which directly call a given subprogram, and *fan-out* the number of subprograms which a given subprogram calls.

A subprogram may be called from a large number of places in a program for one of two reasons. The first possible reason is that the subprogram is performing some very simple and straightforward operation which is fundamental to the software's specification. In this case the subprogram is being used almost as an extention to the standard package facilities, or even the programming language facilities. As such this represents good design and construction practice and should be encouraged.

The second possible reason why a subprogram should be called from a large number of different places would be because it is performing a number of different operations, which would be better performed by a number of different subprograms. There are two clues to indicate that this might be the case. The first clue would be that the subprogram is itself complex and the second would be the presence of *in only* parameters whose only effect is to control the operation of the subprogram.

The solution to this problem is to divide the original subprogram into two or more separate subprograms each of which performs only a part of the specification of the original subprogram. This redesign will hopefully have the effect of reducing the average subprogram complexity by producing two or more less complex subprograms in place of one complex subprogram. It will also reduce the overall data flow by removing the requirement for the *in only* control parameter. Instead of having to pass a parameter to control the operation of the subprogram, each different possible operation of the original subprogram will be performed by a separate subprogram. As each operation is now performed by a separate subprogram each will have only a part of the fan-in which the original subprogram had.

The limitation on fan-out is a direct consequence of the individual subprogram complexity limitations which were introduced in the previous chapter. A subprogram with a large fan-out is by definition complex and would have been flagged as such at the design stage.

Both of these metrics can be first obtained from a design review or could be automatically generated by a software design tool before the subprograms are constructed. They could also be obtained from a large scale static analysis of the source code or from the call graphs produced from the dynamic instrumentation of the program. In the context of an integrated suite of computer aided software engineering (*case*) tools, the predicted coupling of a subprogram from the design tool can be checked against the actual coupling, as determined from dynamic instrumentation or static analysis, in order to ensure that the implementation is in accord with the design.

Medium scale metrics

Between the scale of the individual subprogram and the scale of the overall software project lies the scales of an individual package and of a class hierarchy of types implemented as a collection of packages. All the considerations which have been introduced so far, both small scale and large scale, can be applied to this medium scale. There are also additional considerations which apply in particular to class hierarchies and which will be introduced in this part of the chapter.

Individual package metrics

Metrics related to an individual package have to be divided into public and private metrics. The public metrics would include the number of types, subtypes, exceptions and subprograms which it exports together with the average and maximal data flow interface complexity of the exported subprograms.

There is one additional metric which can be derived for a package: the number of other packages which it is dependent upon. This is a *package coupling* metric which can be derived from the package dependency diagram and, as with subprogram coupling metrics, the value should be limited. This metric can be used at a larger scale to obtain a measure of the *fragility of a package*. A highly intercoupled set of packages will be highly fragile, and any change in a package specification will have a large number of ramifications in the rest of the packages.

A more loosely intercoupled set of package will be more robust when any changes are made to any of the specifications.

Thus a package coupling metric should indicate for each package produced, or used, in a software project its individual couplings. This should be expressed as the total number of couplings and the number of couplings with other packages which form part of the project. A summary metric of all the packages produced, or used, in the project should indicate the average and maximum amount of coupling and intercoupling. This metric should be reviewed with respect to the possibility of reducing the amount of coupling.

The package coupling metric should also distinguish between couplings with normal packages and couplings with instantiated packages. A coupling with an instantiated generic package is cognitively more complex than a coupling with a non-generic package. Accordingly a coupling to a generic package should be related to the number and types of its generic formal parameters. This value can be obtained by a complexity analysis using a table of complexities, similar to those used in the complexity analysis of individual subprograms as presented in the last chapter. A possible table of generic parameter complexities is as follows:

Generic formal parameters complexity

Parameter	Complexity
limited private	0.5
private	0.5
discrete <>	1.0
numeric	1.0
array	1.5
tagged	1.5
subprogram	1.5+

The + symbol in the subprogram entry indicates that the complexity factor must be increased to take account of the number and types of parameters which the subprogram requires.

These public metrics relate both to the complexity of the construction of the package and, more importantly, to the complexity of using the package. A developer wanting to use a presupplied package should be primarily concerned with the specification of the package, as reflected in its public complexity metrics. Thus the potential for successful reuse of a package is related to its public complexity.

The metrics associated with the private complexity of a package include the average and maximal complexity of the private subprograms and any other private resources which are declared within the package body. As the package body can be coupled with other packages independently of the specification it will have an independent private package coupling metric. These metrics are primarily of interest to the developer of the package, although they may be of some interest to the developer of a client of the package if this developer is concerned about the future reliability and maintenance implications of using a pre-supplied package.

Class wide metrics

In addition to the individual package metrics introduced above a class hierarchy of types, implemented as a collection of packages and child packages, introduces additional metrics. These metrics are known as *object oriented metrics* and relate to the class wide properties of the hierarchy. The most fundamental of these metrics relates to the shape and complexity of the *class hierarchy*. There are three independent considerations to take into account. The first is related to the data attributes of the types, the second to the operations of the type and the third to the overall shape of the class hierarchy.

For a given specification there is a design choice between a larger number of smaller type extensions or a smaller number of larger type extensions. The advantage of having a smaller number of types is a reduced overall perceived complexity at the expense of flexibility, as there will be fewer places in the hierarchy where an extended type can be introduced. For an arbitrary specification the average size of each extension can be related to the number of distinct data attributes which are added on each extention. A large number of data attributes being added would indicate that large types are being declared; a small number of data attributes indicates that small types are being declared.

The design advice advocated in this book is that the value for the average *data attribute extension complexity* metric of a class should be less than or equal to 1.0, indicating that on average only a single data attribute is being added on extension, and in some cases only behaviours are being added. This will result in a rich class hierarchy which consists of a large number of types resulting in a large number of places where additional types can be derived by extension. Consequently this metric can be directly related to the potential reusability of the class.

In addition to the data attributes of a class, the behavioural aspects of the class should also be measured. Each data type in the class hierarchy may introduce actions which can be categorized as being an overloading of an existing action, a new class wide action or a distinct action specific to the extended type. When a class hierarchy of types is considered then summary counts of these three different classes of actions can be maintained.

The most fundamental metric which can be obtained is a count of the number of unique subprogram names in the hierarchy. This will given an indication of the *number of different operations* which are available from the class as a whole.

Each individual operation name can have the number of distinct data types from the hierarchy which can use the operation recorded. This will give an indication of the *generality* of the operation. The number of different signatures which exist for a named operation can also be recorded. This will give an indication of the *cognitive difficulty* associated with using the operation.

For example, a class wide operation declared at the root of the hierarchy will have a single declaration, a single signature and be applicable to every data type in the hierarchy. Thus it can be categorized as a simple operation with a large degree of generality. Alternatively a constructor operation may be redeclared in every package extension and as the data attribute complexity of the types increases, its signature will also increase. This operation can be categorized as a complex operation with a large degree of generality. Finally a named subprogram might only be declared in a small number of packages and be very restricted in the precise types of its parameters. This could be categorized as a specialized operation with a small degree of generality.

The final metric which can be associated with a class of types relates to the overall shape of the type hierarchy. A type hierarchy can be narrow and deep, consisting largely of parent/child relationships. Alternatively a type hierarchy can be wide and shallow, consisting largely of parent/child/sibling relationships. There are two sets of measurements which can be made. The first are the maximum and average *depth* of the hierarchy. This can be computed by determining the length of the hierarchy from the root type to each peripheral type in the hierarchy. This metric will give an indication of the extent to which the concepts have been refined into *is a* relations and a higher value should be favoured.

The second set of measurements which can be made are the average *number of child types* derived from each type, which gives an indication of the width of the hierarchy. This second measurement should exclude the types at the periphery of the hierarchy and will given an indication of the extent to which the object analysis has encouraged specialization in the types. Again a higher value for this metric should be favoured.

The only private metric of a class of types which might be of interest is the number of subprograms which are exported from the private part of the package specification. These subprograms are visible only to the children of the package which exports them and indicate a coupling between the package which exports them and the package which uses them. A high value for this metric would indicate extensive coupling and as such might be regarded as a value to minimize. However, too low a value might indicate a lack of effective design and analysis before the hierarchy was constructed. The absence of such subprograms might indicate needless duplication of operations in the individual package private parts. Perhaps this is an example of a *Goldilocks metric* where the appropriate value is neither too low, nor too high, but just right.

Usability metrics

The final set of metrics which are to be considered in this book relate to the user oriented aspects of software and are known as *usability metrics*. As was emphasized in Section II the usability aspects of software design should be regarded as being as central to successful software development as any other, possibly more technical, aspects. It is not sufficient merely to extol usability as a design consideration and to provide heuristic advice on interface design and construction. Additionally the usability of a software product should be capable of being precisely measured and in order for this to be possible there has to be some standards against which measurements can be made and techniques to make the measurements. This part of the chapter will introduce techniques by which the usability aspects of software can first be specified and subsequently measured.

Usability specifications

A usability specification for a software product must be expressed in a manner which is capable of being measured in order that, once the product is available, the degree of compliance with the specification can be measured. Thus specific criteria must be stated in a way which allows qualitative, or preferably quantitative, targets to be expressed.

An example of a non-specific criterion which is unfortunately far too prevalently stated is the phrase **user friendly**. When this phrase, commonly touted in promotional literature, is carefully analyzed it usually turns out to mean only that the software is **less user hostile** than previous versions of the same, or a competitor's equivalent, product.

More specific and measurable criteria might include **ease of use**, which can be only stated against a named application oriented task and which has subcriteria against which it can be measured. For example, a word processing system may define an initial task as follows:

> Start the system, enter a single paragraph consisting of three given sentences with default character and paragraph formatting, print the document and save it in a named file before exiting from the system.

This is a precise statement of a task which has to be performed but is unclear as to how the performance of the user is to be measured. The simplest measurement to make is the success, or degree of success, in completing the task. However, there are additional aspects of the user's behaviour which are capable of being measured, which include the following: the amount of time which the user takes to complete the task, the number of mistakes (excluding typing errors) which the user makes in completing the task, the amount of assistance which the user asks for, the number of distinct commands which the user issues and, perhaps most importantly, the user's attitude towards the software after completing the task.

There is one further consideration which needs to be included in the task specification before it can be considered a complete usability specification. The amount of general computer and application-specific expertise which the user has will affect the user's performance on the task. Assuming application-specific expertise users can be categorized into: *novice users* who have never or very rarely used a computer, *occasional users* who might be regular users of computers but only occasionally use a computer to perform the specified task, and *expert users* who use a computer to perform the specified task on a daily basis. Thus a fully usability specification might outline precise performance indicators against expertise, for example as follows:

Usability specification for a simple task

	Novice	Occasional	Expert
Time to complete task in seconds	300	120	60
Number of errors made	10	5	2
Number of commands issued	$2n$	$n + 25\%$	$n + 10\%$
Amount of assistance requested	3	1	0
Attitude after completing task	neutral	positive	positive

The time taken to complete the task in seconds, the maximum number of allowable errors and the maximum number of requests for assistance are absolute numeric values and as such should be easy to comprehend. The number of commands issued is related to n, which is the minimum number of commands which an expert user who is very familiar with the system would use to complete the same task. This can be taken as the minimum number of commands which the usability design indicates is required. The final measurement is related to a five point, 1 to 5, attitude measurement scale where 1 indicates complete frustration and dissatisfaction with the experience and 5 indicates total happiness. A positive measurement is regarded as 4 or 5 and a neutral measurement as 3.

The usability specification is now expressed in terms which allow it to be accurately measured. The task and the measurements which are to be made are related only to the application domain of the software and not to the precise interface which will be constructed. Thus, for example, the request for assistance does not indicate if this is to be accomplished by using the on-line help facilities for by making a verbal request to the person supervising the usability trial.

The example above has established a task oriented usability specification; there are other possible specifications which could be produced along similar lines. These include: *learnability* which would specify the amount of effort and experience required to attain a defined level of competence; *retention*, which would specify the extent to which performance would deteriorate over a period when the software was not used; *transferability*, which would specify the extent to which learning to perform one task would improve the learning of a related task in the same, or a related, software package.

Usability measurement

Having established a usability specification it is necessary to establish that the software product, either a prototype of the interface or the completed program, satisfies the specification. This is not as straightforward as it might appear owing to the inherent variability of human responses. It is neither feasible nor possible to measure the actual performance of all possible users of a software product. All that can be done is to measure the performance of a representative subset and extrapolate from the observed performance.

This is a familiar problem to experimental psychologists and statisticians who would emphasize the following considerations. The first relates to the number of users who are to be measured, known as the sample size. This should be as large as possible within the constraints of applying and possibly reapplying the measurements. Although no upper size can be stated, using more than about 20 users is unlikely to result in much additional accuracy of measurement being obtained; however, too small a sample size is unlikely to yield accurate measurement. Ideally between 10 and 20 users from each user category should be included.

The second consideration is that every member of the population of potential users should have an equal chance of being in the sample. This immediately rules out the use of volunteers if meaningful results are to be obtained. Volunteers are by definition an identifiable subgroup of the entire population and as such their characteristics will be different from that of the population of users as a whole. Presumably they might be regarded as being more co-operative and hence more likely to be favourably disposed towards the product. This criterion will also allow for any other demographic biasing of the sample, such as gender, age, education, ethnicity, social class, etc.

The third consideration is that the measurement should be done according to a strict protocol so that it can be meaningfully repeated. The attitude of the person conducting the trial, the location where the trial takes place, the time of day or week when the trial takes place, the precise instructions which are given to the users and many other considerations may have an effect upon the outcome of such an investigation. Although it is not possible completely to control all of these factors as many as possible should be specified, or at least recorded, so that they can be taken into account when an generalization of conclusions is considered.

The fourth consideration is that the act of measurement itself has an effect upon the outcome. This is known as the ***Hawthorne effect*** and was first observed in studies which attempted to discover what factors affected productivity in factory assembly lines. The initial results were found to be contradictory as a proposed change, such as having more frequent but shorter breaks, had a positive effect as did its converse, having less frequent but longer breaks. What was eventually concluded was that what caused the positive effect was not the changes in the production organization but the attention given to the workers by the investigators.

The final major consideration, although there are many other minor considerations, is that even if all the other considerations are allowed for the best that can be obtained is a statistically significant rather than an absolutely significant result. In recognition of this the statement of a usability specification will usually be preceded by a qualifying 'at least 90% of ...'.

These considerations have only touched the surface of the complexities concerned with the specification and measurement of usability considerations. It may seem that the complexity and thus expense of such processes would result in them not being widely used. However, such processes and techniques are being more and more widely used for a variety of reasons, the most fundamental of which are economic. By improving the usability of software products large scale software manufacturers have increased their market share and thus repaid the additional development costs. From the perspective of the user it has been shown that the improvements in usability have led to improvements in productivity, which have repaid the increased purchase costs of such software.

These improvements in usability, initially in large scale generic software products such as word processors, have led to a situation where users who have had experience of ergonomically designed and usability validated generic software have demanded that such care be put into more specialized software products.

Less mercenary considerations are related to the changing role of the workplace and the legislative protection of workers. As more and more economic activity becomes computer based, legislation determining safe and healthy working conditions is starting to specify minimum acceptable environments. These considerations relate not only to the physical organization of the computer workstation but also the quality of the software's user interface, which can only be assured by usability specification and measurement. These changes are leading to a new specialization in software production teams – that of a ***usability engineer.***

A usability engineer ideally should be a full member of the production team taking a role in all parts of the software production process. This would consist of establishing or negotiating the usability specification as the product is specified, designing the user interface in the design phase and measuring its usability in the testing phase. It is important that the usability engineer is a full member of the production team for two reasons. The first is that, as with quality, it has been repeatedly shown that usability cannot be bolted on to a product at the end of the production process, but has to be designed in from the outset. The second reason is to produce a usability ethos throughout the team by ensuring that due consideration is given to usability and to provide a point of expert reference if any questions relating to it are raised. This will also lead, over a period of time, to a dissemination of the usability engineer's skills to the rest of the production team.

Metrics in context

The previous three chapters have provided an initial introduction to the major techniques of software measurement and have indicated the benefits and advantages which accrue from their use. There are much wider consequence of the rigorous use of metrics which have been identified within software production organizations, and which by analogy can apply equally to an individual developer.

The *software crisis* is a term introduced to describe a situation which was once, and in many cases still is, prevalent in the software production industry. The crisis was initiated by the increased complexity and economic importance of software products. The symptoms of the crisis were that software products suffered from a variety of faults including: being very expensive to produce, being produced vastly over budget, being delivered late, being delivered with an unacceptable number of faults, being inflexible and requiring extensive re-engineering to meet even small changes in specification or environment, being as user friendly as a cornered rat, as well as many other symptoms.

The causes of the crisis were varied but two major factors predominated. The first was the nature of the software product, which is highly abstract and intractable requiring a great deal of cognitive effort and little physical effort. The second was that the software industry is, in historical terms, very recent and has had a phenomenal rate of growth. This had led to a situation where the vast majority of people concerned with the production of software have had very little, if any, training in engineering in general and software engineering in particular. The consequence of this is that standard engineering practices concerned with quality assurance and quality control have had to be painfully reinvented by software engineers, rather than being adapted from existing practice.

There are many software engineering initiatives directed towards alleviating the software crisis, many of the ideas from which have already permeated this book. One of the most useful concepts is that of *software production capability* (SPC). This categorizes the process maturity of an organization on a five point nominal scale:

> initial or chaotic
> repeatable
> defined
> managed
> optimized

The initial stage is categorized by an inability to organize the production process with almost no control over product quality. It is typified by an absence of design techniques and production consists of putting code together until it appears that the product seems to work. The second stage contains few qualitative differences, but largely through experience allows a sequence of similar projects to be completed. However, any significant differences in the specifications will cause performance to revert to the initial level.

Progress beyond the repeatable level is dependent upon a number of factors including rigorous use of a variety of design techniques and the ability to manage

subject to a white box analysis. The white box techniques introduced in Chapter 31 were shown to be only partially effective in ensuring that all aspects of the implementation were tested.

This part of the chapter will commence by introducing additional white box techniques which can be used to increase confidence in the coverage of implemented code. The testing of software throughout the development process will then be considered before this part of the chapter will conclude with an introduction to statistical techniques for estimating the effectiveness of the testing process and the number of remaining faults in a software product.

Condition testing

A representation of the flow of control within a subprogram is the basis of the white box techniques already introduced. The construction of a flowgraph effectively treats the places in the flowgraph where control diverges as black boxes, it only notes that flow of control can diverge at these locations and is not concerned with the precise circumstances which cause it to diverge. The first improvement to white box techniques is to ensure that the Boolean controlling expressions are adequately tested, a process known as *condition testing*.

The process of condition testing ensures that a controlling expression has been adequately exercised whilst the software is under test by constructing a *constraint set* for every expression and then ensuring that every member of the constraint set is included in the values which are presented to the expression. This may require additional test runs to be included in the test plan.

To introduce the concept of constraint sets the simplest possible Boolean condition, a single Boolean variable or a negated Boolean variable, will be considered. These conditions may take forms such as

```
if DateValid then          while not DateValid then
```

The constraint set for both of these expressions is {t, f} which indicates that to test these expressions adequately they should be tested twice with *DateValid* having the values true and false.

Perhaps the next simplest Boolean condition consists of a simple relational expression of the form *value operator value*, where the operator can be one of: *is equal to* (=), *is not equal to* (/=), *is greater than* (>), *is less than* (<), *is greater than or equal to* (>=) and *is less than or equal to* (<=). It can be noted that the negation of the simple Boolean variable above has no effect upon the constraint set and that the six relational operators can be divided into three pairs of operators and their negations. *Is equal to* is a negation of *is not equal to*, *is greater than* is a negation of *is less than or equal to* and *is less than* is a negation of *is greater than or equal to*. Thus the condition set for a relational expression can be expressed as {=, >, <}, which indicates that to test a relational expression adequately it must be tested three times with values which ensure that the two values are equal, that the first value is less than the second value and that the first value is greater than the second value.

More complex control expressions involve the use of the Boolean operators **and, or** and **xor**, which combine the values of two Boolean values. To construct a constraint set for a simple Boolean expression of the form *BooleanValue operator BooleanValue* all possible combinations of true and false have to be considered. This gives the constraint set for the expression as {{t, t} {t, f} {f, t} {f, f}}. If both *BooleanValues* are simple or negated Boolean variables then no further development of this set is required. However, if one or both of the *BooleanValues* are relational expressions then the constraint set for the relational expression will have to be combined with this constraint set. The combination takes the form of noting that the equality condition is equivalent to true and the both inequality conditions are equivalent to false. Thus every true condition in the condition set is replaced with '=' and every false replaced twice, once with '>' and once with '<'.

Thus if only the left hand *BooleanValue* is a relational expression the condition set would be {{ =, t} {=, f} {>, t} {<, t} {>, f} {<, f}}. And if both *BooleanValues* are relation expressions this would become {{=, =} {=, >} {=, <} {>, =} {<, =} {>, >} {>, <} {<, >} {<, <}}.

An increase in the complexity of the Boolean expression by the addition of more operators will introduce implicit or explicit bracketing of the order of evaluation which will be reflected in the condition set and will increase the number of terms in the set. For example, a Boolean expression of the following form

BooleanValue1 **operator1** *BooleanValue2* **operator3** *BooleanValue3*

has the implicit bracketing

(*BooleanValue1* **operator1** *BooleanValue2*) **operator3** *BooleanValue3*

The constraint set for the complete expression would be {{e1, t} {e1, f}}, where e1 is the condition set of the bracketed subexpression and when it is used to expand this constraint set gives {{t, t, t} {t, f, t} {f, t, t} {f, f, t} {t, t, f} {t, f, f} {f, t, f} {f, f, f}}. If any of the *BooleanValues* are themselves relational expressions this will increase the number of terms in the condition set. In this example the worst case would be if all three values were relational expressions and would produce a total of 27 terms in the condition set. This would imply that 27 tests are required to test the expression adequately. As the number of Boolean operators increases the number of terms in a condition set increases exponentially and comprehensive testing of the expression becomes more complicated and less likely. It is this consideration which led to the advice, initially given in Section I, to keep Boolean control expressions as simple as possible, and one way to do this is to use Boolean variables rather than expressions within such control conditions.

Data life cycle testing

Keeping control expressions simple can be argued simply to distribute the complexity from the control expressions to the other parts of the subprogram and an effective testing strategy should recognize this and account for it. One approach to this consideration is known as *data life cycle testing*, and it is based upon the consideration that a variable is at some stage created, and subsequently may have its value changed or used in a controlling expression several times before being destroyed. If only locally declared Boolean variables used in control conditions are considered then an examination of the source code will indicate the place in the code where they are declared and possibly given an initial value, where they have a new value assigned, where they are used in a control expression and where they are destroyed.

This approach to testing requires all possible feasible life cycles of the variable to be covered whilst the module is under test. In the case of a Boolean variable this should include the possibility of a Boolean variable being given the values true and false at each place where it is given a value. A typical outline sketch of a possible lifecycle of a controlling Boolean variable within a subprogram might be as follows:

```
~~~ SomeSubProgram( ~~~ ) is
    ControlVar : BOOLEAN := FALSE;

begin -- SomeSubProgram
    ~~~
    while not ControlVar loop
        ~~~
        ControlVar := SomeExpression;
    end loop;
    ~~~
end SomeSubProg;
```

In this sketch ~~~ indicates the parts of the subprogram which are not relevant to the life cycle. In this example there are two places where the variable *ControlVar* is given a value: the location where it is created and the assignment within the loop. Additionally there is one place where it is used as a control expression. There are two possible life cycles to consider, one which can be characterized as {f, t} indicating that the variable is created with the value false and given the value true upon the first iteration of the loop. The other life cycle can be characterized as {f, f, .., t}, which differs from the first by indicating that the variable is given the value false on the first iteration, following which there is the possibility of more iterations where it is also given the value false, being given the value true on the last iteration.

Other possible life cycles such as {f} or {f, t, f, .., t} can be shown from a consideration of the source code not to be possible. The first is not possible as the default value will ensure that the loop iterates causing the variable to experience at least two values during its life cycle. The second is not possible because, as soon as the variable is given the value true within the loop, the loop and subsequently the subprogram will terminate, causing the variable to be destroyed.

This quick look at the *variable life cycle* approach only indicates the basis of this approach to white box testing. It should also indicate that this is one of the most laborious and thus expensive and difficult techniques to apply. As it is expensive and does not add a great deal to the testing considerations which have already been discussed, it is not widely used.

Testing loops

The final white box consideration which will be introduced is the testing of loops, which have been shown to be the most common cause of faults in subprograms. If a loop, definite or indefinite, is intended to iterate n times then the test plan should include the following seven considerations and possible faults:

> That the loop might iterate zero times.
> That the loop might iterate once.
> That the loop might iterate twice.
> That the loop might iterate several times.
> That the loop might iterate $n - 1$ times.
> That the loop might iterate n times.
> That the loop might iterate $n + 1$ times.
> That the loop might iterate infinite times.

All feasible possibilities should be exercised whilst the software is under test. The last possibility, an infinite loop, is a very noticeable and common fault. All loops should be constructed in such a way that it is guaranteed that they will at some stage come to an end. However, this does not necessarily guarantee that they come to an end after the correct number of iterations; a loop which iterates one time too many or one time too few is probably the most common loop fault. Of these possibilities an additional iteration may hopefully cause a CONSTRAINT_ERROR exception to be raised announcing its presence. Otherwise the $n - 1$ and $n + 1$ loop faults can be very difficult to detect and correct.

A loop executing zero times may be part of the design, in which case it should be explicitly tested that it does so when required and does not do so when it is not required. Otherwise, if the loop should never execute zero times, and it does, this can also be a very subtle fault to locate. The additional considerations, once, twice and many, are included to increase confidence that the loop is operating correctly.

The next consideration is the testing of nested loops. One approach to this is to combine the test considerations of the innermost loop with those of the outermost loop. As there are seven considerations for a simple loop, this will give 49 considerations for two levels of nesting and 343 considerations for a triple nested loop, which is clearly not a feasible proposition.

What is possible is to start by testing the innermost loop, with all other loops set to iterate the minimum number of times. Once the innermost loop has been tested it should be configured so that it will iterate the minimum number of times and the next outermost loop tested. Testing of nested loops can continue in this manner, effectively testing each nested loop in sequence rather than in combination, which will result in the number of required tests increasing arithmetically (7, 14, 21, ..) rather than geometrically (7, 49, 343, ..).

Testing throughout the production process

The testing considerations which have been introduced so far have concentrated mostly upon the testing of individual units, although the black box considerations in Section II did briefly consider the testing of an entire application. A complete testing strategy consists of testing at various points in the production process and can be described by the *test vee* shown in Figure 34.1.

The left hand side of the vee indicates the processes involved in the construction of the software, starting with the determination of requirements which are subsequently refined into a precise specification. The design phase in this model is taken to indicate the design of modules and the code phase the detailed design and construction of subprograms.

The right hand side of the vee indicates the testing actions which correspond to each stage on the left side. *Unit testing* is concerned with the testing of the individual subprograms, *integration testing* with the assembly of the modules to produce the application, *validation testing* with ensuring that the application meets its specification and *system testing* that it serves its requirements and fits into its environment. Although this model presents these four actions as distinct

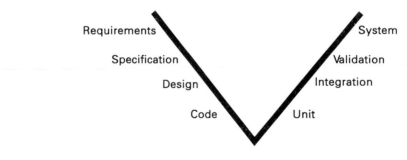

Figure 34.1 The test vee.

stages, in practice the stages overlap to a considerable extent. Consequently it is often difficult to state explicitly that a particular operation fits into a particular stage, and operations often reappear in different stages. This consideration will be clarified in the discussion below.

The first two of these test stages have already been adequately covered in the discussion of white box and black box testing. Unit testing primarily relies upon white box techniques, although black box testing of individual subprograms is also valuable. Integration testing and the first stages of validation testing make much more use of black box techniques although at the integration stage there is still a role for white box techniques when the major paths of control through an application are considered.

Integration testing

Integration testing can proceed in a number of different ways, which can be broadly characterized as *top down* or *bottom up*. In *top-down integration testing* the high level control routines are tested first, possibly with the middle level control structures present only as *stubs*. Subprogram *stubs* were presented in Section II as incomplete subprograms which are only present to allow the higher level control routines to be tested. Thus a menu driven program may have the major menu options initially only present as stubs, which merely announce that they have been successfully called, in order to allow the high level menu driver to be tested.

Top-down testing can proceed in a *depth first* or a *breadth first* manner. For depth first integration each module is tested in increasing detail, replacing more and more levels of detail with actual code rather than stubs. Alternatively breadth first would proceed by refining all the modules at the same level of control throughout the application. In practice a combination of the two techniques would be used. At the initial stages all the modules might be only partly functional, possibly being implemented only to deal with non-erroneous data. These would be tested in breadth first manner, but over a period of time each would be replaced with successive refinements which were closer to the full functionality. This allows depth first testing of a module to be performed simultaneously with breadth first testing of all the modules.

The other major category of integration testing is *bottom-up integration testing* where an individual module is tested from a test harness. Once a set of individual modules have been tested they are then combined into a collection of modules, known as *builds*, which are then tested by a second test harness. This process can continue until the build consists of the entire application.

In practice a combination of top-down and bottom-up testing would be used. In a large software project being developed by a number of subteams, or a smaller project where different modules were being built by individuals, the subteams or individuals would conduct bottom-up testing of the modules which they were constructing before releasing them to an integration team which would assemble them together for top-down testing.

Validation and system testing

Validation testing is a concern which overlaps with integration testing. Ensuring that the application fulfils its specification is a major criterion for the construction of an integration test. Validation testing also overlaps to a large extent with *system testing*, where the application is tested with respect to its typical working environment. Consequently for many processes no clear division between validation and system testing can be made. Specific tests which can be performed in either or both stages include the following:

Regression testing. This version of the software is tested with the automated test harnesses used with previous versions to ensure that the required features of the previous versions are still working in the new version.

Recovery testing. The software is deliberately interrupted in a number of ways, for example taking its hard disk off-line or even turning the computer off, to ensure that the appropriate techniques for restoring any lost data will function.

Security testing. Unauthorized attempts to operate the software, or parts of it, are attempted. This might also include attempts to obtain access to the data, or harm the software installation or even the system software. As with all types of security it is recognized that someone sufficiently determined will be able to obtain unauthorized access and the best that can be achieved is to make this process as difficult as possible.

Stress testing. Abnormal demands are made upon the software by increasing the rate at which it is asked to accept data, or the rate at which it is asked to produce information. More complex tests may attempt to create very large data sets or cause the software to make excessive demands on the operating system.

Performance testing. Here the performance requirements, if any, are checked. These may include the size of the software when installed, the amount of main memory and/or secondary storage it requires and the demands made on the operating system when running within normal limits or the response time.

Usability testing. The process of usability measurement was introduced in the previous chapter. Even if usability prototypes have been tested whilst the application was constructed, a validation test of the finished product will always be required.

Alpha and beta testing. This is where the software is released to the actual end-users. An initial release, the *alpha* release, might be made to selected users who would be expected to report bugs and other detailed observations back to the production team. Once the application has passed through the alpha phase a *beta* release, possibly incorporating changes necessitated by the alpha phase, can be made to a larger, more representative set of users, before the final release is made to all users.

The final process should be a *software audit* where the complete software project is checked to ensure that it meets production management requirements. This ensures that all required documentation has been produced, is in the correct format and is of acceptable quality. The purpose of this review is: first, to assure the quality of the production process and by implication the product; and second, to ensure that all is in order before the initial project construction phase concludes and the maintenance phase commences. A formal handover from the development team at the end of the audit will mark the transition between the two phases.

Statistical testing

The intention of statistical testing techniques is to attempt to predict the quality of the software product. There are a number of different techniques which can be used, of which only one will be introduced here. A model of the processes of testing and debugging is shown in Figure 34.2.

The graph illustrates that faults are introduced into the software product almost as soon as the project commences; the number of faults introduced is shown on the

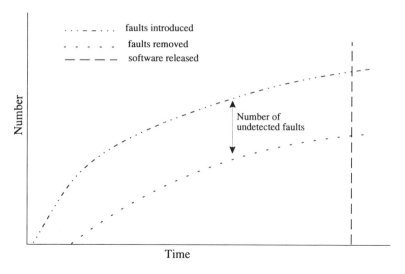

Figure 34.2 Testing and debugging during production.

upper line. Shortly after the first fault is introduced the process of debugging starts to remove faults as they are located; the number of faults removed is shown on the bottom line. The gap between the two lines indicates the number of undetected faults which are present in the product and, as the graphs show, it is assumed that the product is released with some faults still not discovered.

The quality assurance process during the production phase can attempt to limit the height of the upper curve by insisting upon a rigorous design/design review and code/code review process. A complementary approach is to increase the height of the lower curve by insisting upon rigorous and thorough testing throughout the production process. Despite all of these approaches it seems that it is impossible, or at least extremely unlikely, for any software to be produced which is totally free of undiscovered faults.

Metrics on the number of faults detected and the number of faults removed can be obtained from a managed production process which requires all faults discovered during testing to be recorded. However, this will gives no indication of the number of faults which were introduced and thus the number of undiscovered faults which remain.

One technique which can be used to attempt to obtain an estimate for the number of remaining faults is deliberately to introduce faults into a copy of the software and require all testing to be repeated on the faulty copy. The number of faults discovered by this process will then give some indication of the effectiveness of the test processes, and from the records of the faults discovered in the real software product an estimation of the number of remaining faults in the real software can be obtained.

For example, assume that 200 faults were removed from the software during the integration testing phase, and that 100 deliberate faults were introduced into the copy made at the end of this stage. If a repeat of all the integration tests only detects 80 of these deliberate faults then it can be assumed that the integration testing process is only 80% effective. Returning to the 200 faults in the original copy, it can now be assumed that these represent only 80% of the faults which were actually present, this indicates that there may be 40 as yet undiscovered faults in the actual software at the end of the integration phase.

The types of fault which are deliberately introduced should reflect the types of faults which have been shown to be present by the testing process. The faults which could easily be introduced might include: a small change to the value of a constant, the replacement of an **and** with an **or** in control expressions, the insertion or removal of a **not** in control expressions, the insertion or removal of brackets within expressions, changing the bounds of a definite loop to start or terminate one value too low or too high, changing an *in only* or an *out only* parameter to *in out*, rearranging the order of operations within a sequence, removing the initialization of a declared variable, and many other possibilities.

This process is made feasible only if automated tools for the application and recording of tests are used to apply the integration tests. It also requires the project management processes to have effective techniques for the recording of errors detected during integration testing. The process can also be used as a quality control check by insisting that integration testing should continue until 95% (or 99%) of all introduced faults have been removed.

Techniques such as this are required for the process maturity of a software development organization to be assessed as defined or managed on the process maturity scale introduced in the previous chapter. The collection of such reports and the tracking of the causes of the faults can also be used as an indication of those parts of the production process which are introducing the most faults, and thus are the most deserving of management attention. Such a collection of statistics over a number of different projects can also be used to indicate if the quality of the development process is improving. Historical statistics can also be used to estimate the number of undiscovered faults in the current product from records of the number of faults reported by end-users of previous similar products.

Production processes

The waterfall model of software production is so called as it is analogous to descending a river through a number of waterfalls. Between waterfalls it may be possible to move backwards and forwards, although it would take much more effort to move backwards. However, having passed down a waterfall it is tremendously difficult but not impossible to travel back up over it, and thus is something to be definitely avoided. The waterfalls in software production are the completion of the requirements statement, the completion of the detailed specification, the completion of the high level module design, the construction of the software and finally verification and system testing.

This is a very powerful, and successful, technique for managing a production process in the situations where it can be applied. Unfortunately these situations are comparatively rare and are virtually unattainable by a novice developer. The waterfall process is possible for experienced developers if all the following apply. The application domain is very well understood by the developer. The sponsor of the software has a full awareness of the effects which the automation of a process will have on the way in which that process is performed. The developer has a detailed knowledge of and practised skills in using the production tools, which include the language which will be used. And finally the developer has previous experience of the successful development of similar products.

These circumstances are relatively rare in the real world, and by definition are impossible for a novice developer. When these circumstances do not apply then it is not possible even to obtain a complete specification as the process of design will most probably reveal aspects of the specification which are missing or ambiguous. Likewise the process of implementing and testing a design will reveal considerations which are missing from the design, and possibly also from the specification.

Before considering alternatives to the waterfall method a justification for the implicit advice given throughout this book – always to complete program designs before commencing construction – will be given. Although the pure waterfall method represents an ideal situation which a novice developer should strive to attain, it is a situation which few developers actually ever achieve. The greatest virtue of the method is the emphasis on taking the design process seriously, rather than attempting to hack code together in the hope of achieving a useful subprogram. As such the initial advice to attempt to produce complete and comprehensive designs before commencing any coding can be justified.

The first alternative to the waterfall method recognizes that the process of design will reveal problems with the specification and the process of construction and testing will reveal problems with the design. Accordingly it plans for this and allows for the successive refinement of the specification and design to proceed as the software is constructed. This process of construction is known as the *spiral method* and one possible interpretation of it is compared with the waterfall method in Figure 34.3.

The key to the successful use of the spiral method is to ensure that the spiralling is controlled and produces an effective refinement on each cycle, leading towards the complete product. Each cycle is also expected to increase the complexity of the implementation, the initial cycles should be concerned with a simple implementation of the most central and complex part of the specification and each cycle thereafter should add further functionality.

The major problem with the method is that it can become a justification for endless fiddling with the code in the hope that an effective design will emerge at some stage. However, within the scope of the method there is provision for

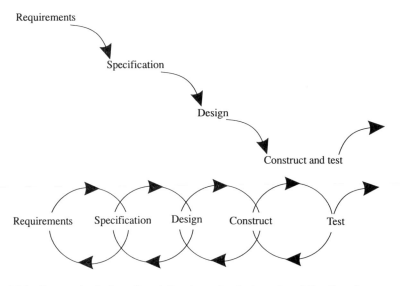

Figure 34.3 The waterfall method (top) and spiral method (bottom) compared.

experimentation with different implicit designs by the production of different possible implementations. To be effective this stage must be carefully monitored to ensure that progress continues to be made towards a finalized design and product.

This technique of experimental, exploratory coding followed by consolidation in a design has led to a further production method known as *prototyping*. There are several possible prototyping approaches. The first is *exploratory prototyping* where a model of the product is produced in order to allow design ideas to be tried out, and to allow end-users to comment on the implementation. At the end of this stage the prototype is thrown away and more traditional techniques are then used to produce the actual product. A variation on this technique, known as *rapid prototyping*, has one team of developers working on the prototype. A second, larger team follows the prototyping team producing the actual product, before the prototype is completely finished, using lessons learned from the prototype.

The third prototyping technique is *incremental prototyping* where the intention is to produce the product directly from the prototype. Here the comments of the sponsors on the prototype lead to the developers implementing the changes, and then presenting the revised prototype for further comments. A dialog develops between the developers and the sponsors which will hopefully lead to the development of a product which satisfies the user's requirements. The danger with this approach is that documentation and testing may be sacrificed in order to maintain the dialog with the user and this may result in future maintenance problems. However, this technique does not regard development as ever being finished and what would be the maintenance phase is simply the continuation of the refinement of the prototype, though at a less intense rate.

In practice most development teams use *opportunistic techniques*, where the most appropriate method for the project, or the current stage of the project, is used. This technique may be used within the *incremental development* method when the product is planned from the outset to be delivered in a number of phases. The first deliverable version, not a prototype, will be a bare bones version of the required product but will be sufficiently functional as to be useful to the end-user. In consultation with the sponsors the most urgently required additional functionality is decided upon and this is then incrementally added to the deliverable for the next release. The production method used for each increment is decided opportunistically using whichever method seems the most appropriate for the particular stage of implementation. What is not left to chance, however, is the necessity of documenting all the design changes and testing, and most importantly regression testing, each deliverable before handing it over. One other feature of this technique is a short timescale between each deliverable, which is intended to ensure that the development team never lose contact with the users' needs and opinions.

It is a variation of this technique which is advocated as the most appropriate for novice developers. Production of a software product should be done in a planned incremental manner, with each incremental version thoroughly tested before proceeding to the next stage. In the context of a novice developer this provides small manageable development objectives, which can be subsequently evaluated both for product and process quality, before the next increment is attempted. This process can be summarized as the ***design–build–test–evaluate*** cycle.

Whatever production process method is used, one overriding requirement is to develop skills which allow secure software to be rapidly and economically constructed. The only way in which this can happen is to think about software assembly by adapting or extending pre-supplied components rather than the development of the program from scratch.

EXERCISES

34.1 Revisit the test plans for the four sorting algorithms in Exercise 31.2 and extend them again to include condition testing considerations.

34.2 Choose one of the sort algorithms in Exercise 34.1 and attempt to determine if life cycle testing of all of its variables and parameters would produce any useful additional considerations.

34.3 Review the test plan from Exercise 34.2 with regard to the loop testing considerations given in this chapter. For a sorting algorithm which includes a double loop, for example the insertion sort, is it possible to apply the loop testing as suggested?

34.4 For a package for which you have an automated test harness, attempt to determine its statistical effectiveness by having someone else introduce a known number of errors into the source code and find out how many of the errors are detected by your harness.

34.5 For a software production which you have already produced, tested and consider satisfactory, subject it to recovery and stress testing. Are you still satisfied with it?

APPENDIX A
Other resources

The LAW (Learn Ada on the Web) project contains a collection of resources directly supporting this book, including a draft of the complete text, one complete section which was not included for reasons of space, all the source code and much else besides. It will also contain a list of errata in this book!

The LAW project is hosted at: http://www.scism.sbu.ac.uk/law

The LAW project contains a page of links to other Web services, the most important of which are:

- The ACM SIGAda server: http://info.acm.org/sigada

- The Home of the Brave Ada programmers: http://lglwww.epfl.ch/Ada

- The complete text of the Ada '95 Language Reference Manual (LRM) is at: http://lglwww.epfl.ch/Ada/LRM/9X/rm9x/rm9x-toc.html

- A list of Ada software repositories is maintained at: http://lglwww.epfl.ch/ Ada/Resources/Repositories.html

A very comprehensive software engineering textbook is: *Software Engineering*, 5th edition, by Ian Sommerville, Addison-Wesley 1995, ISBN 0-201-42765-5. Support for this book is available at: http://www.comp.lancs.ac.uk/computing/resources/ser

A comprehensive text on usability engineering is: *Usability Engineering* by Jacob Nielsen, Academic Press 1993, ISBN 0-12-518405-0

Information on software engineering metrics tools can be found at: The Center for Systems and Software Engineering (CSSE): http://www.sbu.ac.uk/csse

If you do not have an Ada '95 compiler, you can use one across the Web. WebAda is at: http://se-eng.falls-church.va.us/AdaIC/compilers/webada/

Or you can obtain a free MS Dos Gnat Ada '95 environment from:

ez2load
        ftp://ftp.gwu.edu/pub/ada/ez2load/

Gnat versions for other platforms, including Solaris, OS2 and Linux, are available.

The Gnat project home page: http://cs.nyu.edu/cs/projects/gnat/

Mirrored in Europe at: http://lglwww.epfl.ch/Ada/Resources/Compilers/GNAT.html

Should you not have Internet access much of the material described above is available on a regularly updated series of CD roms, available from:

Walnut Creek CDROM
1547 Paltos Verdes Mall
Suite 260, Walnut Creek
CA 94596, USA (http://www.cdrom.com)

Index

+ (addition)   186, 193
=> (aggregate array value)   382
.. (aggregate array value)   382, 401
| (aggregate array value)   382, 401
:= (assignment)   14, 31–2
' (attribute mark)   176
(base literal)   178
<> (box, generic parameter)   624
<> (box, generic subprogram default)   648
<> (box, unconstrained array)   383
| (case selector, and)   111
.. (case selector, range)   111
& (catenation arrays)   386
& (catenation strings)   212, 274
. (component of access types)   437
** (exponentiation)   186, 193
> (greater than)   186, 192
>= (greater than or equal to)   186, 192
= (is equal to)   182, 196
<> (is not equal to)   182, 192
! (JSP exception notation)   153, 242
=> (JSP i/o notation)   26
* (JSP iteration notation)   118
? (JSP posit/admit)   242
o (JSP selection notation)   94
< (less than)   186, 192
<= (less than or equal to)   186, 192
* (multiplication)   186, 193
=> (named parameter association)   180
. (record component of)   69, 400
7 ± 2 (seven plus or minus two)   713
– (subtraction)   186, 193
=> (when clause of case statement)   111

abed   266, 277
abs   186, 193
abstract   514, 615

abstract data type (ADT)   183, 247
  c.f. EDT   536, 612
  c.f. ESV   517, 536, 612
abstract subprograms   642, 644
abstract types   537, 539, 565
  and access types   569
access types   434–55
  and abstract types   569
  restrictions on subprograms   585
  subprogram access types   451, 455, 576
access   435
  access all   446
  access constant   448
ACCESS (attribute)
  variables   454
  subprograms   446, 584
actions of an object   536
actual parameter   45, 47
  and arrays   387
  and extended types   81
  and generic   620
  and variant records   646
ADA   343
ADA.CALENDAR   262, 277, 346–9
ADA.CALENDAR.HANDLING   205, 318
ADA.CHARACTESR.LATIN_1   204, 262, 277
ADA.COMMAND_LINE   349–52, 360–70
ADA.DIRECT_IO   500, 601
ADA.EXCEPTIONS   680
ADA.NUMERICS.DISCRETE_RANDOM   352–5
ADA.NUMERICS.ELEMENTARY_FUNCTIONS   356
ADA.NUMERICS.FLOAT_RANDOM   352–5
ADA.NUMERICS.GENERIC_COMPLEX_TYPES   342

ADA.NUMERICS.GENERIC_
    ELEMENTARY_FUNCTIONS 356
ADA.SEQUENTIAL_IO 487, 601
ADA.STREAMS 601
ADA.STREAMS.STREAMS_IO 601
ADA.STRINGS 357–60
ADA.STRINGS.CONSTANTS 359
ADA.STRINGS.FIXED 360
ADA.STRINGS.MAP 359
ADA.TEXT_IO 14, 342, 456, 457, 467, 468,
    601
ADA.TEXT_IO.DECIMAL_IO 197
ADA.TEXT_IO.EDITING 371
ADA.TEXT_IO.ENUMERATION_IO 225,
    459
ADA.TEXT_IO.FIXED_IO 196
ADA.TEXT_IO.FLOAT_IO 190, 459
ADA.TEXT_IO.INTEGER_IO 178, 459
ADA.TEXT_IO.MODULAR_IO 188
ADA.TEXT_IO.PICTURES 197, 237
ADA.WIDE_TEXT_IO 457
adaptive user interfaces 531
admit 242, 263, 275, 471
ADT *see* abstract data type
AFT 190
aggregate array value
    one dimensional named 382
    one dimensional positional 382
    two dimensional named 401
    two dimensional positional 401
algorithm 6, 667–72
    order of 685–97
    standard 668
aliased 434, 446
    dangers of 447
all 440, 574
allocator statement 435
alpha testing 760
and, boolean 106, 120
and, modular bitwise 188
and then 549
APPEND_FILE 461
arrays 377–415
    as generic parameter 624
    constrained one dimensional 377
    constrained two dimensional 396
    element type 378
    index type 378
    more than two dimensional 402
    one dimensional 377–90
    one dimensional aggregate values 382
    one dimensional attributes 384

one dimensional unconstrained 377
    two dimensional 395–401
    two dimensional aggregate values 401
    two dimensional attributes 402
    two dimensional unconstrained 401
ASCII 199, 456
assertions 296, 298, 671
    formal assertions 670–2
    post-assertions 671
    pre-assertions 671
automated testing 286, 302

BASE 180
base type 182
before common era (BCE) 248
begin
    exception block 243
    procedure 69
    program procedure 14
beta testing 760
black box diagram 287, 290, 325, 714
black box testing 281–303, 667, 714–15, 753
    c.f. white box testing 718
BOOLEAN 229–31
bounded lists 644
build test, build test … 552, 611

call depth 736
call graph 736
case 109–13, 154
catenation (&)
    of arrays 386
    of strings 212
CHARACTER 198, 207
class 613–14, 616
class hierarchy 84, 143, 536, 538, 561,
    564
    generic 657–61
class wide types 434, 536–41, 572
    access types 448, 451, 569
    c.f. definite types 541
    as type of function 588
client 45, 58
CLOCK 278, 346
CLOSE
    DIRECT_IO 501
    SEQUENTIAL_IO 489
    STREAM_IO 602
    TEXT_IO 462
cognitive chunk 114, 236, 713
cognitive complexity 114, 124, 404, 419
COL 464, 466

collating sequence   198
command line   32, 235
command line arguments   349–52,
    360–70
comments   15, 338
    density of   729
compilation unit   178
complexity   610, 711
    analysis   733
    of expression   730
    of operations   731
    of specification   726–8
    of subprogram call   732
composite test method   296, 299
computer aided software engineering
    (CASE)   742
computer science   4
condition testing   754
consistency   236
constant
    ADT   295
    integer   25, 29, 30
    string   14, 16–17, 22–3
constrained
    one dimensional arrays   377
    STRINGs   207
    two dimensional arrays   396, 400
CONSTRAINT_ERROR   49, 65, 180, 182
    185, 187, 189, 204, 212, 222, 250,
    263, 385, 463
constraint set   754
context clause   15
coupling   742–3
CREATE
    DIRECT_IO   501
    SEQUENTIAL_IO   489
    STREAM_IO   602
    TEXT_IO   462
CURRENT_INPUT   467
customization   237

data attribute   66, 523, 536–7
DATA_ERROR   49, 180, 233, 241, 277,
    463, 481, 490, 502
data flow diagrams   41, 56, 75
data life cycle testing   756
data type   175
debugger   332
debugging   284, 305, 311, 315–32
decimal types   196, 371
declare/define   42, 45, 56, 67, 68, 75, 137
defensive programming   266

definite types   541
delay   349
DELETE
    DIRECT_IO   501
    SEQUENTIAL_IO   489
    STREAM_IO   602
    STRINGS_FIXED   368
    TEXT_IO   466
delta   197
demonstration (c.f. testing)   281
density of comments   729
dependencies in production   306, 312
dependency diagrams   170
designation   435
design review   28
desk check   285
development by extension   595, 601
digits   196
DIGITS   189
direct files   456, 485, 499–513
discrete types
    case   111
    for   131
    as generic parameters   626
    INTEGER   177
    random values   355
dispatching to a parent's action   546, 548
documentation
    technical   333–40
    user   238–9
DURATION   699
dynamic data structures   434
dynamic dispatching   451, 536, 578, 615

EDT *see* extended data types
effectiveness of an algorithm   669
efficiency of an algorithm   669
egoless programming   310
elegance of an algorithm   669
element type of an array   378
else   96, 98
elsif   98
empty string   212
encapsulated static variable (ESV)   517–34
    c.f. ADT   536, 517, 612
    c.f. EDT   563, 612
encapsulation   613
end
    case   111
    exception block   243
    if   96, 98
    loop   119

end *continued*
  package 58
  procedure 69
  program procedure 17
END_ERROR 463, 466, 490, 502
END_OF_FILE
  DIRECT_IO 501
  SEQUENTIAL_IO 489
  STREAM_IO 602
  TEXT_IO 466
END_OF_LINE 465
END_OF_PAGE 466
enumeration types 220–9
  overloaded literal 406
error management 237
error recovery 237
ESV *see* encapsulated static variable
exception 49, 65, 182, 240–6
  developer declared 149, 151, 250, 263
  explicit 240
  implicit 240
EXCEPTION_IO 680
EXCEPTION_MESSAGE 680, 681
EXCEPTION_NAME 680
executable file 32
exit status 352
EXP 190
explicit qualification 460, 488, 600, 659
extended data types (EDT) 536
  c.f. ADT 536, 612
  c.f. ESV 536, 612
extension aggregate 547
external filename 460

fan in 742
fan out 736, 742
feature point analysis 726–8, 741
FILE 461, 464
FILE_MODE 461, 501
file pointer 460, 485, 495–9
FILE_TYPE 460, 501
FIRST (attribute)
  CHARACTER 203
  enumeration 223
  FLOAT 189
  INTEGER 176
  one dimensional array 384
  STRING 209
  two dimensional array 402
fixed types 196
flag 218
FLOAT 189–95

FloatIO 190
flowgraphs 705–13
  complexity of 711
  exceptions in 719–22
  iteration 709
  selection 708
  sequential 707
flow of control 46
FLUSH 467
for 131
FORE 190
FORM
  DIRECT_IO 501
  SEQUENTIAL_IO 489
  STREAM_IO 602
  TEXT_IO 467
formal methods 301, 682
formal parameter
  and arrays 387
  and extended types 81
  and generic 620
  and variant records 645
formal specification 670–2
fragile base class 537
function 56
  c.f. procedure 89
  recursive 427–30
  returning class wide type 588

generality of an algorithm 669, 671, 672
generic 30, 344–6, 585, 614, 617–39
  design 623
GET
  enumeration 227
  FLOAT 190
  from a file 463
  from a string 216, 277
  INTEGER 30–1, 179
  overloading 275
  STRING 214
GET_IMMEDIATE 467
GET_LINE 214
glass box testing 281
  see also white box testing
gnat 37, 767

'has a' 537, 542, 561, 611
Hawthorne effect 749
heterogeneous data structures 564–616
heuristic user interface rules 234
hidden support 237
homogeneous data structures 564, 641–63

how c.f. what   45, 69, 303

identifiers   19–21
if   96, 98
IMAGE
   CHARACTER   203
   enumeration   223
   INTEGER   177, 181
in   186, 205, 224
   class membership   639
incremental development   764
indentation   96, 105, 112, 120
INDEX (ADA.DIRECT_IO)   503
INDEX (ADA.STRINGS.FIXED)   368
indexed files   500
INDEXED_IO (non–standard
      package)   342
INDEX_NON_BLANK   368
index type of array   378
IN_FILE   461
infinite recursion   17, 417, 421
infix notation   257
inheritance   613
in only mode   52, 54, 407
   subprogram parameters   447
in out mode   52, 54, 407
INOUT_FILE   501
INPUT   602
instantiation   30, 178, 190, 344–6, 617
   of a generic hierarchy   657–62
instrumented code   734
INTEGER   25
   modular   185–8
   signed   175–85
IntegerIO   20, 178
integrated development environment
      (IDE)   32
integration testing   331, 758
intelligent agent   237
INTERFACES   343
internal filename   461
internationalization   205, 237, 249
inverse test method   296,
'is a'   537, 542, 561, 611
IS_ALPHANUMERIC   206
IS_BASIC   206
ISBN   556, 562
IS_CONTROL   206
IS_DECIMAL_DIGIT   206
IS_DIGIT   206
IS_GRAPHIC   206
IS_HEXADECIMAL_DIGIT   206

IS_OPEN
   DIRECT_IO   501
   SEQUENTIAL_IO   489
   STREAM_IO   602
   TEXT_IO   466
IS_ISO–646   206, 217
IS_LETTER   206
IS_LOWER   205
IS_SPECIAL_GRAPHIC   206
IS_UPPER   206
ISO, 646 (ASCII)   199
ISO, 8652:1995 (Ada, 95)   199
ISO, 8859–1 (Latin_1)   199
iteration   92, 116–40
   compared   138–9
   definite   128–38
   indefinite   117–28

JSP schematics
   cross referencing   58
   data structure diagrams   66, 335
   enumeration   220
   iteration   118, 129
   of a sequential file   486
   of a string   207
   of text files   458
   of variant records   647
   one dimensional array   377
   recursive data structure   428
   recursive program structure   420
   refinement   26
   selection   44, 94
   sequence   26
   subprogram parameters   454
   subtypes   181
   two dimensional array   395
Julian dates   248–79, 542, 559, 607

k8 (krunched to 8 characters)   xvii, 260
key
   direct file   499
   ordered list   596, 650
   sort   689

large scale metrics   740–3
LAST
   CHARACTER   203
   enumeration   223
   FLOAT   189
   INTEGER   176
   one dimensional array   384
   STRING   209

LAST *continued*
    two dimensional array   402

latin_1   199
    table   200–3
layout conventions   18
LAYOUT_ERROR   466
learnability   236
LENGTH
    one dimensional array   384
    STRING   209
    two dimensional array   402
limited private   90, 258, 260
LINE   464–5
LINE_LENGTH   464–5
lines of code   729
linking   34
listing file   35, 260, 360
literal
    BOOLEAN   229
    CHARACTER   204
    enumeration   221
    FLOAT   190
    INTEGER   177
    STRING   18, 209
LOCALE   371
LOOK_AHEAD   467
loop   119
loop parameter   130–1
loops   116
    testing   757
LOWER_CASE   226
LRM   342

McCabes cyclomatic complexity   713
maintenance   285, 333, 388, 562, 600, 611
make utility   171
mathematical functions   356
medium scale metrics   743–6
memory load   236
memory packages   518
menu/dispatch standard design   317, 415, 580
menu driven user interfaces   235
metrics   685–704, 724–38
    call depth   736
    call graph   736
    complexity/resource scattergraph   741
    coupling   742
    data attribute extension   745
    density of comments   729

dynamic   698–702
    expression complexity   730
    fan in   742
    fan out   736
    function point   726–8
    generic parameter complexity   744
    Goldilocks metrics   746
    hierarchy depth   746
    large scale metrics   740–3
    lines of code   729
    medium scale metrics   743–6
    McCabes cyclometric complexity   713
    operation complexity   731
    static   685–98
    usability metrics   746–50
milestone   306, 308
MODE
    DIRECT_IO   501
    SEQUENTIAL_IO   489
    STREAM_IO   602
    TEXT_IO   467
MODE_ERROR   463, 466, 490, 502–3
MOVE   368

NAME
    DIRECT_IO   501
    SEQUENTIAL_IO   489
    STREAM_IO   602
    TEXT_IO   467
named notation
    allocation aggregate   436
    array aggregate   382
    record aggregate   436
    subprogram calls   46
NAME_ERROR   462
NATURAL   176, 181, 389, 405
new
    access types   435
    character types   203
    enumeration types   221
    inheritance   613
    integer types   183–5
    string types   208
    type extension   77, 145
NEW_LINE   23, 24, 29, 30, 464
NEW_PAGE   464, 466
not, BOOLEAN   230
not, bitwise modular   188
noun phrases   182, 538
null
    allocator value   436
    statement   112, 127, 164

null record   555, 577

object (defined)   615
object diagram   40, 53, 75, 250
object file   32
object oriented design (OOD)   537
object oriented programming (OOP)   612–16
OPEN
    DIRECT_IO   501
    SEQUENTIAL_IO   489
    STREAM_IO   602
    TEXT_IO   461
opportunistic development   765
or, bitwise   188
or, boolean   104
order of an algorithm   685–97
ordinal   499
others
    arrays   382
    case   111
    strings   209
OUT_FILE   461
out only   52, 54, 407
    and subprogram access parameters   447
OUTPUT   602
overloaded   257, 613, 615, 620
overriding   144, 149, 595
    and class wide actions   541

package
    body   45, 68
    child   40, 344
    generic   626–37
    parent   40, 344
    private child   613
    specification   43, 57
PAGE (ADA.TEXT_IO)   464, 466
PAGE (pragma)   339
PAGE_LENGTH   464, 466
parallel test method   295
parameter modes   52
parent/child   344, 536
peer review   310
performance testing   760
PIC   372
PICTURE   371
plural   262, 378
polymorphic   613, 615
POS   177, 203, 223, 272
posit   242, 263, 275, 471
positional
    allocator aggregates   436

array aggregates   382
record aggregates   436
subprogram calls   46
POSITIVE   176, 181
post condition   671
pragma   339
pre condition   671
PRED   177, 203, 223
prefix notation   257
primitive operations   90, 144, 610, 614
private   45, 58, 66, 258, 260
    child packages   613
    generic parameters   619
procedure   42, 56
    c.f. **function**   89
    generic   618–26
    recursive   419–25
production management   610, 724, 740
production plan   308, 312, 335
production planning   305–15
program heading   15
programming by contract   667, 672–83
    enforcement   676–83
programming in the large   667
programming in the small   667
program procedure   14
proof   282, 301
propagation   240, 244, 263
prototype
    exploratory   765
    incremental   765
    rapid   765
    usability   234
public   45, 57, 258, 261
PUT
    enumeration   226
    FLOAT   190
    INTEGER   179
    overloading   272
    STRING   31, 214
    to file   462
    to string   216, 274
PUT_LINE   14, 17, 214
    to file   463

quit   242, 263, 275, 471
quality
    assurance   719, 724
    control   719
    indicator   729

raise   65, 241, 283

RAISE_EXCEPTION   680–1
random access   499
random number generator   355–54
range   131
RANGE
    one dimensional array   384
    two dimensional array   402
range diagrams   287, 291, 293, 352, 714
rationale   282
READ
    DIRECT_IO   520
    SEQUENTIAL_IO   489
real time control   517
record   66
recovery testing   760
regression testing   760
recursion   417–32
    function   427–30
    head   430
    c.f. iteration   432
    mutual   430–2
    procedure   419–25
    tail   430
    termination   421
redirection   300, 457
regression testing   337
relational operators
    arrays   387
    enumeration   224
    equivalencies   213, 261, 265
    FLOAT   192
    INTEGER   185
    programmer declared   249
    STRING   212
relational test method   296, 298
rem   186, 193
repetition   92, 116, 125
REPLACE_SLICE   364
reserved words   19
RESET
    DIRECT_IO   501
    SEQUENTIAL_IO   489
    STREAM_IO   602
    TEXT_IO   466
return   70
    multiple   228
reuse   611, 668
reverse   132, 137
reverse engineering   334
root integer   184
rounding error   193–6

scope   137, 480
    local   169
    global   169
    of encapsulated variable   523
    of instantiation   226
Seaprinksi triangle   418
search   568, 573–4, 574
    binary chop   686
    generic   620–6
    sequential   686
security testing   760
SEED   354
selection   92, 115
    multi way   98, 100
    nested   101, 105
    one way   100
    sequential   100
    three way   97–8
    two way   93–6
sequence   92
SET   226
SET_COL   29, 30, 464–5
SET_INDEX   503
SET_INPUT   467
SET_LINE   464, 465
SET_LINE_LENGTH   464–5
SET_PAGE_LENGTH   464–6
singular   262, 378
short circuit operators   549
SIZE   504
skin subprogram   634
SKIP_LINE   51, 246, 464, 481
SKIP_PAGE   464, 466
slice
    of array   386, 575
    of string   211
software artifact   4–6
software assembly   8, 303, 342
software audit   761
software construction   8, 303, 242
software crisis   751
software production capability   751
software repository   8, 247, 286, 303, 340,
        342
sort
    bubble   691
    generic   629–33
    insertion   689
    merge   703
specification   6, 281–4, 335
    usability   748
spiral production   8–11, 764

stack frame   424
STANDARD   182, 229
standard designs
  binary chop search   687
  bubble sort   691
  insertion sort   629
  menu/dispatch   317, 415, 580
  sequential search   686
STANDARD_ERROR   457
STANDARD_INPUT   457, 467–8
STANDARD_OUTPUT   457, 468
standard packages   279, 303, 342–72
static variables   517
statistical testing   761
STATUS_ERROR   462, 466
STREAM   602
STREAM_ACCESS   602
streams   456, 486, 601–6
stress testing   760
STRING   207–20
  array of constants   522
  constrained   207
  literal   18
  recursive processing   428–30
  standard packages   357–60
  unconstrained   207
strong type checking   182
structured files   456, 485–513
stubs   314, 320, 759
style guides   236, 730
subprogram   40, 46
  data flow interface diagrams   41
  map   168, 236, 333, 482
  nesting   162–3, 169
subprogram parameters   451–5, 584
  generic   628
  restrictions   634, 638
subscript
  array   211
  one dimensional array   385
  two dimensional array   397, 398
subtype   43
  cast of array slice   383
  CHARACTER   203
  enumeration   221, 390
  FLOAT   191
  INTEGER   181–3
  STRING   208
SUCC   177, 203, 223
swap   618–20
SYMBOLS   372
SYSTEM   343

system testing   758

tagged   58, 74, 536, 545
technical writer   333
termination
  algorithm   669
  loop   125
  recursion   421
testing   281–304, 715–18
  alpha testing   760
  beta testing   760
  black box testing   281–304
  condition testing   754
  data life cycle testing   756
  c.f. demo   58, 281
  exhaustive   281
  harness   286
  integration testing   758
  of generic hierarchies   660
  performance testing   760
  recovery testing   760
  regression testing   760
  security testing   760
  statistical testing   761
  stress testing   760
  system testing   758
  testing loops   757
  test vee   758
  unit testing   758
  usability testing   760
  validation testing   578
  white box testing   715–18
test cases   283, 288, 291, 293, 325, 714
test log   283, 290
test methods   283–95
  compared   302
  composite   296, 299
  inverse   296
  parallel   295
  relational   296, 298
test plan   283, 288, 292, 293, 296, 325, 715
test runs   283
text files   456–83
TIME   277, 346
TO_BASIC   207, 217
TO_ISO_646   207, 217
TO_LOWER   206, 216
TO_UPPER   206, 217
trace table   121, 124, 245, 315, 327–31
  access types   441–5
  bubble sort   693–4
  heterogeneous data structure   572, 576, 599

trace table *continued*
    insertion sort   630–3
    recursive   424, 427, 429
    sequential file   495–9
trigonometric functions   356
TRIM   368
type   43
type conversion   132, 185, 212, 224
    263, 386–8
type qualification   147, 224, 406

unbounded   464
unbounded lists   644
UNBOUNDED_STRINGS   357
unconstrained
    one dimensional arrays   377, 383
    STRINGS   207
    two dimensional arrays   401
    variant records   647
unit testing   758
UNIVERSAL_FLOAT   189
UNIVERSAL_INTEGER   176, 189
until   349
UPPER_CASE   226
usability
    engineer   234, 750
    measurement   749–50
    metrics   724
    specification   747–8
    testing   760
use   14, 178
    and class hierarchies   554, 578
USE_ERROR   462–3, 466, 490, 503
user categorization   748
user interface design   233–9

VAL   177, 203, 223, 272

validation testing   760
VALUE   177, 203, 233
variables   25
variant records   645, 647, 651
verb   182, 538
version number   338
view conversion   546, 566, 590
visibility
    of instantiations   178, 226
    of packages   67
    of subprograms   236, 323

walk through   285, 310
waterfall production   8–11, 764
what c.f. how   45, 69, 303
when   111
where, why, when, what, who   15, 20, 58
while   119–28
white box testing   667, 753, 715–18
    c.f. black box testing   718
WIDE_CHARACTER   199, 457
WIDE_STRING   207
WIDTH   179–80, 191, 226
Windows, Icons, Mice and Pointer
    (WIMP)   235
with
    class hierarchy   554
    context clause   14
    type extension   77, 146
wrap around enumeration functions   228
WRITE
    DIRECT_IO   502
    SEQUENTIAL_IO   489

xor, bitwise modular   188